The Norton Introduction to Music History

BAROQUE MUSIC

O che d'alti fofpir vaga,e di pian   ti Spar'or di doglia

Music in Western Europe, 1580–1750

JOHN WALTER HILL

University of Illinois, Urbana-Champaign

John Michael Cooper
Georgetown, Texas
27 October 2014

W·W·NORTON & COMPANY

New York · London

W. W. Norton & Company has been independent since its founding in 1923, when William Warder Norton and Mary D. Herter Norton first published lectures delivered at the People's Institute, the adult education division of New York City's Cooper Union. The Nortons soon expanded their program beyond the Institute, publishing books by celebrated academics from America and abroad. By mid-century, the two major pillars of Norton's publishing program—trade books and college texts—were firmly established. In the 1950s, the Norton family transferred control of the company to its employees, and today—with a staff of four hundred and a comparable number of trade, college, and professional titles published each year—W. W. Norton & Company stands as the largest and oldest publishing house owned wholly by its employees.

Library of Congress Cataloging-in-Publication Data

Hill, John Walter, 1942–
    Baroque music: music in Western Europe, 1580–1750 / John Walter Hill.
        p. cm. — (Norton introduction to music history)

ISBN 0-393-97800-1

    1. Music—17th century—History and criticism. 2. Music—18th century—History and criticism. I. Title. II. Series.

ML193.H54 2004
780'.9'032—dc22

2004058144

W. W. Norton & Company, Inc., 500 Fifth Avenue, New York, N.Y. 10110
www.wwnorton.com

W. W. Norton & Company Ltd., Castle House, 75/76 Wells Street, London
W1T 3QT

1 2 3 4 5 6 7 8 9 0

For my loving wife,
Laura Callegari Hill

CONTENTS

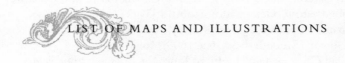

LIST OF MAPS AND ILLUSTRATIONS

PHOTO CREDITS

Title page: Jacopo Peri, detail from *Le Musiche di Jacopo Peri Nobil Fiorentino sopra l'Euridice* (Florence, 1600), facsimile edition published by Arnaldo Forni Editore, Bologna, 1969; Fig. 1.1: The Conway Library, Courtauld Institute of Art; Fig. 1.2: MIT Collection/Corbis; Fig. 1.3: Bridgeman Art Library; Figs. 1.5–1.6: Facsimile from Jacques Callot, *Das gesamte Werk, II*, Durckgraphik, ca. 1620 (Munich: Verlag Rogner & Bernhard); Figs. 2.1–2.2: Uffizi Gallery, Gabinetto dei Disegni, Florence; Fig. 2.2: Gabinetto dei Disegni, Florence. Photo: Foto Marburg/Art Resource, NY; Fig 2.3: Galleria Sabauda, Turin. Photo: Scala/Art Resource, NY; Fig. 2.4: From a facsimile in series *Bibliotheca musica Bononiensis; Sezione IV,* n. 11, Forni Editore, Bologna; Fig. 3.1: École Nationale Supérieure des Beaux-Arts, Paris. Photo: Scala/Art Resource, NY; Fig. 3.2: From Emanuel Winternitz, *Gaudenzio Ferrari: His School and the Early History of the Violin* (Varallo Sesia: Società Conservazione Opere Arte Monumenti Valsesia, 1967); Fig. 3.4 box: From a facsimile edition of Michael Praetorius, *Syntagma musicum,* Vol. 2 (Wolfenbüttel, 1619); Fig. 4.1: Staatliches Institut für Musikforschung, Berlin; Fig. 4.2: Biblioteca Nazionale Marciana, Venice, Italy; Fig. 5.1: Courtesy of the Rare Book and Special Collections Library, University of Illinois at Urbana-Champaign; Fig. 5.2: Musée des Beaux-Arts de Rennes. Photo by Louis Deschamps; Fig. 5.4: From Thoinot Arbeau, *Orchésographie* (1588/89), facsimile edition, Dover Publications; Fig. 5.6: Musée du Louvre, Paris. Photo: Réunion des Musées Nationaux/Art Resource, NY; Fig. 5.7: Los Angeles County Museum of Art. Photo: Erich Lessing/Art Resource, NY; Fig 5.8: Staatliche Museen zu Berlin, Kupferstichkabinett, Ms. 78, C 12, p. 43. Photo: Jörg Anders/BPK; Fig. 5.10: From a facsimile *Les pieces de clavessin y livre premier.* Paris, 1670; Fig. 6.2: Kunstsammlung der Veste, Coberg; Fig. 6.3: Musikinstrumentenmuseum, Universität Leipzig; Fig. 6.5: Museo del Prado, Madrid. Photo: AKG Images, London; Fig. 7.1: Photo archives of the National Gallery, Washington; Figs. 7.2–7.8: The Devonshire Collection, Chatsworth. Reproduced by permission of the Duke of Devonshire and the Chatsworth Settlement Trustees. Photographs: Photographic Survey, Courtauld Institute of Art; Fig. 8.1: Museo Correr, Venice. Photo: Fotoflash Mario; Fig. 8.2: From *Apparati scenici* (Venice, 1644). Biblioteca Nazionale Marciana, Italy;

PREFACE

Baroque Music takes its place in The Norton Introduction to Music History series between the volumes entitled *Renaissance Music* and *Classical Music*, already published. Thus its scope and its title were determined by the overall plan of the series. The title is a conventional way to refer to the period marked off by the years 1580–1750 and limited to the high-culture art music tradition of Western Europe.

This book attempts to provide an even and balanced account of the music of all decades within the seventeenth century and the early–eighteenth century and of all national cultures in Western Europe. It includes mention of developments before the year 1600 when they are needed to explain the innovations of the early seventeenth century. And it encompasses the cultivation in the early eighteenth century of genres already established before 1700 and modifications of those genres occurring shortly after that year. Coverage begins to taper off at about the year 1720, as it does not discuss the emergence of the new genres—symphony, solo keyboard sonata, accompanied sonata, keyboard concerto, string quartet and related types of chamber music, national varieties of comic opera, and symphonic church music—and the associated stylistic innovations that define the beginning of the Classical Era.

This volume is intended for serious readers who understand musical notation in score form and who have learned the nomenclature of musical intervals and key signatures. A background in the theory of tonal harmony will be useful in the later chapters. Students, graduates, and faculty in history, art history, and literature who have that musical background should find this book appropriate for broadening their knowledge of seventeenth-century European culture. The primary readership, however, will be current or former university students of music.

For many readers, the book will seem rather densely provided with information and explanation, and it should not be read quickly. When used as the text for a university course, it should be read over the span of a semester or quarter. It is designed to serve as the text for an upper-level period survey course for music majors, following a one-year survey of the whole of music history. Or it could be used, with the other volumes of The Norton Introduction to Music History, during the Baroque segment of a two-year survey.

For best results, this book should be read at a steady pace. In my course at the University of Illinois, which meets three times a week for an hour, I assign about fifteen pages of the text for each class session. I also recommend that readers keep the Anthology open and refer to the scores as they are discussed in the text. Marking the score to reflect the discussion in the text is a good way to connect the two and to understand each better.

Baroque music is approached here from several perspectives: social history, historical cultural anthropology, period music theory, musical style history, and historical narrative. Social history is useful because music making was and is a social activity, and musical works are, among other things, artifacts of such activity. Historical cultural anthropology focuses on the cultural values of past societies and their expressions in writing, the arts, abstract thought, and other forms of symbolic behavior. As products of culture, musical works can be explained, in part, as embodiments of cultural values. Period music theory provides us with an entrée into the mind-set of the participants in the creation of music in the past—the composers, performers, listeners, patrons, critics, and teachers who shaped it. It helps us to follow the course of the music in terms that would have been comprehensible to those participants in its creation, and it helps to rid us of anachronistic expectations that can only lead to disappointment and misunderstanding. Style history provides a means for us to organize in our minds a variety and multiplicity of genres and a span of style change that never confronted seventeenth-century participants in music making. Historical narrative provides a framework for chronology, allows us to avoid mistakes in explanation, and imposes that degree of shape and sense that we require when reviewing the past.

If the Baroque Era is so named because its music was baroque by virtue of its creation during the Baroque Era, we would be caught up in circular reasoning. Music historians have tried to find a way out of this circularity by discovering common features shared by all or most music of this period that distinguish it from the music of the previous and following eras.

The entry "Baroque" in The New Grove Dictionary of Music and Musicians, 2nd edition, explains that the term was applied to music during the eighteenth century, with the implication of "bizarre, irregular, extravagant, unnatural, and impassioned." But these words describe only a small portion of seventeenth-century musical works. Consequently, it would be misleading to use the word baroque, without the capital, to designate music of the Baroque Era. Another term or other principles of historical unity are needed. Chapter I includes my alternative suggestion for a unifying principle that relies more upon social, political, and cultural dimensions and less upon musical-stylistic features.

Although historians of art and literature refer to a Baroque Era, general historians today tend to favor broader, more neutral terms for periods in the history of Western Civilization—Antiquity, the Middle Ages, the Early Modern Period, and the Modern Period. The Early Modern Period is thought to begin with the Renaissance, the start of which historians tend to place roughly at the fall of Constantinople in 1453. This period is marked by the rediscovery and understanding of ancient learning independent of church dogma, a resurgence of cultural innovation, new growth of social mobility, the development of stronger central governments, and the creation by Europeans of overseas colonial empires. The end of the Early Modern Period is conventionally placed at the death of the French king Louis XIV in 1715, very near to the point at which we begin to see signs of epochal change in European music and musical culture. For the general historian, the end of the Early Modern Period is signaled by the start of the gradual collapse of absolutism, the beginning of the gradual rise of constitutional government, the first signs of the cultural, economic, and political ascendency of the commercial or middle classes, and the rise to dominance of Enlightenment cultural values (utility, naturalness, liberty) and ideas (empiricism, humanity, progress) over those of the outgoing Age of Reason. If we were to follow this lead, we would entitle this book *Music during the Later Early Modern Period*. For the sake of familiarity and in conformity with the tiles of earlier volumes in the Norton series, however, we have chosen to stay with the more traditional title *Baroque Music*.

In the first chapter of this book, the unity of music composed during the Baroque Era is sought in its cultural meaning, rather than in any specific set of technical, stylistic, or expressive features. The seventeenth century is presented as the period in which the European court nobility, guided by its vital ideology, Monarchy, arrived at its historic apogee of influence over music and high culture generally, and in which conflict and competition between the Catholic and Lutheran religions was most strongly reflected in church music of various kinds. This book as a whole will show that the interconnected influences of court culture and church Reformation and Counter-Reformation can be found in the background of most seventeenth-century music, even if those influences are not always manifested in the same way. Those influences are offered here as the main components of a unifying principle that justifies treating the period ca. 1580–1750 as the subject of a single volume.

ACKNOWLEDGMENTS

The Norton music editor who very ably attended the birth of this book was Michael Ochs, who retired before it was finished. His successor, Maribeth Payne, and assistant music editor Allison Benter expertly guided the project to port with firm hands on the wheel. Art director Neil Hoos lent his valuable expertise during the late stages, and Richard Wingell served very ably as copyeditor.

Early drafts of individual chapters were substantially improved through the precise corrections and invaluable suggestions provided by Michael Dodds, Mary Fransen, Bruce Gustafson, Barbara Hanning, Rebecca Harris-Warrick, Robert Kendrick, Jeffery Kurtzman, Lowell Lindgren, Carol Marsh, Curtis

Price, Ellen Rosand, Lois Rosow, Alexander Silbiger, and Louise Stein. Among my very fine colleagues at the University of Illinois, I wish to mention Tom Ward in particular, for his support and encouragement. I owe these outstanding scholars a very large debt of gratitude.

The graduate research assistants at the University of Illinois, Urbana-Champaign, who helped create and correct the scores in the *Anthology of Baroque Music* were Gregory Hellenbrand, Sharon Hudson, Sonia Lee, Patrizia Metzler, and Kenneth Smith. I hope that this experience will help each one of them as they launch their promising careers.

I am grateful to the Research Board of the University of Illinois, Urbana-Champaign, who contributed the salaries of research assistants and funds for acquisition of microfilms and photographs.

Above all, I wish to thank my dear wife, Dr. Laura Callegari Hill, a musicologist of very high attainments, who provided translations from Spanish and Latin, many basic ideas and suggestions, and her unwavering support, understanding, and encouragement during the long and arduous labor that this book required.

REFERENCES TO MUSIC

Throughout this book will be found references to musical works followed by the abbreviation "A." and a number in parentheses. These abbreviations refer to the scores in the *Anthology of Baroque Music*, edited by John Walter Hill and published by W. W. Norton as a companion to the present volume. Some other titles of musical works are followed by the abbreviation "W." and a number in parentheses, referring to a Web-based supplement maintained by W. W. Norton and accessible through their Web site at www.wwnorton.com/college/music/hill. This supplement consists of additional scores that can be viewed with the Adobe Acrobat Reader, available without charge from www.adobe.com.

The musical staff below shows the system of pitch identification used throughout this book.

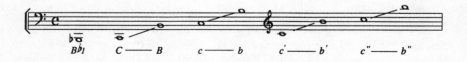

CHAPTER 1

Introduction:
Monarchy, Religion, and the Rhetoric
of the Arts

In the late afternoon of Saturday, October 11, 1687, a large ceremonial barge slipped through the waters of the Thames River and landed at the stone stairway fronting Whitehall, the largest palace in Europe (Fig. 1-1). To the sound of trumpets, cannons, and the cheers of the assembled household, King James II of England and Queen Mary (formerly Maria d'Este of Modena) made their way to the central banquet hall.

The palace had been planned for King James's grandfather, James I, by the famous court architect and stage designer Inigo Jones, and the ceiling of its banquet hall (Fig. 1-2) had been decorated in 1634 by the celebrated Flemish painter Peter Paul Rubens. The proportions, dimensions, and layout of the palace were modeled on those of the biblical temple of Solomon, as it was then conceived. Rubens's allegorical ceiling paintings—typically Baroque in their turbulent movement, strong contrast of light and dark, and theatrical expression—carried out the same theme, depicting James I as a wiser, modern Solomon, uniting the kingdoms of England and Scotland under one crown rather than dividing them, as the biblical Solomon offered to divide a baby of disputed birth between two rival mothers (Fig. 1-3).

Once inside the banquet hall, the king and queen were seated among their many courtiers to hear court musicians perform the customary welcome song, this one titled *Sound the Trumpet, Beat the Drum* (W. 29), newly composed for the occasion by Henry Purcell, Organist of the Chapel Royal and Keeper of the King's Instruments. The string orchestra began with a French overture: twenty-two measures in majestic dotted rhythm followed by a lively fugal section in

Figure 1-1. Whitehall Palace

Figure 1-2. Banquet Hall,
Whitehall Palace

triple meter. Imitating instrumental flourishes with their singing, the coun-
tertenor and bass soloists proclaimed:

> Sound the trumpet, beat the drum,
> Caesar and Urania come.
> Bid the Muses haste to greet 'em,
> Bid the Graces fly to meet 'em
> With laurel and myrtle to welcome them home,

The text compares James to a Roman conqueror and Mary to the Roman
goddess of spiritual love, the muses and graces of ancient Greek mythology
crowning them both. The other movements of the work extolled James's victo-
ries over Discord and Rebellion.

The rebellion that James put down had been led by the Duke of Monmouth
and the Duke of Argyll in June of 1685, just four months after James inherited
the throne from his older brother. The rebels, largely farmers and artisans, were
led by members of the nobility. The nobles fought to defend England's liberties
and parliamentary constitution and to oppose James's Catholic religion, which
they feared he would impose on them, along with French political and military
domination. Although James's army quickly put down the revolt, dissension
remained. In fact, on that Saturday in October, James was returning from a
summerlong tour of his realm aimed at lining up support before a crucial parliamentary election.

But instead of mending fences with the nobility, James promoted the interests of fellow Catholics and other opponents of the Church of England. In
reaction to this effort, seven powerful English noblemen appealed for help to
James's Protestant daughter Mary and her husband, William of Orange, ruler of

Figure 1-3. Rubens, *The Judgment of Solomon*, on the ceiling of the banquet hall at Whitehall Palace

Holland and enemy of France. William landed his army at the port of Brixham on November 5, 1688, and, aided by massive defections of English officers and soldiers, captured James without a fight and sent him into exile.

Purcell's *Sound the Trumpet, Beat the Drum* was James's last welcome song. William and Mary were crowned by order of Parliament on April 21, 1689, and nine days later, on the new queen's birthday, the same musicians performed the ode *Now Does the Glorious Day Appear*, likewise composed by Henry Purcell. This work begins with an Italian overture (with neither dotted rhythms nor fugal section) and contains these words in praise of Queen Mary:

> Her Hero to whose conduct and whose arms
> The trembling Papal world their force must yield;
> Must bend himself to her victorious charms,
> And give up all the trophies of each field.
> Our dear Religion with our Law's defence,
> To God her zeal, to man benevolence
> Must her above all former monarchs raise
> To be the everlasting theme of praise.

The story of the Glorious Revolution of 1688 exposes several ironies: James II considered himself an absolute monarch, ordained by divine right to rule the British Empire, and yet he was deposed by Parliament on account of his religion; he received fawning praise from the very nobility who opposed him; and Henry Purcell's settings of poetic expressions of servility could be directed at King James I or at Queen Mary within the short span of eighteen months. The key to these ironies is, of course, that divine right, parliamentary loyalty, and praise did not adhere to King James II personally, but to monarchy as an institution and to an ideology. Henry Purcell, as court composer, was expected to contribute to institutional goals and could certainly not communicate any personal feelings he may have had through his music. The fact that most of Purcell's music served the monarchy (or the supporting nobility) and the state religion resulted from his employment as a member of the royal chapel and household.

In this respect Purcell was typical: nearly every important composer during the seventeenth and early eighteenth centuries was employed by a court, by a church, or by both. While the same can be said of medieval and Renaissance composers, it cannot be said of Classical period composers. Although court and church patronage of music was no more prevalent in the Baroque than it had been during the Renaissance, important changes in the institutions of monarchy and religion affected the arts, especially music, with particular force during the Baroque period.

MONARCHY AND NOBILITY

Like other monarchs, James II expected to rule as head of state for life. In Europe during the Early Modern Period (roughly 1450 to 1715), monarchs—whether called emperor, king, duke, or some other title—were either designated by birth, as they normally were in France, England, and parts of the Italian peninsula, or were elected by an assembly of nobles, as was typical of the German-speaking regions, Venice, and Rome, where the pope ruled a considerable territory like a secular monarch.

At various times and places, monarchs had to deal with assemblies of clergy, nobles, and non-nobles. Like James II, most monarchs did not answer to any higher governmental authority—except in the German lands, where regional monarchs were united into a loose confederation called The Holy Roman Empire. The ruling emperor was chosen by the permanent electors—three archbishops and four princes who would vote for one of their number.

Monarchy had been the prevailing form of government in Europe since the fall of the Roman Empire in the fifth century AD. Although republics ruled by trade-guild councils emerged in Italy during the Renaissance, nearly all had been replaced by monarchies by the beginning of the seventeenth century.

The nobility, including monarchs, represented the privileged class everywhere in Europe until the end of the Early Modern Period. Although nobles constituted only one or two percent of the European population during the seventeenth century, this relatively small group sponsored nearly all artistic activity outside the sphere of religion—and most of it within the religious sphere as well.

Noble status was most often conferred by birth, less often granted by a monarch. It was defined by privileges originating in custom, confirmed by law, and supported by religion. Nobles usually enjoyed a near monopoly on high governmental, military, and church positions; exemption from taxes; the exclusive right to inherit land; the unique right to bear arms, a right often symbolized by a ceremonial sword; the right to be tried by special courts; freedom from certain criminal penalties; the exclusive right to wear certain types of clothing; the expectation of receiving signs of deference such as ceremonial bows or special seating in church; and the exclusive prerogative of using titles of nobility, such as duke, count, marquis, and baron, or at least a special name form, usually including the word *of* or its equivalent in other languages (*de, di, von,* or *van*).

Vestiges of the highly developed noble hierarchy of medieval feudalism remained in central and eastern Europe at the beginning of the seventeenth century. For example, the king of Bohemia (located roughly where the Czech Republic is today) owed allegiance to the emperor in Vienna but in turn ruled over five regions, each with its own duke or margrave. One of those five regions, Silesia, contained sixteen principalities, each with a local ruler who had jurisdiction over a number of estates of noblemen who, in their turn, had certain rights of legal and administrative jurisdiction over the village people and tenant farmers living on the nobles' properties. At the other extreme, many noble landholders in other parts of Europe—notably France—came directly under the jurisdiction of the national monarch.

In spite of local differences, European nobility had a well-established international character at the beginning of the seventeenth century. James II of England is typical is this respect. His mother was the sister of the king of France, and he himself married the daughter of the Duke of Modena in Italy. At various times during the English Commonwealth period, James II led troops for the armies of Spain and France. In the lives of many lesser nobles, foreign diplomatic service also created international ties. The effect on the arts was to foster both the cross-fertilization of styles and deliberate references to specific national genres—witness the French and Italian overtures in the two Purcell works mentioned above.

In the seventeenth century the nobility was divided into higher and lower categories according to relative wealth and power. A typical French duke in the seventeenth century had an income one hundred times greater than that of a Paris merchant and five hundred times greater than that of a successful artisan. Cardinal Richelieu, prime minister to King Louis XIV of France, died with a fortune equal to that of twenty thousand middle-rank nobles. The king's wealth, of course, greatly exceeded even that.

Monarchy in the Seventeenth Century

Important changes in the institutions of monarchy and nobility in Europe occurred during the late sixteenth and early seventeenth centuries. These changes underlie the developments in music and the other arts that mark the beginning of the Baroque period.

New forms of warfare—larger armies, extensive use of gunpowder, new systems of fortification—eroded the nobles' independent power and helped bring about centralized governments and accumulation of revenues. During the 1500s, nobles still fought personally in wars, and the king himself often took part as first among equals. Not so in the 1600s, as the monarch's status became considerably higher than that of other nobles, who increasingly became administrators in a national bureaucracy.

Absolutism is the political doctrine that justified and characterized the trend toward concentrating power in the hands of a monarch. With roots in the sixteenth century, absolutism became the dominant political ideology in Europe during the seventeenth. Of course, no European monarch actually achieved absolute power. Parliaments and local nobles continued to provide some internal checks, but the principal restraints were international competition and conflict.

In fact, the seventeenth century was, by some measures, the most bellicose period in European history, largely because of the changes and tensions associated with the rise of absolutism. The 1600s and early 1700s saw almost continuous war between Spain and its neighbors England to the north and France to the northeast; between France and its neighbors England and the Netherlands to the north, Spain to the southwest, and the Holy Roman Empire to the east; and between the Empire and its neighbors France to the west and the Ottoman Turks to the east. (See the map, Fig. 1-4.) The most bloody and protracted conflict of the period, the Thirty Years' War (1618–48), pitted the Holy Roman Emperor, Spain, Poland, and the German Catholic nobles on one side against France, Denmark, Sweden, the Netherlands, and the German Protestant nobles on the other. It resulted in perhaps the highest casualty rate of any war in history. In addition, major civil wars erupted in England (1642–49) and France (1648–53) that tried in vain to reverse the trend toward absolute monarchy. The English Civil War resulted in the beheading of Charles I and the temporary creation of a Commonwealth, 1649–60, during which there was no king of England. Still, in the midst of these conflicts, court culture flourished.

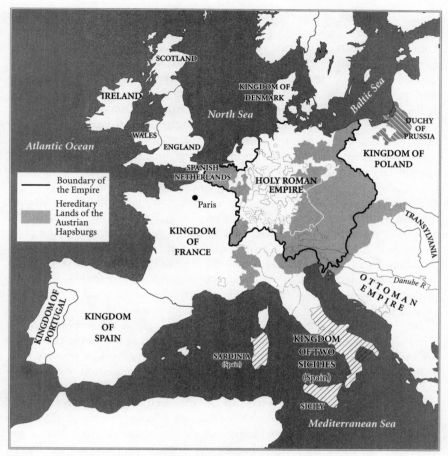

Figure 1-4. Europe at the end of the Thirty Years' War, 1648

Court Life

The court of a monarch or nobleman consisted of an extended family and a group of salaried individuals numbering from about a half dozen in the case of minor nobility to several hundred for the ruler of a large country. To these were added a larger number of long-term guests and officials with regular access to the ruler. The salaried men and women constituted what was often called the household; the household of James II of England, for example, numbered over 1,500. In addition, each member of the king's extended family normally had a separate household, which in turn was part of the larger court establishment. A household consisted not only of servants in the usual sense but also of men and women of all social classes, including sons and daughters of important noble families. About six hundred members of the household of James II were of noble birth and held administrative or honorary offices; the other nine hundred were considered servants. Members of a noble household of even moderate size might include political advisers, diplomats, a physician, scientists, writers, philosophers, poets, painters, architects, musicians, dancing instructors, ladies-in-waiting, pages, guards, cooks, waiters, cleaners, stable hands, and so on. The high-ranking and learned members of the household not only offered their professional skills to their patron but also provided company, conversation with important guests, audiences for each others' performances, and many miscellaneous services.

The noble or royal patron of the household enjoyed the fruits of the servants' talents and shared in the glory and prestige of their artistic and intellectual accomplishments. Patrons normally gave only general suggestions, for example about subject matter, to household artists and musicians but relied on expert advice when it came to choosing among available talent and styles.

A royal household and its long-term guests constituted a miniature community for which the patron provided food, housing, clothing, and entertainment. The term *court* refers primarily to this group of people but also to the place where they resided—usually a large palace together with a number of smaller buildings. To a great extent, the products of the fine arts from the seventeenth and previous centuries that we value and enjoy today—painting, sculpture, poetry, and music—were influenced by court culture and were in most cases created by and for members of noble or royal households.

Beginning in the sixteenth century and increasingly in the seventeenth, the trend among nobles was to leave their country estates in the hands of caretakers and to reside in cities or at the court of a monarch or wealthy regional lord, either as a member of the household or as a guest. The migration of the nobility to royal courts and the elevation of the monarch's relative status brought about changes in court life. Access to the monarch became subject to strict rules and controls, and the monarch increasingly became a ceremonial figure, a remote presence. Life at court brought about elaborate rules of behavior and etiquette, spelled out in printed handbooks. These guides fostered the official courtly values of education, eloquence, dignity, self-control, grace, ease (*sprezzatura*), pride, authority, glamour, elegance, idealization of women and of love, accomplishment, and dissimulation (hiding under a false appearance). We will see in the following chapters that these aristocratic court values are reflected in several Baroque musical styles.

Courts and the Arts

The rise and growth of royal courts gave new importance to the display of culture and learning. Standards of education among nobles increased markedly toward the end of the 1500s in response both to their new roles in governmental administration and to the effects of living together at court. In the course of the 1600s, the lead in cultural matters passed from the merchant class and university scholars to the class of courtiers and nobles. The ideal, classically educated "Renaissance man" gave way to the elegant noble amateur unburdened by pedantry. The cultivation of wit and personal style also offered new prominence to women in seventeenth-century court culture.

Higher levels of education brought with them more patronage of the arts and greater appreciation of artistic innovation. During the seventeenth century, European nobles supported and participated in the cutting edge of culture. Many wrote poetry and established art galleries in their homes. Among the distinguished noble painters of the period we may count Giuseppe Cesari (Cavaliere d'Arpino, 1568–1640), Diego Velazquez (1599–1660), Anthony van Dyck (1599–1641), Francisco de Zurbarán (1598–1664), Georges de la Tour (1593–1652), and Louis Le Nain (1593–1648). Many of the composers and poets who took part in the emergence of opera were aristocrats as well. Furthermore, portraits and literary character sketches of noblemen that convey individuality and personal complexity became the fashion. In the seventeenth century, more than ever before or since, the aristocracy dominated culture, the arts, and learning, by direct participation and through patronage. Because of this domination, complicated allusions and forms of argument gained favor in several artistic areas.

Indeed, display of culture and learning, as well as adherence to distinctive modes of behavior and dress, became ever more important to European nobility during the seventeenth century, as more and more of them obtained their status not by birth but as gifts from monarchs, who granted titles of nobility in order to preserve and increase their own power by rewarding their allies. This increase in the number of newly created nobles explains in part the exaggerated elegance of noble costume (Figs. 1-5 and 1-6), including elaborate wigs for men during the later part of this period (Fig. 1-7).

Figure 1-5. French nobleman ca. 1620—Jacques Callot

Figure 1-6. French noblewoman, ca. 1620—Callot

Figure 1-7. French wig,
ca. 1690

At the same time, seventeenth-century painting and literature became increasingly occupied with aristocratic themes. Also, music in many genres absorbed influences from the kinds of music conceived for extravagant court pageantry, which often used allegory to support political theories of absolutism. For example, several movements of Purcell's *Sound the Trumpet, Beat the Drum* allude to musical styles and forms typical of the allegorical ballets and operas performed at the French royal court, where James II had resided from 1646 to 1656. Court pageantry also influenced the lives of nobles, which became increasingly theatrical—mannered, exaggerated, and artificial. In this way, products of artistic culture, which were used as propaganda to establish and support monarchical authority and legitimacy, permeated the lives of seventeenth-century nobles as never before or since.

Because of the nobles' wealth, power, education, and refinement, their large numbers at courts, and their desire for esteem and deference, their taste dominated the arts in the seventeenth century, and European culture had a much more aristocratic character by the end of the seventeenth century than it had during the late sixteenth.

The end of the seventeenth century marked the high point in the grandeur of court life in Europe. Beginning about 1700, the importance of courts and their culture began a rapid decline. Sustained challenges to the legitimacy of monarchs and nobles emerged with the Enlightenment of the early eighteenth century. The most progressive artistic styles soon lost their distinctively aristocratic character and increasingly reflected middle-class values and sensibilities, signaling the end of the Baroque era.

RELIGION

The religious strife that dethroned James II pitted Protestants against Catholics. This conflict, which originated in the early sixteenth century, reached its climax in the seventeenth. The arts in the Baroque era were as much involved in religious discord as they were in the struggle to maintain absolute monarchy.

Until the early sixteenth century, the overwhelming majority of western Europe's people were of the Catholic religion. The Jews formed the major non-Christian group, accounting for a little over 1 percent of the population. (Eastern Europe, where the Hussite, Orthodox, and Muslim religions held sway, does not figure prominently in the history of European art music in the seventeenth century.) This relatively simple picture became much more complicated as a result of the Reform movements of the sixteenth century, when the seeds were sown for the religious strife that deeply affected sacred and even secular music as well as the other arts in the Baroque period.

Catholicism

At the beginning of the sixteenth century, virtually all Christians in western Europe recognized the ultimate religious authority of the pope as Christ's representative on earth and spiritual heir of the apostle Peter. The western Christian world was divided into archdioceses headed by archbishops. Archdioceses were divided into dioceses, each roughly the size of a county and administered by a bishop, whose church was designated a cathedral. Each diocese was in turn divided into neighborhood parishes, each administered by a priest. Parallel to this structure and outside the jurisdiction of the bishops were numerous orders of monks and nuns with their monasteries and convents, each order governed by its own administrative hierarchy under direct papal authority. In addition to cathedrals, parish churches, and monastic churches, there were a variety of independently endowed or privately supported churches belonging to monarchs, noble families, lay confraternities, educational institutions, hospitals, civic governments, and other groups. As a consequence, the historic city centers in Italy, for example, might accommodate two or three Catholic churches in each block.

Catholics viewed their church as the institution in which God approaches humanity through grace and humanity approaches God through worship. Through grace they hoped for salvation, without which they would be condemned for their sins. They believed that the salvation offered by the incarnation and crucifixion of Christ became actual through faith, good works, and the seven sacraments administered by priests: baptism, confirmation, Eucharist (communion), penance, extreme unction, holy orders, and matrimony. Worship and the administration of the sacraments (except penance and extreme unction) took place in organized church services whose forms and content made up the Catholic liturgy, which was controlled and prescribed by the church hierarchy. The major daily Catholic church services consisted of the Mass and the Divine Office. Although the Mass, which culminates in holy communion, could be celebrated on any day, most of the faithful attended Mass only on Sundays and on important church holidays such as Christmas, Easter, and days dedicated to the commemoration of certain saints. The Divine Office consisted of a daily series of eight church services called hours: Matins, Lauds, Prime, Terce, Sext, None, Vespers, and Compline. Most of these were celebrated only by monks; typical church members attended only Vespers and Compline on the eve of a Sunday or holiday. Although sermons were preached in Catholic churches, they did not constitute a regular part of the liturgical services, which were conducted in Latin.

Catholicism was closely allied with monarchy for several reasons. The Catholic hierarchy of pope, cardinals, archbishops, bishops, and priests was modeled on that of feudal government. Catholic church leaders were recruited largely from the ranks of the nobility. Also, instead of always praying directly to God, Catholics frequently appealed for intercession to the Blessed Virgin and the saints, just as they appealed to lesser nobles for recommendations to greater lords. Thus, monarchy was seen as a reflection of the heavenly realm, and its acceptance was thought to be necessary for an individual's salvation. Some Catholic theologians even argued that the monarch served as an intermediary between his subjects and Christ, that the king's person and authority were sacred, and that his power derived from God and was therefore absolute. Indeed, the Catholic and English monarchs of Europe, particularly during the Baroque era, used religious ceremony and symbolism as powerful tools of persuasion in their continuous quest for ever more far-reaching authority.

Lutheranism

The first significant challenge to the Roman Catholic Church came from Martin Luther (1483–1546). As an Augustinian friar, Luther had been sent by his order in 1511 to Rome, where he became disillusioned by the worldly behavior of Roman prelates. He was most upset by the sale of indulgences, which enabled wealthy people to avoid the consequences of their sins by donating money to the Church. Luther nailed a document to the door of the Wittenberg Cathedral in 1517, detailing ninety-five theological theses questioning the authority of the pope. His bold act led to excommunication in 1520 and subsequent imprisonment. But Luther's ideas spread; in time, some noblemen and entire monasteries were won ever. Regional princes tended to embrace Lutheranism—after all, it reduced the authority of the Church and allowed them to confiscate monastic lands—and German and Scandinavian townspeople and peasants were drawn to it because it appealed to middle- and working-class values.

Lutherans believed that the key to salvation was to be born again by embracing the Gospel, that is, the account of Christ's life and teaching found in the New Testament, and the redemption from sin that it offers through the office of the Holy Spirit. This pathway was supposed to produce a series of

strong emotions beginning with remorse and ending in joy. Thus, it was crucial for Lutherans to read the Bible and to hear it explained in their own language. For the same reason, the emotional appeal of preaching and of
inspirational music played an important role in their church services.
Seventeenth-century Lutherans honored Martin Luther's words, "True
preaching is the living voice of the Gospel, and likewise true music is the living voice of the Gospel: the [musical] notes make the text come alive" (*Tis-
chreden*, no. 2545b).

The sacraments held less importance for Lutherans. Neither did the Lutherans have monks, nuns, monasteries, or convents. Because they believed in the
heavenly dominion over all earthly things and aspects of life, Lutherans rejected
the Catholic dualism between the spiritual and the worldly. Without central
authority, they maintained no standardized liturgy, only a tendency to conform
to local traditions. During the seventeenth century Lutheran theology was not
completely formalized but only partially articulated in response to specific situations. Whether a Lutheran preacher's sermons were acceptable was determined by the congregation of born-again believers.

Other Protestant Groups

Luther was followed by several other religious reformers during the sixteenth
century. The most influential among them was John Calvin (1509–1564). In
1541 Calvin was invited to assume the religious leadership of Geneva, Switzerland, which had become officially Protestant in exchange for military aid from
the city of Bern. In the course of the sixteenth century, Calvinism gave rise to
the Puritan religion in England, the Presbyterian Church in Scotland and the
New World, the Huguenots in France, the Reformed Church in the Netherlands, and the Calvinist Church in parts of Germany.

Calvinists shared many Lutheran beliefs, but they thought that since an individual's salvation was predetermined by God, human activity could not change
a person's fate. But people destined for salvation showed it by their rigorous
Christian deportment. Calvinists nevertheless dedicated themselves to a patient
struggle to bring the present world under God's law. These factors in combination with the considerable authority given to their clergy led many Calvinist
groups into forms of Puritanism, which rejected luxury, worldly behavior, religious images, and elaborate forms of church music.

The Church of England, although created under the influence of the
Lutheran Reformation, became independent of Rome more for political than
religious reasons. When King Henry VIII could not persuade Pope Clement
VII to annul his marriage to Catherine of Aragon, he nullified the pope's
authority over the English clergy and in 1534 established the Church of England, with the monarch as its head. English monasteries were suppressed, their
lands were taken by the king, and church services were held in English rather
than Latin. However, the Church of England maintained many aspects of the
Catholic religion, such as the priesthood and the forms of worship.

The Church of England contained both a Protestant-leaning wing, which attracted commoners of a parliamentarian political persuasion, and a more orthodox contingent associated with the nobility and royalist politics. Only extreme English Protestants—Puritans, Presbyterians, Congregationalists, Baptists, and Quakers—favored the foundation of separate churches. In the seventeenth century, these Protestant Separatists did not favor the use of elaborate music in church services, so we will hear little of them in the chapters that follow.

The Counter-Reformation

Beginning in the second half of the sixteenth century, the Roman Catholic Church mustered considerable resources to combat the spread of the Protestant Reformation. The principal impulse to this Catholic Reformation, or Counter-Reformation, came from the Council of Trent (1545–63). The Council reaffirmed certain Catholic doctrines and drew sharp distinctions between them and the beliefs of Protestants. It also provided for a renewed emphasis on teaching and preaching, as opposed to ceremony and ritual. Several new orders of priests were commissioned or created to carry out these new educational and inspirational objectives: the Theatines (founded in 1524); the Society of Jesus, or Jesuits (founded in 1540); the Fathers of the Oratory of Saint Phillip Neri, or Oratorians (recognized in 1612); and the Congregation of the Oratory of Jesus and Mary Immaculate (founded in 1613), to name the most important. All of these orders, but especially the Jesuits and the Oratorians, used several related means of instruction—rhetorically embellished preaching, drama and pageantry, the newer dramatic styles of music, and the visual arts—to communicate their message, especially to the young and to the nobility. Although the Jesuits were heavily involved in missionary work in the New World, east Asia, the western Pacific, and elsewhere, they used the arts to maintain and strengthen the faith of populations that were already Catholic, while meeting the Protestant challenge through emotionally charged spiritual renewal. Meanwhile, the Lutherans were engaged in parallel efforts on behalf of their denomination. These competing efforts in the seventeenth century account, in no small measure, for the vehement and persuasive aspects of the arts, especially the visual arts and music, during the Baroque era.

Unfortunately, competition and conflict between the Catholic and Lutheran religions was not confined to the arts. The seventeenth century saw the greatest concentration of wars over religion of any period in European history. The Thirty Years' War (1618–48) was merely the largest and most devastating. The English Civil War (1642–49) was as much about religion as about politics. Although the major religious wars in France took place earlier (1562–98, culminating in the War of the Three Henrys), Protestants remained a viable force there until the defeat of the Huguenots at the siege of La Rochelle in 1628. Half a century later, the French revoked the Edict of Nantes, depriving French Protestants of religious and civil liberty and causing their mass emigration.

Meanwhile, the Holy Roman Emperor in Vienna—often in alliance with other major Catholic monarchs—carried on a fundamentally religious war against the Islamic Ottoman Turks to the east that lasted nearly the entire seventeenth century. It seems almost fitting that one of the last armed religious conflicts in Europe took place toward the end of the Baroque era: the Catholic grandson of Charles II, Charles Edward, called Bonnie Prince Charlie, landed with a tiny force of about a dozen men on the west coast of Scotland in July 1745 and raised the Highlands in revolt. He advanced as far as Derby, England, before his defeat on April 16, 1746, after which he escaped to France.

On top of the political dislocations of emerging absolutism, incessant religious conflict, and almost perpetual war, seventeenth-century Europeans experienced major economic depressions, terrible famines, outbreaks of plague, violent extremes of weather, and such social pathologies as witch hunting and other forms of persecuting women. It was a century of crisis and violent transition. This atmosphere of crisis found its way into the exaggerated expression, radical experimentation, and exhortative or rhetorical character that music and the other arts frequently took on during the Baroque era.

THE RHETORIC OF THE ARTS

To the educated European of the seventeenth century, the word *rhetoric* meant the systematic study of persuasive speaking and writing based on outlines, principles, and nomenclature inherited from ancient Roman civilization, mostly through the writings of Cicero and Quintilian, which were widely read, taught, and imitated during the 1600s. By extension, the word *rhetoric* could also refer to the art of communication, the techniques of persuasion, and the products of writers, orators, preachers, lawyers, and others.

Rhetoric was one of the core subjects taught in seventeenth-century schools to prepare of noble youths for careers as courtiers, diplomats, bureaucrats, lawyers, and preachers. In addition to its practical value, knowledge of rhetoric could provide undeniable prestige to non-nobles because of its association with the aristocracy. This prestige, along with natural affinities and inherent similarities between rhetorical language and artistic expression, led many writers on painting, sculpture, architecture, and music to employ the terms and concepts of rhetoric in discussing both verbal and nonverbal arts. They realized that any of the arts could be used as a means of persuasion through a calculated appeal to the emotions of audiences.

The expression *rhetoric of the arts*, if not actually used during the seventeenth century, would have been easily understood by literate people of the time. Writings that describe and explain music and the visual arts in terms of rhetorical lore abounded in the Baroque era. This use of rhetoric is a powerful indication of how educated people of that time thought about the arts and how the arts were influenced by the turbulent events that surrounded monarchy and religion. A clear way to summarize this body of thought is to look at what the standard rhetoric books of the period say about the activities of the orator, the typical parts of an oration, and the most important ways of projecting meaning, argument, and emotion, and to explain how writers of that time found parallels in the activities of poets, artists, and composers.

"All the activity and ability of an orator falls into five divisions.... He must first hit upon what to say; then manage and marshal his discoveries, not merely in orderly fashion, but with a discriminating eye for the exact weight, as it were, of each argument; next go on to array them in the adornments of style; after that keep them guarded in his memory; and in the end deliver them with effect and charm." These words of Cicero from the first century BC were repeated and explained by innumerable writers down the centuries following and were traditionally reduced to these five activities of the orator:

1. Invention
2. Disposition (or Arrangement)
3. Elocution (or Style)
4. Memory
5. Delivery

Invention in classical rhetoric means deciding on the content of the speech, the arguments and evidence to be presented, the topics to be covered, and the strategies and tactics to be employed. Rhetorical invention relied heavily on the so-called topics, or *topoi*, conventional frameworks into which content was molded. For example, Aristotle's *Rhetoric* mentions as *topoi* "what can and cannot happen; what has and has not happened; what will or will not happen." Cicero begins his list of sixteen basic topics with "Argument from definition; Argument from partition; Argument based on etymology."

For a composer, invention meant deciding on the basic purposes, features, and motives of a work before planning its form or actually composing. For Purcell, the act of invention that preceded the composition of *Sound the Trumpet, Beat the Drum* (W. 29) would have included deciding on the number and types of the movements, choosing the overall prevalence of minor modes, selecting the specific references to national styles and courtly dances, settling on the instrumentation (including the lack of trumpet and drum), planning the keys, meters, and tempos of all the movements, and determining any other features that could contribute to the prevailing expression of emotions or to the communication of meaning.

Disposition (or arrangement) for the orator meant organizing the speech using all or some parts of a traditional design. Although treatises differ on the number of these parts, a common scheme of rhetorical Disposition divides the oration into these seven parts:

Exhortation (*Exordium*)—attracts the audience's attention and favorably disposes it to listen; for example, "Friends, Romans, and countrymen, lend me your ears!"

Narration (*Narratio*)—sets forth the facts.

Exposition (*Explicatio*)—defines the terms and opens the issues to be proved.

Proposition (*Partitio*)—clarifies the points at issue and states exactly what is to be proved.

Amplification (*Amplificatio*)—sets forth the arguments for and against and offers proof.

Refutation (*Refutatio*)—refutes opponents' arguments and restates the accepted conclusions.

Conclusion (*Peroratio*)—sums up arguments and makes a final appeal to the emotions of the audience.

Various shorter schemes were proposed from time to time, one by Torquato Tasso, the greatest Italian poet of the later sixteenth century:

Exhortation (*Exordium*)—introduction, during which the poet proposes and defines the state of things with language that "will capture the attention of the reader and his expectation."

Narration (*Narratio*)—where tension is built up.

Confirmation or Reversal (*Confirmatio* or *Rivolgimento*)—a change from good to ill or from ill to good fortune.

Conclusion (*Peroratio*)—the ending, which marks the completion of the action.

About the exhortation, Tasso writes, "The beginning of poems should be full of grandeur, magnificence and splendor, like the facade of palaces." There are seventeenth-century writers who discuss the design of buildings, the layout of series of painted scenes, or even the composition of individual paintings as if the viewer's experience should be controlled and planned by the artist or architect according to rhetorical principles. Several Baroque writers explain the exhortation of a speech by comparing its function to that of a musical prelude or introduction.

Most rhetorical disposition schemes include the functions of introduction, presentation, elaboration, contrast or conflict, recapitulation, and conclusion— a basic scheme that could easily be applied to many musical forms. The earliest writer to do so was Joachim Burmeister, in his *Musica poetica* of 1606. Burmeister's plan for the rhetorical disposition of a musical composition was simple:

Exhortation (*Exordium*)—the portion of the composition up to the first major cadence, in which each voice enters with the subject being imitated, or, at least, in which the principal expressive character of the work is established.

Body of the Composition (*Corpus Carminis*)—the central portion of the composition, consisting of several periods, in which, "by means of various rhetorical arguments, the text is insinuated into the souls [of the listeners] in order that its meaning be better understood and considered." The *Corpus Carminis* might contain further subdivisions, such as a *Narratio*, *Explicatio*, *Partitio*, *Amplificatio*, and *Refutatio*.

Conclusion—the final cadence, sometimes with a "supplement," in which additional melodic activity lets the emotions "more clearly penetrate into the souls of the listeners."

The most elaborate comparison of musical form with rhetorical disposition is found toward the end of the Baroque era in *Der vollkommene Capellmeister* ("The Complete Music Director") of 1739 by Johann Mattheson.

Elocution (or Style) included the choice among the Plain Style, Middle Style, or Grand Style, but especially relied on the use of *rhetorical figures*, which give a speaker's points their emotional coloring and render them memorable. Two examples of rhetorical figures are *antithesis* and *parenthesis*.

Antithesis, mentioned in virtually all treatises from Quintilian's onward, meant "the conjoining of contrasting ideas." In Athanasius Kircher's *Musurgia Universalis* of 1650, it is called "a musical passage in which we express opposing affections, as [the composer] Giacomo Carrissimi contrasted Heraclitus's laughing with Democritus's weeping." In Purcell's *Now Does the Glorious Day Appear*, musical antithesis is created when the alto's flowing melisma to the words "By beauteous softness mix'd" is followed immediately by energetic dotted rhythms that syllabically set the continuation of the text, "with majesty an empire over ev'ry heart she gains."

Parenthesis, according to Quintilian, "occurs when the flow of the oration is interrupted in the middle by another thought." Mattheson writes that when a parenthesis in a text is set to music, "the melody should drop to the point of sounding like another voice." This is exactly what Purcell does in *Now Does the Glorious Day Appear* at the words "Our dear Religion (with our Law's defence)/ to God her zeal to man benevolence / must her above all former monarchs raise."

In musical treatises of the Baroque era we find scores of rhetorical figures discussed, with musical examples supplied. It is true that in some cases the name of a rhetorical figure is simply assigned to a feature of harmony or counterpoint for no apparent reason. But in most instances, we find a conventional pattern of repetition, similarity, contrast, digression, recurrence, or progression in the text mirrored faithfully by the composer. Often, a rhetorical figure not actually present in the poetic text is created by the composer, who might, for example, insert a sudden and unexpected silence in the middle of a sentence. Purcell uses this figure, called *aposiopesis*, in *Sound the Trumpet, Beat the Drum* at the words "To Caesar [silence] all hail, [silence] all hail [silence] to Caesar unequaled in arms."

In some cases, a musical pattern is so similar to a verbal pattern and is so strongly associated with it that it can retain its identity even in textless instrumental music; the *gradatio*, or *climax* (as in "I came, I saw, I conquered"), for example, became so closely associated with a rising melodic sequence that the sequence alone, without any text, could have a rhetorical function. Appendix A contains a list of rhetorical figures often mirrored or created by Baroque composers.

Memory relates to performance rather than to composition, so we will pass over it here and proceed to delivery.

Delivery of a spoken text requires the effective use of inflection, selective accentuation, and pacing. The analogies to the melodic contours, accents, and rhythms of vocal music are so obvious that they received little commentary until the end of the Baroque period. On the other hand, some seventeenth-century Spanish Jesuits used musical notation to teach priests how to deliver impassioned sermons. Despite a lack of a precise vocabulary to describe it, musical control of delivery pervades Baroque music. All recitative, for example, controls rhetorical delivery in order to project the meaning and passions of the text. We can see, in Example 1-1, from Purcell's *Sound the Trumpet, Beat the Drum*, how the composer selectively emphasizes the words "morning" and "British," rather than "star" and "sphere," through melodic leaps, dissonance, certain rhythms, and metrical downbeats, and how the incompleteness of this dependent clause is made clear by the upward melodic inflection at its end.

Example 1-1. Purcell, *Sound the Trumpet, Beat the Drum*, "While Caesar, like the morning star"

Thus, Baroque composers of vocal music could help communicate the meaning and emotions of the text through interpretive declamation in the act of delivery. They could intensify its force with rhetorical figures in the act of elocution. Or they could summarize its prevailing passions, imagery, or conceits by making large-scale strategic choices in the act of invention. All three approaches to musical-rhetorical interpretation of text can be found in the Baroque era, but, as we will see in the following chapters, composers in the early part of the period, ca. 1600–1630, tended to concentrate on delivery. In the middle of the period, ca. 1630–70, their focus turned more toward elocution, whereas in the later part, ca. 1670–1750, we find a noticeable trend toward summarizing textual meaning in the act of musical invention.

In this chapter, we have seen how composers, artists, poets, and commentators in the Baroque era conceived of the arts in terms of classical rhetoric. It has been suggested that this rhetorical conception of the arts, which was certainly concentrated in that era although not unique to it, reflects the fact that the arts were frequently used as a means of persuasion and inspiration in a period of cultural, social, political, economic, and religious conflict, change, and turbulence. This connection between the rhetorical conception of the arts and its uses helps explain the dominant position of the nobility and its monarchical ideology in seventeenth-century culture. These factors, rather than any particular set of stylistic criteria, are what define the Baroque era in music and the other arts.

In the following chapter, these ideas will be illustrated concretely as we see how opera—the new, defining genre of the era—emerged in the context of an early absolutist cultural program in Florence, ca. 1600.

BIBLIOGRAPHICAL NOTES

Monarchy and Nobility

The most useful study is Jonathan Deward, *The European Nobility, 1400–1800* (Cambridge: Cambridge University Press, 1996). Another book with a more theoretical approach is Paul Kléber Monod, *The Power of Kings: Monarchy and Religion in Europe, 1589–1715* (New Haven: Yale University Press, 1999). More factual detail but less sweeping interpretation can be found in Michael Laccohee Bush, *Noble Privilege* (Manchester: Manchester University Press, 1983). Two very useful collections of specialized essays are Ronald G. Asch and Adolf M. Birke, eds., *Princes, Patronage, and the Nobility: The Court at the Beginning of the Modern Age, c. 1450–1650* (Oxford: Oxford University Press, 1991), and H. M. Scott, ed., *The European Nobilities in the Seventeenth and Eighteenth Centuries*, I, *Western Europe* (London: Longman, 1995). Specific detail about the Holy Roman Empire has been drawn from Charles W. Ingrao, *The Habsburg Monarchy, 1618–1815* (Cambridge: Cambridge University Press, 1994). Details concerning King James II of England are found in Michael Mullett, *James II and English Politics, 1678–1688* (London: Routledge, 1994). For the history and interpretation of Whitehall Palace and its decorations, see Roy Strong, *Britannia Triumphans: Inigo Jones, Rubens, and Whitehall Palace* (London: Thames and Hudson, 1980). Information about Purcell's odes and welcome songs can be found in Peter Holman, *Henry Purcell* (Oxford: Oxford University Press, 1994), and Rosamond McGuinness, *English Court Odes, 1660–1820* (Oxford: Oxford University Press, 1971).

Religion

Reliable and disinterested overviews of the history and beliefs of the religions mentioned in this chapter can be found in the *Encyclopaedia of Religion and Ethics*, ed. James Hastings (New York: Scribner, 1908–27), 12 vols.; and in the *Encyclopedia of Religion*, ed. Mircea Eliade (New York: Macmillan, 1987). More recent, specialized articles on the Protestant Reformation are found in Pierre Chaunu, ed., *The Reformation* (New York: St. Martin's Press, 1986); and the *Oxford Encyclopedia of the Reformation*, ed. Hans J. Hillerbrand (New York: Oxford University Press, 1996). Useful detail about the Catholic Counter-Reformation is contained in Martin D. W. Jones, *The Counter-Reformation: Religion and Society in Early Modern Europe* (Cambridge: Cambridge University Press, 1995).

The Rhetoric of the Arts

A seminal and provocative treatment of this subject is Gerard LeCoat, *The Rhetoric of the Arts, 1550–1650*, European University Papers, Series XVIII: Comparative Literature, Vol. 3 (Bern: Lang, 1975). A useful and brief summary of rhetorical nomenclature is Richard A. Lanham, *A Handlist of Rhetorical Terms* (Berkeley and Los Angeles: University of California Press, 1969). The idea that the arts often had a distinctly political purpose in the seventeenth century is developed by Roy Strong, *Art and Power: Renaissance Festivals, 1450–1650* (Berkeley and Los Angeles: University of California Press, 1984). The theory that musical spectacle can be considered as ritual sacrifice in a cult of monarchy is advanced by Kristiaan P. Aercke, *Gods of Play: Baroque Festive Performances as Rhetorical Discourse* (Albany: State University of New York Press, 1994). A useful survey of Baroque music treatises that pursue analogies between music and rhetoric is Dietrich Bartel, *Musica Poetica: Musical-Rhetorical Figures in German Baroque Music* (Lincoln: University of Nebraska Press, 1997).

CHAPTER 2

The Birth of Opera, Monody, and the Concerted Madrigal

COURT CULTURE, POLITICS, AND SPECTACLE IN FLORENCE

Every Medici family wedding since the beginning of their reign as grand dukes in 1537 had been celebrated with elaborate musical pageantry, almost all of it based on themes from ancient Greek mythology, supporting through allegory a contemporary political myth: that the Medici were not recent non-noble usurpers of power (the reality) but a noble clan with an ancient right to rule (the myth). The myth foretold that their dynasty would usher in a new golden age, as in Greek mythology, a renewal symbolized by the rediscovery of the arts, literature, and philosophy of ancient Greece under the patronage of their founding fathers (actually distant relatives), Cosimo and Lorenzo the Magnificent, leading citizens in the fifteenth century, who in reality were never official rulers of Florence.

In order to foster this political mythology, Grand Duke Cosimo I organized an Academy of Art (1563) to design and execute paintings, sculptures, and temporary architectural structures based on favored themes of mythological allegory. Cosimo I earlier (1541) had deputized the Florentine Academy to invent the conceits, scripts, and poetry for his public pageants. In many cases, research into the public celebrations of ancient Greece and Rome was carried out by the grand duke's courtiers in preparation for each of his spectacles.

Intermedi

The most elaborate and artistically adventurous of these Medici spectacles were the *intermedi* performed regularly for important state occasions since Cosimo's marriage in 1539. These intermedi were performed between the acts of spoken plays, but within them all the words were sung. Actually, the music in the intermedi was not really continuous, the sung words did not actually form extended dialogue, and there were hardly any plots. Instead, an intermedio was something of a living picture, static or nearly so, of an episode drawn from mythology. The vocal music, often sung by a solo voice accompanied by chordal instruments, usually added explanatory commentary.

Intermedi of particular importance were performed between the acts of the play *La pellegrina* ("The Pilgrim Woman") produced to celebrate the marriage of the second Medici Grand Duke, Ferdinando I, and Cristina of Lorraine in 1589. Each of these six interludes depicts an ancient myth concerning the power of music:

1. Dorian Harmony sings an ornate solo, which is answered by the Fates, Sirens, and Planets, all praising the wedding couple, whose reign will usher in a new Golden Age foretokened by an appearance of the goddess Astrea.
2. The Pierides claim to sing better than Arion and Orpheus, but the Muses claim to please the Nymphs who, as judges, decide in favor of the Muses, while the Pierides are changed into magpies.
3. Apollo's victory over the Serpent Python is danced in pantomime and narrated by a chorus.
4. A prophecy of the New Golden Age is sung by a Sorceress descending on a flying chariot, after which the Demons of Envy and Wrath are banished forever to the underworld (Fig. 2-1).
5. Aphrodite and her nymphs sing of the wedding couple and the coming Golden Age. A ship appears, carrying the famous singer Arion (Fig. 2-2), who leaps overboard in the face of a mutiny. The Sirens believe he is drowned, but Arion reappears, riding on the back of a dolphin.

Figure 2-1. *La pelligrina* (Florence, 1589), Intermedio 4

Figure 2-2. Jacopo Peri as Arion in
La pelligrina (Florence, 1589),
Intermedio 5

6. A group of gods, Graces, Muses, Cupids, and the personification of Harmony and Rhythm descend on clouds and are welcomed by the nymphs
and shepherds of Tuscany. The heavenly visitors proclaim that the reign of
Ferdinando and Cristina will usher in a new Golden Age, in token of which
they bring the gift of music and dance, presumably of the ancient kind.

Several of these musical numbers were composed by Emilio de' Cavalieri, (ca.
1550–1602) including the ornate solo "Godi turba mortal" sung by the God
of Love in the sixth intermedio. Giulio Caccini (1551–1618) contributed the
song of the Sorceress in Intermedio 4, "Io che dal ciel cader farei," which was
sung by his wife, Lucia. And Arion's solo in the fifth intermedio was composed and performed by Jacopo Peri (1561–1633), whose costume is shown
in Figure 2-2. All three composers were members of the grand-ducal court
household of Ferdinando I.

The allegorical meaning of the 1589 intermedi is that the reign of Ferdinando and Cristina will usher in a new Golden Age symbolized by a revival of
the miraculous powers of ancient music, which produce victory for the protagonists of each intermedio. Music and the other arts were employed as vehicles
and symbols contributing to the political rhetoric of Medici Florence. The
novelty of these productions, the rare skill of the singers, and the astonishing
scenic effects contributed to the message directed at the courtiers and important visitors that always formed the audiences for such spectacles: Medici Florence had a rich history, had made significant contributions to European
culture, was in the process of political resurgence, could muster and coordinate
the most advanced activities in several arts, and had the discernment and
resources to employ the very best performers and designers available.

The Camerata

The inventor of the scenarios for the 1589 intermedi was the noble Florentine courtier Giovanni Bardi (1534–1612), who for more than fifteen years had sponsored and led a group of intellectuals and musicians—known as the Camerata—in research, discussion, and experimentation aimed at learning about ancient Greek music, the sources of its legendary power to move the emotions, and how it was deployed in the performance of Greek tragedies. Thus, the activities of this unofficial Camerata were parallel to those of the official Academy of Art and the Florentine Academy.

Much of what we know about the discussions of Bardi's Camerata comes from letters written to the group from Rome by the Florentine humanist Girolamo Mei (1519–1594) during the 1570s and from a book, *Dialogo della musica antica, et della moderna* ("Dialogue of Ancient and Modern Music"), published in 1581 by the noble Florentine musician Vincenzo Galilei (ca. 1520–1591), father of the famous astronomer Galileo Galilei. The principal conclusions of Mei and Galilei were that (1) ancient Greek vocal music was always a single melody; (2) its rhythms were based on those of its words; (3) it was confined to a narrow range—low, middle, or high—which helped determine its expressive character; (4) with this kind of music the ancient Greeks sang their tragedies throughout; and (5) the polyphonic music of the modern world cannot achieve the marvelous effects of ancient music because its words are sung simultaneously in all registers and with different rhythms and melodic contours by several voices that cancel each other's expressive effects. Galilei also ridicules musical pictorialism—for example, using rapid notes to set the words "to flee" or "to fly," as often happens in earlier polyphonic madrigals. He even objects to using dissonances to set a line of text like "Bitter heart and savage, cruel will." Instead he maintains that the expressive power of music comes from its ability to use pitch and rhythm to imitate the precise speech patterns, intonations, accents, and inflections that actors use to distinguish the diverse characters in a drama, their relations with other characters, and their emotional state at each moment. Galilei claims that he put these theories into practice in two works—a set of lamentations and responses for Holy Week and the lament of Count Ugolino from Dante's *Inferno*—which were performed for the Camerata in 1582. Neither survives, however.

Giulio Caccini, in the Preface to his publication *Le nuove musiche* (Florence 1602), gives Bardi's Camerata credit for encouraging him to fashion a kind of music that "conformed to that manner so lauded by Plato and other philosophers (who declared that music is naught but speech, with rhythm and pitch following it, not vice versa) with the aim that it enter into the minds of men and have those wonderful effects admired by the great writers [of antiquity]."[1] Caccini calls this kind of music *in armonia favellare* ("speaking in [musical] harmony"), and claims that it was the "very style" that he had "employed for the

---

[1]Preface to *Le nuove musiche* (Florence, 1602).

fables performed in song at Florence." Those "fables performed in song" were *La Dafne* (1597–98), *L'Euridice* (1600), and *Il rapimento di Cefalo* (1600), which are today called the first operas. The style to which Caccini refers was later called recitative.

It might be tempting to conclude from this that opera and recitative were invented by the Florentine Camerata in their attempt to recreate the music and drama of Greek antiquity, but that would be incorrect. It would be better to consider their discussions and experiments contributing factors rather than pre-cipitating causes. After all, the Camerata never staged an opera nor, as far as we know, ever considered doing so. Its activities did not extend beyond 1589. The earliest operas were conceived as pastoral tragicomedy, a type of spoken drama with no special connection to Florence. And the recitative styles of Peri and Caccini, as we shall see, were developed out of recitational "aria" formulas whose history can be traced back more than a century. Vincenzo Galilei actually recommended traditional "aria" formulas as models for this new type of singing. Furthermore, Jacopo Peri, the principal composer of *La Dafne* and *L'Euridice*, was too young to have played any role in the Camerata. His recitative style con-tinued a development begun well before Caccini composed his earliest works.

THE FIRST OPERAS

After Giovanni Bardi was transferred to a diplomatic post in Rome in 1592, another group of poets and musicians replaced his Camerata in Florence. Its patron was Jacopo Corsi (1561–1602), a noble courtier, wealthy silk merchant, and amateur composer. Although Camerata stalwarts Giulio Caccini and Vin-cenzo Galilei were part of Corsi's group, its central figures were younger men—Jacopo Peri and the aristocratic poet Ottavio Rinuccini (1562–1621). Corsi's group did not discuss Greek music or philosophy but was oriented toward producing musical stage works. An early experiment of theirs was enti-tled *La Dafne*, on a libretto by Rinuccini. This was the first entirely sung stage work with a plot divided into scenes. It underwent development from 1594 to 1598, at first with music by Corsi himself, then with settings by both Caccini and Peri, until the final version, mostly by Peri, was privately performed during carnival of 1598 and repeated for the grand-ducal court several times after that. Although only six fragments of *La Dafne* survive, they are enough to show that the work included at least two types of recitative.

After the success of *La Dafne*, in 1600, Corsi offered the grand duke a more extended work, *L'Euridice*, again on a libretto by Rinuccini. It survives in two complete settings by Peri and Caccini. At the first performance, October 6, 1600, about 75 percent of the music was by Peri, while the rest was by Caccini. Another opera, mostly by Caccini, *Il rapimento di Cefalo*, was performed in Florence a few days after *L'Euridice*, but only a half dozen of its numbers survive today.

L'Euridice was performed as part of an elaborate celebration with profound importance for the political future of Tuscany—the marriage of the grand duke's daughter, Maria de' Medici, and Henry IV, king of France. At this time, Spain ruled parts of the Italian peninsula both north and south of Tuscany, and it had a long-standing claim to Tuscany itself, which it enforced by maintaining military bases in the southwestern part of the grand duchy. The Medici grand dukes of Tuscany maintained their relative independence through bribery, appeasement, and, when possible, counterpoising alliances, in this case with France, which was almost continuously at war with Spain at this time. Thus, the Florentine wedding of 1600 between Maria de' Medici and Henry IV of France was first and foremost aimed at preserving the independence of Tuscany from Spain by gaining an alliance with France.

As a drama, *L'Euridice* belongs to the tradition of the pastoral play, or more precisely, the subgenre of the pastoral tragicomedy, since its characters are the noble shepherds, shepherdesses, nymphs, gods, and demi-gods of ancient Greek myths. The plot is serious, but the story ends happily:

I. Nymphs and shepherds celebrate the wedding of Orfeo and Euridice.

II. Orfeo expresses his contentment but is interrupted by Dafne, who brings news of Euridice's death by snake bite. Orfeo vows to join his bride in the underworld.

III. Arcetro recounts that, as Orfeo lay weeping, Venus, goddess of love, carried him off in her chariot.

IV. Venus leaves Orfeo at the gates of the underworld, exhorting him to win back Euridice through the power of his singing. Orfeo succeeds in charming Pluto, god of the underworld, who agrees to restore Eurdice to the living.

V. Orfeo and Euridice return to the pastoral scene of the opera's beginning amid rejoicing.

The novelty of *L'Euridice* was that instead of using spoken dialogue to link its songs and choruses, as in earlier pastorales, it was entirely sung.

The style of singing that replaced spoken dialogue was given the name *stile recitativo* forty years later by the Florentine courtier Giovanni Battista Doni (1595–1647). From Doni's term comes the English word *recitative*. Doni distinguishes three types of recitative: (1) recitative style proper, or narrative style, (2) expressive style, and (3) special recitative.[2] It is narrative style that Peri and Caccini generally use for dialogue, and as an example of it, Doni cites the passage in Peri's *L'Euridice* in which Dafne reports the death of Euridice (A. 1).

The characteristics of the **narrative style** illustrated in Dafne's report are:

• syllabic text setting without decorative melismas,
• abundant use of pitch repetition (monotone recitation),
• usually a rather narrow vocal range within phrases,

[2] Giovanni Battista Doni, *Annotazioni sopra il compendio de' generi e de' modi della musica* (Rome: Fei, 1640), pp. 60–63.

- a lack of any memorable patterning or directional growth in rhythm or melodic contour,
- generally diatonic melody and harmony, and
- an accompaniment of chords defined by a slowly moving bass line that has no independent melodic or rhythmic activity.

In his preface to his score of *L'Euridice*, Peri claims to have composed his recitative "having in mind those inflections and accents that serve us in our grief, in our joy, and in similar states," meaning that he controls rhetorical delivery through choice of melodic contours, intervals, rhythmic durations, and accents so as to project meaning and expression much as an actor would. In addition, we know that the singer was expected to take considerable liberties with the notated rhythm, in order better to follow the cadence of dramatic speech. In the same preface, Peri says that he wanted movements of the bass line to coincide, when possible, with the principal accents of the text, and he succeeded in this example, if not perfectly. Beneath the notes of the bass line there are sometimes numbers or sharp signs that indicate the intended harmonies that must be added. Caccini referred to this kind of figured bass part as *basso continuato*, while later composers called it *basso continuo* (see the box).

The **expressive style** of recitative is similar in many ways to the narrative style, except that it uses less monotone recitation and more chromatic intervals, strong dissonances, and dramatically interpretive declamation in order to project strong emotions. A good example of the expressive style is the lament "Non piango e non sospiro," sung by Orfeo after he has heard Dafne's full report (A. 1). Peri begins this lament with slow delivery of the syllables and little inflection, suggesting Orfeo's initial shock—"I do not weep and do not sigh, oh my dear Euridice." He recovers with short, almost breathless phrases— "for to sigh, to weep, I am unable, unhappy cadaver"—using a more impassioned delivery, faster pace, strong dissonance, chromatic cross-relations, and at first a rising voice, which, however, sinks back after a brief pause for reflection. The long, sighing melodic descent that sets the words "Oh my heart, oh my hope, oh peace, oh life, oh me!" begins with a high exclamation delayed until after the beat—a syncopated accent that is a trademark of Peri's style of musical declamation. In the next phrase, Orfeo becomes argumentative as he repeats his urgent question with new emphasis—"*Who* took you from me? Who *took* you from me? *Where* have you gone?" After a long pause for reflection, his mood changes again, as with more rapid delivery of the text and eventually a more energetic bass he declares, "*Soon* you will see that, *dying*, you did not call on your *husband* in vain. I am not, *I am not* far." And then falling off in pitch and pacing: "I come, dear life, oh dear death."

Thus, in Orfeo's lament Peri does not merely reflect in his music the natural or correct inflections of the text, as a Renaissance composer might have, but he uses rhetorical delivery to interpret the text dramatically, projecting on it a series of changing emotions, which, in their range, order, and relation, form a representation of the character of Orfeo—sensitive, tender, excitable, and

BASSO CONTINUO, as a notational device, includes a written bass line above which one or more performers add chordal harmony in order to create all or part of an accompaniment. Instruction books and some fully written-out basso continuo accompaniments from the period show us that early opera composers expected plain chords, without independent parts, in the basso-continuo accompaniment of recitative. The accompanying instruments used in the first performance of *L'Euridice* were a harpsichord, a large lute, a chitarrone (a kind of lute with extra-long neck and unfretted bass strings, shown in Fig. 2-3), and a lira da gamba (an upright, bowed instrument with nine to fourteen strings, on which four-part chords could be played). In Baroque church music, the basso continuo was normally realized on an organ, and in music for several instruments or singers, a bass instrument such as viola da gamba or bassoon would often play the bass line for reinforcement, while a keyboard or fretted instrument played the bass line together with its chordal realization. Basso continuo as a notational device emerged at the end of the sixteenth century out of an earlier practice of improvising chordal harmony above the lowest-sounding part of vocal or instrumental ensemble music. A special bass part created out of the lowest-sounding ensemble parts and used for this purpose was often called a *basso seguente*. The novelty of the basso continuo parts in the music of Peri, Caccini, and Cavalieri is that the bass was not composed as a member of a contrapuntal complex of parts but as a strictly subordinated part conceived exclusively for a chordal-accompanying role. As such, it normally has much less melodic and rhythmically active than the vocal or instrumental part(s) that it accompanies.

courageous—that corresponds to and motivates his subsequent actions, propelling the plot to its conclusion. This is truly dramatic music, which is why Doni asserts that it "alone is really proper and suited for the stage."

Special recitative, according to Doni, has more musical patterns and formulas than the narrative style but is less emotional than the expressive style. He traces its origins to the musical reciting formulas, called "arias," with which Italians had sung long poems of many stanzas for over a century. Considering dramatic music of his day, Doni reports that special recitative is confined to prologues, and his example of it is the prologue to Peri's *L'Euridice* (A. 1). The text of this prologue, sung by the personification of Tragedy, consists of seven four-line stanzas, each stanza having the same rhyme scheme and each line having eleven syllables. Peri provides music for only the first stanza, but he intended that the singer, following a long-established custom, would use the same music for each successive stanza, varying the vocal line each time in order to conform as closely as possible to the correct declamation of the poetry. In special recitative, Peri uses monotone recitation, as he does in the narrative style, but there is less naturalistic inflection added to it. Each line of its poetry is marked at its end by two long notes, whether or not the meaning of the text calls for a pause in that place. In these respects, Peri's prologue resembles those recitation formulas ("arias") mentioned by Doni that survive in written form from the sixteenth and early seventeenth centuries, although they were sung even earlier.

The performance of these earlier recitational "arias" was described as resulting in a style midway between speech and song as early as the fifteenth century. And that is exactly how Peri characterizes his own recitative. It would appear that, in creating his narrative and expressive styles, Peri modified the approach used in the older recitational "arias" by making the written rhythms more flexible, the melodic contours more varied and interpretive, and the chords represented by the bass more sparse and spread out, in order that the voice "might not seem, in a certain way, to dance to the movement of the bass," as he put it. The sparseness of the chords not only helps to free the voice from the restrictions of measured rhythm but also opens the way to bold dissonance. Still, Peri seems to have kept the earlier recitational "arias" in mind when he wrote that, in his recitative, the ordinary singing voice "could in part be hastened and take an intermediate course between the suspended and slow movements of song and the swift and rapid movements of speech, and could be adapted to my purpose (as they [the ancient Greeks] adapted it in reading poems and heroic verses) approaching that other kind of speech which they [the Greeks] called 'continuata,' *a thing our moderns have already accomplished in their compositions, although perhaps for another purpose*" (emphasis added). Compare, in this regard, Peri's prologue (A. 1) with a recitational "aria" composed about 100 years earlier (Ex. 2-1).

EXAMPLE 2-1. Michele Pesenti, Sapphic ode *Integer vitae*, from *Frottole libro primo* (Venice: Petrucci, 1504), lower voices simplified and untexted

The texts of *L'Euridice* that are not set in recitative style are organized into standard closed poetic forms, and the music in these places is similar in style to corresponding forms of chamber vocal music of the time. For example, "Nel pur ardor," sung by the shepherd Tirsi in the second scene of *L'Euridice* (A. 1), is a strophic canzonetta in poetic form. Its vocal line has distinct melodic shapes and recurring rhythms. Its bass is melodically and rhythmically active throughout. It was meant to be sung in strict time.

Before Peri's first operas, Emilio de' Cavalieri, nobleman and superintendent of all the arts at the court of the Tuscan grand duke, had composed three brief, all-sung pastorales for Florence, *Il Satiro* and *La disperazione di Fileno* in 1591 and *Il giuoco della cieca* in 1595. No music from these works survives, but Caccini claims in a letter of 1614 that they contained no recitatives. On the other hand, Cavalieri's *Rappresentatione di Anima, et di Corpo*, which was performed in Rome in January of 1600, is preserved in a printed score. This work was sung throughout with staging and costumes. Its moralistic, allegorical libretto relates to the earlier traditions of *sacra rappresentazione* and Italian religious dialogue songs (dialogue *laudi*). The musical style of Cavalieri's dialogues fits best into Doni's category of special recitative. For example, in the short statement of the Soul (A. 2), the rhythms are stereotyped, each poetic line is punctuated by two long notes, individualized inflection is sacrificed to a prevailing monotone, the bass marks the time rather than sustaining a chord without obvious measure, and the bold dissonances of which Peri was so proud are notably absent. Whether Cavalieri's *Rappresentatione* has a unified, coherent plot can be debated.

In the prefaces to their scores, which were printed within a year of one another, Peri, Caccini, and Cavalieri each claimed to have been the first to adapt contemporaneous ("modern") musical traditions and practices to a continuously sung drama, with the aim of emulating the expressiveness imputed to ancient Greek stage music.

LE NUOVE MUSICHE (1602)

In his preface to *Le nuove musiche* ("New Pieces of Music," Florence, 1602), Giulio Caccini asserts that this publication includes three works "composed by me more than fifteen years ago"—i.e., about 1585—"in that very style I later employed for the fables performed in song at Florence." The works in question (*Perfidissimo volto, Verdò'l mio sol,* and *Dovrò dunque morire*) do contain monotone recitation, even if they are not quite in the recitative style later used in Peri's *Euridice*. But *Le nuove musiche* has historical importance of another kind: it was the first printed music collection to include all major varieties of Baroque monody—Italian songs for solo voice and *basso continuo*. Its publication therefore symbolizes the beginning of a new era in vocal chamber music as much as Peri's *Euridice* signals the beginning of opera. Dozens of similar collections were published in Italy during the following twenty-five years.

The name that Caccini gives to the style of his "New Pieces of Music" in this collection and its sequel, published in 1614—*Nuove musiche e nuova maniera di scriverle* ("New Pieces of Music and a New Way of Writing Them")—is "speaking in [musical] harmony" (*in armonia favellare*). Caccini mentions two defining characteristics of this style, to which we may add a third:

1. "Nonchalance in singing" (*sprezzatura di canto*), by which Caccini means rhythmic freedom in performance, a form of tempo rubato, by means of which the singer aims to approximate the unmeasured rhythms of speech.
2. Bass notes with added chords in the accompaniment that are held while the voice moves freely from note to note, creating dissonances that would not have been allowed by the rules of counterpoint.
3. A narrow range of pitches within many phrases of a piece and frequent multiple repetitions of single pitches, which contribute further to the impression of a style of singing somewhat more like speech than ordinary song.

These features come close to describing Jacopo Peri's operatic recitatives. However, at the beginning of the seventeenth century, operatic recitatives included faster delivery of the words and excluded the melodious and ornamental passages that are found in many of Caccini's earliest monodies.

Caccini's claim to have been innovative in 1585 must be placed in historical perspective. In reality, each of the three major types of monody in *Le nuove musiche* is to some extent a written-out version of a kind of earlier, sixteenth-century solo singing that was either partially improvised or whose true soloistic character is not represented to us in the notated forms in which it is preserved. These are the three types of monody in *Le nuove musiche*:

1. **Solo madrigals.** The term "madrigal" refers primarily to a type of poem that has no stanzas or strophes, no predictable rhyme scheme, and an irregular sequence of seven- or eleven-syllable lines with no recurring pattern of accentuation. Poetic lines with these characteristics are called *versi sciolti* ("loose verses"). A madrigal in *versi sciolti*, when read out loud, sounds very much like normal speech or prose, which is why most of Caccini's "speaking in [musical] harmony" is found in his settings of madrigal texts. Before Caccini, madrigals were always written for several voices, most often four or five, but they were frequently performed by a solo voice accompanied by a lute that played the parts written for the other voices. Solo singers of sixteenth-century polyphonic madrigals frequently improvised embellishments to the vocal line, and several instruction books from the time show us exactly how that was done (Ex. 2-2). Furthermore, some degree of "nonchalance in singing" would have been allowed by the fact that the lute accompaniments were normally played by the solo singers themselves. There is occasionally some hint of this rhythmic freedom in the notation of an earlier type of polyphonic madrigal called *madrigale arioso*.

EXAMPLE 2-2. The beginning of the madrigal *Vestiva i colli* by Palestrina as it was published for five voices in 1566 and as it would have been sung with the embellishments by Giovanni della Casa, published in 1585, and the lute accompaniment by Cosimo Bottegari of Florence in a manuscript dated 1574

The composer of a solo madrigal projects an interpretation of the text largely by controlling musical declamation (delivery), that is, by using musical rhythms, pitch contours, accents, and pacing that imitate the pacing, inflection, and accents of spoken poetic recitation. Caccini's *Deh, dove son fuggiti* (A. 3), for example, begins slowly and pensively, "Ah (pause), *ah* (higher and more emphatically), to where have you fled (first rushing, then slowing and inflecting upward at the end)? Ah (still higher and more emphatically), to where have you disappeared (similarly, but descending somewhat more deliberately)? Your eyes (pause), by whose rays (suddenly lower in pitch, as if lowering the voice for a subordinate clause), *I* (emphasized by a higher, longer note) am burnt to a cinder by now (wilting, losing energy)? Breezes (exclaimed, as if calling), divine breezes, which go wandering about (Caccini writes here, "without measured rhythm, speaking in [musical] harmony, with the aforesaid nonchalance"; more rapidly and lower, as for a subordinate clause), in this place and in that (more deliberately and coming to a conclusion). Ah (exclaimed), bring news (high throughout, as if pleading) of their sweet light (lower, subordinated), breezes (calling as before, but now in a lower voice), for which I die (Caccini says, "in a slower tempo," as if dejected). Ah, bring news of their sweet light, breezes (as before), *breezes* (more urgently, with wider inflection), for which *I* (exclaimed and more prolonged than before) die (much more prolonged and with a sobbing ornament called a *trillo*)."

We have seen this method of projecting the text already in the operatic lament of Orfeo composed by Jacopo Peri in expressive recitative style. However, in solo madrigals like Caccini's *Deh, dove son fuggiti*, the declamatory writing is combined with broader melodic lines and recurring phrases, which are usually avoided in recitative. Many solo madrigals have elaborate embellishment written in, although this is not found in *Deh, dove son fuggiti*. Finally, the bass line is more active in a typical solo madrigal than in recitative, which means that harmonic shape and direction also play a larger role in the musical interpretation of the madrigal text.

Caccini's principal innovation in his solo madrigals was to mold the rhythms and contours of the vocal line more closely to the poem than had been done in earlier polyphonic madrigals and to write out the ornamental runs (melismas) that had been improvised earlier. It is worth noting that Caccini passed up the opportunity to use musical figures to illustrate his text. A polyphonic madrigal composer might have set the word "fuggiti" ("fled") to rapid, fleeing runs in the various voices. But this approach had been severely criticized by Vincenzo Galilei, as we have seen earlier, and Caccini appears to have taken his advice to heart.

2. **Strophic canzonettas.** These are the least novel of Caccini's monodies. The poems are strophic—that is, all stanzas have the same rhyme scheme and pattern of line-lengths. Groups of poetic lines establish regular patterns of accentuation. The same music is sung for each stanza, and the pat-

terns of poetic accentuation are reproduced exactly by the music. The results are the very opposite of "speaking in [musical] harmony." Caccini's *Udite, udite, amanti* (A. 4) is an example. Here the music does not interpret the text through declamation but rather reflects its shape and structure.

LINE	RHYME	SYLLABLES	TRANSLATION
1. Udite, udite, amanti,	A	7	Hear ye, hear ye, lovers,
2. Udite. o fere erranti,	A	7	hear ye, oh wild beasts,
3. O cielo, o stelle,	B	5	oh heaven, oh stars,
4. O luna, o sole,	C	5	oh moon, oh sun,
5. Donn'e donzelle,	B	5	ladies and maidens,
6. Le mie parole	C	5	hear my words,
7. E s'à ragion mi doglio	D	7	and if my complaint is just
8. Piangete al mio cordoglio.	D	7	weep for my sorrow.

Lines 1 and 2 have the same rhyme, the same syllable count, and parallel messages ("Hear ye, hear ye, lovers. / hear ye, oh wild beasts"), and so Caccini set them to two phrases that are alike except for their first three notes. Lines 3–6 form a second unit, set apart by rhyme scheme, line length (five-syllable lines), and, in lines 3–5 at least, a pattern of pairing two objects of appeal ("oh heaven, oh stars, / oh moon, oh sun, / ladies and maidens"). The music for these lines is organized into two pairs of one-measure phrases that form two sequential patterns. Finally, the last two lines, likewise set apart by rhyme, length, and meaning, are sung to longer phrases that set up the final cadence. Each of the following stanzas of the poem has a similar shape and structure, so that Caccini's music fits them as well as it fits the first stanza.

The melodies and harmonies of Caccini's strophic canzonettas are very similar to those of earlier sixteenth-century canzonettas, which, although almost always written out for three voices, were very often sung by a solo voice with lute accompaniment. Caccini's principal innovation in his strophic canzonettas was to reduce the inner voices to a series of chords, often shown by figures added to the untexted bass line.

3. **Strophic variations**. Some of Caccini's strophic variations are settings of canzonetta texts in which he has varied the vocal line for each stanza by slightly changing its rhythms, adding different embellishments, or

modifying its melodic contours, while maintaining the same bass line and harmonies from stanza to stanza. In other cases, sudden shifts from a melodious to a recitational style and constantly changing embellishments make the vocal line seem quite different from stanza to stanza. Caccini's *Torna, deh torna* (A. 5) is an example of the latter type. Its text is not a canzonetta but a stanza of *ottava rima*, an old poetic form with serious, classical associations. The defining characteristics of *ottava rima* are stanzas of eight lines each, a rhyme scheme of ABABABCC within each stanza, and lines of eleven syllables with no regular patterns of accentuation. Stanzas of *ottava rima* (as well as several other classical poetic types) were sung, in the sixteenth century and before, by soloists who spun out variations, either ornamental or declamatory, on traditional melodic and harmonic formulas, called "arias," that were only rarely written down. In *Torna, deh torna* Caccini employs the "aria" called the Romanesca, (see Ex. 2-3), which was traditionally associated with the improvised singing of poems in *ottava rima*. Here, as usual in settings of this poetic form, the Romanesca pattern is repeated for each two lines of text. Some of Caccini's strophic variations are ornamental in style, like *Torna, deh torna*; others have enough "speaking in [musical] harmony" to resemble solo madrigals, while still others are more simi-

EXAMPLE 2-3. The bass pattern in Caccini's *Torna, deh torna* (1602) compared with the normal Romanesca bass pattern and the typical harmonies that accompany that pattern in early seventeenth-century music

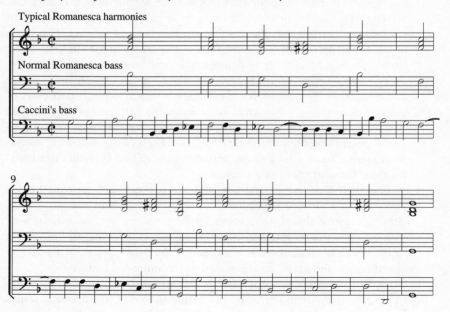

lar in style to strophic canzonettas. Caccini's innovation in his strophic variations was to capture in notation the improvised embellishment and "nonchalance in singing" that formerly belonged to a largely unwritten tradition.

Singing to the accompaniment of one's lute was listed among the necessary accomplishments of the ideal Renaissance nobleman in *Il cortegiano* ("The Courtier," 1514) by Baldassare Castiglione, who popularized the concept of "nonchalance" (*sprezzatura*) in aristocratic behavior. This helps to explain why Caccini described his self-accompanied "singing with nonchalance" as the "noble style." The revival of this ideal in Florence can be understood in the context of Grand Duke Ferdinando de' Medici's court. Ferdinando awarded many new titles of nobility and encouraged courtly behavior in order to continue the transformation of Florence from a republic into the capital of an absolutist grand duchy, a transformation begun by his father, Cosimo I. It is worth noting the unprecedented number of participants (composers or poets)

Performance of Monody

CACCINI GIVES many performance indications in the prefaces to his two books of monody of 1602 and 1614. He requires a flexible tempo and rhythmic freedom in the florid or recitational madrigals and strophic variations. He counsels the use of dynamic contrasts and gradations for expressive purposes. And he specifically describes several ways of beginning or attacking notes. But he places particular emphasis on the articulation of notes in very rapid ornamental passages. The key to all passage work, he says, is the *trillo*, which consists of very rapid reiterations of the same pitch, each repetition articulated by a light glottal stop, "ah." All the notes in the ornamental melismas must be articulated in exactly that manner. These melismas contain many sixteenth notes and even some thirty-second notes to be sung at the tempo of ca. ♩ = 120.

Realizations for lute and for keyboard of many of Caccini's basso continuo accompaniments are found in Florentine manuscripts from the composer's period, and they indicate the same practices prescribed by the earliest instruction books for accompaniment from a figured bass: The added chords should be rendered simply and without any contrapuntal or rhythmic independence from the vocal and bass parts. Although ordinary lutes, harpsichords, and even organs were used to accompany early seventeenth-century monody, the preferred instrument was the chitarrone, illustrated in Figure 2–3. It was thought best that the singer played the accompaniment in order to facilitate the rhythmic freedom so characteristic of "speaking in tones."

in the emergence of opera and monody, in Florence and elsewhere, who were noblemen. These include three of the four known members of the Camerata—Giovanni Bardi (Count of Vernio), Vincenzo Galilei, and Piero Strozzi—as well as Jacopo Peri, Ottavio Rinuccini, Emilio de' Cavalieri, Sigismondo d'India, Cesare Marotta, Ippolito Macchiavelli, Ferdinando Gonzaga, Giovanni del Turco, Jacopo Corsi, Battista Guarini, and Giambattista Marino, among others. The "noble style" of singing, even if done by professionals, helped to support the courtly etiquette that Ferdinando and other rulers required. The notion, promoted by Giovanni Bardi, that somehow Caccini's "speaking in [musical] harmony" was related to the lost musical practices of ancient Greece further corresponded to the Medici family political mythology.

MONODY AND THE SERIOUS CANZONETTA IN NAPLES, ROME, AND ELSEWHERE

When Giulio Caccini was recruited into the service of the Medici court in 1565, he was a boy soprano in the choir of St. Peter's Basilica in Rome. The Medici grand duke, Cosimo I, had instructed his agent in Rome to find a boy with "a beautiful voice and good grace in singing with embellishments in the Neapolitan manner," and this is exactly what the agent found in the fourteen-year-old Caccini. Once Giulio arrived in Florence, the Grand Duke put him under the instruction of Scipione del Palla, who had recently been brought to Florence from Naples. Caccini says in his 1602 preface that he learned the "noble style" of singing from Palla.

One of Scipione del Palla's few surviving works, *Che non può far donna leggiadra e cara* (Ex. 2-4), was sung as part of an intermedio produced in Naples in

EXAMPLE 2-4. Scipione del Palla, *Che non può far donna leggiadra* (1558), soprano with text and bass without

1558, and a contemporary description of that production says that it was performed "in a style midway between singing and reciting," which foreshadows Peri's description of recitative. The written music, however, is rhythmically square and melodically stereotyped: it is an "aria" formula. Extemporaneous "nonchalance in singing" must have transformed this aria into proto-recitative, perhaps with the suppression of pitch repetitions in a chordal accompaniment.

In and around Palla's Naples in the second half of the sixteenth century the five-string Spanish guitar (see Fig. 2-3) was sometimes used to accompany singing with simple chords nearly as sparse as those indicated by the basso continuo parts in the earliest Florentine operas. Early precedents for this kind of accompaniment can be found in Spain, e.g., Alonso Mudarra's *Si por amar, el hombre se amando* and *Claros y frescos rios* (both 1546). Since Spain ruled the Kingdom of Naples from 1502 to 1738, Spanish music circulated widely there during those years.

Figure 2-3. A Roman gentleman, ca. 1615, playing a chitarrone. On the table are a five-course Spanish guitar and a book of Italian monodies.

Two fully written-out examples of pre-1600 monody from Naples and Rome are known to survive, and they come close to the style of the madrigals in Caccini's *Le nuove musiche*. They are by Bartolomeo Roy (ca. 1530–1599) and Sebastiano Raval (ca. 1550–1604). There are also a number of undated pieces by the Roman Giuseppino Cenci (d. 1616) that contain actual recitative style; his contemporary Vincenzo Giustiniani credits him with developing this style at the same time as Caccini. What makes Cenci's works especially interesting is their juxtaposition of recitational and songlike writing, as shown in his setting of the sonnet *Io che l'età solea viver nel fango* (A. 6).

Perhaps the most artistically ambitious of the early monody composers was Sigismondo d'India (ca. 1582–1629), who moved among various Italian courts before settling into a position in the household of the duke of Savoy in Turin in 1611. India's most characteristic monodies are his solo madrigals, which are generally full of expressive chromaticism, augmented and diminished intervals, unusual harmonic progressions, sharp dissonances, harsh contrasts, bold contours with wide leaps, abrupt changes in pacing, and dramatic pauses. Most of these features can be found in his *Riede la primavera* (1609, A. 7) on a text by his colleague at the court of Savoy, Giambattista Marino (1569–1625), the most influential Italian poet of the early seventeenth century. The poem and its musical setting revolve around an antithesis between the joys and promises of springtime and the frigid grip of winter. These are intended as metaphors for two aspects of the beloved—kindness and cruelty—the one reflected in diatonic intervals, lilting phrases, and bright rhythms, the other by anguished moans, tortured leaps, pungent dissonances, sharp contours, breathless stammering, and violent outbursts.

The kind of highly expressive solo-voice madrigal that India composed rapidly faded out of fashion during the second decade of the seventeenth century. After about 1620 very few madrigals are included in monody collections, which are henceforth almost completely dominated by settings of canzonetta texts. At the same time, important changes occur in the canzonetta.

During the 1620s and 1630s canzonetta texts with a serious content become more prevalent, while silly and playful poems appear less frequently. The new serious canzonetta texts tend also to be longer and more complex in their rhyme schemes and patterns of line lengths within each strophe. The music of these new canzonettas is often varied and complex, too. Canzonettas with repetitive triple-meter rhythms do not entirely disappear, but they are increasing crowded out of later monody collections by canzonettas that feature contrast between metrical, aria-like sections and passages in recitative or in styles that explore the grey areas between recitative and aria. In most canzonettas, these contrasts or shifts between metrical and recitational styles occur within the block of music that is repeated for each strophe of text. In a few of them, however, these contrasts occur between the independently composed settings for each strophe of text. In Girolamo Frescobaldi's *Così mi disprezzate?* (1630), Martino Pesenti's *O Dio, che veggi?* (1633), and Giovanni Felice Sances's *Misera hor sì ch'il pianto* (1633), the aria-like sections employ an ostinato figure in the basso continuo part, a technique that rose to popularity among Italian composers during the 1630s.

Pesenti's and Sances's works are called "cantata" in their printed sources. This term, which literally means "something sung," is parallel to the term *sonata* ("something played"). Its first use can be traced to Alessandro Grandi's *Cantade et arie* (1620). Until about 1650, the term *cantata* can be found applied to all sorts of monody, ranging from simple, strophic canzonettas to works entirely in recitative style. A significant number of the earliest pieces called "cantata" are strophic variations with nearly constant quarter-note motion in the bass. Another group of early cantatas include discrete sections of recitative and aria but often within a block of music repeated exactly for each strophe of music. Many other similarly sectional works, even those that are not strophic, are still called "canzonettas" in their sources.

Orazio Michi dell'arpa (1594–1641), a Roman musician, made a speciality of setting canzonetta texts with contrasting sections of recitative and aria styles. Twenty-one of these are preserved with only one strophe of text, and in every case where the additional strophes can be found in collections of poetry, the additional text cannot be sung to the music composed for the first strophe. In effect Michi composed monostrophic serious canzonettas with internal sectional contrast. An example is *Sù l'oriente* (A. 8), a setting of the first strophe of a four-strophe serious canzonetta text, moralizing on the brevity of human life, by Francesco Balducci (1579–1642) published in 1630. In this work, the sudden shift from the lively, triple-meter aria style to a forceful recitative style (at m. 28)—a shift underscored by an equally dramatic harmonic juxtaposition—corresponds to the antithesis in the text between descriptions of the laughing, victorious Dawn and the sudden appearance of a black cloud that carries away the sun. The second aria section (mm. 41–67) introduces the moral with irony underscored by harmonic tension and a cross relation (mm. 54–55) and driven home by the analogy to Tantalus of Greek mythology, set in a florid arioso style.

In a few of the serious canzonetta texts set in this way by Michi, the shift from recitative to aria corresponds to a change in the poetry from unpatterned, prosaic declamation to metrical poetry. An example is the text *Empio cor, core ingrato*, in which the fifth and sixth lines, where Michi breaks into aria style, establish the metrical rhythm — ∪ ∪ — ∪ — ∪:

1. Empio cor, core ingrato	Wicked heart, ungrateful heart,
2. M'han le tue colpe à questo legno affisso,	your strokes have nailed me to this cross,
3. E'l mio petto svenato	and my eviscerated breast
4. Apre per te, d' ogni tesor l'abbisso	opens, for you, the greatest of all treasures.
5. Strale d'amor più forte	Love's strongest arrow
6. M'hà già ferito à morte	has already mortally wounded me.
7. Già languisco, già moro e non rispondi	I already languish, already die, and you do not respond.
8. Cor ingrato empio cor dove t'ascondi	Ungrateful heart, wicked heart, where are you hiding?

During the 1630s and 1640s a few poets in Rome began to devise texts that deliberately alternate groups of metrical verses with unmeasured *versi sciolti*. Even though texts of this new type were not strophic, they continued to be called canzonettas, probably because they included metrical verses, typical of the canzonetta.

A musical setting of such a monostrophic, sectionalized, serious canzonetta is *Hor che l'oscuro manto* (A. 9) by Luigi Rossi (ca. 1597–1653), an important composer from Naples who served in the households of two powerful papal families (the Borghesi and the Barberini) in Rome and who had significant contact with Orazio Michi. Its text consists of six sentences, to which Rossi's musical sections correspond almost exactly. Sentences 1, 3, and 4 are written in *versi sciolti*, whereas sentences 2 and 5 use metrical verses in canzonetta style. The last sentence is split between the two. Rossi sets the canzonetta-like verses in triple-meter aria style, while the *versi sciolti* of sentence 3 are in recitative style. Sentence 4 is set in a quasi-aria style and in duple meter. In much of it Rossi employs rapid syllabic declamation, as in recitative. This section (mm. 51–78) is marked "aria" in the manuscript score, perhaps in order to clarify the composer's intention to go against the usual correlation between *versi sciolti* and recitative in this type of work. The first sentence is set in the style that Marco Scacchi (ca. 1600–1662), in his *Breve discorso sopra la musica moderna* ("Brief Discourse about Modern Music") of 1649 called *imbastardito* ("bastardized"): "It will go on for a while interpreting the text in recitative style and then, suddenly, will vary this with melismatic passages (*passaggi*) and with other melodic shapes (*modulazione*)." The portions of the text that Rossi set in triple-meter aria style can be classified as lyric in nature, since in those places the words express strong feelings and are addressed to "my heart" and to "martyrs" only metaphorically. The portion of the text that Rossi set in pure recitative style is dramatic, since the words of the singer are addressed to actual lovers. Sentences 1 and 4 and the first half of sentence 6 are basically narrative, since they serve to recount events or the state of affairs. However, in sentence 1 and 4 the narrative style is mixed with the lyric, and in both the aria style is mixed with features of recitative (sentence 4) or the recitative style is mixed with melismas more typical of an aria (sentence 1). It is typical of Italian chamber cantatas of the middle decades of the seventeenth century to correlate musical and poetic styles and to explore the grey areas between them, as is done in this work.

STANZA	SYLLABLE COUNT	TRANSLATION
[1] Or che l'oscuro manto	7	Now that the dark mantle
della notte ricopre il ciel d'intorno,	11	of night recovers the sky all around,
alla cruda beltà ch'adoro tanto,	11	to the cruel beauty whom I adore so much,
fortunato amator, faccio ritorno.	11	a fortunate lover, I return.

STANZA	SYLLABLE COUNT	TRANSLATION
[2] Sù, mio cor, con dolci accenti	8	Come, my heart, with sweet words
fa' che desti i vaghi rai	8	awaken those beautiful eyes
per cui perdono i tormenti	8	for which all torments lose
la crudeltà che non si stanca mai.	11	that cruelty that never tires.
[3] Amanti, o voi che siete	7	Lovers, oh you who are
pien' di cure e d'affanni,	7	full of cares and anxieties,
se trovar non sapete	7	if you know not how to find,
in un guardo gentil conforto al core,	11	in a glance, gentle comfort for your heart,
sempre, sempre a languir con vario stile	11	always, always to languish in various ways
vi condanni Amore.	7	does Love condemn you.
[4] Mentre sanno influir due luci belle	11	While two beautiful eyes know how to gather in
tutto il ben che quaggiù piovon le stelle,	11	all that is good which rains down from the stars,
da due nere pupille	7	from two dark eyes
io sol chiedo un sguardo,	7	I ask only a glance,
poi sen vada in faville	7	then may go up in flames
l'alma trafitta da sì dolce dardo:	11	my soul wounded by such a sweet arrow:
beltà che sia negl'occhi armata e forte	11	such beauty in the eyes, armed and strong,
ha saette di vita e non di morte.	11	has arrows of life and not of death.
[5] Godete, martiri,	6	Rejoice, martyrs!
trionfi il mio core,	6	Let my heart triumph!
dal regno d'Amore	6	From the kingdom of Love
nessun si ritiri;	6	let no one retreat;
quest'alma lo sa:	6t★	my soul knows it:
bellezza, fierezza	6	beauty has no wrath
in seno non ha.	6t★	in its bosom.
[6] Hor che Lilla mi rimira	8	Now that Lilla looks at me
il mio cor più non sospira,	8	my heart no longer sighs,
ond'io pur godo se per lei tanto ardo:	11	whence I take pleasure that I burn so much for
a chi si strugge è gran conforto un sguardo.	11	her: for one who is destroyed one glance is a great comfort.

★The "t" in the symbol "6t" means *tronco* ("truncated")—that is, the final, unaccented sylla-ble has been chopped off, leaving an accented syllable at the end of the line, but the verse is still considered to have six syllables, according to Italian poetic theory. A line with the nor-mal, single unaccented syllable at its end is termed *piano* ("plain"), and a line with an extra unaccented syllable at its end is termed *sdrucciolo* ("sliding").

SECONDA PRATICA AND THE CONCERTED MADRIGAL

The rise of monody did not mark the end of the polyphonic madrigal, which continued through at least two major phases of development during the first half of the seventeenth century: the cultivation of the *seconda pratica* and the introduction of the concerted madrigal.

The term *seconda pratica* ("second practice") arose in the context of a dispute between the Italian theorist and composer Giovanni Maria Artusi (ca. 1540–1613) and Claudio Monteverdi (1567–1643). In one of his theoretical treatises, *L'Artusi overo Delle imperfettioni della moderna musica* ("Artusi, or the Imperfections of Modern Music," 1600), Artusi pointed out passages in Monteverdi's madrigals *Anima mia, perdona, Cruda Amarilli*, and *O Mirtillo* where the composer breaks several rules governing the preparation and resolution of dissonances, use of accidentals, coordination of parts, and mixture of modes. For example, Artusi shows that in the passage from Monteverdi's *Cruda Amarilli* given in Example 2-5 the soprano's high *a''* creates an unprepared dissonance against the bass and is followed by a leap instead of a step on the way to a second unprepared dissonance, *f''*. Artusi rejects the explanation that the soprano part in bar 13 is really an abbreviation of the phrase given in Example 2-6, which would conform to the established rules of dissonance treatment. Of course, the difference between the soprano parts in Examples 2-5 and 2-6 has a lot to do with the declamation and emotional expression of the words "ahi lasso" ("oh, alas"). But Artusi does not even print the words in his treatise.

Artusi elaborated on these criticisms and raised the debate to a philosophical level in *Seconda parte dell'Artusi overo Delle imperfettioni della moderna musica* ("Second Part of Artusi, or the Imperfections of Modern Music," 1603), written in response to letters he received from an anonymous supporter of Monteverdi, or perhaps from Monteverdi himself. When Monteverdi got around to publishing *Cruda Amarilli* in his Fifth Book of Madrigals (1605), he added a

EXAMPLE 2-5. Monteverdi, *Cruda Amarilli*, mm. 12–14

EXAMPLE 2-6. Monteverdi, *Cruda Amarilli*, mm. 12–14, with Artusi's soprano

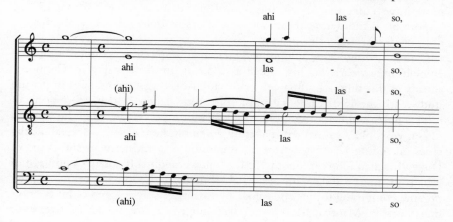

brief preface, in which he claimed that "I wrote a reply [to Artusi] to let it be known that I do not do things by chance, and as soon as it is rewritten it will be published under the title *The Second Practice* [*seconda pratica*], *or, The Perfection of Modern Music.* Some will wonder at this, not believing that there is any practice other than that taught by Zarlino"—referring to Gioseffo Zarlino (1517–1590), whose treatise *Le istitutioni harmoniche* (1558/1573) was still accepted as the most authoritative summary of strict counterpoint as exemplified by the works of Palestrina. "But let them be assured concerning consonances and dissonances that there is a different way of considering them from that already established, one that defends the modern manner of composition with the assent of reason and of the senses." In 1607, Claudio Monteverdi's brother Giulio Cesare published an extended commentary on his brother's reply to Artusi, in the course of which he claims that in the second practice "the poetry is ruler over the harmony," meaning that musical text expression justifies bending the rules.

Monteverdi did not claim to be the first to use this second practice, and his brother includes a substantial list of earlier madrigal composers who made use of it, starting with Cipriano de Rore (1515/16–1565) and concluding with Jacopo Peri, Giulio Caccini, and members of the Academia degli Elevati in Florence, which was led by Marco da Gagliano. Although we do not have Monteverdi's treatise, a theoretical explanation of the second practice had already been provided in a counterpoint study left in manuscript by Vincenzo Galilei, one of Caccini's colleagues in the Florentine Camerata. Furthermore, many of Monteverdi's contrapuntal liberties are demonstrated in several manuals of the late sixteenth and early seventeenth centuries that taught improvised counterpoint and the kind of florid embellishment that are found written out in many monodies—e.g., Ex. 2-2). Thus, the controversy between Artusi and Monteverdi once again illustrates how formerly improvised practices were finding their way into written compositions and how strong emotional expression of the words in vocal music was now given more importance than observing the rules of counterpoint. Both factors are important in the definition of the new styles in Italian music at the beginning of the seventeenth century.

Claudio Monteverdi undoubtedly learned improvised counterpoint and embellishment early in his career as a string instrumentalist in Cremona, already at this time a leading center of violin-making. On the basis of private study with the local cathedral music director, Claudio had his first book of motets published, with the sponsorship of a local nobleman, when he was still fifteen years old. As member of a string ensemble, he traveled to several nearby cities, including Mantua, where he was hired as a musician in the court of Duke Vincenzo Gonzaga about 1591. Monteverdi quickly rose to a position of leadership in the duke's musical establishment, and soon his principal duty became composing for his colleagues' performances. By the end of his twenty-one years in Mantua, Monteverdi had published five books of five-voice madrigals and a substantial collection of church music, and he had composed the music for two operas and two ballets. When Duke Vincenzo died in 1612, his son Francesco dismissed Monteverdi along with a number of other court artists. A year later, however, Claudio was able to secure the position of music director at the basilica of San Marco in Venice, where he remained until his death in 1643.

During his thirty-one years in Venice, Monteverdi's music underwent a remarkable development. He had used an independent basso continuo part already in his fifth book of madrigals (1605), and his sixth book (1614) incorporates recitative style. In his seventh book (1619), entitled *Concerto*, some of his chamber monodies are found for the first time, along with concerted madrigals.

The Italian term *madrigale concertato* is usually translated as "concerted madrigal," although a more apt translation would be "arranged madrigal," since the verb *concertare* was used at this time to mean "to put together or prepare for performance." This preparation included assigning parts and passages within parts to specific combinations of singers and instruments. Thus, for example, madrigals that were performed in Florentine intermedi during the second half of the sixteenth century were "concerted" by this process, although they were published as plain polyphonic vocal music without instruments. In his title *Concerto*, Monteverdi was advertising "something already arranged." Today, the term "concerted madrigal" is normally reserved for polyphonic madrigals in which ensemble instruments are assigned an obligatory role, although it is sometimes applied to madrigals in which contrast between few voices and many is made possible by an independent continuo part.

The expressive and dramatic potential of the concerted madrigal is most fully realized in Monteverdi's Eighth Book of Madrigals, *Madrigali guerrieri et amorosi* ("Warlike and Amorous Madrigals," 1638). In the important and informative preface to this collection, Monteverdi alludes to rhetorical lore going back to Plato, which designates three styles (or *genera*) of oration—high, middle, and low—and he asserts that these correspond to the agitated, moderate, and soft in music. He claims that, up to this point, music has had only the moderate and soft *genera*, lacking the high or agitated, which he now intends to rediscover. Following Plato, he says that the high genus would be characterized by expressions of anger. But in order to move listeners more profoundly, he deploys strong contrast between expressions of anger and expressions of love, hence the title of this collection, "Warlike and Amorous Madrigals." His initial inspiration for this, he says, came from an episode in the epic poem *La Gerusalemme liberata* ("Jerusalem Liberated" [from the Turks by the Crusaders]) by Torquato Tasso (1544–1595), the most famous Italian poet of the late Renaissance, whom Monteverdi had met in Mantua. In fact, much of what Monteverdi writes in the preface to his Eighth Book of Madrigals is an expansion of and response to a challenge to Italian madrigal composers that Tasso had issued in his treatise *La cavaletta overo de la poesia toscana* ("The Grasshopper, or Tuscan Poetry," 1587): Leave aside "all that music which through degeneration has become limp and effeminate" and "summon it back to that gravity from which it has strayed." Tasso was also the author of an extensive treatise on rhetoric and its application to poetry (*Discorsi dell'arte poetica e in particolare sopra il poema eroico*, 1587/94), in which the entire tradition of invention, disposition, elocution, and delivery is treated in detail. Hence, Monteverdi's invocation of Tasso and the classical *genera* places the composer's thought squarely within the tradition of classical rhetoric, even if he felt it unnecessary to rehearse the rest of what his readers had learned in school and took for granted.

Monteverdi's *Hor ch'el ciel e la terra* (A. 13) from his Eighth Book of Madrigals shows the extent of his involvement with rhetoric, especially with elocution (the use of rhetorical figures). The text (a sonnet by Petrarch) begins with an extended adverbial clause, "Now that heaven and earth and wind are silent, and sleep holds in check the animals and birds. . . ." Monteverdi sets the twenty-two syllables of this clause to twenty-two mostly slow reiterations of a single low-pitched and darkly voiced A-minor chord. This is extraordinary. It is not simply a matter of illustrating the poetic image that comes in the fourth line of the text, "the sea lies waveless in its bed." The effect of this hushed, majestic, and mysterious opening is to underscore the tension and anticipation of such a long introductory clause, to convert it into a rhetorical figure, procatascene, "giving an audience a gradual preparation and buildup before telling them about something done." Just when the text reaches the subject, the harmony changes for the first time (to E major, eventually cadencing to A major): "*Night* is circling in its starry chariot, and the sea lies waveless in its bed." At this point the poet introduces antithesis ("conjoining contrasting ideas"): "I awake, I think, I burn, I weep." Not only is waking contrasted with sleeping, but drawn-out syllables of long, languorous phrases of poetry are suddenly replaced by staccato, two-syllable words (in Italian). The rhetorical figure is brachylogia, "brevity in speech or writing caused by omission of conjunctions between words." And, of course, Monteverdi underscores this contrast by introducing repetitions of a more rapid, two-chord motive separated by rests and rising higher each time, so as to produce the effect of auxesis, "words or clauses placed in climactic order." For the words "and she who undoes me is always before me," Monteverdi introduces a new, more flowing phrase whose repetitions are abruptly punctuated by recurrences of the staccato two-chord motive, so that the total effect is approximately this: "and she who undoes me . . . I wake! . . . and she who undoes me is always before me to my sweet pain . . . I wake! . . . always, always before me . . . I think! . . . always before me to my sweet pain . . . I burn! . . . she who undoes me is always before me to my sweet pain . . . I weep!" In other words, Monteverdi intersperses fragments of poetic lines 5–6 to comment upon each of the two–syllable verbs of line 5, part 1. The rhetorical figure is epanodos, "a general statement expanded by discussing it part by part, with the further qualification that the terms used in the initial summary are specifically repeated in the fuller discussion that follows. "At measure 42 the musical motive of the two–syllable verbs returns in the form of rapid, dotted rhythms without rests between them (anacephalaeosis, "a summary or recapitulation, intended to refresh the listener's memory"). At measure 59 another antithesis results when the text "war is my state" inspires Monteverdi to deploy repetitions of rapid dotted rhythms for "war! war! war! war! war! war! war! war! war!" (epizeuxis, "emphatic repetition of a word with no other words between") and, eventually, agitated imitations of trumpet calls in the two violins (mm. 65–67). Just when the excitement reaches its height, a sudden, astonishing silence (aposiopesis, "stopping suddenly in midcourse, leaving a statement unfinished") introduces a third antithesis—slow, consonant chords in the high voices with a smooth, conjunction melodic line, "and only in thinking of her do I have some peace" (antanagoge, "ameliorating a fault or difficulty implicitly admitted by balancing an unfavorable aspect with a favorable one"). Then returning to a more extensive elaboration of the dotted rhythm of "war!" and its associated trumpeting in the violins (mm. 76–87) creates rhetorical figures not present in the original poetry: apaetesis, "a matter put aside in anger and resumed later" which, when added to the contrasting antanagoge, creates anacephalaeosis, "a summary or recapitulation. . . ."

All these rhetorical figures are either present in the text, or else Monteverdi created them by rearranging the text. In every case, his music conforms to the pattern created by the figure or produces a comparable effect. The reason for naming and defining these Greek terms for these rhetorical figures is to emphasize that they were recognizable, time-tested devices for moving the passions of the orator's audience—now transferred to music to an unprecedented extent.

COURT OPERA IN MANTUA, FLORENCE, AND ROME

The Duke of Mantua attended the first performance of *L'Euridice* in Florence along with a number of his household musicians, almost certainly including Claudio Monteverdi, who is named in a contemporary account as one of the musicians who frequented the house of Jacopo Corsi. Since the scores of both Caccini's and Peri's settings of *L'Euridice* were printed in 1600, Monteverdi had the opportunity to know them.

Mantua

Monteverdi's first opera, *L'Orfeo* (Mantua, 1607) bears a very close resemblance to *L'Euridice* and to Peri's setting of it. Its plot and characters are nearly the same, except that in the new libretto by Alessandro Striggio, Orfeo fails to return Euridice to the world of the living because he looks back while leading her out of the underworld, in violation of his agreement with Pluto. The general musical style is very similar to both Caccini's and Peri's settings in the deployment of special, narrative, and expressive recitative, and in such details as the use of syncopated exclamations it resembles Peri's exactly. Monteverdi treats several episodes just as Peri did. Compare the scenes of the messenger's report followed by Orfeo's lament from the two operas in the Anthology (nos. 1 and 10). Monteverdi, however, expanded on his Florentine model by increasing the role of dance and of instrumental music in his opera. The prologue to Monteverdi's *Orfeo* provides a very interesting study in musical declamation because one basic aria is varied differently for each strophe of text in order to produce a clear and moving delivery—but this is more or less a written-out version of the sort of performance that Peri would have expected his singer to improvise.

During the year after *L'Orfeo*, 1608, the court of Mantua presented Monteverdi's second opera, *L'Arianna*, of which the surviving lament (W. 1) was regarded by Doni as the most perfect example of expressive recitative. Earlier in the same year the court produced the first opera of Jacopo Peri's most important follower in Florence, Marco da Gagliano (1582–1643), entitled *La Dafne*, on the old libretto revised and expanded by Rinuccini, the poet of the original version.

Florence

Gagliano frequently collaborated with Francesca Caccini (1587–after 1641), the daughter of Giulio Caccini, an important composer and poet, who initially earned a position in the household of Grand Duke Ferdinando de' Medici because of her outstanding ability to sing. Francesca became the leading composer for the Florentine court during the regency of Cristina of Lorraine and Maria Maddalena of Austria, the widow and daughter-in-law of Grand Duke Ferdinando. These two women ruled Tuscany from 1621 to 1628, between the early death of Cosimo II and the maturity of Ferdinando II.

Whereas the early Medici grand dukes had to struggle to maintain power as self-promoted monarchs with a non-noble ancestry in a historically republican city, the regents in the 1620s had the additional problems of being foreigners and women. So, like their male predecessors, they deliberately controlled the medium of musical spectacle in order to bolster their claims to political legitimacy. However, finding few models of powerful but admirable women in ancient mythology, they turned to the Bible and the lives of saints for the female protagonists of their operas and other musical pageants. Thus the characters in Florentine operas of the 1620s tend to be portrayed as fully rounded human beings rather than the stereotyped, mythical gods and demi-gods of earlier opera.

Francesca Caccini's *La liberazione di Ruggiero dall'isola d'Alcina* ("The Liberation of Ruggiero from the Island of Alcina," 1625), although not on a sacred subject, features a female protagonist, Melissa, who wins a victory over lascivious love in freeing Ruggiero and his fellow crusaders from the magic spell of the witch Alcina. The story and characters of this opera were taken from the book-length epic poem *Orlando furioso* by Ludovico Ariosto (1474–1533). Francesca Caccini's recitative style is more melodious, less monotone, rhythmically smoother, and more frequently embellished than that of Peri, Monteverdi, or Gagliano. At the same time, her harmony is more adventurous, although she tends to use harmonic contrast together with the other features of expressive recitative in order to portray such negative characteristics as excitability and suggestibility. This is nicely illustrated by the confrontation between Melissa and Ruggiero, the central event in the opera (A. 11), where Melissa's exhortations are set to music that exhibits melodic, rhythmic, and harmonic self-control, while the lovesick Ruggiero's replies are characterized by musical confusion and inaction.

Rome

In Rome, Cavalieri's *Rappresentatione di Anima, et di Corpo* (1600) was followed by a number of other religious musical dramas performed in churches or seminaries, of which *Eumelio* (1606) by Agostino Agazzari (1578–1640) alone survives. It resembles Cavalieri's *Rappresentatione* in its extensive use of special recitative. The first secular opera known to have been performed in Rome was *Amor pudico* (1614), music by Cesare Marotta and others, produced at the Chancellery Palace for Cardinal Montalto. This opera and the next one done in Rome, Filippo Vitali's *Aretusa*, were produced with some personnel from Florence and were derived in part from Florentine models.

A distinctly Roman style of opera began to emerge after the poet and scholar Cardinal Maffeo Barberini became Pope Urban VIII (ruled 1623–44). His cardinal-nephews began producing operas in 1632 with a performance of *Sant'Alessio* by Stefano Landi (1587–1639); in 1639 they added a 3,000-seat theater to their family palace. Whereas the earliest operas in Florence and Mantua drew their stories from ancient mythology, Roman opera of the Barberini era, like that of the Florentine regency of the 1620s, tended to use plots with characters presented as real human beings. Similarly, a number of Roman operas in this period, beginning with *Sant'Alessio*, are based on stories drawn from the lives of saints, while others draw on the historical epic poems of Tasso, Ariosto, and Marino.

Some of the earliest comic scenes in opera appeared in Landi's *Sant'Alessio*. Also in this opera the heterogeneous collection of winds and strings used to accompany earlier court opera is replaced by an orchestra of violin-family and continuo instruments. Its recitatives, in general, feature more repeated pitches and less variety in rhythmic details than those of Florence and Mantua (see Act I, scene 3, A. 12). Its choruses are more prominent and more elaborate, reflecting the full range of styles and approaches found in the polyphonic madrigal of the early seventeenth century. The choral scene of devils (Act I, scene 4, A. 12) is shown in Figure 2-4, an engraving included in the original printed score of the opera. Act I, scene 2 (A. 12), in which Sant'Alessio contemplates the vanity of men and the frailty of mortal things, culminates in an aria of two strophes at a place where in earlier opera we would expect a recitative soliloquy. This use of an aria to portray private reflection is an early manifestation of a trend that will grow during the next few decades.

The libretto of *Il Sant'Alessio* was written by Giulio Rospigliosi (1600–1669), who later became Pope Clement IX (ruled 1667–69) and who also wrote for the Barberini theater *Chi soffre speri* ("He Who Suffers May Hope," 1637, revised in 1639, also known under the titles *L'Egisto*, *Il falcone*, and *L'Alvida*) with music by Virgilio Mazzocchi (1597–1646) and Marco Marazzoli (ca. 1602/1608–1662). The plot of *Chi soffre speri*, based on a moralizing fable recorded first in Boccaccio's *Decameron* in the fourteenth century, is about a poor nobleman who proves his love for a wealthy widow by sacrificing his most prized possessions. The story is extended through the addition of some unrelated subplots and built-in intermedi, requiring an enlarged cast of thirty-two, as

Figure 2-4. The chorus of devils in Stefano Landi, *Il Sant'Alessio* (1632). Act I, scene 4

is typical of Barberini operas. Its comic scenes revolve around the servants Coviello and Zanni, roles modeled on stock characters from *commedia dell'arte*, originally a type of improvised street entertainment using masks, exaggerated costumes, and traditional songs.

At the beginning of the seventeenth century, the values and fashions of court culture, absolutist aspirations, formal rhetoric, and the transformation of unwritten practices into notated genres converge dramatically in Italian secular vocal music—opera, monody, cantata, and *seconda pratica* and concerted madrigals. In Italian instrumental music of the same period we will find similar aristocratic *sprezzatura*, rhetorical gestures, and notational control of improvisation alongside the traditions of town musicians and the modal structures of church music.

BIBLIOGRAPHICAL NOTES

General

Translations of the prefaces and other writings by Artusi, Bardi, Caccini, Galilei, Monteverdi, and Peri are conveniently collected in *Source Readings in Music History*, ed. Oliver Strunk, rev. ed., IV, *The Baroque Era*, ed. Margaret Murata (New York, W. W. Norton, 1998). A more detailed overview of the material covered in this chapter is found in Tim Carter, *Music in Later Renaissance & Early Baroque Italy* (London: Batsford, 1992).

The First Operas

A useful overview of the emergence of opera with a very good discussion of musical styles is Howard Mayer Brown, "How Opera Began: An Introduction to Jacopo Peri's *Euridice* (1600)," *The Late Italian Renaissance*, ed. Eric Cochrane (New York, 1970), pp. 401–444; reprinted in *The Garland Library of the History of Western Music*, ed. Ellen Rosand, XI, *Opera*, I, *Up to Mozart* (New York, 1985), pp. 1–44. A more detailed study, which emphasizes the Florentine and pan-Italian traditions of classical (Greek and Roman) studies, is Barbara Russano Hanning, *Of Music's Power: Humanism and the Creation of Opera* (Ann Arbor, 1980). Detailed information about Peri's opera *L'Euridice* can be found in Tim Carter, *Jacopo Peri, 1561–1633: His Life and Works* (New York: Garland Publishing, 1989). The study that best puts the emergence of opera in the context of earlier musical spectacle, especially the Florentine intermedi, is Nino Pirrotta, *Music and Theatre from Poliziano to Monteverdi*, trans. Karen Eales (Cambridge, 1982). The best summary of what is known concerning the Florentine Camerata is Claude V. Palisca, "The 'Camerata Fiorentina': A Reappraisal," *Studi musicali*, I (1972), 203–36; reprinted in *The Garland Library of the History of Western Music*, ed. Ellen Rosand, XI, *Opera*, I, *Up to Mozart* (New York, 1985), pp. 45–80.

Court Culture, Politics, and Spectacle

For the political context of early Florentine opera, see John Walter Hill, "Florence: Musical Spectacle and Drama, 1570–1650," *The Early Baroque Era from the Late 16th Century to the 1660s*, ed. Curtis Price, Music and Society, ed. Stanley Sadie (New York: Prentice Hall, 1993), pp. 121–145. For background to Florentine politics and society ca. 1600, three articles by Samuel Berner are especially useful:

"Florentine Political Thought in the Late Cinquecento," *Il pensiero politico*, III (1970), 177–99; "Florentine Society in the Late Sixteenth and Early Seventeenth Centuries," *Studies in the Renaissance*, XVIII (1971), 203–46; and "The Florentine Patriciate in the Transition from Republic to *Principato*, 1530–1609," *Studies in Medieval and Renaissance History*, IX (1972), 203–46.

*Le nuove musiche (*1602*)* and Monody in Naples, Rome, and Elsewhere
Specific studies of Giulio Caccini and his early monodies include Howard Mayer Brown, "The Geography of Florentine Monody: Caccini at Home and Abroad," *Early Music*, IX (1981), 147–168; Tim Carter, "Giulio Caccini (1551–1618): New Facts, New Music," *Studi musicali*, XVI (1987), 13–32; Carter, "On the Composition and Performance of Caccini's *Le nuove musiche* (1602)," *Early Music*, XII (1984), 208–217; H. Wiley Hitchcock, "Vocal Ornamentation in Caccini's *Nuove Musiche*," *The Musical Quarterly*, LVI (1970), 389–404; reprinted in *The Garland Library of the History of Western Music*, ed. Ellen Rosand, V, *Baroque Music*, I, *Seventeenth Century* (New York, 1985), pp. 131–47; and Stephen Willier, "Rhythmic Variants in Early Manuscript Versions of Caccini's Monodies," *Journal of the American Musicological Society*, XXXVI (1983), 481–97. The only published overview in English of early monody remains Nigel Fortune, "Italian Secular Monody from 1600 to 1635: An Introductory Survey," *The Musical Quarterly*, XXXIX (1953), 171–195; reprinted in *The Garland Library of the History of Western Music*, ed. Ellen Rosand, V, *Baroque Music*, I, *Seventeenth Century* (New York, 1985), pp. 47–71. A detailed study of the emergence of monody in Rome and Naples and of the origins of the chamber cantata is John Walter Hill, *Roman Monody, Cantata, and Opera from the Circles around Cardinal Montalto*, 2 vols. (Oxford: Clarendon Press, 1997). A very important treatment of the new serious canzonetta and the early Roman chamber cantata is Robert Rau Holzer, "Music and Poetry in Seventeenth-Century Rome: Settings of the Canzonetta and Cantata Texts of Francesco Balducci, Domenico Benigni, Francesco Melosio, and Antonio Abati," Ph.D. diss., Univ. of Pennsylvania, 1990.

Seconda Pratica and the Concerted Madrigal
The dispute between Artusi and Monteverdi is summarized by Claude V. Palisca, "The Artusi-Monteverdi Controversy," *The Monteverdi Companion*, ed. Denis Arnold and Nigel Fortune (New York, 1968), pp. 133–66. In addition to the two recent books on Monteverdi cited earlier, there are two additional treatments of the composer's madrigals: Nino Pirrotta, "Monteverdi's Poetic Choices," *Music and Culture in Italy from the Middle Ages to the Baroque: A Collection of Essays* (Cambridge, MA: Harvard University Press, 1984), pp. 271–316; and Gary Tomlinson, *Monteverdi and the End of the Renaissance* (Oxford: Oxford University Press, 1987).

Opera Continues in Mantua, Florence, and Rome
Two recent books devoted to Claudio Monteverdi are useful in placing his opera *L'Orfeo* in context: Paolo Fabbri, *Monteverdi*, trans. Tim Carter (Cambridge: Cambridge University Press, 1994); and Silke Leopold, *Monteverdi: Music in Transition*, trans. Anne Smith (Oxford: Oxford University Press, 1991). A detailed study of the opera is John Whenham, *Claudio Monteverdi: Orfeo* (Cambridge: Cambridge University Press, 1985). Operas and other musical spectacles in Florence after *L'Euridice*, particularly performances during the regency of the two women, are

explored in Kelley Ann Harness, "*Amazzoni di dio*: Florentine Musical Spectacle under Maria Maddalena d'Austria and Cristina di Lorena (1620–30)," Ph.D. diss., Univ. of Illinois, 1996. The beginnings of opera in Rome are explored by Hill, *Roman Monody, Cantata, and Opera*; by Margaret Murata, "Classical Tragedy in the History of Early Opera in Rome," *Early Music History*, IV (1984), 101–34; and by Murata in *Operas for the Papal Court, 1631–1668* (Ann Arbor, 1981). An outstanding study of music in the context of early seventeenth-century Roman culture and of Barberini family patronage is Frederick Hammond, *Music & Spectacle in Baroque Rome: Barberini Patronage under Urban VIII* (New Haven: Yale University Press, 1994). A study of the opera *Chi soffre speri* with text, translation, and score of the *Fiera di farfa* episode from it is Hammond, "Bernini and the 'Fiera di Farfa,'" *Gianlorenzo Bernini: New Aspects of His Art and Thought*, ed. Irving Lavin (University Park, PA: Pennsylvania State University Press, 1985), pp. 115–78.

CHAPTER 3

New Genres of Instrumental Music

FRESCOBALDI AND STYLE CHANGE IN LUTE AND HARPSICHORD MUSIC

T he virtuoso singers and composers of early monody and opera introduced in Chapter 2 served side by side in the courts of Italian noblemen
with composers and performers on keyboard and instruments of the lute
family. In both areas of composition and performance—vocal and instrumental—early seventeenth-century Italians sought to capture in notation the spontaneous effect of improvised performance, and both employed striking
contrasts and broad rhetorical gestures to stir the passions of listeners. An
important difference, however, is that improvisational style appeared much earlier in the written collections for keyboard and lute. The principal types of keyboard work—toccata, variations, dances, and contrapuntal elaboration—had
been composed for a century or more before Frescobaldi put the stamp of the
early Baroque and of his personal manner on them.

The teacher of Girolamo Frescobaldi (1583–1643, Fig. 3-1), Luzzasco Luzzaschi (ca. 1545–1607), was the leading composer at the court of Alfonso II d'Este,
duke of Ferrara. Luzzaschi was a famous keyboard virtuoso who composed

Figure 3-1. Drawing of
Girolamo Frescobaldi by
Claude Mellan

madrigals in the *seconda pratica* style earlier than Monteverdi and solo madrigals before Caccini. Frescobaldi's studies with Luzzaschi and his prodigious talent led to his employment at the Este court, where he met Carlo Gesualdo (ca. 1561–1613), composer of highly chromatic and dissonant polyphonic madrigals. When Duke Alfonso died without an heir in 1597, Ferrara was taken over by the pope, and the court was disbanded. After a few years, Frescobaldi moved to Rome, where he served in the households of several cardinals. In 1608 he won the important position of organist at St. Peter's basilica, which he held, with some interruptions, for the rest of his life.

Frescobaldi's most important compositions are included in two printed collections of toccatas (1615 and 1627; the second was republished in 1637, with the addition of variations, dances, etc.), five books of contrapuntal keyboard works (canzonas, ricercars, fantasies, capriccios, versets), a collection of ensemble canzonas (1628/1635), a book of five-voice madrigals (1608), two books of monodies (1630), two Mass settings, and numerous motets for one to four voices with basso continuo.

Toccatas

Frescobaldi's toccatas derive in style mainly from the Venetian school, as exemplified by the works of Claudio Merulo (1533–1604). The toccatas of earlier

Performance of Frescobaldi

FRESCOBALDI WROTE four prefaces to publications of his keyboard music (in 1615, 1616, 1624, and 1635) in which he included valuable remarks on the proper performance of his compositions. These can be supplemented by knowledge gained from contemporaneous instruction manuals and markings in works by Frescobaldi and others of his time. In contrapuntal works and variation sets, Frescobaldi expected a steady tempo. However, works with rapid passages might be played at a slower tempo than works without them. In toccatas the "manner of playing must not be subject to a beat, as we see practiced in modern madrigals, which, however difficult, are facilitated by means of the beat, conducting it now slow, now rapid, and even suspending it in the air, according to their passions" (1616). Keyboard fingering in Frescobaldi's day deliberately promoted a very slight lengthening of notes on the strong parts of the beat. Sustained notes, especially at suspensions, should often be repeated, and chords should be arpeggiated "so as not to leave the instrument empty" (1616), as happens when the sound dies away. Frescobaldi sometimes wrote out his trills, but at other times he simply marked them with the letter "t." His trills normally begin on the main note and oscillate upward.

Venetians such as Andrea Gabrieli (ca. 1532/3–1585) had consisted of little more than a rambling series of episodes with chords in one hand and runs in the other—a kind of piece that organists could improvise. Merulo gave the toccata more predictability of form, variety of textures, subtlety of rhythm, and expressive resources. A typical Merulo toccata may be divided into five sections: (1) chords with trills; (2) figural passage work with rhythmic variety and broad contours; (3) imitative counterpoint; (4) dissonances and chromaticism; (5) climactic return to figural passage work. Viewed in another way, these sections have been considered as embodying five different ways of varying an underlying madrigal-like composition for four or five continuous, vocally conceived voices, using patterned or unpatterned diminution. According to this view, one point of origin for the emergence of the keyboard toccata is the practice of playing a madrigal or motet on an organ or harpsichord with the addition of idiomatic keyboard diminutions. In this view, Merulo's toccatas are embellished, newly composed madrigals that were never texted and never sung.

Passages in triple or compound meter—found occasionally in polyphonic madrigals as well—were added to toccatas by composers in the generation after Merulo, as for example the toccata for chitarrone published in 1604 (A. 14) by the Venetian nobleman Giovanni Girolamo Kapsberger (ca. 1580–1651), a colleague of Frescobaldi in Rome for many years. Triple meter sections, suddenly slow phrases full of chromaticism and dissonance, and dramatically erratic figuration are typical of the toccatas by two Neapolitans, Ascanio Mayone (ca. 1565–1627) and Giovanni Maria Trabaci (ca. 1575–1647), published in 1603. These works, too, had an influence on Frescobaldi.

In spite of these influences, Frescobaldi's early toccatas were surprising and novel when his first collection of them was published in 1615. For the enlarged second edition of this collection in 1616, Frescobaldi wrote a preface that describes their style as "the manner of playing with *affetti cantabili* ("lyrical embellishments") and a *diversità di passi* (meaning both "variety of figural passages" and "contrasts between the structural divisions of the piece").

Frescobaldi presented his second book of toccatas (1627) as "conceived and carried out with novelty of artifice" in a "new manner" requiring "grace, ease, flexibility of tempo, and elegance" in performance. Meter change, not found in the first collection, is now included. The component sections tend to be more numerous, shorter, and more clearly set apart. Melodic, rhythmic, and harmonic formality is mixed into the informal figural passages, while seemingly whimsical variants of subject motives make the imitative sections less formal.

The ninth toccata from Frescobaldi's second book (A. 15) is both representative and, like most of the others, special in certain ways. Some of the sections of this work are so short that one might think of them as subsections of longer segments. The wide variety of textures, rhythms, and degrees of formality, the sudden dramatic juxtapositions between contrasting passages, and the constantly changing shape of related ideas make this work fresh, spontaneous, and bizarre. On the other side of the balance, most of its sections are internally unified by a small number of musical ideas, and the whole derives some coherence

EXAMPLE 3-1. Two conventional motives found in various guises in later passages, in Frescobaldi's *Il secondo libro de toccate* (1727), Toccata nona

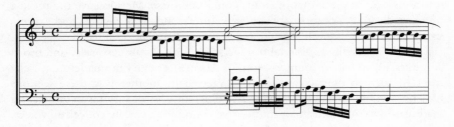

from the recurrence in many guises of two conventional motives that appear in the left-hand figure that crosses the first barline (Ex. 3-1).

In Frescobaldi's ninth toccata, the five types of passage established by Merulo are present, along with the triple-meter episodes added to the genre by Kapsberger and the Neapolitans. The traditional chordal opening is richly embellished, but its underlying harmony is easy to follow (Ex. 3-2). In fugal passages (mm. 12–15, 27–29, 31–34), the subject is stretched and pulled in various ways, never stated exactly the same way twice. The *ligature e durezze* section (mm. 25–26) is very brief. Several of the triple- or compound-meter passages feature conflicting time signatures, which appear to represent deliberate superimpositions of duple and triple divisions of the beat. This is probably the feature of the toccata Frescobaldi meant in the remark added to the end of the work: "Not without toil is the end attained."

Variations

Like toccatas, variations may be thought of as arising out of an extemporaneous performance practice captured and refined by musical notation. Variation

EXAMPLE 3-2. The chordal outline that is embellished in Frescobaldi's *Il secondo libro di toccate* (1727), Toccata nona, mm. 1–9

technique can be found in music as early as the fourteenth century, and formal variation sets for keyboard instruments date back to the early 1500s. Frescobaldi and his Italian contemporaries continued the earlier tradition of composing variations upon well-known melodies and upon the same chordal/bass patterns, such as the Romanesca, that were used in monodic strophic variations such as Caccini's *Torna, deh torna pargoletto mio* (A. 5). Variations on these traditional patterns in the seventeenth century tended to repeat a standard bass line in every variation far more often than was customary in the previous century. This is especially characteristic of variations on the short ostinato basses—the passacaglia and the ciaccona. Example 3-3 shows common—although not invariable—chord patterns represented by a bass line associated with the individual genre of composition.

The **Passamezzo (antico and moderno)** was originally an Italian duplemeter dance of the period ca. 1550–1650. In written variations, passing notes or auxiliary harmonies may be inserted between the chords of these frameworks or the associated bass notes. This process is shown in Example 3-3.

The **Romanesca** was a musical formula used in the sixteenth and seventeenth centuries for singing poetry (especially *ottava rima*) and for instrumental variations. A family of chordal/bass patterns is the most conspicuous feature that Romanesca variations have in common. Although some authorities maintain that two phrases of descending melody, note-against-note above the bass, formed part of the Romanesca tradition, those melodic phrases are found in no written music. In vocal and instrumental variations of the early seventeenth century, the Romanesca is almost always written in duple meter but with a predominant pattern of organization that suggests triple meter. The basic chordal/bass framework is normally expanded by means of passing notes and replacement harmonies like those of the basso continuo part for Caccini's *Torna, deh torna pargoletto mio* (A. 5).

The **Passacaglia** arose from the popular music of Spain and first appears as a chord pattern in guitar books. A passacaglia pattern was often used as a brief interlude between strophes of a song or between different songs. The name, which derives from the Spanish words *pasar* ("to walk") and *calle* ("street"), suggests that it was once played by street entertainers as they walked from place to place. In early seventeenth-century Italian guitar books, passacaglias most often are given as a pattern of four chords (the primitive pattern shown in Ex. 3-3). On the other hand, in early Italian variations, the passacaglia usually employs a repeating bass ostinato that traces, with some deviations, a minor scale descending from the eighth down to the fifth degree (the developed pattern), as we see in the variations by Frescobaldi (1627, A. 17). Many passacaglia variations add chromatic intermediary steps to this pattern, and in some the pattern is inverted melodically, producing a four-note rising scale segment.

Ciaccona: To judge from Spanish literature and songs of the late sixteenth century, the ciaccona was originally a popular dance associated with the West Indies and accompanied by castanets. It first appears in guitar collections as the primitive chord pattern shown in Example 3-3. In later variants the final V

EXAMPLE 3-3. Common chordal/bass patterns used in seventeenth-century music

chord was often extended by a standard cadential formula (the developed form shown in Ex. 3-3). One of the earliest known sets of instrumental variations on this ostinato (1623, A. 16) was composed for chitarrone by Alessandro Piccinini (1566–ca. 1638), a colleague of Frescobaldi at the Este court in Ferrara. This work is typical of early ciaccona variations in the persistence of the bass melody, the use of a repeating chord progression with each recurrence of the bass, and the unified rhythm within each variation, which sways between the patterns ♩♩ and ♩♩.

Other patterns used for variations in seventeenth-century music include those derived from the Ruggiero (a singing formula), the Folia (originally a folk dance in Portugal), and La Monaca (a popular song). Although these patterns are of diverse origins and have tunes or tune families associated with them, they all give rise to chordal/bass patterns that are used as the basis of variations having little or no connection with the musical genres or practices in which the patterns originated.

Two of Frescobaldi's passacaglias appear as the third movement of short sets of dances. In two of these sets, the first movement in duple meter and the second movement in triple use the same motives. This is a vestige of a Renaissance compositional practice that probably originated in an unwritten tradition of modifying a duple-mater dance extemporaneously to make it go in triple meter. The gagliarda and corrente in Frescobadi's *Aria detta la Frescobalda* (1627) are completely parallel in this traditional manner.

Contrapuntal Works

Likewise traditional in basic format are Frescobaldi's contrapuntal keyboard works—ricercars, canzonas, fantasias, and capriccios. The traditional keyboard ricercar that Frescobaldi inherited began in the 1540s with various transferences of Renaissance motet procedures to the medium of instrumental ensemble and organ. Like motets, ricercars were usually pervasively imitative in texture, serious in character, stately in rhythm, and conjunct in melody. Some of them exhibit chromaticism and dissonance. Although many of Frescobaldi's ricercars employ a series of imitated subjects, like a motet, others use a single or predominant subject, an approach introduced by Jacques Buus in his *Recercari . . . da cantare et sonare d'organo et altri stromenti* (1547 and 1549).

Canzonas derive from Parisian chansons of the sixteenth century, either as embellished arrangements for instruments of specific songs or as imitations of the Parisian chanson style in general. By contrast with the ricercar, canzonas tend to be lively in melodic contour and rhythm, typically beginning with some variant of the pattern ¢♩♩♩. They usually feature some form of repetition, often of the initial duple-meter subject after a homophonic triple-meter middle section. Although Frescobaldi's fantasias and capriccios most often belong to the ricercar family, the title "capriccio" can also appear over canzonas and variations.

It is typical of Frescobaldi's works bearing the titles "fantasia" or "capriccio" to incorporate such intriguing features as simultaneously stating several subjects, presenting subjects in rhythmic augmentation or diminution or in melodic inversion, and limiting the composition by imposing certain obligations, such as avoiding all steps, resolving all suspensions upward, or requiring the organist to sing a cantus firmus indicated by a verbal rule (a "canon") but not notated. Among these devices one also finds the *inganno* ("deception"), which transforms a subject by replacing one or more of its notes with different

EXAMPLE 3-4. The gamut of hexachords

pitches that happen to have the same syllable in a different hexachord (see Ex. 3-5). Some words of explanation are required here.

Musicians of the early seventeenth century continued to name and organize the pitches of the normal ranges of voices (the "gamut") according to a set of three six-note scales called "hexachords" in three octaves, as shown in Example 3-4. The gamut could be continued into higher and lower octaves if needed, and it could be transposed by adding a key signature or by consistently employing accidentals. At this time, musicians were trained by singing the solmization syllables of the hexachords as a way of learning intervals and positions within the gamut.

The other method of accounting for the structure of the pitch material of melodies and contrapuntal textures in use during the seventeenth century was mode, which remained the system of pitch organization for contrapuntal works throughout the century. Yet some types of composition seem to operate outside the modal tradition and to rely on chords and chord patterns. An explanation of these two approaches is required before they can be applied to individual works.

EXAMPLE 3-5. Transportation of Subject 3 by augmentation and *inganno* in Frescobaldi's Fantasia 10 (1608)

CHORDAL COMPOSITION

The sound of the triadic chord had already been common in music for more than a century when in 1558 Gioseffo Zarlino gave it theoretical recognition as the basic building block of music. However, Zarlino recognized two different musical triads: (1) the bass note with the third and fifth above, and (2) the bass note with the third and sixth above.

Theoretical recognition of triadic inversion can first be found in the *Artis musicae delineatio* ("The Art of Music Outlined," 1608) by Otto Siegfried Harnisch (ca. 1568–1623), in the *Synopsis musicae novae* ("Summary of New Music," 1612) by Johannes Lippius (1585–1612), and in *A New Way of Making Fowre Parts in Counter-point* (ca. 1613/14) by Thomas Campion (1567–1620).

Harnisch, drawing on earlier work (1581) by Johannes Avianius (d. 1617), describes the triadic chord as consisting of a root (*basis*), a third (*medius*), and a fifth. A triad is "perfect," according to Harnisch, "when the *basis* or lower part of the fifth is written in its usual place, or an octave below. It is "imperfect" when the *basis* is written only in the upper octave, so that the *medius*, the third, which lies between the top and the bottom of the fifth, is left as the lowest part of the chord. If the bass has the note that would normally stand a fifth above the *basis*, then that note will form a fourth with one of the upper voices. Harnisch considers this last triadic inversion a dissonance.

Lippius uses terms similar to Harnisch's: the *trias radicalis* ("root triad") consists of a bass note (*basis*) and the notes a third (*media*) and a fifth (*ultima*) above it. "The bass voice may sometimes, although rarely, use the *ultima* or *media* of the triadic root," he explains. Thus, any triad can be inverted by placing in the bass a note belonging to any one of the triad's three constituent pitch classes. In addition, the notes of the triad can be transposed and doubled in any octave. Lippius even taught beginners to start a new composition by writing the bass line on a great staff, then placing dots above each bass note to indicate members of the corresponding root triad (Ex. 3-6a), and finally connecting the dots without violating the rules of counterpoint in order to form the tenor, alto, and soprano voices (Ex. 3-6b). Lippius's theory had many followers in Germany, including Baryphonus (1615, 1630), Alsted (1620, 1630), Crüger (1630, 1754), Herbst (1643), Printz (1676–77), Ahle (1695–1701), and Werckmeister (1702).

Campion likewise teaches a way of composing against a bass, but he also adds a method and terminology for analyzing existing music. He explains that when a chord contains a sixth above the lowest voice, that lowest voice is not the "true base," which is found a third lower than the written bass. Campion's "true base" is the root of an invertible triad.

The fundamental and invertible nature of triads finds its clearest practical recognition in the notation and performance of dances and song accompaniments for the five-string Spanish guitar, which was the rage in Italy during the early decades of the seventeenth century. Spanish guitar music was notated in a simple tablature, each chord voicing represented by a letter of the alphabet and the number of repetitions of the chord sometimes shown by slanted pen strokes.

EXAMPLE 3-6a. Bass with dots showing the notes of triadic chords, from Lippius (1612)

EXAMPLE 3-6b. Three upper parts realized from chordal notes chosen, from Lippius (1612)

This system was first printed in Girolamo Montesardo's *Nuova inventione d'intavolatura per sonare li balletti sopra la chitarra spagnuola* ("New Invention of a Tablature for Playing Dances on the Spanish Guitar," 1606), although it was found in manuscripts at least a decade earlier. In this notation, patterns such as the romanesca, passamezzo moderno, ciaccona, and passacaglia were shown simply as a series of chords, some of them sounding as root triads, some of them in first inversion, and some of them in second inversion. The succession of chords in guitar tablature went ahead without regard to the melodic shape of the bass line or to the inevitable consecutive fifths, producing purely chordal music.

MODAL COMPOSITION

Modality was originally a system for classifying plain chant antiphons in order to choose the correct psalm tone. It became a system for classifying and composing chants of all types by the late Middle Ages. It was first applied to polyphonic music by Tinctoris in 1476, and by the end of the sixteenth century it was a topic treated in every book about counterpoint. Throughout the seventeenth century, modality remained the only comprehensive theory of musical pitch structure, even if certain types of music—those based on established chordal/bass patterns and those that used an improvisational style, for example—seem not to conform to the norms of modal composition.

Modality was invoked as both a system of classification of existing music, independent of composer's intentions, and as a framework for composition that could be followed more or less closely. A composition was assigned to the mode with which it shared the most notable characteristics, in spite of occasional counterindications. Likewise, a given composition might reflect the chosen mode in some ways and not in others.

By the later sixteenth century and throughout the seventeenth century, there were three essential criteria for determining the mode of a composition and three secondary features. The three essential criteria were:

1. The pattern of whole and half steps in relation to the final note (actual or expected) in a melody or individual voice. This was usually described in treatises as **the species of fifth** (i.e., pattern of whole and half steps within the fifth) above the final and **species of fourth** (i.e., pattern of whole and half steps within the fourth) either above the fifth or below the final, depending on whether the melody or voice is cast in an authentic mode or in a plagal mode. Potentially these patterns of whole and half steps could be transposed to any pitch level through the use of key signatures, but in practice only one or two transpositions (key signatures) were used for each mode during the seventeenth century.

2. **The position of the final** of the composition (most readily identified as the final pitch class of the bass) **within the** (possibly hypothetical) central octave or **ambitus** of each voice. The ambitus extends either an octave above the final in the case of authentic modes or a fifth above and a fourth below the final in the case of plagal modes. Theoretically, a polyphonic texture was thought to contain four essential voices—soprano, alto, tenor, bass—sharing the same final but alternating between authentic and plagal form of the mode from highest to lowest voice. The ambitus of the tenor and of the soprano relative to the final determine whether the composition as a whole is classified as authentic or plagal.

3. **The type of motive** or **melodia** heard at the beginning of the composition. Although important for the judgment of mode in chant, melodia is less essential than the first two criteria in determining the mode of polyphonic works.

The three secondary features of a mode in polyphony were:

1. The compositional definition of a second-most important pitch class, after the final, called **the repercussion**, which corresponds to the reciting pitch (tenor) of the associated psalm tone formula. In authentic modes, this repercussion is a fifth above the final, except that the note C replaces the note B when the final is E. In plagal modes, the repercussion is a third below the repercussion of the authentic mode sharing the same final, except that C replaces B when the final is G.

2. **Melodic and contrapuntal framing of the modal octave** during the exordium (generally, the portion of the work from the beginning up to the first important cadence) through a special emphasis on the final, the boundary notes marking off the characteristic fourth and fifth of the mode, and the repercussion (if different from both boundary notes). This framing is usually accomplished by the melodic shape of

the most important motives and melodic lines, especially a motive that is imitated, the pitch levels of imitative entries, and/or the way each two adjacent voices divide the modal octave between them.

3. **The hierarchy of cadences** according to the pitch class of the note of resolution in relation to the final. By the seventeenth century, the order of this hierarchy is usually final, repercussion, boundary notes, and third above the final. Some theorists **also** mention the **type of final cadence**— whether authentic, plagal, or phrygian—as a guide to modal classification.

In addition, many sixteenth- and seventeenth-century theorists and composers associated specific combinations of clefs and key signatures with the representation of specific modes. These combinations, however, are a matter of convenience—clefs are chosen to avoid ledger lines and key signatures are selected in order to avoid unsingable tessituras. Neither clefs nor key signatures should be thought of as intrinsic to the modes.

Most composers and theorists in the seventeenth century continued the tradition of naming eight modes. However, ever since Heinrich Glarean proposed it in his *Dodecachordon* (1547), a twelve-mode system appeared in theory and compositional thought from time to time, usually in certain musical centers, such as Venice. To the traditional eight modes, Glarean proposed four more: Mode 9 (Aeolian) and Mode 10 (Hypoaeolian) with their final A, and Mode 11 (Ionian) and Mode 12 (Hypoionian) with their final on C. In the eight-mode system, which remained the predominant one throughout the seventeenth century, compositions ending on A were thought to represent transposed E modes, and compositions ending on C were considered to represent transposed F modes.

There were three methods of naming these modes: by number, by maniera and ambitus (for the original eight modes), and by Latinized Greek name, as follows:

Mode 1	authentic protus	Dorian
Mode 2	plagal protus	Hypodorian
Mode 3	authentic deuterus	Phrygian
Mode 4	plagal deuterus	Hypophrygian
Mode 5	authentic tritus	Lydian
Mode 6	plagal tritus	Hypolydian
Mode 7	authentic tetrardus	Mixolydian
Mode 8	plagal tetrardus	Hypomixolydian
[Mode 9]		[Aeolian]
[Mode 10]		[Hypoaeolian]
[Mode 11]		[Ionian]
[Mode 12]		[Hypoionian]

Designation by number was by far the most common.

The specific features of each mode changed slightly over the sixteenth and seventeenth century. The effects of these changes tended to disturb the regular

EXAMPLE 3-7. The octave structure of the modes according to late-Medieval and early-Renaissance theory

symmetry and diminish the variety of pitch patterns in use. In Examples 3-7, 3-8, and 3-9, the final of each of the traditional eight modes is shown as a whole note, the boundary notes as half notes, and the repercussion by a quarter note.

Under the influence of Zarlino, many theoretical treatises in the seventeenth century present the modes as a set of abstract designs that have little relation to actual practice: the modal finals are D, E, F, G, A, and C; typical transpositions and modifications of scale patterns via key signatures are not recognized; and the principal cadence pitches are uniformly the final, the third above the final, and the fifth above the final, with no special recognition of the repercussion. A more complex and realistic accounting of modal practice can be found in *L'organo suonarino* (1605) and *Cartella musicale* (1614) by the Bolognese organist and composer Adriano Banchieri (1568–1634). Banchieri's explanation, or at least his conclusions, are repeated in an important series of treatises stretching almost to the end of the seventeenth century. More importantly, Banchieri's more sophisticated account of modes corresponds to seventeenth-century practice far better than the rigid and mechanical twelve-mode system deriving from Zarlino. Banchieri's account is of great significance because the compositional practice that it reports and explains remained important during the entire seventeenth century.

The modal octave structures that result from Banchieri's theory are summarized in Example 3-9, where the octave framework to be emphasized at the beginning of the movement or work is shown by half notes, the most important cadential goals are shown in quarter notes, and the final is shown as a whole note. Notice that works or movements cast in either of the two deuterus (or phrygian) modes, numbers 3 and 4, begin as if in a minor mode on A, and both of them include the note C among the significant cadence goals. But mode 3 concludes on A, whereas mode 4 ends on E. The principal cadence goals, according to Banchieri, are drawn from a mixture of final, boundary tone, third degree above the final, and repercussion, according to practical musical convenience rather than following any logical principal. The finals of modes 3 and 7 are quite different from those assigned by earlier modal theory, and this requires some explanation.

EXAMPLE 3-8. A typical late sixteenth-century formulation of modal octave structure, based on Gallus Dressler, *Praecepta musicae poeticae* (1563)

EXAMPLE 3-9. Typical pitch structures used in the seventeenth century to represent the eight tones, based on Adriano Banchieri, *Cartella musicale* (1614)

*Lorenzo Penna, *Li primi albori musicali* (1672), says that some composers represent the 7th mode with the final D and a key signature of two sharps, while others represent it with the final E and a signature of one sharp. Similar reports are found in other treatises. The explanation offered is that the final D with two sharps represents a different alternative psalm-tone ending.

In Banchieri's more sophisticated account, a series of eight modes for polyphony are explained by merging the main features of the eight ecclesiastical modes for chant with other features derived from some of the corresponding eight psalm tones. In the structures of Banchieri's polyphonic modes that accommodate psalm tones (Ex. 3-9), the final of each mode or "tone" and the boundary notes of the fifth and fourth are given as in older, conventional modal theory. Mode 2 is shown in the traditional transposition upward by fourth with one flat, as it was in Example 3-8. Mode 6 is given the signature with B♭, also as in Example 3-8. Mode 5 is transposed to C, but since the untransposed Mode 5 was considered to have a B♭ (again as in Ex. 3-8), the transposition to C results in removal of the flat. For each mode, Bancieri also restores recognition of the repercussion or reciting tone from the associated psalm tone formula—a feature suppressed by Zarlino when it did not fit into his modal triad consisting of scale-degrees 1, 3, 5, and 8. However, in the cases of Modes 3 and 7, Banchieri incorporates a feature of the associated psalm tone never previously used in modal theory—the final pitch of the psalm-tone termination formula. Thus, Psalm Tone 3, which has a reciting tone of C, does not end on the modal final, E. Actually, chant books give five possible termination formulas for Psalm Tone 3, one that ends on B, two that end on A, and two that end on G. Of these, Banchieri arbitrarily selects one of them that ends on A (shown in Ex. 3-10), and he uses this pitch in substitution for the modal final, E, in his display of the third mode in Example 3-9. For Mode 7, Banchieri takes as his modal final the note A, which is the final pitch from one of the five alternative termination formulas available for Psalm Tone 7. But then he transposes the resulting structure down a fifth to D, with a signature of one flat. Although Psalm Tone 5 also terminates on A, Banchieri ignores this and maintains the traditional modal structure based on F, which he transposes to C.

It is clear, then, from Banchieri's selection of concluding pitches that his objective was not solely to provide composers with the means of matching the pitch structure of their vocal settings and organ versets to the structure of the psalm tone when they compose psalm-verse settings and organ versets for alternation with plain chant. He apparently aimed, instead, to restore recognition of the reciting pitch (repercussion) to all the modes and to give a theoretical home

EXAMPLE 3-10. The structure of Psalm Tone 3a applied to the first verse of Psalm 109

to music written in an A minor mode, a C major mode, and a D minor mode with one flat, without adding to the traditional number of chant modes.

Although theory treatises usually present the modes as if they were something static—established at the beginning of the composition and never altered thereafter—it is clear in practice that the techniques used to establish the reigning mode at the outset of a work are often applied later in the composition to outline or suggest a different modal octave in preparation for a cadence on another pitch class. Note that cadences on the principal and subsidiary modal degrees do not signal a change of mode by themselves. A series of theorists from the fifteenth and sixteenth centuries discuss change of mode, including the authoritative Gioseffo Zarlino, who mentions cases in which the ranges of both authentic and plagal modes with the same final are used, as well as cases in which melodic shapes repeatedly emphasize a fifth different from the one that defines the original mode (*Istitutioni harmoniche*, 1558, Part IV, Chapter 14). Pietro Pontio, *Dialogo . . . ove si tratta della theorica et prattica di musica* (1595) shows in detail how new points of imitation and cadences can remove a polyphonic piece from one mode to another. Change of mode figured prominently in the controversy between Artusi and the Monteverdi brothers. Christoph Bernhard, a student of Heinrich Schütz, in his *Tractatus compositionis augmentatus*, written during the 1650s, presents a detailed analysis of mode changes in an Offertory by Palestrina. In the early eighteenth century, Jean-Philippe Rameau called change of mode, logically enough, "modulation."

Cadences are integral to modal composition because the selection of pitches on which they conclude, relative to the final, help to determine the mode.

Like their predecessors, seventeenth-century musicians continued to view the cadence as a particular kind of musical articulation or conclusion based upon a two-voice framework and its typical harmonic elaborations. The two-voice framework of a cadence normally involves stepwise contrary motion from an imperfect consonance (major sixth, minor third, or minor tenth) to an octave or unison, in which the note that is followed by an ascent is usually delayed by a suspension. The normal attributes of a cadence include conclusion on the strong beat of a measure, some degree of rhythmic stoppage at the resolution, and, in vocal music, the completion of a unit of meaning in the text.

In theory, the two-voice cadential framework involved the soprano and tenor, although it could actually be formed by any two voices. By the sixteenth century, typical harmonizations became so closely associated with the two-voice cadential structures that two or even one of the harmonizing voice patterns could, under certain circumstances, replace the theoretically normal two-voice structure. The absence of the typical harmonization of the final octave of a cadence (bass note, third, and fifth) was viewed as an indication of avoidance of full cadential closure.

Example 3-11, taken from the *Mostra delli tuoni della musica* ("Presentation of the Musical Modes") by Orazio Vecchi (1550–1605), shows cadences on all the diatonic pitches of the natural system. Names of the final pitch classes and lines showing the contrary motion of the soprano and tenor have been added. The leap of a fourth or fifth in the bass should be regarded as typical. Notice that when the major sixth does not occur in the natural system, a sharp has been added to the soprano. The cadence on E is created by a half step descending in the tenor, rather than by a half step ascending in the soprano. In this example, the conclusion of the cadence to E in the soprano and tenor is harmonized by an A, rather than by an E, in the bass. This results in a progression of a D chord to an A chord at the cadence, which is the only way the plagal cadence was recognized theoretically at this time. In other E cadences, the descending stepwise motion of the tenor can be found transferred to the bass with the final note harmonized

EXAMPLE 3-11. Cadences on all the pitches of the natural system, from Orazio Vecchi, *Mostra delli tuoni della musica* (ca. 1600)

with a major chord on E. In Example 3-12, from the same treatise by Vecchi, we see yet another harmonization of the E cadence as well as a brief coda following the final cadence on C, which concludes with a plagal chord progression.

Distinct theoretical and practical methods of thinking about music and chordal and modal composition gradually merge in the course of the seventeenth century, until by about 1680 these two principles can be found working in tandem to form what today is sometimes called "harmonic tonality." For the present, it will serve our purposes to examine modal composition at work in the church organ music of Frescobaldi.

CHURCH ORGAN MUSIC IN EARLY SEVENTEENTH-CENTURY ITALY

Since organs in seventeenth-century Italy did not generally have independent pedalboards, Italian organ music of that period is largely indistinguishable from harpsichord music in notation and musical idiom. The principal genres of

EXAMPLE 3-12. Additional examples of cadences from Orazio Vecchi, *Mostra delli tuoni della musica* (ca. 1600)

seventeenth-century Italian keyboard music—toccatas, partitas, canzonas, ricer-cars, fantasies, dances—were played on either instrument. The only music that was intended only for organ performance was that written specifically for the Roman Catholic liturgy, and even in this case certain works playable by the harpsichord could also be played on the organ in church.

Virtually every church in Europe had an organ during the seventeenth cen-tury, and the instrument played a major role in most church services. In Catholic churches at this time, the use of the organ during the Mass was regu-lated by the *Ceremoniale episcoporum* ("Ceremonial of Bishops") issued by Pope Clement VIII in 1600:

> At the solemn Mass the organ is played *alternatim* for the Kyrie eleison and the Gloria in excelsis . . .; likewise at the end of the Epistle and at the Offer-tory; for the Sanctus, *alternatim*; then more gravely and softly during the Ele-vation of the Most Holy Sacrament; for the Agnus Dei, *alternatim*, and at the verse before the post-Communion prayer; also at the end of the Mass.

From collections of church organ music such as Frescobaldi's *Fiori musicali* ("Musical Flowers," 1635) or the *Annuale* (1645) by the Venetian organist Gio-vanni Battista Fasolo (ca. 1598–after 1664), we can see that "at the end of the Epistle" (that is, during the silent recitation of the Gradual) it was normal to play a canzona. "At the Offertory" (that is, during the silent recitation of the Offer-tory) it was customary to play a ricercar. During the Elevation of the consecrated Host the organist usually played a toccata or a short, somber "modulation." And a canzona was customarily played while communion was offered ("before the post-Communion prayer"). A canzona or toccata could be performed following the Mass. There were also specific places in the Vespers service where the organ was played, particularly in place of alternate verses of the Magnificat.

The organ alternated with the plainchant choir during the singing of four of the five parts of the Mass Ordinary—Kyrie, Gloria, Sanctus, and Agnus Dei, but not the Credo. This is the meaning of the word *alternatim* in the "Ceremo-nial of Bishops." In this practice, the organist played short movements, called versets, in replacement of specific portions of the plainchant. The result of this alternation of chant and organ was called an Organ Mass. During the first half of the seventeenth century, each of these versets normally incorporated the replaced portion of the plainchant in some way. An example of this is the set of versets for the Kyrie of the normal Sunday Mass (A. 18), from the *Ricercari a quattro voci, canzoni francesi, toccate, et versi* (1641) by the Neapolitan organist Giovanni Salvatore (early seventeenth century to about 1688).

In a performance of Kyrie versets, the plainchant choir begins by chanting the Kyrie once. Salvatore's first verset replaces the repetition of the Kyrie; it incorporates the replaced chant melody as cantus firmus in long notes in the bass. After the third Kyrie, which is chanted, Salvatore's second and third versets replace the first and third Christe, incorporating the first five notes of the Kyrie melody as the basic motive for elaboration. Salvatore's fourth verset, which replaces the second return of the Kyrie chant, prefigures the melody for the penultimate Kyrie, which the choir chants immediately afterward. The final verset has no apparent relation to the chant.

The organ canzona was the genre selected to replace the Gradual after the reading of the Epistle, probably because of its liveliness, in keeping with the public character of the Liturgy of the Word, the educational portion of the Mass between the Introductory Rite—Introit, Kyrie, and Gloria—and the consecration of the communion host. The first of Banchieri's *Fantasie over canzoni alla franceses* ("Fantasias or Canzonas in the French Style," 1603, A. 19) employs the typical dactylic rhythm (— ∪ ∪), lively melodic style, and opposition of contrapuntal and homophonic textures mentioned in the previous section. In addition, the return in bar 35 of the opening motive, after a relatively homophonic episode, is common in canzonas of the early seventeenth century.

This canzona serves as a relatively uncomplicated example of Mode 2 in its typical transposition to G by means of a signature of one flat (refer to Ex. 3-9). The final, G, can be found in the alto, tenor, and bass of the last chord. The soprano (canto) and tenor voices do not extend upward beyond the half step neighbor (E♭) to the upper boundary note of the characteristic fifth of the mode (G–D). At the beginning, the octave framework of Mode 2 on G, D–G–D, is outlined by the soprano and alto together and by the tenor and bass together, as is typical when the imitated motive emphasizes the boundary notes of the fifth or fourth. And all the cadences are on the final, G, except the two on B♭ (bars 19 and 30). B♭ is the repercussion or reciting tone of Mode 2 transposed to G, and a cadence on the repercussion does not necessarily signal a change of mode. However, in the measures leading up to this cadence, Banchieri emphasizes the pitches F and B♭, particularly in the soprano and bass parts. This suggests a momentary change to the mode that Banchieri identifies as number 6, transposed here to B♭. The same brief change of mode occurs in measures 28–30, as part of a large-scale repetition; mm. 12–22 are repeated in mm. 22–34.

The less familiar structure of Mode 4 is illustrated by Frescobaldi's *Canzon quarti toni dopo il post comune* ("Canzona in the fourth mode after the post communion") from his *Fiori musicali* of 1635 (A. 20). The initial outline of A–E–A, projected in Banchieri's display of the modes (Ex. 3-9), is presented in the combination of the soprano and alto voices in measures 1–3. This is illustrated in Example 3-13a, in which the first cadence on the final, E, is also marked. This is a Phrygian cadence, in which the major sixth formed by the D and the F expands to an octave (E–E) by means of a half-step *descent* (F–E) and a whole step *ascent* (D–E). Compare this with the cadences on E in Examples 3-11 and 3-12. Other Phrygian cadences on E appear in measures 17, 21, 26, and 59; in the last case, the expected E in the soprano voice is replaced by a rest. The other cadences in this work are Phrygian cadences on B and normal (authentic) cadences on E, A, and C, exactly as Banchieri's model predicts. None of these cadences is associated with a change of mode.

Frescobaldi's *Canzon quarti toni dopo il post comune* also illustrates the variation canzona, a subtype that can be traced back to Giovanni Maria Trabaci's

EXAMPLE 3-13a. The framework of Mode 4 and Phrygian cadence at the
beginning of Frescobaldi's *Canzon quarti toni dopo il post comune* (1635)

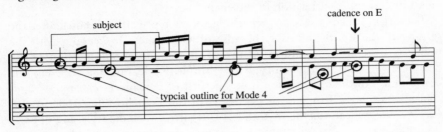

Ricercate, canzone franceses, capricci . . . of 1603. In this subtype of canzona, the initial subject returns in one or more transformations, usually in at least one new
meter. In the case of Frescobaldi's *Canzon quarti toni dopo il post comune*, a first
variant of the original subject, rhythmically and metrically transformed, is
introduced in measure 18. This is shown in Example 3-13b. Essentially the
same variant is presented soon after in triply augmented rhythm (mm. 22–25
in the soprano, to begin with). Measure 39 begins a final section based on a
second major variant of the subject, shown in Example 3-13c.

The genres cultivated by Frescobaldi and his contemporaries remained typical of Italian keyboard music throughout the seventeenth century and well into
the beginning of the eighteenth.

Canzonas were typically used in a seventeenth-century Mass during the
Liturgy of the Word (the portion of the Mass devoted to biblical readings and
general prayers) and after the communion. During the Liturgy of the Eucharist
(the preparation, transubstantiation, and distribution of the communion bread
and wine), a more somber ricercar was played instead. An organ ricercar tends
to be slower in rhythm and often is more chromatic and dissonant than a canzona. In his *Fiori musicali* (1635), Frescobaldi provides ricercars to be played
"after the Credo," which means in place of the Offertory, and during the Elevation of the host.

The genres cultivated by Frescobaldi and his contemporaries remained typical of Italian keyboard music throughout the seventeenth century and well into
the beginning of the eighteenth.

EXAMPLE 3-13b. The first major variant of the subject in Frescobaldi's *Canzon
quarti toni dopo il post comune* (1635)

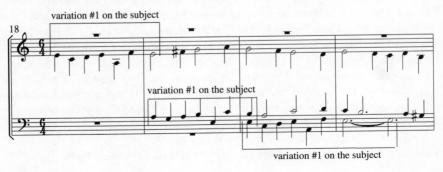

EXAMPLE 3-13c. The second major variant of the subject in Frescobaldi's *Canzon quarti toni dopo il post comune* (1635)

variation #2 on the subject, incomplete

variation #2 on the subject, complete

THE VIOLIN AND ITALIAN INSTRUMENTAL ENSEMBLE MUSIC

The earliest known written compositions that specify violins are two dances for five-part ensemble (two violins, two violas, and bass, all of them considered to be "violins," i.e., members of the violin family) that were played by ten Italians as part of a French court musical spectacle called the *Balet comique de la royne* (1581). There are many earlier references to the use of violins for dancing and outdoor serenading going back to 1523.

Jambe de Fer, who is the earliest (1556) to describe a four-string violin tuned in fifths, expressed the common opinion that the violin was a low-class instrument because "there are few persons who use it save those who make a living from it through their labor," whereas with the viola da gamba "gentlemen, merchants, and other virtuous people pass their time."

Actually, instruments of the violin family began to participate in art music by the middle of the sixteenth century, at least in northern Italy (Fig. 3-2). This is best documented in Brescia. There, as in most cities of Europe, the civic government contracted with instrumentalists for their participation in ceremonial occasions. Whereas the instrumentalists were salaried in most cities, the Brescians played in civic processions and in church in return for certain exclusive privileges as protection against competition. In Brescia several stable ensembles, called "companies," were covered by this agreement, rather than a single municipal band, as in most other towns.

The earliest petition from the Brescian instrumentalists in 1508 expresses their desire to associate their trade with "worthy and eminent" accomplishment, with what is "elevated and lofty," and with products of "sublime and excellent" talents, and it refers with scorn to "base, vile, and inexpert" players of crude and unrefined instruments. The ensemble companies covered by the agreement with the city were selected by a panel of experts on the basis of an audition. In a petition of 1546, one of the ensembles, consisting of six musicians, attested that they played trumpets, shawms, cornetts, crumhorns, recorders, flutes, and violins (*viole da braccio*) "in consorts, with the organ, and extemporaneously" (*in concerti et nell'organo, come all'improviso*). By 1562, the city

Figure 3-2. Gaudenzio Ferrari, Angel playing a violin, from a group of wood figures in the church of the Sacro Monte in Varallo, Italy, before 1549

recognized three specialized ensembles: a corps of trumpets, a wind band, and an ensemble of violin-family instruments (probably five).

A corps (*compagnia*) of trumpets in seventeenth-century Italy, and probably in the rest of Europe, made music through a combination of improvisation together with tunes and procedures normally learned by rote but occasionally written out. Two instruction manuals that explain this are Cesare Bendinelli, *Tutta l'arte della trombetta* ("The Whole Art of the Trumpet," 1614) and Girolamo Fantini, *Modo per imparare a sonare di tromba* ("Method for Learning How to Play the Trumpet," 1638). Two similar but less detailed manuals were written earlier by the Danish court trumpeters Hendrich Lübeck (ca. 1596–1609) and Magnus Thomsen (1598). From these manuals and several further printed treatises it becomes clear that trumpet corps normally involved five parts, whose range, function, character, and name were determined by well-established tradition. The highest of these, the *clarino* ("clarion"), improvised a rapid, embellished countermelody. Example 3-14 shows a sonata with its clarino part written out by Bendinelli, to which have been added the *alto e basso*, *vulgano*, and *grosso* according to his instructions. Trumpet sonatas like this one were heard in the battlefields, streets, courtyards, banquet halls, and churches of Europe on a daily basis, and one can hardly overestimate their presence in the soundscape of the Baroque period. When they are imitated in vocal and instrumental music of other types, powerful associations with pomp, ceremony, warfare, and the nobility were invoked.

From just about the time of the Brescia petition of 1546 come the earliest datable surviving instruments that correspond to the modern violin in every detail, made by Gasparo da Salò in Brescia and by Andrea Amati in nearby Cremona. During the 1550s and 1560s entire ensembles of violinists from Brescia were hired by the city of Parma, religious confraternities in Venice, and the

EXAMPLE 3-14. A sonata from Bendinelli, *Tutta l'arte della trombetta* (1614), realized for five-part trumpet corps

electoral court of Dresden. The first widely noted traveling violin virtuoso, Giovanni Battista Jacomelli (ca. 1550–1608), came from Brescia, as did the first two violinists to become well-known composers for their instrument, Biagio Marini (1594–1663) and Giovanni Battista Fontana (ca. 1589–ca. 1630). Early in the seventeenth century, violin-family ensembles were established in several cities in the plain between the Alps to the north and the Apennines to the south, drained by the Po and its tributaries; the earliest composers of music for such ensembles came from the same cities, where the earliest depictions of violins are also preserved (Fig. 3-3).

As with solo vocal music, early seventeenth-century music for violins seems to fix in notation practices that in the sixteenth century belonged to unwritten traditions. The wording in the Brescian petition of 1546 seems to hold the key: "in consorts, with the organ, and extemporaneously."

When instruments played in consorts in the middle of the sixteenth century, they could play canzonas, ricercars, dances, or vocal music. Brescia had several composers producing such music, and production continued into the seventeenth century all over the Po valley. The innovations of the early seventeenth century in consort music depended upon the introduction of basso continuo. In some cases, this merely meant that the bass part in the ensemble could be played by an organ, with added chords. In the case of the earliest instrumental ensemble work to specify the violin—the *Sonata con tre violini* ("Sonata with Three Violins," published in 1612; W. 2) by the Venetian organist Giovanni Gabrieli (1551–1612)—the organ continuo part opened the way for an ensemble of soprano instruments. But the most radical innovation fostered by the use of basso continuo in ensemble music is the introduction of works for accompanied solo violin, cornett, or other ensemble instrument.

The earliest dated work for solo violin and basso continuo is the *Sonata: violino e violone* ("Sonata: Violin and Bass," 1610; A. 21) by Giovanni Paolo Cima (ca. 1570–1630), an organist and church music director in Milan. While the sonata for violins by Gabrieli is actually a ricercar in musical style, Cima's violin sonata is like a canzona, as can already be detected in the rhythm of the opening motive (♩ ♩. ♪ | ♩). The typical homophonic middle section before the return of the opening motive is replaced here by a passage (bars 59–71) in which the violin and the accompanying bass instrument take turns playing written-out "diminutions" (rapid passages) of the type that instrumentalists were trained to improvise in replacement of slower written notes. In keeping with the nature of the canzona, the expected tempo of this work was probably in the range of ♩ = 70–80, which would make the separately bowed sixteenth notes quite brisk. As commonly happens in early seventeenth-century canzonas or ricercars for solo instrument and basso continuo, multivoice imitation is suggested by sequences in which a given motive is heard successively in different parts of an octave, as if played by different instruments (bars 13–15, 26–27, or 98–105).

There were several kinds of instrumental performance *all'improviso* reflected in the early written repertoire of violin music. One type appears to be preserved in

Early Seventeenth-Century Wind Instruments

The **cornett** (cornetto, zink) is played with a cupped mouthpiece, like a brass instrument, but it is made of wood and has six or more holes like a recorder. It was made in soprano, alto, and tenor sizes. The bass cornett is called a serpent.

Cornett

Trombone

The Baroque **trombone** (sackbut) was used in alto, tenor, and bass sizes. By comparison with the modern trombone, the Baroque instrument had a much narrower bore and smaller bell.

The **trumpet** of the Baroque period had neither valves nor slide to change the length of the windway. It produces its variety of pitches through overblowing to various partials. Its tubing is twice as long as that of the modern valved trumpet, which brings its partials closer together in a given octave. Thus it can play a major arpeggio in its lower octave and a complete major scale, plus raised fourth degree, in its upper octave.

Trumpet

Shawms were made in alto, tenor, and bass varieties. The shawm uses a double reed, either enclosed in a windcap like a bagpipe, or in contact with the player's lips, like a modern oboe, in comparison with which its bore is much wider and its sound louder and less refined.

Shawm

Recorders create their sound through the oscillations in the airstream engendered by the eddies created by a hole in its beak. They were made in many sizes.

Recorder

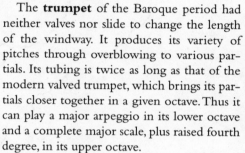

toccata-like pieces such as the *Sonata 6* published posthumously in Giovanni Battista Fontana's *Sonate a 1. 2. 3. per violino. . .* (1641), but probably composed during the 1620s or earlier (A. 22). The elements of this work that seem particularly improvisatory are the combination of typical diminution figuration against sustained notes (chords) in the continuo accompaniment and the lack of such form-building devices as recurrence or points of imitation. Such works are frequent, for example, in the early printed collections of Biagio Marini's violin music.

Figure 3-3. The cities in Italy where violin playing, violin making, and violin music first emerged in the Po valley

Written variations on familiar tunes or standard chordal-bass patterns surely capture the results of improvisation as well. An example is variations on the popular song "La monica" ("The Nun") in Biagio Marini's *Sonate, symphonie . . . e retornelli*, Op. 8 (1629); (A. 23). Marini's piece inserts a ritornello, unrelated to the tune, between each of the variations.

Improvisatory technique seems to be preserved in the many echo sonatas of the early seventeenth century, in which two or three violins take turns playing simple ornamental figures over a relatively inactive continuo accompaniment. Early collections of violin music also contain many simple dances, which historically belong to a category of music that was often improvised. The earliest such dances for violins with basso continuo, and the earliest examples of the trio setting with two violins and continuo, are found in *Il primo libro delle sinfonie e gagliarde* (1607) by Salamone Rossi (1570–ca. 1630), the leading musician in Mantua's artistically prominent Jewish community in the early seventeenth century, whose theatrical and musical activities attracted the support of the ducal court.

A separate category of improvised performance is evoked by the phrase *nell'organo* ("with the organ"). Musicians of the early seventeenth century continued to improvise above a cantus firmus or chordal pattern provided by an organ, another chordal instrument, or a melodic bass instrument. An extensive demonstration of this technique is found in the mid-sixteenth-century instruction manual for players of the viola da gamba by Diego Ortiz, *Trattado de glosas sobre clausulas y otros generos de puntos en la musica de violones* (published in Rome, 1553, and in an Italian translation; the title means "Treatise on Discants over Chant Melodies and Other Kinds of [Improvised] Musical Counterpoint for Viols"). Example 3-15 shows Ortiz's demonstration of "improvised" counterpoint above an "Italian tenor" (as he called them) that we recognize as the Romanesca. Although many of his other examples show only a bass under the solo instrumental line, Ortiz teaches that the keyboard accompanist should add chords to the bass notes; he writes out the chords for his readers in this example. This kind of extemporaneous counterpoint, consisting of a steadily paced bass (cantus firmus) and florid upper part (discant) was called contrapunto alla mente ("mental counterpoint") or *sortisatio* in Italy. The manual by Ortiz is one of the earliest and most explicit of many that teach this technique. The counterpoint that results can be very rudimentary. Notice that in the variation shown in Example 3-15 the improvised upper part consists mostly of four one-measure patterns, each corresponding to the length of a bass note. The one-measure pattern labeled B, for example, is used nine times in twenty-four measures. It always begins a fifth above the bass note and ends a third above it. If the bass (or cantus firmus) consists of equal note values (dotted whole notes in this case), the improviser could, at minimum, use a simple figure like this one for every measure within a passage. As long as the pitch of the first note of the figure stands at the proper interval from the bass note, the rest will take care of itself. If the bass notes form a sequential pattern, the solo part above it will also. Example 3-16 shows two such sequences, both created by *sortisatio*-style counterpoint above evenly paced stepwise motion in the bass. This kind of counterpoint is very common in early sonatas by musicians who, like the Venetian Dario Castello, were leaders of a company of instrumentalists.

More intricate and learned counterpoint and construction techniques can be found in the early seventeenth-century instrumental ensemble music composed by church music directors, such as the Franciscan monk Giovanni Battista Buonamente (d. 1642), who held posts in Mantua, Vienna, Bergamo, Parma, and Assisi. He published at least seven books of ensemble pieces, of which the first three are lost. The canzona-style *Sonata quarta* from his fourth book of sonatas (1626, A. 24), features a constant intermixing of new and recurring motives.

EXAMPLE 3-15. The final variation (on the Romanesca pattern) from the Recercada segunda in the *Tratado de glosas sobre clausulas* (1553) by Diego Ortiz, illustrating improvised counterpoint above a given bass pattern

Like many works of its kind to follow, it consists of several substantial sections set off by changes of meter (i.e., proportions), the last of which brings back two prominent motives from the first section, a standard procedure in the instrumental canzona. Buonamente's instrumental lines are unified by sequences and melodic inversion, and the bass participates in the imitative counterpoint.

Buonamente's service as chamber musician at the court of Emperor Ferdinand II in Vienna, 1626–29, was not the first by an Italian violin composer in the German-speaking lands. Biagio Marini was music director at the Wittelsbach court at Neuburg an die Donau from 1623 to 1649; and Carlo Farina (ca. 1604–1639) served as concertmaster at the electoral court in Dresden, 1625–29, during which time he published five books of violin music, which include many surprising programmatic works that call for such effects as *col legno, sul ponticello*, glissandos, scordatura, and multiple stops.

EXAMPLE 3-16. Dario Castello, Sonata 3 from *Sonate concertate in stile moderno* (1621), illustrating *sortisatio*-like counterpoint

The last important composer with roots in the traditions of civic and court string ensembles of the Po valley was Marco Uccellini (ca. 1603–1680). After studying with Buonamente at Assisi, from 1641 to 1662 he led the Company of Violinists at the court of Modena, a typical string ensemble of five parts— two violins, two violas, and a *violone*, a large variety of cello. From 1665 to 1680 he led the Parma court and civic string band that had been founded by five players from Brescia in the middle of the sixteenth century.

Uccellini's sonatas are notable for the extensive notation of very rapid and difficult ornamental diminutions, extended sequences, extreme high register, very long sections, defined by meter, and changes of mode and system (even using A♭ and D♭ chords). His sonata entitled *La vittoria trionfante* ("Triumphant Victory," 1645, A. 25) combines intensive elaboration of a small number of motives (using rhythmic augmentation and diminution, and melodic and contrapuntal inversion) with passages reflecting the tradition of informal improvisation above a bass or cantus firmus. Instructional manuals of this period make it reasonably clear that rapid ornamental passages and even trills, which frequently combine oscillation with some pitch repetition, were customarily performed with separate bows or articulation syllables on wind instruments, such as "le re le re," "de ler de ler," or "de re te re." Since in other places Uccellini is unusually careful to mark such slurs as he intends, the sixteenth and thirty-second notes in *La vittoria trionfante* were certainly meant to be bowed separately at about ♩ = 60–70.

Composers of keyboard and instrumental ensemble music in Italy in the first half of the seventeenth century, therefore, created new genres, in part by bringing to musical notation several practices that had developed earlier in unwritten or partially notated traditions. Once reduced to notation, these genres were often enriched by cross-fertilization from the more learned forms of written music. A new type of professional keyboard player and virtuoso lutenist replaced the general-purpose performer and noble amateur in church and court venues, while instrumental ensembles, particularly ensembles of violins, became more elevated in artistry and in social prestige and began to spread out from their place of origin in the Po valley of Italy. Several of these developments ran parallel with innovations in the area of court and theatrical vocal music, and, as we shall see in the next chapter, some can be traced in the development of church music in early seventeenth-century Italy as well.

BIBLIOGRAPHICAL NOTES

Frescobaldi, Lutenists, and Style Change in Harpsichord Music

The standard book on Frescobaldi's life and works is Frederick Hammond, *Girolamo Frescobaldi* (Cambridge, MA: Harvard University Press, 1983). A useful survey that includes chapters on Frescobaldi's Italian contemporaries is Alexander Silbiger, ed., *Keyboard Music before 1700* (New York: Schirmer Books, 1995), which replaces Willi Apel, *The History of Keyboard Music to 1700*, trans. Hans Tischler (Bloomington, IN: Indiana University Press, 1972). A book with more detail about minor composers is Alexander Silbiger, *Italian Manuscript Sources of 17th-Century Keyboard Music* (Ann Arbor, MI: UMI Research Press, 1980). The idea that the Italian keyboard toccata originated in notated diminutions of madrigal-like polyphonic background structures is advanced by Alexander Silbiger in "Is the Italian Keyboard Intavolatura a Tablature?" *Recercare* 3 (1991, 81–104; and "From Madrigal to Toccata: Frescobaldi and the *Seconda Prattica*," *Critica Musica: Essays in Honor of Paul Brainard*, John Knowles, ed. (Amsterdam: Gordon & Breach, 1996), pp. 403–28. An extensive and detailed account of the origins and history of the chordal/bass patterns found in seventeenth-century music for keyboard and lute-family instruments is the series of four volumes *The Folia, the Saraband, the Passacaglia, and the Chaconne* by Richard Hudson, Musicological Studies and Documents, 35 (Neuhausen-Stuttgart: American Institute of Musicology, 1982). A contrasting view, that chordal/bass patterns are aspects of various specific musical genres and practices, inseparable from other features such as rhythm, meter, texture, and purpose, is advanced by Alexander Silbiger, "Passacaglia and Ciaccona: Genre Pairing and Ambiguity from Frescobaldi to Couperin," *Journal of Seventeenth Century-Music*, 2 (1996), http://sscm-jscm.press.uiuc.edu/jscm/v2no1.html. Also see the entries on specific chordal/bass patterns in *The New Grove Dictionary of Music and Musicians*, 2nd ed. (London: Macmillan, 2001).

Chordal versus Modal Composition

The most thorough introduction to modal theory focuses on the sixteenth century, but it forms an indispensable foundation for understanding mode in the seventeenth century: Bernhard Meier, *The Modes of Classical Vocal Polyphony Described According to the Sources*, trans. Ellen S. Beebe (New York: Broude Brothers Limited, 1988). A less detailed discussion of mode together with the gamut of hexachords and the potential meanings of mutation and change of system underlies the analyses in Eric Thomas Chafe, *Monteverdi's Tonal Language* (New York: Schirmer Books, 1992). Banchieri's exposition of modal composition, fundamental for the seventeenth century, is translated in Clifford A. Cranna, Jr., "Adriano Banchieri's *Cartella Musicale* (1614): Translation and Commentary," Ph.D. diss., Stanford Univ., 1981. The chordal theories of Lippius and his contemporaries are presented in Benito V. Rivera, *German Music Theory in the Early 17th Century: The Treatises of Johannes Lippius*, Studies in Musicology, 17 (Ann Arbor, MI: UMI Research Press, 1980). A stimulating book that contains useful information but which comes to erroneous conclusions because of faulty methodology, placing the rise of tonality far too early, is Carl Dahlhaus, *Studies on the Origin of Harmonic Tonality*, trans. Robert O. Gjerdingen (Princeton: Princeton University Press, 1990).

Church Organ Music in Early Seventeenth-century Italy

The books by Apel and Hammond mentioned under the first heading are relevant to this category as well. The entry "Organ Mass" in *The New Grove Dictionary of Music and Musicians* provides a valuable overview. Donald Karl Marcase, "Adriano Banchieri, *L'organo suonarino*: Translation, Transcription and Commentary," Ph.D. diss., Indiana University, 1970, gives a convenient point of entry into the details of organ use in the Italian Catholic Church at the beginning of the seventeenth century.

The Violin and Italian Instrumental Ensemble Music

The standard work on the subject, although now somewhat outdated, is David D. Boyden, *The History of Violin Playing from its Origins to 1761 and its Relationship to the Violin and Violin Music* (London: Oxford University Press, 1965). Details concerning the violin in Brescia are reported in John Walter Hill, "The Emergence of Violin Playing into the Sphere of Art Music in Italy: *Compagnie di Suonatori* in Brescia during the Sixteenth Century," *Musica Franca: Essays in Honor of Frank D'Accone*, ed. Irene Alm, Alyson McLamore, and Colleen Reardon (Stuyvesant, NY: Pendragon Press, 1996), pp. 333–366. The most extensive listing and overview of early composers of violin music is still William S. Newman, *The Sonata in the Baroque Era*, 4th ed. (New York: W. W. Norton, 1983), even though it is outdated in some respects. More details about a smaller number of composers is found in Willi Apel, *Italian Violin Music of the Seventeenth Century*, ed. Thomas Brinkley (Bloomington, IN: Indiana University Press, 1990), and Peter Allsop, *The Italian 'Trio' Sonata from its Origins until Corelli* (Oxford: Clarendon Press, 1992). Very valuable insights into styles and genres of early violin music are found in Eleanor Selfridge-Field, *Venetian Instrumental Music from Gabrieli to Vivaldi*, 3rd ed. (New York: Dover Publications, Inc., 1994).

CHAPTER 4

Church Music in Italy, 1600–1650

CHURCHES AND OTHER RELIGIOUS INSTITUTIONS

The number and variety of churches in Italian cities of the seventeenth century was greater than at any other place or time in European history. On a walking tour of the historic center of any Italian city, one often encounters several churches within a few blocks of each other, nearly all of which were in use during the seventeenth century. In Bologna, for example, a city of about 64,000 inhabitants during the seventeenth century, there were more than two hundred churches, occupying about one-sixth of its total land surface. Obviously, the number of churches in Bologna and most other Italian cities was not the result of rational planning for the pastoral needs of the population. In fact, the single cathedral and its parish churches accounted for a relatively small portion of churches in any Italian city of even moderate size during the seventeenth century. In most cases, cathedrals and parish churches were not the main centers of musical activity.

In many cities, especially in northern Italy, the principal church for music was the civic or governmental basilica, which often overshadowed the cathedral in importance. San Marco in Venice, San Petronio in Bologna, Sant'Andrea (civic) and Santa Barbara (ducal) in Mantua, Sant'Antonio in Padua, Santa Maria dei Miracoli in Brescia, and Santa Maria Maggiore in Bergamo were civic churches, not the cathedrals of their cities. A civic basilica normally had a stable, salaried polyphonic musical ensemble, called a *cappella* (literally, a "chapel"), in addition to a plainchant choir of priests or clerics in minor orders. Whereas the permanent salaried musicians in the *cappella* of an Italian basilica during much of the sixteenth century were normally singers, by the seventeenth century, especially in northern Italy, this group often included instrumentalists as well. At the beginning of the seventeenth century, Santa Maria Maggiore in Bergamo had a *cappella* made up of about 16 singers and 14 instrumentalists (1–2 violins, 3 violas, 1 violone, 2 cornetts, 4–6 trombones, and 2 organists). In 1605, San Petronio in Bologna had 36 singers, 4 trombones, 1 cornett, and 1 violin; by 1610 its instrumental component had increased to 7 trombones, 2 cornetts, and 1 violin. At the beginning of the seventeenth century, San Marco in Venice employed about 20 singers as well as 4 trombones and cornetts; at the start of Monteverdi's tenure there as *maestro di cappella* in 1613, the *capella* was augmented to 16 instrumentalists, including at least 3 violins, 3 trombones, and a contrabass violone. At the end of Monteverdi's term, in 1643, the *cappella* of San Marco included 35 singers and 15 instrumentalists.

Figure 4-1 depicts a typical Italian *cappella* of about 1595, in this case divided into two antiphonal choirs of voices with instruments (cornetts and trombones)—about twenty-four musicians in each choir, suggesting that this is a performance for a special holiday, for which extra musicians have been hired—reading from choir books that display each part as a separate block of notation on each pair of facing pages. The instruments appear to be doubling the voices, a common method of "concerting" church music in the early seventeenth century. On a lower level, we can see a few members of the plainchant choir, seated on benches. The kneeling figures in the right foreground are canons of the chapter. The celebrant, a bishop, appears to be in the midst of the Offertory prayers, prior to the elevation of the communion host, which is being held by the priest directly behind him. It remained customary during the seventeenth century, as it had been during the sixteenth century, to perform non-liturgical vocal or instrumental music during the Offertory of the Mass (see the table on pages 88–89).

Cathedrals generally had smaller *cappelle* than the largest civic basilicas. The Modena cathedral in 1615 had fifteen singers, a cornett, a trombone, and an organist on salary. The music director (*maestro di cappella*) of a cathedral was normally obligated to maintain a school for the choirboys who customarily

Figure 4-1. Engraving by Adrian Collaert (1595) of a sketch by Johannes Stradanus of a Mass at an unnamed (imaginary?) Italian cathedral

The Catholic Mass in liturgy and musical performance in the seventeenth century

IN THE CATHOLIC LITURGY:	IN MUSICAL PERFORMANCE:
	An organ work or vocal concerto may be performed before the Mass begins.
Introit	The liturgical words sometimes set to polyphonic music; also a favorite place for *contrapunto alla mente*. Often recited softly or mentally by the celebrant while a non-liturgical motet, organ work, or ensemble sonata is performed.
KYRIE	Often sung to polyphonic music of either the seventeenth or sixteenth century or chanted in alternation with organ versets.
GLORIA	Often sung to polyphonic music of either the seventeenth or sixteenth century or chanted in alternation with organ versets.
Collect	Spoken or chanted to a formula.
Epistle	Spoken or chanted to a formula.
Gradual	Often recited softly or mentally by the celebrant while a non-liturgical motet, organ work, or ensemble sonata is performed.
Alleluia or Tract	Usually chanted.
Gospel	Spoken or chanted to a formula.
Sermon (optional)	
CREDO	Often sung to polyphonic music of either the seventeenth or sixteenth century or chanted in alternation with organ versets.
Offertory	Often recited softly or mentally by the celebrant while a non-liturgical motet, organ work, or ensemble sonata is performed. If this is done, the music can continue until the Sanctus, in which case the next three items would be recited softly or mentally by the celebrant.
Offertory prayers	Often recited softly or mentally while the Offertory music continues, or another motet or organ work is performed.
Secret	Often recited softly or mentally while the Offertory music continues.
Preface	Often recited softly or mentally while the Offertory music continues.

SANCTUS (with Benedictus)	Often sung to music of either the seventeenth or sixteenth century or chanted in alternation with organ versets. The Elevation of the host occurs between the Sanctus and its continuation, the Benedictus. The Elevation is often accompanied by a non-liturgical motet, organ work, or ensemble sonata.
Elevation of the host	If music is performed during the Elevation, the music may continue while the celebrant softly or mentally recites the Benedictus, Canon, and Pater noster; or it may be followed by the Benedictus, especially if a polyphonic setting of the Sanctus is used. Because Elevation music became very important during the seventeenth century, Mass Ordinary settings of this period often have very brief Sanctus and Agnus Dei movements or none at all.
Canon	Recited softly or mentally when an Elevation motet or organ work is performed.
Pater noster	Recited softly or mentally when an Elevation motet or organ work is performed.
AGNUS DEI	Often sung to polyphonic music of either the seventeenth or sixteenth century or chanted in alternation with organ versets.
Communion	Usually chanted, but sometimes recited softly or mentally by the celebrant while a non-liturgical motet, organ work, or ensemble sonata is performed.
Post-communion	Often recited softly or mentally by the celebrant while a non-liturgical motet, organ work, or ensemble sonata is performed.
ITE MISSA EST	Usually chanted.
	A vocal or instrumental work may be performed after the Mass.

made up the bulk of the soprano section of the cathedral's *cappella*. Women were still forbidden to sing in church and would be for the next 250 years.

After major basilicas and cathedrals comes a large, miscellaneous category including collegiate churches (those controlled by a chapter of canons), monastic churches, and churches of the newer non-monastic orders of priests. Most parish churches fall into this category. It is difficult to generalize about this group of churches: some had only an organist on salary in addition to a plainchant choir of priests or friars, but many retained at least a small *cappella* and hired extra musicians—even the entire *cappella* of the local cathedral or major basilica—for special holidays. A recent survey has concluded that in the Po Valley (essentially northern Italy) during the seventeenth century there were seventy-three churches that employed a composer as music director, half of these belonging to the present category and half to the category of major basilicas and cathedrals.

Churches of convents for women were also extremely numerous in seventeenth-century Italy. For example, in the city of Pavia, which at that time had about 12,000 inhabitants old enough to take communion, there were twenty convents for women typically housing about 680 nuns and religious. In other words, in Pavia more than 11 percent of the women were in convents.

Many convents populated by women of the nobility had a large and well-developed musical *cappella* in seventeenth-century Italy. In many cases, these noblewomen nuns had extensive musical training at home before entering the convent. At certain times and places, nuns also received musical training, both vocal and instrumental, within the convent, either from sister nuns or from outside music teachers. The rule prohibiting women from singing in church was frequently circumvented by constructing a double church for the convent, with an outer church where the Mass and Office were celebrated by priests, often with other men present, and an inner church for the nuns, separated by a grill-work "wall." In this way, the musical performances by the nuns were heard in the outer church, but the nuns were technically not in that church and were kept separate from the priest and from other men. This arrangement, as well as the instructional activities that supported the performances, were either supported or suppressed at various times and places in the course of the seventeenth century, as bishops came and went and vied for control over the convents with the hierarchy of the associated male monasteries or with the civic authorities, who often represented the wishes of the noble families of the nuns.

Although nuns composed or received dedications for numerous works written for high voices, usually with continuo and often with other instruments, the *cappelle* of women's convents often performed the same music that was heard in other types of church. When tenor and bass voices were required by the compositions, four methods of performance can be documented. (1) The entire composition could be transposed at sight upward by a four or fifth through substitution of clefs and key signatures; if the composite range of the voices did not exceed two and a half octaves, this was considered feasible. (2) The bass part was sung an octave higher while being played in the original octave by the organ or other continuo instruments; if the tenor part was not within the compass of some of the female singers, the work could also be sung at a higher pitch. (3) The tenor and bass parts could be played by ensemble instruments, such as viola da gambas or trombones, while only the upper parts were sung. (4) A few women could actually sing bass parts as written or at a slightly higher transposition.

Women's convents in Italy boasted many well-known singers, instrumentalists, and composers.[1] The *cappella* of an aristocratic convent could attain sub-

---

[1] For example, the composers Raffaella Aleotti (ca. 1570–after 1646), Caterina Assandra (ca. 1590–after 1620), Rosa Giacinta Badalla (ca. 1662–ca. 1703–19), Maria Caterina Calegari (1644–ca. 1662), Francesca Caterina Cellana (ca. 1634–after 1690), Chiara Margarita Cozzolani (1602–ca. 1676–78), Sulpitia Cesis (fl. 1619), Isabella Leonarda (1620–ca. 1700), Claudia Francesca Rusca (ca. 1593–ca. 1641), Claudia Sessa (ca. 1570–ca. 1617–18), and Lucrezia Orsina Vizzana (1589–1662).

stantial size and importance: from time to time during the seventeenth century, the largest *cappella* in Milan was at a convent, not the cathedral.

Several non-monastic orders of priests, especially the Jesuits and Oratorians, cultivated music as part of the special educational missions they were given in connection with the objectives of the Catholic Counter-Reformation. The most important of these was the Jesuit order, the Society of Jesus. They maintained schools for sons of the nobility, whom they identified as crucial to their aim of renewing the Church. In larger cities they established seminaries: by the year 1600 there were more than four hundred all over Europe, three in Rome alone. In both their schools and colleges, the Jesuits employed music and drama for inspirational and didactic purposes, always stipulating the use of Latin instead of the local vernacular. The Jesuit college for Germans in Rome became famous for its elaborate music under the directorship of Giacomo Carissimi (1605–1674), whose works were spread by the Jesuit network throughout Europe.

The Oratorians—Fathers of the Oratory of Saint Philip Neri (who founded his original congregation in Rome in 1554)—likewise pursued a mission of teaching and preaching, aided by music and drama. Like the Jesuits, the Oratorians tended to recruit their members from the nobility, but the Oratorians normally organized adult laymen and women into satellite organizations for informal religious education rather than educating boys or training priests. The Oratorians made a specialty of evening "oratory" services, in which the central event was a sermon, preached in the vernacular, preceded and followed either by congregational unison singing of religious songs (called *laudi* in Italy), also in the vernacular, or by didactic religious dialogues or stories set to music (sacred dialogues and, later, oratorios).

The number and variety of churches per capita were never greater in Italy than in the seventeenth century. Although hard figures are not available, it appears that the number of active musical *cappelle* was also greater in this century than before or after. Thus, combined with innovations in musical style, these numbers resulted in an upsurge in the publication of church music in early seventeenth-century Italy; nearly 1,500 collections of printed music containing motets issued from the Italian presses between 1600 and 1650. A marked increase in the commissioning of paintings and sculptures for Italian churches took place at the same time. The amount of church music produced in this period probably exceeds even the amount of secular music composed, and its variety is no less expansive, encompassing both persistent traditions and seminal innovations.

PERSISTENCE OF TRADITIONS

The most commonly heard music in Italian churches during the seventeenth century was plainchant, as was true during the preceding ten centuries. While every church had a plainchant choir, relatively few of them used figural music (polyphony) on a daily basis.

EXAMPLE 4-1. Psalm Tone 6 fitted with the first verse of Psalm 109

The most common addition to plainchant was the organ. The concept and performance of the organ Mass was explained in Chapter 3. Since nearly every church employed an organist, we may conclude that the performance of versets in alternation with plainchant during the Mass Ordinary and the Magnificat of Vespers, as well as canzonas, ricercars, and toccatas in place of the Introit, Gradual and Offertory, during the Elevation, and during or after the Communion at Mass and in place of antiphons during Vespers were very common supplements to the ubiquitous chant.

One type of simple polyphony that was often performed by plainchant choirs, as well as by *cappelle*, is *falsobordone*. *Falsobordone* is an uncomplicated method of singing psalms in harmony by using a chord in place of the recitation tone of a plainchant psalm tone and by employing brief cadential passages in place of the mediation and termination formulas that punctuate the singing of each verse of the psalm. Although these harmonizations could be improvised, there are many written-out examples from the late sixteenth and early seventeenth centuries. One, representing Psalm Tone 6, published by Giovanni Valentini (1582/3–1649) in 1618, is given as Example 4-2. Psalm Tone 6 from the plainchant tradition is given as Example 4-1, fitted with the first verse of Psalm 109, the first psalm sung at most Vespers. As you can see, virtually all that remains of the plainchant Psalm Tone 6 in the *falsobordone* by Valentini is the polar opposition between the reciting tone, A, and the conclusion on F. Valentini's *falsobordone* formula was printed without text and could have been used to sing any psalm whatsoever. Inasmuch as psalm verses have no prescribed length, a variable number of syllables would

EXAMPLE 4-2. Giovanni Valentini's falsobordone for Psalm Tone 6 (1618)

The Vespers service of the Catholic Church in liturgy and musical performance in the seventeenth century

In the Catholic liturgy:	In musical performance:
Salutation and response	The liturgical text, *Deus in adjutorium*, etc., could be sung in a polyphonic setting or chanted.
Five psalms framed by 5 antiphons	The five psalms for Vespers varied between different categories of feast. Some or all of the required psalms were frequently set by composers of the seventeenth century, and one or more of these settings were often performed at Vespers. One or more of the antiphons were often replaced by motets with non-liturgical texts. What was not sung in polyphony or replaced was chanted, either entirely or in verse-by-verse alternation with organ versets, or sung to *falsobordone* formulas.
Scriptural reading	Spoken or chanted to a formula.
Hymn	The hymn was chanted, or the prescribed hymn text was sung in a polyphonic setting, or a motet with non-liturgical text was substituted.
Magnificat framed by an antiphon	Seventeenth-century composers made many settings of the Magnificat text, and one of these was often heard in Vespers, sometimes in verse-by-verse alternation with plainchant; or organ versets alternated with chant. Settings of Magnificat antiphon texts for important feasts were composed in the seventeenth century, but often motets with non-liturgical texts were substituted here as well.
Prayers and benediction	The concluding plainchant benediction, *Benedicamus Domino*, was frequently followed by music for organ or instrumental ensemble, which could substitute for the response *Deo gratias*. The seasonal Marian antiphon or the Litany of the Virgin frequently was sung at the conclusion of Vespers.

be sung to the chords in measures 1 and 4 of Example 4-2, which stand in place of the reciting tone of the chant formula. In actual use, a *falsobordone* formula would be repeated for each verse of the psalm, or it would be sung in alternation with a plainchant psalm-tone formula. The rhythm with which the syllables would be sung would be determined by the singers' understanding of the normal pronunciation of Latin and would not conform to any meter or steady beat. *Falsobordone* can be traced back to the late fifteenth century, and it practically disappeared by about 1650. However, in its last decades it was in wide-spread use, perhaps because it happened to conform to the early seventeenth-century aesthetic of spontaneous expression through metrically free declamatory singing. For the same reason, composers often added passages resembling *falsobor-done* to their church compositions, both for voices and for organ—compositions that in other respects conformed to other generic norms.

Another long-established church music tradition that stood outside the boundaries of formal composition and corresponded to the early seventeenth-century predilection for spontaneity was *contrapunto alla mente* (literally, "mental counterpoint"), a kind of semi-improvised performance also called *sortisatio*. In some of the most prestigious *cappelle* of Italy, particularly intricate *contrapunto alla mente* was created by three or more singers improvising rapid melismatic vocal lines above a slow and steady cantus firmus in the bass part. Here is what Adriano Banchieri had to say about this practice in his *Cartella musicale* (1614):

> In Rome at the chapel of the pope, in the Holy House of Loreto, and in countless other chapels, when they sing *contrapunto alla mente* over a bass, no one knows what his companion is going to sing, but rather they all, with cer-tain restrictions agreed upon amongst themselves, create a most tasteful sound. And it is a general maxim that if a hundred voices (so to speak) sing consonantly over the bass, they will all be in accord. And those bad fifths and octaves, excesses, and discords that occur are all graces that create the true effect of *contrapunto alla mente*.

Then Banchieri gives an example of "certain restrictions agreed upon" among the singers and transforms them into instructions for writing out a sample of *contrapunto alla mente*:

1. The bass from the plainchant is written down on a music sheet. . . . This is put in whole notes, for it must be sung one note per measure.
2. Over this cantus firmus is woven a solo soprano voice that creates descending effects with half notes, quarter notes, rests, and eight notes, as desired. And this soprano part is copied down exactly.
3. Similarly, over the same [bass] cantus firmus, a tenor part is written that creates ascending effects and notes similar to the soprano. And this is copied down.
4. There remains the contralto, which can make syncopated notes—that is, whole notes that sing against the downbeats in thirds or fifths above the bass, or in half notes, leaping up and down. And this part is copied down.

Banchieri's instructions are put to the test in Example 4-3, for which the florid passages in the upper voices have been created using examples from another early seventeenth-century treatise on *contrapunto alla mente* by the Roman composer Giovanni Bernardino Nanino (ca. 1560–1618). Nanino gives dozens of formulas that can be used above cantus-firmus notes, organizing them according to their suitability for accompanying each of the possible ascending or descending intervals or repeated pitches in the bass cantus firmus. Passages of this kind are found frequently in seventeenth-century motets, and it would

EXAMPLE 4-3. Banchieri's instructions for *contrapunto alla mente* (1614) carried out using formulas written down by G. B. Nanino, ca. 1600

be no exaggeration to say that the use of simultaneous passage work or diminutions of this kind produced a fundamental and lasting change in compositional norms during the early seventeenth century.

The *a cappella* style associated with prestigious sixteenth-century composers remained viable throughout the seventeenth century. But it would be a mistake to associate it automatically with what Monteverdi called the "first practice." There continued to be stylistic growth in *a cappella* music. The Holy Week Responsory *Vinea mea electa* (A. 26) for voices alone by the Florence cathedral *maestro di cappella* Marco da Gagliano (1582–1643) is an example of this growth. Here, typical early seventeenth-century concern over declamation is evident in the emphasis on pitch repetition and in the series of syncopated chords in measure 2, which momentarily obscure the beat and meter. Departures from the norms of Palestrina's style, a prime example of the "first practice," are evident in the three leaps of a diminished fourth (mm. 26 and 27), the melodic outline of a diminished fifth (m. 30, Tenor I), the cross relation between F natural and F sharp (m. 30), and the barely concealed consecutive octaves (D to B, Altus and Bassus, mm. 30–31).

A considerable amount of *a cappella* music was written in Rome during the seventeenth century. The leading representative was Orazio Benevoli (1605–1672), *maestro di cappella* at St. Peter's basilica from 1646 until his death. His *a cappella* Masses and motets part company with Palestrina in their distinctly chordal conception, less reliance on imitation, use of formalized repetition schemes, emphasis on textural contrasts, and antiphonal writing on an exaggerated scale, employing up to six choirs and twenty-four independent voices.

In addition, *a cappella* church music in early seventeenth-century Italy exhibits several other changes in musical style, such as frequent cadences, musical illustration and expression of the text, and extended triple-meter, aria-like passages. It is a misconception that this body of music merely perpetuated the "first practice" of Palestrina.

THE SMALL-SCALE SACRED CONCERTO

The Italian church vocal compositions of the early seventeenth century that appear to break most decisively with the past are the Latin-texted motets, psalm settings, and liturgical items (including of the Mass Ordinary) for solo voices (typically one, two, or three) with basso continuo (sometimes with one to three ensemble instruments, as well). In printed collections a work of this category was almost always called a *concerto* (pl. *concerti*), *concerto sacro* (*concerti sacri*), *concerto ecclesiastico* (*concerti ecclesiastici*), *psalmo concertato*, or *messa concertata*.

As with the *madrigale concertato*, these terms imply that the planning and arranging has already been done by the composer. Just like the *madrigale concertato* (and monody, and the violin sonata), the church concerto of the early seventeenth century thus arises, in part, out of a process of reducing to precise notation aspects of actual performance that were formerly not reflected in the written music.

We know from contemporaneous descriptions that as early as the 1550s it was customary in certain *cappelle*, in Rome and elsewhere, to arrange four- to seven-voice motets by assigning the upper parts to solo singers while performing the bass and at least an approximation of the other voices on the organ. Lodovico Viadana (ca. 1560–1627) refers to this practice in the Preface to his *100 Concerti Ecclesiastici* (1602), the first printed collection of small-scale sacred concertos, a collection that is historically parallel to Giulio Caccini's *Nuove musiche*, also published in 1602.

> Seeing that any singer who, from time to time, wishes to sing either with three, two, or one voice to the accompaniment of an organ was constrained, by the lack of compositions suitable to his purpose, to extract one, two, or three parts from motets composed for five, six, seven, or even more voices, [motets] which should have, for the ensemble, other parts, which are

required for the points of imitation, cadences, counterpoint, without which the singing is full of long and repeated rests, deprived of cadences, and without melody, and has insipid progressions, in addition to suffering occasional interruptions of the words in the silent parts and occasional discontinuous connections between parts, which rendered the style of the singing either imperfect, boring, or inept and little pleasing to those who were listening as well as very inconvenient for those who were singing. Thus, having given not a little consideration to such difficulties at various times, I gave myself much trouble to investigate the means of remedying, in some measure, such a notable lack. And, thanks be to God, I believe to have finally found it, having for this purpose composed some of these *concerti* of mine, with one solo voice for sopranos, for altos, for tenors, and for basses, and some others for the same parts accompanied in various ways, having regard to giving satisfaction in these to every sort of singer, combining the parts together with every sort of variety, in such a way that whoever wants a soprano with a tenor, a tenor with an alto, an alto with a soprano, a soprano with a bass, a bass with an alto, two sopranos, two altos, two tenors, or two basses, they will have all of this very well accommodated.

The motet *Duo seraphim clamabant* (A. 27), for two sopranos and basso continuo, from Lodovico Viadana's *100 Concerti Ecclesiastici* (1602), is typical of early seventeenth-century church concertos in several ways. It employs a trio texture that became very common in small-scale concertos: two upper voices of equal range and importance, sharing material imitated at the unison, continually crossing over one another, and frequently moving in parallel thirds, supported by a basso continuo part that is far less active rhythmically and melodically and which usually does not participate in the imitation. The bass part is often stationary, creating moments of static harmony typical of several early seventeenth-century genres. There is a pattern of motivic recurrence, rare in earlier motets but common in later ones: in this case the descending motives of the first period, C–B♭–A and C–B♭–A–G (mm. 5–7), are echoed in the last section (mm. 59–61); and two motives from the third section, the falling third in half notes (mm. 15–16 and 25–26) and the scale segments in quarter notes (mm. 17–18 and 26–34) are heard in the penultimate part (mm. 49–58). A melodic sequence is used in two places (mm. 30–31 and 55–56). The harmony, especially in the outer sections, is dominated by successions of chords whose roots move predominantly in fourths and fifths. The text is dramatized in several ways: the two angels are represented by two voices until the text mentions "three," whereupon the organist has to sing the third voice (mm. 44–48); the calling of the two voices is illustrated by echoing imitation (mm. 6–7); there is a dramatic pause after *tres sunt* ("there are three"); the trinity of "Father, Word, and Holy Spirit" is underscored by rhythmic and textural contrast (mm. 38–41).

The text of *Duo seraphim clamabant*, a combination of Isaiah 6:3 and John 5:7, served as a Matins response. But this motet was probably not intended for the Matins office, which rarely used polyphony in the seventeenth century. Matins texts like this one were frequently recycled in motets meant to replace items of the Mass Proper or the antiphons of Vespers on a day for which the text would be generally appropriate.

As might be expected, sacred concertos with obbligato parts for ensemble instruments often incorporate features of instrumental genres, especially in northern Italy, where ensemble music first flourished. For example, the Elevation motet *O salutaris hostia* of 1609 (A. 28) by the Pavese nun Caterina Assandra begins with a variant of the typical canzona rhythm played in imitation by the violin and violone. As usual in the canzona, the instruments bring back an altered version of this motive in the final section (mm. 61–71) after the triple-meter, homophonic interlude (mm. 37–41). A concerted Mass Ordinary in the *Motetti et dialoghi* (1615) of the Brescian *maestro di cappella* Giovanni Francesco Capello, for three voices and five instruments, actually incorporates two canzonas by fellow Brescian Antonio Mortaro.

The incorporation of instrumental pieces, forms, and styles into church vocal works is one of the modern features of Claudio Monteverdi's lavish collection *Sanctissimae Virgini missa senis vocibus ac vesperae pluribus decantandae* . . . ("Of the Most Holy Virgin: Mass for Six Voices and Vespers for Several Singers . . .") published in 1610. His setting of *Domine, ad adiuvandum*, the response that opens every Vesper service, incorporates the opening trumpet fanfare ("Toccata") from *L'Orfeo* (A. 10), to which has been added the choir's harmonized monotone chanting, which resembles slow-motion *falsobordone*. The *Sonata sopra Sancta Maria, ora pro nobis* is a variation canzona for very large instrumental ensemble, to which have been added eleven statements of a vocal cantus firmus taken from the Litany of the Saints. Monteverdi's setting of Psalm 109, *Dixit Dominus Domino meo* ("The Lord said unto my Lord") alternates a dance-like instrumental ritornello with cantus-firmus and *falsobordone* settings of Psalm tone 4A in a symmetrical structure of interlocking repetitions and similarities, thus conforming to one new trend in Italian church music.

Monteverdi's 1610 collection begins with a *prima pratica* Mass based on the sixteenth-century polyphonic *Missa In illo tempore* by Nicolas Gombert. The rest of the collection consists of a grab bag of five Psalm settings, five concerted motets, two Magnificats, and the Marian hymn *Ave maris stella*, from which a music director might select several pieces for a particular Vesper service. The pieces are about evenly divided between those which require substantial instrumental and vocal resources and those accompanied by nothing more than an organ continuo. The motets, whose texts are not liturgical, were evidently intended to replace one of the two statements of the antiphons that precede and follow both Psalms and Magnificats in chanted Vespers.

One of these motets, *Nigra sum* ("Black I am," A. 29) illustrates how Monteverdi transferred his rhetorical approach from madrigal composition to church music. The text is from Song of Songs 1:4; 2:10–12:

Nigra sum, sed formosa filia Jerusalem.	Black I am, but lovely, daughter of Jerusalem.
Ideo dilexit me Rex	Therefore, the king loved me
et introduxit me in cubiculum suum,	and brought me into his chamber,
et dixit nihi: surge, amica mea, et veni.	and said to me, "Arise, my love, and come.
Iam heims transiit, imber abiit et recessit,	Already the winter and rains are past;
flores apparuerunt in terra nostra,	and flowers have appeared in our land;
tempus putationis advenit.	the time of pruning is coming.

The love poems of the Song of Songs were especially popular as motet texts in the seventeenth century, probably because they afforded composers the opportunity to express strong passion. Allegorical interpretations of the these poems abound in Catholic tradition, but the prevailing tendency was to identify the bridegroom with God or Christ and the bride with God's chosen people (i.e., parties to the Old or New Covenant), with the Christian Church, or with an individual soul. Hence, this text would be seen to refer to salvation in spite of sinfulness (blackness) and to resurrection at the time of the Last Judgement ("the time of pruning"). This would seem to have been Monteverdi's understanding, as he intones the words "tempus putationis advenit" in an unusually solemn and foreboding manner.

The first section of Nigra sum (mm. 1–7) captures one's attention as the exordium of an oration, by means of the enigmatic incantation "Nigra sum" (procatascene: a preparation, whose drama is heightened by the following silence—aposiopesis), alternating with the musically contrasting antithesis "sed formosa filia Jerusalem," which makes it clear that "black" and "lovely" are considered opposites—probably standing for "sinful" and "saved," in this context. The brief exposition of facts—the narratio (mm. 8–13)—uses the same rhetorical figures, plus iteratio (the heightened repetition of "Ideo") and hyperbole (the exaggerated statement "dilexit me Rex" reflected in the precipitous rise in the vocal line). Measures 14–20 can be likened to an explicatio, in which issues are opened and intensified, here by means of congeries (the word heaps created by Monteverdi's rapid text repetitions). The climax of the piece comes in measures 21–22, where the text "Iam heims transiit, imber abiit et recessit, flores apparuerunt in terra nostra" is interpreted as words or clauses placed in climactic order (auxesis) by Monteverdi's drive to the cadence on D. The rivolgimento (sudden change from good to ill) implied by the text "tempus putationis advenit" is underscored by the solemn intonation mentioned before (noema—obscure, subtle speech). After the textual and musical anthesis (mm. 28–32), the repeat of "tempus putationis advenit," now with an ironic meaning (ploce), serves as the peroratio (final appeal to emotions).

Another example of a Song of Songs motet is *Veniat dilectus meus* (W. 3) by Alessandro Grandi (1586–1630), who was Monteverdi's assistant at Saint Mark's in Venice, 1617–1627, and was probably the most influential composer of small-scale motets during the first half of the seventeenth century. This work belongs to the subgenre of the dialogue motet, which rose to popularity during this period. The text is arranged from excerpts taken from the fifth, sixth, and seventh stanzas of the Song of Songs so as to form a dialogue between Christ and a soul, with some commentary by a chorus. In it, the soul welcomes Christ, who in turn promises salvation. The music offers a series of contrasts between melodically and rhythmically patterned triple-meter passages against duple-meter sections in which the syllabic setting approaches recitative style, giving fluid text declamation precedence over metrical shape. Similar contrast can be found in secular chamber monody (early cantatas), including those written by Grandi. And as in the secular genre, texts for motets were sometimes also arranged so that rhymed verses with regular accentuation patterns, meant to be set to triple-meter aria passages, alternated with prosaic verses, for example from Psalms, meant to be set to duple-meter recitational passages.

Another influential Italian composer of church music during the seventeenth century was Giacomo Carissimi (1605–1674). He served as *maestro di cappella* of the Jesuits' German and Hungarian College in Rome for forty-four years (1630–1674), during which time his music was disseminated to Jesuit churches all over Italy and was carried to the German-speaking lands by generations of seminarians who studied at the College.

Although Carissimi's church music spans both sides of the year 1650 about equally, the style of his motets for two or more solo voices appears to have been stabilized before that date. His motets for solo voice all appear to have been composed after the middle of the century.

The texts of most of Carissimi's motets are Latin paraphrases of Biblical passages, to which rhetorical figures have been added as a stimulus to the creation of musical parallels. The texture of the music is often imitative, but long and difficult melismas, taken up in turn or sung in parallel thirds by the solo voices, diminish the impression of contrapuntal style.

In many of Carissimi's motets, the first voice to enter sings in a recitational style approaching operatic recitative. This recitational passage may be repeated, immediately or later on, by a second voice at a different pitch level, usually removed by a fourth or fifth. After the opening recitational passages, the voices of the full ensemble make their entrances, either in homophonic texture or one by one, in imitation. In this way, recitational style is integrated into ensemble singing.

Nearly all of Carissimi's motets have an independent basso continuo part for the organ, while a minority of them employ ensemble instruments, most commonly two violins or a bass viola da gamba. Recurring passages are uncommon, but subtle transformations of melodic or harmonic features frequently unify his longer motets. Most of Carissimi's motets are divided into sections defined by contrasting meters and motives. A significant number of these works are dialogue motets or have some dialogue elements.

SACRED DIALOGUES AND ORATORIOS

Some Italian dialogue motets resemble small dramatic scenes, in which case their genre blends into that of the sacred musical dialogue and early oratorio. But sacred dialogues were not generally intended for insertion into a Mass or Vespers service. Instead, they were performed at evening sermon assemblies in the churches or oratories of confraternities.

One difference between a sacred dialogue and a dialogue motet is that the former goes further in telling a complete story, often using one singer as narrator in order to accomplish this. An example is *Vivean felice* (1619; W. 4) composed by Giovanni Francesco Anerio (ca. 1567–1630) for the Congregation of the Oratorio of St. Philip Neri in Rome. Intended for the edification of the boys and laymen who attended the evening prayer and sermon services at the church of the Congregation, it tells the story of the temptation of Eve in the Garden of Eden with simple moral and religious commentary. In this work, the role of the narrator is taken by a chorus that sings in a simple, homophonic style so as to make the words easily understood. Eve and the Serpent are represented by solo singers, but their passages rarely approach operatic recitative in style, more often resembling two voices in a polyphonic texture. These two voices are represented in notation only by the vocal line and the bass part (basso continuo). The bass part in this sort of writing, although untexted, has the same degree and type of rhythmic and melodic activity as the solo vocal line, while the inner voices are represented by the choral realization of the basso continuo part. Such a texture, with one or two vocal lines and a basso continuo part having an essentially vocal character, has been called "reduced polyphony."

The Latin sacred dialogues or oratorios composed by Giacomo Carissimi were intended for the sophisticated audiences of the Jesuits' German College and for the aristocratic Archconfraternity of the Most Holy Crucifix in Rome. As a consequence they are much more up-to-date and complex than most Italian sacred dialogues of the early seventeenth century. Most of them are based on stories from the Old Testament in which the language of the Latin Vulgate Bible is augmented and rhetorically intensified. Carissimi's oratorio *Historia di Jephte* (before 1650; A. 30) is an example.

In Judges 11, Jephthah is called back from exile to defend Israel against the Ammonites. On the eve of the crucial battle, he vows that if God should grant him a victory, the first person who comes from his house to meet him afterward will be sacrificed as a burnt offering. After the victory, it is his daughter who first greets him. When she understands the reason for Jephthah's distress, she accepts her fate but first asks to spend two months wandering on the mountains with her companions to bewail her fate, to die a maiden. In the end, Jephthah fulfills his vow.

Carissimi's librettist expands the story in two places—the victory of the Israelites and the lamentation of Jephthah's daughter. Carissimi dramatizes this large-scale opposition of passions—rejoicing versus lamentation—through his choice of modes, as was observed by Athanasius Kircher (1601–1680), a Jesuit professor at the Roman College, in his encyclopedic music treatise *Musurgia universalis* (Rome: 1650):

> [Carissimi] first began and continued the dialogue [*Jephte*] in a festive and triumphant mode, which is the eighth mode. Then he composed his lament in a very different mode, or the fourth mixed with the third. And to represent a tragic story, in which the soul's sorrow and distress were to dominate over its joy, he put the lament very appropriately in that mode [i.e., the fourth mixed with the third], which, as they say, is completely different from the eighth [mode], in order, thus, better to express the difference of the affections, according to their opposite natures.

Indeed, in the first part of the oratorio, which is made up of rhythmically lively choruses with trumpet-like motives, metrical arias, and narrative recitatives, the notes G (the final of the eighth mode) and C (the repercussion of the eighth mode) predominate as the basis of initial and concluding harmonies of major sections and mid-length periods. In the second part, which begins at measure 196 (Jephthah's return from victory), the harmonic centers are E (the final of the fourth and third modes) and A (the repercussion of the fourth mode and often the final of the transposed third mode); the second part contrasts with the first also in its reliance on expressive recitative, slow-paced, lamenting choruses, and the absence of metrical arias.

The large-scale contrast in words and music between the two halves of *Jephte* produces an antithesis at the beginning of Part 2, where celebration suddenly is replaced by foreboding and sorrow, and the energetic chorus in the major mode on G is followed by a subdued recitative beginning with an A-minor triad. Kircher, who uses two synonyms for this textual and musical rhetorical figure, explains it this way:

> The *antitheton* or *contrapositum* is a musical passage in which we express opposing affections, as Giacomo Carissimi contrasted Heraclitus's laughing with Democritus's weeping, or as Leonus Leoni said, "I sleep, but my heart wakes" (*Musurgia universalis*, Rome 1650, VIII, 145).

Later, Kircher returns to musical antithesis (antitheton or contrapositum) from Carissimi's cantata *A piè d'un verde alloro* and explains it with reference to the "metabolic style," a term that he borrows, again, from rhetoric, where it means frequent and abrupt changes by the speaker from, for example, a serious tone to a comic one, thence to an expression of sorrow, to wrath, and so on. In music, Kircher explains, the metabolic style means one in which the composer frequently changes mode or transposes the diatonic system from one to another pitch level through the introduction of accidentals. Kircher prints the passage from Carissimi's cantata as an example of the metabolic style, given here as Example 4-4.

EXAMPLE 4-4. Carissimi, excerpt from the cantata *A piè d'un verde alloro*; cited in Kircher, *Musurgia universalis*, VII 673–74, as "Example 1 of the Metabolic Style"

EXAMPLE 4-5. Carissimi, *Jephte*, mm. 221–223

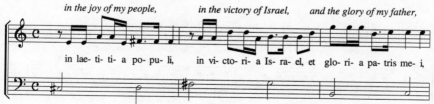

In addition to antitheses, Carissimi's *Jephte* contains many other rhetorical figures. In several places the figure auxesis in the text ("words or clauses placed in climactic order") is set to a rising sequence, as in Example 4-5. Or, as in Example 4-6, Carissimi himself chooses to bring back the words *quid poterit* ("what can") after the intervening words *animam tuam* ("your spirit"), creating the rhetorical figure diacope ("repetition of some words with one or a few words in between"). Naturally, in doing so, he repeats a melodic motive. The verb at the end of the question set in this passage governs the meaning of the whole sentence; saving it until last creates the figure hypozeugma, to which the anticipated Phrygian cadence corresponds, upwardly inflected in the voice part to correspond to the figure interrogatio. Elsewhere in *Jephte* Carissimi's music parallels or creates the textual figures anaphora, antistrophe, aposiopesis, apostrophe, conduplicatio, epandiplosis, epizeuxis, hypotyposis, iteratio, parechesis, and procatascene. It should be possible to locate these using the "List of Rhetorical Figures Often Mirrored or Created by Baroque Composers" in Appendix A.

Rhetorical figures like those in Carissimi's *Jephte* can, of course, be found in many vocal works, both for church and for secular purposes, from the seventeenth century, although not often deployed as abundantly or as effectively. It is easy to imagine that Carissimi was aware that in choosing texts or arranging them to maximize rhetorical content, and in shaping his music to a variety of rhetorical figures in those texts, he was correlating this aspect of his motets and oratorios with the training in rhetorical preaching being received by the young noblemen in the Jesuit German College who formed his audience.

LARGE-SCALE CONCERTED CHURCH MUSIC

Large-scale sacred concertos or concerted Mass settings are works involving at least a full choir, rather than only soloists and a basso continuo part realized on an organ. The works of this category that are most clearly distinguished from small-scale concertos and from the choral works of the sixteenth century use a small group of soloists and an instrumental ensemble in addition to one or more choirs of singers. Works on this scale were often reserved for special occasions when extra musicians were hired by the church.

EXAMPLE 4-6. Carissimi, *Jephte*, mm. 256–260

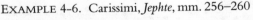
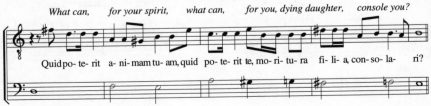

Works for two or more choirs (in which instruments often doubled or replaced voices) appeared in Rome, Venice, and elsewhere during the sixteenth century and remained common in every major Italian city throughout the seventeenth century. Printed and manuscript accounts of church celebrations relating to weddings, state visits, royal births, the feasts of patron saints, and such holidays as Christmas and Easter speak of music for four, eight, twelve, even twenty choirs, sometimes positioned on every available balcony and platform—even high up around the base of the cupola. Yet scores for such musical representatives of "the colossal Baroque" are surprisingly hard to find, because normally music for such large numbers of choirs was actually arranged ("concerted") from works originally written for one or two choirs. Ignazio Donati explains, in the preface to his *Salmi boscarecci*, Op. 9 (Venice, 1623):

> Being persuaded (kind readers) by the entreaties of those who command me to publish the present work, which I call *Psalms of the Forest*, claiming that they are apt for minor feasts, I have thought it necessary to accompany them with some instructions, since it is a large-scale and abundant collection that can be sung in few parts or in many, in various ways. However, I have compressed it into just twelve part books, in addition to the basso continuo, in order to save work and to minimize the expense for those who will want to buy it.
>
> First, therefore, it can be sung by only six voices using the first six books, although none of these six parts can be left out. But for lack of sopranos, the first soprano part can be sung in the tenor octave, separated by a good distance, however, from the actual tenor. And if nuns want to use it, they can sing the bass an octave higher, which would become an alto part.
>
> Second, the other six books, which I call *ripieno*, contain another six voices, which simply double the others [at times], and six instruments, three low and three high. One can use all of these, if one wishes, or part of these additional voices and instruments, which can make up another choir above the choir stalls, doubling, at will, the *ripieno* voices only where they are marked *tutti*.
>
> Third, if one wishes to make more choirs, the soprano, alto, sixth voice, and bass of the first six books can be placed in the organ loft. The first tenor with the low instruments can serve for the second choir. The fifth voice with the high instruments can form a third choir. And if you have several copies of these books, you can also add two further choirs, making one choir out of the three lower voices and instruments and the other out of the three high voices and instruments, singing the two sopranos in the tenor octave, if necessary, and doubling the voices in the *ripieni*. Or else one can make a single choir with the last six books, which would serve as the fourth choir and the *ripieno*. I rely on the taste and judgment of him who is pleased to use this work.
>
> Fourth, if one wishes, one may use the last six books for the voices and for the instruments together—taking care that where it says "solo" only the singer, without the instrument, should sing; and where it says "trombone" or "violin" only that instrument should play. And where it says "tutti" they all should sing and play together. But if one of these books has to serve for a solo voice or for a solo

instrument, it will be necessary to warn the performers to sing or play at the proper time and place, marking the notes that are to be left out and numbering the rests, to show the musicians where to enter.

Fifth, in the Credo of the Mass, when one arrives at the verse "Et resurrexit," which is in triple time, if there are instruments in the performance, they can play there alone, which will create an interlude. And then one would repeat it with the voices and instruments together. And similarly in the second *ripieno* added to my other Mass for 6 voices concerted, recently printed along with my a capella masses. And in the same way, one can play an instrumental interlude in the first Magnificat at the verse "Suscepit Israel," taking care, also, in the above-said Credo that when you arrive at the verse "Et iterum" for four voices, that there are appropriate parts in the second choir which sing it. To give satisfaction, the bass, tenor, and alto of the first choir will drop out and the soprano of the first choir will sing with the three voices of the second choir, which have the said verse.

Sixth, the Sanctus and the Agnus Dei are set very simply and briefly in the Venetian manner, so that they can be finished quickly in order to leave time for the vocal music to be performed during the Elevation and for some instrumental music during the Communion. Thus, it suffices for me to have given directions to the wise singers, for whom, with luck, this work will bring some pleasure; for if it does, perhaps soon some other work of mine will be published to please him who shows favor even to small things from one who cannot do better. Meanwhile, live happily.

Not all large-scale concerted church music was arranged from a one- or two-choir source. Some of the most characteristic works in this category use different styles or idioms for the solo voices and for the ensemble instruments, and many employ a true basso continuo that is not merely constructed out of the lowest voices sounding in the vocal or instrumental ensemble. The most celebrated large-scale concerto of this type is the motet *In ecclesiis* (A. 31) by Giovanni Gabrieli (ca. 1554–1612), organist at St. Mark's basilica in Venice.

It appears that *In ecclesiis* was composed for an annual procession of Venetian governmental dignitaries and church prelates from St. Mark's to the votive Church of the Redeemer. The rulers of Venice had vowed to build this church if the city were delivered from a plague, which it was. The first procession of 1577 was then re-enacted each year. The same thing happened in 1631 when the church of Saint Mary of Health (Santa Maria della Salute) was ordered built at the mouth of the Grand Canal in thanksgiving for the end of another plague. An imaginary procession to the latter church, modeled on the older tradition of the Church of the Redeemer, is shown in Figure 4-2. In this illustration the procession is beginning to enter the brightly illuminated church, where, we may imagine, an enlarged *capella* of voices and instruments is just starting to perform a work like *In ecclesiis*.

Gabrieli's *In ecclesiis*, published in 1615 after the composer's death, but probably composed after 1600, is among the earliest sacred concertos in which the

Figure 4-2. Marco Boschini, engraving of an imaginary procession to Santa Maria della Salute in Venice (1644)

instruments are specified—three cornetts, violin, two trombones, and a basso continuo part for organ—in addition to a four-voice choir and four vocal soloists (SATB). Its text consists of five one-sentence verses drawn from various antiphons sung by soloists, alternating with the choral refrain "Alleluia." This refrain form and the distinctly symmetrical overall shape of the work (soprano verse–refrain–bass verse–refrain–instrumental interlude–alto and tenor verse–refrain–soprano and bass verse–refrain–tutti verse–refrain) are typical of early seventeenth-century sacred concertos. The work is a good example of Kircher's metabolic style, inasmuch as striking harmonic shifts, often coordinated with contrasts of tempo, meter, pacing, and texture, give it consistently strong expression and feelings of expansiveness. In it, Gabrieli highlights or creates a number of rhetorical figures (anaploce, antistrophe, antithesis, aposiopesis, apostrophe, auxesis, epizeuxis, hyperbole, noema). The declamatory writing in the first two solo verses approaches recitative style. Second-practice dissonance is heard in the instrumental interlude. The simultaneous embellishments in the solo parts toward the end of the last (tutti) verse are reminiscent of *contrapunto alla mente*. Thus, *In ecclesiis* is a compendium of innovations that distinguish early seventeenth-century Italian music. This work was apparently well-known at the time; it and works like it seem to have had considerable influence in and outside of Italy.

Gabrieli's death in August 1612 occurred one year before Claudio Monteverdi's appointment to the post of *maestro di cappella* of St. Mark's in Venice. As *maestro di cappella* of St. Mark's, Monteverdi was responsible for composing large quantities of liturgical music as well as the music for the most important state occasions. Such an occasion was the Mass of Thanksgiving for the end of the plague, November 21, 1631. The Gloria presumed to be from that Mass (W. 5) was published in Monteverdi's *Selva morale e spirituali* ("Moral and Spiritual Anthology") in 1641. The printed music specifies seven-voice choir, seven

solo voices, two violins, basso continuo for the organ, and either four trombones or four viols to double the tenor and bass parts of the choir. The
payment records and descriptions of the event make it clear that two trumpets
also played in this Gloria, perhaps improvising without written music, as was
the custom of trumpeters at this time. Music like this was a sounding emblem
of civic tradition, governmental authority, glorification of the state, communal
piety, and belief in divine intervention in a mixture as typical of the seventeenth century as it is difficult for us to imagine today.

BIBLIOGRAPHICAL NOTES

The best concise overview of this subject is Jerome Roche, *North Italian Church
Music in the Age of Monteverdi* (Oxford: Clarendon Press, 1984). Three important
studies of leading or representative churches are Thomas D. Culley, *Jesuits and
Music: A Study of the Musicians Connected with the German College in Rome during the
17th Century and of Their Activities in Northern Europe*, Sources and Studies for the
History of the Jesuits, 2 (Rome: Jesuit Historical Institute, 1970); James H. Moore,
*Vespers at St. Mark's: Music of Alessandro Grandi, Giovanni Rovetta, and Francesco Cav-
alli* (Ann Arbor: UMI Research Press, 1981); and Colleen Reardon, *Agostino Agaz-
zari and Music at Siena Cathedral, 1597–1641* (Oxford: Clarendon Press, 1993).
Three outstanding recent studies of music in women's convents reveal a wealth of
astonishing detail: *The Crannied Wall: Women, Religion, and the Arts in Early Modern
Europe*, ed. Craig A. Monson (Ann Arbor: Univ. of Michigan Press, 1992); Craig A.
Monson, *Disembodied Voices: Music and Culture in an Early Modern Italian Convent*
(Berkeley and Los Angeles: Univ. of California Press, 1995); and Robert L.
Kendrick, *Celestial Sirens: Nuns and their Music in Early Modern Milan* (Oxford:
Clarendon Press, 1996). Three outstanding genre studies are Howard E. Smither, *A
History of the Oratorio*, I, *The Oratorio in the Baroque Era: Italy, Vienna, Paris* (Chapel
Hill: Univ. of North Carolina Press, 1977); Murray C. Bradshaw, *The Falsobordone: A
Study in Renaissance and Baroque Music*, Musicological Studies & Documents, 34
(Neuhausen-Stuttgart: Hänssler-Verlag, 1978); and Frits Noske, *Saints and Sinners:
The Latin Musical Dialogue in the Seventeenth Century* (Oxford: Clarendon Press,
1992). Two wide-ranging books on the contributions of individual composers are
Jeffrey G. Kurtzman, *The Monteverdi Mass and Vespers of 1610: Music, Context, Perfor-
mance* (Oxford: Oxford University Press, 1999); and Andrew V. Jones, *The Motets of
Carissimi* (Ann Arbor: UMI Research Press, 1982). Masses, motets, psalms, hymns,
and Magnificats of the seventeenth century are published in *Seventeenth-Century
Italian Sacred Music*, vols. 1–20, ed. Anne Schnoebelen and Jeffrey Kurtzman (New
York: Garland Publishing, 1995–2002) The books about Monteverdi mentioned in
the note to Chapter 2 are also relevant to this chapter. In addition, a large portion
of the information available on Italian churches and church music of this period is
found in journal articles, many of them cited in the bibliographies of the books
mentioned here. In addition, there are many books and articles devoted to music at
individual churches published in Italian; again, many of these are cited in the books
listed here.

CHAPTER 5

Stage, Instrumental, and Church Music in France to 1650

THE *BALET COMIQUE DE LA ROYNE*

The kingdom of France was far larger, richer, and more powerful than the Grand Duchy of Tuscany or any other realm in Italy, and its political and tax systems made its government and wealth more centralized than those of Spain, England, or the Holy Roman (Austro-German) Empire. The French kings of the sixteenth and seventeenth centuries strove to increase their power even further at the expense of the regional nobilities and the estates of the parliaments. To help further this aim, musical spectacle in seventeenth-century France contained more obvious propaganda than did early opera in Italy.

The central type of musical spectacle in seventeenth-century France was the court ballet (*ballet de cour*), the basic structure of which was created by a series of entries of costumed dancers (normally courtiers) representing allegorical personages, often from mythology. Although these ballets were performed in great halls or ballrooms, rather than in theaters, elements of scenery and even theatrical machinery were normally employed. Often these scenic elements were brought in and out of the hall on pageant carts like those used in parades. In some of these ballets, the entries were tied together by explanatory texts sung by professional singers or printed in program booklets. In a few ballets, spoken dramatic scenes provided some of the story line, in which case the ballet entries would appear to be interludes between the acts of a play. Although the French court ballet was based on an Italian spectacle called *mascherata* ("masquerade") or *festa da ballo* ("dance festivity"), specifically French characteristics grew up around it early in the seventeenth century

In 1581 the *Balet comique de la Royne* ("The Dramatic Ballet of the Queen") initiated a series of court ballets that became the central tradition of French musical spectacle for the entire Baroque era, eclipsed only temporarily by opera during the 1670s and 1680s. During the nineteen years from the performance of this work until the death of Henry IV, at least eighty new court ballets were written and staged, about four per year, whereas operas at Italian courts were produced far more rarely. The *Balet comique de la Royne* had more dramatic continuity than most of the court ballets that followed it.

In fact, it was organized into five brief acts of spoken drama mixed with songs, each followed by an intermedio (they used the Italian term) featuring singing and dancing without spoken dialogue.

The *Balet comique de la Royne* begins with an astonishing stroke, as a knight bursts upon the scene to address the king, who is seated in the audience (Fig. 5-1). He begs for help in defeating the wicked witch Circe's plot to prevent the return of the Golden Age to France. In a later scene (see A. 32) it is revealed that Circe is changing men into monsters by depriving them of reason. After the god Mercury fails to defeat Circe, the goddess Pallas Athena explains that all attempts to combat the witch independently through virtue are doomed without the help of the king of France and his wise laws. In the end, the chief god, Jupiter, conquers Circe and presents her magic wand to the king, "the Jupiter of France."

The plot and events of this court ballet obviously embody a political message, stated explicitly and reinforced by allegory. The message was even clearer because all the speaking and dancing roles were taken by the noblemen and ladies who formed the inner circle around the royal family at court. To understand this message, we must digress to a bit of French history.

Henry III, who presided over this court ballet, was king of France from 1574 to 1589. During his reign the Wars of Religion were fought between French Catholics and Protestant (Calvinist) Huguenots. Matters were made worse by dynastic rivalries arising because the male line of the Valois dynasty was going to die out with Henry. The Peace of Bergerac (1577) ended the hostilities temporarily; the Huguenots lost some of their liberties in the Edict of Poitiers, and the Holy League of Catholic nobles aided by the King of Spain and other Catholic princes was dissolved. During this respite, but in the knowledge that the underlying conflicts had not been resolved, the *Balet comique de la Royne* was written and performed.

Figure 5-1. A knight begs the king's help

The French Wars of Religion spawned competing political philosophies that outlived the wars themselves. The Huguenots advocated their right to attack the king if he would not guarantee them tolerance, and they raised fundamental questions about a monarch's power and the rights of his subjects. Deeply opposed to this contractual theory of the Huguenots was the doctrine of ultramontanism, the philosophy of the Catholic extremists. The ultramontanists feared that a strong national monarchy would mean the subordination of papal authority. Between these extremes was the Politique party, convinced of the need to support a strong monarchy that could resist both ultramontane and Huguenot excesses and the divisive influence of noble factions. This is the philosophy expressed by the *Balet comique de la Royne*. From its emphasis upon passive obedience emerged the theory of the divine right of kings. The first written statement of this theory in France is contained in the works of Pierre de Belloy, especially his *De l'Autorité du roi* (1588), in which he asserted that the monarchy was created by God, to whom alone the king was responsible. There can, therefore, be no contractual relationship between the king and his people. He considered the king's authority to be absolute.

In many respects, the Politique position was the creation of the Queen Mother mentioned in the ballet booklet, Catherine de' Medici, the daughter of Lorenzo de' Medici, duke of Urbino. As tutor and chief political advisor to three sons who became, in their turn, kings of France, she waged a long struggle with the Catholic extremists who, supported by Spain and the papacy, sought to dominate the French crown and extinguish its independence.

Catherine had been instrumental in bringing a large number of artists and musicians from her native Italy to the royal court of France. Among these was Baltzarini da Belgiojoso, who came in 1555 as a member of a company of violinists from the Piedmont region of Italy (in the extreme north, near Turin). Having frenchified his name to Baltasar de Beaujoyeulx, he became a gentleman in Catherine's household, and it was he who designed and produced the *Balet comique de la Royne* as well as its two important predecessors, the *Paradis d'amour* (1572) and the *Ballet polonis* (1573).

The music for the *Balet comique de la Royne,* by the courtier and singer Lambert de Beaulieu (fl. ca. 1559–90), is, on the other hand, quite un-Italian. The vocal numbers, both ensemble and solo, reflect a unique development of the homophonic French chanson of the sixteenth century called *musique mesurée.* This parallels a type of poetry called *vers mesurés à l'antique* ("verses made metrical in the ancient style") invented in 1567 by the noble poet and scholar Jean-Antoine de Baïf and fostered by the members of the Académie de Poésie et de Musique, which Baïf and the noble musician Joachim Thibault de Courville founded in 1571; the composer Lambert de Beaulieu was a member.

The stated purpose of the Académie de Poésie et de Musique was almost identical to that of the Florentine Camerata, founded at almost precisely the same time: to rediscover and revive the fabled moral and spiritual effects of the music, poetry, and drama of the ancient Greeks and Romans. But Baïf came to a radically different conclusion. He thought that the key lay in the patterns of long and short syllables that organized classical Greek and Latin poetic verse, patterns that he attempted to impose upon French poetry.

These patterns of long and short syllables, when translated into half notes and quarter notes in musical settings of *vers mesurés à l'antique*, yield rhythmic patterns that defy grouping into regular musical meters. The ensembles of the *Balet comique de la Royne* show these traits most clearly, but they are present also in the solo *récits* ("recitations" for solo voice), such as the first part of the dialogue of Glaucus and Thethys and in its second part, where this feature is only partially disguised by the brief, written-out ornamental divisions that have been added. This is illustrated in Example 5-1, in which the solo vocal lines of the last portion of the dialogue between Glaucus and Tethys (A. 32) are stripped of their embellishment.

Most of the musical numbers in French court ballets, however, were dances, especially if we add the choruses and airs that were essentially dances with texts. Dances and solo airs had other uses as well, and they circulated and were performed independently of the court ballets.

TYPES OF DANCE IN COURT BALLETS, OTHER SPECTACLES, AND SOCIAL CONTEXTS

Dance was a very important social and cultural activity at the royal court and in most noble households in France during the seventeenth century. It encom-

EXAMPLE 5-1. The solo vocal lines of a portion of the dialogue between Glaucus and Tethys, stripped of its embellishment

passed aspects of art, recreation, social ritual, political affirmation, and entertainment. A high degree of skill in dancing was expected of all noblemen and ladies, and several kings of France distinguished themselves as solo dancers on stage. Choreography involved step types and sequences, geometrical patterns of floor movement, and intricate upper-body gestures, such as bows and hand signals, that mimicked stylized courtly behavior. Various dance types were distinguished musically by their meter, tempo, type of formal organization, and underlying rhythmic patterning. Differences that may seem subtle and difficult to grasp today were at that time considered fundamental.

Choreography holds an essential key to distinguishing the musical characteristics of dance types. For the early part of the seventeenth century, the single best source of information on French choreography is *Orchésographie* (1588/89) by Jehan Tabourot, the vicar general of the diocese of Langres, who wrote under the pseudonym Thoinot Arbeau. Arbeau describes the kinds of step that were used in each dance, illustrates them with drawings, and plots them against musical rhythms. In many cases, the grouping of steps, preparations, and pauses illuminates the typical phrasing, flow, and points of arrival in specific dances. The underlying rhythmic patterns of dances are also brought to the surface by the strumming patterns in tablatures for the five-string Spanish guitar.

Additional information about underlying rhythmic patterns comes from the system of rhythmic analysis explained by the French mathematician, philosopher, and music theorist Marin Mersenne (1588–1648) in part of his multivolume music treatise *Harmonie universelle* ("Universal Harmony," 1636–37). Mersenne distinguished the underlying rhythmic patterns of dances by adapting the symbols, terminology, and concepts of the poetic scansion used by Greek and Roman scholars and poets. When applied to poetry, this system identifies short and long syllables with the markings U and — and groups them into metrical feet.

When Mersenne applied the classical theory of poetic meters (the theory that he called *rythmique*) to music, he translated the abstract concepts of short and long musical *temps* into quarter notes and half notes, respectively, where the musical meter permitted. Even so, he knew that patterns of quarter notes and half notes corresponding to the classical metrical feet were not normally repeated in music the way patterns of short and long (or unaccented and accented) syllables are repeated in certain kinds of poetry. He recognized that the actual rhythms of even the simplest dance were usually far more varied than that. He therefore considered the shorter notes in the dance music to be divisions of hypothetical background quarter notes or half notes, while longer note values could result from the elision of two or more of these.

Mersenne's insight was that certain patterns of longs and shorts underlie the actual surface music of dances. Sometimes these patterns are reflected in the harmonization of the dance melody or in the rhythms of accompanying parts. At other times, the pairing of one or several shorts with one or two longs seems to reflect a linkage of an extended upbeat (arsis) with a downbeat (thesis) on the measure-to-measure level, of motion with repose, of instability with stability, or the ebb and flow of energy created by the interaction among surface rhythm, meter, melodic shape, and harmony. In some cases, Mersenne related a certain pattern of longs and shorts to a specific, well-known drum cadence used for marching. He implied that the corresponding drum cadence would fit appropriately with a dance based on the corresponding pattern of longs and shorts, although he does not say that drums actually accompanied court or theatrical dances. Where violin or viol bowing for a dance is marked in the score, the phrasing and pattern of accentuation implied by the bowing often corresponds to the movement that Mersenne assigns to the dance. And in many cases the typical dance step reported by Arbeau reflects Mersenne's pattern of longs and shorts as well.

"The PASSEMEZZE," according to Mersenne, ". . . is danced while making some tours around the hall with certain alighting steps, and then in crossing the middle, as the word [*passemezze*, "step in the middle"] implies. Or else it takes its name from the step and one half in which it is measured. . . . It is connected with the choreobachic foot ∪ ∪ ∪ ∪ — —. Its meter is binary." Example 5-2 is the passemezze melody that Mersenne uses to illustrate; in this example, the choreobachic foot has been superimposed in the form of quarter and half notes above the musical staff. The quarter notes of the choreobachic foot generally line up with more rapid motion in the actual dance melody, while the half notes of Mersenne's rhythmic movement correspond to relatively slower rhythms in the melody. A. 33a is an early seventeenth-century passemezze for the standard five-part string orchestra of the French royal court (one violin part, three viola parts, and a part for bass violin [a large-size cello]) by Pierre Francisque Caroubel (d. 1611), a violinist at the court of King Henry IV.

Arbeau writes that "A cavalier may dance the PAVAN wearing his cloak and sword, and [ladies] . . . dressed in their long gowns, walking with decorum and measured gravity." Mersenne thought that the pavan came from Spain and was named for the strutting peacock (*paon*), but most modern scholars trace its early sixteenth-century origin to Italy. Mersenne assigns it the same poetic foot as the passemezze. Example 5-3 is the first strain of a *Pavane de Spaigne* ("Pavan of Spain") by Caroubel, upon which has been superimposed Arbeau's choreography for a Spanish Pavan and Mersenne's choreobachic foot, represented again by quarter and half notes. Notice that the choreography at the beginning and end of the example forms two-bar units set off by a *pied joint* ("feet together" = FT), in one case with a *pied en l'air* ("foot in the air" = FA) added. Repeated pitches or harmonies likewise articulate the music into the same two-bar units. The middle section of this choreography consists of *fleurets*, each of which is made up of three kicks with alternate feet in the rhythm ♩♩♩; thus, in this part of the dance the steps do not mark off two-bar phrases.

"The ALLEMANDE," writes Mersenne, "is a dance from Germany [*Allemagne*] that is measured like the pavan. Arbeau writes, "You can dance [the allemande] in a group, because when you have joined hands with a lady, several others may fall into line behind you, each with his partner. And you will all dance together in duple time, moving forward, or if you wish, backward, three

EXAMPLE 5-2. Mersenne's passemezze melody

steps and one *grève* . . . and in certain parts by one step and one *grève*. . . ."
Arbeau's choreography, superimposed on his example of an allemande melody,
is given as Example 5-4. Notice that walking alternations of left (L) and right
(R) feet are normally marked off into two-measure phrases by a stylized kick,
called a *grève*, with right (GR) or left (GL) foot. In Example 5-4, three of these
two-measure phrases end with two half notes on the same pitch, corresponding to the two half notes in Mersenne's choreobachic foot, which has also been
superimposed over the music. This phrasing seems to be typical of early
seventeenth-century allemandes intended for dancing. Allemandes for purely
musical performance exhibit a much greater variety and are, in fact, the least
regular in rhythm of all the common dance types. See, for example, the two
allemandes in A. 34, a suite of dances by Michel Mazuel (1603–1676), a violinist at the French royal court from 1636 to 1674.

EXAMPLE 5-3. The first strain of a Pavane de Spaigne by Caroubel

The SARABANDE is a triple-meter dance. Mersenne assigns it an underlying poetic foot that covers two measures: ∪ ∪ ∪ — ∪. The surface rhythm of Mersenne's example of a sarabande melody conforms to this poetic foot very closely, with only a simple division of the long "syllable" of each foot. Example 5-5 is a brief five-part sarabande by Mazuel from the *Ballet du roy des festes de Baccus* ("The King's Ballet of the Feasts of Bacchus"), danced at the French royal palace in 1651. The underlying poetic foot, shown by the overlay of quarter and half notes, is evident in the composite rhythm of the ensemble, with minor variants; the second strain introduces the prolonged second note in measures 5 and 7, a feature that seems to grow in importance in sarabandes from the middle of the seventeenth century onward. The same features are found in the two sarabandes by Mazuel in his suite, A. 34. All remarks on the subject from the first two-thirds of the seventeenth century indicate that the sarabande was a lively dance.

The VOLTA is a lively triple-meter dance to which Mersenne assigns three possible poetic feet: ∪ ∪ ∪ —, ∪ — ∪ —, and ∪ ∪ — —. He adds, "It has this name also because, after several steps to the right, the man makes the woman leap while turning, and, after having led her around for a certain time, he takes her with his left arm by her waist and turns her several times while holding her up high, as if he wanted to make her fly" (see Fig. 5-2). Arbeau complained that "in dancing [a volta] the ladies are made to bounce about in such a fashion that more often than not they show their bare knees, unless they

EXAMPLE 5-4. Arbeau's allemande choreography

keep one hand on their skirts to prevent it." Example 5-6 is a fairly typical
volta by Caroubel, over which the three rhythmic feet named by Mersenne
have been marked.

Mersenne reports, "The COURANTE is, of all the dances, the most frequently employed in France, and it is danced by only two persons at a time,
since it makes one run (*courir*) to a tune measured by the iambic foot ∪ −, so
that the entire dance is nothing but a leaping race of coming and going
from beginning to end. It is composed of two steps in one measure, that is,
of one step for each foot, alternating with the step with three movements,
that is, the bend, the rise, and the fall. Its movement is called sesquialtera [$\frac{3}{2}$]
or triple [$\frac{3}{1}$] . . . ."

Mersenne's example of a courante melody (Ex. 5-7) begins with a pickup
note that establishes the predominant iambic pattern that occasionally gives
way to the trochaic foot — ∪ ; the tied notes at the end of each strain show
that the rhythm really falls into metrical units of six half notes. This six-beat
unit is reflected in the barring of those early seventeenth-century courantes
that carry a proportion sign of $\frac{6}{2}$, but it is also implied in the music of courantes
with the equally common proportion of $\frac{3}{2}$.

EXAMPLE 5-5. A sarabande by Mazuel from the *Ballet du roy des festes de Baccus*, 1651

EXAMPLE 5-6. A volta by Caroubel

Iambic rhythm (U —) predominates in early seventeenth-century courantes, resulting in the division of the six-beat metrical units into two groups of three beats (see Fig. 5-3). Increasingly toward the middle of the century one finds the six beats divided 2 + 2 + 2 in irregular alternation with 3 + 3 groupings. Often the subdivision of the six beats appears to be different among the various instrumental lines in the same measure. Examples are found in the two courantes by Mazuel in A.34. When Mersenne says that "two steps in one measure" alternate with "the step with three movements," we may assume that he is referring to a measure of six beats and that this alternation of steps is identical with the fluctuation between 3 + 3 and 2 + 2 + 2 groups of beats in the music.

The GALLIARD was danced with caprioles, which are high leaps with a quick backward and forward movements of the feet (see Fig. 5-4). Its music is in triple meter, and Mersenne assigns to it the rhythmic foot U U U U —. This foot is not clearly found in the melody of any galliard. It seems, rather, to relate to the choreography, of which Arbeau gives eleven variants, all of which have five steps in three movements. The common feature of all Arbeau's galliard pat-

EXAMPLE 5-7. Mersenne's courante melody

Figure 5-2. Dancing the volta
at the court of King Henry III
of France, ca. 1585

terns is a series of four even steps or kicks, on the beats, followed by a high leap
and a pose: 1 2 3 / 1 2 pose (see Fig. 5-5). In the early seventeenth century, as
in the sixteenth, a triple-meter galliard was often paired with a duple-meter
pavan or passemezze of which the galliard was a musi-
cal variation: Anthology 33a and b is an example of
that sort of dance pairing. Galliards were written with
the proportion signs 3 or $\frac{3}{2}$, but never $\frac{6}{4}$, although their
six-beat dance-step patterns always yield a six-beat
(two-bar) musical unit. Like a courante, a galliard
often features shifts between 3 + 3 and 2 + 2 + 2
groupings at both the half-note level and the quarter-
note level.

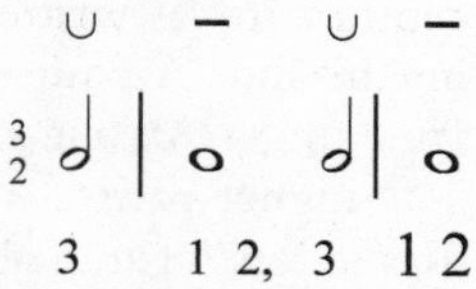

Figure 5-3. Iambic
courante rhythm

Mersenne presents the GAVOTTE as a type of
branle in duple meter characterized by the rhythmic
foot ∪ ∪ ∪ ∪ — —. According to Arbeau, it was
danced in a line or circle with a sideways motion created by crossing the feet and a hop. The steps tend to
mark off pairs of quarter notes, and each four-bar
phrase may be set off by a leap.

The BOURRÉE was a fast duple-meter dance
with a quarter-note pickup. The typical choreography
of the bourrée appears to have been very closely connected to the rhythm and phrasing of its music, as is
shown in Example 5-8. The *pas de bourrée* ("bourrée
step") was one of the basic building blocks of many
choreographies for various dances.

Figure 5-4. Arbeau's
illustration of a
capriole

THE *AIR DE COUR*

Air de cour ("Court Air") was the name used in France, ca. 1571–1660, for
strophic songs, usually of narrow range, either for an ensemble of three to five
voices treated homophonically or for solo voice with lute accompaniment. The
majority of *airs de cour* were printed in dual versions for ensemble and for

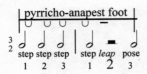

Figure 5-5. Typical galliard
steps

accompanied solo voice, although in the seventeenth century it appears that
the solo-voice version was considered the primary one. Over 1000 *airs de cour*
were printed during the genre's peak period, 1608–43, primarily for use in
noble households.

The lute accompaniment of an *air de cour* usually resembles a composite
score of all the voices of the ensemble arrangement, except for the highest,
which is sung. These lute accompaniments were written using a system of
notation called "intabulation" that originated at the beginning of the sixteenth
century. It was written on a six-line staff, each line representing one "course"
on the lute. A course consists of one or two adjacent strings stopped by the
same finger. All but the highest course on a lute are made up of pairs of strings.
The higher pairs are tuned in unison, the lower in octaves. Lute intabulation
uses letters written above the lines of this staff to show the fret to be fingered
and the strings to be plucked for every note (*a* represents open strings).
Rhythm is shown by note symbols or stems with flags written above the staff.
A given note value is repeated until replaced by another. Example 5-9 shows
the beginning of an *air de cour* with a solo vocal line in staff notation, a staff-
notation transcription of the lute tablature, and a lute accompaniment in tablature. The pitch of this vocal line requires a lute tuning of (top to bottom) *a' e'
b g d A*. The tablature for the first chord shows that the first string (*a'*) is
stopped at the first fret, making the note *b♭'*; the second course (*e'*) is stopped at
the third fret, making the note *g'*, and so on.

Figure 5-6 shows a painting by Nicolas Tournier (1590–1639) entitled *Le
Concert* ("The Concert"), depicting a performance, probably of an *air de cour*.
The players of the lute and the violin appear to be young noblemen, to judge
by their clothing. The lady is also noble, but the older man playing the bass viol
appears to be a cleric, very likely the priest in charge of educating the young
lady and perhaps the boy. If they are really in the act of performing, then the

EXAMPLE 5-8. The melody of Mazuel's first bourrée, with the choreography

EXAMPLE 5-9. Beginning of *Lorsque lè andre* from Gabriel Bataille, *Les Airs de differents autheurs mis en tablature de luth*, 1608

music in the boy's hand would be the soprano part of an *air de cour*. The violin, small harpsichord, and viol would be playing the four lower parts of the polyphonic version of the air, and the lute would be playing the intabulated accompaniment from the solo-voice version.

While the vocal line of a solo *air de cour* almost always appears to be syllabic as represented in musical notation, it was customary to embellish it extemporaneously. This is shown in an illustration from Mersenne's *Harmonie universelle* (Ex. 5-10), in which the solo vocal line of *N'esperez plus* by Antoine Boesset, Sieur de Villedieu (1586–1643), is provided with one set of embellishments for

Figure 5-6. Nicolas Tournier, *The Concert*

EXAMPLE 5-10. The vocal line of *N'esperez plus* by Antoine Boesset with embellishments by Le Bailly and Boeset

the second strophe by the composer and another by Henry Le Bailly (d. 1637), composer, singer, and co-superintendent with Boesset of music for the French royal chapel. The airs in the *Balet comique de la Royne* were printed with embellishments of this kind. Like Beaulieu, the composer of the *Balet comique de la Royne*, both Boesset and Le Bailly were noblemen.

Like earlier polyphonic music, *airs de cour* were printed without barlines, whether the music was inherently metrical or not. Although the modern transcription shown in Example 5-10 is barred almost entirely in $\frac{4}{4}$, the internal musical indications of metrical grouping are quite weak in some places. Example 5-9 has similar characteristics but is transcribed without bar lines. The *airs de cour* in the Anthology are transcribed with barlines that may seem arbitrary in some cases but are included for the convenience of students.

Examples 5-9 and 5-10 are representative of one type of *air de cour* in which the note values of the unornamented melody may be limited to mostly half and quarter notes, rather than the wider range from thirty-seconds to double-whole notes found in Italian solo madrigals on this period. The influence of *musique mesurée* in these airs is sufficient to defeat clear meter, even if the distinction between long and short syllables is not always followed exactly according to Baïf's theory. These examples are similar in this respect to the *récits* in the *Balet comique de la Royne*.

A second, earlier type of *air de cour* employs clearly metrical rhythms and regular phrases. Some of these, like the anonymous *Ma belle si ton ame* ("My Beauty, Your Heart" A. 35), are actually adaptations of traditional melodies (*Une jeune fillette* in this case) belonging to the category of *vaudeville* and circulated largely through oral tradition.

The third type of *air de cour* features dramatically interpretive declamation of the text resulting from the composer's setting. Airs of this type show the influence of Italian monody. An example is *Quel excès de douleur* ("What an Excess of Sorrow," A.36), a *récit* from an as-yet-unidentified court ballet by Pierre Guédron (after 1564–1619/20), royal chamber composer and a dominant figure in the early history of the *air de cour*. Among the Italian features of this air are the wider range of note values to which syllables are set, the occasional use of monotone recitation, sudden changes of register for emphasis, dramatic pauses, long syncopated notes, expressive chromaticism, and the rapid three-note ascending ornament. In 1617 Guédron became the first French composer to employ a basso continuo accompaniment—another Italian trait—although he abandoned the experiment immediately and returned to intabulated lute accompaniments.

The probable source of this Italian influence was Giulio Caccini and his family. In 1604–5 the Caccini family was summoned from Florence to the French royal court by Maria de' Medici, for whose wedding in 1600 to King Henry IV of France the first operas by Caccini and Peri had been performed. The Caccinis' visit created a stir at court. The two composer-singer sisters, Francesca and Margherita Caccini, were invited to remain in the queen's service, but they declined.

LUTE MUSIC

The fashion among the nobility of Europe for playing the lute, which began in the early sixteenth century, peaked during the first half of the seventeenth century and probably reached its highest point in France during the reign of Louis XIII (1610–1643). We know the names of several dozen professional players and teachers of the lute residing in Paris during this period. It appears that virtually every nobleman and quite a few noblewomen studied the lute at some point.

The lute shown in Figure 5-6 is typical of this period, with its ten courses, each course except the highest having two strings. In addition to the six courses of the Renaissance lute, an instrument such as this would have four bass courses tuned to the next four notes of a diatonic scale descending from the sixth course (usually *A* or *G*). The transcribed tablature shown in Example 5-11 calls for the unstopped seventh course of such an instrument, producing the note transcribed as *G*. During the seventeenth century composers and performers introduced a variety of new lute tunings that facilitated music in which chords are more important than polyphonic textures.

A printed collection of lute music by Anthoine Francisque (ca. 1575–1605)—a face in the crowd of Parisian lutenists—entitled *Le trésor d'Orphée* ("The Treasure of Orpheus," 1600) shows the main trends in French lute music in the first half of the seventeenth century. Instead of the polyphonic fantasias and ricercars and the transcriptions of vocal music typical of sixteenth-century lute books, *Le trésor d'Orphée* contains mostly court dances—the same types used in court ballets. The style of Francisque's works also departs from that of the previous century. Instead of maintaining the continuity of individual lines or voices in a polyphonic texture, Francisque, like most of his French contemporaries, wrote only a sketch of the lower voices of the texture, discontinuing and resuming them many times in the course of a piece and frequently delaying their notes with syncopation so as to increase the number of separate attacks and to disperse them throughout each phrase; even the uppermost line may disappear for a time. Example 5-11 demonstrates this point by constituting the hypothetical continuous voices of a courante by Francisque. The complete piece, with the Prelude that precedes it in the collection, is transcribed in the usual manner—on two staves—as A. 37.

An allemande by Louis XIII's finest player, René Mesangeau (d. 1638), A. 38, carries further the tendency to break up the voices in the texture, and it adds some slurred ornaments executed by the left hand alone without plucking

EXAMPLE 5-11. A lute courante by Francisque resolved into its individual lines

by the fingers of the right hand, a newly important technique in the seventeenth century.

A piece written in memory of his teacher—*Tombeau de Mesangeau*, A. 39—by the nobleman Ennemond Gaultier, Sier de Nèves (1575–1651), probably composed soon after Mesangeau's death in 1638, avoids recurring rhythmic patterns, reinforcing the impression of spontaneous discontinuity and aimlessness already suggested by the broken texture. Pieces in the genre of the tombeau were meant to be played slowly, and this slow place created silences as each note was allowed to decay before the next one was plucked. This silence also contributed to the impression of discontinuity, and it was prized for its hypnotic effect, as we learn from René François's *Essai des merveilles de nature* ("Essay on the Marvels of Nature," 1621):

> One makes the lute speak as one wishes, and one controls one's audience as one wishes. . . . If [the lute player] chooses to let the strings die away under his fingers, he transports all these people and charms them with a gay melancholy, so that one of them lets his chin fall upon his chest, another on his hand, which slowly extends full length as if pulled by his ear, another with eyes wide open or with mouth half agape, as though all his attention were riveted upon the strings.

The transport of the soul to a state of extreme absorption through contemplation that François and other writers of the time describe can be seen in a number of contemporaneous French paintings, especially those by Georges de La Tour (1593–1653)—for example, his *Repentant Magdalene* of ca. 1640 (Fig. 5-7). Absorption through contemplation was also the goal of

Figure 5-7. La Tour, *Repentant Magdalene*

Quietism, a doctrine of Christian spirituality important in early seventeenth-century France that held that perfection consists in passivity (quiet) of the soul and in the suppression of effort so that divine action may have full play. A political form of Quietism seems to be the object of the discourse in the *Balet comique de la Royne*.

The spontaneous-seeming style of discontinuous lines, delayed entrances, syncopation, dispersal of attacks, left-hand ornaments, and hypnotic dying away—today often called *style brisé* ("broken style")—reached its furthest development in the works of the nobleman Denis Gaultier (1597 or 1603–1672), cousin of Ennemond Gaultier. Denis Gaultier was also one of the first Frenchmen to group his dances into suites—for example, prelude, pavan or allemande, courante(s), sarabande—rather than placing all the dances of each type together in his collections. The elaborate, annotated, and illustrated manuscript from which Gaultier's suite in the Anthology (no. 40) is taken is entitled *La Rhetorique des dieux* ("The Rhetoric of the Gods"), compiled between 1648 and 1652 for the wealthy noblewoman Anne de Chambré. It contains eleven suites, ordered and designated by mode, using C rather than D as the starting point in its ordering and employing the Latinized Greek names favored by late Humanists. Thus, the suite in A. 40 is designated as "Mode Ionien," but it is in a minor mode and has *A* as its final.

The suite begins with an unmeasured prelude, in which the beginnings of notes are shown in the tablature without rhythmic values attached to them (see Fig. 5-8). These notes are normally transcribed as whole notes today, although they were intended to be played with spontaneously varied, often quite brief durations.

The second, third, and fifth pieces in Gaultier's suite carry titles alluding to the evocative poems that accompany them. For example, the fifth piece, *L'Homicide* ("The Murderess") is accompanied by a poem that can be translated, "This beauty, by her charms, causes death to whomever sees her and listens to her; but this death is unlike ordinary deaths in that it is the beginning of life rather than being the end." If the poem has any connection to the music, it would be the word *charms*.

The second and third pieces in Gaultier's suite are found in other manuscripts; in some of these they are called allemandes, while in others they are called gigues. At mid-century, the French gigue, a recent importation from England, was normally written in a compound meter such as $\frac{12}{8}$ or $\frac{6}{4}$, and its prevailing rhythm was generally some variant or diminution of an iambic pattern such as $\frac{12}{8}$ ♪♩♪♩, following the rhythm of the alternations between bends and steps in the choreography. An allemande, on the other hand, is always written in duple meter with steady eighth-note rhythm. A later explanation of this anomaly (Perrine, *Pièces de luth en musique*, ca. 1680) makes clear that when a piece is notated as an allemande in duple meter, it can be performed as a gigue (becoming an *allemande giguée* or *allemande en gigue*) through the application of *notes inégales* ("unequal notes"). Later seventeenth-century French sources give very precise directions for creating *notes inégales* by performing conjunct passages of eighth or sixteenth notes unequally, as pairs of long-short or, more rarely, short-long. One of the earliest and simplest explanations of this per-

Figure 5-8. The original lute tablature notation for Gaultier's unmeasured prelude from the Ionian suite in *La Rhetorique des dieux* (ca. 1648–52). The stylized letters refer to the frets to be stopped, and the lines on which the letters are placed show the strings to be plucked. The absence of rhythmic notation, normally present in the form of stems and flags above the staves, shows that this is an unmeasured prelude.

formance tradition comes from the "Instructions for the Lute" written about 1670 by the English woman Miss Mary Burwell, who was familiar with French lutenists and was probably taught by one. She writes:

> You may get the art by breaking the strokes; that is, dividing of them by stealing half a note from one note and bestowing of it upon the next note. That will make the playing of the lute more airy and skipping.

Example 5-12 shows how Miss Burwell's "breaking the strokes" could produce *notes inégales* that transform the first strain of Gaultier's second allemande (entitled *Echo*) into a gigue. A further clue to performance practice in Gaultier's *Rhetorique des dieux* is the inclusion of written-out diminutions, called "doubles," for the repetitions of each strain of his last courante.

HARPSICHORD MUSIC

Although the harpsichord was in use at least as early as the lute and in the sixteenth century its literature was in many ways comparable to the lute's, in seventeenth-century France it appears that the harpsichord followed the lead of

EXAMPLE 5-12. Gaultier's *Echo allemande*, first strain (A) transformed into a gigue (B) through the application of *notes inégales*

the lute in terms of repertoire and musical style. Surviving manuscripts and prints of French music for the harpsichord from the first half of the seventeenth century are surprisingly rare, whereas they are relatively abundant for the lute. It seems that the bulk of harpsichord music from this period in France consisted of dances imitating the idiomatic lute texture that we call *style brisé*. In the early eighteenth century François Couperin called it *style luthé* ("lute style"), still referring to its origins a century after its transfer to the harpsichord. The sarabande by René Mesangeau, A. 41, from about 1630 certainly employs this texture to the same degree as the composer's lute music (A. 38), if, indeed, it is not simply a keyboard transcription of one of Mesangeau's lute pieces.

The typical French harpsichord of the early seventeenth century was, by contrast to the single-keyboard Italian models, a two-manual instrument about eight feet in length with two sets of strings at written pitch (8-foot) and one sounding an octave higher (4-foot). Normally, each of the keys of the lower manual pushed up two vertical jacks fitted with quills that could pluck a 4-foot string or an

8-foot string or both, depending on how the jack slides were pulled. The upper manual played the second set of 8-foot strings, but this manual could be coupled to the lower keyboard by a set of coupler dogs—small posts on the far ends of the keys that push up the corresponding ends of the upper keys (see Figure 5-9). Consequently, a French harpsichord could produce three different sonorities and could combine or rapidly juxtapose any two of them.

The earliest in the series of distinguished French harpsichordist-composers and the only one whose career unfolded primarily during the first half of the seventeenth century was Jacques Champion, Sieur de Chambonnières (1601/02–1672). Champion's title of nobility, "Sieur de Chambonnières," refers to a small manor in the countryside near Paris, although he grew up at the royal court, where his father held a post as salaried musician, a post which Jacques inherited when he was only nine. By the 1630s Chambonnières was the most famous harpsichordist in France, a frequent dancer in court ballets, and an organizer of public concerts in Paris. Although he lived until 1672, Chambonnières's personal fortune declined markedly in 1652 as a consequence of the civil wars (the Frondes, 1648–52) between the parliamentarians and the royalists. He fell out of favor at court by about 1657. His reputation as a composer, however, remained strong enough that two volumes of his collected works were published in 1670.

In these volumes Chambonnières brought together pieces from all periods of his life and arranged them into suites (e.g., A. 42). In most cases we have no clue as to the date of composition and no way of knowing when the pieces were combined into suites. One exception is a courante whose title, *Les Baricades* ("The Barricades"), probably refers to the Paris uprising of 1648. In addition to a moderate form of *style brisé* and some motivic connections among them, these dances are marked by intensified use of small ornaments represented by marks explained in the composer's "Demonstration des Marges" (Fig. 5-10). They also have broader melodic contours than earlier lute music, a spontaneous variety

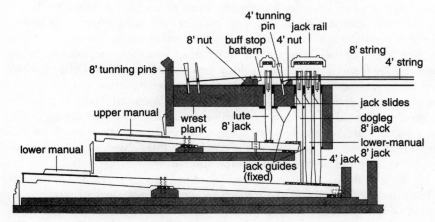

Figure 5-9. The action of a French harpsichord of the seventeenth century

Figure 5-10. Chambonnières's table of ornaments, 1670

of rhythms (avoiding the continuous recurrence of or variations upon a single pattern more typical of earlier ballet music), and more continuous and explicit counterpoint than found in lute music. Actually, among the various manuscripts preserving the harpsichord music of Chambonnières, there are many variants of the same pieces, differing as to the degree of continuity of contrapuntal voices and in details of ornamentation, suggesting that these versions record a variety of spontaneous and freely adapted performances.

INSTRUMENTAL ENSEMBLE MUSIC

In Paris during the first half of the seventeenth century, there were three categories of instrumental ensemble at the French royal court and another in the city of Paris, outside the precincts of the court. The ensemble that played at court ballets, other types of musical spectacle, and ordinary balls was called the *Vingt-quatre Violons du Roi* ("The Twenty-Four Violins of the King") or less formally the *Grande Bande* ("Large Orchestra"). As noted earlier, it played music scored in five parts: (1) six violins, (2) four violas, (3) four violas, (4) four violas, (5) six bass violins (large cellos). The musical repertoire of this ensemble during the first half of the seventeenth century seems to have been limited to dances. Sonatas and canzonas for violins with continuo accompaniment such as were cultivated in Italy at this time were apparently unknown in France.

The Music of the Chamber was under an administration separate from that of the *Grande Bande*: it included solo singers, lutenists, keyboard players, virtuoso cornett soloists, and an ensemble of viols. The repertoires of the singers, lutenists, and keyboard players have already been discussed. The viol ensemble typically consisted of three to six instruments of the three sizes shown in Figure 5-11. Figure 5-6 also includes a bass viol. The characteristic genre for viols in France during this period was the ensemble fantasie with imitative, contrapuntal texture and no continuo accompaniment.

A. 43 is a fantasie for four viols, published in 1610, by Eustache Du Caurroy (1549–1609), composer to the royal chamber, superintendent of music at the court of Henry IV, and member of the minor nobility. The work is based on a subject that is almost always present in its original form, melodically inverted, or

Figure 5-11. Treble, alto/tenor, and bass viols

fragmented. Related to compositions in the learned style of the late Renaissance, works like Du Caurroy's also illustrate a tendency of the early seventeenth century by the intensity and thoroughness with which their contrapuntal plans are worked out. We saw this tendency in some contrapuntal works of Frescobaldi.

A. 44 is a somewhat later fantasie (1639) by Étienne Moulinié (ca. 1600–1669), an important composer of *airs de cour* who directed music in the household of the younger brother of Louis XIII, Gaston Orléans, Duke of Anjou. This work is based on the format of an Italian canzona, with contrapuntal outer sections in duple meter framing a more homophonic middle part in triple meter. Several other passages in the work incorporate contrasts of pacing and texture, which mark it as the work of a composer younger than Du Caurroy, and one in touch with the music of Italy.

A third administrative unit at the French royal court included the Music of the Great Stable, which consisted of players of trumpets, cornetts, trombones, shawms, dulcians, bagpipes, fifes, drums, crumhorns, and trumpet marine, a large, one-stringed, bowed instrument that played harmonics. These instruments were sometimes played on horseback and for ceremonies involving the palace military detachments, as well as for other sorts of outdoor pageant and spectacle. Music for this ensemble survives only from the second half of the seventeenth century.

Instrumental ensembles in the city of Paris were regulated by a guild called the Confrérie de Saint-Juilien-des-Ménétriers ("The Confraternity of St. Julian of the Minstrels"), headed by an all-powerful "King of the Minstrels" or "King of the Violins." This organization controlled all music contracted for weddings, engagement parties, banquets, masquerades, street serenades, and formal concerts. Pierre Francisque Caroubel, whose dances were discussed earlier, was a member of this guild, and his works can be taken as representative of the music played at these social events in the city.

ORGANS AND ORGAN MUSIC

Organs in France and in the rest of northern Europe differed fundamentally from those in Italy, and their characteristics explain some of the differences between the organ music of northern Europe and that of Italy. These northern characteristics appeared first in Flanders (portions of present-day Holland and Belgium) and spread, during the course of the sixteenth century, to France and the German-speaking lands.

By 1600 all European church organs had several sets of pipes arranged in rows (ranks), normally parallel with the keyboard. Depressing a key on an organ keyboard lets air into the channel that runs under the bottom hole of one pipe in each of the parallel ranks. Most of these pipes produce the same pitch or a displacement of it by one, two, or three octaves; a few produce a faint pitch, like an overtone, two octaves plus a third or two octaves plus a fifth above the main note, for the sake of tone color. Only rarely would all the pipes controlled by a given key sound at the same time, because the manually operated bellows could not provide enough wind for that. Only those pipes would sound that belong to ranks whose pipes had been opened to the airstream by drawing a stop. Thus, the organist controls the sound of the instrument by selectively drawing stops in typical combinations. Variety of sound came also from the diversity of pipes—flue or reed, metal or wood, open or closed, wide or narrow, cylindrical or conical—in various combinations.

Whereas Italian organs in the seventeenth century had only one keyboard and one chest containing several ranks of pipes, organs in northern Europe, including France, normally had two, three, or four keyboards and a set of pedals, and each keyboard and the set of pedals had its own chest of pipes. The largest of these chests, containing a dozen or more ranks of pipes, was placed in front of the organist (who faces the wall of the church), behind the main keyboards. This chest extended upward about sixteen feet from the floor of the organ loft. In France this chest was called the *Grand Orgue* ("Large Organ"). Directly behind the organist, hiding him from view, was a second, smaller chest with perhaps a half dozen ranks of pipes rising about eight feet above the floor. This was called the *positif* ("in position," as opposed to portable). In the early seventeenth century it was sometimes controlled by a keyboard in back of the organist, who had to turn around to play it, but by the middle of the century, the *positif* was normally actuated by a keyboard in front of the organist. The pipes controlled by the pedals were normally placed in front and on either side of the *Grand Orgue*. In many cases, a smaller chest of pipes was positioned under the *Grand Orgue*, and it was managed by its own keyboard placed above the main one.

The purpose of multiple keyboards and chests was to enable the organist to produce two or three distinct tone qualities and volumes simultaneously. Thus, a cantus firmus, typically played by the pedals in the upper or middle register, or a songlike melody might be projected by the penetrating tone of a combination including reed stops doubled by upper octaves and overtones, while the subordinated voices or chordal accompaniment could be rendered more softly on wooden flue pipes, which produce tone when the air current strikes the lip, creating vibrating eddies, as in a recorder. Rapid and frequent shifts among various combinations of stops were also facilitated by organ designs of this sort, since the player could easily shift from one keyboard to another.

These features of French organs are reflected in the organ versets for hymns (1623) and for each of the Magnificat tones (1626) by Jehan Titelouze (1562/3–1633), the organist at the cathedral of Rouen. Like Italian versets, these were intended to by played in verse-by-verse alternation with plainchant during Vespers. Each of the hymns by Titelouze has three or four versets. The first one always has the chant melody set as a cantus firmus in one voice, usually the bass, normally in steady whole notes. Typically, in the subsequent versets the cantus firmus is distributed between two or more voices of the texture, sometimes in a two-voice canon, or else each phrase of the chant melody is treated imitatively. In the Magnificat versets, Titelouze may use the chant formula as a cantus firmus, especially in the first verset, but he also often derives one subject for imitative treatment from each of the two halves of the chant reciting formula—a different but related subject for each half of each verset. This happens, for example, in his Magnificat versets for the first reciting tone (A. 45), as shown in Example 5-13.

A gap of nearly a century separates the publication of the organ hymns and Magnificats by Titelouze from the previous known collections of French keyboard music, and the next keyboard collection after them printed in France came out thirty-four years later, in 1660. Consequently, a great deal of historical importance attaches to the fantasie for organ by Charles Racquet (1597–1664) preserved as a manuscript addition to Marin Mersenne's personal copy of his *Harmonie universelle* (1636). Racquet was organist at the cathedral of Notre Dame in Paris from 1618 to 1643 and was Mersenne's source for the abundant information about the organ reported in his treatise. Racquet's Fantasie (A. 46) is remarkably long and complex. In it, the composer develops one subject in several sections, sometimes ornamented and once rhythmically augmented. The subject is joined by several countermotives, themselves used in imitation, in the first section. The work ends with a toccata-like section. It resembles some fantasies by the Dutch composer Sweelinck, but by the time French organ works reappear in any numbers after 1660, most such traces of foreign influences have disappeared from the music as well as from the organs themselves.

EXAMPLE 5-13. The subjects derived from the reciting tone in the Magnificat versets for Tone 1 by Titelouze (1626)

Magnificat Tone 1 adapted to the second verse of the Magnificat text:

Et ex- sul- ta- vit- sou- ri- tus me- us In De- o sa- lu- ta- ri me-   o.

Magnificat

Quia respexit

Et misericordia ejus

Deposuit potentes

Deposuit potentes (alternate)

Suscepit Israel

Gloria patri et filio

VOCAL MUSIC FOR CHURCH

The composer who set the tone for church vocal music in France at the beginning of the seventeenth century was the previously mentioned Eustache Du Caurroy, who was promoted from the position of codirector of the royal chapel to that of general superintendent of music at the French court in 1595. The large-scale motets by him published in the year of his death (1609) appear to be the earliest in France to use two choirs antiphonally, in the manner that we associate with Venice. In other respects, however, the motets of Du Caurroy do not incorporate the following innovations from Venice, seen in Giovanni Gabrieli's *In Ecclesiis*: basso continuo, extended solo voice passages, written-out embellishments (divisions or diminutions), recitational style, second-practice dissonance treatment, and independent parts for ensemble instruments. However, Du Caurroy's motets do have some of the newly intensified verbal expression associated with Italian concertos. In his Sequence for the Easter Mass, *Victimae paschali laudes* (A. 47), significant words are isolated by rests ("Christus," "Patri," "Mors," and "Scimus Christum surrexisse"), and the rhythms and inflections of text declamation often influence the vocal lines (see "Agnus redemit oves" and the many places were pitches are repeated). Still, the texture is almost continuously imitative, the dissonances are mild and controlled, and contrasts of any kind are subdued—ways in which Du Caurroy's church vocal works preserve features of late Renaissance style.

Nicolas Formé (1567–1638), Du Caurroy's successor as co-director of the French royal chapel, is thought to have been the first in his country to publish polychoral motets and Masses that specify soloists for one of the two choirs. After Formé, the combination of soloists and chorus remained a standard feature of large-scale motets in France for the rest of the Baroque period. Formé's motet *Ecce tu pulchra es* (W. 6), published in 1638, is noticeably more oriented toward text declamation than is Du Caurroy's *Victimae paschali laudes*. The continuously shifting meter in Formé's motet represents a vestige of *musique mesurée*. Its texture is far more homophonic, and it presents most of the words in rhythmic unison at some point. Repeated pitches are still more common than in Du Caurroy's work. Syllables are now set to sixteenth notes, whereas Du Caurroy's limit was the eighth note. There is far more text repetition in Formé's works, and it is sometimes arranged to create rhetorical figures, as at the beginning: "Behold, you are beautiful, my love, behold, you are beautiful, my love, my love, my love, behold, you are beautiful!" (epizeuxis and conduplicatio); and at the end: "Lead me, lead me, lead me, lead me, lead me, lead me, lead me; I will run after you, I will run after you in the fragrance, in the fragrance of your perfume" (epizeuxis, explanatio, and procatascene).

During his lifetime, Formé enjoyed a royal monopoly on composing polychoral motets, but after his death, his musical manuscripts fell into the hands of Jean Veillot (d. 1662), who copied some features of Formé's style in the large-scale motet *Angeli archangeli* (1644); in the surviving score, the parts for the solo voices are missing. In two of Veillot's later works, *O filii et filiae* and *Sacris solemnis* (ca. 1659–60), a continuo part for organ supports extended passages for solo voices, perhaps for the first time in French large-scale motets, although Henry Du Mont had published small-scale motets with continuo in 1652. Formé's use of a string ensemble of two violins and violoncello that plays alone in interludes is another innovation with respect to earlier French practices.

The most estimable French church music composer of the early seventeenth century was undoubtedly Guillaume Bouzignac (ca. 1587–after 1642). Unlike nearly all the other composers mentioned in this chapter, Bouzignac never held a post at the royal court and, indeed, never lived in Paris. Instead, he held a series of relatively minor church positions in various cities across southern France (Grenoble, Carcassone, Rodez, and Angoulême) until concluding his career in Tours on the Loire River in the west-central part of the country. Bouzignac did not imitate the latest Italian music, beyond using antiphonal choirs and soloists. Instead, using purely vocal resources, he projected his texts dramatically by means of extreme contrasts of style, texture, rhythm, and pacing, and by creating or emphasizing rhetorical figures. His motet *Ecce homo* ("Behold the Man" A. 48), takes the form of a dialogue between Pilate (an unaccompanied solo voice) and the crowd (singing text fragments drawn from the Gospels of Matthew, Mark, and John). The words of Pilate are intoned with gravity and caution, whereas the crowd responds with frenetic vehemence. In other works, Bouzignac uses dramatic silences, diminished intervals, staccato rhythms, wide leaps, and vivid text illustration.

Bouzignac, however, had little influence on later French church composers, who more or less followed in the path of Du Caurroy, Formé, and Veillot and who accepted, especially after 1650, some important elements of Italian style while also absorbing into their church music some features of the music used in French court spectacles.

BIBLIOGRAPHICAL NOTES

General

The most thorough and recent survey of early seventeenth-century French music is contained within James R. Anthony, *French Baroque Music from Beaujoyeulx to Rameau*, rev. ed. (Portland, OR: Amadeus Press, 1977), which contains an extensive bibliography.

The Balet comique de la Royne

A facsimile edition of the text, description, and music, with commentary, is Margaret M. McGowan, *Le Balet Comique by Balthazar de Beaujoyeulx, 1581*, Medieval & Renaissance Texts & Studies, 6 (Binghamton, NY: Center for Medieval & Early Renaissance Studies, 1982). An English translation with a modern edition of the music (lacking texts for all but the first strophes) is Carol MacClintock and Lander MacClintock, trans., *La Balet comique de la Royne, 1581,* Musicological studies and documents 25 (Rome: American Institute of Musicology, 1971).

Types of Dance

An extensive compendium of information, including translated excerpts from Arbeau and Mersenne, is Betty Bang Mather, *Dance Rhythms of the French Baroque: A Handbook for Performance* (Bloomington, IN: Indiana University Press, 1987), which, however, contains errors and omissions. Information in Mather's book should be checked against Meredith Little and Natalie Jenne, *Dance and the Music of J. S. Bach* (Bloomington, IN: Indiana University Press, 1991/1998), which, although focused on a later period in Germany, contains much information about seventeenth-century dance in France. Thoinot Arbeau, *Orchesography*, trans. Mary Stewart Evans (New York: Dover Publications, 1967), provides convenient access to one of the primary documents. Supplementary information that is useful and interesting is found in portions of George Houle, *Meter in Music, 1600–1800: Performance, Perception, and Notation* (Bloomington, IN: Indiana University Press, 1987). Two important anthologies of French dance music from the first half of the seventeenth century are Jules Ecorcheville, ed., *Vingt suites d'orchestre du XVIIe siècle français*, 2 vols. (Paris: L.-Marcel Fortin, 1906; repr. New York: Broude Brothers, 1970); and David Joseph Buch, *Dance Music from the Ballet de Cour 1575–1651* (Pendragon, 1994). Marie Françoise Christout, *Le Ballet de cour au XVIIe siècle* (Geneva: Minkoff, 1987), contains many valuable illustrations of *ballets de cour* and an expanatory text in French and English.

The air de cour
   The standard work on this subject is in French: Georgie Durosoir, *L'air de cour en France: 1571–1655* (Liege: Mardaga, 1991). An important study in English of a major composer is this area is Don Lee, "Pierre Guedron and the *Air de Cour*" (Ph.D. diss., Yale U., 1972). A study of special significance is David P. Walker, "The Influences of *musique mesurée a l'antique*, Particularly on the *airs de cour* of the Early Seventeenth Century," *Musica disciplina*, II (1948), 141–63; repr. in *Baroque Music*, I, *Seventeenth Century*, Garland Library of the History of Western Music, ed. Ellen Rosand, 5 (New York and London: Garland, 1985), 291–313.

Lute Music
   There is no book-length introduction in English to the lute and its music. The best available short overview of the subject is the entry "Lute" in *The New Grove Dictionary of Music and Musicians*. The standard book on the lute is in German: Ernst Pohlmann, *Laute, Theorbe, Chitarrone: Die Instrumente, ihre Musik und Literatur von 1500 bis zur Gegenwart*, 5th ed. (Lilienthal: Eres Edition, 1982). Francisque's *Le Trésor d'Orphée* and most of the other early seventeenth-century French lute-music collections have been published in modern editions as part of the series Corpus des luthistes français from the Centre National de la Recherche Scientifique. A superior transcription of *La Rhétorique des dieux* by David J. Buch is volume 62 of the series Recent Researches in the Music of the Baroque Era (Madison, WI: A-R Editions, 1990). Stephen Hefling, *Rhythmic Alteration in Seventeenth- and Eighteenth-Century Music* (New York: Schirmer Books, 1993), is considered somewhat controversial; the entry on *notes inégales* by David Fuller in *The New Grove Dictionary of Music and Musicians*, 2nd ed., is concise and widely accepted.

Harpsichord Music
   Two surveys of keyboard music that have useful treatments of early French harpsichord music are Willi Apel, *The History of Keyboard Music to 1700*, trans. Hans Tischler (Bloomington, IN: Indiana University Press, 1972); and Frank E. Kirby, *A Short History of Keyboard Music* (New York: Schirmer Books, 1966). A precise investigation into the surviving manuscript sources of this repertoire is Bruce Gustafson, *French Harpsichord Music of the 17th Century: A Thematic Catalog of the Sources with Commentary* (Ann Arbor, MI: UMI Research Press, 1979). The relationship between early French harpsichord music and lute music is treated thoroughly in David Ledbetter, *Harpsichord and Lute Music in 17th-Century France* (London:

Macmillan, 1987). A rewarding discussion of the cultural context of this repertoire is Margot Martin, "Essential Agréments: Art, Dance, and Civility in Seventeenth-century French Harpsichord Music," Ph.D. diss., UCLA, 1996.

Instrumental Ensemble Music
   The basic book on the viol family is Ian Woodfield, *The Early History of the Viol* (Cambridge: Cambridge University Press, 1984). The subject matter treated here is surveyed in Michel Sicard, "The French Viol School before 1650," *Journal of the Viola da Gamba Society of America*, XVIII (1981), 76–93. The statutes of the Confrérie de Saint-Juilien-des-Ménétriers are published in English translation in Oliver Strunk, ed., *Source Readings in Music History*, rev. ed., IV, *The Baroque Era*, ed. Margaret Murata (New York: Norton, 1998).

Organs and Organ Music
   In addition to the treatment of organ music in the surveys by Apel and Kirby cited above, there are two important books that explain the patterns of construction and lines of historical developments that led to the emergence of a distinctive type of French organ during the first half of the seventeenth century: Peter Williams, *The European Organ, 1450–1850*, 2nd ed. (London: B. T. Batsford, 1978); and Fenner Douglass, *The Language of the Classical French Organ: A Musical Tradition before 1800*, 2nd ed. (New Haven, CN: Yale University Press, 1995).

Vocal Music for Church
   The major survey of French church music that includes the early seventeenth century is in French: Denise Launay, *La Musique religieuse en France du Concile de Trente à 1804*, Publications de la Société Française de Musicologie, series 3, vol. 5 (Paris: Société Française de Musicologie, 1993). A study that focuses on Protestant and Catholic church music of the early part of this period is Susan Youens, "Music and Religion in the French Reformation and Counter-Reformation," Ph.D. diss., Harvard Univ., 1975. A recent scholarly reassessment of Bouzignac is by Leroux Martial, *Guillaume Bouzignac (ca. 1587–ca. 1643): Etude musicologique* (Beziers: Société de Musicologie du Languedoc, 1993).

CHAPTER 6

Music in the Empire through the Thirty Years' War

THE ITALIAN INFLUX TO THE EMPIRE AND EASTERN EUROPE

If we consider the overall trend of music history in the German-speaking lands and the regions to the east of them during the Baroque era, we find that the driving force behind most change was the constant influx of Italian musicians and Italian musical styles. During most of the Renaissance, by contrast, musicians and musical styles had flowed from the North into Italy. Why did the tide of musical influence across the Alps reverse itself at the onset of the Baroque era? And why did the Italian influx begin so much earlier and grow so much more rapidly in the German-speaking lands than it did in France, Spain, or England?

In a sense, the Italian presence in the Holy Roman Empire began in the mid-sixteenth century. Orlando di Lasso was hired as music director at the court of Duke Albrecht V of Bavaria in Munich in 1556, and two years later Philippe de Monte took a similar post at the court of Emperor Maximilian II in Vienna. But although both composers had been trained in Italy and composed Italian madrigals, they were actually brought to Munich and Vienna as representatives of the Franco-Flemish tradition of contrapuntal church music, an international, rather than an Italian style.

Elector Moritz of Saxony had already engaged a band of five Italian instrumentalists from Bergamo in 1549. Two of these, Gabriel and Benedetto Tola, were among the group that petitioned the town council of Brescia in 1548. Another member of this band, Antonio Scandello (1517–1580), eventually became the director of church music (*Kapellmeister*) at the Dresden court in 1568. Scandello had to convert to Lutheranism, the official state religion in Dresden, in order to obtain the post.

State religions were established in the Empire in 1555, when one of the early conflicts between the Lutheran and the Catholic rulers in the region (see Figure 6-1) was resolved by the Peace of Augsburg. This treaty established the principle *Cuius regio, eius religio* ("Whoever rules, his religion"), by which the German-speaking lands that made up most of the Empire were divided between Catholic states, mostly in the south, and Lutheran states, mostly in the north. Although Scandello was succeeded by another Italian, Giovanni Battista

Figure 6-1. The Holy Roman Empire and Austrian Habsburg hereditary lands

Pinello (ca. 1544–1587), the Dresden court then reverted to a composer from the Netherlands, Rogier Michael (ca. 1552–1619), who learned Italian style mostly in Graz and Vienna.

Lutheran Dresden notwithstanding, most of the early Italian influx to the Empire was found in its Catholic regions, particularly in those regions ruled by members of the Habsburg family, from which all the Emperors were "elected" from the sixteenth through the nineteenth centuries. These regions included Upper and Lower Austria, Styria, Tyrol, Carinthia, Carniola, Moravia, Bohemia, Hungary, and Silesia (see Figure 6-1). There are two good reasons why Italian music generally arrived earlier and in greater abundance at Catholic rather than Lutheran courts within the Empire: (1) the sacred repertoire from Catholic Italy (and similar works composed by Germans), with its Latin texts and their liturgical and theological content, could be integrated readily into German Catholic worship services; and (2) Italian musicians could live more easily in German Catholic cities than in Lutheran centers, some of which banned their religion entirely. There was probably also a third, geopolitical motive for the Habsburgs' importation of Italian music and musicians: (3) It reinforced, especially in the minds of courtiers, the Habsburg identity as Catholics opposed to the threat from Lutheranism, and their alliance with the Pope against the threat from France and with the Christian West against the threat from the Islamic Ottoman Empire to the East.

Italian inroads into the Habsburg domains took place first in the Styrian capital of Graz and the Imperial capital of Vienna. In 1566 Annibale Padovano (1527–1575) moved from the post of organist at St. Mark's in Venice to the

court of Archduke Charles in Graz, where he continued to compose impro-
visatory toccatas comparable to those of Andrea Gabrieli. At the same court,
Simone Gatto, a trumpeter and trombonist from Venice and Padua, succeeded
Padovano as *Kapellmeister* in 1581. Next came an impressive group of Italian
composers, almost all of them from Venice: Annibale Perini (ca. 1560–1596),
Francesco Stivori (ca. 1550–1605), Francesco Rovigo (ca. 1541/2–1597),
Lodovico Zacconi (1555–1627), Giovanni Priuli (ca. 1575–1626), and Gio-
vanni Valentini (1582/83–1649).

In 1604 Archduke Charles sent two young composers from Graz, Georg Poss
(ca. 1570– after 1633) and Alessandro Tadei (ca. 1585–1667), to Venice to study
with Giovanni Gabrieli. Italian connections were strengthened in 1573, when
the archduke opened a Jesuit college in Graz, and in 1609 when his daughter
Maria Maddalena married Grand Duke Cosimo II de' Medici in Florence.

Archduke Charles's son Ferdinand II inherited the Italian musical chapel in
Graz and took several of its key members—Priuli, Valentini, and Tadei—with
him to Vienna when he became emperor in 1619. After Ferdinand II married
Eleonora Gonzaga, daughter of the Duke of Mantua, in 1622, the court
imported many more Italians and initiated a splendid series of performances in
Vienna of stage works by Monteverdi, whose music Eleonora had known in
Mantua. These factors set the Imperial court in Vienna in an italianate direction
that it followed for more than a century afterward.

Another Habsburg court with early Italian connections was at Innsbruck, the
capital of Tyrol. Here, in 1582, Archduke Ferdinand II brought Jacob Regnart
(between 1540 and 1545–1599), who had previously served Ferdinand's brother
Maximilian in Prague and Vienna and who had been sent to study in Italy in
1568–70. Native Italians who came briefly to Innsbruck included Silao Casen-
tini, Jacopo Flori, Tiburtio Massaini, Giulio Cima, and G. B. Pinello de Gerardi.

The king of Poland, Sigismund III, was a Roman Catholic but not a Habsburg, although in 1602 he married one (Anne of Austria, the sister of Archduke
Charles). Even before that marriage, he brought the famous Italian madrigal
composer Luca Marenzio (1553/54–1599) and twenty-three other Italians
from Rome in 1595. Marenzio was succeeded by a series of Italian music
directors at the Warsaw court, and an opera season was even launched there in
1628. It must be more than a coincidence that the Italian musical chapel was in
place just in time for the church council at Brest-Litovsk (1596), at which
Sigismund hoped to bring his country's Orthodox hierarchy fully into the
Roman Catholic Church. The Orthodox Church of Poland had ties to the
Church of Russia, but Sigismund wanted Poland to become a Western nation.
He used Roman church music as a symbol of his court's Western orientation,
and importing it had the same kind of geopolitical significance as the Habs-
burgs' cultivation of Italian church music.

In 1618, the Thirty Years' War began in the German lands. It pitted the Catholic
states against the Lutheran states in the Empire and provoked an intensification of
religious identity in that region. On both sides of the conflict, the choice and control of church music became a major factor in constructing that identity.

At the (Catholic) Habsburgs imperial court in Vienna, large-scale and grandiose church music presented an exaggeration of the Venetian polychoral, concerted style of Giovanni Gabrieli. It became a symbol of *Pietas Austriaca* ("Austrian Piety"), a political concept that arose during the 1620s, linking religiosity to beneficent government in the person of the emperor. At that time a myth was created that in 1619, during the Protestant siege of Vienna, Christ spoke through a crucifix to the emperor, "Ferdinand, I will not desert you!" This event continued to be commemorated in Vienna long afterward with pomp and ritual. Court functionaries produced quantities of broadsheets and pamphlets repeating this and similar stories for mass consumption. An engraved illustration on one of them pictures Ferdinand II as Christ on the Mount of Olives (Fig. 6-2). A musical symbol of *Pietas Austriaca* was the colossal church music of Giovanni Valentini, such as the *Messa, Magnificat et Jubilate Deo* for seven choirs (1621), which incorporates trumpets—one of the first printed church works to do so—as a symbol of imperial majesty.

Italians were soon brought to chapels in other German Catholic cities, perhaps in imitation of the Habsburgs. Most notable among these cities was Augsburg, where several generations of the Fugger family heavily influenced the course of music. Originally a wealthy family of merchants and bankers, the Fuggers joined the minor nobility when two of its members were knighted early in the sixteenth century. Octavian Fugger, who collected lute music in Bologna while a student there in 1562, evidently developed a friendship with Andrea Gabrieli, who preceded his nephew Giovanni as organist at St. Mark's in Venice. In 1584–85 the Nuremberg-born musician Hans Leo Hassler (1564–1612) studied in Venice with Andrea Gabrieli, along with fellow-student Giovanni Gabrieli; for the next fifteen years he served as organist in the household of Octavian Fugger. Hassler soon became a prolific composer of polychoral church music and Italian madrigals, setting an important example for his generation of German composers, especially since he subsequently moved to posts in Nuremberg (1601–1608) and Dresden (1608–12).

A third member of the Fugger family, Jakob, recruited his nephew's school friend Gregor Aichinger (1564/5–1628) as organist in his household and promptly sent him to study with Giovanni Gabrieli in Venice. Like Hassler, Aichinger composed Venetian-style polychoral church music, and in 1607 he published his *Cantiones ecclesiasticae* ("Church Songs"), the first collection by a

Figure 6-2. Ferdinand II as Christ on the Mount of Olives (1622/23)

German composer of small-scale sacred concertos with basso continuo accompaniment. In the preface to this collection, Aichinger acknowledges the influence of Lodovico Viadana.

In fact, Aichinger's *Tres sunt qui testimonium dant* (A. 49), from the 1607 collection, could be mistaken for a work by Viadana. The basso continuo part is mostly a basso seguente (that is, it doubles the lowest-sounding voice), but in some brief passages for a single voice the continuo is independent. The text, which celebrates the unity of the Holy Trinity, was assembled from the Bible (1 John 5:7–8) and the Catholic liturgy (a modified opening of the Sanctus), probably by the composer, who had studied theology in Italy and was a priest. This text may have been intended to emphasize a theological point of difference with Lutheran beliefs. Aichinger gives rhetorical emphasis to its meaning with arresting acclamations of "Tres sunt" at the beginning and dramatic preparations (procatascene) for the word "heaven" ("There are three that bear witness . . . *in heaven*") and to the key theological phrase "a-a-and these three are, a-a-and these three are *one*." Harmony provides a similar effect: The music setting the explanation of the Trinity elevates tension by expanding from the C and G chords (natural hexachord) to the D and A chords (mutations to the hard hexachord and the sharp transposition of the gamut). Where the theological tension in the text "and these three are one" is resolved, Aichinger resolves the musical tension with a mutation back to the original hexachords and seventh mode.

The text that Aichinger set and the notable rhetorical emphasis that he gave it may well have been motivated by a theological controversy with the Lutherans that became intense where the composer was working at the time. Luther had asserted that when Christ is present in the flesh, as during communion, we are not to think of him in heaven, "like a stork in a nest." Did this statement lead Aichinger to stress the words "in heaven?" Furthermore, other early Lutheran leaders insisted that Christ had two natures, corporeal and spiritual, but in *Tres sunt*, Aichinger emphasized that the parts of the Trinity are one.

THE EARLIEST LUTHERAN COMPOSERS TO ASSIMILATE NEW ITALIAN STYLES AFTER 1600

In many Lutheran cities, Italian church music was confined to a Kyrie or Gloria by Palestrina or other *prima pratica* composers of the Roman school, or an Introit motet in polychoral style. An important anthology of such Introit motets, *Florilegium Portense*, was published in two volumes (1603 and 1621) by Erhard Bodenschatz. The first volume contained Latin-texted polychoral works, mostly by German composers such as Jacobus Handl (1550–1591) and Melchior Franck (ca. 1579–1639) with basso seguente for the organ added by the editor. The second volume introduced motets by Italian composers such as Agostino Agazzari (ca. 1580–1642), Giovanni Croce (ca. 1557–1609), Giovanni Gabrieli, Marenzio, and Lodovico Viadana, but still for full choirs, without soloists or independent instrumental parts. Some of the texts of these motets were altered for Lutheran use by replacing, for example, references to the Virgin Mary with the name of Christ. The Bodenschatz anthologies were used in such Lutheran cities as Leipzig and Lübeck for most of the seventeenth century, so that they served more to preserve an earlier musical style than to introduce the latest Italian innovations.

Early Italian small-scale sacred concertos by Italian composerrs such as Viadana were used in a few German Lutheran cities as well. It took additional time for Lutheran composers to embrace the latest Italian innovations, perhaps because, from the beginning of the Reformation onward, they sought to incorporate the words and melodies of chorales, which were increasingly regarded as important statements of Lutheran belief.

Lutheran chorales were sung in unison by the congregation or in harmony by the choir. Their texts were normally strophic, rhymed, metrical verses using simple vernacular language. The melodies were also simple and easy to sing, and each stanza of text was sung to the same music (strophic form). Some chorale melodies were derived from plainchant, especially from hymns, with metrical rhythms added; some were adaptations of traditional, folk, or secular art songs; and some were newly composed. Individual chorale melodies were often used to set several texts, and some texts were sung to two or three different melodies. Chorales had been sung in Germany for centuries before the Lutheran Reformation (as were their counterparts in Catholic countries, e.g., laude in Italy), usually not as part of a liturgical worship service but rather in non-liturgical assemblies for prayer, singing, and sermonizing. The Lutheran Reformation made chorales a fundamental part of the Sunday worship service, and many Lutheran churches specified the chorales to be sung on each Sunday of the year, making them part of the regular liturgy. The chorale texts and the sermon, both in the local language, helped to shift the focus of the Lutheran worship service away from ritual and the sacrament of communion toward instruction and inspiration. Congregational participation in chorale singing reflected the Lutheran belief in the priesthood of all believers—the congregation of priests, as opposed to the largely passive flock at the Catholic Mass.

There is evidence that women participated in Lutheran congregational singing in the seventeenth century, meaning that St. Paul's prohibition was not fully in effect. On the other hand, there is no evidence that they were admitted to church choirs at this time, and indeed the records of Lutheran chapels of this period uniformly point to the use of boy sopranos and adult male altos, as in Catholic chapels. Women's participation in Lutheran church music was also diminished by the fact that Protestant religious institutions did not include convents.

Polyphonic or harmonized settings of chorale melodies began to appear as soon as Lutheran congregations were organized. Before 1600 there were generally two methods employed in these settings: The chorale melody was given to the tenors while the other voices sang harmony, or the melody was broken up into its component phrases, each of which served as the basis for a point of imitation. After about 1600 it became more common to place the chorale melody in the soprano voice in simple harmonizations, but it was not long before Lutheran composers began to embrace the innovative aspects of Italian style in works with chorale melodies and without.

Lutheran composers viewed the impassioned and rhetorical character of the newer styles of Italian church music as useful for moving the congregants to receive the Gospel through the office of the Holy Spirit, the key to obtaining Grace and salvation according to Lutheran beliefs. Soon after the fashion for early Baroque Italian music began spreading through the Catholic regions of the Empire, Lutheran composers of neighboring principalities sought ways to adapt its styles to their purposes.

Praetorius

One of the first Lutheran composers to assimilate Italian innovations after 1600 was Michael Praetorius (1571–3–1621), who never traveled to Italy but began following Italian styles by studying, parodying, and copying works by Lassus, Marenzio, and Palestrina. Later, he explored more recent Italian styles, including the use of basso continuo. In 1595 he entered the service of Duke Heinrich Julius of Brunswick-Wolfenbüttel. Although Praetorius remained in the service of the Brunswick-Wolfenbüttel family for the rest of his life, he traveled frequently and spent several extended periods as a visitor at other German courts, notably at Dresden, where from 1613 to 1616 he filled in the gap between the tenures of Rogier Michael and Heinrich Schütz. In the course of his rather short life, Praetorius composed over 1,200 vocal works for the Lutheran worship service, most of them based upon chorale texts and melodies.

The earliest printed collections of Praetorius's music (1605–11) contain many Italian madrigals by Lassus and Marenzio fitted out with German or Latin religious texts, and a number of church works by Aichinger, Hassler, and Palestrina that were simply taken over without attribution. His incorporation of chorale melodies, often in polychoral settings, began about 1611. His later works, from 1619 onward, sometimes include both plain and embellished vocal parts, larger forces, contrast of soloists and chorus, instrumental interludes, and striking echo effects.

In the preface to his *Musae Sioniae* (1605), Praetorius enumerates all the ways in which a composer of his time could incorporate a chorale melody into a new composition.

1. According to Treatment of the Chorale Melody

Motet-style	Each phrase of the chorale melody is modified to create a motive that is imitated by the voices or parts in the texture. The motet-style treatment, then, consists of successive points of imitation, each one based on a phrase of the chorale melody.
Madrigal-style	The composer embellishes the chorale melody with diminution figures, and the embellished melody is sung by one voice, or by several in motet style.

| Cantus-firmus-style | The chorale melody is sung, unembellished, by one voice, voice, often in note values longer than those prevailing in the other voices of the texture. |

2. According to Text Use and Overall Form

One stanza	Only a single stanza of the normally strophic chorale is set.
Purely strophic	The same music is used to set each successive strophe, or stanza, of the chorale text.
Variations	Each strophe, or stanza, of the chorale text is sung to different music, normally with a different treatment of the chorale melody.

3. According to Use of Voices

Full choir(s)	One or two choirs, or more, are used, without soloists.
Chorus and soloists	A full choir, with voices doubled, alternates and contrasts with a group of soloists.
Soloists only	No voices are doubled.

4. According to the Way in which the Forces are Deployed

Unvaried forces	The same voices and instruments are used continuously throughout.
Antiphonal	Two or more choirs, soloists, and/or instruments respond to each other in alternation.
Sectional	In some sections (e.g., strophes, or stanzas) unvaried forces are employed, while in other sections the forces are deployed antiphonally.

5. According to Use of Instruments

With instruments	That is, with ensemble instruments.
Only basso continuo	A basso continuo, normally to be realized on the organ, is the only instrumental part provided by the composer.
No instruments	A cappella format.

If we calculate all the permutations, we find that there are 243 types of chorale-based church composition, not including cases in which the choice changes in the course of the work. Praetorius himself tried just about every combination.

A particularly elaborate but instructive example of a chorale-based work by Praetorius is *Als der gütiger Gott* (W. 7b) from his collection *Polyhymnia Caduceatrix & Panegyrica* of 1619. In this composition, Praetorius elaborates upon two chorales in alternation: (1) *Als der gütiger Gott* with its original text, which tells the story of the Archangel Gabriel's annunciation to Mary that she will bear the Christ child; and (2) the melody of *Menschenkind, mark eben*, which is fitted with new text, *gott durch deine güte*. This text is sung by three pairs of solo voices, each pair representing a personage in the dramatic scene: the Evangelist (narrator), Mary, and the Archangel Gabriel. The full chorus sings plain harmonizations of *Menschenkind, mark eben/gott durch deine güte*, without ornamentation (cantus-firmus-style) as a musical refrain that provides commentary on each pair of stanzas of *Als der gütiger Gott*. The solo voices are accompanied by a four-part instrumental ensemble, which can consist of four viols, or viols in alternation with either cornetts and bassoon or trombones. Praetorius also suggests that when the soloists sing, the instrumental ensemble can be replaced by a simple realization of the basso continuo by organ or regal, perhaps alternating with a lute. When a single solo voice sings, as in stanzas 1 and 2, the chorale melody is lightly ornamented in madrigal style and fitted with the flexible rhythms of an Italian solo madrigal. In the subsequent stanzas, which are sung by several solo voices, embellished fragments from the chorale melody are passed among the parts in imitation—a combination of madrigal-style and motet-style elaboration. In the case of a work this long, Praetorius suggests that part can be performed at the morning worship after the Epistle, another part after the Gospel, and a third part after the sermon; or the whole can be sung at Vespers instead of the Magnificat, or in two parts surrounding the Vespers sermon.

Schein

The first collection of small-scale vocal church works for solo voices with basso continuo to incorporate Lutheran chorale melodies and texts was published in 1618: *Opella nova* ("New Work"), Part 1, "composed according to the Italian style now in use" by Johann Hermann Schein (1586–1630). Schein acknowledges the influence of Lodovico Viadana, just as the Catholic composer Aichinger did in his 1607 *Cantiones ecclesiasticae*.

Schein was Cantor of the church and school of St. Thomas in Leipzig and music director of all the city's churches and its municipal instrumental ensemble. Leipzig had been a self-governing city without a noble court since the fifteenth century. Like most such German cities, its people embraced the Lutheran religion, which generally reflected middle- and working-class values and opposed Catholicism, which tended to support the nobility and monarchy. Schein and his musicians were paid by the town council, which had both civil and religious authority.

Schein's church works conform to Leipzig's liturgical calendar, which specified the chorales to be sung on each Sunday and feast day of the year. Thus, *Erschienen ist der herrliche Tag* ("The Glorious Day has Arrived," A. 50b), from the second volume of Schein's *Opella nova* (1626), uses the text and melody of a chorale specified for Easter Sunday (A. 50a). The text of this chorale is a poetic German paraphrase of the Catholic Easter Gradual *Haec dies* (Psalm 118:4) and a response to the Gospel for that day—Mark 16:6: "He said to them, 'Do not be amazed; you seek Jesus of Nazareth, who was crucified. He has risen, he is not here; see the place where you laid him.'"

Schein's *Erschienen ist der herrliche Tag* combines madrigal-style and motet-style treatment of the chorale melody. The presence of a basso continuo part for organ allowed the composer to begin with an extended solo passage, something never heard in chorale-based works before *Opella nova*. The ornamental elaboration in the opening phrases of the chorale melody gives impetus and energy to the upward-reaching contours of the vocal lines. These contours are extended when the opening motive is transposed climactically upward by a fifth (mm. 13–20) in keeping with the optimistic text. In the second major section of the work, imitation and sequence are combined to elaborate on the opening motive, which emphasizes through various rhetorical figures (conduplicatio, enumeratio, and gradatio) the two fundamental text phrases "It has arrived!" and "The glorious day!" In the last section of the piece, which is repeated in the manner of an Italian concerto, Schein's musical setting transforms the exclamation "Alleluia!" into a group of rhetorical figures (exuscitatio, espizeuxis, and brachylogia) that create an emotional climax the likes of which had never before been heard in Lutheran church music.

Works like *Erschienen ist der herrliche Tag*, which apply a mixture of madrigal-style and motet-style treatment to the chorale melody, share space in Schein's *Opella nova* with equally numerous pieces in which the tenor sings the chorale melody as a cantus firmus while the other voices weave imitative entries based on fragments of the chorale melody, treated in motet style. This type is especially prominent in the first volume of *Opella nova*.

Scheidt

The other prolific composer of chorale-based, italianate Lutheran vocal works in the early seventeenth century was Samuel Scheidt (1587–1654), who produced small-scale works without fully intending to. Scheidt published two collections of large-scale church works in 1620 and 1622, while he was music director to Margrave Christian Wilhelm of Brandenburg in Halle. In 1625, when the Margrave abandoned his court to fight on the Lutheran side in the Thirty Years' War, the court chapel was disbanded. In the course of this war, Halle was taken and lost by the opposing armies several times, and half of its civilian population was killed. In 1628 the civic government created for Scheidt the post of music director for the city's most important church, the Marktkirche, although its chapel was much smaller than the one Scheidt had led at the court.

During this period, Scheidt published four volumes of small-scale church works under the title *Geistliche Concerte* ("Sacred Concertos," 1631–40). Although the published form of these works called for two to four solo voices and basso continuo for organ, Scheidt declared that they were originally written for eight to twelve voices in two, three, or four choirs, with introductions and interludes for ensemble instruments. Since the war had decimated musical chapels throughout the Empire, Scheidt published only scaled-down versions of his works. We shall see that the Thirty Years' War had similar effects on the music of Heinrich Schütz.

The most characteristic chorale treatment in Scheidt's *Geistliche Concerte* is variation form, in which each stanza of the chorale text is set to a different treatment of the chorale melody. An example of this is *Nun komm, der Heiden Heiland* (W. 8b). This chorale text is a German paraphrase by Martin Luther of the Catholic hymn *Veni Redemptor gentium*. Its melody (W. 8a) is a simplified version of the plainchant melody for the hymn, arranged either by Luther or by his principal musical adviser, Johann Walther (1496–1570).

Scheidt sets all eight stanzas of *Nun komm, der Heiden Heiland* (they begin in mm. 1, 30, 55, 69, 84, 160, 177, and 197). The two stanzas of Part 1 use the chorale melody in motet style; the three stanzas of Part 2 use it in cantus-firmus style (with imitative or even canonic accompanying voices); and the three stanzas of Part 3 use it mostly in madrigal style, with some imitation. Notwithstanding the strictures of imitation, cantus firmus, and canon, Scheidt imparts rhetorical emphasis to the text in many places. For example, at the words "at which wonders," he builds excitement and anticipation with faster rhythm, a shorter motive, and intensified repetition, leading to the conclusion "all the world." After using a reduced texture for most of stanza 2, he brings in full texture and chordal harmonization to underscore the words "and a fruit bloomed from woman's flesh." In stanza 7, where the text speaks of the manger, Scheidt alludes to a pastoral tradition by creating echo effects through alternation of *forte* and *piano*.

Although neither Schein nor Scheidt studied in Italy, several other German Lutheran composers did, following very closely in the footsteps of their Catholic neighbors. In Kassel, Landgrave Moritz von Hessen, a composer in his own right, sent two of his musicians, Christoph Kegel and Christoph Cornet (1580–1635) to study in Venice. Cornet went on to compose large-scale polychoral Lutheran church works. These two helped to train the boys of Landgrave Moritz's chapel. The most promising of these boys, also sent to study in Venice, was Heinrich Schütz.

HEINRICH SCHÜTZ

Heinrich Schütz (1585–1672) came from a middle-class background; his father was a town clerk and innkeeper. At the Schütz family inn, Landgrave Moritz heard young Heinrich sing and immediately took him to Kassel for musical training and a nobleman's education. Schütz began the study of law at Marburg University, but Moritz sent him to study with Giovanni Gabrieli in Venice for four years (1609–13). He made such progress in composition and organ playing that Gabrieli wanted to keep him on as his assistant, notwithstanding Schütz's Lutheran faith. Back in Kassel, Schütz's reputation spread to the extent that in 1614 Elector Johann Georg I of Saxony requested a visit from him. As his feudal subject, Moritz could not refuse the Elector's subsequent demands to extend this visit, which turned into a permanent position as music director at the Dresden court by 1619.

For the Electoral court at Dresden, the capital of Saxony, Schütz wrote some music for theatrical spectacles and for banquet entertainment, but his principal duty was composing for and directing the chapel, which was the largest and most accomplished musical establishment in Protestant Germany, consisting of sixteen singers and twenty or so instrumentalists. For this group, Schütz composed the large-scale works that characterize his early years.

When Saxony entered the Thirty Years' War in 1628, the accompanying economic crisis and the Elector's payments to support its Lutheran allies led the him to stop paying his musicians. Schütz took a leave of absence for a second visit to Venice, where he encountered Monteverdi and heard "how a comedy of diverse voices can be translated into declamatory style and be brought to the stage and enacted in song," a practice he thought erroneously was "still completely unknown in Germany." After his return from Venice in 1629, the style of Schütz's church music, and even some musical borrowing in it, show that he had also paid close attention to the concertos of Monteverdi's assistant at St. Mark's, Alessandro Grandi.

Soon after Schütz's arrival back from Italy, the Elector of Saxony became fully involved in the Thirty Years' War and even more drastically curtailed the activities of his chapel. Schütz was glad to take advantage of an invitation to spend a year (1634–35) at the court of Crown Prince Christian of Denmark, where he composed music, almost entirely lost, for a ballet and two comedies. According to the composer himself, the small scale of the works that he published after his return to Dresden reflect the strained circumstances of the wartime electoral court.

After three more extended leaves at various courts, Schütz returned at age 60 to find the Dresden court chapel in ruins. He therefore requested and eventually obtained semi-retired status, allowing him to continue visiting various courts as a celebrity, writing large-scale works for special occasions, publishing them in substantial numbers, and growing wealthy and famous in his old age (Fig. 6-3).

About five hundred compositions by Schütz survive, most of them in fourteen collections printed under the composer's supervision. Almost all of this output is vocal ensemble music setting religious texts, and much of it undoubtedly was intended for Lutheran worship services in the chapels of Dresden and other courts. Unlike Schein and Scheidt, Schütz rarely used the texts or melodies of chorales in his works and sometimes set Latin rather than German texts, reflecting the cosmopolitan style of music and worship in the chapels of the most powerful courts in the Lutheran world. Schein's and Scheidt's use of chorales and the vernacular accorded with the provincial or national characteristics of a small-court or civic church, in which congregational participation was more important. Schütz's church works, on the other hand, are more similar to Italian concertos in both text and music.

Schütz's earliest collection of church music, *Psalmen Davids* ("The Psalms of David," 1619), contains German Psalm settings that closely resemble the polychoral works of Giovanni Gabrieli. These works are provided with a basso

Figure 6-3. A portrait of
Heinrich Schütz painted by
Christoph Spetner before 1654
or after 1657

seguente, rather than a true basso continuo for organ, and instrumental parts
that nearly all double vocal lines. The twenty-six Psalm texts, in German, are
mostly declaimed homorhythmically.

Part I of Schütz's *Symphoniae sacrae* ("Sacred Harmonies," 1629), reflects the
latest fashions in the kind of small-scale sacred concertos that Schütz heard in
Venice during his second visit. These works emphasize stylized speech rhythms
and abstract designs, often reflecting or creating rhetorical figures in the text. *O
quam tu pulchra es* (A. 51) may serve as an example.

The Latin text of Schütz's *O quam tu pulchra es* is taken from the Song of
Songs, a typical source for Schütz's Italian models. Like most non-liturgical
Latin texts, this one is drawn from the Vulgate Latin Bible, translated from the
Hebrew by St. Jerome, who had studied rhetoric in Rome during the fourth
century. Because Jerome undoubtedly used the writings of Cicero and Quintilian as a guide, their concepts and terminology are particularly applicable to
the Vulgate. As part of his aristocrat's education Schütz also studied Cicero and
Quintilian in addition to contemporary elaborations on rhetorical lore. A
number of Schütz's German contemporaries wrote at length of the parallels
between music and rhetoric and applied large parts of the rhetorical vocabulary to musical analysis.

The two parts of *O quam tu pulchra es* begin with a nearly identical series of
phrases that features the rhetorical figure antistrophe—"amica *mea*, columba
mea, formosa *mea*, immaculata *mea*" ("my beloved, my dove, my lovely one, my
perfect")—which Schütz treats in a similar fashion each time: each of the four
text phrases is sung to parallel music, and the word *mea* ("my") is set off from
the other words by a falling leap, the imitative entry of the second voice

doubling the number of repetitions. The rising sequence used for this passage in Part 1 (mm. 5–14; 24–33) also brings out the auxesis that is latent in this portion of the text, as the epithets rise by degrees from "beloved" through "dove" and "lovely" to "perfect." Later on in Part 1, the musical-textural refrain (epimone) "O quam tu pulchra es" ("Oh how beautiful you are!") sets off a series of musically contrasting passages in recitational style, where the text provides specific instances of beauty (enumeratio). The instrumental introduction to Part 2, since it presents three of the motives subsequently elaborated in vocal passages, creates the figure digestion (an enumeration of the points to be discussed). Later (mm. 36–40) an effect of breathless excitement is generated by a series of aposiopeses (sudden pauses) created when Schütz repeatedly interrupts the flow of the text with exclamations or rests. This work contains still other rhetorical figures; the second part seems to have been planned along the lines of rhetorical disposition. Part 2, mm. 1–21, functions like an exhortation, mm. 21–44 like a narration, mm. 45–52 like an exposition, mm. 53–58 like a second exhortation, mm. 58–79 like a proposition and amplification, mm. 80–92 like a refutation or confirmation, and mm. 92–104 like a conclusion or peroration.

The purpose of this rhetorical treatment was to move the listeners emotionally, confirm them in their shared beliefs, and dispose them to receive the Gospel through the inspiration of the Holy Spirit and so obtain salvation through grace.

Was hast du verwirket (A. 52), in Schütz's *Kleine geistliche Konzerte*, Part II ("Small Sacred Concertos," 1639), projects its personal, emotion-laden text (from the *Confessions* of St. Augustine) through musical control of rhetorical delivery—that is selective emphasis, pacing, and inflection—rather than through elocution, the musical highlighting or creation of rhetorical figures. The style here is comparable to certain Italian solo madrigals of twenty or so years earlier (e.g., by Sigismondo d'India), extended and enriched harmonically. The choice of the non-biblical German text, which confesses personal guilt for the crucifixion of Christ, reflects the Lutheran belief that deep sorrow for sin is a necessary step toward Grace.

With the economic recovery following the end of the Thirty Years' War, Schütz returned to publishing large-scale works, notably the third book of *Symphoniae sacrae* (1650). Although the size of the chapel at the Dresden court had been restored by the time this collection was published, its members were still not being paid regularly, and we cannot assume that Schütz's late works were composed primarily for that group. They may instead have been written for the special occasions that brought Schütz to various other courts and cities as an honored guest. In these large works, Schütz typically combines the spaciousness of his early antiphonal works with the strong contrasts, idiomatic resources, and rhetorical delivery of text characteristic of his more recent compositions. A good example is the justly celebrated *Saul, Saul* (A. 53).

Like most of the texts for *Symphoniae sacrae*, Part III, the words for *Saul, Saul* are drawn from a narrative in Luther's German Bible. This one consists of the words that Saul reported hearing from heaven, which led to his conversion (as the eventual St. Paul), as recorded in the Acts of the Apostles 26:12–18. Like Part 2 of *O quam tu pulchra es*, this work has certain features of rhetorical disposition.

The repeated invocation "Saul, Saul, Saul, Saul!" gently coaxes on the weak beats while majestically rising by degrees from dark depths (D minor harmony, open fifth between basses) to bright heights (D major harmony, violins in thirds) and finally echoing through the choirs. This exhortation, which asks insistently "Why do you persecute me?" "attracts the audience's attention and favorably disposes it to listen." An abrupt change of meter, tempo, motive, and texture introduces the second pair of phrases, "It will be hard for you to ignore this summons" (literally, "It will be hard for you to kick against the thorn"). These two phrases (mm. 13–22) present material for later elaboration, like the narration or exposition of a formal oration. The abbreviated return of the opening phrases (mm. 23–27) functions like a second exhortation, while the elaboration on the second pair of phrases (mm. 28–49) forms the amplification. The stirring climax, with its rising sequence of triple invocations of "Saul, Saul, Saul!" is, of course, the "final appeal to the emotions of the audience," the peroration or conclusion of this musical speech.

CALVINIST MUSIC

Although he was an early follower of Martin Luther, Jean Calvin (1509–1564), introduced divergent teachings and practices in his writings and in his work as religious leader of the Swiss city of Geneva from 1541 onward. By the time of Calvin's death, his teachings had become the basis of a distinct Protestant sect, often called the Reformed Church, which was especially strong in Switzerland, some German states, the Netherlands, France (where its adherents were called Huguenots), Scotland (where they were called Presbyterians), and England (where they were called Puritans).

Calvin's puritanical distrust of sensual pleasure and the arts led him to ban polyphony from church services, preferring instead monophonic singing of Psalms translated into French or other vernacular languages in rhymed and measured verse. The musical settings were syllabic, strophic melodies with extremely simple rhythm. Polyphonic vocal or keyboard music that harmonizes these melodies or incorporates them as cantus firmi or as the basis of imitative textures has by extension been called "Calvinist music." Despite the name, however, such music was intended for home use or for performance on the church organ during special music hours, outside the service.

The major composer of Calvinist music during the first half of the seventeenth century was Jan Pieterszoon Sweelinck (1562–1621), organist at the Oude Kerk ("Old Church") in Amsterdam for his entire career. Sweelinck's vocal music—French chansons, Italian madrigals, and Psalm settings for several voices—mostly continue the styles and genres of sixteenth-century French, Italian, and Netherlands composers. Sweelinck's most important and influential music is his keyboard music.

Sweelinck's keyboard music consists of improvisational fantasies and toccatas modeled on the works of Andrea Gabrieli, Claudio Merulo, and John Bull; imitative fantasies and ricercars, often with a single motive or subject of imitation; fantasies that were based on bass ostinato figures or that feature echo effects; and variations derived from the English virginalist tradition, either on well-known song melodies or on Lutheran chorales. Sweelinck's *Ricercar del nono duono* [i.e., *tuono*] (A. 54) is an elaborate and extended work of imitative polyphony, in which twelve subjects are introduced in turn, while, at the same time, the first subject is interwoven in all the voices throughout the piece in a variety of rhythmic guises and variations, including through *inganno* (mm.42–50 and 74–84), the technique used by Frescobaldi. Some of his other imitative fantasies or ricercars are monothematic, using only one subject for all points of imitation. Sweelinck was not the only composer in the early seventeenth century to write elaborate imitative works, but his approach to this genre, with its saturation-level use of subjects, its liberal use of augmentation and diminution, and its insistence on single rhythmic figures over the space of several measures, strongly influenced German organ composition because of the success of Sweelinck's many students, including Andreas Düben, Peter Hasse, Samuel and Gottfried Scheidt, Paul Siefert, Ulrich Cernitz, Jacob Praetorius, and Heinrich Scheidemann. These musicians and their students formed the first generation of the so-called North German organ school, which eventually included Dieterich Buxtehude and Johann Sebastian Bach.

LUTHERAN ORGAN MUSIC

Except in Calvinist cities, an organ was built into nearly every German church of any size in the seventeenth century, and many of these instruments were large and elaborate. Typical small organs found in churches all over the Empire at the beginning of the seventeenth century, even those from the early sixteenth century, had at least two keyboards and a set of pedals. Michael Praetorius (1618) describes an organ with three manuals, a pedal board, and fifty-nine stops. One in Prague had four manuals, pedal board, and seventy stops. The trend in German organs of the seventeenth century was toward ever-increasing variety and subtlety of sound color.

Although Luther enthusiastically endorsed the use of organs in church, we are not certain of the way they were actually used and the repertoire they played, because of missing or contradictory evidence. When parts of the Latin Mass were still performed in Lutheran churches, the practice of alternating plainchant with organ versets continued, and a few Protestant composers contributed to the associated literature. We also find organ accompaniments for congregational singing of chorales, in addition to a few collections of chorale melodies with figured basses for organ accompaniment. Beyond these two categories, however, we know very little about the use of organ in Lutheran church services in the first half of the seventeenth century. To be sure, there is a substantial body of works that could have been used in church, especially works that incorporate chorale melodies, but most of these pieces are preserved in collections freely mixed with ricercars, fugues, stylized dances, preludes, toccatas, and arrangements of vocal music—collections apparently prepared for recreational or didactic use.

The most important and influential collection of German organ music from the first half of the seventeenth century is the *Tabulatura nova* (1624) by Samuel Scheidt. The title of the collection, meaning "New Tablature," refers to the staff notation in open score used in the print. Although this format had been employed by Frescobaldi and several Italians before him, it was an innovation in the German regions, where the letter tablature shown in Figure 6-4 remained a common choice for keyboard music throughout the Baroque period.

Scheidt's *Tabulatura nova* contains fantasies, fugues, echo pieces in imitation of similar pieces by Scheidt's teacher, Sweelinck, settings of Latin hymns and Lutheran chorales, song variations, dances, canons, and, in the third volume of the collection, cantus-firmus settings of the Kyrie, Gloria, and Credo, a set of Magnificat versets in each of nine tones, and harmonizations of Latin hymn melodies. The chorale settings are the most numerous type. Twelve of these are canons, eight are variation sets, and two are chorale fantasies.

Scheidt's chorale variations all place the chorale melody, undecorated and in relatively long notes, in one voice at a time as a cantus firmus. In his introduction to *Tabulatura nova*, Scheidt specifies that this cantus firmus should be played by the pedals on a stop "with a piercing sound, so that the chorale can be heard more distinctly." The counterpoint woven around the chorale cantus firmus at times picks up motives from the chorale melody.

Figure 6-4. An anonymous canzona of ca. 1620 written in German keyboard tablature and transcribed into modern staff notation

Scheidt's *Fantasia super Ich ruf zu dir* (A. 63b) is exceptional for *Tabulatura nova*, but it became exemplary for the next generation of Lutheran organ composers. In it, each phrase of the chorale melody (A. 63a) is given two or three distinct treatments, as is summarized in the table below. Features that reflect the influence of Sweelinck are the extensive use of sequence and the extension of rhythmic figures over several measures at a time. The extreme length and complexity of this work, amplified by the great variety of sound available on a North German organ of this time, was unprecedented.

TREATMENTS OF THE CHORALE MELODY IN SCHEIDT'S *FANTASIA SUPER ICH RUF ZU DIR* (1624)

Phrase 1 as points of imitation (mm. 1–12)
Phrase 2 as points of imitation (mm. 12–24)
Phrases 1 and 2 as cantus firmus in S, T, and B with counterpoint based on a rhythmic diminution of phrases 1 and 2 (mm. 24–51)
Phrase 2 in a semi-chordal harmonization (mm. 52–56)
Phrase 3 as point of imitation with sequences based on fragments of it (mm. 57–80)
Phrase 3 as cantus firmus in S, T, and B, as above (mm. 81–93)
Phrase 3 in a chordal harmonization (mm. 94–98)
Phrase 4 as points of imitation (mm. 99–128)
Phrase 4 as cantus firmus in S, T, B, and T, as above (mm. 129–146)
Phrase 5 as points of imitation and sequences (146–179)
Phrase 5 as cantus firmus in S, T, and B, as above (mm. 179–191)
Phrase 6 as points of imitation (mm. 191–200)
Phrase 6 as cantus firmus in S, T, and B as above (mm. 200–209)
Phrase 6 in chordal harmonization (mm. 209–212)
Phrase 7 as points of imitation (mm. 213–227)
Phrase 7 as cantus firmus in S, T, B, and B (mm. 227–244)
Phrase 7 in chordal harmonization (mm. 244–251)

FROBERGER

Most of the major composers of German organ music in the seventeenth century were Lutheran, lived in the northern German lands, and adapted Italian styles and genres to their own purposes. Johann Jacob Froberger (1616–1667), however, worked at the Catholic imperial court in the southern city of Vienna and used both French and Italian genres and styles. Froberger studied with Girolamo Frescobaldi in Rome for several years about 1640 before becoming imperial court organist in Vienna in 1653. His twenty-five keyboard toccatas and his even more numerous canzonas, ricercars, and other fugal works clearly show the signs of his teacher's influence.

EXAMPLE 6-1. The initial subject and its transformations in Froberger, Canzon III, 1649

Like Frescobaldi's, Froberger's toccatas typically juxtapose extended improvisatory displays featuring scales and arpeggios against well-developed sections of imitative counterpoint. Unlike Frescobaldi, however, Froberger usually varies his opening fugal subject in subsequent imitative sections. In a similar vein, he tends to unify his figural passages with recurring motives, and he places considerably less emphasis than Frescobaldi on strong contrast, whimsical spontaneity, and surprise.

All of Froberger's canzonas are of the variation type like Frescobaldi's models. The example from Froberger's autograph collection dated 1649 (A. 56) transforms the opening subject twice—once to form a variant in the traditional triple-meter middle section, and again in the return to duple meter, in which a variant of the opening subject is typically found (Ex. 6-1).

The same 1649 manuscript collection that contains many of Froberger's toccatas also includes sets of dances that use a more extended application of theme transformation (see A. 57). As shown in Example 6-2, Froberger frequently uses the same material at the beginning of his allemandes and courantes in dance sets. Here, however, this tradition does not stem from Frescobaldi or Italy but from the international Renaissance practice of relating pairs of dances, the first duple and the second triple, through metrical transformation of melodic and harmonic material. Although abandoned in France

EXAMPLE 6-2. Metrical transformation linking an allemande by Froberger with its courant, 1649 (A. 57)

and Italy during the seventeenth century, this practice was preserved in the German-speaking regions, especially in instrumental ensemble music.

Froberger's dance sets—normally an allemande, a courante, and a sarabande—show the obvious influence of French *style brisé*. Since Froberger resided in Brussels about 1647, his knowledge of French keyboard music must date from at least that time.

ENSEMBLE MUSIC IN THE EMPIRE

Italian innovations in ensemble music spread to the regions of the Empire almost as quickly as they did in church music. As we noted, the first Italian musicians to serve at the Dresden court were players of violin and cornetto from Brescia.

Biagio Marini (ca. 1587–1663), one of the first composers of violin sonatas with basso continuo accompaniment, spent twenty-six years (1623–49) in the Empire as music director at the Wittelsbach court at Neuburg an die Donau, with extended visits to Brussels and Düsseldorf. His most important collection of ensemble music, the *Sonate, symphonie . . . e ritornelli, a 1–6* ("Sonatas, symphonies, and interludes for one to six parts"), Op. 8 (Venice, 1629) was published in the middle of this period (see A. 23).

Carlo Farina (ca. 1604–1639) from Mantua became a colleague of Schütz at the Dresden court in 1625, where he published his five books of string ensemble music with continuo accompaniment. Some of Farina's works contain bizarre and comical effects. His *Capriccio stravagante* ("Uninhibited Whim") of 1627, for example, includes imitations of animal sounds, folk instruments, gunfire, and so on, sometimes with clusters of dissonant notes and extended techniques, such as beating the strings with the wood of the bow (*col legno*) and glissandos. Since these special effects are not found in Italian ensemble music but later (1673) resurface in a work by Heinrich Biber (1644–1704), we may surmise that Farina learned them from German "beer fiddlers." Two of his works refer to traditional musical styles of Poland and Hungary.

Antonio Bertali (1605–1669) from Verona spent forty-two years as violinist at the imperial court of Vienna before he succeeded Giovanni Valentini as its music director in 1666. Bertali's instrumental music is mostly undated, but if it was written before he turned his attention to opera composition in 1652, then he is the first known composer of sonatas for trumpets and strings; Valentini had incorporated trumpets into his Viennese church music as early as 1621. The early prominence of trumpets and trombones in Viennese music was evidently intended as an emblem of imperial majesty. Bertali's ensemble works are scored for five-part string ensemble, with or without brass or woodwinds. This type of large-scale sonata, derived from the polychoral ensemble canzona cultivated by Andrea and Giovanni Gabrieli, was known in Italy, and it became a favorite genre of composers in Vienna and at courts in those southern parts of the Empire that correspond to Austria and the Czech Republic of today.

Among the earliest native German composers of italianate trio and solo sonatas with basso continuo were the Nürnberg organist Johann Staden (1581–1634) and his student Johann Erasmus Kindermann (1616–1655). The sonatas of both composers include some in the form of dance sets and others in the canzona-sonata format in which the motivically related first and last sections, imitative in texture and lively in rhythm and melodic character, are separated by a triple-meter, homophonic segment. Canons, notational games, and deliberate mistuning of the violin (*scordatura*) are features of Kindermann's sonatas that appear to be a special characteristic of German instrumental ensemble practices.

STADPFEIFERN

While italianate solo and trio sonatas were common in the noble and imperial courts, a distinctly German tradition of music for civic wind bands (*Stadtpfeifern*, literally "town pipers") continued to flourish in relative isolation from Italian influences. Such ensembles, paid by town councils, were a nearly universal feature of urban musical life all over Europe from at least the fifteenth century. As we saw earlier, civic ensembles in northern Italy developed into distinct groups of wind players, violin-family players, and trumpeters. In the Empire, these groups were primarily wind ensembles, usually five to ten in number, who performed in livery or a uniform of some kind (see Figure 6-5). Unlike the civic ensembles in Italy, those in the German lands cultivated types of composition different from those composed for noble courts. Two types of composition make up almost the entire known repertoire of *Stadtpfeifern*—canzonas for four to eight instruments and sets of dances.

The canzonas of the *Stadtpfeifer* repertoire are shorter than the canzona-style sonatas of court composers, simpler in their overall design (fewer sections), and they lack such Italian innovations as written-out ornamental passages, slow sections with expressive harmony, and long, rapid triple-meter movements. The dance sets by *Stadtpfeifer* composers nearly always include a pavan in duple meter and a galliard in triple time. Following a tradition established in the sixteenth century but later forgotten elsewhere in Europe, *Stadtpfeifer* composers used the same material for both dances in their pavan-and-galliard pairs, and often extended this process to include several or all of the other dances in the set. The result has sometimes been misnamed a *variation suite*; however, the term "suite" arises only in the second half of the seventeenth century, and true variations at this time would follow a single chord series or melodic cantus firmus very closely, which the dances in these *Stadtpfeifer* sets do not. The twenty sets contained in Johann Hermann Schein's *Banchetto musicale* (1617) are examples of this genre. The set in the Anthology (no. 58), published in 1611 by Paul Peuerl (1570–1625), includes a "Dantz," the source of the material used also in the "Padouan" and the "Galliarda."

Figure 6-5. A civic wind band on parade, Brussels, 1616. The instruments are, from left to right, a dulcian (curtal), tenor shawm (bombard), cornett, alto shawm, tenor shawm, tenor trombone (sackbut). The black coats worn were probably the specified livery, while the different collars may distinguish masters from journeymen.

THE GERMAN CONTINUO SONG

This chapter began with a discussion of church vocal music, which led naturally to organ music, other keyboard works, and ensemble music. Italian influence could have been illustrated just as easily with the German continuo song, or *Generalbass Lied*, although the influence of French poetry and *airs de cour* quickly became predominant.

At least three developments converged in the creation of the German continuo song: Schein's application of sacred concerto style to secular music, Johann Nauwach's transfer of Italian monody forms to the German language, and Martin Opitz's reforms of German poetry according to French models.

Johann Hermann Schein's three volumes of *Musica boscareccia* ("Rustic Music") of 1621, 1626, and 1628 stand in dramatic contrast to his earlier collection of German songs, *Venus Kräntzlein* ("Little Garland of Venus"), 1609. The latter are mostly five-voice unaccompanied settings of folk-like poems in simple homophonic style with the melody in the soprano, much like the earlier songs of Hans Leo Hassler. The songs in *Musica boscareccia* are for two sopranos and a bass part that is both texted and figured. Performance instructions allow for solo voice with continuo, two voices and continuo, three voices alone, or three voices with continuo. The texts generally relate to the Italian pastoral tradition and are filled with courtly language and rhetorical figures. The voices are scored and managed in very nearly the same way as in Schein's sacred concertos in *Opella nova*, discussed earlier.

Johann Nauwach (ca. 1595–ca. 1630) had trained as a choirboy in Dresden before the Elector sent him to study in Florence from about 1612 to 1618. His Italian *Arie* (1623), heavily influenced by Caccini, India, and other monodists, consist of ornamented solo madrigals and strophic canzonette. His *Teutscher Villanellen* ("German Villanellas") of 1627 include these types as well a set of strophic variations. Nine texts in this collection are by Martin Opitz.

Martin Opitz (1597–1639) was the most influential German poet of the seventeenth century. In his *Buch von der deutschen Poeterey* ("Book of German Poetry"), published in 1624, he initiated the modern era of German poetry by introducing regular meters and rhyme schemes and elevating the tone and language of the poetry, following French poetic models (principally Ronsard) and theory (of the Pléiade). His poems were set strophically with strong accentual meter and regular phrases in collections of 1634 and 1636 by Thomas Selle (1599–1663) and in the *Cantade und Arien* (1638) by Kaspar Kittel (1603–1639).

The most prolific and influential composer of the early German continuo song was Heinrich Albert (1604–1651), who published eight volumes of such works between 1638 and 1650. Although only a few of his texts were written by Opitz, all of them reflect Opitz's reform of German poetry. Albert, who was influenced by the continuo songs of Schein, trained in Dresden under his cousin Heinrich Schütz. His 170 songs were written for weddings, funerals, anniversaries, visits, and private enjoyment in the town of Königsberg, and these events are described and dated in his dedications of individual pieces. Most of these songs are short, strophic, and syllabic. A few incorporate melismas, word painting, and ritornellos. Although Albert always respects the meter of the poetry in his songs, he is not always bound to regular, dance-like rhythms. For example, the text of his 1640 song *O der rauhen Grausamkeit!* ("O, the Harsh Cruelty!" A. 59), which carries a Latin rubric meaning," consists of two stanzas with the same pattern of trochaic tetrameter and trimeter, thus:

— U — U   — U —   — U — U   — U —
O der rauhen Grausamkeit! / Die nur seufzen jederzeit / etc.

Albert's music, however, stretches the long or accented syllables and compresses the short, unaccented ones to such an extent that at times the vocal line retains metrical orientation only through its coordination with the bass part. Repetition and rapid delivery along with wide leaps and chromatic lines give his setting a strong, rhetorical expressiveness that equals Italian monodies and early cantatas of the 1630s.

By the late seventeenth century, the German continuo song had faded in importance, but the many reprints of songs by Schein and Albert fitted out with religious texts gave rise to the genre of religious continuo song, which found its way into the German church cantata during the period of Dieterich Buxtehude.

We have seen, then, that the courts and cities of the Holy Roman Empire, the Habsburg hereditary lands to the east, and Poland experienced a dramatic influx of musical styles and genres from Italy about the beginning of the seventeenth century. Composers brought with them polychoral technique, the use of basso continuo, small-scale concerted church vocal composition, declamatory and florid solo vocal writing, distinctive sectional repetition schemes in concerted church music, reflection or creation of rhetorical figures in music, idiomatic use of the violin, and several types of chamber ensemble with one or two violin parts supported by basso continuo. At the same time, they retained some features of earlier or regional musical practices and styles by incorporating chorale melodies and texts in a variety of organ and vocal genres, employing cantus firmus technique, using few melodic motives, weaving complex imitative counterpoint, making use of pedals and of a wide variety of stops and mixtures in organ music, expanding Renaissance dance-pair practice into the so-called "variation suite," and emphasizing large instrumental ensembles that included trumpets, cornetts, and trombones, in both *Stadtpfeifer* and court music. This combination of innovations from Italy and traditional or regional features begins at this time to define a distinctive range of German musical styles and genres.

BIBLIOGRAPHICAL NOTES

The Italian Influx to the Empire and East

For an overview of the political and social history of this region, see Rudolf Vierhaus, *Germany in the Age of Absolutism*, trans J. B. Knudsen (New York: Cambridge University Press, 1988), and Charles W. Ingrao, *The Habsburg Monarchy, 1618–1815* (Cambridge: Cambridge University Press, 1994). A good overview of church music is provided by Anne Kirwan-Mott, *The Small-Scale Sacred Concertato in the Early Seventeenth Century*, 2 vols. (Ann Arbor: UMI Research Press, 1981), whose focus on Germany is not mentioned in the title. A study that places the church music of Giovanni Priuli and Giovanni Valentini in the context of musical culture at the Viennese court of Emperor Ferdinand II is Steven Saunders, *Cross, Sword, and Lyre: Sacred Music at the Imperial Court of Ferdinand II of Habsburg (1619–1637)* (New York: Oxford University Press, 1995). Another aspect of this topic not treated here is explored by Sara E. Dumont, *German Secular Polyphonic Song in Printed Editions 1570–1630: Italian Influences on the Poetry and Music*, 2 vols. (New York: Garland, 1989). Other specialized articles in English or books in other languages, especially German, can be identified in the bibliographies attached to the articles in *The New Grove Dictionary* on composers and cities named here and by using those names in searches of RILM online.

The Earliest Lutheran Composers to Assimilate New Italian Styles after 1600

In addition to Kirwan-Mott's book cited above, a good general orientation can be found in the relevant parts of Friedrich Blume, et al, *Protestant Church Music: A*

History, rev. Ludwig Finscher, trans. F. Ellsworth Peterson (New York: W. W. Norton, 1974; London: Victor Gollancz, 1975).

Heinrich Schütz

The standard book in English is still Hans Joachim Moser, *Heinrich Schütz; His Life and Work*, trans. Carl F. Pfatteicher (St. Louis: Concordia Pub. House, 1959), although it is quite outdated by comparison to the rich literature in German. Much of that new richness can be gleaned from the periodical literature surveyed in Allen B. Skei, *Heinrich Schütz, a Guide to Research* (New York: Garland, 1981). A brief modern account is Basil Smallman, *The Music of Heinrich Schütz, 1585–1672* (Leeds: Mayflower, 1985). An important contribution on a small scale is Joshua Rifkin, "Heinrich Schütz," in *The "New Grove" North European Baroque Masters* (London: Macmillan, 1985). A large amount of basic source material is available in Gina Gail Spagnoli, trans, *Letters and Documents of Heinrich Schütz, 1656–1672: An Annotated Translation* (Ann Arbor: UM Research Press, 1990). A good source of Schütz iconography is Richard Petzoldt, *Heinrich Schütz und seine Zeit in Bildern = Heinrich Schütz and His Times in Pictures*, with an introduction by Dietrich Berke (Kassel: Bärenreiter, 1972.). The only complete edition of Schütz's music is Heinrich Schütz, *Sämtliche Werke*, ed. Philipp Spitta, Arnold Schering, and Heinrich Spitta (Leipzig, Breitkopf & Härtel, 1885–1927). This edition, however, is being replaced by Heinrich Schütz, *Neue Ausgabe sämtlicher Werke*, Internationale Heinrich-Schütz-Gesellschaft (Kassel: Bärenreiter, 1955–) and Heinrich Schütz, *Stuttgarter Schütz-Ausgabe* ed. Günter Graulich and Paul Horn (Neuhausen-Stuttgart, Hänssler-Verlag, 1971–).

German Organ Music

A general history of the instrument is Peter F. Williams, *The European Organ 1450–1850*, 2nd ed. (London, Batsford, 1978). The best overview for this as well as other aspects of keyboard music in the seventeenth century is Willi Apel, *The History of Keyboard Music to 1700*, trans and rev. Hans Tischler (Bloomington, IN: Indiana University Press, 1972). The keyboard music of Sweelinck is surveyed in Pieter Dirksen, *The Keyboard Music of Jan Pieterszoon Sweelinck: Its Style, Significance and Influence* (Utrecht: Koninklijke Vereniging voor Nederlandse Muziekgeschiedenis, 1997). A useful study of specific organ practices is Pieter van Dijk, *Mattias Weckmann and the Use of the Organ in the Jacobikirche in Hamburg in The Seventeenth Century* (Sneek: Boeijenga, 1991). A complementary book that includes an introduction to the seventeenth-century German organ is Gustav Fock, *Hambrug's Role in Northern European Organ Building* (Easthampton, MA: Westfield Center, 1997).

Ensemble Music in the Empire

The spread of the solo and trio sonata with continuo is surveyed in William S. Newman, *the Sonata in the Baroque Era*, 4th ed. (New York: W. W. Norton, 1983). A complementary study, now rather old, is Albert Biales, "The Sonatas and Canzonas for Larger Ensembles of the Seventeenth Century in Austria," Ph.D. diss., University of California, Los Angeles, 1962. A fascinating study of German *Stadtpfeifern* is Jeinrich W. Schwab, "The Social Status of the Town Musician," *The Social Status of the Professional Musician from the Middle Ages to the 19th Century*, ed. Walter Salmen, trans. Herbert Kaufman and Barbara Reisner, Sociology of Music, 1 (New York: Pendragon Press, 1982), pp. 31–59.

CHAPTER 7

Music in England under the First Stuart Kings and Commonwealth

ENGLAND IN THE EUROPEAN CONTEXT

At the beginning of the seventeenth century, England, still separate from Scotland, occupied only the southern two-thirds of one island situated a short distance off the coast of France. Its population was about four and a half million, compared with twenty million in France and about fifteen million in the German-speaking lands. Although London was nearly as populous as Paris, there were no other large cities in England at this time, and there were no secondary noble courts that could compare with those of the regional sovereigns of the Empire, the Italian peninsula, or Iberia. England at this time was not a wealthy country, and it had relatively little money to spend on music or the other arts. Furthermore, England by the seventeenth century had a sizable Puritan population, who opposed church music and theater on religious grounds. As a consequence of these factors, art music occupied a relatively thin strand in the social and cultural fabric of seventeenth-century England, and the musical history of the country in at this time involves the waxing and waning of several foreign influences—German, French, and Italian—alongside native traditions that submerge and reemerge from time to time.

INSTRUMENTAL ENSEMBLE MUSIC IN ENGLAND

Wind ensembles like those of the Empire were also found in England, where they were called "waits." The same name was given to watchmen, indicating that in England, as in the German lands, civic wind players once served in the town watchtower, where they signaled the hour or the approach of danger. In many places, town instrumentalists continued to play music from the watchtower even after they had relinquished their watchman duties. A connection between the English waits and the German *Stadtpfeifern* is provided by William Brade (1560–1630), an English instrumentalist who served as a civic musician during two periods (1608-10, 1613-15) in Hamburg, where he published several collections of dances and canzonas in the typical German styles.

Italian-style string ensemble music with continuo accompaniment was introduced in England by Angelo Notari (1566–1663), a singer and violinist from Venice who joined the household of Prince Henry in 1610. In 1618 he transferred to the service of Prince Charles and remained with him after he became king in 1625. Notari's surviving works for solo violin and basso continuo include canzonas, one preserved in both plain and ornamented versions, and variations on the Ruggiero, Romanesca, and La Monica chordal-bass patterns. They are comparable to the earliest violin and continuo works printed in Italy between 1610 and 1620.

Actually, an ensemble of violin-family instruments was established in England almost as early as in Italy. In 1540 King Henry VIII brought a company of six string players from Venice, most of whom were from Sephardic Jewish families expelled from Spain or Portugal during the 1490s. Sephardic immigrants are credited with introducing the viol to Italy, and they may well have played a major role in spreading the violin family as well. It is notable that Andrea Amati served his apprenticeship in string-instrument making with a converted Jew in Cremona, and several of the earliest violin makers in Amsterdam were Jewish as well. The original six violinists at the court of Henry VIII had a long service, and their descendants to the fourth generation inherited those positions and continued to constitute the royal violin consort through most of the seventeenth century.

Throughout the sixteenth century and into the seventeenth, consorts of violin-family instruments—typically six—served as ensembles to accompany dancing and theatrical spectacles. An example of the former function is shown in Figure 7-1. Violinists at the English royal court certainly played the latest ensemble music from Italy; English composers of violin sonatas, however, are not known until the last third of the seventeenth century.

Consorts of viols were more popular in England during the seventeenth century, as they were in France. The continued predominance of viols over

Figure 7-1. Courtiers of Queen Elizabeth dance, ca. 1600; musicians play a lute, viola, violin, and bass violin (large cello).

violins in England and France during this period indicates that amateur music making was more widespread there than in Italy. Several period writings tell us that violin-family instruments were considered suitable for professionals, whereas viols were more commonly cultivated by gentlemen amateurs. But professional viol players also performed both at the royal court and in other noble households. Henry VIII had two viol players at his court by 1526, and the string players from Venice played viols as well as violins.

During the sixteenth century a significant body of viol consort music was produced in England. The principal types were the fantasia (as in France), the In Nomine, and dances, particularly pavans and galliards. These genres continued to be cultivated in England throughout the seventeenth century.

Fantasia

An English fantasia for viol consort is a work with a mostly imitative texture resembling a ricercar or canzona. In the sixteenth century, English viol fantasias began to reveal such idiomatic characteristics as extended range, wide leaps, and a variety of rapid ornamental figures. By the seventeenth century, four distinct types of English viol consort fantasia can be distinguished: monothematic fantasias, fantasias with several subjects but a single prevailing mood, fantasias in two contrasting sections, and fantasias with several sections or movements, each one with a clearly defined close. All begin with an extended series of imitative entries, and many of them include melodic inversion, canon, and rhythmic augmentation and diminution. Frequently an organ part is included, which, however, usually doubles the viol parts.

The fantasia for a consort of four viols by John Jenkins (1592–1678), A. 60, is of the fourth type, consisting of six sections defined by change of motive and prevailing rhythm and, in several cases, change of key signature; the sections end in mm. 39, 70, 88, 113, 126, and 156. This fantasia is unusual for the extent of its mutations of hexachord, mode, and system (key signature), although it is not unique in this respect. It belongs to a tradition of pieces with extreme mutations that can be found in England beginning in the early sixteenth century that continued until the end of the seventeenth century.

The mode of Jenkins's fantasia remains stable throughout Section 1 (mm. 1–39), notwithstanding the cadences on E-flat (m. 13) and G (m. 27), because cadences on the third and fifth above the final are normal for Mode 2 and because neither cadence is preceded by melodic and contrapuntal structures that would suggest a new modal framework. Examples 7-2b and 7-2c show the preparation for these cadences. In both, the notes C and G continue to have a prominent place, and the melodic figures continue to fit comfortably into the hexachords of the two-flat system.

Sections 2 and 3 of this fantasia, however, are remarkably unstable in pitch structure. Section 2 begins with a change to Mode 1 on F (Ex. 7-2d). The second half of Section 2 (Ex. 7-2f) contains an extraordinarily rapid and far-reaching series of mutations, in which a sequential transposition of a falling and rising conjunct motive leads to cadences on F, Bb, Eb, Ab, and Db. The concluding note of the last cadence of this series is changed to C#, which requires a mutation to the four-sharp system. This sets the stage for a second series of sequential transpositions (Ex. 7-2g) that leads to cadences on F#, E, A, and D (only B is missing from a complete set of 12 different cadence pitches) and necessitates mutations to the two-sharp, one-sharp, and natural systems.

EXAMPLE 7-2a–e. Highlights from John Jenkins's Fantasia for viols

EXAMPLE 7-2f–j. Highlights of John Jenkins's Fantasia for viols, concluded

Stability is restored to some extent in Sections 4 and 5. Section 4 (mm. 88–113) remains in Mode 3 transposed to D under the one-flat system, changing to Mode 6 on F in preparation for the final cadence of the section (Ex. 7-2h). Section 5 marks out a return to the original mode and system of the piece through a cadence on B♭ (Ex. 7-2i). The note G becomes *la* in the natural hexachord in the two-flat system, leading downward to the cadence on C as final of Mode 2 (Ex. 7-2j), where the piece remains for the final Section 6.

In Nomine

Pieces called "In Nomine" can be as complex as Jenkins's fantasia, although they are always stable as to mode and system because they are all based upon a specific cantus firmus drawn from the Sarum (English) chant antiphon *Gloria tibi Trinitas*. This chant melody was set to the words "in nomine Domini" in the Benedictus of the Mass *Gloria tibi Trinitas* by John Taverner (ca. 1490–1545), and this section of his composition seems to have circulated separately as an instrumental piece. Successive generations of English composers competed with each other to set new and ever-more elaborate counterpoint against that particular cantus firmus. This tradition endured until the end of the seventeenth century.

Dances

An English innovation of the seventeenth century, possibly reflecting Italian influence, was the fantasia-suite, a work in three movements, consisting of a contrapuntal fantasia followed by an almaine (a duple-meter dance) and galliard (a triple-meter dance), often with a brief duple-meter section, called a "close" or "brouch" at the end. Scoring is normally for one or two violins or treble viols, bass viol, and keyboard instrument, most often an organ. The keyboard generally plays alone at the beginning and during linking passages; otherwise it provides a harmonic background not unlike a basso continuo realization, except that it is written out and somewhat more active. The example in the Anthology (no. 61) is by John Coprario (ca. 1570/80–1626), an Englishman who changed his name from Cooper, allegedly after spending time in Italy. Coprario is credited with composing the earliest fantasia-suites while he was a musician in the household of Prince Charles (1622–25). Coprario's fantasia-suites are the first known works by a native English composer to specify the violin.

Another typical sixteenth-century English ensemble that survived well into the seventeenth was the six-part mixed consort consisting of lute, bandora (a strummed, chordal, fretted instrument with metal strings and scalloped outline), bass viol, cittern (another strummed, chordal, fretted instrument with a body shaped like a thin, vertical center slice of a pear), treble viol (or violin), and transverse flute (wooden and without keys). Works for this combination tend to feature lively rhythmic interplay among the chord-playing instruments and competing embellished passages for the treble viol and flute.

An English specialty for solo viol was the improvisation and composition of "divisions." These are figural variations upon chordal-bass patterns, which the English called "grounds." The term "divisions" refers to the effect of dividing each long note of the ground into many faster notes on different pitches. The earliest written-out divisions on grounds are found in *The First Part of Ayres* (1605) by Tobias Hume. The fullest explanation of how to improvise divisions is found in *The Division-violist; or, An Introduction to the Playing upon a Ground* (1659) by Christopher Simpson. Divisions could be played on a consort bass viol, the smaller lyra viol, or the middle-size division viol—all tuned the same way: D–G–c–e–a–d´.

LUTE AND HARPSICHORD MUSIC

Like the viols, the lute and harpsichord were cultivated by both professional and noble amateur musicians in England during the early seventeenth century.

The outstanding composer of English lute music during the first quarter of the seventeenth century was John Dowland (1563–1626), a university-educated gentleman who spent most of his life in the households of various English nobles or in the temporary but highly paid employment of several courts on the Continent, notably those of the landgrave of Hesse (the first patron of Heinrich Schütz) and the king of Denmark. Dowland was unable to gain a position in the English royal household until 1622, near the end of his life because, he thought, of his Catholic religion. His lute music, like that of his contemporaries, falls into three main categories, which parallel some of the main types of viol consort music: fantasias, dances (pavans, galliards, almains, and jigs), and arrangements of popular and traditional songs. *The Frog Galliard* (A. 62) actually combines the dance and popular song categories, since this music was also sung to the words "Now, o now I needs must part." Because the text requires the unnatural repetition of the word "now" in order to match the rhythmic pattern that permeates the whole piece, it would appear that the song was based upon Dowland's galliard, and not the other way around. Dowland's galliard begins with the chordal-bass pattern of the ciaccona, and it includes written-out, varied repeats of each of its two thirty-two-bar strains.

An abrupt and radical change of fashion overtook English lute music just at the end of Dowland's lifetime. Prince Charles's favorite courtier, George Villiers, first duke of Buckingham, brought the famous lutenist Jacques Gautier from Paris in 1617 and procured a place for him in the prince's household by 1619. Then in 1625 Charles married Henrietta Maria, the daughter of King Henry IV of France. Her arrival with a large entourage from her native country generated great enthusiasm among English courtiers for all things French. Gautier's French style of composing for and playing on the lute quickly found English imitators. One of these was John Lawrence, who served as a lutenist to King Charles from 1626 to his death in 1635. His *Coranto* (i.e., Courante,

A. 63) shows the essential features of the new French *style brisé* and makes a striking contrast to Dowland's *Frog Galliard*.

No comparable revolution overtook English keyboard music during the first half of the seventeenth century. The hefty manuscript anthology of Elizabethan harpsichord music called *The Fitzwilliam Virginal Book* (copied in 1609) contains all of the types cultivated for the next forty years: preludes comparable to the intonations of Andrea Gabrieli; fantasias; cantus-firmus settings, especially In Nomines; dances, especially pavans and galliards; transcriptions of songs; and variations on popular melodies, ground basses, and harmonic formulas.

Although the term "virginal" was used in England to describe all types of harpsichord, the most common type was what is today called the "virginal"—a small instrument with a single set of strings strung parallel to the single keyboard. By the seventeenth century, the virginal supplanted the lute as the predominant domestic instrument for amateurs, especially for ladies. Indicative of its wide cultivation is the publication, about 1612, of *Parthenia: or, The Maydenhead of the First Musicke That Ever Was Printed for the Virginalls*, with selections by the principal keyboard composers of that time: William Byrd (1543–1623), John Bull (ca. 1562–1628), and Orlando Gibbons (1583–1625). Although these three composers died within five years of one another, they represent three different generations. Of the three, only Gibbons belongs to the style period under consideration here.

Gibbons was the son of a civic instrumentalist (wait) who served in the university towns of Oxford and Cambridge. He received early training as a choirboy in the chapel of King's College, Cambridge. After graduation from the college in 1606, he received an appointment as Gentleman of the Chapel Royal. By 1615, Gibbons had become organist of the Chapel Royal. He composed vocal music for the church, English madrigals, consort songs for voices and viols, viol consort music (fantasias, pavans and galliards, and In Nomines), and virginal music (fantasias, pavans and galliards, variations, and transcriptions of stage songs).

Gibbons's set of variations on "Peascod Time" or "The Hunt's Up" (W. 9) illustrates the interesting connections among court music, popular music, oral tradition, and social practices at this time. The Hunt's Up refers to a ground (chordal-bass pattern) that can be traced back to the mid-to-early sixteenth century. Several tunes were sung and played to the accompaniment of the Hunt's Up ground during this period. Each of these tunes gave rise to its own family of variants as it was passed from lip to ear. One of these tunes is shown on the top staff of Example 7-3 (number 1) as it is preserved in, e.g., Anthony Holborne, *The Cittharn* [i.e., *Cittern*] *School* (1597) under the title "Peascod Time". This form of the tune appears in the treble voice of Gibbons's Variation 11, and it forms the basis of all the other variations. The words given as number 2 in the example come from *England's Helicon* (1600), an anthology of poems then preserved in oral tradition. The ground bass line given as number 4 in the example is the version upon which William Byrd composed variations under the title *The Huntes Upp* in *The Fitzwilliam Virginal Book*. Slightly

EXAMPLE 7-3. (1) The melody of "Peascod Time," (2) the test of "Peascod Time," (3) a chordal harmonization of the ground, (4) the Hunt's Up ground, (5) four sets of words for "The Hunt's Up"

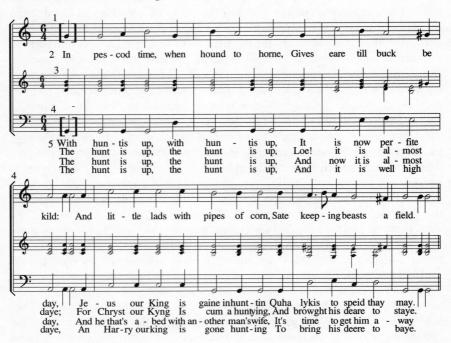

different versions of this ground are preserved under similar titles in earlier sources. The texts given as number 5 in the example are from sixteenth- or seventeenth-century sources, except for the last, which is a nineteenth-century attempt to reconstruct the original. A chordal harmonization that would have been added to the ground is given as number 3.

The Hunt's Up ground is so called probably because of its association with a text that speaks of daybreak. It gave rise to a type of unnotated instrumental ensemble music traditionally performed as a morning serenade under the window of someone who was expected to pay the musicians. These serenades were such a good source of income that in the sixteenth century the Worshipful Company of Musicians of London established a rule whereby anyone who played a "huntsup" without a license from the Company's officers was assessed a substantial fine.

The text of "Peascod Time," which also refers to hunting, was just one of several sets of verses associated with this particular Hunt's-Up tune. Another text sung to that tune was "The Lady's Fall," and under that title this tune became one of the most frequently named on broadside ballad sheets in the seventeenth century. Broadside ballads were poems that told of sensational news—crimes, scandals, executions, elopements, ghosts, witches, and so on.

These ballads were printed on large broadside sheets and sold on the streets. The sheets contained no musical notation but only the name of the tune to which the ballad was to be sung. Because the tune of "The Lady's Fall" ("Peascod Time", "The Hunt's Up") was often cited on broadsides, it is apparent that it was widely known. In fact, the tune has remained in oral tradition up to the present day in rural northern England.

Gibbons's variations on "Peascod Time" are more numerous and complex than was typical of variations from Byrd's generation. Each variation elaborates on its own distinct motive, often used in imitation between the voices of the texture, as happens in the three-bar introduction. The harmonic outline that unifies the variations is less simple than the basic Hunt's Up ground; it is rather a harmonization of the "Peascod Time" tune. The passagework goes very rapidly, and the texture is often complex. To this are added frequent trills and mordents, shown as double and single slashes across the stems of notes.

Similarly dense ornamentation, along with intricate, often syncopated rhythm, lends stylistic brilliance to the *Fancy* (i.e., *Fantasia*), dated 1648 (W. 10), by Thomas Tomkins (1572–1656), Gibbon's successor as First Organist of the Chapel Royal. This piece is typical of Tomkins's late works in that it takes music of earlier generations as its model but exaggerates its contrapuntal complexity. The same exaggeration of late-Renaissance polyphonic style has already been noted in the ricercars and canzonas of Frescobaldi, the ricercars of Sweelinck, the chorale fantasies of Scheidt, the ricercars of Froberger, the viol consort fantasias of John Jenkins, and the English In Nomine tradition.

CHURCH MUSIC UNDER THE STUART KINGS

As mentioned in Chapter 1, the Church of England was proclaimed in 1533 when the pope would not grant King Henry VIII an annulment of his marriage to Catherine of Aragon. In 1549 the Act of Uniformity established English as the normal language of worship in the church, and *The Booke of the Common Prayer* fixed the Anglican liturgy. Communion, or Second Service, corresponds to the Catholic Mass, Matins is a conflation of Catholic Matins and Lauds, and Evensong or Evening Prayer is an amalgam of Catholic Vespers and Compline.

The vocal music for an English Communion Service consisted of the Kyrie, Gloria, Creed, Sanctus, and Agnus Dei, all in English, from the Catholic Mass Ordinary, together with anthems, which are settings of English religious texts to be sung during the Offertory and post-Communion, two places in the Catholic Mass where motets were frequently sung in Italy at this time. There is relatively little English Communion music from the first half of the seventeenth century, and what there is tends to be short, simple, and syllabic.

By contrast to the Catholic Church, the Church of England gave less importance to the Communion Service and more to Matins and Evensong, in which the usual musical items (canticles) carried Latin names (Venite, Te Deum,

Benedicite, Benedictus, Jubilate, Magnificat, Cantate Domino, Nunc dimittis, Deus misereatur) but were sung in English. Settings of these canticles were also called anthems, a term that roughly corresponds to the terms "motet" or "concerto" in the Italian and German traditions. Frequently in the seventeenth century a single composer set all the musical items for the Communion, Matins, and Evensong in the same mode and in a similar style under the collective heading "Service."

English anthems that use the full choir throughout are called "full anthems," and those that use a verse-by-verse alternation between full choir and soloists, accompanied either by an instrumental ensemble (typically a consort of viols) or by the organ, are termed "verse anthems." Verse anthems, which are similar in effect to Italian concerted motets or sacred concertos, can be found fully notated as early as the 1550s, when the practice of "concerting" motets was still an unwritten tradition in Italy. However, Italian basso continuo practice was rarely used in English verse anthems, even by the middle of the seventeenth century. If an organ accompaniment was used, it was fully notated and normally consisted of three to five contrapuntal lines, as continuous as if they were written for viols. Indeed, it was more common to accompany the solo verses with a consort of viols.

Italian influence on the musical style of verse anthems comes through the English importation of the Italian polyphonic madrigal in the late sixteenth century. From that tradition, anthems derive their texture—generally contrapuntal but usually not pervasively imitative, their expressive, rhythmically enlivened declamation of the words, their use of mild dissonance and chromaticism, and their reliance on contrasts of texture, tessituras, and pacing. *See, See, the Word Is Incarnate* (A. 64), by Orlando Gibbons, is a masterful example. The text, by a contemporary Anglican churchman, forms a sketchy narrative of Christ's birth, life, passion, and resurrection. Soloists, singly or in groups, sing the narrations, and the chorus reacts, the first time as a choir of angels. The lack of musical repetitions is unusual for the genre, but there is some motivic reworking in the second, third, and fourth choruses.

Of the many capable church composers in early seventeenth-century England, the most prolific and, after Gibbons, the most important was Thomas Tomkins. His anthems and madrigals are generally less adventurous than Gibbons's, retaining more of the formal counterpoint and careful dissonance treatment of his teacher, William Byrd. At the other extreme stands Walter Porter (ca. 1587/95–1659), the only English composer to have studied with Claudio Monteverdi. His verse anthem *O Praise the Lord* employs basso continuo accompaniment and florid solo vocal writing.

MADRIGALS, AYRES, AND SONGS

The introduction of the polyphonic madrigal was one of the first and clearest signs of Italian influence on English music. It began with the publication of two anthologies of Italian madrigals with texts translated into English—

Musica transalpina (1588) and *Italian Madrigalls Englished* (1590)—and continued with a flood of native imitations, both of the canzonetta type and of the serious type. Madrigals fell out of favor quickly after the turn of the seventeenth century. Thomas Campion's criticism of them in 1613 exactly reflected the attack launched thirty years earlier in Italy by Vincenzo Galilei, representing the Florentine Camerata: "[A polyphonic madrigal] is long, intricate, bated with fuge, chaind with sincopation, and where the nature of everie word is precisely expresst in the Note . . . such childish observing of words is altogether ridiculous."

Continuo-accompanied monody, which replaced the polyphonic madrigal in Italy, was known in England from an early date. Several English manuscripts preserve early versions of monodies by Caccini and other Italians. Angelo Notari, mentioned earlier in connection with early violin music, published a collection of his own monodies in London about 1613. But these are isolated examples. The place of the madrigal in English-language music was actually taken by lute songs or "ayres."

As with most terms for nonreligious vocal genres, "ayre" refers to a type of poem as well as to its musical setting. An ayre is poetry with a regular pattern of meter and line length and a predictable rhyme scheme and is most often strophic, whereas a serious English madrigal, like its Italian model, is nonstrophic and irregular in accents, line length, and rhyme. The term "ayre" became a popular designation for vocal works with the publication in 1597 of *The Firste Booke of Songes or Ayres of Foure Partes with Tableture for the Lute* by John Dowland. Dowland's ayres, of which we have about eighty-four, were normally conceived as solo songs with intabulated lute accompaniment, but they were generally published in a multiple format that also allowed them to be sung by four voices. Lute ayres, when compared with madrigals, are more treble-dominated, have less activity in the lower voices (whether played or sung), use less text repetition, and focus the musical support of text in the area of declamation rather than texture, contrast, harmony, and pictorialism.

Many of Dowland's lute ayres are strongly metrical, evenly phrased, and strophic in design, mirroring the poetry. But some—the more serious or melancholy—are of an opposite character in all three respects. Although a few earlier lute ayres are known, Dowland essentially created the genre by adapting the essential characteristics of the earlier consort song, such as those by William Byrd, by placing in his intabulated lute part the accompanying strands that formerly were entrusted to a viol consort.

Dowland had visited Florence in 1595, while Jacopo Peri was at work on the first opera, *La Dafne*. The declamatory style of continuo-accompanied solo madrigals like Peri's and Caccini's, if not their recitative style, left traces in some of Dowland's lute ayres and in those by a few of his contemporaries. An example is Dowland's *Far from Triumphing Court* (A. 65), first published by his son Robert in an anthology that also included a solo madrigal by Caccini.

The text of Dowland's *Far from the Triumphing Court* was written by Sir Henry Lee, a favorite of Queen Elizabeth, on the occasion of Queen Anne's visit to his estate in 1608, eighteen years after his retirement from court and five years after the death of Queen Elizabeth. Like all ayres, this one has regular scansion (iambic pentameter) and rhyme (ababcc):

U — U — U — U — U — U etc.
Far from triumphing court and wonted glory
He dwelt in shady unfrequented places,
Time's prisoner now, he made his pastime story;
Gladly forgets court's erstafforded graces.
The goddess whom he served to heaven's gone,
And he on earth in darkness left to moan.

Dowland's music, however, runs counter to the poem's scansion, creating a tension that calls attention to its prose-like declamation. In fact, Dowland's music is so closely molded to the natural declamation of the first stanza of the text that the other three stanzas printed with the music can scarcely be sung to the same music. The nearly syllabic setting, the occasional monotone recitation, especially at the beginning, the narrow range of most phrases, and the static harmony at the beginnings of each half of this ayre all resemble features of the new solo madrigal from Italy. Even such a detail as the delayed, syncopated entries of some long syllables ("far," "time's," "glad-") corresponds to the style of Peri and Monteverdi. But by comparison with Caccini's *Deh, dove son fuggite* (A. 3), for example, Dowland's ayre uses a smaller range of note values for the delivery of syllables—no sixteenth notes, only two eighth notes, and mostly half notes or combinations of dotted halves and quarters. This and the active rhythm of the accompaniment, which would not be found in an Italian realization of Caccini's basso continuo parts, give Dowland's ayre less *sprezzatura* (rhythmic freedom) than Caccini's madrigal. When compared with Caccini's, Dowland's melodic contours seem more conditioned by musical values and less by the syntax of the text. And, of course, there is no florid passagework here or anywhere in Dowland's lute ayres, as there often is in Caccini's solo madrigals.

Dowland's lute ayres were followed by a flood of imitations that receded only by about 1620. In 1612 Prince Henry had eight singer-lutenists in his household, and by 1618 Prince Charles had twelve in his. All these musicians composed ayres. The Italianate features of recitational declamation and florid passagework are more marked in the works of these younger composers. Many of their songs were sung in plays. The prolific Robert Johnson (ca. 1583–1633) was the house composer for the King's Men and in that capacity wrote songs for plays by William Shakespeare (1564–1616), such as "Full Fathom Five" and "Where the Bee Sucks" for *The Tempest* (1610). But a much more important theatrical employment of lute ayres was found in court masques of the Stuart period.

THE MASQUE AT THE COURTS OF
THE FIRST STUART KINGS

The court masque was the most important and common form of musical spectacle in England during the first half of the seventeenth century. Briefly stated,
a court masque was an entertainment combining aspects of theater and social
ritual and presented in a social setting such as a banquet hall, rather than a theater. It was made up of theatrical and social dancing, singing, speaking, pantomime, scenery, machinery, and properties, conforming to a general outline
and the specific traditions that are part of the definition of the genre. Related
to the French *ballet de cour*, the masque likewise had its origins in the Italian
mascherata, which was introduced to the English court in the time of Henry
VIII. An idea of the mascherata of that time can be gleaned from this English
court chronicle report of 1512:

> On the date of the Epiphanie at night, the kyng with xi others wer disguised,
> after the manner of Italie, called a maske, a thyng not seen afore in Englande,
> thei were appareled in garementes long and brode, wrought all with gold,
> with visers and cappes of gold, and after the banket doen, these Maskers came
> in, with sixe gentlemen disguised in silke bearynge staffe torches, and desired
> the ladies to daunce, some were content, and some that knewe the fashion of
> it refused, because it was not a thyng commonly seen. And after thei daunced
> and commoned toghether, as the fashion of the Maskes is, thei toke their leave
> and departed, and so did the Quene, and all the ladies.

In the course of the sixteenth century the English court masque became
increasingly theatrical and normally included scenery, which was often brought in
with the masquers on a festival cart on which was mounted a ship, a castle, a
mountain, or a similar setting. After a spoken prologue followed by a song or chorus or both, the masquers would descend to the floor and dance with the spectators. After a speech or song calling them back, the masquers made their exit, on
the cart if one was used. The scenery, costumes, speeches, and vocal texts were
normally unified by some theme, which was usually allegorical or symbolic.

By the early seventeenth century, even more elaborate theatrical elements
were added to the portion of the entertainment preceding the masque proper.
This part, staged before the entry of the main, or "grand" masquers, was called
the "antimasque." It often was comical or satirical. At this time one can usually
find the following twelve elements in an English court masque: (1) a procession
of the minor masquers and/or antimasquers; (2) a speech or dialogue; (3) antimasque songs and dances; (4) revelation of the fixed scenery of the masque, for
example, by drawing aside a curtain, if this was not already done before the first
speech; (5) a song, ending the antimasque; (6) start of the masque proper with
the entry of the grand masquers, dancing or riding on a festival cart, and their
descent to the floor; (7) another song; (8) the main dance of the masquers; (9) a

third song; (10) dancing with the spectators of the opposite sex ("revels"); (11) a fourth song; (12) the masquers' return to the cart or stage and final dance or chorus. Often the masque was followed by a banquet.

During the reigns of the first Stuart kings, James I (1603–25) and Charles I (1625–49), the masque was enriched by the talented court poet Ben Jonson, the gifted architect Inigo Jones, and several of the court lute composers, such as Robert Johnson, Alfonso Ferrabosco, and Thomas Campion. Masques were traditionally presented on certain holidays, such as Twelfth Night (i.e., Epiphany, January 6, as mentioned in the report of 1512) and Shrovetide (the last three days of carnival, immediately preceding Ash Wednesday), and to celebrate marriages, births, treaties, and important visits. At this same time, the increased political content of court masques was undoubtedly due to the difficult position of the Stuart kings.

James Stuart was king of Scotland when Queen Elizabeth of England died childless in 1603. His claim to the English throne derived from the fact that an aunt of Queen Elizabeth (Margaret Tudor, sister of Elizabeth's father, Henry VIII) was the paternal grandmother of James's mother, Mary Queen of Scots, whom Elizabeth had put to death. As king of Scotland, James strove to consolidate the power of the crown at the expense of the feudal lords. He had little understanding of the role played by Parliament, and he tried to promulgate an absolutist doctrine whereby all political rights were granted by and could be revoked by the king. He dissolved Parliament in 1611 when it refused to fund his extravagant expenditures, forcing him to adopt unpopular fiscal expedients. James's son Charles followed closely the policies of his father, and to an even greater extent, he used the masque for political purposes, as a concrete example will illustrate.

The masque *Britannia triumphans* was presented by King Charles I to the royal court and the ambassadors from Spain and France on the first Sunday after Twelfth Night, January 7, 1638. The text was by William Davenant, Ben Jonson's successor as poet-laureate. Scenes and costumes were as usual designed by Inigo Jones, Surveyor of the King's Works. The music was composed by William Lawes (1602–1645), a longtime member of Charles's household and today considered the leading English composer of dramatic music before Purcell. The masque was performed in a new, specially built hall (112 feet long, 57 feet wide, 59 feet high) in Whitehall Palace.

"The Subject of This Masque" is stated in the libretto as follows: "Britanocles [meaning "Glory of Britain," as Heracles, or Hercules, means "Glory of Hera"], the glory of the western world hath by his wisdom, valour, and piety, not only vindicated his own, but far distant seas, infested with pirates, and reduc'ed the land, by his example, to a real knowledge of all good arts and sciences."

A raised stage was erected at one end of the hall, decorated by the allegorical figures of "Naval Victory" and "Right Government" and by the inscription *Virtutis Opus* ("the work of virtue").

A curtain flies up to expose a scene representing "all Great Britain" (Fig. 7-2). The allegorical personages of Action and Imposture, in Puritan dress, come on stage.

Figure 7-2. The scene of
"all Great Britain" by
Inigo Jones for *Britannia
triumphans* (1638)

Action accuses Imposture of imputing a tyrannous intent to God by his attempts to banish dance, music, perfume, and brightly colored clothing in the name of God's word. Imposture claims to have more followers than "these mighty lords of reason" have.

Merlin, the sorcerer at the legendary court of King Arthur, enters, and Imposture asks him to show how little Action's "small and neglected stock of wisdom" has prevailed on earth. Merlin conjures up an inferno (Fig. 7-3) containing "the great seducers of this Isle" who strove to increase the population of hell. These are represented in six French-style "entries" ("antimasques") of costumed dancers: mock musicians, a ballad singer with servants, dishonest tradesmen, charlatans, "old-fashioned parasitical courtiers," and "rebellious leaders in war" (Fig. 7-4). Afterward, Merlin conjures up the personages of a "Mock Romanza": a dwarf, a damsel, a squire, a knight, and a giant (Fig. 7-5). As the giant and knight prepare to fight, Merlin changes their combat into dancing, and they depart. The scene changes to the Palace of Fame (Fig. 7-6). The allegorical personification of Fame sings "Breake forth!" When the grand masquers come on stage, one sees that they are actually members of the royal family with their intimate friends and counselors. The gate of the palace opens to reveal Britanocles, who is played by King Charles (Fig. 7-7). The chorus of

Figure 7-3. The scene of hell
designed by Inigo Jones for
Britannia triumphans (1638)

Figure 7-4. Sketches by Inigo Jones for *Britannia triumphans* (1638), showing some of the antimasquers from hell

[ancient] poets sings "Britanocles, the great and good appears" (W. 11a) to a courante rhythm, which implies that it was accompanied by dancing. Fame sings "Why move these princes of his train so slow" (W. 11b) as a declamatory ayre, approaching recitative style, followed by a brief italianate aria, marked "ciacona." This is followed by a brief chorus (W. 11c) beckoning the grand masquers, who descend to the floor. The scene returns to that of Britain. Additional masquers dance their entry. A chorus of modern poets, raised by Merlin, sings the praises of the queen.

The scene changes to a seascape (Fig. 7-8). The mythical sea nymph Galatea arrives on a dolphin, probably during the introductory "simfony," and sings, "Soe well Britanocles o'er seas doth Raigne" in two declamatory ayres alternating with ensemble passages (W. 11d). Some ships sail into the harbor, moving about on stage, as the masquers dance with the spectators. The masquers are called back to the stage by "The Valediction" (W. 11e), which wishes the king ever more blessings and bids the company go to bed.

Much of this masque alludes to current events and the political ideology of King Charles I. The antimasque ridicules the Puritans, who hoped to purify the Church of England of remnants of Roman Catholicism. Strict in their observance of the Sabbath and in their hostility to the arts, they sought through church reform to make their severe lifestyle the pattern for the whole nation. Although James I was a Calvinist, he proved no friend to the Puritans, who were generally parliamentarian rather than royalist in their politics. In

Figure 7-5. Designs by Inigo Jones for the second set of antimasquers in *Britannia triumphans* (1638): the damsel, knight, squire, dwarf, and giant of "The Mock Romanza"

1618 the enforced reading from pulpits of James's *Book of Sports*, dealing with recreations permissible on Sundays, was an affront to the Puritans. When the Puritan William Prynne published his attack on the theater entitled *Histrio-Mastix; or, The Scourge of Players* (1633), in which he called women actors "notorious whores," he was convicted of treason, fined five thousand pounds, had both his ears cut off, and was imprisoned for life. In reaction to persecutions like these, Separatist groups of Puritans had already fled to Holland and to Plymouth Colony in America on the Mayflower in 1620.

In effect, Merlin's two apparitions portray the lower classes as heedless of wisdom and the old nobility as ridiculous. The caricatures of these two groups, which represent democracy and feudalism, reduce to triviality the alternatives to absolute monarchy. They are easily dispelled by the arrival of Britanocles and his courtiers, the grand masquers.

The allegorical figure of Naval Victory, the reference to King Charles's naval exploits in the introduction to the libretto and the maritime scene with Galatea, who sings that the king rules over the seas, also refer to current events. In the previous year the king had proclaimed himself "sovereign of the seas," and he sought to exact a tribute from anyone engaged in shipping or fishing in the North Sea. This proclamation was at the root of the ongoing dispute between King Charles and Parliament over taxes for the navy ("Ship Money") that the king had been collecting since 1634. These taxes were widely viewed as unconstitutional because they were not approved by Parliament. Charles's

Figure 7-6. Design for the Palace of Fame in *Britannia triumphans* (1638) by Inigo Jones

Figure 7-7. King Charles I as Britanocles in *Britannia triumphans* (1638), design by Inigo Jones

Figure 7-8. Seascape by Inigo Jones for *Britannia triumphans* (1638)

claim of maritime sovereignty was challenged by the powerful navies of Holland and France, against which Charles had been preparing for war with his Ship Money for several years.

Clearly *Britannia triumphans* was conceived to justify Charles's actions and to assure his courtiers that, despite the rebellious spirit of the times, the king in his "secret wisdome" would combat the forces of evil, restore order, and bring about a lasting peace in the region. But by 1638 Archbishop Laud's campaign to root out nonconformity and impose high church orthodoxy in the Church of England was becoming ever more unpopular with the citizens. The Puritans considered it blasphemy that *Britannia triumphans* was staged on a Sunday, and they would not forget the ridicule it heaped upon them. As late as 1698, Jeremy Collier dedicated nineteen pages of his *The Stage Condemn'd* to denouncing *Britannia triumphans.* The production of this masque was one of the provocations that led to the Civil War.

MUSIC, THE ENGLISH CIVIL WAR, AND COMMONWEALTH

As we have seen, the first two Stuart kings, James and Charles, experienced conflicts with an opposition that coalesced around Puritan religion and parliamentary politics.

The Puritans objected to royal patronage of the arts and support of the high-church policies of Archbishop Laud, who promoted ceremony over preaching, art and music in the churches, and the separation of the congregation from the communion table, all of which smacked of Roman Catholicism. Charles's attempt to introduce a new prayer book in Scotland caused a rebellion (The "Bishops' Wars") in 1639–40, which ended in his humiliation.

With Parliament, Charles I was caught in a squeeze between the costs of wars with France and Spain and a domestic economic crisis caused by bad harvests, dislocations in the cloth trade, and a plague. He tried the same avenues as his father, imposing taxes unilaterally and dissolving Parliament in 1629. When Charles was forced to reconvene it in 1640, Parliament ordered the arrest of Archbishop Laud and the Earl of Strafford, the commander in the Bishops' Wars. Strafford was executed for treason. As matters escalated, Charles sent his family out of the country, and he took refuge in York. Parliament raised its own militia. The Civil War began in 1642. By 1648 the English army rebelled at the bloodshed, marched on London, purged the House of Commons of all but a few members, who were forced to do the army's bidding, and put the king on trial for treason.

On January 30, 1649, King Charles I of England was beheaded in front of his palace. By 1651 the remaining royalist forces were defeated, the king's son Charles II escaped to France, and the army was under the control of Oliver Cromwell. A new constitution was written, and Cromwell, as Lord Protector, ruled the English Commonwealth until his death in 1658. Anarchy reigned after Cromwell's death until the strongest of the various warring military factions engineered the return of Charles II and the Restoration of the British monarchy in 1660.

The Civil War had major consequences for the history of music. When Charles I fled to York in 1642, the hundred or so musicians of the royal household lost their positions. Most had not been paid for several years. Some went abroad, and some found other employment. William Lawes joined the royalist army and was killed in battle. In 1642, Parliament closed all theaters and abolished all cathedral chapels. Under the pervasive Puritan influence, organs were listed among "superstitious monuments to be demolished" in 1644, and nearly all of them were. The anonymous author of *The Actor's Remonstrance or Complaint* (1644) wrote, "Our Musike that was held so delectable and precious now wander with their instruments under their cloaks, I meane such as that have any, into all houses of good fellowship, saluting every roome where is company with *Will you have any musike Gentlemen?*"

Only a few remnants of court music remained during the Commonwealth period. One important masque was performed for the Portuguese ambassador in 1653 at a military compound—*Cupid and Death* with music by Matthew Locke (ca. 1621–1677) and Christopher Gibbons (1615–1676). William Davenant, the librettist of *Britannia triumphans*, deeply in debt when he was released from the Tower of London in 1654, sought to raise money by staging plays and musical spectacles in his house. The most important of the works he produced was *The Siege of Rhodes* (1656/59), a masque with features of both Italian opera (recitative) and French court ballet (entries), with music by Henry Lawes (1596–1662), Henry Cooke (ca. 1615–72), and Matthew Locke. Small-scale masques continued to be produced in schools.

Because of Puritan dominance, music making in England during the Civil War and Commonwealth periods was centered mostly in private homes and was carried out on a small scale. Included were performances of private devotional music, such as Henry Lawes's *Choice Psalms* (1648) for three voices and continuo and Walter Porter's Italian-style *Mottets of Two Voyces* (1657). The music publisher John Playford actually profited from these conditions, bringing out dozens of collections of music for lyra viol, cittern and gittern, and three-part viol consort, as well as rounds and catches, country dances, continuo songs and dialogues, Latin motets, violin tunes, psalms, and recorder music. The shift to domestic music also stimulated the manufacturing of instruments, especially virginals.

In spite of this activity, the Civil War and Commonwealth brought the development of musical styles and genres almost to a halt in England. The exile of Charles II and of many of his musicians to France sowed the seeds for new influences and directions that would make music in England vastly different after the Restoration of the monarchy in 1660.

BIBLIOGRAPHICAL NOTES

Instrumental Ensemble Music in England
    Peter Holman, *Four and Twenty Fiddlers: The Violin at the English Court, 1540–1690* (Oxford: Clarendon Press, 1993), presents an outstanding overview as well as the results of important new research. The basic book on the viol family is Ian Woodfield, *The Early History of the Viol* (Cambridge: Cambridge University Press, 1984). English viol consort music is surveyed in Christopher D. S. Field, "Consort Music, I, Up to 1660," *The Blackwell History of Music in Britain*, III, *The Seventeenth Century*,

ed. Ian Spink (Oxford: Blackwell, 1992), pp. 245–81. The historical and theoretical background to John Jenkins's chromatic viol fantasy and similar contemporary English works is explored by Christopher D. S. Field, "Jenkins and the Cosmography of Harmony," *John Jenkins and His Time: Studies in English Consort Music*, ed. Andrew Ashbee and Peter Holman (Oxford: Clarendon Press, 1996), pp. 1–74; the other essays in the same volume form a further resource for the study of English consort music of this period. A selection of music for mixed consort is *Musica Britannica*, 40, *Music for Mixed Consort*, ed. Warwick Edwards (London: Stainer and Bell, 1977). The fantasia-suite is surveyed in Jane Troy Johnson, "The English Fantasia-Suite, ca. 1620–1660," Ph.D. diss., Univ. Of California, Berkeley, 1971. A detailed study of English waits is George Arthur Stephen, *The Waits of the City of Norwich through Four Centuries to 1790* (Norwich: Goose, 1933).

Lute and Harpsichord

An outstanding general survey of Elizabethan lute music is John M. Ward, *Music for Elizabethan Lutes*, 2 vols (Oxford: Clarendon Press, 1992). The succeeding period is treated in Matthew George Spring, "The Lute in England and Scotland after the Gold Age, 1620–1750," Ph.D. diss., Oxford Univ., 1987. The standard work on the leading English lutenist of this period is Diana Poulton, *John Dowland*, new rev. ed. (London: Faber, 1982). The classic study of Elizabethan virginal music is Charles Van den Borren, *The Sources of Keyboard Music in England*, trans. James E. Matthew (London: Novello, 1913; and various reprints). A more recent but less specialized survey is John Caldwell, *English Keyboard Music before the Nineteenth Century* (Oxford: Blackwell, 1973). Two specialized studies of later repertoires are Barry Cooper, *English Solo Keyboard Music of the Middle and Late Baroque* (New York: Garland, 1989), and Candace Lea Bailey, "English Keyboard Music, ca. 1625–1680," Ph.D. diss., Duke Univ., 1993. The fascinating tale of the Hunt's Up is told by John M. Ward, "The Hunt's Up," *Proceedings of the Royal Musical Association*, 106 (1980), 1–25. The most recent of several important books on the broadside ballad is Claude M. Simpson, *The British Broadside Ballad and Its Music* (New Brunswick, NJ: Rutgers University Press, 1966). One of the most important keyboard composers introduced in this chapter is the subject of Denis Stevens, *Thomas Tomkins*, (London: Macmillan, 1957; repr. New York: Dover, 1967).

Church Music under the Stuart Kings

A standard study with a broad scope is Peter le Huray, *Music and the Reformation in England, 1549–1660* (London: Jenkins, 1967; repr. Oxford: Oxford Univ. Press, 1967; repr. Cambridge: Cambridge University Press, 1978, 1979, 1989). A more specialized book with more emphasis on musical style is Peter Phillips, *English Sacred Music, 1549–1649* (Oxford: Gimell, 1991). A useful study of a major figure is John Harley, *Orlando Gibbons and the Gibbons Family of Musicians* (Aldershot: Ashgate, 1999). A more specific study is Mark Ellis, *Gibbons: Anthems*, Mayflower Study Guides, 6 (Leeds: Mayflower, 1984).

Madrigals, Ayres, and Songs

A general study of English vocal music that includes the early seventeenth century is Winifred Maynard, *Elizabethan Lyric Poetry and Its Music* (Oxford: Clarendon Press, 1986). A complementary study of later repertoire is Elise Bickford Jorgens, *The Well-Tun'd World: Musical Interpretations of English Poetry, 1597–1651* (Minneapolis: University of Minnesota Press, 1982). An impressive study of the consort song is Craig Monson, *Voices and Viols in England, 1600–1650: The Sources and the Music* (Ann Arbor: UMI Research Press, 1982). The most comprehensive study of English lute and continuo songs of the seventeenth century remains Ian Spink, *English Song, Dowland to Purcell* (London: Batsford, 1974; repr. 1986).

The Stuart Masque

A recent survey of this subject is Jerzy Limon, *The Masque of Stuart Culture* (Newark: University of Delaware Press, 1990). Two seminal studies that emphasize the political aspects of the Stuart masque are Stephen Kitay Orgel and Roy C. Strong, *Inigo Jones: The Theatre of the Stuart Court* (London: Sotheby Parke Bernet, 1973), and Orgel, *The Illusion of Power: Political Theater in the English Renaissance* (Berkeley: University of California Press, 1975). A new collection of essays on the political aspects of Stuart theater is *Theatre and Government under the Early Stuarts* (Cambridge: Cambridge University Press, 1993). An excellent study of the music is Peter Walls, *Music in the English Courtly Masque, 1604–1640* (Oxford: Clarendon Press, 1996). The full text, music, and designs for *Britannia triumphans* are collected in Murray Lefkowitz, *Trois Masques a la cour de Charles Ier d'Angleterre* (Paris: Éditions du Centre National de la Recherche Scientifique, 1970). A large anthology of masque music is *Four Hundred Songs and Dances for the Stuart Masque*, ed. Andrew J. Sabol (Providence: Brown University Press, 1978). For music in Shakespeare's plays, see Frederick William Sternfeld, *Music in Shakespearean Tragedy*, 2nd ed. (London: Routledge, 1967), and John H. Long, *Shakespeare's Use of Music* (Gainesville: University of Florida Press, 1955).

Music, the English Civil War, and Commonwealth

The best account of England during the reigns of the early Stuarts is Derek Hirst, *Authority and Conflict: England, 1603–1658*, New History of England, 4 (London: E. Arnold, 1986; Cambridge, MA: Harvard University Press, 1986). An excellent study of court culture is G. E. Aylmer, *The King's Servants: The Civil Service of Charles I, 1625–1642*, 2nd ed. (London: Routledge, 1974). A comprehensive account of the social history of music in early Stuart England is Walter L. Woodfill, *Musicians in English Society from Elizabeth to Charles I*, Princeton Studies in History, 9 (Princeton: Princeton University Press; repr. New York: Da Capo Press, 1969). An illuminating musical biography of this period is Murray Lefkowitz, *William Lawes* (London: Routledge, 1960).

CHAPTER 8

The Diffusion of New Vocal Genres for Theater, Chamber, and Church in Italy, 1635–1680

THE SPREAD OF OPERA FROM ROME

U p to this point, the composers and performers discussed have almost all been salaried dependents of a noble court or household, members of a church choir or chapel, or both, and their work served the purposes of their employers. The main exception is the ensemble instrumentalists employed by a city or organized into companies in search of engagements.

Because of surviving correspondence, we know that highly talented musicians with rare abilities were sometimes recruited eagerly by agents of noble courts, but that at other times a court position was given out of the patron's sense of class obligation. At the outset of their training, most musicians probably hoped to become highly paid and in demand. In reality they could see that typical salaries hovered just above the subsistence level, and the supposed lifetime security of court service could vanish in an instant. Even a celebrity such as Claudio Monteverdi at the height of his career was dismissed from the Mantua court without warning at the death of Duke Vincenzo Gonzaga and the succession of his son Francesco in 1612. He remained unemployed for about a year until 1613, when he was chosen as the new *maestro di cappella* for St. Mark's in Venice. In the case of either the famous star or the ordinary musician given patronage out of a sense of obligation, it can be assumed that a musician was not only pulled by demand but also pushed by his or her desire to make music. After all, many noble men and women studied and performed music without any expectation of payment.

This desire to make music appears to be especially prominent in the spread of opera from Rome to other parts of Italy and northern Europe. An important mechanism in this spread was the formation of itinerant companies of opera performers, both singers and instrumentalists, during the years from 1630 to 1660. These itinerant companies apparently took the initiative in the diffusion of opera. Although they usually included performers from various cities, many of their leaders and other key members were born or trained in Rome, especially during the earlier years of this period. Monteverdi notes the presence of such a group in Parma in 1628. In making their way from city to city up and down the Italian peninsula, these performers followed in the footsteps of the itinerant troops of actors—performers of traditional, semi-improvised *commedia dell'arte.*

An important leader of an early band of theater musicians was Francesco Manelli (ca. 1595/97–1667), who toured with his Roman wife, Maddalena, a singer. At Padua in 1636, the Manellis presented a musical drama that preceded a choreographed joust: *L'Ermiona* with music by the Roman composer Giovanni Felice Sances (ca. 1600–1679), who, in 1649, became assistant Imperial *Kapellmeister*, eventually writing operas for Vienna and Prague. Together with another singer in the Padua production, the Roman-trained composer/librettist/comedian Benedetto Ferrari (1603/04–1681), Manelli produced his operas *Andromeda* and *La maga fulminata* at Venice in each of the following two years, 1637 and 1638, in a rented theater—Teatro S. Cassiano, owned by the Tron family—which was otherwise used for *commedia dell'arte.* The libretti, written by Ferrari, clearly state that the productions were "done entirely at their own expense" and "with his money, aided by five fellow musicians." It is understood that the performers needed to recover their expenses by charging for admission.

During the next twenty years, elements of this troupe and several others like it, often generically called *Febiarmonici* ("Musicians of Apollo"), brought opera productions to virtually every major city of Italy, from Milan in the north to Naples in the south. In many cases they were aided by a local noble who furnished his own or a rented theater out of artistic interest at times mixed with the desire to meet attractive female singers. In some cases, the traveling company contracted with a local association of aristocrats, usually called an *accademia* ("academy"), that owned a theater. In a few cases, a ruling court provided the aegis for the company's productions.

If any of the sponsors or the musicians themselves thought that opera production would be profitable, they soon learned that it would not. Finances were almost always precarious, and the specter of bankruptcy lurked constantly. As might be expected, the itinerant companies tended to perform operas tailored to a tight budget and calculated to draw audiences. This gave rise to a new kind of opera, different from the court operas of Florence, Mantua, and Rome in the following respects:

- Reduced number of roles
- Reduced number of choruses
- Restricted accompanying ensemble, often two violins, or five strings, and continuo group
- Stock scenery with less elaborate machinery
- Expanded range of libretto subjects covering a large range of the types of *commedia dell'arte* scenario, including the comic, tragic, pastoral, heroic, mythological, Spanish, adventurous, historical or pseudo-historical, and magical—and mixtures among these.
- Expanded number and length of arias, usually in $\frac{3}{2}$ meter and featuring broader melodic contours and emotional expression

- Reduced importance given to recitative
- Scenes in which recitative, arioso, and aria styles mix freely
- Repetition and revival of operas in the repertoire of a company and the acquisition of scores by indirect means, with adaptations and changes constantly made in response to circumstances

VENETIAN THEATERS

The city where the Febiarmonici found the most fertile ground in which to transplant opera was Venice. This city already had several established *commedia dell'arte* theaters, which were supported by local aristocrats and well-to-do visitors. The Venetian population included an unusually large proportion of nobles, who, unlike their counterparts in most parts of Europe, engaged in trade and commerce and therefore had significant disposable income. Visitors came to Venice for the famous Carnival celebrations, which lasted for the six to ten weeks from the feast of St. Stephen (December 26) to the day before the start of Lent (Shrove Tuesday or Mardi Gras).

One reason for the high level of theatrical activity and the exuberance of the Carnival celebration was the relative liberality of laws and customs in Venice. The Inquisition had little power there, and papal authority was weak or absent during parts of the seventeenth century. During Carnival the visitors to Venice were almost as numerous as the local population, and this, too, contributed to a general licentiousness.

For their third season in Venice, 1639, Ferrari and Manelli moved to another *commedia dell'arte* theater, Teatro SS. Giovanni e Paolo, owned by the Grimani family and modified for opera. The Teatro S. Cassiano was taken over by a competing company of Venetian musicians headed by Francesco Cavalli (1602–1676), a student of Monteverdi who was named organist at St. Mark's basilica the day before the premier of his first opera, *Le nozze di Teti e di Peleo* (1639). Thus began an unbroken string of opera seasons, extending for at least a century, in which operas by local composers were performed in Venice, where sometimes as many as six opera theaters competed for audiences during a single season. Cavalli composed about thirty operas over the following thirty-four years. His operas and those of his Venetian colleagues soon came to dominate the repertoire of traveling opera companies all over Italy.

In keeping with the practice of the traveling companies, Cavalli and several of his collaborators were at first the principal investors in and organizers of their productions. By the 1650s, however, Cavalli and other musicians seem to have relinquished this role to professional impresarios, who were often librettists with a background in business or law. The impresario rented a theater for an entire carnival season. He contracted with the singers, instrumentalists, dancers, designers, painters, costumers, stage crew, and composer, and paid such expenses as candles for illumination. He rented out boxes by the season, but box holders as well as the audience seated on the benches had to pay admission each evening. The librettist (if he was not the impresario) paid for printing copies of the libretti, but he kept the receipts from their sale.

Although paid admission hypothetically opened opera attendance to all members of the general public, in practice opera in Venice and in the other cities visited by the traveling companies was only slightly more public than court opera, as we can deduce from surviving financial accounts. For instance, Cavalli's opera *Antioco* had a run of 24 performances at the Teatro S. Cassiano between January 25 and February 24, 1659. The average attendance was 272, of which 85 sat on the benches and 187 in boxes. Given the fact that box holders typically saw the opera more than once, the total number of people who saw the opera was probably significantly less than 6,521. In Venice at this time there were about 3,844 adult nobles, 5,450 adult non-noble property owners, 70,860 adult artisans and shopkeepers, 4,643 clergy, and 4,870 Jews. The visitors to Venice during Carnival numbered in the tens of thousands, and all but their servants had significant disposable income. The minimum price of admission was more than a day's wages of a better paid workman, and boxes cost many times that amount. Therefore, the audience at a Venetian opera must have consisted entirely of members of the nobility or the wealthier part of the property-owning class. Although two noblemen paid a quarter of the star singer's salary for *Antioco,* double the composer's share, ticket sales fell far short of expenses.

Opera theaters in Venice and in all the other cities to which the traveling companies brought opera were, for the most part, either originally comedy theaters, or modeled on comedy theaters. They had an oval or horseshoe-shaped floor plan, and their walls were formed by several tiers of boxes extending to the stage (see Fig. 8-1).

A new system of theater architecture was invented by Giacomo Torelli for the Teatro Novissimo, which opened in 1641 in Venice. Torelli placed scenery flats in parallel slots on the two sides of the stage, which, along with a central backdrop, could be changed by drawing back one set to reveal another. This design resulted in the symmetrical layout and central vanishing point typical of seventeenth-century Italian stage design (see Fig. 8-2).

The Teatro Novissimo was built and run by a group of Venetian noblemen who were members of the Accademia degli Incogniti ("Academy of the Unknowns"), a literary society whose members exerted significant influence on public policy and government in mid-seventeenth-century Venice. In their philosophical writings, the libertine intellectuals of this academy pretended to praise vice and deceit out of a pervasive philosophical skepticism and distrust of all political, moral, rational, and religious authority. Their libretti tend at times to reflect this pessimistic amorality, while at other times they promote the glory of Venice.

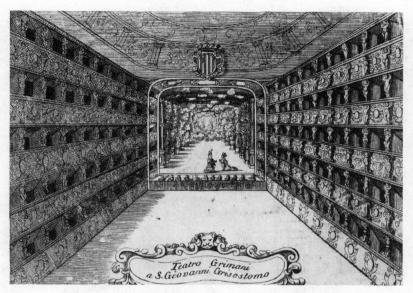

Figure 8-1. Teatro S. Giovanni Grisostomo, built in 1678

INCOGNITI OPERAS

Members of the Accademia degli Incogniti provided Claudio Monteverdi with the libretti for his two surviving Venetian operas, *Il ritorno d'Ulisse in patria* ("The Return of Ulysses to His Homeland") of 1640 and *L'incoronazione di Poppea* ("The Coronation of Poppea") of 1642.

In the Prologue to *Il ritorno d'Ulisse in patria,* Time, Love, Fortune, and Human Frailty come to the conclusion that mortals are frail, wretched, and distressed, and the plot illustrates this. Penelope, awaiting the return of Ulysses from his voyages, blames her husband for abandoning her. Melanto, her lady-in-waiting, tries to convince her to accept one of her new suitors, among whom is Eurymachus, Melanto's own secret lover. Zeus persuades Poseidon to give up his quarrel with Ulysses and let him return home. Ulysses reveals to the goddess Athena that he must wander to escape punishment for a murder he committed. Athena arranges Ulysses's return through her magic because she is grateful for the sack of Troy. Penelope, meanwhile, rejects new suitors not out of loyalty to Ulysses, whom she believes is dead, but out of bitterness and disenchantment with love. Ulysses returns home disguised through Athena's magic as an old beggar. Finally Penelope agrees to marry the suitor who can bend Ulysses's bow. Only Ulysses, still disguised as a beggar, can do this, and with the bow he shoots and kills the other suitors. Penelope is still reluctant to accept him, and even when he resumes his real form she thinks it is a trick of the gods' magic.

Figure 8-2. Giacomo Torelli's stage set for *Venere gelosa* (1643): palace courtyard of the King of Nasso, for the Teatro Novissimo of Venice

Ulysses finally convinces her by describing her silk bedspread, which no one but he has ever seen. The point of the story is that the human characters are petty and fickle, and every turn of events is contrived by the gods.

Monteverdi's music enters into the skeptical and ironic tone of the libretto through the use of satire. An example is the lament (W. 12) for the dead suitors sung at the beginning of Act III by Iro, designated in the libretto as a *parte ridicola* ("comical role"), made into a pathetic stutterer by Monteverdi's music: "Oh grief, oh torment, that saddens the soul! Oh sad memory of a sorrowful sight! I saw the dead suitors. The suitors (*proci*) were killed. The swine (*porci*) were killed. Ah, ah, ah, ah, ah, I have lost my appetite. Who will help the hungry man, who will console him?" He continues to complain about his hunger for the rest of the long lament. Monteverdi begins by sustaining the first exclamation, "oh," for nine whole notes with the bass marking time in eighths, after which Iro requires a new breath. "Oh sad memory of a sorrowful sight!" is set with incongruous frivolity to very rapid notes on one pitch. A high *g'* misplaces the accent in "*I* saw the dead suitors." The repeats of "ah" are excessive, as are the pauses in "Who . . . will help . . . the hungry man?" Later, Iro predicts,

"You will not find anyone who laughs," which he illustrates with a *trillo* annotated by Monteverdi:"Here he lapses into a natural laugh."The music embraces a fluid mixture of expressive recitative, arioso, and aria style typical of mid-century opera.

The fact that *L'incoronazione di Poppea* is based on a historical figure (Emperor Nero) rather than a mythical one (Ulysses) is of little consequence. The underlying themes of frailty and immorality are the same. The libretto by Giovanni Francesco Busenello, an Incognito, tells the story of Poppea's seduction of Nero and abandonment of her lover Ottone, of Empress Ottavia's use of blackmail to procure the murder of Poppea, of the foolish philosopher Seneca's obedient suicide and his disciples' subsequent rejoicing, and of Poppea's manipulation of Nero's love to persuade him to murder his wife, Ottavia, and crown her empress. The plot demonstrates once again the truth of what is said in the prologue, this time by Fortune and Virtue: "There is no human or divine heart that dares to do battle against Love."

Ottone's opening monologue (W. 13) is a naive and idealistic expression of love set to four rhapsodic strophic variations over a walking bass, interrupted once and followed by expressions of sincerity in a naturalistic recitative style. This scene is followed, in an abrupt inversion of theme typical of mid-century opera, by the bitter complaints and wry observations of two low-life sentinels, who fill in plot background while cursing love, Poppea, Nero, Rome, and the army in rapid exchanges sprinkled with comical word painting. The third scene shifts back to the theme of love, but with a cynical twist: saying farewell at dawn to her lover Nero, who leaves two steps ahead of Ottone's return home, Poppea pleads in expressive recitative for his promise to return soon. Nero answers her at first in an off-hand, sing-song aria style until, giving in to Poppea's insistence, he mimics her recitational music. The fourth scene is again comic and satirical. It brings on another character, like the sentinel, from the *commedia dell'arte*—Arnalta, the old nursemaid, who, following tradition, gives frank advice in another set of strophic variations based on her background as a retired courtesan: "You are quite mad if you believe that you can trust in a blind boy [Cupid] and a bald woman [Fortune]." Empress Ottavia has her own aging confidant who advises in Scene 5, "If Nero has lost his senses in his enjoyment of Poppea, choose someone who is happy to embrace you." In all five scenes the most sincere, intimate, and spontaneous expressions are set to recitative, while aria style tends to be used for insincere or sarcastic formulas. Aside from the strophic variations, which are more recitational than songlike, the aria passages in *L'incoronazione di Poppea* tend to be brief and continuous with surrounding recitative.

Monteverdi's Venetian libretti were very much of their time, but his use of recitative for the most expressive moments and his scenes that flow quickly between recitative, aria, and the grey areas in between may be considered a bit old-fashioned by 1642, when the composer was seventy-five years old. On the other hand, the clearer separation of recitative and aria, in form and function, and the delineation of standard types of aria make Francesco Cavalli's *Giasone*

("Jason," 1649; A. 66a–e) a more typical representative of mid-seventeenth-century Venetian opera, and its enduring popularity with touring companies made it a model for Italian opera for forty years, through at least twenty revivals and transformations.

The librettist for *Giasone* was another Incognito, Giacinto Andrea Cicognini (1606–1651), who took to heart the advice given his father, Jacopo, by the Spanish playwright Lope de Vega to abandon the classic unities of time, place, and action, and to allow the story to be told in disconnected episodes, in which characters of both high and low station mix freely. In this respect and on account of his radical revision of the tragic myth of Jason and Medea, Cicognini confessed in his preface to *Giasone,* "I write out of mere caprice, and this caprice of mine has no other aim than to delight."

The Prologue of Cavalli's *Giasone* is a dialogue between the Sun (Apollo, grandfather of Medea) and Love (Amore). The Sun claims that Fate has decreed that Jason (Giasone) will capture the Golden Fleece and marry his secret lover, Medea, Queen of Colchis and guardian of the fleece. Love objects that a marriage cannot take place without his permission. The ensuing story will test which is stronger, Fate or Love.

Act I. In a castle garden at Colchis, Hercules (Ercole) complains that Giasone, having spent a year with Queen Hypsiplyle (Isifile) of Lemnos, who bore him twins, has now fathered a second set of twins with an unknown lady who turns out to be Queen Medea. She leaves her former lover, King Aegeus (Egeo) of Athens, and laughs when he begs her to stab him to death. Orestes (Oreste) has been sent by Isifile to retrieve Giasone, but Demo, Egeo's stuttering, hunch-backed dwarf, tells Oreste that Giasone loves another woman. On the advice of her nursemaid, Medea reveals her identity to Giasone, who vows to marry her. Isifile arrives, having fled a revolution in Lemnos, to seek Giasone herself. Medea, to hold him, conjures up Volano from the Inferno, who brings a ring that will help Giasone get the Golden Fleece (A. 66a).

Act II. Aided by Volano's magic ring, Giasone seizes the Golden Fleece and flees in his ship with Medea. Egeo and Demo pursue him. In the cavern of Eolo, Jove (Giove) asks Eolo, the god of the winds, to take revenge for the theft of the fleece from his altar by sinking the Argonauts' ship. But Amore tricks Eolo into blowing Giasone's ship back to Isifile, sinking Demo's boat instead. Besso, the captain of Giasone's soldiers, connects with Isifile's maid, Alinda (A. 66b).

Act III. In a forest, Giasone and Medea fall asleep together (A. 66c). When Isifile discovers them, Giasone falsely promises to return to her. Medea orders Giasone to murder Isifile (conclusion of A. 66c). Her jealousy is ridiculed by the nursemaid Delfa (A. 66d). Giasone gives the job of killing Isifile to Besso, telling him a secret code word by which his victim will identify herself. By accident, Medea says the secret word and is thrown into the sea. However, Egeo saves her, in gratitude for which Medea marries him. Isifile, feeling disgraced, asks Giasone to kill her, but Giasone, shamed and touched by her moving lament, accepts her as his wife (A. 66e).

VENETIAN OPERA CONVENTIONS

The rambling and improbable plot of Cavalli's *Giasone* creates a large number of contrasting episodes, within which there is room for a virtual compendium of distinct types of aria and scene that were becoming standard conventions in Italian opera.[1]

The Comic Aria

Usually arias of this type serve a realistic function—for example, drinking songs or lullabies—or they contain complaints or advice directed to the audience as well as to characters in the opera. The text is usually two or more stanzas of metrical verse set strophically and syllabically within a narrow range, with many repeated notes, homophonic texture, short, separated and repeated music phrases that parallel the phrases of the text, rhythms derived from the words, and exaggeration of text painting, contrasts, sequences, or repetition. Many arias of this kind include instrumental passages between vocal phrases to accompany comic stage business. "È follia" ("It is madness"), sung by Medea's nursemaid Delfa in Act III, scene 10 (A. 66d), derives much of its humor from the intentionally awkward, rapid, patter delivery of its words to a mechanical sequential pattern already over-elaborated in the introduction. This forced pace is broken in the middle for mock reflection in a recitational style. The text contains typically ribald advice to the heroine and audience: "If one day he enjoys two loves, then oh ladies, do this—enjoy three in less than an hour!"

The Trumpet Aria

Arias of this type can be either comic or heroic; their identity as a type derives from their imitation of the idiom of the natural trumpet—arpeggios, fifths, the diatonic steps *ut* through *sol*, with an occasional raised fourth, and the anapest rhythms characteristic of fanfares. Like most arias of this type, Alinda's "Quanti soldati, ò quanti" ("How many, many soldiers"), Act II, scene 11 (A. 66b), takes its cue from the military motif of the text. This type of aria achieved great popularity during the last quarter of the seventeenth century. It is used in two places in *Giasone* even though in 1649 the trumpet was hardly established as an ensemble instrument in written music.

The Music Scene

As comic arias are often songs that would be sung in the analogous real-life situation, they are often found in scenes that are about music and singing. In a

---

[1] The following discussion is based on Ellen Rosand, *Opera in Seventeenth-Century Venice: The Creation of a Genre* (Berkeley and Los Angeles: University of California Press, 1991), pp. 275–76, 322–86.

continuation of Act II, scene 11, after "Quanti soldati, ò quanti," Alinda suddenly changes the subject after learning that Besso is a soldier but without scars or injuries: "Since you are whole, I want you whole. But how much more you would charm my heart if you were a good musician and a singer!" Besso claims that he is a singer, too—a soprano—although assuredly not a castrato. Actually, Besso is sung by a bass. Next comes a duet ("No more trumpets or drums! Love! Love!") with more trumpet music (A. 66b).

The Love Duet

Act II, scene 11 (A. 66b), is also a love scene culminating in a love duet. The convention here, as in *L'incoronazione di Poppea*, is that lovers united in sentiment should sing the same melodic material. And since the uniting of lovers is usually the goal of action, love duets more often than not mark musical and dramatic closure of a scene complex or act. Musical unity between the male and female characters is helped by the fact that both of them are usually portrayed by sopranos whose vocal lines, therefore, may wind around each other.

The Sleep Scene

This convention, taken over from the *commedia dell'arte*, facilitates sudden and surprising turns of plot because it makes the sleeper vulnerable to assassination, rape, unmasking, discovery, loss of self-control, and exposure of private thoughts. Sleep scenes often begin with a lullaby. Since sleep suspends action, it accommodates static musical numbers. There are five sleep scenes in *Giasone*. In Act I, scene 14, Isifile, dreaming, describes Giasone's departure from Corinth, a scene that took place before the events depicted in the opera; her sleep allows her servant Orestes to press his affections on her for the titillation of the audience. In Act III, scene 17, Egeo attempts to murder the sleeping Giasone. In Act III, scene 2 (A. 66c), Giasone and Medea lie down to sleep together. However, Medea only pretends to sleep, while Giasone, expecting to plant murderous thoughts in Medea's subconscious, pretends to declare his love for Isifile. Two of the sleep scenes involve a lullaby (II, 1 and III, 2). In the second of these (A. 66c), an abrupt harmonic shift in the recitative signals the onset of slumber, which is imitated in the drooping chromatic melody and long rests.

Invocation Scenes

In these, a character with magic powers calls upon supernatural forces, usually with spectacular scenic effects. The example in *Giasone*, the closing of Act I, is Medea's invocation of Volano who brings the magic ring for Giasone (A. 66a). Following a tradition already established in spoken drama, Cicognini provided Cavalli with an incantation consisting of short poetic lines with *sdrucciolo* ("sliding") endings — ∪ ∪, which are reflected in the rhythm ♩ ♪ ♪, highly characteristic of such scenes in Venetian and later opera. During this incantation, the orchestra pounds relentlessly on repeated chords to the rhythm ♩♩♩|♩ – – |, against which Medea's phrases overlap unpredictably. Medea's unusually wide vocal range throughout this scene and the unsettling harmonic juxtapositions in her recitative contribute to its powerful expression, reinforced by the conventional appearance of the chorus of infernal spirits, whose *sdrucciolo* verse endings are spit out aggressively in Cavalli's unusual and off-balance rhythmic diminutions:

Le mu-   ra si squar- ci- no
Let the walls collapse

Madness

Mad scenes were another convention taken into Venetian opera from the *commedia dell'arte*. Their appeal was that they could accommodate a wide variety of musical styles, since madness freed characters from the restrictions of normal behavior. In music as in speech, the portrayal of madness often involved deliberate breaking of rules and violations of customs, creating surprises and discontinuity, which were valued by the aesthetic of mid-seventeenth century arts. In *Giasone* no one actually goes mad, but Giasone convinces Medea that Isifile is mad in order to explain Isifile's rage. Cavalli's increasingly rapid and vehement recitative for Isifile concludes Act II (A. 66b).

The Lament

The earliest operatic laments, as found in *Euridice*, *Orfeo*, and *Arianna*, used expressive recitative. Although they sometimes preserve this tradition, early Venetian operas often introduce aria style into their laments. This is a harbinger of the shift in the focus of emotional expression from recitative to aria that was accomplished gradually in Italian opera during the second half of the seventeenth century. The use of aria style in a lament originates in Monteverdi's *Lamento della ninfa*, published in his Eighth Book of Madrigals (Venice, 1638), which introduced the descending ostinato bass figure covering the interval of a fourth, often described as a "descending tetrachord." Cavalli's repeated use of this convention in his later operas established its emblematic meaning of lamentation, which it retained for more than a hundred years afterward. In *Giasone*, the last of Isifile's three laments, "Regina, Egeo, amici" (in A. 66e) combines expressive recitative with an incomplete aria-like passage in the customary $\frac{3}{2}$ meter that employs a version of the descending tetrachord ostinato at three pitch levels (G–D, B♭–F, C–G) and its inverted, ascending form at two levels (G–C, C–F).

During the 1650s and 1660s the arias in Cavalli's operas tend to be longer, more expressive, and more prominent than they were in his earlier works. Arias with two strophes of text, both sung to the same music, become more common. In his later operas the scenes often conclude with an aria in place of the short arioso passage typically found in the earlier works.

VENETIAN ARIAS

The trend toward increasing the importance of arias appears more clearly in the operas of Antonio Cesti (1623–1669), the leading composer of Venetian-style operas in the generation after Cavalli. This trend can be seen, for example, in Cesti's *Orontea* of 1656.

Orontea begins Act I straightaway with an aria, instead of the conventional long recitative. In *Orontea*, nearly all of the emotional expression is found in the arias, not in the recitatives, which now function almost exclusively to advance the story through dialogue. The texts of the arias are now almost exclusively lyrical in nature—that is, the words express the feelings of the character but are not part of the action being portrayed and are generally not heard by other characters on stage.

The libretto of *Orontea* (by Cicognini, the poet of Cavalli's *Giasone*) was written with the clear distinction between recitative and aria in mind. As before, the recitative text is all in *versi sciolti* (unpredictable alternations of seven- and eleven-syllable lines with no pattern of rhyme), whereas the major arias are accommodated by canzonetta-style verses of fewer than eleven syllables with regular patterns of accentuation and rhyme. The older tendency, found in the operas of Monteverdi and Cavalli, for arias to conclude with a distinctive textual and musical tag, has developed by this point into a predilection to repeat the words and music of the second half of the aria, producing the first more-or-less standard aria form, ABB′, in which the B′ is usually a transposed or differently elaborated form of part B. The penchant toward two-strophe repetition of this ABB′ scheme, sometimes with embellishments, that emerges in Cavalli's later operas is already present in Cesti's *Orontea*.

These general features are illustrated in the conclusion of Act II (scenes 17 and 18) of Cesti's *Orontea* (A. 67). First we must summarize the complicated plot. The prologue once again is an argument in which Love promises to demonstrate his superiority, in this case over Philosophy. Queen Orontea, who initially boasts that she will never love, immediately falls for the painter Alidoro, who, however, lusts for Silandra, who reciprocates by dumping Corindo. It also turns out that Alidoro had another lover, Giacinta, who is pursuing him disguised as a man named Ismero. Giacinta's male disguise has the unintended effect of attracting the attentions of the ribald old nursemaid, Aristea. Consider, for the moment, that a male soprano probably sang the role of the woman Giacinta, who, dressed as a man, makes love with the old woman Aristea, sung by a male tenor. Venetian opera thrived on such sexual ambiguities. When Orontea confronts Alidoro over his affair with Silandra, he faints. In Act II, scenes 17–18, Orontea's love is rekindled as she views Alidoro unconscious, so she leaves him a forgiving love letter, which Alidoro reads upon awakening. In Act III, Alidoro opportunistically gets rid of Silandra. But after Orontea again turns to philosophy instead of him, Alidoro tries to get back with Silandra, who instead decides to return to Corindo. In the end, Orontea finds out that Alidoro is really the long-lost son of the King of Phoenicia, so she finds him to be a worthy groom. All of this is further enlivened by scenes featuring a comic drunkard and a martial arts aficionado.

The elevated role of the aria in Cesti's *Orontea* qualifies it as one of the first singer's operas. Indeed, Cesti himself was a famous and highly sought operatic tenor who frequently toured with traveling opera companies, even though he was a Franciscan friar during the early part of his career.

The leading seventeenth-century opera composers associated with Venice after Cesti were Giovanni Legrenzi (1626–1690), Antonio Sartorio (1630–1680), and Carlo Francesco Pollarolo (ca. 1653–1723). However, as opera theaters became better established in other Italian cities, several important composers fulfilled commissions outside of Venice, and we can distinguish local varieties of opera.

FLORENCE, NAPLES, GENOA

Traveling opera companies performing their increasingly Venetian repertoire made repeated visits to many Italian cities during the middle decades of the seventeenth century. Their activities in Florence and Naples spawned significant local traditions.

Although Florence was the birthplace of opera, performances there had become so rare since the late 1620s that the genre practically had to be imported from Venice in the 1650s. In 1645 Mattias de' Medici, a brother of Grand Duke Ferdinando II, had an opera theater constructed in the Tuscan city of Siena, of which he was governor, and he brought singers and operas from Venice to be heard there. In 1650, another brother, Giovanni Carlo, did something similar in Florence. He served as protector of the Accademia degli Immobili ("Academy of the Immovables"), an organization of noblemen that provided instruction in fencing, horsemanship, and dancing to its members' sons as well as sponsoring theatrical entertainment.

At Giovanni Carlo's command, the Immobili built a small opera theater in Via del Cocomero with just thirty-six boxes on two levels and a stage only twenty-five feet across, on advice of a contact in Venice, who reported that the Grimani theater with its four tiers of boxes was too large for the singers' voices. The small theater, however, did not allow enough room for elaborate scenery and stage machinery, so the Immobili had a second theater built, called the Pergola, which was inaugurated in 1657 with *Il potestà di Colognole* ("The Mayor of the Canaries") by the local composer Jacopo Melani (1623–1676), on a libretto by Giovanni Andrea Moniglia. This work and four other operas that Melani and Moniglia wrote for the Pergola theater are entirely comical in content, continuing the well-established tradition of *commedia dell'arte* and written plays that derive their humor from social satire and the use of rural and low-class dialects. In all, some forty-one similar operas were performed in Florence, including works by Domenico Anglesi (ca. 1610/15–1674) and Antonio Cesti from nearby Arezzo. Many of these were produced at the tiny Cocomero theater, which had been taken over by the less aristocratic Accademia dei Sorgenti ("Academy of the Resurgents") after it was abandoned by the Immobili.

At exactly the same time, 1650, another company of Febiarmonici began making annual visits to Naples, at the invitation of the Spanish viceroy there, the Count of Oñate, who had been Spanish ambassador in Rome during the 1630s, when the first traveling opera companies were being formed. Their first opera in Naples was Cavalli's *Didone*, which had been premiered in 1641 at Venice. By their fourth season in Naples, the Febiarmonici produced the first of a series of operas by the local composer Francesco Provenzale (1624–1704), and works by Francesco Cirillo (1623–1667) from nearby Aversa, and Giuseppe Alfiero (1630–1665) from Naples. The works of these three composers, especially their comic operas, are typical of early Neapolitan opera, featuring dance-like arias with a popular flavor.

Alessandro Stradella (1639–1682) composed three operas for Genoa and two or three for Rome, where he also wrote a large number of shorter stage works called serenades and many new prologues and revised scenes for revivals of earlier operas. Like Cesti, Stradella had a colorful career with its share of scandals and scrapes. Although he worked in the households of cardinals and royalty, including Queen Christina of Sweden after she abdicated, converted to Catholicism, and moved to Rome, Stradella also pursued an independent lifestyle based upon his private means and noble status. He was an important composer of oratorios and chamber cantatas, as we will see later. His operas, although few in number, were well known and influential.

Stradella's recitatives continue the trend away from expressivity; they are written largely in quarter notes and eighth notes, using mostly stepwise motion, without attempts to construct real melodic lines. Repetition is used only rarely to underscore dramatic effects. Sequences are almost never found. Cadences are reserved for only the most important punctuations of the text. Arioso can appear as a refrain within a recitative or as a connection at the end of a recitative to link it with the following aria, in which case it often is an extended passage marked by a change of meter and tempo.

The most common formal scheme in Stradella's arias is ABB', as in Cesti's operas. This is sometimes modified as ABCC. Binary form, AB or AABB, is also found. Further, ABA form is common, occasionally with contrast of tonality and of tempo in the B section. A few of Stradella's arias have refrains, ABABA or ABACA. Many arias with one of these formal designs have two strophes, but a small number have no repetition within strophes. Basso ostinato and domination of the melodic line by a single rhythmic motive are encountered frequently in Stradella's arias.

Like Cavalli's and most of Cesti's, all of Stradella's opera scores call for two violins and continuo. This ensemble is limited mostly to ritornelli before and after the arias. Although the singer in most cases is accompanied by continuo alone, composers began to use the violins along with the voice. Stradella's texture is typically more contrapuntal than that found in Venetian operas.

Comic effects in Stradella's *Il Trespolo tutore* (ca. 1677) include rapid recitative of the patter type and running eighth notes or square phrases in the arias. Each act concludes with an ensemble; the Act III ensemble has episodes in different meters and tempos.

Stradella's *Corispero*, apparently a later opera, calls for the full range of serious roles—a female soprano, female mezzo soprano, male soprano and alto, and bass—and comic roles—female alto, two tenors, and two basses. This gives ample opportunity for contrast between serious and comic styles. In this opera, ostinato figures in arias are transposed to various pitch levels, and in some arias, an ostinato-like motive is developed at different times in the bass, in the violin parts, and in the vocal line. One aria employs six different ostinato figures in the bass. The ostinato principle is found also in the insistent rhythmic figures that occur in the violin parts in several of these arias.

With *La forza dell'amor paterno* (1678) Stradella reached a new stage of development. The vocal parts are more integrated into the texture of the aria in two ways: The voice holds one note for several measures while the instruments play several phrases, or the voice and instruments engage in a rapid exchange of phrases. Both devices suggest an instrumental use of the voice. The texture is contrapuntal, but the material imitated is defined more rhythmically than melodically. Mechanically repeating motor rhythm is the dominant characteristic of the entire opera. The sequence is used as the principal means of extension of material. The aria form ABA displaces ABB′ as the most common, although the middle section is quite short in proportion to the outer sections. There are a few arias of greater length than any in preceding operas. Sometimes this effect of extension is achieved by giving the same singer two successive arias. Ostinato bass arias are still in abundance, with the same devices for variation used earlier. The comic scenes are not especially funny, merely simple and lyrical.

In *Moro per Amore*, probably Stradella's last opera, his harmonic style seems completely crystallized and rather rigidly consistent. All arias are clearly in a major or minor mode. Opening themes tend to outline the triad of the final tonic. The hierarchy of subordinate cadence points in major modes is, in order, the first, fifth, fourth, and sixth degrees. In minor modes, cadence points are the first, third, fifth, and fourth degrees. Consistent chord associations are maintained between recitatives and arias. Root progression by fifths is found in extended passages in the recitatives. ABA form now completely dominates in the arias. Many of the arias begin with a motto or device stated in the continuo, repeated by the voice, then taken up again by the continuo. Imitative counterpoint is the prevailing texture. Some arias have active bass parts unrelated thematically to the voice, exemplifying a new treble-bass polarity. The orchestra assumes a larger role in accompanying the arias, often playing a key role in underscoring the sense or expression of the text. A single expressive theme or rhythmic motive tends to provide material for elaboration by both voice and instruments throughout the aria. This theme or motive usually relates to the sense of the whole text, rather than to a single word or phrase to be underscored rhetorically, as in earlier operas.

An example of this expressive unity is provided by "Dimmi Amor che fia di me?" from Stradella's *Moro per Amore*, of ca. 1680 (A. 68). The energetic anapest rhythm (ᴗ ᴗ —) that dominates this aria, together with its rapid tempo, wide leaps, strong accents, insistent word repetition, and minor mode appears to be motivated by the overall thrust of the text, "Tell me, Cupid, what are you doing to me? In such cruel bondage I can endure no longer; my faith is under assault," with special reference to the military metaphor of assault. However, Stradella makes no attempt to react musically to the words "cruel," "bondage," "endure," or "faith," as a composer in the early and middle seventeenth century might have. Further, the ABA' form and the framing of the first question by instrumental ritornelli opens the way to a rhetorical organization or disposition: The instrumental introduction is like an exordium, in which the composer vies for the listeners' attention. The first question, which closes with a cadence on the final, C, is like the narratio, in which the basic idea (both textually and musically) is set forth. The balance of the text, in its first setting, is like a propositio, in that both words and music are an expansion and elaboration of the basic idea. After the third ritornello (mm. 22–23), the point of maximum tonal removal or contrast is found, as in a confutatio, where opposing ideas are stated and refuted. The return of the text and music of the narratio in measures 33–41 form the confirmatio or restatement of the initial arguments. The concluding instrumental ritornello is the final appeal to emotions, or peroratio. Thus, in Stradella's last opera, rhetorical invention and disposition can be seen displacing delivery and elocution.

THE SPREAD OF THE CHAMBER CANTATA

Until roughly the middle of the seventeenth century, the center for the cultivation of the Italian secular chamber cantata was Rome, and the majority of the city's cantata composers were associated with the Barberini family. About the middle of the century, however, the genre spread to other cities, more or less as opera spread. This phase is marked by stylistic parallels with opera and the influence of Marinist poetry.

The works of Barbara Strozzi (1619–1677) include important examples of the mid-century cantata. At a time when most cantatas were preserved in manuscript only, Strozzi published eight volumes in which this genre figures prominently. She was the most extensively published cantata composer of her time. Her life and career illustrate how the social and artistic milieu of the genre expanded along with its geographic range.

Barbara Strozzi was probably the illegitimate daughter of Giulio Strozzi, an impoverished Florentine nobleman living in exile in Venice, and his servant Isabella Griega. Giulio Strozzi lived off his small inheritance, wrote opera libretti and other poetry, and was a member of the Accademia degli Incogniti. Barbara must have developed very rapidly as a singer, for by the age of fifteen she was singing for guests in her father's home. Three years later, in 1637, Giulio Strozzi founded the Accademia degli Unisoni ("The Academy of the Unisons") as an offshoot of the Accademia degli Incogniti. The members of this academy gathered for evenings of frivolous debate on such subjects as whether slander stimulates or inhibits love, whether tears or song is the more potent weapon in love, etc., mixed with performances by Barbara, who also judged the debates and handed out prizes. Almost immediately after its founding, Giulio Strozzi's academy was the subject of eight anonymous satires that clearly implied that Barbara had by the age of eighteen become a courtesan, a type of cultured, high-class prostitute associated with theatrical life and with Venice in particular. There is a provocative portrait of Barbara at about the age of eighteen (Fig. 8-3). By the age of twenty she was lending and investing large sums of money. Soon Barbara was the principal provider for Giulio Strozzi, and she was able to place her own daughter in a good convent. One of her sons became a priest and the other a painter.

Nearly all Barbara Strozzi's pieces called "cantata" are lengthy, varied works containing several sections and a mixture of vocal styles, whereas those marked "aria" are usually shorter and often strophic or enclosed by a refrain. Of her eighty-two printed pieces, twenty-five are large and complex enough to be called cantatas, comparable to those by Carissimi, Rossi, and Cesti.

Strozzi's texts are mostly limited to the Marinist love poetry (influenced by the style of Giambattista Marino, 1569–1625) and typical of the mid-seventeenth century. It was marked by affectation, wit, elegance, circumlocutions, extravagant metaphors, hyperbole, fantastic word play, and original myths, and written with great sonority and sensuality, with the aim of *far stupire* ("stupefying"), dazzling the reader or listener. The forms of her arias may be strophic with internal divisions, strophic variations, full or partial da capos,

Figure 8-3. Barbara Strozzi,
1637, by Bernardo Strozzi

refrain, and rondo structures. Her cantatas may be continuous, cumulative, or sectional. Like her teacher, Cavalli, Strozzi likes to shift fluidly between recitational and metrical styles in ways that reflect the changing voices and expressions of the poetry. She favors the lyrical more than the declamatory and employs many word repetitions and long, sensual melismas, which are not mere technical displays of virtuosity but often unfold slowly and make extreme demands on breath control. She provides more indications of expression and tempo change than any earlier or contemporaneous composer.

Many of these features are found in Strozzi's cantata *Udite amanti* (A. 69, published in 1651), which carries the rubric *L'Eraclito Amoroso* ("Heracleitus in Love"), referring to the ancient Greek philosopher who claimed that there is an hidden connection between opposites, so that things that seem to be moving apart are actually being brought together. This rubric explains the text, which is a lament of betrayal expressed with typical Incognito irony, through oxymoron (condensed paradox), dialysis (arguing from a series of disjunctive propositions), and isocolon (repetition of phrases of equal length and usually corresponding structure): "I long only to weep, I feed only on tears, sorrow is my delight, and moans are my joy; I relish every martyrdom, I delight in every sorrow; sobs heal me, sighs console me." Compare this Marinist text with the much more straightforward *Hor che l'oscuro manto* set by Luigi Rossi, A. 9. Strozzi sets the first quatrain of *versi sciolti* as recitative, the second half of which recurs as a partial refrain (mm. 79–89). The other quatrains, which are isometrical (*settinari sdruccioli*) but not regularly rhymed, are set in aria style to the four-note descending ostinato bass that Monteverdi and Cavalli made into an emblem of lament. The last two lines return to recitative style.

Giulio Strozzi's Accademia degli Unisoni was not an isolated phenomenon. Every Italian city had several academies, and most of them included among their activities performance of chamber music, especially cantatas, along with their ritualistic orations, recreational debates, sponsorship of operas, and training for sons in fencing, horsemanship, and dancing. There is even a collection of cantatas from Modena for which the texts are the words of academic debates over frivolous subjects. The composers are Giovanni Marco Martini (ca. 1650–1730), Antonio Maria Pacchioni (1654–1738), and Giovanni Battista Vitali (1632–1692).

Style trends in the chamber cantata toward the end of the period treated in this chapter are well illustrated by the works of Giacomo Carissimi, Antonio Cesti, and Giovanni Legrenzi (1626–1690). The most important among these trends was an ever clearer separation between recitative and aria: both recitatives and arias become longer as time passes, they become more frequently and more clearly closed off at their terminations, and they become ever more distinct in their features. These results are found Antonio Cesti's *Languia già l'alba* (A. 70), which is preserved in an undated manuscript but probably was composed during the period 1657–1661, when Cesti was in Rome.

The text of Cesti's *Languia già l'alba* is the poet's account of a dream of his beloved. The narrative portions of the text (e.g., "Already dawn was languishing . . .") are written in *versi sciolti* and set as simple recitative—rapidly paced with rather steady rhythms and largely predictable phrase articulations at the end of each line of text, without interpretative inflection, chromaticism, dissonance, or other expressive details. Aria style is used to set the actual words spoken by the beloved in the dream (e.g., "Do you not know me?") and the lyrical reflection of the poet (e.g., "Kindly Fate paints for me a lovely vision . . ."). The poetic lines of these aria passages have even numbers of syllables (4, 6, 8), metrical scansion, and regular rhyme schemes. These correlations and distinctions become mixed only in the last section of the cantata (mm. 97 to the end), where the poet addresses the beloved in the dramatic mode, but at the same time recounts events in the narrative mode and expresses feelings in the lyrical mode. The two major aria segments of the cantata ("Non mi consci, no?" mm 19–46, and "Mi dipinge amabil Sorte," mm. 68–95) are unified internally by recurring rhythmic figures that are maintained even when they run counter to good declamation and interpretive emphasis. The first of these two arias is strophic, and each strophe has the internal repetition pattern ABA, requiring a somewhat illogical repetition of text. Thus, in a reversal of the situation that prevailed two generations earlier in Italy, formal and rhythmic design is here given precedence over elocution and delivery of the text; instead, the content and expression of the text is reflected in the general expressive features of each aria (invention) rather than in local details. The same observation could be made about the arias in the operas and oratorios by composers of Cesti's and Stradella's generations.

THE ORATORIO IN ROME AT MID-CENTURY

Music and the other arts in Rome had been given decisive encouragement by Pope Urban VIII (reigned 1623–44), particularly through the patronage of his nephews, Cardinals Francesco and Antonio Barberini and Princes Taddeo, Matteo, and Urbano Barberini, into whose treasuries the pope channeled considerable wealth. Several of the composers of operas and cantatas in the Barberini households also wrote dramatic vocal works that we now call "oratorios" for several congregations and confraternities in Rome. A leading poet among those who supplied librettos for these oratorios, Giovanni Ciampoli, was brought to the papal household from Florence, where this genre seems to have originated.

A 1638 visitors' guide to Rome lists five major oratories where oratorios were performed on a regular basis in conjunction with evening sermon assemblies during the winter season between All Saints' Day (November 1) and Easter. Four of these oratories were the churches of religious societies or confraternities of wealthy and often noble laymen. The fifth oratory was the newly constructed prayer hall attached to the Chiesa Nuova ("New Church"), the home church of the Fathers of Oratory of St. Philip Neri. A sixth site of oratorio performances in mid-seventeenth-century Rome was the church of the

Jesuit college for Germans in Rome, where performances were sponsored by the seminarians, and the music director was Giacomo Carissimi.

By the 1650s the term "oratorio" began to be used to describe Italian-texted vocal works in which a religious subject or story is presented by solo voices individually and in ensembles, using recitative, arioso, aria, and polyphonic madrigal styles. These oratorios last from ten minutes to an hour; a typical duration is about twenty-five minutes. The shorter works are in one part, whereas those that last twenty minutes or more are typically in two parts, separated by a sermon.

The texts of mid-seventeenth-century oratorios can be either reflective or dramatic. The dramatic type, in which solo singers portray specific characters engaged in dialogue, almost always includes narration delivered in recitative by a personage called *Testo* ("Text"), *Historia* ("History"), or, in the case of a story from the Gospels, *Evangelista* ("Evangelist"). The stories of the dramatic oratorios are derived from the Old Testament, the New Testament, the lives of saints, or spiritual and moral allegory. The biblical stories are usually filled out with freely invented dialogue and episodes, and they rarely quote directly from scripture.

The music and poetry of mid-seventeenth-century oratorios resemble those of operas and cantatas of the same period, insofar as *versi sciolti* ("free verse") are used for dialogue and are set in some variety of recitative style or madrigal-arioso style, while canzonetta verses with regular metrical and rhyme schemes are used for lyrical moments of reflection or emotional expression and are set as arias or ensembles with regular musical meters. Such choruses as are found in these oratorios are sung by the same solo voices that take the individual roles. The influence of sacred concertos can be found in the style of the ensembles and in the occasional use of a musical refrain within a single number or linking musically distinct solo passages.

An example of the mid-seventeenth-century Italian oratorio is *San Tomaso* ("St. Thomas"), composed for the Fathers of the Oratory of St. Philip Neri by Marco Marazzoli (ca. 1602/05–1662), a singer in the Sistine Chapel choir and musician in the household of Cardinal Antonio Barberini, a nephew of Pope Urban VIII, for whom Marazzoli also composed parts of the opera *Chi soffre speri*.

The story presented in Marazzoli's *San Tomaso* is based on John 20:19–29. In Part 1, Thomas, who missed seeing the resurrected Christ when he appeared to the other apostles, will not be convinced of the resurrection unless he can see and touch the body of Jesus. In Part 2, the narrator (Evangelist) describes how Jesus appears again. In dialogue, Jesus then invites Thomas to touch him and to believe, and the apostles reflect on the blessedness of faith.

Marazzoli's setting calls for five solo voices—representing Jesus, St. Thomas, St. Peter, and three other unnamed apostles—and basso continuo, likely played by organ, chitarrone, and, perhaps, viola da gamba. The music is balanced between recitative, nine arias, two duets, two trios, and a chorus of soloists at the end of each Part. Although the arias and ensembles are brief, they are clearly differentiated from the recitative.

Formal design in *San Tomaso* contributes to the forceful projection of the oratorio's religious message in two places. The concluding portion of Part 1 is introduced by St. Peter's admonition in the aria, "Believe, believe, oh Thomas! Blessed is he that sees not but only hopes and believes." This lesson is taken up by the other apostles in two musically distinct ensembles that frame a series of arias connected by a ritornello in which each of the apostles describes a famous case of blind faith (A. 71). And in Part 2 Peter upbraids Thomas in a full stanza of *ottava rima* set in the traditional manner to a series of four strophic variations on the Romanesca pattern, here linked by ritornelli. The relentless pressure represented by these four variations brings Thomas to understand his error and to beg forgiveness in an expressive arioso that is the emotional climax of the work.

The Spread of the Oratorio throughout Italy

During the seventeenth century, the Fathers of the Oratory of St. Philip Neri established congregations in several Italian cities, such as Brescia (1620), Bologna (1621), Florence (1632), Venice (1661), and Turin (1675). Although in some of these places, confraternities of laymen were already sponsoring performances of sacred musical dialogues and oratorios, the Congregations of the Oratory provided an important network for the dissemination of musical works and consequently for mutual influence among Italian oratorio composers, which resulted in greater standardization of the genre.

The general features of Italian oratorios from the 1660s are similar to those in Marazzoli's *San Tomaso*: three to five solo voices, which perform both the dramatic roles and the choruses; accompaniment often limited to basso continuo occasionally with two or three strings; fluid alternation between recitative, arioso, aria, and ensemble passages; and occasional structures created by repetition or refrains. New trends during the period include growth in length of arias, some standardization of aria forms (especially ABB' and ABA'), a shift of expression from recitatives to arias, an increase in the size and role of the instrumental ensemble, and use of ostinato basses.

These features can be illustrated by *San Giovanni Battista*, (A. 72), composed by Alessandro Stradella for a religious confraternity of Florentines living in Rome in commemoration of the Holy Year of 1675. The libretto dramatically portrays the imprisonment and death of John the Baptist as recounted in three of the Gospels—Matt. 14:3, Mark 6:17–28, and Luke 3:19–20.

John the Baptist leaves his hermit's existence to deliver God's command that Herod give up his brother's wife. For this, Herod imprisons him. In Part 2 Herod's daughter Salome dances for her father, who offers her anything she wishes. John reproaches them from his prison cell. This kind of imaginary split scene is often found in oratorios, which were not staged. Salome asks for John's head, which Herod reluctantly promises; note the contrast of expression and personality in their recitatives. John looks forward to the liberation of his soul. In the final duet, Salome rejoices with elaborations on energetic rhythms in minuet style, while Herod expresses anxiety and fear with long, scalewise descending lines of sustained dotted half-notes, an early instance of an ensemble in which opposing feelings are expressed at the same time, illustrating the degree to which emotional expression can now be projected through such abstract elements of musical design as rhythm and melodic contour, capable of projecting their meaning even without text. At the end of this duet, Herod and his daughter both ask the reason for their feelings—fear and rejoicing—the question "Why?" pressed home by numerous repetitions. The question was undoubtedly intended to be educational, and the answer according to Church doctrine is that John's death was a prefiguration of the crucifixion of Christ, which paradoxically can be the subject of both anxiety on personal grounds and joy, because it meant mankind's salvation.

CHANGES IN LITURGICAL MUSIC IN ITALY

Fundamental changes overtook the musical *cappelle* of Italy and their music for Mass, Vespers, and other offices of the official liturgy about the middle of the seventeenth century. These are illustrated nowhere more dramatically than in Bologna. In 1657 the board that administered the basilica of San Petronio for the city government hired a new *maestro di cappella*, Maurizio Cazzati (1616–1678), an up-to-date composer whose previous experience had been at courts and religious confraternities in northern Italy and as *maestro* of the progressive civic basilica of Santa Maria Maggiore in Bergamo. At the time of Cazzati's arrival, the *cappella* of San Petronio consisted of a *maestro*, two organists, and forty-two musicians designated as "singers and instrumentalists"—the instrumentalists were mostly players of cornetti and trombones, which generally doubled the voices of the choir. Cazzati immediately fired thirty-three of these and absorbed the others into a completely reorganized *cappella*, which consisted of the *maestro* (himself), two organists, a male soprano soloist (probably a castrato) and a male alto soloist, boy sopranos and altos who are not listed in the payment roster, five tenors, four basses, three violins, two alto violas, one tenor viola, two violoni (specifically, a viol halfway between the size of a bass viola da gamba and a modern contrabass, which plays at times in the written octave and at times an octave lower), a theorbo, and a trombone. Thus, the newly reorganized *cappella* of San Petronio was about equally divided between a group of singers consisting of soloists and a small choir on the one hand, and a string orchestra designed, like Venetian opera orchestras of the time, around the typical five-part scoring of mid-seventeenth-century music. Several members of the new orchestra were composers in their own right. For major holidays, additional winds, especially trumpets, were brought in from the civic instrumental ensemble, called the Concerto Palatino ("Ensemble of the Palace"), headquartered in the city hall building just across the main piazza of the city.

Similar changes took place more gradually at St. Mark's in Venice and in other cathedrals and civic basilicas of northern Italy. The Mass Ordinaries, concerted motets, psalm settings, and Magnificats composed for these *cappelle* typically feature alternations and combinations of two choirs, one or two sets of vocal soloists, and orchestra. The weighty and solemn tutti sections of large-scale works, including Mass Ordinaries, normally make use of emphatic, repeating rhythmic patterns that animate the essentially homophonic texture. These are set against lighter solo sections with virtuosic melismas and sketchy imitation. Orchestral introductions and interludes often set these contrasting sections apart.

A well-known example of this mid-century style is the *Messa concertata* ("Concerted Mass," published in 1656) by Francesco Cavalli, Monteverdi's eventual successor as *maestro di cappella* of St. Mark's in Venice (W. 14). It is lavishly scored for two four-voice choirs; two sets of four vocal soloists; two violins and one violoncello, to be doubled by *ripieni* ("reinforcements") during the instrumental sections (*sinfonie*) and choral passages; a continuo group, probably consisting of two organs, bassoon, and chitarrone; and three trombones, which play independently during the instrumental sections and double the voices of the choirs. Apparently the original two viola parts were left out of the printed parts, or perhaps they are absorbed into the trombone parts.

The Gloria and Credo of Cavalli's Mass are very long and actually consist of subsections that are so extensive, internally elaborated, closed off, and different from one another that they can be considered separate movements; the Gloria has five of them, and the Credo has fourteen. In each of these sections, the prevailing musical material seems to gather up the sense of the portion of the text set there. The organization of the Gloria is outlined in the table on page 210 and in Example 8-1. This is different from musical reflection of rhetorical delivery, in which the music mimics the accents, inflections, and pacing of speech. It is also different from musical reflection of rhetorical elocution, in which the music parallels certain figures of speech. The means of relating music to text in Cavalli's Gloria and Credo is, instead, musical-rhetorical invention, as the term is used by Athanasius Kircher in his *Musurgia universalis* (1650), discussed in Chapter 4: the composer determines certain general, overall features of the music which reflect the thrust of the whole text, rather than the pronunciation of any word or the figures used in any localized part of the text.

W. 14 contains the Kyrie from Cavalli's Mass, which, following tradition, has just three sections. Each of these is unified through extensive elaboration of a few basic motives, defined above all through characteristic rhythms and extended through sequencing, transposition, exchange of mode, imitation, and repetition. The first Kyrie and the Christe are introduced by a fully closed instrumental introduction, called "sinfonia."

Frequent and extreme contrasts of texture, sonority, range, and especially pacing link Cavalli's Mass to such earlier Venetian polychoral works as Gabrieli's *In ecclesiis*. Also traditional are its use of written-out *falsobordone* in the Credo and the call for improvised embellishment indicated by the fermatas in the second Kyrie. But the new techniques of extension and elaboration, internal subdivision, and use of the flowing melodic style in $\frac{3}{2}$ meter, reminiscent of

A SUMMARY OF TEXT AND MUSIC IN THE GLORIA OF CAVALLI'S *MESSA CONCERTATA* (1656)		
Gloria in excelsis Deo	Glory to God in the highest	Energetic triple-meter rhythm, major mode, fanfare-like triadic motive, rising contours.
et in terra pax hominibus bonae voluntatis.	and on earth peace to men of good will.	Suddenly slower, with harmonies expanding in both the sharp and flat directions in system and hexachord mutations.
Laudamus te. Benedicimus te. Adoramus te. Glorificamus te. Gratias agimus tibi propter magnam gloriam tuam.	We praise Thee. We bless Thee. We adore Thee. We glorify Thee. We give thanks to Thee for Thy great glory.	A series of long phrases in a smooth triple meter; tender and affectionate but growing in strength and animation.
Domine Deus, Rex coelistis, Deus Pater omnipotens. Domine Fili unigenite, Jesu Christe. Domine Deus, Agnus Dei, Filius Patris	Lord God, King of heaven, God, Father almighty, Lord only-begotten Son, Jesus Christ. Lord God, Lamb of God, Son of the Father	Lyrical, tender, evoking pastoralism ("Lamb of God") with its dotted triple-meter rhythm.
Qui tollis peccata mundi, miserere nobis. Qui tollis peccata mundi, suscipe depracationem nostram. Qui sedes ad dexteram Patris miserere nobis.	Who takes away the sins of the world have mercy upon us, receive our prayer. Who sits at the right hand of the Father, have mercy upon us.	Dissonances and chromaticism, becoming momentarily energetic at *suscipe* ("receive") with a fanfare motive.
Quoniam tu solus Sanctus. Tu solus Dominus. Tu solus Altissimus. Jesu Christe, cum Sancto Spiritu, in gloria Dei Patris. Amen.	For Thou only art holy. Thou only art the Lord. Thou only art most high, Jesus Christ. With the Holy Ghost, in the glory of God the Father. Amen.	A rhythmically crisp motive reminiscent of the canzona tradition returns in an instrumental ritornello. Slower at *Jesu Christe*. Even more energetic at *In gloria*.

mid-century Venetian opera arias, set Cavalli's Mass apart from earlier Venetian church works.

The same tendency to create closed sections of contrasting meters and styles can be found in Italian small-scale sacred concertos in the second half of the seventeenth century. Many of the widely circulated and influential motets for one, two, and three voices by Giacomo Carissimi, which date from about 1650 to 1674, contain a fluid mixture of aria, arioso, and recitative styles. Carissimi's three-voice motets typically begin with one voice in recitative style, shifting to arioso, followed by a responding passage for all three voices. A second voice may then begin another cycle with recitative.

In Carissimi's *Suscitavit Dominus* (1665), A. 73, the first voice to enter begins a narration in recitative style and continues with melismas in response to the word *ventum* ("wind") and with rhythmically patterned measures, underscoring with rigor the words *misi ventilatores* ("he sent judges"). This combination of styles creates what Marco Scacchi called *stile imbastardito*. In the balance of the motet, other passages of narration in *stile imbastardito* are framed by a recurring three-voice ensemble representing the Babylonian people, whose music is made up of a homophonic and illustrative segment (*Fugite, fugite*, "Flee, flee") followed by an imitative passage (*et salvet unusquisque animam suam*, "and save your souls"). This motet was later (1666) printed in Cologne with an introductory Symphonia and an interlude for two violins and violone (bass violin).

Even more extended passages in each of these contrasting styles, clearly distinguished, are found in the solo motets of Bonifatio Gratiani, or Bonifazio Graziani (1604/5–1664), which were published in seven collections at regular intervals from 1652 to 1678.

An example of rather elaborate sectionalization is *Ave, suavis dilectio* (A. 74) from the 1676 collection *Motteti a voce sola, parte con istromenti, e parte senza* ("Motets for Solo Voice, Part with Instruments and Part without") by the nun Isabella Leonarda (1620–1704). The text—a Latin poem in honor of the Blessed Sacrament (the consacrated Communion waver and wine, mystically transformed into the body and blood of Christ) but not part of the official liturgy—contains the cues for a series of sectional contrasts. The first line, "Hail, sweet love," is set as a melismatic arioso suggesting delirious passion. The second two sentences are set as a complete aria in two parts, fully closed. Beginning in B minor, the first part cadences on D major, while the second part concludes in the original B minor. In each half, the voice enters with a brief phrase (a "motto") set off from the principal vocal section by a short ritornello for the two violins, which is heard at the beginning and conclusion of each part as well. In the first part, the minor mode and gently pulsing fifth degree with minor sixth degree neighbor tones lend an air of tenderness to the introduction, which tends to carry over into the vocal sections in keeping with the meaning of the text, "Hail, o tender fullness." The second part of the aria is written with a different proportion ($\frac{12}{8}$), which denotes a faster pace. This, together with the dotted rhythms, lends this section a more lively expression, reflecting the text "To drink of thee is to live, to eat of thee is to be born." At

EXAMPLE 8-1. Musical motives from the Gloria of Cavalli's *Messa concertata* (1656), referring to the table on page 210.

the text *Salve lumen animarum* ("Hail, light of our souls"), Leonarda returns to the impassioned melismatic arioso style of the opening and adds some text painting, such as the rising chromatic line at the word *peccatoris* ("for sinners"). The text "In thee is salvation, life, all of Paradise," brings another aria in $\frac{12}{8}$ with lively expression, but it is interrupted by a gentler and smoother aria section in $\frac{3}{2}$ time and a sudden change to arioso style with expressive leaps and sighing figures at the text "from death, life." The return to $\frac{12}{8}$ brings exuberant and impassioned expression to the text "for mortals, life through death, o wondrous fate, for the truly faithful!" In effect, in this motet Leonarda has paralleled the procedure of the Italian chamber cantata by alternating closed sections in contrasting styles, and she has brought into her church music some of the features (extensive elaboration on a small family of rhythmic ideas) and forms (binary) typical of Italian opera of the 1670s.

Isabella Leonarda was born in Novara, in the northwestern area of Italy known as Piedmont, to a wealthy noble family. The convent she entered at age 16, the Virgins of Saint Ursala, was founded toward the end of the sixteenth century. At the time of her entry into the convent, its guardian was her uncle. In fact, the convent was not under the control of a central authority, and its rules were comparatively liberal, allowing Leonarda to maintain a musical *cappella* and training school for young female musicians as the central activity of the institution. Eventually, she published over two hundred works in twenty collections of her own, mostly motets but also a concerted Mass with string ensemble and a collection of ensemble sonatas for strings.

While north-Italian composers such as Isabella Leonarda favored the combination of solo voices with ensemble instruments in their motets, Roman composers appear to have led the way toward incorporating clearly defined sections of recitative and aria, even in non-dialogue motets, during the third quarter of the seventeenth century, perhaps because these same Roman composers were writing chamber cantatas at the same time.

The conclusion seems inescapable: as opera and oratorio production spread over Italy in the second half of the seventeenth century, and as the chamber cantata became the most frequently heard type of music in noble households, church music was drawn into the same stylistic orbit. The same techniques are found in these vocal genres in Italy during this period: the musical expression of the prevailing affect of a section of text by means of unifying musical factors, especially rhythmic and melodic features that become the subject of extensive elaboration, yielding more extended, unified, and closed sections, movements, or arias. Thus, the composer relates the music to the text in the act of invention, rather than in musical elocution (creating or reflecting rhetorical figures in the text) or in delivery (using the rhythms, contours, accents, and pacing of the music to imitate or control those same features of interpretive speech), as composers of the early seventeenth century had done. This newer approach tends to yield longer, more elaborated and unified closed sections of contrasting styles, especially sections in which the distinguishing features of recitative and aria are ever more exaggerated.

BIBLIOGRAPHICAL NOTES

The Spread of Opera from Rome

Two books cited at the end of Chapter 2 are also relevant to this chapter: Margaret Murata, *Operas for the Papal Court, 1631–1668* (Ann Arbor, 1981), and Frederick Hammond, *Music & Spectacle in Baroque Rome: Barberini Patronage under Urban VIII* (New Haven: Yale University Press, 1994). The notion that Venetian opera resulted from the same process of dissemination from Rome that transplanted the genre to many other Italian cities was originally and most forcefully argued by Nino Pirrotta in a series of articles translated as "Early Venetian Libretti at Los Angeles," "The Lame Horse and the Coachman: News of the Operatic Parnassus in 1642," "Falsirena and the Earliest *Cavatina*," and "*Commedia dell'Arte* and Opera," *Music and Culture in Italy from the Middle Ages to the Baroque: A Collection of Essays* (Cambridge, MA, 1984), pp. 317–360. Further important details to this story have been added in an article by Lorenzo Bianconi and Thomas Walker, "Dalla *Finta pazza* alla *Veremonda*: Storie di febiarmonici," *Rivista italiana di musicologia*, X (1975), 379–454, which has been promised in English translation as "Tales of the Febiarmonici: On the Spread of Opera in the 17th Century," the projected introduction to Volume 1 in the series Drammaturgia musicale veneta.

Venetian Theaters, Incogniti Operas, Venetian Opera Conventions

The principal source and best overview of these subjects are found in Ellen Rosand, *Opera in Seventeenth-Century Venice: The Creation of a Genre* (Berkeley, 1991), and in several articles by the same author, such as "The Bow of Ulysses," *The Journal of Musicology*, XII (1994), 376–95; "Iro and the Interpretation of *Il ritorno d'Ulisse in Patria*," *The Journal of Musicology*, VII (1989), 141–64; Seneca and the Interpretation of *L'Incoronazione di Poppea*," *Journal of the American Musicological Society*, XXXVIII (1985), 34–71. "Aria as Drama in the Early Operas of Francesco Cavalli," *Venezia e il melodramma nel seicento*, ed. Maria Teresa Muraro, Studi di musica veneta, 5 (Florence, 1976), pp. 75–96. An interpretation of the Incogniti operas, different from both Rosand's and the one presented here, is advanced in Iain Fenlon and Peter N. Miller, *The Song of the Soul: Understanding* Poppea, Royal Musical Association Monographs, 5 (London: Royal Musical Association, 1992).

Florence, Naples, Genoa

The introduction of Venetian opera to these cities is treated in the article by Bianconi and Walker, "Dalla *Finta pazza*" ("Tales of the Febiarmonici") mentioned above. Robert Lamar Weave and Norma Wright Weaver, *A Chronology of Music in the Florentine Theater, 1590–1750* (Detroit, 1978), provides great detail, specific listings, and useful narrative about Florence in this period. Opera in Naples is discussed by Michael F. Robinson, *Naples and Neapolitan Opera* (Oxford, 1972). The major book on the most important opera composer discussed in this section is Carolyn Gianturco, *Alessandro Stradella (1639–1682): His Life and Works* (Oxford, 1994).

The Spread of the Chamber Cantata

While there is no book-length treatment of the Italian chamber cantata, there are several useful articles and dissertations. Early cantata composers in Venice are the subject of Roark Thuston Miller, "The composers of San Marco and Santo Stefano and the development of Venetian monody (to 1630)," Ph.D. diss., Univ. of Michigan, 1993. Gloria Rose [Donnington], "The Cantatas of Carissimi," Ph.D. diss., Yale Univ., 1959, remains an excellent guide to developments in the genre about mid-century, as does David L. Burrows, "The Cantatas of Antonio Cesti," Ph.D. diss., Brandeis Univ., 1961. General information from her dissertation are included in Gloria Rose [Donnington], "The Italian Cantata of the Baroque Period," *Gattungen der Musik in Einzeldarstellungen: Gedenkschrift Leo Schrade*, ed. Wulf Arlt, Ernst Lichtenhahn, Hans Oesch, and Max Haas (Bern, 1973), pp. 655–77. Another useful treatment of a single composer is Kathleen Chaikin, "The Solo Cantatas of Alessandro Stradella (1644–1682)," PhD. diss., Stanford Univ., 1975. Many cantatas from the decades covered here are published in facsimile volumes in the series *Italian Cantata in the Seventeenth Century*, ed. Carolyn Gianturco. The key articles on Barbara Strozzi are Ellen Rosand, "Barbara Strozzi, *virtuosissima cantatrice*: The Composer's Voice," *Journal of the American Musicological Society*, XXXI (1978), 241–81; Ellen Rosand and David Rosand, "Barbara di Santa Sofia and *Il prete genovese*: On the Identity of a Portrait by Bernardo Strozzi," *Art Bulletin*, LXIII (1981), 249–58; Ellen Rosand, "The Voice of Barbara Strozzi," *Women Making Music* (Urbana, IL, 1986), 168–90; and Beth L. Glixon, "New Light on the Life and Career of Barbara Strozzi," *The Musical Quarterly*, LXXXI (1997), 311–35.

The Spread of the Oratorio Throughout Italy

The master study here again is Howard E. Smither, *A History of the Oratorio*, I: *The Oratorio in the Baroque Era, Italy, Vienna, Paris* (Chapel Hill, 1977). A study of a sub-category important in the earlier part of this phase is Fits Noske, *Saints and Sinners: The Latin Musical Dialogue in the Seventeenth Century* (Oxford, 1992). Two recent studies of the oratorio in a city outside Rome are by Victor Crowther, *The Oratorio in Modena* (Oxford, 1992), and *The Oratorio in Bologna (1650–1730)* (Oxford, 1999). Denis Arnold, *the Oratorio in Venice* (London, 1986), is also useful. Stradella's oratorios are discussed in Carolyn Gianturco's book on the composer mentioned above.

Changes in Liturgical Music in Italy

Among the few studies in English of this topic are Denis Arnold, "The solo motet in Venice (1625–1775)," *Proceedings of the Royal Musical Association*, CVI (1980), 56–68; James H. Moore, "The *Vespro delli cinque laudate* and the Role of *salmi spezzati* at St. Mark's, *Journal of the American Musicological Society*, XXXIV (1981), 249–78; and "*Venezia favorita da Maria*: Music for the Madonna Nicopeia and Santa Maria della Salute," *Journal of the American Musicological Society*, XXXVII (1984), 299–355. Of special interest is Stewart Arlen Carter, "The Music of Isabella Leonarda (1620–1704)," Ph.D. diss., Stanford Univ., 1982).

CHAPTER 9

Music at the Court of Louis XIV to the Death of Lully

POLITICAL, ECONOMIC, AND CULTURAL CENTRALIZATION IN FRANCE

By contrast to the Italian and German parts of Europe, where a large number of cities were home to local and regional courts, civic basilicas, churches of Oratorians and Jesuits, academies, and commercial theaters that employed significant numbers of musicians, France in the seventeenth century had relatively few of these venues. Most of its musical activity was concentrated in the capital, Paris, and most of that in the large musical establishments of the royal court. As a consequence, the history of music in France during this period is largely the history of music in Paris and at the royal court. The reasons for this are found in the political and economic history and systems of the French nation.

The processes of political, economic, and cultural centralization in France began as far back as the fifteenth century, when the first steps were taken to fashion a French army. In 1523 Francis I founded a central treasury, and gradually the crown established its right to collect taxes nationally, using an ever-growing and more professional central bureaucracy. Henry II gave four of his secretaries the official title of Secretary of State, and in 1561 they became full members of the royal council.

Henry IV relied heavily on Maximilien de Béthune, Duke de Sully, who was admitted to the king's financial council in 1596. Sully encouraged agriculture, promoted road building, planned a national canal system, and directed the construction of frontier defense works. Henry's reign was followed by the regency of his widow, Maria de Medici, who ruled on behalf of their young son Louis XIII (1610–43). But the real power and initiative during this period belonged to the most powerful minister, Armand-Jean du Plessis, Cardinal de Richelieu. The objectives of Richelieu's policies were absolute obedience to the king at home and increased prestige abroad. Richelieu crushed aristocratic conspiracies with quick executions. He abolished the medieval military dignities and prevented the great lords from sitting in the king's council. He created a system of local government whereby each of thirty-two districts had a royal intendant who had complete responsibility for justice, police, and finances under the king's authority. Richelieu aimed at national economic self-sufficiency for strategic reasons, and sought a favorable balance of trade by promoting the manufacture of tapestry, glass, silk, linen, and woolen cloth for export while using tariffs to discourage the importation of luxuries.

Richelieu died in 1642 and Louis XIII the following year. France was once again ruled by a regent, the queen mother, Anne of Austria. But the task of governing the country fell increasingly to another cardinal, Jules Mazarin (Giulio Mazzarini), an Italian Jesuit friendly to papal authority and, perhaps with a view to its cultural-political symbolism, Italian music and art.

Louis XIV's youth was troubled by a series of civil wars called "The Frondes" (1648–1653). The first of these was a revolt by magistrates and the Parliament of Paris in reaction to Mazarin's use of the intendants, especially in matters of taxation. The second involved elements of the old nobility who resisted the elimination of their financial, political, and military power.

At the death of Cardinal Mazarin in 1661, Louis XIV took the reins of government in his own hands, but by 1665 Mazarin's former secretary, Jean-Baptiste Colbert, had risen to the position of first minister. Colbert pushed Richelieu's economic policies further toward outright mercantilism—the central direction of the national economy and trade to promote self-sufficiency and advantage over competing nations. For this purpose he continued to improve the infrastructure, grant monopolies, raise import tariffs, subsidize exports, and import skilled workers.

Louis XIV sought constantly to expand the borders of France, ostensibly in order to make it secure from attack. There can be no doubt that Louis's personal pride and hunger for glory played its role, too, and this had important consequences for the arts, as we shall see. France was almost continuously at war during his reign.

Louis XIV was an autocratic ruler, and he strove to consolidate and increase his power. He buttressed his authority with the divine-right doctrines elaborated by Bishop Jacques-Bénigne Bossuet and proclaimed it across Europe by force of arms. No class of subject could escape his supervision.

But in neither theory nor practice was Louis's power truly absolute. He was supposed to rule under laws, both civil and religious. He was expected to take counsel. He needed to respect and uphold the privileges and customs of such peripheral provinces as Brittany, Normandy, and Provence. He was bound by the need to raise revenue from his country, and he understood that his own authority rested upon the prestige and privileges of the nobility.

However, Louis constantly pressed against these limits, and for this reason as well as for reasons of pride and thirst for glory, he and his ministers directed the arts and branches of learning to promote an ideology that can be described, with the reservations mentioned here, as absolutism.

All of the policies and programs, economic, political, military, and administrative, conspired to channel resources and the attention of the nobility toward Paris and the royal court. The financial and cultural life-blood was drained away from the regional courts and provincial capitals. During the reign of Louis XIV, the epicenter of national focus became the Palace of Versailles.

The Palace of Versailles and its surrounding city are located about ten miles west–southwest of Paris. The palace was originally built between 1631 and 1634 as a hunting lodge for Louis XIII. Under Louis XIV it was expanded (1661–1710) into an immense complex surrounded by elaborate and sprawling formal gardens (Figure 9-1), every detail of which was calculated to glorify the king. It was finally declared the official royal residence in 1682 and soon became the object of imitation throughout Europe.

Louis de Saint-Simon, Duke of Rouvroy (1675–1755), reports in his *Mémoires* (covering the early 1690s through 1723) that Louis reduced his nobility to subjugation by requiring them to stay frequently at court and to attend and participate in theatrical spectacles that glorified him.

Each French monarch and several of their ministers cultivated specific areas of culture and the arts. Henry IV was concerned with town planning. Louis XIII took a personal interest in music. Louis XIV was passionate about theater, dancing, and landscape gardening. Richelieu's importance lay in the establishment in 1634 of the Académie Française to regulate and maintain the standards of the French language—another aspect of his policies of national unification and standardization. Richelieu also patronized a number of dramatists, including Jean de Rotrou and Pierre Corneille. Mazarin collected paintings and promoted the introduction of opera to the French court.

As with many other aspects of the French royal court, music making was bureaucratically organized into several discrete organizations: the Musique de la Grande Écurie ("Music of the Great Stable"), the Musique de la Chambre ("Music of the Chamber"), the Chapelle Royale ("Royal Chapel"), and the Académie Royale de Musique ("Royal Academy of Music").

MUSIQUE DE LA GRANDE ÉCURIE

The wind and percussion ensembles of the Grande Écurie played mostly outdoors, at weddings, receptions, contests, proclamations, processions, fireworks displays, and pageants. Its members accompanied the king on journeys, at military reviews, and on hunts. The musicians of the Écurie played trumpets,

Figure 9-1. The
Palace of Versailles

drums, fifes, bagpipes, oboes, horns, and bassoons. They were relatively well paid, receiving either 120 or 180 *livres* annual salary, large bonuses for many categories of celebration, free meals at the royal banquet hall, exemption from several forms of taxation, and freedom from in-kind services to church wardens and mayors and from the obligation to provide living quarters to soldiers in wartime. The twelve trumpets of the Écurie, four of whom were also assigned duties in the Chapelle Royale, enjoyed the highest status of all, and their privileges included the right to pass their position on to a son.

The creation of the oboe in France about the middle of the seventeenth century enabled the Écurie ensemble for the first time to play elaborate, fully developed music, comparable to that played by string ensembles. The creation of the oboe is generally credited to Jean Hotteterre (ca. 1610–ca. 1690), a musician of the Écurie beginning about 1650, and his son and nephews. The oboe emerged as a new type of shawm with a free-standing reed, allowing greater control of intonation and timbre than an enclosed reed; a narrower, more precisely graduated bore, made possible by a three-joint construction; an improved disposition of undercut holes and a short, vented bell section, allowing a full set of chromatic pitches and much improved intonation; and keys for playing middle c' and $d\sharp'$ (see Fig. 9-2). The oboe was able to perform almost anything played on a violin at that time, and it was useful in a mixed ensemble for alternating with the trumpets, which cannot play continuously for long stretches.

Also at the French royal court at about the middle of the seventeenth century, a three-keyed bassoon in four detachable sections was developed to take the place of the older dulcian (Fig. 9-3).

Figure 9-2. An early
two-keyed French oboe

Figure 9-3. An early three-keyed
bassoon

One typical employment of Écurie ensembles was to accompany a carousel, a special type of outdoor pageant developed by combining aspects of the equestrian ballet and the ceremonial, staged joust. In a carousel, allegorically costumed riders and horses moved in a large circle in front of the king and his invited guests (Fig. 9-4) to the accompaniment of wind music, usually in the form of a suite of dances.

The example in the Anthology (no. 75) is a suite for the trumpets, oboes, bassoons, and timpani of the Écurie written by Jean-Baptiste Lully (1632–1687) for the royal carousel of 1686. Its opening movement (Prelude) is an entry march based upon typical figures used in the fanfares (or "sonatas") of the ubiquitous trumpet corps described in Chapter 3. Here and in the other movements, the oboes alternate with the trumpets, providing an echo, as if representing a far-off corps returning the signal. The oboes, capable of playing a complete set of pitches, also offer tonal relief by transposing material by the interval of a fifth.

Every reference to trumpet music carried inferences of glory, pride, and military valor. In many other respects too, the boundaries between social occasion, pageantry, and warfare were deliberately blurred: noblemen rode into battle and in carousels bedecked with plumes and ribbons to the sound of trumpets; they wore swords and boots at social occasions; many types of outdoor pageant included military-style maneuvers; and illustrations of foot positions for sword combat and dancing were practically identical. Music for pageants, theater, concerts, and church that evokes the characteristic sound and textures of the trumpet corps is typical of the seventeenth and early eighteenth centuries—the Baroque period. Like the pageantry with which it was associated, it is closely related to the strong influence of monarchy and nobility, a defining characteristic of culture during this historical epoch.

MUSIQUE DE LA CHAMBRE

The music of the royal chamber was organized under the direction of two superintendents of music and two masters of the chamber. Most of the musicians in this organization served for a quarter of the year, for which

Figure 9-4. The Grand Carrousel given by Louis XIV on June 5, 1662 at the court of the Tuileries in Paris

they were paid 400 *livres*; they were free to pursue their profession in the city of Paris for the rest of the year. Thus, four duplicate bodies of chamber musicians played at court.

Under the administration of the Musique de la Chambre came the *Vingt-quatre Violons du Roi* ("Twenty-four Violons of the King) and the *Petits Violons* ("Small Violins"). An official court publication of 1686 explains, "The *Grand Bande* of the *Vingt-quatre Violons*, always so labeled although they are at present twenty-five . . . plays for the dinner of the king, for ballets, and for comedies. The *Petits Violons*, which number twenty-four . . . follow the king on his journeys to the country, usually play for his supper, for balls, and the recreation of His Majesty." Both these ensembles consisted of six violins, four first violas (*haute-contre*), four second violas (*taille*), four third violas (*quinte*), and six *basses de violon* (large-size violoncellos). Members of the two violin "bands" were paid the handsome salary of 400 *livres* per year, considerably more than musicians of the Grand Écurie. In addition, the Musique de la Chambre included players of viols, lutes, theorbos, guitars, harps, harpsichords, and flutes, as well as solo singers. Oboe players from the Écurie were brought into the chamber as needed.

Figure 9-5. At the king's apartments ca. 1680; two oboes, bass violin, and two violins play as guests mingle and converse

Harpsichord Music

Louis Couperin (ca. 1626–1661), although a famous keyboard player and composer, held the position of treble viol player in the Musique de la Chambre,
having refused in 1657 the post of harpsichord player out of loyalty to Chambonnières, who was eased out because he could not play from a figured bass.
Couperin's music for viol consort is interesting principally for its use of dance
rhythms in imitation of the violin bands. His greater importance lies in his keyboard music, which generates unprecedented drama and passion.

Couperin's *Tombeau de Mr. de Blancrocher* (A. 76) commemorates the passing
of a lutenist who died in 1652 from a fall caused by drunkenness. Like most
works of this genre, it is essentially a special kind of allemande, featuring at its
beginning the pyrrhico-anapest rhythm (♪) that reminded
Mersenne of drums in a funeral cortege. Some of the features of this work that
are typical of Louis Couperin are the startling intervals heard in the bass line of
the first strain, the abrupt contrasts created by changes of register, texture,
mode, rhythms, and tempo (*plus viste*, "faster," marked at m. 15), the intricate
chain of suspensions (mm. 16–22), and the shocking harmonic deceptions
(mm. 21, 26, 46).

The spontaneity implied by so many sources of abrupt contrast in Couperin's
Tombeau is the explicit basis of his unmeasured preludes (e.g., A. 77) derived
from the unmeasured lute prelude but incorporating a written-out imitative
section in triple meter as in the Italian keyboard toccatas of Frescobaldi.

French harpsichord music from the later seventeenth century generally
shows more emotional restraint, unity, and continuity than we find in the earlier works of Louis Couperin. The best representative of this later style in
France is Jean-Henri D'Anglebert (1629–1691), who succeeded his teacher,
Chambonnières, as *ordinaire de la chambre du Roy pour le clavecin* ("regular [musi-
cian] of the king's chamber for the harpsichord") in 1662.

D'Anglebert's single surviving printed collection, *Pièces de clavecin* (1689), contains pieces grouped by "modes": G major, G minor, D minor, and D major;
D'Anglebert's preface claims that he had also composed in all the other "modes"
as well. Each group contains an allemande, courante, sarabande, and gigue, preceded in the first three groups by a semi-notated unmeasured prelude, and followed in all four instances by other dances and arrangements of overtures and
numbers from Lully's stageworks. W. 15 includes the allemande, two courantes,
sarabande, and gigue from the D major group in the original, engraved notation.

D'Anglebert continued the tradition of relating pairs of dances by theme or
motive; the allemande and first courante of the D-major group begin with a
similar melodic outline, as do the second courante and sarabande. This type of
correspondence is also carried out within each dance, as each reprise is normally dominated by a single rhythmic figure played out with variations over
sundry melodic contours and harmonic digressions.

D'Anglebert's counterpoint is also more consistent than was typical earlier
in the century, especially his motivic bass lines, less broken and sketchy than

would be found in Chambonnières or Louis Couperin. On the side of variety, D'Anglebert increases the number of standard ornaments represented by special signs; he explains twenty-nine of them in a prefatory table. The ornaments are not deployed haphazardly—they usually intensify the direction and purpose of the melodic lines and emphasize the most important notes in their structures. Far beyond compensating for the rapid decay of the harpsichord's tone, D'Anglebert's ornaments exploit the instrument's full and magnificent sonority with swirling, rustling, and purling sonorities.

Music for Viols

The most notable *musique de la chambre* of Louis XIV for ensemble instruments is certainly that for viols. Earlier in the seventeenth century the most characteristic genre of French viol music was the ensemble fantasie for three to six instruments of various sizes, with contrapuntal, imitative texture. However, the most important French music for viol in the later part of the century was for one or two bass instruments, using multiple stops and ornamental figures, almost in the manner of a lute. This newer, virtuosic solo viol idiom was pioneered by André Maugars (ca. 1580–ca.1645), of whom no compositions are known, and Nicolas Hotman (before 1613–1663), of whom fifty works for solo viol survive. A more important composer of solo viol music was Hotman's student, Jean de Sainte-Colombe (fl. ca. 1640–1690), of whom 188 pieces for solo viol and 67 for two viols have been located.

Although Sainte-Colombe was very well known among French viol players during the second half of the seventeenth century, he never held a position at the royal court, and little has been discovered about his life, other than that he taught the most important players of the next generation and that at his house in Paris he held concerts that featured the viol playing of his two daughters, Brigide and Françoise.

Sainte-Colombe's music for one or two unaccompanied viols shares with the keyboard works of Louis Couperin the traits of irregularity and surprise. These features are promoted by Sainte-Colombe's often unpredictable harmony and frequent mutation of mode and system through chromaticism (see, e.g., the first section of his Concert "Le Tendre," A. 78). They are also reflected in his general avoidance of rhythmic and melodic patterning and his frequent and extreme shifts in register.

Although Sainte-Colombe's *concerts* mostly take the form of dance suites, apparently to be played without pauses between the movements, his phrases are almost always irregular, usually avoiding groupings of two and four measures. The concert "Le Tendre" is among several of his works that feature contrasts between loud and soft. Some of the others use unmeasured rhythms. Small ornaments slurred under a single bow stroke are marked with special signs and are found, on average, more than once per measure. Older-style trills and slides requiring separate bow strokes for each note are written out using small unbeamed notes that have single flags but are not counted in the time of the measure. These works maintain the illusion of spontaneity and contemplative absorption associated with earlier French lute music.

If the style of Sainte-Colombe's music is parallel to Louis Couperin's, the viol works of his best-known student, Marin Marais (1656–1728), might be compared with the keyboard works of D'Anglebert for their greater regularity, continuity, and unity. As shown in Example 9-1, it is relatively easy to analyze the underlying rhythm of Marais's suite movements using the system explained by Mersenne, even in movements that are not dances, such as the Prélude in Suite no. 6 from Marais's first book of pieces for two viols and continuo of 1686 (W. 16). The harmony, too, is far more predictable in Marais's music than in Sainte-Colombe's. And although they still retain significant vestiges of *style brisé*, there is far less discontinuity in texture and motivic material in Marais's viol suites than in Sainte-Colombe's works.

The variety of treatment of viol idiom found in the music of Marais and his contemporaries was reduced to two opposing categories by Sainte-Colombe's other famous student, Jean Rouseau (1644–ca. 1700), who described *jeu de melodie* ("play of melody") and *jeu d'harmonie* ("play of harmony") in his important and influential *Traité de la viole* ("Treatise on the Viol," 1687). Essentially, *jeu de melodie* uses multiple stops sparingly and focuses attention on melodic and rhythmic features, as happens in Sainte-Colombe's concert "Le Tendre" (A. 78) and in the Sarabande and Gigue of Marais's Suite no. 6 (W. 16). *Jeu d'harmonie*, on the other hand, emphasizes multiple stops and the variety of

EXAMPLE 9-1. Mersenne's "Bacchian foot" in the Prélude of Suite no. 6 in the *Premier livre des pieces a deux violes* (1686) by Marin Marais

harmonies and textures associated with them, as in the Prélude, Allemande, and Courante of the suite by Marais.

The major development in accompanying French solo vocal music in the second half of the seventeenth century was the replacement of lute tablature by figured bass and the corresponding substitution of the theorbo for the simple lute as the accompanying instrument of choice. The most representative composer of vocal chamber music at the royal court during this period was Michel Lambert (ca. 1610–1696), who in 1661 succeeded the *air de cour* composer Jean de Cambefort (ca. 1605–1661) as *Maître de musique de la chambre du Roi* ("Master of the King's Chamber Music"). Although Lambert is reported to have composed at least twenty books of *airs*, only two that were printed in his lifetime are now known. Still, these books, together with manuscripts and printed anthologies, preserve more than three hundred of his compositions. Most of them are in binary form followed by an ornamented *double*, or in rondeau form, in which a refrain alternates with various couplets. Some explore various degrees of recitational style and became important models for the formation of French operatic recitative in the works of Cambert and Lully, Lambert's son-in-law. But more of them conform to a standard dance meter and rhythmic type. A few incorporate dialogues between personages represented by solo voices.

THE CHAPELLE ROYALE

For Louis XIV, perhaps more than for any other Catholic monarch in this age, religion—its beliefs, ideas, practice, ceremony, and symbolism—was thoroughly integrated into the apparatus for preserving and expanding his royal authority and glory. This idea is summarized in Charles Le Brun's painting *The Resurrection of Christ*, Figure 9-6. In it, Christ rises above the worshipful figures of Louis XIV and his ancestor Saint Louis. The French king, kneeling upon the treasures of his realm and dominating over defeated enemies, offers up the symbols of his royal authority while reaching beyond the veil of the tabernacle that divides the heavenly and earthly realms. Christ himself blesses the king's sovereignty, without the mediation of the church, while Louis's prime minister, Colbert, stares out at us, proudly pointing to his sovereign.

Considering the official view of the divinity of the king and his role as anointed intermediary between France and Christ, it is understandable that Louis XIV placed great importance in his Chapelle Royale ("Royal Chapel") and invested heavily in its maintenance and expansion.

At the death of Louis XIII in 1643, the Chapelle Royale consisted of six boy sopranos, two falsettists, eight high tenors, eight normal tenors, eight basses, and two cornettists and was led by two *sous-maîtres* ("co-directors"), who alternated six-month tours of duty. It was an ensemble suited above all to the performance of polychoral music of the kind left by Formé and Veillot. Its venue was the chapel of the Tuileries Palace, essentially an annex to the Louvre Palace. In 1663 Louis XIV reorganized the Chapelle Royale under the direction of four

Figure 9-6. Charles Le Brun,
The Resurrection of Christ
(1676)

sous-maîtres: Henry Du Mont, Gabriel Expilly, Pierre Robert, and Thomas
Gobert, of whom only Du Mont (ca. 1610–1684) and Robert (ca. 1618–1699)
remained after 1669 and were active composers of church music. The Chapelle
Royale by that time included six boy sopranos, nine adult male sopranos, thirteen countertenors, eighteen tenors, twenty-one baritones, eight basses, and a
small orchestra.

The style history of French church music during the second half of the seventeenth century consists of two processes: the absorption of the features of
Italian small- and large-scale concerted motets and Masses, and the incorporation of features identified with French court pageant and ceremonial music. Its
incorpration of pageant and ceremonial styles meant that the music of the
Chapelle Royale became another emblem of the king's glory, which increasingly became identified, at least metaphorically, with the glory of God.

The absorption of Italian features into French church music during this
period was aided by two related factors—the cultural politics of Cardinal
Mazarin, an Italian, and the activities of the Jesuit order in Paris (Mazarin was
originally a Jesuit). The decisive impetus came from another source—the early
training and subsequent career of Henry Du Mont (ca. 1610–1684), the first
composer in France to publish small-scale motets (*petits motets*) with continuo
accompaniment (in 1652) and one of those who established the basic features
of the French large-scale motet (*grand motet*) for the rest of the seventeenth and
most of the eighteenth centuries.

Du Mont was born near Liège, started his training in Maestricht, and returned to Liège to study composition with Léonard de Hodemont (ca. 1575–1636), the music director at the cathedral of Liège. The musical repertoire of this cathedral included large- and small-scale concerted works—some for one to three voices and continuo by Alessandro Grandi, Antonio Cifra, Felice and Giovanni Francesco Anerio, and others. The cathedral also had a salaried ensemble of two cornetts, two bassoons, bass viol, violins, lute, and two organs. Hodemont's own *Sacri concentus* (1630) contains motets for one to five voices, violin, and basso continuo, perhaps the earliest motets of this sort composed in a French-speaking city.

Liège at this time was the capital of a papal state ruled by a prince-bishop, which would explain the presence of Italian music in the cathedral repertoire. Maestricht was an isolated outpost of the Republic of the United Netherlands, at that time ruled by the princes of Orange-Nassau.

After completing his training, Du Mont moved to Paris, where, from 1643, he was organist at the church of St. Paul in the fashionable Marais district. From 1652 to 1660 he was a keyboard player in the household of the Duke of Anjou, brother of Louis XIV. And in 1660 he joined the household of Queen Marie-Thérèse. In 1663 he was one of the four selected as *sous-maîtres* of the Chapelle Royale. After the death of his wife, Du Mont became Abbot of Notre Dame de Silly in Normandy, around the same time that he received the title of Music Master to the Queen, 1673.

Du Mont's *Cantica Sacra* of 1652 can be considered the first French church music with basso continuo. Although Constantijn Huygens published his *Pathodia sacra et profana occupati* for solo voice and continuo earlier (1647) in Paris, he lived in the Netherlands, never in France.

Italian features of Du Mont's *Cantica Sacra* are the use of the basso continuo, false relations, chains of suspensions, affective melodic intervals, and word-painting. Some motets in the collection have short contrasting sections. These features show the influence of the Venetian and Roman repertoire that Du Mont encountered in Liège. The settings are for two, three, and four voices with continuo; nine have optional viol or violin parts.

Du Mont's *Trisitia vestra* (A. 79) is based on the rhetorical figure antithesis. The text itself, drawn from John 16:20, embodies antithesis, but the jarring interruptions of its syntax by the Italian-style refrain "Alleluia" exaggerates the effect: "Your sorrow, *Alleluia*, shall be transformed into joy, *Alleluia*; while the world shall rejoice, so shall you be made sorrowful; but it shall be transformed into joy, *Alleluia*." With every shift of the text between references to sorrow and to joy, Du Mont changes the character of his music from slow, chromatic, and dissonant to fast, diatonic, and consonant, and back again. Including the repetition of measures 19–36 at the end, there are four such contrasts in a work lasting only about two and a half minutes.

Du Mont's twenty *grands motets*, published after his death, were probably written during his service in the Chapelle Royale, 1663–ca.1673. In these, he extended the models of Formé and Veillot by creating several chains of contrasting sections, each consisting of instrumental introduction or interlude, solo vocal passages, ensemble phrases, and full choir statements. In *Quemadmodum desiderat cervus* (W. 17) there are six sections that more or less conform to that pattern (starting in measures 1, 59, 81, 122, 132, 183, and 202), each one introducing musical features that contrast with the preceding section and project the general sentiment suggested by each new segment of the text. In this respect, this motet is comparable to an Italian work as up-to-date as Cavalli's *Missa concertata*. The extended binary-form introduction for five-part string ensemble has the character of an allemande, and the triple-meter section (mm. 132–179) elaborates extensively on a few rhythms, most of which place the accent on the second beat in the manner of a sarabande. These are early instances of crossover from stage music to church music, which becomes a special feature of French *grands motets* during the later seventeenth century.

With works as long as *Quemadmodum desiderat cervus*, the Mass at the king's chapel became essentially a choral concert, with the liturgical text whispered or read silently by the celebrants, as becomes clear in the introduction to a volume of Latin motet texts written by the court opera librettist Pierre Perrin in 1665:

> For the king's Mass, there are ordinarily three motets sung: a *grand*, a *petit* for the Elevation, and a *Domine salvum fac regem* ("God Save the King"). I have made the [texts for the] *grands* long enough to last a quarter of an hour . . . and they occupy the beginning of the Mass up to the Elevation. Those of the Elevation are shorter and can last until the Post-Communion, where the *Domine* begins.

Covered as it was by continuous music, the royal Mass under Louis XIV became another form of state pageant, an emblem of his glory. And so the prevailing style of the *grands motets* of the Chapelle Royale quickly evolved into something overstated and theatrical. A good example of this is *Plaude Lætare Gallia* ("Applaud, rejoice, Gaul [i.e., France]"), composed by Jean Baptiste Lully to celebrate the birth of Louis XIV's first son in 1668. This *grand motet* sets a newly written Latin text for two choruses, soloists, and five-part string orchestra. The opening symphonie, which leads without pause into the first chorus, uses the stately dotted rhythms that invariably begin Lully's ballet and opera overtures and which had become a musical emblem of glory. In this first chorus, the number of repetitions of the words *plaude* and *lætare* becomes overwhelming when combined with the repetitions and elaborations of the dotted and anapest rhythms tossed between choruses. The bass solo, answered by chorus, at *Sacro Delphinus fonte laratur* ("The dauphin is anointed in the sacred font") is a second distinct movement, in the meter and style of a minuet. After a second orchestral interlude, brief solos marked "récit" alternate with choral responses until the final exclamations, beginning with *Vivat regnet princeps fidelis* ("May the faithful prince live and rule"), which begin with further minuet rhythms and conclude with the dotted rhythms of the opening. This motet demonstrates how closely the glorification of the king and the worship of God were identified and how the musical styles of the theater and ballroom were incorporated into French church music under Louis XIV.

An explanation of how and why French musical spectacle in the theater was transformed by the introduction of opera in the second half of the seventeenth century requires brief accounts of Italian opera at the French royal court, Louis XIV's use of spectacle as propaganda, and the system of royal academies under his reign.

ITALIAN OPERA AT THE FRENCH ROYAL COURT

Attempts to introduce Italian opera at the French royal court were initiated by individuals of Italian birth who shared the aims of the Ultramontanist party. The first to attempt this importation was Maria de' Medici, queen consort of King Henry IV, for whose wedding in 1600 the earliest surviving opera, *Euridice*, had been performed in her native Florence. Once installed in Paris, the queen summoned Giulio Caccini and his family to her court, where they remained for the winter and spring of 1604–05. In addition to chamber monody, they sang at least excepts from *Euridice,* presumably with Caccini's music.

A much later and more successful attempt to introduce Italian opera was initiated by Cardinal Mazarin, the Italian Jesuit priest, at the time when he exercised broad powers during the Regency (1643–1661), while Louis XIV was a minor. Mazarin had been a member of the Roman household of Cardinal Antonio Barberini, a nephew of Urban VIII. When, at the death of Urban VIII in 1644, the Barberini were forced to flee Rome, Cardinal Mazarin invited them, along with many of their musicians, to Paris. Included in this group were the composers Luigi Rossi, Marco Marazzoli, Atto Melani, and Carlo Caproli. The theater architect and set designer Giacomo Torelli was also hired, along with several famous female singers, a dozen or so castrati, several librettists, and a troupe of instrumentalists.

Cardinal Mazarin's aims were to boost the prestige of Italian music and art as a means of inducing support for the Ultramontanist party, which favored concessions to papal authority, always a goal of the Jesuits. In a more practical way, Mazarin hoped to use his Italians at the French court as spies and agents of influence, and he hoped that impressive spectacles might distract attention from his political machinations. It appears that Mazarin, like his predecessors at the French royal court, appreciated the potential of musical theater to sway opinion.

There were only a few scattered performances of Italian opera at the French court after the death of Cardinal Mazarin (1661). In the meantime, French opera had taken root, encouraged by Louis XIV, who wanted the French to assert themselves against the Italians in all cultural matters and who personally sent the Italian musicians away in 1666.

SPECTACLE AS PROPAGANDA AT
THE COURT OF LOUIS XIV

In Chapter 5 we encountered political allegory in the *ballet de cour* of the late sixteenth and early seventeenth centuries. This genre continued under Louis XIV, an expert dancer who often portrayed an allegorical symbol of himself (Hercules, Apollo, the Sun) in ballets during his youth (Fig. 9-7). During his reign, the propaganda aspect of court spectacle became even more obvious and exaggerated. An example will make this clear.

In 1685 the court presented stage works for a visiting group of ambassadors from Siam (modern Thailand), a country where the French hoped to compete with the Dutch and the English for lucrative trade. The reactions of these ambassadors, as reported in the court newspaper, the *Mercure galant*, probably mirrored the intentions of the court planners more than anything else. In reaction to the ballet *Clovis*, which extolled the exploits of Hercules, the Siamese ambassadors are supposed to have remarked, "This Hercules must represent the king, since he triumphs over all his enemies and carries victory everywhere he goes." When they saw a palace burn in Lully's opera *Armide*, they are quoted as saying, "Let us leave. The palace has fallen. We can sleep here no longer." At the end of a royal Mass, the choir sang the standard *Domine salvun fac regem*, and "it seemed as if they also prayed for the king." The climax of the visit came when the ambassadors were brought to Versailles and marched in a procession to the foot of a grand staircase. There, thirty-six drums and twenty-four trumpets heralded the king, who appeared on his throne, high above, at the top of the long staircase.

Figure 9-7. Louis XIV as Apollo in the *Ballet du Roy des Festes de Bacchus* (1651)

THE SYSTEM OF ROYAL ACADEMIES

In keeping with the policy of centralization, regulation, and self-sufficiency, the goals of mercantilism, Louis XIV's minister of finances, Jean–Baptiste Colbert, created a system of royal academies. The older academies were the Académie Française, established in 1634 to create a comprehensive dictionary of the French language and to regulate matters of spelling, vocabulary, and literary style; and the Académie Royale de Peinture et de Sculpture, established in 1648 as a guild of painters and sculptors. To these were added five other academies created after the death of Cardinal Mazarin, when Louis XIV began to rule on his own: the Académie Royale de Danse (1661), the Académie des Inscriptions et Belles-lettres (1663), the Académie Royale des Sciences (1666), the Académie Royale de Musique (1669), and the Académie Royale d'Architecture (1671). There were two main purposes for these academies: (1) to make France an exporter rather than an importer of arts and scholarship, and (2) to coordinate the imagery, mythology, and language through which the French monarchy was portrayed, directly or through allegory.

The first of the new academies created by Colbert under Louis XIV was the Académie Royale de Danse in 1661, reflecting the central position of dance in court pageantry and entertainment. The king himself was the academy's protector, and he personally appointed its original thirteen directors and dance instructors. These thirteen were to meet once a month in order to confer about dance and how to advance it. They enjoyed a national monopoly on dance instruction. Documents surrounding the creation of this academy emphasize the connection between dance and the arts of combat.

The Académie des Inscriptions et Belles-lettres was established in 1663, initially to devise subjects for the king's tapestries and to design vouchers, coins, and medals. Its work on emblems and insignia soon expanded into the creation of designs and plans for paintings, sculptures, and architectural decorations; the oversight of themes for all types of spectacle and pageant; and supervision of the content of histories, accounts, and eulogies. In effect, it became the master academy in charge of unifying the imagery and mythology employed by all the arts under the patronage and control of the court.

Although the Académie Royale de Peinture et de Sculpture was founded before the reign of Louis XIV, Colbert reorganized it with a new charter in 1663. Under the new charter, this academy functioned as a school of art, rather than an artists' guild. Its purpose was to control the style and development of the visual arts through training, directives, and competitions. The subject matter of paintings and sculpture prescribed by this academy centered around interpreting and immortalizing the glory of the king and his exploits, either directly or through allegory.

Although the Académie Royale des Sciences contributed mostly to industry and commerce, it occasionally assisted in politically motivated activities such as the research and writing of histories in support of the king's territorial claims.

The Académie Royale de Musique (1669) had a predecessor of a kind in the Académie de Musique et de Poésie founded in 1570 by Jean-Antoine de Baïf, whose purpose was to guide the development of music toward the goals of stirring the passions, instilling morality, and "ensuring the stability of the state" by allowing poetry to control musical rhythms. The new Académie Royale de Musique was a court opera company with a national monopoly on the creation and production of musical dramas. The content—language, imagery, and allegory—of these was controlled by the Académie des Inscriptions et Belles-lettres.

Under the same supervision, the Académie Royale d'Architecture (1671) designed new buildings, fountains, and gardens for the king, always with a view toward proclaiming his glory through the use of what today is often called "power architecture," which strives for grandeur by imposing the edifice and the will of its creators upon the environment and the people who visit and use it. The palace and gardens at Versailles (Fig. 9-1) embody this ideal.

THE BEGINNINGS OF FRENCH OPERA

The first French musical drama entirely sung, *Le Triomphe de l'Amour sur des bergers et bergères* ("The Triumph of Cupid over the Shepherds and Shepherdesses"), with music by Michel de La Guerre, was performed in 1655. Although this experiment was undoubtedly launched in response to the Italian opera productions of the previous ten years, its libretto actually belongs to an earlier French tradition of pastoral plays with songs, choruses, and dances, such as *Arimène* by Nicolas de Montreux, performed in 1597.

A collaboration of more lasting importance was initiated in 1659 with the production of the *Pastorale d'Issy* with music by Robert Cambert (ca. 1628–1677) on a text by Pierre Perrin (ca. 1620–1675), who hailed his creation as a victory for "our poetry and our music over a foreign language, poetry, and music." With the encouragement of Cardinal Mazarin, Perrin and Cambert followed this with *Ariane ou Le Mariage de Bacchus* ("Ariadne; or, The Marriage of Bacchus") later in the same year.

It was Perrin's aim to found a national opera tradition and to establish an academy to promote it. As part of his ambitious plan, at the age of twenty-three, he had married a wealthy widow of sixty-one. With her money he purchased a position at the court of the king's brother. When his elderly wife left him, he was imprisoned for debts in 1659. After his release from prison in 1666, Perrin continued his campaign with another collaboration with Cambert in *Ariane* (1669) and with intensive lobbying directed at Colbert. These efforts bore fruit with the grant of a royal monopoly over the establishment of "academies for opera or musical spectacles in the French language on the footing of those of Italy." He was allowed to charge admission and to include ladies and noblemen in his productions without hazard to their social or legal status.

The first production under the new monopoly was *Pomone* (1671) by Perrin and Cambert, a mixture of tentative recitative (brief and Italianate) and airs (short, syllabic, and relatively unexpressive), both in keeping with developments in Lully's *ballets de cour* of the 1660s. With *Les Peines et les plaisirs de l'amour* ("The Pains and Pleasures of Love") in 1672, Cambert, with the poet Bariel Bilbert, introduced more rhythmic and harmonic variety, to the extent that music began to contribute to the expressive ends of the drama. In this work, a distinctive type of French recitative begins to emerge, including more melodic design, wider range, and more varied rhythm than found in the recitatives of the Italian operas that had been performed in Paris. In Act I, scene 1, there are stretches of monotone syllabic declamation over a static bass alongside more generously contoured phrases, some with active bass lines—features probably derived from the more declamatory *airs de cour* by Lambert and other composers of his generation and later found in Lully's operatic recitatives. Furthermore, it seems that Cambert attempted a realistic imitation of speaking inflections with his syllables that begin on a weak sixteenth or eighth note and slur to a longer, accented note, almost a mannerism with him, and one which has no echoes in later French recitative.

BALLETS DE COUR AND COMÉDIES-BALLETS

Perrin's monopoly on opera production in France had the unintended effect of preserving two older forms of French musical spectacle—the *ballet de cour* and the *comédie-ballet*—that were not covered by Perrin's patent. In these types of musical spectacle, Perrin's eventual successor, Jean-Baptiste Lully, initially advanced his career.

Lully was born in Florence in 1632, the son of a prosperous miller. He was brought to Paris at the age of thirteen as a pageboy to a noblewoman. In that post he had an incentive to learn guitar, violin, composition, and dancing. At the age of twenty, he met the fourteen-year-old king Louis XIV when they both danced in the *Ballet de la nuit* (1653), for which Lully composed some music. This led to a friendship and Lully's appointment as Composer of Instrumental Music to the King later that year. He soon became well known for composing and performing in court ballets. In 1656 he was made leader of the *Petits Violons*, where he established a new level of ensemble discipline. Under the leadership of Lully as conductor, winds were added to the strings of this ensemble, and the musicians learned to strike the opening notes of a piece exactly together and to use uniform bowing. Lully's leadership was a reflection of absolutist ideology, a ceremonial pageant by itself, and a model for future orchestras.

In the wake of the vast political changes that occurred with Mazarin's death and Louis's majority in 1661, Lully was made Superintendent of Music and Composer of Chamber Music to the King, becoming a naturalized French citizen in the same year. In 1662 he was named Music Master to the Royal Family. When Lully made the major career move of marrying the daughter of the older court composer Michel Lambert, his marriage contract was signed by the King and Queen of France.

Figure 9-8. Comic bandit,
Ballet de la nuit, 1653

Up to this point, Lully's compositions had all been in the well-established genre of the *ballet de cour*. He composed music for nineteen of them between 1653 and 1663. In each case he wrote overtures, interludes, pantomimes, dances, solo airs, ensembles, and choruses.

During the 1650s, the *ballet de cour* encompassed two types: the dramatic (*ballet mélodramatique*, i.e., with a story line) and the non-dramatic (*ballet à entrées*, i.e., ballet made up of loosely related choreographed entries of costumed dancers). The non-dramatic ballets almost always celebrated the glory of the king through allegory in a serious vein. Dramatic *ballets de cour* could be serious and allegorical, comic and satirical, or a mixture (as was the *Ballet de la nuit*, "Ballet of Night," of 1653, mentioned earlier; see Fig. 9-8). In the period 1653–73, the general trend in the *ballet de cour* was toward the dramatic type.

In both kinds of *ballet de cour*, the dances are of two general kinds: those that mime action and those that develop abstract geometrical patterns. In both cases, the music and the choreography are extensions of and elaborations upon the standard courtly social dances. The table on page 235 lists the types of dance in Lully's stage works with some of their principal defining characteristics. The sarabande, gavotte, courante, galliard, and bourrée were described in Chapter 5. Other dances described there (pavan, allemande, volta, branle) were out of fashion by the 1650s. Some, especially mimed dances, did not belong to any of these standard categories.

Choreographies for fifty-six of Lully's dances were written out and printed early in the eighteenth century by three dancing-masters who served at the court of Louis XIV—Raoul-Auger Feuillet (1659/60–1710), Louis Guillaume Pécour (?1651–1729), and Anthony L'Abbé (?1667–?after 1756)—using a system of notation invented by Pierre Beauchamp (1631–1705), Louis's personal dancing-master. Although these notated diagrams may not show precisely how

DANCES IN LULLY'S STAGEWORKS	
Allemande	c ♩ = 66–80 No longer danced. A derivative is the initial, slow part of Lully's overtures, c ♩ = *ca.* 80 or ¢ ♩ = 66–80.
Bourrée	¢ ♩ = 112–160 The typical rhythmic module comes to rest on beat 7: ¢ | ♩♩♩♩|♩♩ ♩|♩♩♩♩|♩
Canarie	Meters include 3, ⁶⁄₄, ³⁄₈, or ⁶⁄₈. ⁶⁄₄♩. = 128; ⁶⁄₈♩. = 108. Usually begins with a group of upbeat notes equal to a dotted half or dotted quarter.
Chaconne	Triple meter with one of these bass ostinatos: 8–7–6–5; 8–5–6–5; 1–5–2–5; 1–2–3–4–5. Always in a major mode. After two statements of the ostinato, there is often a contrasting bass for an equal time. ♩ = 121–159
Courante	³⁄₂♩ = 82–90; if sixteenths are present, ³⁄₂♩ = *ca.* 60. Usually with an eighth-note upbeat and frequent hemiola.
Entrée grave	¢ ♩ = 64–67. Music often characterized by dotted and over-dotted iambs, anapests, and pyrrhico-anapests. A slow and stately dance for a man. Similar to the first part of a French overture; see Allemande, above.
Gailliarde	³⁄₂ with no upbeat.
Gavotte	¢ ♩ = 98–128. A typical rhythmic module, always with two quarters as upbeat: ¢ | ♩♩|♩♩♩♩|♩♩
Gigue	Meters include 3, ⁶⁄₄, or ⁶⁄₈. ⁶⁄₄♩. = 105–121. Although actual gigue rhythms tend to be complex, a typical rhythmic module for a gigue is: ⁶⁄₄ ♪♪|♩. ♪♪♩.♪♪|♩
Loure	Meters and rhythms the same as the gigue, but tempos slower.
Marche	2 ♩ = 95–120. Shows a wide variety of rhythm and phrase characteristics.
Minuet	³⁄₄♩. = 71–78. Typical rhythms include ³⁄₄ ♩♩ |♩♩ and ³⁄₄♩.|♩♩♩
Passacaille	3 ♩. = 63–106. The usual bass pattern is 8–7–6–5, always in a minor mode.
Passepied	³⁄₈♩. = 86–100. Typical rhythmic patterns are ³⁄₈ ♪|♪♪♪♪|♪♪ ³⁄₈ ♪|♪♪♪|♪ ³⁄₈ ♪♪|♪♪♪♪|♪
Rigaudon	The usual meters are 2 and ¢. ♩. h = 116–148. Step and music often mark this rhythm: ¢♩ ||♩♩♩♩|♩
Sarabande	³⁄₂♩ = 72–96. The note beginning on the second beat of the first and third measures of four-bar phrase may be elongated or emphasized. The faster type of sarabande is notated in ³⁄₄ and moves in steady quarter notes.

these dances were performed in Lully's time, each choreography represents general features belonging to the given type of dance. Fig. 9-9 is a page of choreography; Fig. 9-11 is a picture of a dance in progress on stage. In addition, arm and upper-body movements were carefully prescribed and could even be notated (Fig. 9-10).

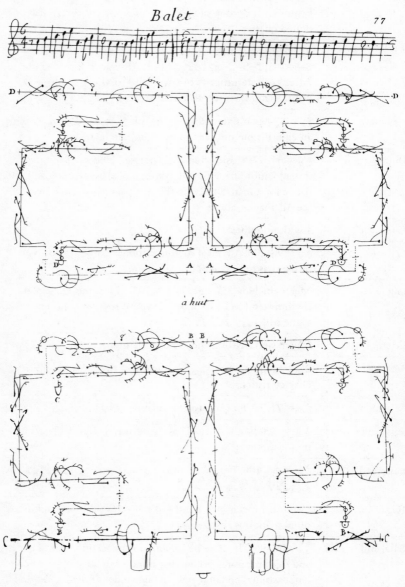

Figure 9-9. A page from Feuillet's choreography for a canarie from Lully's *Bellèophon* (1679), showing steps and floor patterns for eight dancers

Figure 9-10. Dancer with arms extended and notation of the same

The dances that were used in pageants and theatrical works were also danced at the frequent court balls. Of these, the courante was the most important. Noble men and women residing at the court spent significant time learning the latest choreographies, because many dances required precise unanimity and coordination among participants, while others were danced by single couples under the watchful gaze of the court. This regimentation and conformity was of course symbolic, as were the position of the king at one end of the room and the requirement that each couple make a formal bow to him at the end of each dance.

Figure 9-11. *Ballet de Psyché* (1656), Entrée 12, "Pluto appears upon his throne, surrounded by demons"

In keeping with the social and political function of dancing—to promote respect, honor, and obedience to authority and custom—foot, body, and arm gestures for dancing corresponded closely to those belonging to the elaborate technique of etiquette studied assiduously by all noble men and women, above all by courtiers. For example, the French dancing-master Pierre Rameau advised, "When entering a room, remove your hat with your right hand, advance two or three steps to clear the door, slide the back foot forward to the fourth position without transferring any weight, direct your bow while taking everyone present into your field of view, and make a bow forward, followed by a bow backward. The foot that closed to the third position after the bow forward now opens to the second position for the bow backward." In this connection, observe that the courtier depicted at the extreme right in Figure 9-5 is standing in the same position (the fourth position) as the dancer in Figure 9-10.

It was mentioned earlier that fencing used the same foot and body positions as dancing and social etiquette. So did other martial arts, such as handling the pike. Likewise, the movements and designs of the horse ballet and the carrousel resembled both the dance and cavalry maneuvers. All of these—swordsmanship, personal combat, horsemanship, dancing, and etiquette—were distinguishing accomplishments and attributes of the nobility. By extension, the music of courtly dancing must have taken on similar associations, as did the musical idiom of the trumpet corps. In this way, musical compositions and genres that incorporated dance styles and features of other music belonging to courtly ceremony, entertainment, and pageant carried an association with nobility, monarchy, and the values that they espoused and that supported their claims, such as majesty, prestige, honor, respect, grace, formality, ease, and civility. Thus, the *ballet de cour* was a central link in a complex of artistic expressions and social behaviors that helped to define court and noble culture in the period of Louis XIV.

One of the most powerful and widely understood of the musical emblems of monarchy and nobility that developed out of the *ballet de cour* was the French overture. Its defining features were its construction in two parts: (1) moderately slow and (2) fugal and faster. The first part, which carried the ideological message, featured the iambic dotted rhythm (∪ —) and several variants of it, such as the anapest (∪ ∪ —) and pyrrhico-anapest (∪ ∪ ∪ —), possibly exaggerated through over-dotting, an unnotated performance practice thought to be related to *notes inégales*. It is clear from commentary and from the use of this style in conjunction with certain texts and situations in vocal music, especially dramatic music, that there was a widely understood association between this rhythmic style and the concepts of glory, majesty, triumph, and nobility. The source of this association may perhaps be found in the traditional sonatas of the European trumpet corps, which features such rhythms, although it was also known in poetry, as Torquato Tasso in the sixteenth century associated the "ascending feet" (iambs and anapests) with the elevated style, suitable for noble and warlike subjects. Although other models and precedents have

been suggested, the earliest unequivocal instance of this type of French overture was composed by Lully for the *Ballet d'Alcidiane* (1658).

As the second decade of Lully's *ballet de cour* composition progressed (1663–73),
vocal music became more prominent in these productions, primarily at the
expense of spoken dialogue and secondarily in replacement of some dances.

Solo vocal numbers, always a part of *ballet de cour*, were called *récits*. In Lully's
earlier *ballets de cour*, many of these *récits* were in Italian, while the spoken dialogue remained in French. The most obvious Italian feature of these airs by
Lully is the adoption of the form *ABB'*, which had become common in Italian
opera arias by this time. The *récits* took on the characteristics of French airs de
cour of various types: dance-like, ornamental, declamatory, chromatic, and
expressive (the *air sérieux*). Lully's principal models at that time were the airs by
his father-in-law, Michel Lambert.

As spoken dialogue was gradually displaced from the *ballet de cour*, three related
forms of musical theater arose in which its role was much greater: the *comédie-
ballet*, the *tragédie-ballet* and the *tragédie à machines*. In all three, a complete play was
performed with *divertissements* containing dances and vocal music interspersed as
interludes or as integrated scenes. The earliest of these was the *Les Fâcheux* ("The
Bores"), a *comédie-ballet* of 1661 combining a play by Jean-Baptiste Poquelin
(1622–1673), called Molière, with music by Pierre Beauchamps.

Divertissements can occur in nearly every type of French musical theater in
the seventeenth and early eighteenth centuries. A *divertissement* is a coherent
group of songs, vocal ensembles, choruses, and dances that forms a separate
scene within a larger stage work. In most types of stage work, the *divertissements*
are usually ancillary to the main action. But in many of Lully's *tragédies en
musique*, discussed below, they are a decorative but integral part of the drama.

In 1664 Lully began a series of collaborations with Molière that produced
twelve *comédies-ballets* over the next seven years. The best known of these is *Le
Bourgeois gentilhomme* ("The Middle-Class Nobleman") of 1670, for which
Lully supplied music for four extended *entrées* of airs and dances and five individual dances, all woven into the plot of the play, either as activities of the characters (dancing lessons, etc.) or as ceremonial pageant ("The Turkish
Ceremony to Ennoble the Bourgeois").

TRAGÉDIE EN MUSIQUE

When Perrin went back to debtors' prison in 1671, he sold part of his opera
monopoly to the composer Sablières and the librettist Guichard. A year later
(1672), he sold the entire privilege to Jean-Baptiste Lully, who, with the back-
ing of prime minister Colbert, immediately established the Académie Royale
de Musique, which was granted a royal monopoly on the performance anywhere in France of any dramatic work that was sung throughout and used
more than two singers and six instrumentalists. Thus, Colbert's mercantile policy of using monopolies and academies for the encouragement and control of

commerce, industry, and cultural activity for national purposes and the promotion of royal glory was extended to musical theater.

Lully quickly chose his librettist, Philippe Quinault (1635–1688), with whom he had already collaborated on two *ballets de cour* and with whom he would produce eleven *tragédies en musique;* the genre is now often called *tragédie lyrique.* The first result of their collaboration in this new genre was *Cadmus et Hermione* (1673).

The basic features of Lully's *tragédies en musique* were drawn from the older genres of *ballet de cour, comédie-ballet,* and spoken tragedies with elaborate scenic effect (*tragédie à machines*) and were fixed from the outset:

- The drama is unified by a main plot (with subplots, in some cases) and a consistent group of characters, although the story normally unfolds in various places and over an extended period of time.
- The main plots, always serious in character, are derived from mythology and legend, so that the cast includes deities and allegorical figures; intervention of deities is a common method of resolving the plot.
- The plots revolve around conflicts between the virtues, with honor, glory, and duty typically showing the proper direction to love.
- The plots were conceived as allegories promoting the glory of the king and often contain symbolic references to recent or current events; the allegory is usually framed in a long prologue consisting of singing and dancing.
- The work is sung throughout; there are no spoken words.
- It is divided into five acts (not three, as Italian opera was).
- Spectacular scenic effects, machines, and elaborate, sometimes bizarre, costumes form a predominant element.
- Dances, which are numerous, are found in *divertissements* in every act, normally performed by collective secondary characters (shepherds, demons, rivers); they generally arise directly from the plot and contribute to the drama by depicting action, defining collective characters, or expressing passions.
- Orchestral numbers often accompany action or scenic effect, frequently in a descriptive manner, while actors perform pantomime.
- Choruses, normally standing off to one side, participate in the drama, representing the collective voice of groups of personages whose bodies are represented by dancers.
- Solo airs, stemming from the *air de cour* tradition and from Italian opera, are shorter and less melismatic than Italian arias. Those that occur in the main dialogue typically either take their ABB′ form from Italian arias or are in binary form like dances. Monologue airs are usually in ternary or rondeau form. Airs in *divertissements* are sometimes strophic and often adopt the rhythmic patterns of the surrounding dances. The text of airs for confidants or other minor characters often are based upon maxims—general truths or generic advice.

- French recitative, having developed gradually from the declamatory *air de cour*, can be quite similar to the air; compared with Italian recitative, its vocal lines may have more variety of pitch, rhythm, and meter, more rhythmic and melodic patterning, and a bass that is more active. However, some of Lully's recitatives use more monotone recitation and sustained bass than those of his French predecessors, perhaps revealing some Italian influence.
- In Lully's early operas, recitative is accompanied only by the continuo group; beginning with *Bellérophon* (1679) Lully added recitative in which the orchestra accompanies continuously.
- Many scenes achieve musical continuity through a fluid alternation between recitative, air, ensemble, chorus, and orchestral passages, while action continues and the plot is advanced. Tonal coherence within scenes, harmonic transitions marking stages in the action, and tonal contrast between scenes contribute to one's impression that music keeps pace with the unfolding of the plot. In Lully's later operas, recurring motives or a bass ostinato can promote musical unity or continuity within a scene.

These features are illustrated in Lully's second opera, *Alceste* (1674).

LULLY'S *ALCESTE*

Alceste was written to celebrate the return of Louis XIV in January 1674 from his brief participation in the Dutch War. Its prologue explicitly connects this opera with the military campaign in Holland and with the glory of the king. According to the usual procedure, the subject of the opera and the details of its treatment were submitted for approval to the Académie des Inscriptions et Belles-lettres, which certified its conformity with the official line, and the completed libretto was reviewed for purity of language by the Académie Française.

Since the days of Mazarin, the French had desired the annexation of the Spanish Netherlands as an enhancement of national security. The conditions that led Louis XIV to invade Holland in 1672 included the mortal illness of Charles II of Spain, political shifts within the Holy Roman Empire, and a secret treaty with Charles II of England. To cover his aggression, Louis cited specific rights that had become his with the capture of certain frontier cities in a previous war and his shaky claim to the throne of Spain. Although the Dutch had a strong navy, its army was quickly overpowered by the French. In order to cover its retreat, the Dutch opened a series of dikes and let sea water flood the fields ahead of the advancing French. The high point of the war for the French was the siege and conquest of Maestricht, a Dutch city on the Rhine at the border with France. During the war, official versions of its events and of the roles of the king and his military commanders were reported in court newspapers. At the same time, paintings, poems, pageants, and theatrical spectacles at court projected compatible visions.

Figure 9-12. The open-air performance of Lully's *Alceste* on the Marble Courtyard at Versailles, July 4, 1674; the orchestra divided to give Louis XIV an unobstructed view of the stage

Lully's *Alceste* allegorically depicts the principal events of the war as reported in official accounts and interpretations. In addition, Louis's war minister, Michel Le Tellier, and his son, the Marquis de Louvois, are portrayed obliquely in the opera, as both of them rose and fell in stature at court with the shifting French fortunes in the war. In the course of the conflict, Louvois gradually supplanted his father in authority, and it was he who pressed for more attention to the development of the French navy.

Quinault loosely based his libretto on Euripides's *Alcestis*, in which it is ordained that Admetus, king of Thessaly, must die because he failed to sacrifice to the god Artemis at his marriage to Alcestis. Apollo intervenes and arranges that Admetus will be spared if someone will die in his place. Alcestis volunteers, but she is saved from death by Hercules.

Quinault's free elaboration on this outline begins in Act I. At the wedding of Alceste and Admète, Alcide (the original name of Hercules in his youth) confesses that he, too, loves the bride, although he will honor her marriage to Admète. However, Alceste is also loved by Lycomède, who, less honorable than Alcide, abducts her by ship to his island fortress at Scyros. When Admète and Alcide give chase, the deity Thétis blocks them with a storm. When Eole sends the Zephyrs to chase away the Four Winds, the storm abates, and Admète and Alcide follow Lycomède to his island.

In Act II, Alcide provides decisive leadership during a successful siege of the enemy capital of Scyros. Only after the battle, Admète's aging father, Phérès, arrives, barely able to walk in his armor. He discovers his son mortally wounded. Apollo descends to declare that Admète will be lost unless someone is willing to die in his place. The god orders the Arts to erect a monument, upon which will miraculously appear the image of whoever agrees to be sacrificed.

Shortly after the start of Act III, the image of Alceste appears on the monument. Alcide offers to save Alceste's life if Admète will give her up to him. The bargain is struck, and Alcide enters Hades through a passage opened by Diana, goddess of the hunt.

Act IV opens with Charon demanding payment from the spirits of the dead for passage across the River Acheron. A caricature of a greedy merchant, he ridicules those who cannot pay. Alcide, however, leaps into the boat and demands passage. At the palace of Pluto, god of the underworld, Alcide defeats the many-headed dog, Cerebus, and impresses Pluto's wife, Proserpine, to the extent that she convinces Pluto to allow Alceste to go back with Alcide.

In the final act Alcide claims Alceste as his bride, but, on seeing the grief this would cause, he relents and allows Admète to remain wed to her. Apollo descends again and initiates a celebration of love and glory.

In Lully's opera, Alcide represents Louis XIV, since Hercules was one of the main figures of mythology used to personify the king in paintings, poems, and pageantry. The central conflict with Lycomède refers to the Dutch War then in progress—the prologue practically tells us that. Therefore, the siege and defeat of Scyros refers to the capture of Maestricht. The storm conjured up to block Alcide's pursuit of Lycomède represents the breach of the dikes and flooding of Holland's fields. Alcide's subsequent success in pursuit by sea argues Louvois's case for improving the French navy. Lycomède is portrayed as a jealous usurper of legitimate authority, self-interested and brash—traits imputed to the Dutch in French wartime propaganda. The mercenary Charon, trying to extract money from navigation, is a satirical reference to the Dutch as a nation of seafaring merchants. Admète's role in the opera parallels that of Louvois in the Dutch War, even to the detail of the comic father, Phérès, who in his old age has become irrelevant, like Le Tellier at the French court. Finally, the bride, Alceste, the prize won by Alcide in battle, personifies Glory, which Alcide (Louis) nobly concedes to his subordinate, Admète (Louvois), thereby increasing his own honor.

The contrasting characterizations created by Quinault's libretto for *Alceste* are musically reinforced by Lully's recitative. In this respect, the composer advanced significantly over his French models, having made a detailed study of the dramatic declamation of French actors, especially of the famous tragedienne Marie Champmeslé (1642–1698).

For example, in Act I, scene 5, Lycomède reveals his character clearly enough in his first speech, "Straton, give the order to be prepared to begin the feast. At last, thanks to spite, I enjoy the sweetness of feeling the calm that has returned to my heart. I should have been preferred to [Admète,] the king of Thessaly; and if, for his glory, it is said that Apollo once served him as a shepherd, I am king of Scyros. Thetis is my sister. I have found some consolation for this marriage that offends me. I am organizing these games with cool tranquillity."

The interpretation of these lines that Lully provides to his actor/singer reveals a proud, arrogant king, who, contrary to his claim of cool tranquility, actually feels anger at the offence to his honor. In fact, at Lycomède's words "cool tranquillity," Lully writes a cross-relation between E-flat and E-natural. Mostly, however, Lully projects Lycomède's character through musical control of rhetorical declamation. Typical vocal intonations expressing anger are reflected in the melodic contours and phrasing of Lully's setting (A. 80): level, average pitch except for leaps upward of about a fourth or fifth on stressed syllables; unstressed syllables remain at an even pitch level; the distinctive pitch contours last about the length of a breath group. Notice, in fact, that there are several unnaturally short segments toward the beginning of Lycomède's discourse, showing breathlessness. On the other hand, there are some impetuous run-on phrases, when he begins to express his resentment of the king of Thessaly, climaxing in wide leaps upward at "*I* am king of Scyros, *and* Thetis is my sister. *I* have found some consolation. . . ."

In direct contrast to Lycomède stands the truly noble Alcide, who, in Act I, scene 1, expresses restrained and wistful sadness at having lost Alceste to Admète (the beginning of the passage is in Ex. 9-2; the entire sequence is in A. 80). One of the defining traits of his speech is the prevalence of low accents, where the pitch descends, rather than ascends, to the principal accent of a phrase, as at "Ah! Ly*chas*," "J'aurai beau me pres*ser*," "je partirai trop *tard*," "Ce n'est pint avec *toi*," "que je prétens me *taire*," "Alcest est trop ai*mable*," "C'en est *fait*," "qu'une âme ja*louse*," etc. These accents, approached downward, project Alcide's sincerity, melancholy, and moderation.

Lully's recitatives cannot mimic normal speech in every way because the text is poetry, not prose. Quinault wrote his recitatives in *vers libres* ("free verse," the equivalent of Italian *versi sciolti*), with an unpredictable mixture of line lengths, mostly of eight, ten, and twelve syllables. The texts of airs are also written in *vers libres*, but they tend to have a predictable pattern of accentuation, as in Italian arias. In a poetic line intended for recitative, the principal accent comes at the end and may be followed by an unaccented syllable that is not included in the syllable count. In a twelve-syllable line (called an "alexandrine"), another principal accent comes on the sixth syllable, which is followed by a break or caesura. Each half line ("hemistitch") of an alexandrine and each six-syllable line has an additional secondary accent, whose position is variable. Some eight-syllable lines have two such moveable, secondary accents.

Following Mersenne's approach, the accented and unaccented syllables may be grouped into poetic feet. This has been done in Example 9-2, where the feet are marked in the scansion analysis by a single slash (/), a caesura by a double slash (//), and a poetic line by a triple slash (///). In the poetry itself, caesuras are marked by an asterisk (*), and a line ending is shown by a single slash (/), under which is given the theoretical number of syllables in that line just concluded.

Example 9-2 shows that the rhythm of Lully's recitative is generally faithful to the structure of the poetry, whereas pitch accent is often used to interpret the text dramatically. Only occasionally Lully gives greater weight to a secondary accent over a primary one. Where scansion of the text favors grouping into iambs (∪ –) and anapests (∪ ∪ –), Lully tends to follow suit with his music, creating patterns that would not be characteristic of Italian recitative.

Airs, too, can be used to portray character and create expression. Act I, scene 3, contains a minuet air, "Je prétends rire" ("I mean to laugh"), which is part of

EXAMPLE 9-2. Alcide's recitative in Act I, Scene 1, of Lully's *Alceste* (1674); scansion is marked above the French text, and syllable counts (excluding the occasional weak final E) are marked below the end of each line of poetry.

246

EXAMPLE 9-2. (continued)

a comic scene that pokes fun at the preceding serious scene. Previously Alcide sighed for Alceste; here Straton asks Lychas, "Cephise, as you know, has me under her spell; you are always at her side: what do you mean to do?" to which Lychas replies, "I mean to laugh," a sentiment well served by a minuet, described by a long series of French writers as a dance with a "gay" affect.

When Straton has the opportunity to complain to Cephise of his unrequited love for her (I, 4), she replies "Un ton grondeur et sévère/ N'est pas un grand agrément" ("A complaining and severe tone is not a fine ornament"), a typical maxim air, in which a general truth or lesson is stated, usually with a notable degree of emotional detachment, promoted here by the predictable, patterned rhythm and uncomplicated descending contours. The form ABB´ is another typical feature. In keeping with his comical melancholic character, Straton replies (also in I, 4) with the expressive air "Par un espoir doux et trompeur" ("With a sweet misleading hope"), which Lully treats with frequent change of mode, mild chromaticism, and dissonance.

As with most of Lully's airs, these begin and end without orchestral framing or other formality to separate them from the surrounding recitative. Together with their almost completely syllabic text setting, instead of the melismatic setting that creates contrast between arias and recitative in Italian operas, the lack of interludes contributes to the musical continuity that is a major feature of Lully's scenes and acts. Continuity is further promoted by the fluid succession of brief chorus interjections, short ensemble segments, and abbreviated airs, as well as the tonal organization of acts.

In *Alceste* as in most of Lully's operas, each act is divided into scenes, or groups of scenes, each normally centered on a single tonality and set off from the following scene by a rapid shift of harmony, usually signaled by an accelerated scalewise descent of the bass (Ex. 9-3), called a *chute* ("fall") when it occurs as an ornament in keyboard music. The tonal organization of Lully's *Alceste*, Act I, is shown in Table 9-2. In this act, it appears that the wedding celebration correlates with C major, the character of Alcide with A minor, and the personage and influence of Lycomède with D minor.

An example of descriptive orchestral music that coordinates with a scenic effect—and probably with a pantomime dance—is entitled "Les Vents" ("The Winds," Act I, scene 8), marked "Viste" ("Fast"). It is full of rushing scales of sixteenth notes. This is immediately followed by a calmer ritournelle, which accompanies the entrance of Eole and the Zephyrs and the exit of the Aquilons. This ritournelle may be considered purely descriptive music, without dance, as Eole and the Zephys calm the stormy sea and allow Alcide and Admète to pursue Lycomède.

Even a conventional dance number may contribute to the action. In Act I, scene 7, "The sea nymphs and tritons put on a sea festival, in which sailors and fishermen are brought together." At the end of this *divertissement*, the celebrators dance a loure, traditionally thought to project mirth and cheerfulness, but often with a heavy beat, perhaps in reference to the manner of dancing to the folk bagpipe of Normandy for which the dance is named.

EXAMPLE 9–3. The *chute* that connects Act I, Scenes 2 and 3 in Lully's *Alceste*

From 1673 to 1687, Lully produced one *tragédie en musique* each year. His success in musical theater and in court politics brought him a noble title in 1681. Because of his royal monopoly over opera production, his talent for innovation, his instinct for musical drama and spectacle, and his personal relationship with Louis XIV, Lully became the most influential French musician of the seventeenth century.

LULLY'S HARMONY

The harmonic organization of Lully's operas section relies upon the way common patterns of chords contribute to the impression of movement from one stable zone to another in his music. In order to explain this in terms appropriate to France in the later seventeenth century, it will be useful to invoke French theory of the period.

In his *Traité d'accompagnment pour le théorbe, et le clavecin* ("Treatise on Accompaniment for the Theorbo and the Harpsichord") of 1690, Denis Delair explains that "the natural chord is varied by beginning with the octave, the third, or the fifth." This must have been common knowledge among French composers and continuo accompanists, whether or not they were acquainted with the German theory of roots (*bases*) or the English theory of "true bases." Delair's concept of the "natural chord," which maintains its identity through all inversions, was further developed by the harpsichordist known as Monsieur de Saint Lambert, in his *Nouveau traité de l'accompagnement de clavecin, de l'orgue, e des autres instruments* ("New Treatise on Accompaniment by the Harpsichord, the Organ, and by Other Instruments"), published in 1707; and it forms an important basis for the later and more famous theory of Jean-Philippe

The Tonal Organization of Lully's *Alceste*, Act I

SEGMENT	ACTION	TONAL ORGANIZATION	ENDS WITH A *CHUTE*?
Scenes 1 & 2	Amidst wedding celebrations, Alcide confesses to his friends is love of Alceste.	*C* and other closely related harmonies at the beginning and end. An internal *chute* leads temporarily to *a* to set off Alcide's dark reply to his friends' questions.	yes
Scene 3	Straton loves Céphise and begs Lychas not to pursue her; Lychas torments Straton with is cynicism and scorn.	Begins and ends with *a* and elaborates on other closely related harmonies.	yes
Scene 4	Céphise carelessly admits that she now loves Lychas and no longer Straton.	Begins and ends with *F* and elaborates on other closely related harmonies.	yes
Scene 5, except for the last speech by Straton	Lycomède expresses anger and disdain that Alceste is wedding Admète.	Begins with *d* and elaborates on harmonies closely related.	yes
Scenes 6 & 7, preceded by the transitional speech by Straton	*Divertissement* in the form of a wedding celebration. Toward the end, Lycomède abducts Alceste by ship.	Moves from *a* to *e* and alternates between *a* and *C*; changes to *F* when Lycomède abducts Alceste.	yes
Scene 8	Thetis blows up a storm to stop Alcide and Admète from pursuing Lycomède's ship.	Begins and ends with *d*.	no
Scene 9	Eole calms the sea.	Begins and ends with *a*.	no

Rameau. Delair's concept of the natural chord and its inversions will help explain the regularities of Lully's harmony illustrated in Example 9-4.

Example 9-4 is a minuet that Lully composed in 1670 for Moliere's comédie-ballet *Les amants magnifiques* ("The Magnificent Lovers"). It is in a major mode, probably Mode 6 transposed to D by means of a signature of two sharps. Like

EXAMPLE 9-4. Lully, "Les Hommes et femmes armés," from *Les Amants magnifiques* (1670), reduced to two staves, with the "natural chords" shown sccording to Delair's theory

most dances of this time, it is divided into two reprises (repeated sections), the second cadencing on the final, D, and the first cadencing on the boundary note, A. There is also a cadence on E in measure 18. The mode is established melodically at the beginning through emphasis on the final D, the A above, and the A below in the first violin part. The cadence on A is prepared by an elaborated descent from the E above in measures 7–10. Likewise, the cadence on E concludes a section (mm. 14–18) in which the fifth from E up to B is exploited in the melody; and a longer, more elaborated descent from A to D (mm. 19–24) reestablishes the reigning mode and prepares for the final cadence on D. But mode does not seem to structure the other voices in the texture. Rather, certain regularities of harmony seem to coordinate with melodic shapes, meter, phrasing, and cadences in the creation of four distinct modal areas.

At the beginning, the rhythmically and metrically regular alternation of "natural chords" based on D and A contribute to the establishment of the reigning mode, even though there is no formal cadence on D in this part of the minuet. A succession of three chords, on G, E, and A, produces the effect of movement to a new final, A, confirmed by a typical series of cadential chords, in this case based on D, E, and A. After the chord on A is allowed to resolve back to D at the beginning of the second reprise, a new departure from the G chord, G—F♯—B, prepares for the cadence on E. The return to D is accomplished by a series of fifth/fourth chordal progressions, E—A—D—G, which overshoots the mark, bracketing D between A and G.

As often happens in dance music, even much earlier, the natural chords in this minuet are mostly related by "true base" movements of fourth or fifth—equivalent intervals since one is the inversion of the other. But something more is operating here. Only the G chord is found upward from D in a series of ascending fifths: The dance uses chords based on G, D, A, E, B, F♯, and C♯, but not on C♮, F♮, or B♭. These seven chords are not distributed haphazardly: in each of the four sections of the minuet, once the fifth above the eventual cadence note is attained by the melody, the chords are normally limited to four—the one based on the cadence pitch, the chord founded on the pitch a fifth below that note, and the two chords based on the two pitches in the series ascending by fifths from the cadence pitch. An exception occurs in measure 22, where a chord founded on C-sharp is included in the section leading to a cadence on D; however, chords founded on the leading tone are often treated like the seventh chord based on the fifth scale degree, inasmuch as these two chords share three notes in common. Also, whereas any number of chords in the series based on *descending* fifths or ascending fourths can be found in this practice (e.g., mm. 17–21 contains a series of five chords arranged in this manner, based on B, E, A, D, and G), no more than three chords from the series of *ascending* fifths or descending fourths will normally be found. Furthermore, three of the four non-fourth/fifth chord movements belong to stereotyped patterns common in Lully's music: the descending third followed by an ascending fourth (mm. 6–8), the descending second followed by an ascending fourth (mm. 14–15), and the descent by a third from the fourth scale degree in preparation for a cadence (m. 21).

Seemingly purposeful harmonic regularities such as these are more common in Lully's dances than in his airs, and far more common in either than in his recitatives. Meter and phrasing seem to coordinate with harmonic shapes to create the impression of stability or goal-oriented movement. There are, of course, other dances that conform to these regularities less than this one, but the trend is clear. Younger composers increasingly took dances with this sort of regular harmony as their models.

MUSIC IN THE CITY OF PARIS IN THE AGE OF LOUIS XIV

The music of the court and the music of the city were not, of course, entirely separate. As mentioned earlier, the chamber musicians of the court were free to ply their trade in Paris during three quarters of each year. Although a theater was built at Versailles about 1681–85, Lully's *tragédies en musique* were most frequently performed in the theater of the Palais-Royal in Paris, home to Lully's Académie Royale de Musique from 1674 to 1683. The audience capacity was about thirteen hundred; offering multiple performances of each opera to an elite public for paid admission, the theater of the Palais-Royal served the wealthy and aristocratic citizens of Paris, although the works performed there were cultural products of the royal court.

The keyboard players of the royal court typically held positions as organists at churches in the city. In fact, with the growth in the length and importance of the *grand motet*, little place remained for organ music during Mass and Vespers in the royal chapel. Thus, it is not surprising that, when books of French church organ music began to be published again in 1665, after a hiatus of nearly forty years since the last publication of Titelouze (1626), nearly every one of the composers of these new publications held a position in a church of the city— Guillaume Gabriel Nivers (ca. 1632–1714) at Saint-Suplice and St. Louis-des-Invalides, Nicolas Antoine Lebègue (ca. 1631–1702) at Saint-Merri, and Nicolas Gigault (ca. 1627–1707) at Saint-Nicolas-en-Champs.

The content of printed French organ books, from Nivers's first volume in 1665 onward, was standardized by the *Ceremoniale parisiense*, a church order published in 1662 that restricted the range of form and content of worship services in the Paris archdiocese. It required organists to incorporate the appropriate chant melodies into the versets they played in alternation with the plainchant choir during the Kyrie, Gloria, Sanctus, Agnus Dei, and Domine Salvum. During the other parts of the Mass Ordinary and in place of alternate verses of the Magnificat at Vespers, organists were permitted to play short *récits*, duos, trios, and similar items. The names and typical characteristics of these short pieces refer directly to the construction and resources of the classic French organ, which emerged as a highly standardized type during the decades from 1660 to 1690.

By about 1670, a typical newer French organ had four keyboards and a pedal board, with five separate chests of pipes. The *grand orgue*, attached to the wall of the church and faced by the organist, was the largest of these—it contained the largest number of ranks or stops in the 16-, 8-, 4-, and 2-foot octaves, as well as several that sounded an octave and a fifth, or two or three octaves and a third above the note played on the keyboard. In back of the organist, facing the congregation, was the *positif* chest, which contained a smaller number of ranks but representatives of all types found in the *grand organ*, except for those of the 16-foot octave. The chest of the *grand orgue* sat on top of a much smaller chest called the *echo*, which had a narrower selection of stops, mostly reeds, covering only the soprano register and controlled by a short keyboard. Another short keyboard controlled the pipes of the *récit*, a very small chest placed on top of the *grand orgue* and hidden by its largest pipes. The *récit* usually held only one or two ranks of reed pipes, confined, as those of the *echo*, to the upper range. The pipes controlled exclusively by the pedal board were normally of the 8-foot octave only; they were not the largest, lowest pipes of the instrument as they were in German and Dutch organs. Typically the pedal chest of French organs held only two ranks of pipes, one of reeds and the other of wood. The purpose of the pedal board of French organs was to play prominent melody lines in the lower register, and in this way it functioned as the lower-range counterpart to the *récit*.

The titles given to the short pieces that make up the all-purpose suites and sets of versets in French organ books of this period usually refer at the same time to the keyboards, chests, and typical combinations to be used, often explained in the composer's preface, and to certain features of style and form. Thus, the pieces in Nivers's Book 3, Suite 3 in Mode 2 (1675, W. 18) that are entitled *Récit* or *Dialogue de Récits* feature a vocal-style melody to be played in the soprano register on one or two of the prominent reed stops of the *récit* chest, a melody introduced and accompanied by softer stops or mixtures from the *grand orgue* or *positif*. In the piece called *basse*, the melody line is played on the trompette (reed) stop of the pedals. The *Dialogue à 2 choeurs* requires alternation between the *positif* and a complex mixture on the *grand orgue*, called *grand jeu*, which included stops that sound two octaves and a third above the note played. Even the title *Fugue grave*, which at first appears to refer only to musical structure and style, implied a specific combination of metal flute pipes and reeds of the *grand orgue*, according to instructions published by Legègue.

The musical style of the short pieces and versets in these French organ books reflects three sources of influence. *Style brisé* from lute music via the harpsichord works of Chambonnières, Louis Couperin, and others can be found in many of these pieces, particularly in the preludes and echoes. Dance rhythms crop up frequently in *récits*, *duos*, and *dialogues*, where the ornamental style of opera and chamber airs is also found. Although subjects are passed from voice to voice in the fugues, the slight extent of rhythmic differentiation among the parts in the texture and the sparing use of dissonance renders even these pieces rather more homophonic than polyphonic.

The Sainte-Chapelle on the Île de la Cité was a church that belonged in part to the royal court and in part to the city. Built in the thirteenth century as the palace chapel of Louis XI and a splendid example of Gothic architecture, it remained under the direct protection of the king even after the royal court moved to other buildings—to the Palace of the Louvre by the time of Louis XIV. Although the chapel masters of the Sainte-Chapelle were not officers of the court, the musical establishment there was supported by endowments established by the crown and by direct payments from the king. The music directors at the Sainte-Chapelle during the reign of Louis XIV were Eustache Gehenault, 1657–63; René Ouvrard, 1663–79; François Chaperon, 1679–98; Marc-Antoine Charpentier, 1698–1704; and Nicolas Bernier, 1698–1726. The prevailing style of music performed there inclined toward the Italian, the principal model being Giacomo Carissimi.

In fact, Charpentier (1643–1704) studied with Carissimi in Rome, 1666–67, and the motets that he composed upon his return reflect his teacher's style very clearly, as well as that of some younger Roman composers. This influence is most obvious in his thirty-five dramatic or dialogue motets, often called Latin oratorios, many of which Charpentier composed for the Jesuits in Paris, first at their Collège de Clermont and then at their principal Parisian church, St. Louis (called Collège de Louis-le-Grand after 1683).

In Charpentier's *Filius prodigus* ("The Prodigal Son," 1680), for example, the recitatives, with their frequently static bass, unchanging meter, and liberal use of monotone alongside dramatic inflection and rhetorical organization, and the interjections of many brief aria-like segments, recall the oratorios of Marco Marazzoli. The first narrative chorus, however, is full of pictorial details that resemble an older style of madrigal.

Among the other churches in Paris with Italianate musical traditions was Sainte-Anne-la-Royale, the church of the Theatine priests, who were so dedicated to music that they were called "the fathers of song." The Roman composer Paolo Lorenzani (1640–1713), who had been in France since 1678, served as the Theatines' music director from 1685 to 1687. The Congregation of the Oratorians, established in Paris in 1611, served as another conduit for Italian music. These institutions contributed to a building pressure for a continuation of the accommodation with Italian styles that was begun by Du Mont in the 1650s. But Lully largely held this tendency in check.

Although Lully held a monopoly on the public performance of opera, several means were employed for circumventing his restrictions outside of the royal court. From 1672 to 1686 Charpentier composed music for the spoken plays staged by the Comédie-Française, many of them by Molière. As music director in the large household of Marie de Lorraine, known as Mademoiselle de Guise, Charpentier composed a series of eight small-scale stage works, 1684–87, that were performed privately. The creative outlets of such major talents as Marc-Antoine Charpentier and the curiosity of the Parisian public about Italian music remained pent up for as long as Lully lived. At Lully's death in 1687, this pressure was released, with consequences that will be explored in Chapter 15.

255

BIBLIOGRAPHICAL NOTES

Political, Economic, and Cultural Centralization in France
Two books about Louis XIV's reign that best reflect recent thought are David J. Sturdy, *Louis XIV* (New York: St. Martin's Press, 1998); and William F. Church, *The Impact of Absolutism in France: National Experience under Richelieu, Mazarin, and Louis XIV* (New York: John Wiley and Sons, 1969). A book that focuses on the economic aspects of centralization is Charles Woolsey, *Colbert and a Century of French Mercantilism* (New York: Columbia University Press, 1939; repr. London: F. Cass, 1964).

Musique de la Grande Écurie—Musique de la Chambre—The Chapelle Royale
The book that presents most thoroughly the political, social, and economic aspects of the administrative divisions of French court music making is Robert M. Isherwood, *Music in the Service of the King: France in the Seventeenth Century* (Ithaca: Cornell University Press, 1973). Additional information on this subject is summarized in James R. Anthony, *French Baroque Music from Beaujoyeulx to Rameau*, rev. ed. (Portland, OR: Amadeus Press, 1977).

Spectacle as Propaganda at the Court of Louis XIV
The basic work on this subject is Isherwood, *Music in the Service of the King*. A more general exposition of the use of spectacle for political ends by European monarchs of the Early Modern Era is by Roy C. Strong; it was originally published under the title *Splendour at Court: Renaissance Spectacle and Illusion* (London: Weidenfeld and Nicolson, 1973) and immediately reissued as *Splendor at Court: Renaissance Spectacle and the Theater of Power* (Boston: Houghton Mifflin, 1973). A revised edition with the title *Art and Power: Renaissance Festivals, 1450–1650* was published in 1984 (Berkeley: University of California Press and Woodbridge: Boydell Press). Two books with more theoretical approaches to the subject are Peter Burke, *The Fabrication of Louis XIV* (New Haven: Yale University Press, 1992); and Kristiaan P. Aercke, *Gods of Play: Baroque Festival Performances as Rhetorical Discourse* (New York: State University of New York Press, 1994).

The System of Royal Academies
Here again the basic text is Isherwood, *Music in the Service of the King*. Additional information can be found in Woolsey, *Colbert and a Century of French Mercantilism* and in Gilette Ziegler, *At the Court of Versailles*, trans. Walter Taylor (New York: I. P. Dutton and Co., 1966).

The Beginnings of French Opera—Ballets de cour and Comédies-Ballets
The best summaries of these topics are in Anthony, *French Baroque Music*. Most of the specialized writings on this subject are in French and are cited in Anthony's book. The most reliable guide to the musical and choreographic characteristics of French court dances is Meredith Little and Natalie Jenne, *Dance and the Music of J. S. Bach* (Bloomington: Indiana University Press, 1991/1998). Further detail about choreography is found in Wendy Hilton, *Dance of Court & Theater: The French Noble Style, 1690–1725* (London: Dance Books and Princeton: Princeton Book Co., 1981), reprinted, with other writings, in Hilton, *Dance and Music of the Court and*

Theater: Selected Writings of Wendy Hilton, Dance & Music, 10 (Stuyvesent, NY: Pendragon Press, 1997). A detailed study of a single ballet spectacle, with additional general information, is Rebecca Harris-Warrick and Carol G. Marsh, *Musical Theatre at the Court of Louis XIV:* Le Mariage de la Grosse Cathos (Cambridge: Cambridge University Press, 1994). *Dance & Music in French Baroque Theatre: Sources and Interpretations,* ed. Sarah Yuill McCleave and Geoffrey Burgess (London: Institue of Advanced Musical Studies, King's College London, 1998), contains specialized articles on this subject. Two earlier books on the choreography and musical style of Lully's dances contain much that is useful but should be used with caution: Helen Meredith Ellis, "The Dances of J. B. Lully (1632–1687)," Ph.D. diss., Stanford Univ., 1967; and Betty Bang Mather, *Dance Rhythms of the French Baroque: A Handbook for Performance* (Bloomington, IN: Indiana University Press, 1987). A videotape illustrating the principal court dances of France as they were notated in the early eighteenth century is Paige Whitely-Bauguess, *Introduction to Baroque Dance: Dance Types* (New Bern, NC: Down East Dance, 1999). Lully's music for *comèdies-ballets* is studied in Stephen Harlan Fleck, "Molière's Comedy-Ballets: A Dramatic and Musical Analysis," Ph.D. diss., Univ. of California, Davis, 1993. The most recent biography of Lully in English is Ralph Henry Forster, *Jean-Baptiste Lully* (London: Owen, 1973). New biographical research on Lully by Jérôme de La Gorce is reported in *Lully Studies,* ed. John Hajdu Heyer (Cambridge: Cambridge University Press, 2000) and in the entry in *The New Grove Dictionary of Music and Musicians,* vol. 15, 2nd ed. (London: Macmillan, 2001).

Tragédie en Musique—Lully's Alceste

Anthony, *French Baroque Music,* contains a fine overview. The principal book in English is Caroline Wood, *Music and Drama in the* Tragédie en Musique*, 1673–1715: Jean-Baptiste Lully and His Successors* (New York: Garland, 1996). Caroline Wood and Graham Sadler, *French Baroque Opera: A Reader* (Burlington, VT: Ashgate, 2000), is a very useful collection of translated excerpts from period writings on this subject. The most recent and thorough treatment in French is Manuel Couvreur, *Jean-Baptiste Lully: musique et dramaturgie au service du Prince* (Brussels: Vokar, 1992). A key discussion of Lully's recitative style is Lois Rosow, "French Baroque Recitative as an Expression of Tragic Declamation," *Early Music,* XI (1983), 468–77. The theaters in which Lully's operas were performed are described in Barbara Coeyman, "Theatres for Opera and Ballet during the Reigns of Louis XIV and Louis XV," *Early Music,* XVIII (1990), 22–37. An extended argument for the allegorical interpretation of *Alceste* presented here is in Kenneth O. Smith, "Jean-Baptiste Lully's *Alceste* as an Allegory for Louis XIV's Dutch War," M.M. thesis, Univ. of Illinois, Urbana-Champaign, 2000.

Music in the City of Paris in the Age of Louis XIV

There are many detailed studies of French organs of this period. A useful overview is Fenner Douglass, *The Language of the Classical French Organ,* rev. ed. (New Haven: Yale University Press, 1995). An excellent guide to the life and works of Lully's worthy rival is H. Wiley Hitchcock, *Marc-Antoine Charpentier* (Oxford: Oxford University Press, 1990).

CHAPTER 10

Music in Spain, Portugal, and their Colonies

THE SPANISH EMPIRE AND ITS CHURCH

At the outset of the seventeenth century, the King of Spain ruled the entire Iberian Peninsula (present-day Spain and Portugal), part of the Netherlands, the southern half of the Italian peninsula, Sicily, Sardinia, the Canary Islands, the Philippine Islands, major portions of North, South, and Central America, and a number of other colonies. Spain was one of the four major powers of Europe, along with France, England, and the Holy Roman Empire, and it had a proud history of accomplishment in music, painting, and literature.

The Spanish Empire in the seventeenth century was larger and more diverse than that ruled by the Habsburgs and was more centrally controlled, although less so than France. The core of the Spanish Empire was created by the unification of Aragon and Castile through the marriage of Ferdinand II and Isabella I in 1479. As the other regions of the Iberian Peninsula—Catalonia, Navarre, Valencia, and, eventually, Portugal (from 1580 to 1640)—were absorbed into this empire, they were governed as provinces, each ruled by a viceroy appointed by the king, exactly the same as non–Iberian Spanish provinces or colonies.

In many parts of Spain and its provinces and colonies, significant power continued to be shared with local and regional nobility, who were very numerous. Thus, government, economy, and patronage of the arts were less centralized in the Spanish empire than they were in England and France. Because Spain's New World colonies were set up on the same footing as its Iberian provinces, and because Spain pursued Christianization of its New World subjects more vigorously than the other European colonial powers, musical chapels were established in Spanish America far earlier than in any other place outside of Europe—in the early sixteenth century in some cases.

When Ferdinand II died in 1516 without a male heir, the crown passed to Charles I, the son of Ferdinand's daughter and her Habsburg husband. Charles also inherited the Habsburg dominions and the Imperial crown in 1519, briefly uniting the Spanish and German empires as Emperor Charles V. In 1556, Charles gave the throne of Spain and part of the Netherlands to his son, Philip II, and the Holy Roman Empire to his brother, Ferdinand I. Charles himself retired to a monastery. As a consequence, a series of Spanish kings during the seventeenth century began their public lives as rulers of the Spanish Netherlands before ascending to the throne of Spain, bringing a degree of Flemish influence to Spanish music and painting. Another consequence was that, for most of the seventeenth century, Spain and the Holy Roman Empire were allies, generally against France.

Although Spain derived enormous quantities of silver and gold from its New World colonies, these riches led ironically to economic crises and military reversals during the seventeenth century. In its pursuit of New World treasure, Spain neglected its agriculture, manufacturing, and infrastructure, in striking contrast to the national mercantilism of France. Yet during most of the seventeenth century, Spain remained a world power with a rich cultural heritage of which its nobility was confident and proud.

Most of the seventeenth century is included in what is commonly reckoned Spain's Golden Century in architecture and painting and its Golden Age in literature. In the visual arts, it boasted El Greco, Bartolomé Esteban Murillo, Francisco de Zurbarán, Diego Velázquez, and Juan Carreño de Miranda. In literature, the crises in Spain beginning in the later sixteenth century gave rise to a reaction in the works of writers called the *arbitristas* ("projectors"), such as picaresque novels, which tell stories of young men who make their way by cleverness and roguery rather than by honest work. Although Miguel de Cervantes (1547–1616) wrote several picaresque novels, his most famous work, *Don Quixote* (in two parts, 1605 and 1615), is a satire of his contemporaries' exaggerated quest for honor. On the other hand, the comedies of the court poets such as Lope de Vega (1562–1635) and Pedro Calderón de la Barca (1600–1681) present conflicts that are resolved in ways that preserve the prevailing social order.

Although the social and economic vicissitudes of seventeenth-century Spain may be reflected in the history of its music, as in its literature, they did not diminish its quantity or quality, which are high by any measure. Spanish composers confidently strode a path different from that of their contemporaries in the other major European nations. Enough music survives to make that judgment, even though most of the Iberian music of the seventeenth century listed in documents has been lost.

The documents that catalog the lost music of Spain and Portugal are mostly inventories of libraries and descriptions of court festivities. The most important inventory is the first volume of a projected multi-volume printed list of the royal music library belonging to King John IV of Portugal (ruled 1640–56), a composer in his own right. Although incomplete, the first volume, published in 1657, runs to 521 pages. This massive collection was destroyed by the earthquake and fire that ruined Lisbon in 1755. Likewise, the royal music collection at the court of Spain was destroyed by the fire of 1734 in Madrid. As a consequence of these two disasters, Spanish and Portuguese music of the seventeenth century is represented by a relatively small number of examples, while the vast quantity that once existed is lost.

LATIN LITURGICAL MUSIC

At the beginning of the seventeenth century, the musical repertoires, styles, and ensembles heard in Spanish cathedrals closely resembled those of the cathedrals and major basilicas of central and southern Italy. The chapels of Spanish cathedrals generally consisted of about sixteen singers and a smaller or equal number of instrumentalists, mostly players of shawms, dulcians, cornetts, and trombones. The music for the Mass Ordinary, the motets performed in place of most of the Mass Proper, and the psalm settings, Magnificats, responsories, and motets for Vespers, Compline, and sometimes Matins were written in large choir books in which all the parts were texted, as if to be sung and not played. A great deal of this music was written for two or more choirs. The psalms and Magnificats were usually arranged so that verses sung by the polyphonic choirs alternated with verses sung in plainchant. Falsobordone was also in widespread use for psalms, hymns, and Magnificats.

The similarity between cathedral music in Spain and the southern parts of Italy during the early seventeenth century was the result of contacts established during the sixteenth century, a period when many Spanish musicians spent at least part of their careers in Italy, most often in Rome. Among the most famous examples were Francisco de Peñalosa (ca. 1470–1528), Cristóbal de Morales (ca. 1500–1553), Francisco Guerrero (1528–1599), and Tomás Luis de Victoria (1548–1611). After Victoria's return to Spain in 1595, no major Spanish composers worked in Italy for many decades, during which the church music of Spain flourished independently and on its own terms.

Some features of Italian Latin liturgical music of the late sixteenth century that now seem the most innovative and progressive—polychoral arrangement, chordal declamation approaching a recitational style, new freedom in dissonance treatment, and frequent cadences—are almost more pronounced in Spanish cathedral music of about 1600. Polychoral composition is found in Spain as early as 1572 in the works of Victoria. To his beloved royal monastery of El Escorial, Philip II between 1563 and 1584 gave eight organs for the accompaniment of separated choirs. By the middle of the seventeenth century, polychoral music predominated in Spain, and it is not uncommon to find Spanish works of that period calling for five and six choirs.

A good example of polychoral composition with progressive features is the *Dixit Dominus* (W. 19) by Mateo Romero (1575/6–1647), who was born Mathieu Rosmarin in Liège (Spanish Netherlands). Often called "Maestro Capitán," he was the music director at the Spanish royal court in Madrid, 1598–1634. The amount of monotone recitation in his *Dixit Dominus* (W. 19) is striking. Nearly every short interjection by a different choir ends in a cadence. The dissonance in measure 29 (Ex. 10-1) is striking but not unusual in Spanish music of the seventeenth century.

Looking back on this period from a perspective of several decades, the Spanish composer and theorist Francisco Valls (1665–1747), in his *Mapa armónico*

260

EXAMPLE 10-1. Dissonance in Mateo Romero, *Dixit Dominus*

d, e, f, a, b

(1742), defended his countrymen's use of unusual dissonance as justified by the needs of expressive melody and part of what made their music different from French and Italian music.

Although works like Romero's *Dixit Dominus* seem to be written for several similar choirs of voices, they were apparently performed with soloists doubled by organ in the first choir and with various combinations of voices and wind instruments in the other choirs. In some cathedrals at least, the wind instruments played alone in preludes, postludes, processions, and during otherwise silent moments, such as the Elevation of the Communion host. The sound of shawms and dulcians was so strongly identified with church music in Spain that these instruments were used in musical plays to evoke the theme of religion.

Beside instrumentation, other unnotated features of Spanish church music included embellishment by diminution, mentioned in documents from the cathedral of Granada as early as 1552, and organ accompaniment of solo voices, mentioned by Juan Bermudo in 1549. Although chordal accompaniment, especially by harp, had been used in Spain since the sixteenth century, specific continuo accompaniment, rather than a vocal bass part, is found in Spanish church music only after the harpist/composer Juan Hidalgo (1614–1685) joined the royal chapel in Madrid. Parts idiomatically composed for solo voice with written-out diminution, specifically designated ensemble instrumental parts, and figured bass can be found in Spain by the second half of the century, for example in works by Miguel de Irízar (d. 1684) of Segovia dating from 1656, by Diego de Pontac (1603–1654) from Santiago, and by Romero's successor as *maestro* of the royal chapel in 1634, Carlos Patiño (1600–1675).

Patiño's antiphon *Maria, Mater Dei* ("Mary, Mother of God," A. 81, ca. 1640) juxtaposes a soprano soloist supported by basso continuo accompaniment and two four-voice choirs. In addition to the contrast between soloist and choruses, there are several striking changes in the pace of declamation, which place the gentle, pleading phrases replete with sighing appoggiaturas and expressive harmonies in relief against moments of emphatic declamation marked by dotted rhythms, pitch repetition, and sequential elaborations that almost reach the intensity of shouts. A third style of text setting is reserved for the melismatic climax of the work, in which the auxesis figure in the text *o clemens, o pia, o dulcis virgo Maria* ("o gracious, o gentle, o sweet Virgin Mary") is projected by means of a parallel series of elaborations on a single rising and falling scale passage introduced each time by a prolonged and tension-filled anacrusis on the syllable "o."

Idiomatic writing for solo voice, using diminutions and other decorative melismas as well as smooth, aria-like melodic lines, entered into Spanish cathedral music rather late in the seventeenth century, as in the solo Lamentations for Holy Week by Irízar and his student José de Vaquedano (d. 1711), who became *maestro* at Santiago in 1681.

However, polychoral music with all parts vocally conceived and texted and with continuo accompaniment continued to represent the mainstream of Latin liturgical music in Spain and Portugal until the end of the seventeenth century.

Opposition to the emotionalism of Italian church music was expressed by King John IV of Portugal in his *Defensa da la música moderna contra la errada opinión del obispo Cyrilo Franco* ("Defense of Modern Music against the Erroneous Opinion of Bishop Cyrilo Franco," 1649), even though he knew and admired the dissonant and chromatic music of the late Italian madrigalists Marenzio, Gesualdo, Striggio, Monte, and Monteverdi. King John's favorite composer and musical confidant was Manuel Cardoso (1566–1650), whose style resembles that of Palestrina. The king's taste and attitude were widely shared among the nobility and church hierarchy of the Iberian peninsula at this time. Nevertheless, music of a far less formal character also found its way into Spanish and Portuguese churches in the form of the villancico, inspired by and appealing to the culture of the lower social classes.

THE VILLANCICO AND OTHER VERNACULAR CHURCH MUSIC

The most distinctive feature of Spanish church music in the seventeenth century is the singing of Spanish-language villancicos in place of the Responsories of Matins at Christmas, during the octave of Corpus Christi, and on various saints' days. There are normally three Responsories in each of the three Nocturns of Matins each day, making nine in all, but it was customary to replace only eight of them with villancicos, leaving the Te Deum in Latin as the ninth Responsory. Since at many churches in Spain, Portugal, and their New World colonies the music director was required to provide new villancicos for each of these holidays every year, the number of these works, both surviving and lost, is very large.

By the time polyphonic villancicos were composed in the fifteenth century, the form paralleled that of the French virelai and Italian ballata. The distinguishing characteristic of this international family of strophic verse-and-refrain song forms is found in the conclusion of each verse, where music from the refrain is sung to lines of poetry that reverse the opening rhyme scheme in order to make a link with the following musical and textual refrain.

Religious villancicos are found alongside their secular counterparts in Spain at every stage in the genre's history. Villancicos were sung in place of the Responsories of Matins in the Granada Cathedral by the late fifteenth century. The spread of this practice during the sixteenth century led to the first publication of religious villancicos by Francisco Guerrero, *maestro de capilla* of the Seville Cathedral from 1574 until his death in 1599. In his large collection of *Canciones y villanescas* [villancicos] *espirituales* (1589), the practice of setting the refrain (*estribillo*) for many voices and the verses (*coplas*) for few or even a solo voice became the norm.

The religious villancico continued to flourish during the second half of the sixteenth century and developed a great variety of forms and styles during the seventeenth century. The vast majority of these religious villancicos still show an alternation between large-ensemble refrains (*estribillos*) and verses (*coplas*) for soloists, but they may precede the first *estribillo* with an *introducción* or *tonada* for soloists, which sometimes is repeated along with the *estribillo* after each of the *coplas*.

Typical in many respects of early seventeenth-century religious villancicos are the seventy-one surviving examples composed by Juan Bautista Comes (1582–1643), *maestro de capilla* of the Valencia Cathedral, 1613–18 and 1632–38, and a prolific composer of Latin church music as well as villancicos.

Bien te puedes alegrar (W. 20) is representative of the genre and of Comes's style. Its text, which refers to the consecrated Communion host, reveals that this villancico was composed for Corpus Christi ("The Body of Christ"), a holiday in which the host, mystically transformed into the body of Christ, is carried through the streets in processions. The text of *Bien te puedes alegrar* ("Well may you rejoice") puts this celebration in direct, familiar language in the first *copla*: "See that God offers you glory in my morsel."

Villancicos for Corpus Christi were sung either during Matins or in one of the special afternoon musical performances, called *siestas*, traditionally presented every day for a week preceding Corpus Christi, in or in front of the church, or during an outdoor procession.

In *Bien te puedes alegrar*, the introduction, called the *tonada*, is sung by one voice, and it is followed by the choral refrain, called the *responsión*, which repeats the words of the *tonada* and elaborates upon its music. The melody originally sung by the solo voice in the *tonada* is taken up in the *responsión* by the Alto I part; it is typical of Spanish part songs of this and the previous century that the melody is found in an inner voice. The two *coplas* are sung by the solo voice and are each followed by the music of the *tonada*, which resembles that of the *responsión*, but with new text, and the *responsión* itself, with its original text. In effect, therefore, this piece preserves a vestige of the older, fifteenth- and sixteenth-century division of the *copla* into the *mudanza,* the repeated musical phrase, and the *vuelta,* in which the music of the refrain is sung with new text with reversed rhyme.

The music of Comes's *Bien te puedes alegrar* preserves several features that can be traced to the secular villancico of a century earlier: syllabic text setting, triple meter, frequent hemiola, and syncopation. These features remained typical of the religious villancico throughout the seventeenth century. Nothing comparable to this syncopated rhythmic style can be found in the music of any other European nation at this time. A new feature of Comes's villancicos—in fact a feature appearing here remarkably early in the context of Spanish music—is the continuo part indicated by the untexted and unfigured bass, presumably to be rendered with appropriate chords, on harp, guitar, or organ.

By the middle of the seventeenth century, three further developments in the religious villancico are evident: (1) a lengthening and elaboration of the *responsión*, typically including a variety of contrasting textures, pitting individual soloists against various combinations of voices and the full chorus; (2) the incorporation of dialogue between specific characters or personages, usually in the *coplas* but sometimes within the *introducción*; and (3) the representation of ethnic stereotypes (the Frenchman, the Portuguese, the Italian, the Negro, the Guinean, etc.), especially in Christmas villancicos, through the use dialects or distortions of Spanish or Portuguese and, perhaps, allusions to folk music.

An example illustrating all three of these mid-seventeenth-century developments is *A siolo flasiquiyo* ("Hey, Mister Flasiquiyo!") by Juan Gutierrez de Padilla (ca. 1590–1664). In this piece (A. 82), the greatest variety of texture and also the dialogue are contained in the *introducción*, which is sung only once. In it, the characters of Mister Flasiquiyo and Mister Thomas are represented by different pairs of texted voice parts, but this may be only a notational expediency, allowing the piece to be performed by voices alone in the absence of an accompanying instrument. At the end of the *introducción* there is an eighteen-bar segment written in only two of the voice parts, marked with the names "Andrea" and "Ynes." There are no corresponding segments, even with rests, in the other voices. The text of this segment is that of the *responsión*, which follows it in all six voices. Perhaps it, too, represents an alternate version for accompanied solo voices, and the six-voice *responsión* is the version to be used in the absence of accompanying instruments.

The texture and harmony of *A siolo flasiquiyo* are typical of those seventeenth-century villancicos that evoke popular or folk style, including villancicos belonging—like *A siolo flasiquiyo*—to the subgenre of the *negrilla*, in which the speech and behavior of black Africans is depicted from a Spanish point of view. There is no imitation in *A siolo flasiquiyo* but an almost exclusively chordal texture relieved only by occasional rhythmic interplay among the voices. In many places, such as in the *responsión*, the *basis* (the term used by Harnisch [1608] and Lippius [1612] for what is called the "root" of the chord in modern theory) oscillates between pitches a fifth apart, C, G, and D, with major thirds, perhaps suggesting the frequent cadences of mid-century Italian music. In other places, such as the *introducción*, the harmony implies successions of chords related by steps and thirds. Generally, the chords seem neither patterned, as in the ciaccona, etc., nor organized to lead to the final chord, as in some of Carissimi's music. In combination with lively, syncopated rhythms and rapid tempos, the harmonic style of seventeenth-century villancicos seems unlike that of any other European music of the period.

The Text of *A siolo flasiquiyo* set by Juan Gutiérrez de Padilla,
Puebla, Mexico, 1653

"¡Ah, siolo Flasiquillo!"	"Hey, Mister Flasiquillo!"
"¿Qué manda, siol Tomé?"	"What's up, Mister Tomé?"
"¿Tenemo tura trumenta	"Do we have all the instruments
templarita cum consielta?"	tuned up as a group?"
"Si, siolo ven, poté	"Yessir, you can
avisa voz a misé,	tell my master

Introducción

que sa lo moleno ya	that the black man is already
cayendo de pula risa	falling down from laughter
y mulliendo por baila."	and dying to dance."

Responsión

"¡Llámalo, llámalo aplisa!	"Call him, call him quickly!
que ha veniro lo branco ya,	for the white men have already
y lo Niño aspelando sa,	come, and the Child is waiting
y se aleglala	and will be gladdened,
ha ha ha ha,	ha, ha, ha,
con la zambambá	by the zambambá,
ha ha ha ha,	ha, ha, ha,
con lo guacambé,	by the guacambé,
con lo cascabé."	by the jingle bell."
"Sí, siñolo Tomé,	"Yes, Mister Tomé,
repicamo lo rabé	we will play the rebec,
y a la panderetillo Antón	and let Antón play the tambourine;
bailalemo' lo' neglo al son."	we Negroes will dance to the *son*.

¡Tumbucutú, cutú, cutú,	Tumbucutú, cutú, cutú,
y toquemos posito, querito!	and let's play slowly and quietly!
¡Tumbucutú!	Tumbucutú!
¡No pantemo a lo Niño Jesú!	Let's not frighten the Child Jesus!

Coplas 1, 2, & 3

1 Turu neglo de Guinea	1 All of us Negroes from Guinea
que venimo combirara:	who are invited come:
Adé tlae su criara,	Adé brings his servant girl;
Mungla ve con su liblea;	Mangla comes in his livery;
y plu que lo branco vea	so that the white man can see
que Re brano nos selvimo,	that we serve a white King,
con vaya Adé un lamo, plimo,	in jest, Adé, with a stick, pokes at
y halemo a lo Niño: "¡Bu!"	and tickles the Child: "Bu!"

Repeat the *Responsión*

2 De mérico y cilujano	2 As a doctor and surgeon
se vista Minguel aplisa,	let Minguel get dressed quickly,
pues nos cula Jesuclisa	for Jesus Christ cures
la helilas con su mano.	our wounds with his hand.
Baile el canario y villano,	Let's dance the canary and the villano;
más no pase pol detlás	but one shouldn't go behind
de mula que da la ¡zas!,	a mule that kicks
de toro que dirá "Mu."	or a bull that says "Moo."

Repeat the *Responsión*

3 Antonilo con su sayo, que tlujo re Puelto Rico, saldrá vestiro re mico, y Minguel re papagayo; y cuando llegue a adorayo, al Niño le diré asi: "Si tú llola pol mí, yo me aleglamo' pol Tú."	3 Antonilo with his sash that be brought from Puerto Rico, will come out dressed as a monkey, and Minguel as a parrot; and when I come to worship him, I'll say to the Child, "If You weep for me, I will be happy for You."
Repeat the *Responsión*	Repeat the *Responsión*

In the dialogue of the *introducción* to *A siolo flasiquiyo*, Mister Flasiquiyo and Mister Tomé sing a distorted sort of Spanish that conventionally represented the speech of Africans as often happens in a *negrilla*. The men discuss preparations for dancing to the music of a "son." The Spanish word *son* is still today applied to various types of folk song and dance featuring the triple meter and hemiola typical of the seventeeth-century villancico. Although the syncopated rhythms and call-and-response format of villancicos of the *negrilla* have been ascribed to African influences, both features were typical of Spanish and Portuguese villancicos of this period as early as the fifteenth century.

What are ethnic stereotypes and references to folk song and dance doing in a villancico written for Christmas Matins? Perhaps the explanation lies in the rise in the seventeenth century of Nativity scenes, especially the folk-art diorama of dolls and models (the crèche, still in use today), in which scenes of everyday life and people of a variety of classes and conditions are included to illustrate the universal importance of the event (see Fig. 10-1). This concept is in keeping with the official policy of the Spanish monarchy, which actively promoted the ideal of a multiethnic empire.

The composer of *A siolo flasiquiyo* was Juan Gutiérrez de Padilla, who wrote the piece for Christmas Matins of 1653 at the cathedral of Puebla, one of the most important cities of that part of New Spain corresponding to present-day Mexico.

As mentioned earlier, Spain and Portugal established mission churches and cathedrals in their colonies on the same footing as the provinces of the Iberian Peninsula. As a consequence, chapels with chapel masters, normally composers of merit, were established very early in Las Palmas in the Canary Islands (1514), Cartagena de Indias (1537), Mexico City (1539), Cuzco (1553), Bogotá (1584), Manila (1586), Puebla (1603), Lima (1612), Rio de Janeiro (1645), and Caracas (1671). At the cathedral of Mexico City, indigenous instrumentalists appear on payrolls as early as 1543. Padilla's successor at the Puebla Cathedral was his student Juan García (ca. 1619–1678), who was perhaps the earliest composer of European art music born in the New World.

Although ensemble instruments other than those of the continuo group are indicated in villancicos as early as a few by Comes, the shawms, dulcians, and cornetts documented in villancico performances throughout the seventeenth

Figure 10-1. Detail showing African musicians in an Eighteenth-Century crèche in the Michele Cuciniello Collection, National Museum of San Martino, Naples

century apparently played from the texted parts, doubling or replacing voices. Specific parts for violins in villancicos became common only with the surge of Italian influence near the end of the seventeenth century. An example of such a work is the villancico *Corazón, que suspiras atento* for solo soprano, two violins, and *accompañamiento* (i.e., continuo) by Sebastián Durón (1660–1716), who worked at the cathedrals of several cities in Spain beginning in 1672 before joining the royal chapel as organist in 1691 and becoming its director in 1702.

As early as 1678, printed books of texts indicate that recitatives and arias had begun to replace *coplas* in some villancicos at the Toledo Cathedral. By the beginning of the eighteenth century, villancicos can be found that resemble Italian cantatas of that time, and they are often called *cantadas* in their sources. An early example is ¿*O quién pudiera alcanzar?* ascribed to a "Juan de Torres." Several musicians of this name are known from seventeenth-century records, but there is no certain connection between any of them and this work. ¿*O quién pudiera alcanzar?* has three da-capo arias alternating with recitatives, rapid violin parts, and a harmonic style comparable to that of Italian composers of the early eighteenth century.

Even before the infiltration of recitatives and arias, religious villancicos had connections with drama and staged spectacle. Documentary evidence shows that at times villancicos were sung during Matins in costume, with scenic elements and movement. This staging seems to have been most common with the Christmas villancicos that contain dialogue between ethnic types. Sometimes villancicos were included in the religious plays called *autos sacramentales*.

AUTOS SACRAMENTALES

An *auto sacramental* ("sacramental act") is a short allegorical play in Spanish (or other vernacular) verse dealing with some aspect of the Holy Eucharist (the consecrated communion host). These plays were performed on carts pulled from place to place during the celebration of Corpus Christi. They are considered an outgrowth of earlier skits that were a traditional part of the Corpus Christi procession. The earliest *autos sacramentales* in written form date from the sixteenth century. By the seventeenth century, many of the texts were written by the major court playwrights of the era, Lope de Vega and Pedro Calderón de la Barca, in whose works the *auto sacramental* was fully realized as a genre of Baroque religious theater, with a codified and expanded role for music. Although always involving the Eucharist in some way, *autos sacramentales* in the seventeenth century include a very wide range of additional subject matter, usually illustrating directly or by allegory the role of Spanish monarchy as the main defender and promoter of the Catholic religion throughout the world.

By the seventeenth century, it became customary to perform an *auto sacramental* using three carts, each with a platform of about 32 by 16 feet—two for scenery (Fig. 10-2) and one for the actors. Several groups of such carts, each one with its own *auto sacramental*, would follow in succession, presenting a series of dramatic presentations to the crowd in the city square. The performers were usually professionals, paid either by the municipal government or by the members of lay confraternities, who normally participated in the Corpus Christi procession.

Although the dialogue of the *auto sacramental* was spoken, the main characters often interpolated expressive songs, and an off-stage chorus typically provided atmospheric commentary. Theater music of this sort will be discussed later. One of the most important composers of music for *autos sacra-*

Figure 10-2. A scenery cart for a Spanish *auto*, 1646

mentales was Cristóbal Galán (ca. 1630–1684), *maestro* at Segovia Cathedral from 1664 to 1667 and then at the Real Convento de las Señoras Descalzas in Madrid, where several ladies of the royal family took vows.

VOCAL CHAMBER MUSIC

Although polyphonic madrigals and settings for three or four voices of Spanish imitations of Italian *ottava rima*, *terza rima*, and sonnets can be found at the end of the sixteenth century, the mainstream of Iberian secular vocal music about the year 1600 derives from a type of Spanish narrative ballad called the *romance*.

Beginning in the 1580s, the poetic style of the traditional romance was replaced by that of the *romance nuevo* ("new romance"), which was considered to be less erudite, serious, and esoteric and more natural, revitalized through renewed contact with traditional and popular verse. The most influential poet in this development was Lope de Vega.

In the sixteenth century, a romance was always a strophic poem in which each stanza has four lines of eight syllables each, and the even-numbered lines have the same final vowel. Soon after the beginning of the seventeenth century, romances are found more often with a poetic and musical refrain (*estribillo*) before or after each strophe of poetry. By the 1620s these refrains can be quite long and elaborate, constituting songs in their own right, with an elaborate, traditional internal formal design.

An example of this hybrid romance of the early seventeenth century (ca. 1625) is *Estávase el aldeana* ("The village woman was returning"), A. 83, by Juan Blas de Castro (ca. 1560–1631), a contemporary of Jacopo Peri and Claudio Monteverdi, a chamber singer and guitarist at the court of Philip III and Philip IV of Spain. In his youth, Juan Blas was a colleague of the poet Lope de Vega at the court of the Duke of Alba near Salamanca.

In *Estávase el aldeana*, a refrain appears between the first and second quatrain of the romance and at the end of the song. This refrain is part of a *letrilla*, which is a sort of villancico with short lines. This *letrilla* interrupts the narrative of the romance with lyrical poetry representing the private thoughts of the young woman who is the subject of the romance's narration. The initial refrain, or *cabeza* ("head"), of the *letrilla* returns at the end of the series of quatrains that make up the romance proper of this work. In addition to the *cabeza*, the *letrilla* contains two sets of *coplas,* each followed by a modified *estribillo* that begins with two variable lines that serve the function of the *vuelta* of a villancico.

The *cabeza* of this *letrilla* is found in poetic sources separately from the rest of the text of *Estávase el aldeana*. It appears, therefore, to have been known as an independent poem or as words to a traditional song of the type known as a *seguidilla*, a type of popular dance-song having as text a quatrain with seven, five, seven, and five syllables, normally in triple meter, in two six-measure phrases in antecedent-consequent relationship, with syncopation toward the end of each phrase. Typically a *seguidilla* features variants of the rhythm (for two lines of text) $\frac{3}{2}$ ♩♩♩♩♩ ♩♩ ♩♩♩ ◌ ♩. In fact, that rhythm appears in its pure form in the invariable part of the *estribillo* of *Estávase el aldeana* (mm. 36–41), which may be a direct quotation of an actual *seguidilla*.

The subject of *Estávase el [la] aldeana*, rustic rather than courtly love, was commonly found among the texts of vocal music in all European countries during the Renaissance. It survived in Spanish and Portuguese courtly song during the seventeenth century after being abandoned by all the other European traditions. It represents, of course, an aristocratic perspective on rustic life, much as do the genre paintings of everyday life (Fig. 10-3) by the great Spanish Baroque painter Diego Velázquez (1599–1664), who combined the realism and dramatic contrast of light and dark of Caravaggio with brushstroke virtuosity, harmony of color, and effects of form and texture, space, light, and atmosphere.

Figure 10-3. Velázquez, *The Water Carrier of Seville* (ca. 1619)

The Text of *Estávase el aldeana* (ca. 1625) by Juan Blas de Castro

Estávase el aldeana a las puertas de su aldea, viendo venir por la tarte los zagales de las eras.	*romance,* *Quatrain 1*	The village girl was at the gate of her village watching the evening return of the lads to the farmyard.
Tañen a la queda, mi amor no viene, *algo tiene e el campo* *que le detiene.*	*The inserted* letrilla *begins* *with its* cabeza ("head")	They are sounding lights-out, my love is not coming, *there is something in the field* *that detains him.*
A la queda tañen, espadas quitan, con su esposo cena quien tiene dicha.	*First pair of* coplas ("couplets") *of the* letrilla	Lights-out is sounding, the swords are put away; the lucky one dines with her husband.
A salir del día se fue mi ausente, *algo tiene en el campo* *que le detiene.*	*First* estribillo ("refrain") *of the* letrilla, *beginning* *with two lines with* *the function of a* vuelta.	At daybreak my absent one left, *there is something in the field* *that detains him.*
Qué mal hizo en irse tan da mañana, si a la media noche venir pesava.	*Second pair of* coplas ("couplets") *of the* letrilla	What trouble is caused by leaving so early in the morning, if by midnight he intended to return.
Cena, esposa y cama non me le buelven, *algo tien e el campo* *que le detiene.*	*Second* estribillo ("refrain") *of the* letrilla, *beginning* *with two lines with* *the function of a* vuelta.	Neither dinner, wife, nor bed bring him back to me; *there is something in the field* *that detains him.*
Cargados los alto carros de espigas doradas llevan, y a sus rústicos cantares van ayundando las ruedas.	*romance,* *Quatrain 2*	The tall carts carry golden sheaves, and to their rustic song the wheels join in.
A todos pregunta Silvia, pero con mucha verguença de que recién desposada, por cuidadosa la tengan.	*romance,* *Quatrain 3*	Sylvia asks everyone, but with much shame, if, though recently married, they consider her watchful.

El zagal de Inés venía, el de Casilda y Lorença; como son amigos suyos crecen su imbidia y su pena.	*romance,* *Quatrain 4*	Inés's lad came, and those of Casilda and Lorença; since they are his friends, her envy and pain increase.
Quando vio que y tañían la campana de la queda a recojer los mancebos, dio llorando a la puerta:	*romance,* *Quatrain 5*	When she saw that they are sounding the bell for lights-out to call in the boys, she said, while weeping at the gate:
Tañen a la queda, mi amor no viene, *algo tiene e el campo* *que le detiene.*	*The* cabeza (*"head"*) *of* *the* letrilla *as closing* *refrain*	They are sounding lights-out, my love is not coming, *there is something in the field* *that detains him.*

The music of *Estávase el aldeana* is written for four voices—the upper two of similar melodic importance, the bass serving as harmonic support, and the remaining voice as filler. As often happens in this repertoire, the quatrains of *Estávase el aldeana* preserve features of the old romance—syllabic text setting, one short phrase for each line, little word repetition, homophonic texture, narrow range, and frequent pitch repetition. These features may be vestiges of an earlier recitational style or even of a musical formula for singing these long narrative poems when they were part of an oral tradition. The refrain-*letrilla*, here as in most cases, is much longer and more varied in texture, rhythm, and melodic shapes. In it we find the syncopations and hemiolas that give much of the seventeenth-century Spanish and Portuguese vocal repertoire its distinctive character. These features are thought to derive from the style of popular songs and dances. It is even possible that specific traditional or popular music, as well as text, has been incorporated into *Estávase el aldeana*.

Spanish romance texts are often found with guitar tablature written above (almost exclusively in Italian manuscripts), evidently for solo-voice performance. When a rare solo-voice version of a romance is found in staff notation, in the partsong elaboration the melody is given to the second voice and the solo-voice tune is expanded somewhat to accommodate counterpoint. In fact, it is presumed that the surviving written repertoire of Spanish vocal chamber music, overwhelmingly for three or four voices, is based upon a widely performed solo-voice repertoire transmitted orally.

Although there are many descriptions of solo singing accompanied by guitar from early-seventeenth century Spain, there are virtually no written guitar accompaniments from Spain before the importation in about 1650 of figured-bass continuo notation. To fill in this gap, scholars have extrapolated from sixteenth-century vihuela accompaniments, which can be either contrapuntal or chordal. An exceptional case is the *Libro segundo de tonos y villancicos a una, dos, tres y cuatro voces, con la zifra de guitarra espannola a la usanza romana* ("Second book of tunes and villancicos for one, two, three, and four voices with tablature for the Spanish guitar in the Roman manner") published by Juan Arañes in 1624 during his brief stay in Rome. His lost first book must have been published there in 1623, shortly after he arrived.

The last of the large collections of chamber vocal music (*cancioneros*) containing three- and four-voice *romances*, including some by Mateo Romero, was compiled in Madrid about 1655. At this time, a new generation of Spanish songwriters were composing *tonos humanos* ("secular songs") for solo voice and continuo. These included Juan del Vado y Gomez (after 1625–1691), Cristóbal Galán (ca. 1630–1684), Juan Francisco de Navas (ca. 1650–1719), and Sebastián Durón (1660–1716), all musicians at the royal court in Madrid. Most of these solo songs retain the alternation of *estribillo* and *coplas* of the earlier villancico as well as pervasive triple meter with hemiola and syncopation. At the end of the seventeenth century, Spanish chamber cantatas with Italian-style recitatives and da capo arias join the traditional *tonos* in the chamber repertoire.

STAGE MUSIC[1]

The thriving commercial theaters of Madrid, Seville, Valencia, and Valladolid during the seventeenth century presented plays belonging to the genre of the *comedia nueva* ("new play"), developed to a great extent by the poet Lope de Vega. These plays had three acts, were spoken in polymetric verse, and mixed comic and serious elements and characters in a verisimilar fashion. The plot of these plays was usually set in the present (i.e., the seventeenth century) without regard for the classical unities of time, place, character, and action.

In the *comedia nueva*, music was supposed to contribute to the effect of verisimilitude. Thus, well-known songs were performed when songs might be sung in real life. In the same way, instrumental music occurs during the portrayal of ceremonies, processions, fanfares, battles, dancing, and so on. On the other hand, supernatural events were usually accompanied by unrealistic music sung or played offstage. Both onstage and offstage music was expected to reflect the subject, mood, or theme of the scene. Vocal music in the *comedia nueva* normally was written in the same forms and styles as the chamber vocal music discussed above. In most cases, however, the songs were sung by a solo voice, most often a woman, accompanied by a guitar.

Although standard *comedias* were occasionally performed for the royal family with elaborate scenery and machinery, musical spectacles were infrequent at the Spanish court during the first half of the seventeenth century, largely because of austere court etiquette and the opposition of Queen Margarita (ruled 1598–1611). On major occasions, such as the birth of Philip III's son in

---

[1]This section is based upon Louise K. Stein, *Songs of Mortals, Dialogues of the Gods: Music and Theatre in Seventeenth-Century Spain* (Oxford: Clarendon Press, 1993).

1605, a *máscara y sarao* ("masque and ball") was produced along the lines of an English masque or French *ballet de cour*. For the celebration in 1605, the hall was hung with tapestries depicting the glories of Spanish kings. Two choirs from the royal chapel sat facing each other and sang, antiphonally, the texts praising the king and his family.

The major break in the history of Spanish theater in the seventeenth century was Philip IV's marriage to Mariana of Austria in 1649. This marriage came at the end of a decade that brought economic, political, and military reversals to the Spanish monarchy. With the return of relative prosperity and with his queen's encouragement, Philip embarked upon a new policy of using theater to influence the important and powerful noble courtiers. Pedro Calderón de la Barca developed a new kind of play with high moral tone, increased symbolism, and a clear political message. Music was given so much more dramatic importance and prominence in these plays that modern scholars often call them semi-operas. Some of the dialogue was sung, rather than being entirely spoken, as in earlier Spanish musical plays.

Calderón's first semi-opera was *La fiera, el rayo y la piedra* ("The beast, the ray, and the stone," 1652), a dramatization of the Pygmalion myth in which the sculptor brings his statue to life, a clear departure from the realism of Spanish comedy. In Act II, "Cupid enters singing in recitative style" according to the libretto (the music is lost), and there are other places where dialogue among the gods was probably also sung as recitative. However, since mortals apparently could not understand recitative, when the gods address them, they sing strophic songs. The mortals converse in plain speech. These distinctions became customary for Calderón's semi-operas.

The music and even the set designs are preserved for Calderón's second semi-opera, *Fortunas de Andrómeda y Perseo* ("The Fates of Andromeda and Perseus," 1653). In this play Calderón apparently collaborated with the most important court composer of that time, Juan Hidalgo (1614–1684), who provided most of the music for Calderón's later works of this kind. Like most of Calderón's semi-operas, this one is based upon an ancient myth. The gods Mercury and Pallas want to relieve the mortal Perseus of his anxiety by revealing to him that his father is the chief god, Jupiter. Discord, out of spite, tries to thwart their plan but is defeated in the end. The story was intended to demonstrate how a monarch (Jupiter) and his nobility (the gods) can create a happy outcome for ordinary mortals by providing security and justice.

In *Fortunas de Andrómeda y Perseo* we find surviving Spanish theatrical recitative (*recitado*) for the first time. Unlike Italian recitative, the Spanish variety tends to employ rhythm that is musically patterned, even in triple meter at times, repetition, wider range, broader melodic contours, and a more active bass. An extreme example of these features is found in the dialogue where "Pallas and Mercury, in a different manner than the mortals, began their conversation in a recitative style, which, being a mixture of declamation and music, was neither really music nor declamation, being rather an intoned consonance, accompanied by the ensemble of instruments," according to the libretto (W. 21a). Although the bass is melodically static and rhythmically inactive and the vocal line includes a great deal of monotone pitch repetition, as in Italian recitative, the rhythms are patterned and repetitious, not attempting to imitate natural speech, a goal of Italian recitative. The models and sources for this recitational style are found in the quatrains of Spanish romances and not in Italian opera or monody.

Following his custom, Calderón indicates the use of ordinary song when the gods communicate with mortals, as when Morpheus, god of sleep and dreams, sings a double strophic air (AABB) to the sleeping Perseus to reveal that his father is Jupiter. The music here (W. 21b) differs from *recitado* in its more active bass line and avoidance of monotone repetition, but the rhythmic style is similar. In this scene, Perseus's answers are spoken, as befits a mortal.

Vocal ensembles in *Fortunas de Andrómeda y Perseo* are sung by the supernatural figures who represent the forces of the universe, the monarchy, and the Christian divinity, and by mortals in realistic situations. An example of the first type is the mysterious "Sí, no: tu lo sabrás presto" ("Yes, no: you will know it soon") referring to Perseus's awareness of the circumstances of his birth. This atmospheric four-part chorus (W. 21c) with the refrain "To say it without saying it, to know it without knowing it" is sung repeatedly, but offstage by disembodied voices, following the established Spanish theater practice for such utterances.

In Act II, the trio of the Furies summoned by Discord (Fig. 10-4) provides another example of powerfully dramatic music. The description in the score remarks, "The three Furies appeared in the distance richly and appropriately costumed, and above all, what was most admired was the dissonance with which they sang, subdued and horrible" (W. 21d). In fact, the trio contains many accented and prolonged dissonances, delayed and irregular resolutions, false relations, and non-diatonic intervals. Such infernal music was a staple on the Spanish stage in the Baroque era, so that Pablo Nassare could advise readers of his *Escuela música segúin la práctica moderna* ("Music Instruction According to Modern Practice") of 1723–24, "In heaven everything is a perfect harmonic concord. In the Inferno, it is total discord, disunion, and confusion."

The Spanish court was not ignorant of Italian opera. In 1627, a group of influential Florentines at the Madrid court commissioned the first opera entirely sung in Spanish, *La selva sin amor* ("The Forest without Love"), with music by a court lutenist from Bologna, Filippo Piccinini (d. 1648) on a text by Lope de Vega. Evidently these Florentines wished to bolster the prestige of the Grand Duchy of Tuscany, which had become a second-rate power by this time, although it had a rich and preeminent cultural heritage. Spain had Tuscany surrounded on the Italian peninsula, so, in addition to pursuing its alliance with Spain's enemy, France, the Florentines sought respect and approval from the Spanish court.

Lope's dedication in the libretto says that the opera "was performed sung, something new in Spain." Although a recitational style native to Spain had long been used in romances, Italian *stile recitativo* was evidently perceived as something entirely different. One of the Florentines wrote home that "It has moved

Figure 10-4. The three Furies summoned by Discord in *Fortunas de Andrómeda y Perseo*, Act II

the king, out of curiosity, to hear recitative style, something so new in these parts that even the *maestro di cappella*, otherwise very capable, has no knowledge of it." Another letter reports that the king (Philip IV), a well-trained musician, had played through the score himself.

Nevertheless, no further opera on the Italian model was attempted in Spain until 1660. One may guess that the influential members of the Spanish court and musical establishment understood the motives of the Florentine representatives quite well, and decided that Spain, too, had a rich musical heritage, whose prestige was equal to Spain's political and military importance. By the time all-sung opera was eventually embraced by the court, new political and military realities had emerged.

The first opera by a Spanish composer was *La púrpura de la rosa* ("The Crimson of the Rose"), music by Juan Hidalgo on a text by Pedro Calderón, produced in 1660. Although the score written for this production is lost, a second musical setting of the same libretto survives and has been recorded. It was composed by Tomás de Torrejón y Velasco (1644–1728) in 1701 for the viceroyal court in Lima, Peru. This was the first New World opera. A second Spanish opera written by Hidalgo and Calderón in 1660 or 1661 does survive: *Celos aun del aire matan* ("Jealousy, Even of the Air, Kills").

The occasion for the first two Spanish operas was the celebration of the Peace of the Pyrenees, a treaty signed in 1659 that ended decades of warfare between Spain and France. It contained an agreement to a future marriage between Philip IV's daughter Maria Teresa and French King Louis XIV. In Paris, this treaty was celebrated with Francesco Cavalli's *Xerxes*, with added ballets by Lully. The first two Spanish operas were commissioned so that the court of Madrid would not be outdone, as Calderón makes clear in his prologue to *La púrpura de la rosa*: "It is to be entirely in music, as it is meant to introduce this style, so that other nations will see their primacy rivaled."

As in their previous collaborations, Calderón and Hidalgo had recourse to ancient mythology for their plot. *La púrpura de la rosa* is based on the myth of Venus and Adonis, in which Adonis is killed by a wild boar because he disobeyed Venus, the goddess of love, and fell under the influence of Mars, the god of war. The blood of Adonis becomes "the crimson of the rose." The reconciliation between Venus and Mars at the end of the opera obviously symbolizes the peace between Spain and France.

Celos aun del aire matan continues many Spanish conventions typical of Hidalgo's semi-operas. Most of the numbers are strophic airs, refrains, homophonic choruses, and several kinds of recitative in duple and triple meter. Choral refrains are used to separate scenes or to underline important messages. Often the chorus represents unseen forces or serves as the collective voice of groups. Narration, exposition, and dialogue are often set to rhythmically repetitive strophic airs, not as recitative, as in Italian and French opera. Hidalgo's true recitatives are generally reserved for monologues or spontaneous outpourings, another departure from Italian usage. In general, Hidalgo relies on the song forms and musical textures that came to theatrical music from chamber songs, and mortals sing songs conforming to their character type. For example, a rustic character sings a *seguidilla*, a type of popular dance-song. The character of Clarín, however, sings a *jácara*, a song-type derived from an urban dance, always associated with the tough and proud *jaque*. It is usually in the minor mode, with a recurring descending minor tetrachord, false relations on the sixth degree, and pervasive and exaggerated hemiola; it would typically be accompanied by guitars.

Although *Celos aun del aire matan* was revived in 1679, 1684, and 1697, no further Spanish operas of this kind were composed during the seventeenth century. The genre that did survive and become predominant, the zarzuela, had connections to popular entertainment.

THE ZARZUELA

Although it has roots in earlier theatrical practices, it may be fair to say that the zarzuela was a new genre of Spanish music theater developed by Calderón after he abandoned semi-opera in 1653. His first zarzuelas, *El laurel de Apolo* ("The Laurel of Apolo") and *El golfo de las sirenas* ("The Gulf of the Sirens"), both written in 1657, combine familiar kinds of music and spoken dialogue in a two-act format with a simple plot in an idealized rustic or pastoral setting, ordinary language, and a more comic tone than in semi-operas or operas. They were also staged much more simply than other kinds of court entertainment.

The earliest zarzuela for which the music survives is *Los celos hacen estrellas* ("Jealousy Makes Stars") of 1672, on a text by Juan Vélez de Guevara with music again by Juan Hidalgo. As was the tradition in Spanish commercial plays, all the songs in this zarzuela and others like it have a realistic function in the action portrayed, while some of them also support dramatic expression or characterization.

With the deaths of the Calderón (1681) and Hidalgo (1685) the era of specifically Spanish musical theater gives way to a period of transition in which native song forms are mixed with Italian elements, such as plain recitative, da capo arias, florid ornamentation, long melismas, and orchestral ritornelli. This mixture is characteristic of the three surviving zarzuelas (1680–1711) and one surviving all-sung opera, *La guerra de los gigantes* ("The War of the Giants," date uncertain), by Sebastián Durón.

The real inundation of Spain by Italian influence, however, came with the accession of Philip V, the grandson of Louis XIV and Philip IV of Spain. This inundation had nothing to do with Philip's French upbringing. French music had been rejected by the Spanish court when, in 1679, Marie-Louise d'Orléans, the wife of Charles II, the last of the Spanish Habsburgs, brought thirty-eight musicians and a stage designer/librettist to Madrid in a futile attempt to bring French opera to Spain. Instead this Italian influx was due to the influence of Philip V's first Italian wife, María Luisa Gabriela of Savoy, and his second, Isabella Farnese of Parma, whom he married in 1714.

Because Louis XIV refused to exclude Philip V from the line of succession to the French throne, England and the Austrian Empire feared that Spain and France, with their extensive possessions, might eventually be united under Philip's rule. To prevent this, they waged the War of the Spanish Succession, in the course of which Philip took command of an army in Naples. After he returned, an Italian opera troupe arrived and performed Antonio Cesti's *Il pomo d'oro* (composed 1668) at Madrid in 1703. In the same year this troupe won the monopoly for performances in the principal theater of Madrid. A few Spanish composers such as Antonio de Literes (1673–1747) and José Nebra (1702–1768) attempted to compete by adapting to the Italian style, but native styles and genres, even the zarzuela, would be eclipsed by Italian music until well past the middle of the eighteenth century.

KEYBOARD MUSIC

The most important keyboard instrument in Spain and Portugal during the seventeenth century was the organ. Although Iberian harpsichords from this period are known, there is no surviving music written specifically for these instruments. On the other hand, much Spanish and Portuguese organ music is equally playable on the harpsichord, since it never calls for pedals.

Although Iberian organs of the Baroque period varied somewhat according to region, they have certain features in common. Normally, they had only a single keyboard and chest. If pedals were provided, there were usually no more than eight or ten, and they simply pulled down the manual keys above them rather than actuating a separate set of pipes. Presumably they were used to sustain bass notes or to provide a contrabass at cadences. Large cathedral organs in Spain and Portugal had up to twelve ranks of pipes, both flues and reeds. About the middle of the seventeenth century the fashion for horizontal trumpet pipes overtook the Iberian peninsula. In general, the sound of an Iberian Baroque organ is robust and brilliant.

One unique feature of Spanish and Portuguese organs is the "divided register" (*medio registro*), allowing the notes below middle *c.* to be played on one set of pipes, while the keys above middle *c'*, on the same keyboard operated a different set of pipes. This made it possible, for example, to have the notes played by the right hand sound lower than those played by the left. The most common use of the divided register was to isolate a bass line, setting it in relief against the other voices by the use of a stronger mixture.

The dominant form of keyboard music in Spain and Portugal during the seventeenth century was the *tiento* ("trial," from the Spanish verb *tentar*, "to try out" or "to test"). The term is parallel to the Italian *ricercare*, and like the ricercar, the tiento may be either figural or contrapuntal.

The earliest tientos are those for solo vihuela (an instrument tuned and played like a lute but shaped like a guitar), for example, Luys Milan's of 1536. The first major composer of tientos for organ was Antonio de Cabezón (ca. 1510–ca. 1566), the blind organist to Charles V. Among Cabezón's tientos one finds strict imitative counterpoint, elaborate diminutions, and cantus firmus technique, sometimes in one and the same work. Many features of the Baroque tiento are already established in the works of Cabezón, who remained a model for composers for several generations.

The first major composer of tientos of the seventeenth century was Sebastián Aguilera de Heredia (1561–1627) of Zaragoza in Aragon (northeastern Spain). Five of the thirteen surviving tientos by Aguilera are considered monothematic—that is, they concentrate on a single motive that provides the basis of imitation throughout the work. His *Tiento lleno de 4° tono* ("Full [not divided] tiento in the fourth mode," W. 22), presents the opening theme in six rhythmic guises (Ex. 10-2), using techniques parallel to those of the variation canzona cultivated by Frescobaldi. In most phrases, one of the voices in the texture contains ornamental diminution. Liveliness is also increased by syncopation figures such as $\frac{3}{4}$ ♩♩♩♩♩♩ and by the cross rhythms in the triple-meter sections, similar to those characteristic of Spanish and Portuguese villancicos and romances. These features are typical of Aguilera's tientos and are taken up by later Spanish composers.

While Aguilera's tientos are still tied to the Renaissance style of Cabezón, those of Francisco Correa de Arauxo or Araujo (1584–1654), are among the earliest considered typically Baroque for their irregular rhythms and startling pitches and harmonies. These features are exemplified by the *Quinto tiento de medio registro de baxones de primer tono* ("Fifth tiento with split register for the

EXAMPLE 10-2. Six forms of the principal motive in Sebastián Aguilera de Heredia, Tiento lleno de 4o tono

bass in the first mode") in Correa's *Libro de tientos y discursos de música práctica, y theórica de órgano intitulado Facultad orgánica* ("Book of tientos and discourses on practical and theoretical music for the organ, entitled Organ Faculty") of 1626, A. 84. The words "medio registro de baxones" refer to the split keyboard and the fact that the leading part, with most of the diminution, is the bass (*baxon*), which should be made more prominent by choice of stops. Correa is careful not to have this bass ascend higher than middle *c'* and to keep all the other voices above that note, so that the division of the keyboard corresponds to the division of registers among the parts. The irregular rhythm, typical for Correa, occurs in measures 98–117, marked by the proportion sign $\frac{7}{2}$[it should be $\frac{7}{8}$]. These measures feature running figures of seven notes to the bar, which, the composer admonishes, should be performed evenly. Unexpected pitches or strained dissonance treatment are found at measures 22 (no proper resolution of the dissonant A), 50 (simultaneous cross relations of C-sharp and C-natural), and 112–113 (the leap from the dissonant *f* in the bass). In the treatise portion of his *Libro de tientos*, Correa discusses the theoretical basis of such dissonance treatment as well as the proper way of adding unmarked ornaments.

The most important among the many students of Francisco Correa de Arauxo was José Jiménez, or Ximénez (1601–1672), who succeeded his teacher as organist at La Seo Cathedral of Zaragoza. The tientos of Jiménez are notable for their contrasting elements in successive points of imitation and for their extended thematic development. His *Batalla de 6° tono* ("Battle piece in the sixth mode") of about 1650 (W. 23) belongs to a widely disseminated genre of lute, keyboard, vocal, and ensemble piece of the sixteenth and seventeenth centuries in which successive points of imitation are based upon trumpet-like triadic motives and fanfare rhythms. This one contains a brief instance of broken texture similar to the rhythmic texture of French lute and harpsichord music of the same time. The cross rhythms associated with Jiménez's insistence on the rhythm ♩♩ in the triple-meter section are typical of Spanish and Portuguese compositions in several genres throughout the seventeenth century.

The most prolific composer of tientos of the late seventeenth century was Juan Bautista José Cabanilles (1644–1712), whose more than one thousand surviving works cover all genres of Iberian keyboard music of this period (tientos, versets, batallas, clarines, toccatas, variations, and dances). Like the other Spanish composers discussed in this section, Cabanilles developed along lines set out by earlier Spanish composers. Thus, the sharp dissonaces, unusual melodic intervals, and astonishing harmonic progressions of those tientos that he called *falsas* actually contain intensifications of features typical of Spanish *falsas* reaching back to Aguilera. Cabanilles's *Tiento XXIV de falses 8. punt alt* ("24th tiento with false notes in the 8th mode, transposed upward") of about 1690 (A. 85) features a chromatically descending subject, augmented and diminished triads, and abrupt departures from expected chord resolutions. Composers in most other parts of Europe were abandoning such audacious pitch relations, which are a development of late-sixteenth-century experimentalism, in favor a more restricted and predictable conduct of harmony. The major exception was England, where composers like Henry Purcell continued the tradition of chromatic modality and cross relations.

Next to tientos, the most common form of Iberian organ music was sets of versets that were played in place of alternate verses of psalms, hymns, Mass Ordinary items, and Responsories, as they were in all parts of Catholic Europe. A simple example of this type is the verset for the hymn *Ave Maris stella* (A. 86) from a 1620 collection by Manuel Rodrigues Coelho (ca. 1555–ca. 1635), the most important organ composer in Portugal during the seventeenth century. Here, the plainchant melody is presented in whole notes by the tenor voice, while the other parts engage in diminution. Coelho's tientos in the same collection are unusually long and varied, while his variations reveal the influence of Sweelinck and Sweelinck's English-virginalist models, as well as Cabezón.

HARP AND GUITAR

Although harps were in use all over Europe from medieval times, they enjoyed a particular cultivation in Spain from the middle sixteenth through the eighteenth centuries. The treatises of Alonso Mudarra (*Tres libros de música en cifras para vihuela*, 1546) and Juan Bermudo (*Declaración de instrumentos musicales*, 1555) discuss harp-playing techniques and provide music for the instrument. Luis Venegas de Henestrosa's *Libro de cifra nueva para teclas, harps y vihuela, canto llano de órgano y contrapunto* ("Book of new tablature for keyboard, harp, and vihuela, plainchant on organ, and counterpoint") of 1557 and Antonio de Cabezón's

Obras de música para tecla, arpa y vihuela ("Musical works for keyboard, harp, and vihuela") of 1576 contain pieces notated in a single tablature system, equally playable on keyboard instruments, harp, and vihuela. Likewise, Coelho's *Flores de musica pera o instrumento de tecla, & harpa* (1620) lists the harp as an alternative to keyboard instruments for his long and elaborate tientos. Cabezón declared that "the harp is so like the keyboard that all music played on the keyboard can be played on the harp without much difficulty." The harp was a favored instrument for the accompaniment of vocal music in Spain and Portugal from the middle of the sixteenth century to the end of the seventeenth. As mentioned earlier, it became an indispensable instrument in Iberian cathedral chapels during the seventeenth century, and it maintained its preeminence as a continuo instrument in this region, almost to the exclusion of the harpsichord.

Diatonic harps required the player to press on a string with the thumb in order to raise the pitch by a half step. During the first half of the seventeenth century, diatonic harps were rapidly displaced in Spanish chamber and church music by double-strung chromatic harps (Fig. 10-5). The diatonic single harp continued to be used in traditional and popular music and has remained important in this context in Latin America until the present day.

During the fifteenth century, when the European lute was developing into a six-course instrument designed for polyphonic music, fretted instruments with a waisted outline began to diverge into the vihuela, which had six courses tuned like a lute's, and into the guitar, which initially had four courses. At the end of the fifteenth century, five-course guitars are seen in paintings, and these became standard by the end of the sixteenth century. Although some polyphonic music, similar to that for the lute and vihuela, was written for the five-string guitar during the sixteenth century, it was usually used, especially in the seventeenth century, as a strummed chordal accompaniment to vocal music.

Figure 10-5. A double-strung, chromatic harp in the painting *The Presentation of Christ in the Temple* (early seventeenth century) by Diego Valentin Diaz

Chord tablature had been developed in Italy at the end of the sixteenth century, but Spanish and Portuguese guitarists used the bass line as their guide, as did keyboard players and harpists.

A new guitar technique and tablature notation emerged about 1630, in which plucked notes written in lute tablature were added to strummed chords shown by alphabet notation (Fig. 10-6). This style of playing and system of

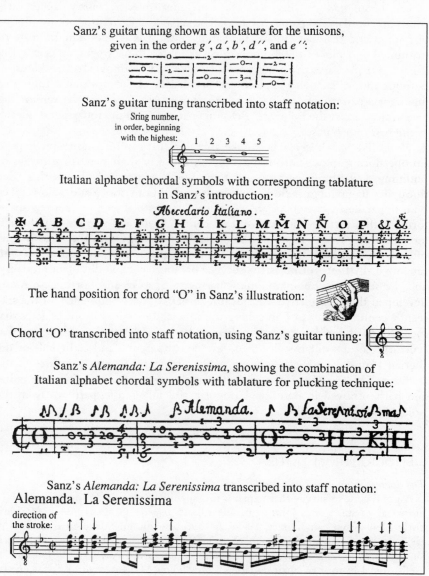

Figure 10-6. Tuning and notation in Gaspar Sanz, *Instrucción de música sobre la guitarra española y método de sus primeros rudimentos hasta tanerla con destreza* (1674)

notation were brought to Spain by Gaspar Sanz, who learned them in Naples and Rome. His *Instrucción de música sobre la guitarra española y método de sus primeros rudimentos hasta tanerla con destreza* ("Musical instruction on the Spanish guitar and method for its first rudiments up to playing it with skill") was printed in eight editions, with additions, between 1674 and 1697, and it spawned a host of imitators.

Sanz's *Instrucción* contains toccata-like preludes, suites of courtly dances, variations on chordal-bass patterns, especially the passacaglia, transcriptions of popular songs and trumpet fanfares, and indigenous folk dances. The mixture of strummed and plucked techniques gives many of these works, especially the dances, a percussive rhythmic profile unlike that found in other kinds of Baroque music. Sanz also exploits the peculiarity of Spanish guitar tuning to highlight a pattern of accents, as in the *jácaras* (A. 87), where the reinforcing harmonies extract the following rhythmic pattern from the foreground of each of the first four phrases: $\frac{3}{4}$ ♩♩.♩♩♩♩.♩♩.

Works like Sanz's *jácaras* are unlike anything that can be found elsewhere in Europe during the seventeenth century because of their percussive means of outlining a rhythmic pattern and their boldly strummed chords that slice through a fragmented melodic line harmonized both above and below. Likewise unparalleled elsewhere are the villancicos with their intricate refrains— forms within forms—the triple-meter compositions and segments with their cross rhythms, syncopation, and hemiola; the partsongs with the melody line, often from a traditional song, in the middle of the texture; the recitatives with repetitive, rhythmic formulas; the survival of chromatic and dissonant modality; and the seemingly free and aimless harmony. Spanish and Portuguese music developed these distinctive features out of native styles and genres of the sixteenth century instead of absorbing the innovations coming out of Italy that increasingly defined the cosmopolitan Baroque style of Europe. When that Italianate cosmopolitan style finally invaded the courts and cathedrals of the Iberian Peninsula at the beginning of the eighteenth century, features of the traditional, indigenous genres and associated instruments, especially the guitar and harp, survived in traditional, popular, and folk music, particularly in the isolated New World colonies.

BIBLIOGRAPHICAL NOTES

The Spanish Empire and its Church
    A good general survey that explains the Spanish empire and puts its creation in historical perspective is John Huxtable Elliott, *Imperial Spain, 1469–1716* (New York: New American Library, 1977). A more specific and detailed treatment of early modern Spain is John Lynch, *Spain under the Habsburgs,*Vol 2., *Spain and America, 1598–1700*, 2nd ed. (New York: New York University Press, 1981/1984). A useful social history of Spain is James Casey, *Early Modern Spain: A Social History* (New York: Routhledge, 1999). The history of religion in Spain is illuminated by E. William Monter, *Frontiers of Heresy: The Spanish Inquisition from the Basque Lands*

to Sicily (New York: Cambridge University Press, 1990); and Henry Arthur Francis Kamen, *The Spanish Inquisition: An Historical Revision*, 2nd ed. (London: Phoenix Press, 1997/2000).

Latin Liturgical Music

The classic study of this subject is Robert Murrell Stevenson, *Spanish Cathedral Music in the Golden Age* (Berkeley: University of California Press, 1976). Two specialized studies are Michael J. Noone, *Music and Musicians in the Escorial Liturgy under the Habsburgs, 1563–1700* (Rochester, NY : University of Rochester Press, 1998); and Mark Brill, "Style and Evolution in the Oaxaca Cathedral: 1600–1800," Ph.D. diss., University of California, Davis, 1998. For the Spanish empire, see Robert Murrell Stevenson, *The Music of Colonial Spanish America* (Cambridge: Cambridge University Press, 1980/1985). *Music in Latin America: An Introduction* by Gerard Béhague (Englewood Cliffs, NJ: 1979), begins with a chapter on "Sacred Music in Spanish America" that focuses on the Baroque period. The two major books in Spanish on Latin liturgical music of this period are José Subirá, *Historia de la música española y hispanoamericana* (Barcelona: Salvat, 1953); and José López-Calo, *Historia de la música española*, Vol. 3, *Siglo XVII*, 2nd ed. (Madrid: Alianza Editorial, 1988).

The Villancico and Other Vernacular Church Music

The major English-language study of this topic is Paul R. Laird, *Towards a History of the Spanish Villancico* (Warren, MI: Harmonie Park Press, 1997). A specific study centering on Mexico but including general information on the villancico is Robert Stevenson, *Christmas Music from Baroque Mexico* (Berkeley: University of California Press, 1974). Concerning the Italianate phase of the villancico in the early eighteenth century, see José V. González Valle, "Italianate Sections in the Villancicos of the Royal Chapel, 1700–40," *Music in Spain during the Eighteenth Century*, ed. Malcolm Boyd and Juan José Carreras (New York: Cambridge University Press, 1998). An English-language book with useful information about the *auto sacramentale* is N. D. Shergold, *A History of the Spanish Stage from Medieval Times until the End of the Seventeenth Century* (Oxford: Clarendon Press, 1967). A more specific study in Spanish by the same author is N. D. Shergold and J. E. Varey, *Los autos sacramentales en Madrid en la epoca de Calderón, 1637-1681: Estudio y documentos* (Madrid: Ediciones de Historia, Geografía y Arte, 1961).

Vocal Chamber Music

There is no book-length general study of this repertoire. The dozen or so manuscripts that preserve the early seventeenth-century repertoire are listed by Judith Etzion, "The Spanish Polyphonic Cancioneros, c. 1580–c. 1650: A Survey of Literary Content and Textual concordances," *Revista de musicología*, IX (1988), 65–107. Introductions to modern editions of those manuscripts are a good source for general discussions of the musical forms and styles. Nearly all of these, however, are in Spanish. An exception is Judith Etzion, *The* Cancionero de la Sablonara *(A Critical Edition)* (London: Tamesis Books, 1996). Studies in Spanish of individual composers can be a useful source of general information about this repertoire, for example, Luis Robledo, *Juan Blas de Castro (ca. 1561–1631): vida y obra musical* (Saragossa: Institución "Fernando el Católico," 1989). There are also many studies of the poetry set in these songs listed in Etzion's bibliography and elsewhere.

Stage Music

There is really only one book necessary for further study of stage music in Spain during the seventeenth century: Louise K. Stein, *Songs of Mortals, Dialogues of the Gods: Music and Theatre in Seventeenth-Century Spain* (Oxford: Clarendon Press, 1993). For the early eighteenth century, see William M. Bussey, *French and Italian Influence on the Zarzuela 1700–1770* (Ann Arbor: UMI Research Press, 1982); Manuel Carlos de Brito, *Opera in Portugal in the Eighteenth Century* (New York: Cambridge University Press, 1989); and Juan José Carreras: "From Literes to Nebra: Spanish Dramatic Music between Tradition and Modernity," *Music in Spain during the Eighteenth Century*, ed. Malcolm Boyd and Juan José Carreras (New York: Cambridge University Press, 1998).

Keyboard Music

The general book on this subject is Robert Parkins, *Spain and Portugal* in the series Keyboard Music before 1700 (London: Prentice Hall International, 1995). Useful discussions of specific works, organized by composer, are found in Willi Apel, *The History of Keyboard Music to 1700*, trans. Hans Tischler (Bloomington, IN: Indiana University Press, 1972). The Spanish organ in the Baroque era is treated by Jesús Angel de la Lama, *El órgano barroco español* (Valladolid: Junta de Castilla y León, 1995). The organ *batalla* as genre is the topic of Mary Ellen Sutton, "A Study of the Seventeenth-Century Iberian Organ Batalla: Historical Development, Musical Characteristics, and Performance Considerations" Ph.D. diss., University of Kansas, 1975. Specialized studies of single composers include J. E. Ayarre Jarne, *Francisco Correa de Arauxo, organista sevillano del siglo XVII* (Seville, 1986) Mary Jane Corry, "The Keyboard Music of Juan Cabanilles: A Stylistic Analysis of the Published Works," Ph.D. diss., Stanford University, 1965.

Harp and Guitar

A brief overview of the harp and its music in Spain is Cristina Bordas-Ibañez, "The Double Harp in Spain from the 16th to the 18th Centuries," *Early Music*, XV (1987), 148–63. The instrument itself is scrutinized in Hannelore Devaere, "An Organological Study of Baroque Double Harps in Spain and Italy," *Zur Baugeschichte der Harfe* (Bankenburg: Harz, 1992), pp. 59–67. The only book-length treatment of the Baroque harp in Spain is in Spanish: María Rosa Calvo Manzano and Mariano Pérez Gutiérrez, *El arpa en el barroco español* (Madrid: Alpuerto, 1992). The best general treatment of the Baroque Spanish guitar in Europe is James Tyler and Paul Sparks, *The Guitar and its Music from the Renaissance to the Classical Era* (Oxford: Oxford University Press, 2002).

CHAPTER 11

Music in the Empire during the Later Seventeenth Century

THE NEW LUTHERAN PIETY AND THE RELIGIOUS ARIA

In the aftermath of the Thirty Years' War (1618–1648), new currents of thought and religious sentiment arose in the German-speaking lands. Among these was a noticeable reaction against dogmatically sanctioned religious revelation, which many blamed for the terrible devastation brought about by the bitter fighting between Catholics and Protestants. Although there was no clear winner of the Thirty Years' War, on balance the Catholics gained territory at the expense of the Protestants. This loss, as well as growing pressure on Protestants in France, saddened many Lutherans and contributed to the reaction against the established leadership of their religion. In some places this reaction took the form of a trend toward secularization and a dramatic increase in crime. In other places Lutherans rejected orthodox belief in favor of a simpler, more emotional approach to religion, characterized by subjectivity, mysticism, and mistrust of authority.

By about 1675 this personal and emotional approach to the Lutheran religion gave rise to the movement known as Pietism, under the intellectual leadership of Philipp Jakob Spener (1635–1705), whose book *Pia Desideria* ("Pious Desires," 1675) advocated group bible study, family devotions, the rights and responsibilities of the laity, love of one's neighbor, avoidance or moderation of religious controversies, spiritual commitment of pastors, and edification and inner piety as the goals of preaching. Even before Spener's codification of Pietism, the trend toward the personal and emotional approach to religion led to a renewed interest in the writings of such earlier Lutheran mystics as Johann Arndt, who in 1612 had written of the crucifixion in these terms:

> Ah, my love! You were wounded for the sake of my love, wound my soul with your love. Ah! Your precious blood, shed out of great love, is so fine, so penetrating, that it might soften a heart of stone: ah, let it penetrate my heart, so that your love might also penetrate my heart, for your love is in your blood. Ah! That my heart might open up, to receive and to drink in your fragile and fine little drops of blood, which fell on the ground during your struggle with death.

This sort of emotional intensity can be traced in German religious song texts as early as 1627 in the rhymed and metrical paraphrases of the biblical Song of Solomon by Martin Opitz, whose importance in the history of German poetry and secular continuo song was discussed in Chapter 6. Andreas Hammerschmidt (1611/12–1675) included twelve settings of these texts in his *Geistlicher Dialogen* ("Spiritual Dialogues") of 1645. But the precise kind of personal and emotionally charged religious poetry that contributed to Pietism is first found in the texts of two poets born in 1607, Paul Gerhardt (1607–1676) and Johann Rist (1607–1667). The emotional intensity of these texts is often attributed to the childhood experiences of these two poets during the Thirty Years' War. Gerhardt is particularly important as a poet of chorale texts in a Pietist vein, such as *O Haupt voll Blut und Wunden* ("O head, full of blood and wounds"), published in 1656.

Chorale (*Kirchenlied, Kirchengesang*) texts like Gerhardt's, intended for use in the Lutheran church service, were usually published without music, and in many cases became associated with several different tunes. Although these tunes were often harmonized or set polyphonically, chorales were typically sung in unaccompanied unison by the congregation, and during the seventeenth century their music was sometimes notated without rhythmic note values. Chorale texts usually describe or narrate something, state a general proposition, such as an article of faith, or express the collective feelings of the congregation. The text and music of chorales were strophic. In a large number of chorales, especially the older ones, each strophe has seven lines of text, of which the first four form two rhymed pairs. In the most traditional musical settings, the music for the first pair of lines is repeated for the second pair, and this is followed by different music for the last three lines. This creates the traditional "bar form," which can be traced back to the fifteenth century in German secular song.

On the other hand, a Lutheran German religious aria (*geistliche Arie, geistliche Lied*) was intended principally for private devotional use in middle-class homes and secondarily for professional singers to perform in church. It was sung to newly composed music, most often for solo voice with continuo accompaniment, frequently with an optional ritornello for two violins to be played before, between, and after the strophes of the aria. The text and music of a Lutheran religious arias was strophic, like those of the chorale. Unlike the chorale, however, the aria did not make use of the traditional bar form. The texts of a religious aria (sometimes called "ode") was often written in the first person, and it tended to focus in a personal way on Jesus and the torments of the cross, solace in times of stress, or renunciation of the vanities of the world. Like a secular continuo song in the Opitz tradition, the music written to such a text was strophic, almost exclusively syllabic, and usually molded to the rhythm of the poetry. This music often strove for expression by using unusual intervals and selective word emphasis.

Among the earliest religious arias of this type are the *Gottliche Liebesflamme, das ist Christliche Andachten, Gebet und Seufftzer* ("Godly Flames of Love, That Is, Christian Worship, Prayer, and Sighs," 2nd edition with music, 1651) by Johann

Erasmus Kindermann (1616–1655) on texts by Johann Michael Dilherr (1604–1669); and the two volumes of *Geistlicher Arien* ("Spiritual Arias," 1660/61) on texts by Johann Rist set by Kindermann's colleague in Nuremberg, Wolfgang Carl Briegel (1626–1712).

The example given as A. 88 is from a later collection of sacred arias by Briegel, the *Geistliche Oden Andreae Gryphii* ("Spiritual Odes of Andreas Gryphius," 1670). Gryphius was one of Germany's leading poets in the seventeenth century. He was orphaned early in life, and the horrors of the Thirty Years' War cast a shadow over his childhood. His plays are full of melancholy and pessimism, and they deal with the themes of stoicism, religious constancy, illusion versus reality, and human emotions in adversity. These are exactly the themes of Gryphius's text for *Was frag ich nach der Welt!* ("What do I care about the world!"). Briegel's setting of this text uses almost the same rhythm for each line of poetry, while the rhetorical trajectory of the poem is faithfully traced by the succession of concluding pitches of these phrases, and selective accentuation within the phrases intensifies the meaning of the words. An overall feeling of emotional torment is promoted by Briegel's use of diminished intervals.

SACRED CONCERTOS FOR SOLO VOICE

More difficult and varied settings of religious texts for solo voice are found in German-language sacred concertos (*geistliche Konzerten*) of this period. In order to distinguish this genre from the sacred aria, the definition in Martin Fuhrmann's *Musicalischer-Trichter* ("Musical Hopper," 1706), although published in the early eighteenth century, is valid and useful. Fuhrmann writes, "The concerto is a piece for voices and instruments in which the vocalists and instrumentalists, as it were, fight or contend with one another. For a church concerto, a composer must take nothing but biblical texts, and indeed, those that are well known, if they are to be understood by the congregation." The features that generally distinguish German sacred concertos during the second half of the seventeenth century are:

- Prose texts, especially from Psalms or other books of the Bible
- One or more voices
- Phrases and rhythms that follow the irregularities of the text
- Imitation, antiphonal treatment, and musical-rhetorical figures
- Instruments freely mixed with the voices
- Sectional treatment of the text
- Some portions of the text possibly set in aria style

"If an aria is sung, rhyming texts or verses are laid under the notes," according to Fuhrmann. These are the typical features of German sacred arias from the second half of the seventeenth century:

- Strophic poetry with regular rhyme and meter
- One or more voices

- Regular rhythm and phrase structure
- Homophonic texture
- Domination by a single emotional expression (affection) in the music
- Instruments reserved for ritornelli
- Sections defined by the stanzas of the text; strophic, strophic variations (with or without refrain), or sectional form
- An instrumental, or vocal introduction, or a contrapuntal conclusion (e.g., an "Alleluia") may be added in concerto style

An early example of a German sacred concerto for solo voice is *Was hast du verwirket* (A. 52) from the 1639 volume of the *Kleine geistlichen Concerten* by Heinrich Schütz discussed in Chapter 6, a setting of a German translation of a passage from the *Confessions* of St. Augustine (354–430). The recitational (*recitativo arioso*) style of *Was hast du verwirket* is based on Italian secular monody of the early seventeenth century, and it was typical of German solo-voice sacred concertos during the first half of the century. On the other hand, developments that took place during the 1630s and 40s in the Italian chamber cantata are reflected in the juxtaposition of flowing triple-meter aria style against duple-meter declamatory writing in some German solo sacred concertos beginning in the 1650s. An example of this is *Natus est Jesus* (A. 89b) from the 1651 *Partitura sacra* ("Sacred Score") by Philipp Friedrich Böddecker (1607–1683), an Alsatian musician employed in Frankfurt, Strasbourg, and Stuttgart churches at various times.

Böddecker's *Natus est Jesus* is highly unusual in that its text is a mixture of Latin and German. The Latin text has biblical and liturgical overtones and is narrative, communal, and doctrinal. The German words are put in the mouth of Mary and serve to personalize the message of the Latin text. The German text is derived from a traditional Christmas song whose words were written down as early as the fourteenth century. They are found in a number of variant forms in manuscripts from the following centuries, reflecting a process of oral transmission. The earliest written source of the melody comes from a publication of 1543 with a Latin Christmas text; the German words "Joseph, lieber Joseph mein" are set to versions of the same melody in a series of prints beginning in 1545. A reconstruction of the song, using its oldest text, a dialogue between Mary and Joseph, and the phrases of early versions of the melody arranged to fit it, is given as A.89a. Böddecker begins the setting of the German words with a quotation of the beginning of this tune, and he alludes to fragments of it in the other passages that set the German text in later parts of the work.

Sacred concertos for one or few voices with Latin texts that have similar opposition between duple-meter recitational music and aria-like passages in triple meter were composed by Schütz's successor as music director at the Dresden court, Vincenzo Albrici (1631–1690 or 1696) and his Roman compatriot Marco Gioseppe Peranda (ca. 1625–1675). Some have thought that these Latin works introduced the arioso/aria contrast to Germany, but they were actually composed after the publication of Böddecker's *Natus est Jesus*. We detected this element of style in Italian sacred concertos as early as 1619 in Alessandro Grandi's *Veniat dilectus meus* (W. 3). Many German composers learned about this type of contrast from the mid-century concerted motets of Giacomo Carissimi, which were disseminated by the Jesuit order to the Catholic German-speaking lands and then to Lutheran areas.

SACRED CONCERTOS FOR SEVERAL VOICES

Sacred arias and sacred concertos were composed for vocal ensembles or choruses with texts of the same types used for solo arias and concertos. Ensemble arias have musical characteristics very much like those of the solo arias in the German sacred tradition: they are strophic, syllabic, and rhythmically bound to the text; in addition the texture is almost exclusively homophonic. On the other hand, the music of German sacred concertos for several voices from the later seventeenth century encompasses a considerably wider variety of styles, not always paralleling those of solo concertos.

When compared with the sacred concertos for several voices by Schütz, those of the later seventeenth century tend to be more sectional, and their texts, still biblical, tend to be selected to include introspection, meditation, and strong emotions, reflecting the tendencies of Lutheran Pietism, like the newly written poetic texts for solo arias.

The trend toward creation of longer, self-contained, and contrasting sections, which is very important in all types of German religious vocal music in the second half of the seventeenth century, is particularly pronounced in the sacred concerto for several voices. Examples of this sectionalization are found in the sacred concertos by Matthias Weckmann (ca. 1616–1674), a student of Heinrich Schütz who served as organist at the Jacobikirche in Hamburg and produced weekly instrumental and vocal concerts in the cathedral refectory.

Weckmann's *Zion spricht: Der Herr hat mich verlassen* ("Zion says, 'The Lord has Abandoned Me'"), published in 1663, is given as A. 90. This sacred concerto draws its text from Luther's German translation of Isaiah 49: 14-16. The mournful and lamenting character of the text is reflected in the prevailing musical expression of the piece, as seen in the composer's performance indication, "NB: This entire piece must be performed slowly and expressively." Weckmann's use of pervasive chromaticism and dissonance also contributes to the general impression of gloom. This generalized expression of emotion, rather than reliance on declamation, rhetorical figures, or changing musical expression for each few words or phrases, reflects a trend in both sacred and secular music of all nations during the second half of the seventeenth century. The string ensemble of two violins and three viols in this work, typical of much German music at this time, provides long introductions and interludes in several places. The vocal textures and styles cover a wide range: motet-like imitation in the first section, recitational in the second, and antiphonal and declamatory in the third.

In another of his sacred concertos, *Wie liegt die Stadt so wüste* ("Now the City Lies So Deserted"), also of 1663, Weckmann introduces recitative, perhaps for the first time in German church music. In this work, Weckmann alternates recitatives with aria-style sections in triple meter (as shown in Ex. 11-1) to set off narration from the reflection and introspection found in his text, taken from Lamentations.

Sectionalization and introspection tend to be associated with dialogue texts and texts that combine poetry of differing types and sources. When part of the text comes from the Bible and other parts from strophic poetry, the work is usually called a "concerto-aria." An example is *Euch ist's gegeben zu wissen das Geheimnis* ("Unto You Is Given to Know the Mysteries," 1665) by Christoph Bernhard (1628–1692), A. 91. In this work, passages from the gospel according

EXAMPLE 11-1. Recitative and aria in Weckmann, *Wie liegt die Stadt* (1663)

to Luke (8: 10–15) are set in a florid arioso style characterized by ornamental melismas, avoidance of rhythmic patterning, and consequent lack of a clear musical meter. These biblical passages alternate with strophes of newly written poetry that meditate upon the gospel verses and personalize their message through the use of the first person. These aria strophes are set, in contrast to the biblical passages, in triple meter with clear rhythms that are undisturbed by ornamental passagework.

Christoph Bernhard, the composer of *Euch ist's gegeben zu wissen das Geheimnis*, had been a student of Heinrich Schütz in Dresden. When Johann Georg II succeeded his father as Elector of Saxony in 1656, he added his musical chapel to that of the Dresden court. Schütz retired with the title of chief or senior *Kapellmeister*. Bernhard, who had risen to the office of vice-*Kapellmeister*, was passed over in favor of the Italians Giovanni Andrea Bontempi (1625–1705) and Vincenzo Albrici. In order to help Bernhard fit into this new musical regime, Johann Georg II sent him twice to Rome, where he learned about the latest styles of Italian music and singing. Bernhard wrote about what he learned in Italy in his very important *Tractatus compositionis augmentatus* ("Extended Treatise on Composition," ca. 1657), which will be discussed in the section on German music theory.

CHORALE CONCERTOS

Lutheran sacred concertos based on chorale texts and melodies followed a path of development during the later seventeenth century parallel to that of the sacred aria and biblical concerto. This path led toward increasing sectionalization, in which musical closure at the end of each stanza became ever more pronounced; ever stronger contrast between sections; and combining features of various genres. Style features drawn from the concerto, the motet, and the aria, together with simple chorale harmonizations, can be found in the sections of a single work.

An early example of this sectionalization and contrast of styles can be found in *Ein' feste Burg ist unser Gott* ("A Mighty Fortress Is Our God," A. 92b) by Franz Tunder (1614–1667), organist at the Marienkirche in the Baltic port city of Lübeck, at the extreme northern reaches of the German-speaking lands. The text consists of all four stanzas of Martin Luther's famous Reformation chorale (A. 92a). The first three stanzas are set off from each other by a full close and change of style and scoring, and sectionalization also occurs within each of the stanzas.

The instrumental accompaniment of Tunder's *Ein' feste Burg ist unser Gott* consists of a normal trio of two violins and organ continuo along with five viols, ranging from the treble to the contrabass violone. This combination of violins and viols was common in Germany during this period. The introductory Sinfonia in two sections incorporates three motives that are used in the first verse setting.

Each of the verse settings incorporates the chorale melody in decorated form (Praetorius's term was "madrigal style") or in imitative treatment ("motet style" according to Praetorius). Verse 1, for soprano and strings, begins and ends in aria style, with a middle section at the mention of "the old, evil foe" in contrasting concerto style and slow ("lento") tempo, with frightful, breathless interruptions. Verse 2, for the vocal quartet doubled by the viols with two violins and continuo, uses both homorhythmic and imitative textures within the concerto style, introducing trumpet fanfare figures at the words "[Christ] fights for us," which are interrupted by a solemn Adagio at the words "whom God himself has elected." Verses 3 and 4 mix aria and concerto styles while changing motives and textures in response to each line of text.

Chorale concertos that set each stanza of the original text were not new with Tunder, of course. The earliest datable example is Samuel Scheidt's *Nun komm, der Heiden Heiland* (1635), W. 8b. Although they were written only fifteen years apart, comparison of Scheidt's concerto with Tunder's illustrates Tunder's more extensive use of rhythmic elaboration of small motives, extremes of contrast, rhetorical devices, and sectionalization, all of which serve to dramatize the text in ways not found in Scheidt's composition or elsewhere during the first half of the seventeenth century.

Combination of texts from different sources and of different structures, typical of the aria-concerto combination—for example, in Bernhard's *Euch ist's gegeben zu wissen das Geheimnis*—is also found in some chorale concertos during the second half of the seventeenth century. An example is *Ihr lieben Christen, freut euch nun* ("Dear Christians, Rejoice Now"), W. 24b, by Dieterich Buxtehude (ca. 1637–1707), Franz Tunder's successor as organist at the Marienkirche in Lübeck and the most important German composer of the later seventeenth century.

The first and last sections of Buxtehude's *Ihr lieben Christen, freut euch nun* (BuxWV51, ca. 1680) set the words from the first and last stanzas of the chorale. The chorale melody that Buxtehude uses is, however, not the one generally sung to this text, but an anonymous melody (W. 24a) first published by Georg Rhau in 1544 with the words *Nun laß uns den Leib begraben* ("Now let us lay to rest the body"). This melody is sung in half notes by the soprano voice in the first vocal section of Buxtehude's work, and it returns, set homophonically for all the voices in triple meter, in the last section ("Ei lieber Herr, eil zum Gericht"). The first stanza of the chorale calls for Christian rejoicing over the imminent second coming of Christ. This is followed by an extended, fully closed section for all voices with full instrumental ensemble in concerto style, using antiphonal responses and some imitation, setting the words "See, the Lord comes with many thousand saints to judge everyone" from The Letter of Jude, 14–15. After a fanfare for trumpets, cornetts, and trombones, alluding to the seven trumpets of judgment day, the bass sings an arioso to the words "See, I am coming soon, and my recompense with me" from Revelation 22: 12. The text of the fourth section of the work is an aria text, calling on Christ to return on judgment day. After a short self-contained "Amen," the sixth, chorale-based section contains the same message as the fourth, "Oh, dear Lord, hasten to the judgment, show your glorious face, the essence of the Trinity, so that God may help us into eternity."

Although the last three sections of *Ihr lieben Christen, freut euch nun* ("So komm doch, Jesu," "Amen," and "Ei lieber Herr, eil zu Gericht") are in concerto style, the first of these (the fourth section overall) contains significant vestiges of aria style in the way its rhythm reflects the scansion of the poetry. This poetry, as we noted earlier, is a strophe of an otherwise unidentified aria. In the following table, the accented and unaccented syllables and divisions of poetic feet are marked above the German words, using Marin Mersenne's system of rhythmic analysis.

U — / U —/U — /U — So komm doch, Jesu, komme bald	So come, then, Jesus, come soon
U — / U — / U — U uns gänzlich zu befreien,	to free us completely,
U —/U —/U —/U — komm, unser Seelen Aufenthalt,	come, dwelling of our souls,
U —/U —/U — U uns ewig zu erfreuen.	to delight us eternally.
U —/U — / U —/U — Komm, Jesu, komm und säume nicht,	Come, Jesus, come and tarry not,
U — /U —/U — / U — laßt uns in deines Himmels Licht,	that in your heavenly light
U — / U — / U — U dein ewiges Lob ausschreien.	we may sing your eternal praises.

Examination of the patterns of rhyme and scansion indicate that a sixth line of the text is missing; if the missing line were restored, the poem would consist of two stanzas of four lines each.

Rather than follow the scansion of the poetry exactly, as Albert (*O der rauhen Grausamkeit!*, A. 59) or Briegel (*Was frag mich der Welt!*, A. 88) did, Buxtehude stretches, compresses, and elaborates on the rhythm of the verse. A contemporaneous theory of "rhythmopoeia" that recognizes these techniques and provides a vocabulary and set of concepts for its analysis was included in *Phrynis Mitilenaeus, oder satyrischer Componist* ("Phrynis Mitilenaeus, or the Satirical Composer") by the German composer and music theorist Wolfgang Caspar Printz (1641–1717), a treatise that was published in 1696, when Buxtehude was composing.

Printz recognized that the segments of melody that correspond to individual syllables of poetry are not always single notes but are often made up of groups of notes. He also knew that the melodic segments that correspond to poetic feet were often varied and ornamented by composers. Accordingly, he described and named seven techniques for varying the "sound feet" (musical accent groups) in melodies:

incitati = the addition of a dot to the long notes
dilatorio = delay

contractio = abridgment
commutatio = alteration
decuratio = shortening by leaving out a note or a part of a note
prolongatio = increasing the duration of a note
expletio = adding a note

Thus, Printz would analyze the alto part in Buxtehude's setting of the stanza "So komm doch, Jesu, komme bald," in *Ihr lieben Christen, freut euch nun* as shown in Example 11-2.

The significance of Printz's theory of rhythmopoeia is that it recognizes and emphasizes the fact that music written by composers of Buxtehude's generation tends to be based upon short rhythmic ideas or modules that become the subject of extended elaboration through repetition, variation, embellishment, extension, abbreviation, sequencing, and so on. In many cases, the rhythmic module helps the music project a single emotion or affection in addition to providing a source of unity and the basis of variety. The theory of rhythmopoeia can also help performers of late Baroque music, instrumental as well as vocal, to find recurring patterns that should be grouped together through vocal phrasing, bowing, or articulation.

EXAMPLE 11-2. Modification of "sound feet" in Buxtehude's setting of the aria strophe "So komm doch, Jesu, komme bald," using the terminology and theory of Printz (1696)

Because of its length and large ensemble, Buxtehude's *Ihr lieben Christen, freut euch nun* was probably composed not for a regular Sunday church service but for the special *Abendmusik* ("Evening Music") concerts, a tradition at the Marienkirche in Lübeck since Franz Tunder began them about 1646. These free concerts were originally held on Thursdays but later under Buxtehude's directorship changed to the second, third, and fourth Sundays of Advent. They were sponsored by an association of Lübeck businessmen and eventually included works for chorus and orchestra, such as oratorios. This tradition continued throughout the seventeenth and eighteenth centuries.

RELIGIOUS VOCAL MUSIC AT THE CATHOLIC GERMAN COURTS

The Catholic courts of the Empire were concentrated in the southern German-speaking lands, especially in the hereditary territories of the Habsburg family. The religious vocal music written for the chapels of these courts included Latin-texted liturgical items, such as Masses, Psalms, and Magnificats, as well as non-liturgical concertos. They included both a cappella works and works with organ continuo in what Bernhard called the *stylus luxurians communis* as well as concerted works, often with large instrumental ensembles that include trumpets and trombones, evoking the imperial style initiated by Valentini during the reigns of Ferdinand II and III. The culmination of the grandiose style of German Catholic church music is the large-scale Masses and Vespers written for the prince-archbishop of Salzburg for performance in that city's cathedral.

The most colossal of the works for the Salzburg cathedral ascribed to Biber are the *Missa Salisburgensis* ("Salzburg Mass") and ceremonial motet *Plaudite tympana* ("Beat the Drums"), both apparently composed in 1682 to celebrate the eleven hundredth anniversary of the founding of the archbishopric of Salzburg by St. Rupert. Anonymous in their sources these works are today thought to be by either Heinrich Ignaz Franz Biber (1644–1704) or Andreas Hofer (1629–1684), the two principal composers at the Salzburg cathedral at that time. These two works are written in scores of fifty-four staves each. The voices and instruments are divided into seven groups: Choro 1 (eight singers and organ), Choro 2 (two violins and four viols), Choro 3 (two oboes, four flutes, and two trumpets), Choro 4 (two cornetts and three trombones), Choro 5 (eight singers, two violins, two violas, and organ), Loco I, and Loco II (each with four trumpets and timpani, Loco 2 also providing the basso continuo). A performance of these or similar works is depicted in an engraving of 1682 shown in Figure 11-1. Details of this engraving given as Figures 11-2 and 11-3 show four of the seven choirs of performers.

Plaudite tympana (W. 25) depends on simple rhythmic and chordal material reinforced through repetition, antiphonal echoes, and accumulation of sonorities. The first section (mm.1-42), which is repeated at the end, grows out of the two rhythmic figures of the first measure and the timpani-like

Figure 11-1. An engraving of 1682 possibly depicting the performance of the *Missa Salisburgensis* or *Plaudite Tympana* in celebration of the eleven-hundredth anniversary of the dedication of the first Salzburg cathedral

Figure 11-2. Choirs with trumpet (foreground) and trombones (background), Salzburg, 1682

pounding of fourths and fifths in the bass, out of which the composer builds the first climax. The second climax of the first section adds a rumbling, frenzied bass ostinato, against which the cries and blasts of the voices and instruments recur with increasing impatience. A different set of rhythms and quasi-ostinato treatment of the bass begin the middle section with sparser texture, the climax delayed but inevitable, punctuated by exclamations of "long live!" and "rejoice!"

Works as massive in scale as the *Missa Salisburgensis* and *Plaudite tympana* survive in far smaller numbers than reports of music for six, twelve, even twenty-four choirs in Austria and Italy during the seventeenth and well into the eighteenth centuries. It seems apparent that many works performed by a large number of choirs were actually scored for four to eight voices in one or two choirs and were arranged by assigning the parts to voices and instruments

Figure 11-3. Choirs of singers, trumpet, and organs, Salzburg, 1682

in various octave transpositions. Performances of that type must be considered far more typical of the Catholic Baroque than the surviving scores would suggest. They created massive sonorities through doubling and spatial expansion. On the other hand, works like Biber's, in which all the parts are composed individually, add to this massive effect a profusion of detail amounting at times to heterophony. In practice, details would be heard differently according to the relative location of each listener. This combination of massive scale and power together with overwhelming amounts of detail is exactly the defining feature of the monumental Austrian imperial style of architecture, called the *Kaiserstil*, which emerged toward the end of the seventeenth century under the leadership of Bernhard Fischer von Erlach (1656–1723). This style is illustrated in Figure 11-4.

In Vienna the reign of Emperor Leopold I, 1658–1705, marks a particularly brilliant period for music. The emperor was a trained musician and a composer of some distinction. Following the lead of his father, he continued to favor Italian musicians as he expanded his court chapel through the addition of Giovanni Felice Sances (ca. 1600–1679), Antonio Draghi (1634/35–1700), Giovanni Bononcini (1670–1747), and Francesco Conti (1681/82–1732). At the same time, Emperor Leopold nurtured a new generation of native German composers, notably Johann Heinrich Schmelzer (ca. 1620–1680), Johann Caspar Kerll (1627–1693), Ferdinand Tobias Richter (1651–1711), and Johann Joseph Fux (1660–1741). All of these court composers wrote Latin-texted church music for large forces in the grandiose style.

Another distinctive type of religious vocal music at the court of Leopold I is found in the forty-two sacred dramatic works that Antonio Draghi composed between 1668 and 1699. These include sixteen oratorios, comparable to those by Giovanni Legrenzi and Alessandro Stradella, and twenty-six *sepolcri*, musical dramatizations of events between the burial and Resurrection of Christ as narrated in the Gospels, emphasizing the laments of disciples and the fulfillment of the Old Testament prophecies. They were presented either on Maundy Thursday in the chapel of the emperor's widowed mother, with a costumed cast acting around a replica of the holy sepulcher, or on Good Friday in the imperial chapel, with additional painted scenery as a backdrop. In keeping with the somber sub-

Figure 11-4. The Karlskirche in Vienna, designed by Johann Bernhard Fischer von Erlach, begun 1716

ject matter, Draghi composed expansive recitatives with short, syllabic aria-like and arioso sections, and accompanied them with lower-pitched violas and viols.

KEYBOARD MUSIC

The common types of keyboard music in the German-speaking lands during the second half of the seventeenth century remain those of the earlier period: organ chorale settings, preludes, and toccatas in the Protestant North; and the Italian forms of ricercar, canzona, capriccio, toccata, verset, passacaglia, and chaconne in the Catholic South. French-style suites could be found in all parts of the Empire, in continuation of the tradition initiated by Johann Jakob Froberger.

Style change in Lutheran organ chorale fantasies is clear in a comparison of Franz Tunder's *Komm Heiliger Geist, Herr Gott* ("Come Holy Spirit, Lord God," ca. 1650, A. 93b), with Samuel Scheidt's earlier *Fantasia super Ich ruf zu dir, Herr Jesu Christ* (A. 55b). Both of these works are chorale fantasies, since they both use several different techniques (cantus firmus, paraphrase, imitation, ornamentation, variation) in treating successive phrases of the chorale melody. Tunder's piece, however, is far richer in contrasts between various textures, styles, and dynamics, and in dramatic gestures, including toccata-like passages such as those that begin and end the composition. Tunder also creates more intense expression through his use of extreme chromaticism and dissonance—e.g., the treatment of the eighth phrase of the chorale in measures 87–100.

The slightly later organ chorale settings by Matthias Weckmann, all of them variation sets, use a wide variety of approaches—cantus firmus, echo, imitation, figural variation—to make each variation contrast with its neighbors. Several settings are extraordinarily long. *Es ist das Heil* ("It Is Salvation") takes about a half hour to perform—even longer if the choir or congregation was expected to sing alternate stanzas of the chorale between Weckmann's variations. Extended organ chorale settings in fantasy form were composed by Jan Adam Reincken (1623–1722) of Hamburg, whose *An Wasserflüssen Babylon* ("On the river of Babylon") extends to 330 measures and encompasses every known approach to elaboration of a chorale melody.

During the last quarter of the seventeenth century, with the crystallization of conventional means of projecting specific states of emotion by controlling features of music, especially rhythmic features, it became possible for a composer like Dieterich Buxtehude to suggest the emotional aspects of a chorale text even in an organ setting, when the text is not heard. This is shown in excerpts from his chorale-motet-style organ setting of *Ich dank dir, lieber Herre* ("I Thank You, Dear Lord"), BuxWV 194, shown in Example 11-3. In this setting, Buxtehude seems to reflect the unheard chorale text, line by line, through contrasting musical features.

In addition to about sixty-eight organ chorale settings of every type known to the seventeenth century, Buxtehude's surviving keyboard works include twenty-three preludes and toccatas. Like Italian toccatas going back to

EXAMPLE 11-3. Buxtehude, *Ich dank dir, lieber Herre,* sample of the treatment of each phrase with translation of the relevant chorale verses

Frescobaldi, these works combine free, improvisatory passages alternating with imitative or fugal sections. Several, like the Praeludium, BuxWV 137 (A. 95), include virtuosic writing for the organ pedals, a special feature of North German organ music.

When compared with the toccatas by Frescobaldi and his Italian and Austrian followers, the free passages in Buxtehude's preludes appear to be much more rationally organized. The opening passage in Buxtehude's Praeludium, BuxWV 137 (mm. 1–11), exposes a sixteenth-note figure that traces an overall descent by means of an alternation between rising steps and descending thirds, a pattern incorporated into the fugal and free passages later in this work. The arpeggiation in the first measure leaves a gap between G and C that is filled in gradually by the pedal part in measures 5–11. The first fugal section (mm. 12–22) is based on a subject that appears to be derived from the upper component of the rising pedal line in measures 4–5. Models for the various configurations of sixteenth notes in the second free section (mm. 23–36) can also be found in the opening section. The second, more extended fugal passage (mm. 36–65) uses a subject taken directly from the steps and thirds of the first section. The third free section (mm. 66–74) combines motives used in the previous two free passages. The chaconne ostinato figure, repeated in measures 75–99, is once again derived from the pattern of undulating sixteenths in the first passage, with the repeated pitches relating to the oscillating sixteenths of measure 3. Each of these sections is organized by extended processes of climax building and tension and release, while the bass part often traces long segments of ascending or descending scales.

Virtuoso passagework in a free toccata style, technical challenges on the pedals, and rigorous counterpoint—all typical traits of North German organ music in this period—can be found in monumental *Passacaglio* [*sic*] Buxtehude's. This work, A. 94, presents seven variations over the seven-note ostinato in modes founded on each of the four pitches of the D-minor chord—D, F, A, and D. Within each set of seven variations, there is a consistent pattern of rhythmic growth as well as a subdivision of each set into subgroups of four and three variations, a grouping created by the cohesion among the last three of every set of seven variations. This pattern is shown below.

Mode 2 on D:
1. Declamatory syncopation, quarters and halves
2. Similar to #1 but with rhythm pressing ahead a bit more
3. Similar to #1 and #2 but with longer strings of quarters, continuing the contour further downward
4. Still longer strings of quarters with single eighths
5. Groups of three eighths introduced
6. Longer strings of eighths, at first as composite rhythm between adjacent voices, then in a single voice
7. Still longer strings of eighths, continuing the contour downward, with thicker texture, reaching a climax in the two transitional measures

Mode 6 on F:

1. Similar to the first variation above but with eighths
2. Similar to #1 but with fuller texture
3. More rhythmic activity distributed among the voices
4. Continuing the motives and contour direction of #3, but with an acceleration of rhythm at the end
5. Steady eighths forming a measured trill
6. A continuation of #5 but with fuller texture
7. Cascades of eighths resolve the c... downward to the f..; longer patterns in the transition measures

Mode 10 on A:

1. Quarters and eighths, similar to the beginning
2. Continuing with the motives and downward contour of #1, then introducing more rhythmic motion
3. Longer series of eighth notes
4. Eighth-note runs transferred to the tenor voice, with connective groups of eighths in the soprano
5. A new, broken texture with continuous eighth notes as composite rhythm
6. As above but with thicker texture, descending
7. Continuing the descent

Mode 2 on D:

1. Triplet eighths introduced for the first time
2. Triplets with more variety in melodic contours
3. Still more frequent changes of melodic direction, sixteenth notes introduced; an animated pedal on the fifth degree, A.
4. Like #2, but lower
5. A repeat of #3, pedal on A
6. A contrapuntal inversion of #3 (= #5), pedal on A
7. A repeat of #3, pedal on A

The significant features of the organization of Buxtehude's *Passacaglio* outlined above are the use of consistent rhythmic patterns to create unity within each variation; the ordering of rhythmic patterns, variation by variation, within each major section to create a series of accelerations or other processes of intensification of directional movement and growth; the schematic organization of the whole through transposition of the ostinato pattern to each note of the modal triad; and the allegorical references to the numbers 3 for the Trinity and 7 for the days of creation, the sacraments, the gifts of the Holy Spirit, virtues and vices, the trumpets and seals of the apocalypse, and many other things.

The leading composer of keyboard music in Central Germany during the second half of the seventeenth century was Johann Pachelbel (1653–1706), who held posts as organist in the main churches of Erfurt, Stuttgart (at the Württemberg court), Gotha, and Nuremberg. The bulk of Pachelbel's keyboard music consists of organ chorale settings and fugues; he also composed keyboard suites and vocal music, both sacred and secular.

Although Pachelbel wrote organ chorale settings of every known type, he also devised his own unique form, called "combination form," in which a fugue whose subject is derived from the first phrase of the chorale melody is followed by a cantus firmus setting of the entire melody, phrase by phrase, often with prior imitation—*Vorimitation* in German, the process whereby each phrase of the cantus firmus is anticipated by an imitative section based upon a motive derived from that phrase. It is thought that these long and elaborate chorale settings were composed for Pachelbel's obligatory annual organ recitals in Erfurt, rather than as introductions to congregational chorale singing. An example of Pachelbel's combination form organ chorale setting is *An Wasserflüssen Babylon* ("On the River of Babylon," A. 121b).

The fugue subject for the first part of Pachelbel's *An Wasserflüssen Babylon* is taken from the first phrase (mm. 1–3) of the chorale melody (A. 96a) with the rhythm altered, especially after the first statement. In addition, there is a four-note scale fragment that appears in both quarters and eighths, ascending as well as descending, which may refer to various phrases of the chorale melody. Like the fugal passages in Buxtehude's Praeludium, the fugal section of *An Wasserflüssen Babylon* contains statements of the subject in two transpositions, centering on the first and fifth degrees of the scale (i.e., the final and repercussion of the mode) with short episodes linking the statements of the subject. This limitation is typical of German keyboard fugues, canzonas, and ricercars of this period. Pachelbel's fugal section has the character of an introduction, partly because he achieves seamless continuity by avoiding all cadences.

In the second part of Pachelbel's *An Wasserflüssen Babylon* (mm. 41–96) the chorale tune is found in the soprano voice as a cantus firmus, mostly in whole and half notes. Phrases 2 and 3 of the cantus firmus are preceded and accompanied by the same four-note scale fragment that was found in the fugue. Only Phrase 4 of the cantus firmus is preceded by a decorated outline of its particular melodic shape.

INSTRUMENTAL ENSEMBLE MUSIC

By the second half of the seventeenth century, Italian varieties of instrumental ensemble music were composed by German composers in all regions of the Empire, and suites of dances for instrumental ensembles can also be found that resemble those extracted from stages works at the French court. The most distinctive instrumental ensemble music in the German-speaking region was produced in the Habsburg hereditary lands; the center of this production was, of course, the imperial court of Vienna.

Music at the imperial court was fostered by a succession of Habsburg emperors who were productive composers in their own right: Ferdinand III (ruled 1637–57), Leopold I (ruled 1658–1705), and Charles VI (ruled 1711–40). Musical ties between the imperial court and Italy remained very strong, as the second wife of Ferdinand II, Eleonora Gonzaga of Mantua, continued to influence music and the other arts until her death in 1655, when her place was taken by the third wife of Ferdinand III, also from Mantua, whose name was also Eleonora Gonzaga.

Although the musicians of the imperial court were not divided into several administrative units as they were at the French royal court, the same venues of music making were associated with particular kinds of instrumental music. What is said here about the imperial court in Vienna can be said to a lesser extent of the major regional courts of the Empire.

The most public of venues for instrumental music were streets, plazas, and courtyards where processions, ceremonies, and pageants took place. Every time the emperor returned from travels, a tightly organized ceremonial *Einzug* ("entrance") was staged, in which a long procession of military units, groups of court officials, ambassadors, and the emperor himself were each preceded by a trumpet corps of a specific size, whose sonatas were interspersed with cannon fire and musket volleys. For particularly important occasions, such as victory celebrations and weddings, allegorical parade wagons, often with wind ensembles aboard, joined the procession. The parade always ended at the cathedral, where a *Te Deum* was performed by imperial court musicians. Many features of street processions are found in various types of outdoor pageants, including choreographed jousts, staged battles, and horse ballets, which, although originating in Italy, soon became a Viennese specialty.

One of the most elaborate Viennese horse ballets of this period was *La contesa dell'aria e dell'acqua* ("The Contest between the Air and the Water"), produced as part of the celebration of the marriage of Leopold I and Princess Margarita of Spain in 1667. In a pageant of this sort, the horses step and leap in time to the music while representing symbolic actions and forming geometric patterns or spelling out names (Fig. 11-5). The music for the 1667 ballet took the form of dances played by twenty-four trumpets, four timpanists, and over one hundred string instruments. A sample is the "Courante for the Entrance of His Imperial Majesty and All the Knights" for six-part trumpet ensemble, A. 97, by Johann Heinrich Schmelzer, a violin and cornett player at the court since about 1635 who had become its director of instrumental music in 1658. The dances use metrical forms that were standardized in France earlier in the century.

The instrumental ensemble music played in the imperial court chapel during Mass and Vespers could be as festive and brilliant as the music for outdoor ceremonies, because the church was as much a venue for projections of majesty as the procession route, the triumphal arch, or the courtyard ceremony. Indeed, at the Habsburg imperial court elaborate church music remained a symbol of *Pietas Austriaca* through the use of exaggerated scale and evocation of military ceremony and majesty. For example, in 1660 to celebrate the end of a short war, a Te Deum was sung. According to the printed descriptions, the musicians were divided into six choirs consisting of dulcians, theorbos, lutes, recorders, violins, viols, clarini [trumpets in the high register], trumpets, and timpani, along with side drums and shawms as well as two choirs of voices.

Figure 11-5. *La contesa dell'aria e dell'acqua* (1667)

During the period of Leopold I we find descriptions of sonatas played in the imperial chapel by an orchestra of twenty strings; others report various divisions of the components of the ensemble into antiphonal choirs:

> At the beginning of the entrance, trumpets and timpani played for the emperor and the crown prince. Chant as well as polyphony were performed along with a sonata composed by the emperor himself. . . . After the sermon, four choirs without voices played, the first of strings, theorbo, and viols, the second of trombones and cornetts, the third of trumpets and timpani, and the fourth of clarini. Afterward the Mass continued.

Any Viennese sonata from this period written for the forces named in the foregoing report could be effectively performed with its subgroups of related instruments dispersed in separate choirs, because these subgroups tend to be treated antiphonally. Johann Heinrich Schmelzer's three-choir *Sonata Natalitia* ("Christmas Sonata," A. 98) of 1675 serves as a representative example.

Schmelzer's *Sonata Natalitia* resembles northern Italian ensemble sonatas of about 1675 in its division into a relatively small number of long, closed sections or movements distinguished from one another by changes of tempo, meter, and musical material. Schmelzer's choice of tempos is unusual; they are all fast, so that the triple-meter movements have the character of dances; there is no expressive slow movement, as would be typical of an Italian sonata. Also, the large number of instruments and the mixture of woodwinds, brass, and strings have no parallel in the Italian repertoire. On the other hand, the short-winded effect produced by the succession of many brief periods punctuated by frequent cadences, sometimes on unexpected pitches, can be found in contemporaneous sonatas by, for example, Legrenzi or Stradella.

Schmelzer, Biber, and several of their colleagues maintained close connections with Karl Liechtenstein-Castelkorn, the Bishop of Olmütz (Olomouc). Biber had been in the bishop's service in Kroměříž (Moravia) from 1668–70. This bishop, who ruled the surrounding territory from 1664 to 1695, maintained a large chapel that included several prolific composers. It was headed by Pavel Vejvanovský (ca. 1633/39–1693), who was originally a trumpet player. Among the 1,400 works in the bishop's library, of which 1,152 survive, there were 137, both vocal and instrumental, by Vejvanovský. Most of these feature one or more trumpets, but they also include an unprecedented array of instruments: recorders, shawms, oboes, dulcians, bassoons, cornetts, trumpets, horns (perhaps their earliest appearance in ensemble music), trombones, violins, violas, violoni, viols of all sizes, organ, and harpsichord.

Since Vejvanovský's ensemble sonatas with trumpets resemble works by Schmelzer, Biber, and other composers at the courts of Vienna and Kroměříž, the example given as W. 26, *Sonata vespertina* ("Sonata for Vespers," 1665), represents a large repertoire of Austrian and Moravian trumpet sonatas. This work, for two high trumpets (*clarini*), three trombones, two violins, and basso continuo, is divided into three sections, like the Italian repertoire of the early and middle seventeenth century. The opening imitative duple-meter section returns in a variant form after a middle section in triple meter with homophonic texture and antiphonal repetitions. The outer sections are based upon a special type of theme common in works entitled "Intrada," commonly used at the beginning of outdoor pageants at the imperial court. The middle section achieves its unusual length largely by repeating a series of cadential phrases with changes of instrumentation and transposition. Occasionally, as in measures 23–29, the brass instruments imitate the style of music for trumpet corps by employing a tonic drone in the bass.

Trumpet-based works such Vejvanovský's *Sonata vespertina* helped establish a style characterized by extensive elaboration of a few simple rhythmic motives in combination with a limited vocabulary of cadential chord progressions. Music for other instruments and even voices began to copy this trumpet style, down to the emphasis on the first five degrees of the major scale, in all countries of Europe, at least by the 1680s.

The most important printed collection of Johann Heinrich Schmelzer's ensemble music was entitled *Sacro-profanus concentus musicus* ("Sacred-Secular Musical Harmony," 1662). As this title implies, there was substantial overlap between church and secular instrumental music in the Empire (and in Italy) at this time. That is, any ensemble work played in church or in outdoor ceremonies could as readily be played in a banquet hall or in any other indoor social venue.

The custom of dining to the sound of music seems to have been particularly associated with German courts in the seventeenth century. Dozens of printed seventeenth-century collections of German instrumental ensemble music include the word *Tafelmusik* ("table music") or a similar expression in their

Figure 11-6. A banquet with trumpet corps and string ensemble at the Vienna court, 1651

titles, whereas parallel terms in French, English, and Italian are rare before the eighteenth century. Normally the musicians performing *Tafelmusik* were present in the banqueting hall as part of the display that often included gold and silver serving plates and trays, even if not in use, and the scarce and expensive food served to the ruling nobleman of the court (Fig. 11-6). Sometimes, however, the musicians were not visible. A visitor to the court of Dresden in 1617 and 1629 wrote, "Behind every picture it is hollow and set up in such a way that behind one can perform special music. When one dines in the upper hall, the musicians are positioned in the lower hall as well, the doors are closed, and so the resonance ascends delightfully through the ventilators. Above, under the ceiling, there is also an arrangement for hidden music, so that one can hear such music from thirty-two different locations, each separated."

Table music at German courts included the full range of ensembles used for church and outdoor ceremonies, including trumpet music (Fig. 11-6), along with suites of dances, which seemed to have been especially favored. The German ensemble repertoire of the seventeenth century is especially rich in ensemble dance suites composed independently of any theatrical occasion, as opposed to the French ensemble suite repertoire at this time. About 550 ensemble suites were published in the German-speaking lands during the seventeenth century.

One of the leading German composers of ensemble dance suites was Johann Rosenmüller (ca. 1619–1684), an organist in Leipzig who was about to become director of the city's music and cantor of its Thomasschule when, in 1655, he was arrested on suspicion of homosexuality. He escaped from jail and fled to Venice, where he played trombone in the ensemble at St. Mark's basilica and composed music for the orphan girls in the Ospedale della Pietà, until he returned to Germany as music director at the court of Wolfenbüttel in 1682. Although Rosenmüller is credited with bringing elements of the latest Italian ensemble styles to Germany in his last sonata collection of 1682, his suites published in 1645, 1654, and 1667 include mostly German and French features not yet found in Italian sonatas.

In all three of Rosenmüller's collections of ensemble suites, a series of short dances, most often arranged in alternating duple and triple meter, such as allemande, courante (or correnta), ballet (or ballo), and sarabande, are preceded by a longer introductory movement in duple meter. In the 1645 and 1654 collections, this movement is the traditional pavane, as in the suites of the *Banchetto musicale* ("Music Banquet," 1617) by Samuel Scheidt, but without the usual galliard. In the 1667 *Sonate da camera* ("Chamber Sonatas"), however, the first movements, called "sinfonia," take the form of an Italian multi-sectional sonata, as in the 1658 *Epidigma harmoniae novae* by Matthias Kelz (ca. 1635–1695) of Augsburg.

In Rosenmüller's 1667 sonatas, the second section, in slow $\frac{3}{2}$ meter, is always recapitulated at the end. Actually, in the second sonata of this collection (A. 99) the two duple-meter sections are somewhat related in the manner of a canzona, and these allegro flourishes in trumpet style are framed by brief adagio cadential segments with fermatas that appear to invite improvisation. The dance movements in this sonata are notable for delicate rhythmic interplay among the parts and irregular phrasing: each half of the Alemanda has nine measures; each half of the Correnta has six pairs of measures; each half of the Ballo has seven; and only the Sarabanda has eight bars in each reprise.

The German ensemble suite with a substantial introductory movement in some ways parallels the English fantasia-suite, which, however, opens with a thoroughly imitative fantasia unrelated to the Italian sonata.

The ensemble suite with an introductory movement became a German specialty. Nearly three hundred such works were published in twenty-seven collections during the second half of the seventeenth century by at least nineteen composers, including Heinrich Biber, Georg Muffat (1653–1704), Johann Adam Reincken (1643–1722), and Philipp Heinrich Erlebach (1657–1714). In the ensemble suites of his *Florilegium primum* (1695) and *secundum* (1698), Muffat's introductory movements are normally in the style of a French overture, perhaps reflecting his early studies with Lully in Paris (1663–69), although this innovation also appears at Ansbach in the *Composition de musique suivant la méthode françoise* of 1682 by a later (ca. 1675) German student of Lully, Johann Sigismund Kusser (1660–1727).

Programmatic or descriptive instrumental ensembles and keyboard works were another German specialty in the later seventeenth century. Carlo Farina's *Capriccio stravagante* of 1627, mentioned earlier, which imitates such things as dogs, cats, guns, and organ grinders, and other descriptive works were written in Dresden, although Farina ended up at the court of Vienna. In 1631 David Cramer (ca. 1590/95–ca. 1666) of Hamburg published ensemble pieces with titles like "Melancholy," "Patience," "Inconstancy," "Greed," "Joy," and "Sorrow." The Dresden violinist Johan Jakob Walther (ca. 1650–1717) imitated a tremulant organ, bagpipes, trumpets, timpani, hurdy-gurdy, guitar, roosters, hens, and various birds in his 1676 *Scherzi* ("Jokes"). In 1682, Walther's Dresden colleague Johann Paul Westhoff (1656–1705) published a nine-movement programmatic violin sonata entitled "The War." The largest concentration of descriptive ensemble music was written by the composers of the Vienna court.

In a letter of 1669, a Count Wenzelberg wrote to the bishop of Kroměříž, "On the fifth I invited Herr Schmelzer to dinner and used all diligence to get the desired bird song; thus he revealed that he had indeed reduced the "aria" to notes, with the imitated birdsong set among the calls and cries of all sorts of animals." Later Schmelzer sent the count a chaconne for unaccompanied violin with the advice that "there are many more such bizarre things in Vienna." For example, an anonymous Viennese *Musikalisches Uhrwerck* ("Musical Clockwork") uses a bass ostinato to represent the ticking and whirring of the clock, while the violin periodically chimes each quarter hour. On the full hour, it tolls ten times—*hora decima*, or the tenth hour after sunrise, the traditional time for a tower concert by the city musicians; and indeed a regular sonata movement follows.

The subtitle of Heinrich Biber's *Battalia* ("Battle") for string ensemble (A. 100) translates "Imitating the slovenly troops of the musketeers, Mars [god of war], the battle, and lament of the wounded, with arias and dedicated to Bacchus [god of wine]." The second movement, entitled "The slovenly association of all kinds of humors" requires the instrumentalists to play several unrelated melodies simultaneously, and it creates such incredible dissonance that Biber took the precaution to add an inscription in Latin, which translates "Here there are dissonances everywhere, for indeed diverse melodies are clashing." The movement entitled "Der Mars" contains imitations of fife with drum and trumpet corps. "Die Schlacht" ("The Battle") contains the instruction "The battle must not be struck with the bow, but rather the string must be snapped with the right hand as if with a pick, and hard!" The "Lamento der Verwundten Musquetirer" ("Lament of the wounded musketeers") features exaggerated chromaticism and dissonance.

Biber's *Battalia,* composed in 1673, is apparently a satire directed at the French army, since he uses the French term *musquetirer* in his inscriptions. In 1672, the year before this work was composed, Emperor Leopold I entered into an alliance against France for the defense of Holland. This war in Holland formed the basis of Lully's allegorical opera *Alceste* (1674); here we have an Austrian perspective on the same events.

Biber's other instrumental works are more serious but just as fanciful. Especially notable are his works for solo violin and continuo—the sixteen Mystery (or Rosary) Sonatas, completed about 1676, and the eight sonatas published in 1681. These works make unprecedented demands on the violin by including elaborate multiple stops—some requiring scordatura tuning—very rapid passagework, and a range that extends to the seventh position. The Mystery Sonatas are preserved in a manuscript decorated by engravings depicting each of the fifteen Mysteries of the Rosary. They were probably written for Biber to play at special services devoted to these mysteries during the month of October in the Salzburg Cathedral. It seems doubtful, however, that the music attempts to depict the mysteries in any way, beyond creating a mood of contemplation. On the other hand, a later manuscript copy of the tenth Mystery Sonata, falsely ascribed to Schmelzer, with a seventh movement added at the end, includes programmatic titles for all the movements relating to the Turkish siege of Vienna in 1683:

1. The Turkish advance
2. The Turkish siege of the city of Vienna
3. The Turkish attack
4. The advance of the Christians
5. The engagement of the Christians
6. The retreat of the Turks
7. The victory of the Christians

The music seems perfectly fitting in each movement.

It is tempting to see a connection between German aristocrats' fascination with description and bird-call imitations in instrumental music and their enthusiasm for maintaining a type of private palace museum called a *Wunderkammer* ("Chamber of Wonders"), in which all manner of things, from natural produce to skillfully wrought artifacts, were displayed. These might include minerals, samples of ore, precious and semi-precious stones, and fossils; botanical items, such as woods, fruits, nuts, and dried plants; and zoological items such as stuffed or mounted animals, horns, teeth, mollusc shells, eggs, skins, and shells or husks (see Fig. 11-7).

Thus, when the Vienna court organist Alessandro Poglietti (d. 1683) included in his "Nightingale" suite a series of variations "upon the age of your majesty" that imitate a hurdy-gurdy, Bohemian bagpipes, a Dutch flute, a Bavarian shawm, a procession of old wives, an ancestors' honor dance, a French hand-kisser, a bumpkin's rope dance, a Polish magic trick, a soldier's whistle, a Hungarian fiddle, and a Steyermark horn, we might say that he created a musical *Wunderkammer*.

SEVENTEENTH-CENTURY OPERA IN THE GERMAN LANDS

Italian operas were performed in Salzburg in 1614 (*Orfeo* and *Andromeda*, both probably by Monteverdi), Vienna in 1619 (*Orfeo*, probably Monteverdi's),

Figure 11-7. Ole Worm, *Museum Wormianum* (1655): a depiction of a seventeenth-century *Wunderkammer*.

Prague in 1627 (an anonymous *Calisto e Arcade*), Warsaw in 1628 (an anonymous *Acis*), and Innsbruck in 1654 (Cesti's *Il Cesare amante*).

In 1627 Heinrich Schütz set Martin Opitz's German adaptation of Rinuccini's *Dafne* libretto for the court of Dresden; although the music is lost, later comments by Schütz suggest that his setting contained no recitative. Sigmund Theophil Staden (1607–1655) wrote the earliest surviving German-language opera, *Seelewig* ("Soul's Immortality"), probably for a school in Nuremberg, sometime before its publication in 1644. Johann Caspar Kerll's *Oronte* inaugurated the Munich opera house in 1657.

Continuous opera production in the Empire began in Vienna about 1660, during the reign of Leopold I, under long-term associations with the composers Antonio Cesti, Marc'Antonio Ziani (ca. 1653–1715), Giovanni Felice Sances (ca. 1600–1679), and Antonio Bertali (1605–1669), and the librettists Francesco Sbarra and Nicolò Minato. The culmination of this early phase of Viennese court opera came in 1668 with a performance of Cesti's monumental *Il pomo d'oro* ("The Golden Apple"), with its five acts, enlarged orchestra, expanded cast, and twenty-four stage sets (Fig. 11-8); the performance was spread over two days. After this, most of the Vienna court operas were written by resident, salaried composers, the most important and prolific of whom was Antonio Draghi.

From 1666 to 1700 Draghi composed about 120 operas or similar stage works for the imperial court of Vienna, many of them on his own librettos. Draghi's musical style in these works is in line with what prevailed in Venice during this period, but with more ballets, ensembles, and choruses. The subject matter of his librettos is drawn from Greek and Roman history and mythology, treated allegorically so as to promote the glory, majesty, and historic claims of Emperor Leopold I.

During the later seventeenth century, opera theaters were established in several Protestant cities in northern Germany, the most important of which was Hamburg, a free city without a ruling noble court and a prosperous sea-trading partner in the Hanseatic League. Here the first public opera house in Germany opened in 1678 with *Der erschaffene, gefallene und auffgerichtete* Mensch ("Created, Fallen, and Risen Man") by Johann Theile, on a religious theme in deference to the city's watchful and critical Lutheran clergy. During the 1690s operas in French style sung in German prevailed in Hamburg, the leading composers being Johann Georg Conradi (d. 1699) and Johann Sigismund Kusser. In 1697 the leadership of the Hamburg theater passed to Reinhard Kaiser (1674–1739), the most important German opera composer of the period.

The themes of Kaiser's operas are more diverse than would be found in court theaters or even in the commercial theaters of Venice; in addition to mythological, historical, and pastoral plots, there are biblical stories, exotic adventures dealing with, for example, pirates, dramas built around traditional German festivals and holidays, and at least one based on recent history. Although some of Kaiser's operas mix arias in Italian with German recitative dialogue, the composer expressed particular concern for the relationship between music and text. He wrote that the principal aim of operatic music was to express the actual emotions of the characters in the drama. In this he was aided by a quickly developing, international vocabulary of conventional musical devices that allowed composers to communicate specific mixtures of passions in precise proportions.

Figure 11-8. Antonio Cesti's *Il pomo d'oro* performed at the court theater in Vienna, 1668, the imperial family front and center

GERMAN MUSIC THEORY

In his *Tractatus* of ca. 1657, Christoph Bernhard, building on an earlier work (1649) by Marco Scacchi (ca. 1600–1662) written in Warsaw, describes three styles of music then in use—the *stylus gravis* ("Serious Style"), *stylus luxurians communis* ("Common Embellished Style"), and *stylus luxurians theatralis* ("Theatrical Embellished Style").

The *stylus gravis* imitates Palestrina, makes the music master over the text, and employs dissonance only in passing notes, auxiliary notes, suspensions, and prepared appoggiaturas.

In the *stylus luxurians communis* the words and music rule as equals, and there are fifteen additional types of dissonance allowed. Monteverdi, Cavalli, Bertali, Carissimi, Albrici, Peranda, Schütz, and Kerll are among the composers named as leading practitioners of this style. Actually, a great deal of seventeenth-century church music, even for voices, employs these types of dissonance, although their imitative texture, smooth melodic lines, and restricted rhythmic vocabulary may cause these a capella works to be mistaken for examples of Palestrinian *stylus gravis*.

Finally, in the *stylus luxurians theatralis* the text is the master over the music; its techniques include recitative. This style uses all the categories of the dissonance enumerated for the previous two styles and admits eight more.

In his discussion of the *stylus gravis*, Bernhard demonstrates how Palestrina changed mode within a work by defining a series of different finals and repercussions by means of melodic figures and their contrapuntal combinations. His chapters on the *stylus luxurians communis* and *theatralis* contain valuable instruction for the improvisation of melismatic embellishments.

Many of the Latin terms that Bernhard uses to categorize dissonance treatments are traditional names for rhetorical figures. Bernhard is trading on the prestige that Germans attached to the study of rhetoric and to its application by analogy to musical composition. This can lead to confusion because categories of dissonance are not really rhetorical figures. Other German theorists of this time use the names of rhetorical figures more correctly—to point up more significant parallels between music and speech. The names of rhetorical figures were explained as analogues to verbal rhetoric by several German musicians during the second half of the seventeenth century and early eighteenth century, including Athanasius Kircher (1601–1680), Johann Georg Ahle (1651–1706), Mauritius Johann Vogt (1669–1730), Johann Gottfried Walther (1684–1748), and Johann Mattheson (1681–1764).

Mode was another important topic treated by German theory during this period. Most musicians in Germany as elsewhere continued to explain the modes either in the way Adriano Banchieri had in his treatises of 1605 and 1614 or else in the way Gioseffo Zarlino had in his *Istitutioni harmoniche* (1558/1573). However, several German writers in the seventeenth century struck out in new directions in reaction to one or more of the following practical developments in actual composition:

- Instrumental music, especially for violins, normally obscured the distinction between authentic and plagal modes by extending the range of a single voice to more than two octaves.
- Music that was chordal and had little or no imitation made the division of the octave into a fifth and a fourth less evident.
- The frequent or consistent use of B flat in the D and F modes (1, 2, 5, and 6) made them often indistinguishable from Zarlino's modes on A and C; likewise the constant use of F sharp made the G modes (7 and 8) practically the same as C modes.
- The use of the E modes (3 and 4) and their transpositions declined steadily, until they became mostly limited to internal sections within sonatas written in C modes or their transpositions.
- The number of transpositions applied to modes continued to increase, so that the signatures of flats or sharps at the beginning of compositions were of more practical importance than the designation of mode.
- Frequent change of mode within a composition meant that the relative frequency and weight of cadences on specific notes could not be predicted as easily from the manner in which the composition began.

In reaction to these practical developments, several German theorists, beginning with Johannes Lippius in 1612, emphasized the classification of all the modes into the categories *naturalior* ("natural") and *mollior* ("soft") according to the quality of the triad—major or minor—formed upon the final of the mode. Although this type of classification can be found in Zarlino, Lippius and his followers seem to give it more importance than the designation of the individual modes themselves.

Throughout the seventeenth century, most music books recognized the most common transposition of each of the eight traditional modes as the primary keys, often called *Kirchen Thon* ("Church Tone") in German treatises of that period and "church keys" or "pitch-key modes" in modern writing, based Adriano Banchieri's presentation:

TONE NUMBER	FINAL PITCH	SIGNATURE
1	D	none
2	G	one flat
3	A	none
4	E	none
5	C	none
6	F	one flat
7	D	one flat
8	G	none

Although Zarlino had noted that any mode could be transposed to any pitch if necessary, Johann Crüger (1598–1662), in his *Synopsis musica* (1630 and 1654), presented transposed modes as if original in their own right. In this vein, the *Rudimenta musices* (1685–86) by Wolfgang Mylius (1636–1712/13) lists the twelve modes in the fashion of Zarlino, then the modes based on B flat and E flat, and finally an assortment of modes built around the triads of D major, E major, F-sharp minor, A major, B major, and B minor. A similar series is shown in the *Idea boni contoris* (1688) by Georg Falck (1630–1689). In his *Unterricht der musicalischen Kunst* (1687/1697), Daniel Speer (1636–1707) lists six "natural keys" on A, C, D, E, F, and G; five "hard" or "sharp keys" on A (with two sharps), B (with two sharps), D (with two sharps), E (with one sharp), and G (with one sharp); and five "soft keys" on F (with three flats), G (with one flat), B flat (with one flat), C (with two flats), and E flat (with two flats).

The most radical German theorist in the seventeenth century was Andreas Werckmeister (1645–1706), who, although insisting on knowledge of the traditional modes for good understanding of chorale melodies, proposed in his *Musicae mathematicae* (1687) to do away with the church modes and their terminology altogether and to replace them with just two—the "natural mode" or "perfect mode" modeled on the triad C–E–G and the diatonic scale based on C, or their transpositions, which would be called C *dur* ("hard C"), D *dur*, etc.; and the "less natural mode" or "less perfect mode" modeled on the triad D–F–A and the diatonic scale based on D, or their transpositions, which would be called D *moll* ("soft D"), C *moll*, etc. In his last treatise, published in 1707, Werckmeister offered the triad and scale on A, rather than on D, as the model for the "less perfect mode." He recognized all twelve possible transpositions of his two modes and insisted that all the necessary flats or sharps be included in the key signatures and not just added as accidentals. In several of his treatises he refers to a "musical circle" of chords, and in one place (*Hypmnemata musica*, 1697) he writes, "The world-famous Froberger already some thirty years ago composed a canzona [now lost] in which he transposed, varied, and artfully conducted the theme through the entire keyboard in all twelve keys, passing through the circle of fifths or fourths until he returned to the key in which he had begun" (p. 37).

It must be emphasized that Werckmeister was a radical theorist who wished to tidy up what he regarded as messy and irregular traditional practice. His view that the E modes were already out of use was incorrect. Yet in spite of his radical views, Werckmeister still recognized the enduring validity of the most basic modal principles—the correlation between final pitch and interval pattern in determining a mode; and the correspondence between the mode and typical melodic shapes, cadence forms, hierarchy of cadences according to their final pitch, and modulatory possibilities.

SUMMARY

German-language Lutheran vocal church music can be divided into two large groups with parallel subdivisions as follows:

Works with non-chorale text:	Works with chorale text:
Arias	Plain, strophic harmonizations of chorales for 1–4 voices
Concertos	Chorale concertos, especially chorale variations setting several or all strophes in distinct sections; the chorale melody treated in cantus firmus style, madrigal style, or motet style
Concerto-aria	Chorale concertos using Biblical or other non-chorale texts in distinct sections

The texts of Lutheran church works in this period often reflect the more personal, emotional approach fostered by the New Piety. With time, one finds ever longer, more closed, and more internally unified musical sections; in a few cases, recitative and aria styles are contrasted.

Vocal music for Catholic churches in the German-speaking lands continues to set Latin texts, including the liturgical texts for the Mass and Office. In small-scale works for solo voices, the Catholic German repertoire follows closely developments in Italy, especially in the trend toward longer and more self-containing contrasting sections, including occasional contrast of recitative and aria styles. In large-scale polychoral works, German and especially Austrian composers occasionally employ a larger number of voices and a much wider variety of instruments than their Italian and French contemporaries. This grandiose style of German Catholic church music serves the political mythology known as *Pietas Austriaca* and shows parallels to the *Kaiserstil* in architecture.

Organ chorale settings such as Tunder's, coming just after mid-century, tend to be richer in contrasts and in dramatic gestures, creating more intense expression, when compared with earlier works. Later chorale settings show greater length and division into longer and more self-contained sections. Conventional means of projecting affects can create parallels between organ music and the unheard chorale text, possibly changing section by section.

North German organ toccatas, preludes, and ostinato variations, such as Buxtehude's, show more rational organization late in the seventeenth century, including extensive elaboration of short, rhythmically defined motives and a tendency toward number symbolism. Pachelbel's organ chorale settings, especially those in his unique two-fold combination form, reflect the tendency toward motivic unification.

German solo and trio sonatas for violin and continuo in the later seventeenth century parallel trends in Italy. Large-scale, even polychoral sonatas by German, Austrian, and Moravian composers often include brass and woodwind instruments; they carry older Venetian forms to extremes never explored in Italy or elsewhere in Europe. Also particular to this repertoire is the fascination with musical description, onomatopoeia (sound imitation), and narration (program). A somewhat standardized ensemble suite, including allemande, courante, ballet, and sarabande, with an introductory non-dance movement, is another German speciality at this time.

Italian opera performances, heard in isolated occurrences in several German-speaking cities during the first half of the seventeenth century, became a regular feature of court culture in Vienna about 1660. The first public opera house in Germany opened at the commercial city of Hamburg in 1678 with French-style operas in German.

German music theory of the later seventeenth century included Bernard's precise classification of three styles according to dissonance use, Printz's expansion on Mersenne's theory of musical rhythmopoeia, extensive discussions by several writers of parallels between rhetorical figures in speech and music, a general tendency to give more importance to the categories of major and minor rather than to the distinction between eight or twelve modes, a practical recognition of ever more key signatures, and Werckmeister's radical theoretical projection of twelve major and twelve minor keys.

BIBLIOGRAPHICAL NOTES

German Lutheran sacred arias, concertos, concerto-arias, and chorale concertos
An overview, now somewhat dated, can be found in the relevant chapters of Friedrich Blume, et al., *Protestant Church Music: A History* (New York: W. W. Norton, 1974). Geoffrey Webber, *North German Church Music in the Age of Buxtehude* (New York: Oxford Univ. Press, 1996), is limited to music preserved in the Düben Collection in Uppsala, Sweden. Kerala J. Snyder, *Dietrich Buxtehude, Organist in Lübeck* (New York: Schirmer, 1987), summarizes a large literature in German and provides a framework for the study of Buxtehude's Lutheran predecessors and contemporaries. The transformation of the Lutheran sacred concerto in Dresden under Schütz's successors Vincenzo Albrici and Marco Gioseppe Peranda is explored in depth by Mary Frandsen, "The Sacred concerto in Dresden, ca. 1660–1680," Ph.D. diss., Univ. of Rochester, 1996. Three important books in German on this subject are Friedhelm Krummacher, *Die Choralbearbeitung in der protestantishen Figuralmusik zwischen Praetorius und Bach*, Kieler Schriften zur Musikwissenschaft, 22 (Kassel: Bärenreiter, 1978); Michael Märker, *Die Protestantische Dialogkomposition zwischen Heinrich Schütz und Johann Sebastian Bach: Eine stilkritische Studie*, Kirchenmusikalische Studien, 2 (Cologne: Tank, 1990); and Irmard Scheitler, *Das Geistliche Lied in deutschen Barock*, Schriften zur Literaturwissenschaft, 3 (Berlin: Dunckler & Humblot, 1982). A musical supplement to the latter book is R. Hinton Thomas, *Poetry and Song in the German Baroque: A Study of the Continuo Lied* (Oxford: Clarendon Press, 1963), which contains discussions of the sacred and secular *Lied*.

Catholic German Sacred Vocal Music

A key work in this area is Eric Thomas Chafe, *The Church Music of Heinrich Biber*, Studies in Musicology, 95 (Ann Arbor: UMI Research Press, 1975). The *sepolcri* and related genres in Vienna are the subject of Rudolf Schnitzler, "The Sacred-Dramatic Music of Antonio Draghi," Ph.D. diss., Univ. of North Carolina, 1971.

Keyboard Music

Once again, a reliable overview can be found in the relevant chapters of Willi Apel, *The History of Keyboard Music to 1700*, trans. Hans Tischler (Bloomington, IN: Indiana Univ. Press, 1972); and in the parallel chapters in Alexander Silbiger, ed., *Keyboard Music before 1700* (New York: Schirmer Books, 1995). Buxtehude's non-chorale keyboard works and their context are treated in Lawrence Archbold, *Style and Structure in the Praeludia of Dietrich Buxtehude* (Ann Arbor: UMI Research Press, 1985). The books by Webber, Snyder, and Krummacher cited earlier, relate to this subject as well.

Instrumental Ensemble Music

A survey of many German composers of instrumental ensembles can be found in William S. Newman, *The Sonata in the Baroque Era*, 4th ed. (New York: W. W. Norton, 1983. The political use of musical ceremony and pageantry in Vienna is analyzed in Herbert Seifert, *Der Sig-pragende Hochzeit-Gott: Hochzeitsfeste am Wiener Hof der Habsburger und ihre Allegorik, 1622–1699* (Vienna: Musikwissenschaftlicher Verlag, 1988). The distinctive large-scale ensemble music of the Viennese court and its satellites is treated in Albert Biales, "Sonatas and Canzonas for Larger Ensembles in Seventeenth-Century Austria," Ph.D. diss., UCLA, 1962; Michael Grant Vaillancourt, "Instrumental Ensemble Music at the Court of Leopold I (1658–1705)," Ph.D. diss., Univ. of Illinois, 1991); and Gary Don Zink, "The Large-Ensemble Sonatas of Antonio Bertali and their Relationship to the Ensemble Sonata Traditions of the Seventeenth Century," Ph.D. diss., Washington Univ., 1989. A bibliographic study of this repertoire is Paul Alister Whitehead, "Austro-German Printed Sources of Instrumental Ensemble Music, 1630–1700," Ph.D. diss., Univ. of Pennsylvania, 1996). A German-language classic that explores many otherwise inaccessible aspects of this topic is Ernst Meyer, *Die mehrstimmige Spielmusik des 17. Jahrhunderts in Nord- und Mitteleuropa* (Kassel: Bärenreiter, 1934/1982). Articles about the ensemble suite with introductory movement in Germany are collected in Günther Fleischhauer, ed., *Die Entwicklung der Ouvertüren-Suite im 17. und 18. Jahrhundert* (Michalestein, 1996). Descriptive, onomatopoetic, and narrative instrumental music in historical context is the subject of Leslie Orrey, *Programme Music: a Brief Survey from the Sixteenth Century to the Present Day* (London: Davis-Poynter, 1975). In German, a more specific study focusing on the material of this chapter is Hubert Unverricht, "Hörbare Vorbilder in der Instrumentalmusik bis 1750: Untersuchung zur Vorgeschichte der Programmusik," Ph.D. diss., Free Univ. of Berlin, 1953.

Seventeenth-Century Opera in the German Lands

The general survey of opera in Vienna during this period is Herbert Seifert, *Die Oper am Wiener Kaiserhof im 17. Jahrhundert* (Tutzing: Schneider, 1985). This and several other aspects of music at the court of Vienna are touched upon in Theophil Antonicek, "Vienna, 1580–1705," in *The Early Baroque Era*, ed. Curtis Price, Music and Society (Englewood Cliffs, NJ: Prentice Hall, 1994), pp. 146–163. The general treatment of the early Hamburg opera theater is Hellmuth Christian Wolff, *Die Barockoper in Hamburg 1678–1738* (Wolfenbüttel: Möseler, 1957). A more recent political interpretation of this activity is Dorothea Schröder, *Zeitgeschichte auf der Opernbühne: barockes Musiktheater in Hamburg im Dienst von Politik und Diplomatie (1690–1745)* (Göttingen: Vandenhoeck & Ruprecht, 1998)

German Music Theory

An overview of German music theory in this period is provided by George J. Buelow, "Symposium on Seventeenth-Century Music Theory: Germany," *Journal of Music Theory*, 16 (1972), 36–49. Bernhard's treatises are translated by Walter Hilse, "The Treatises of Christoph Bernhard," *The Music Forum*, 3 (1973). Printz's theory of musical rhythmopoeia is explained, with translations and examples, by George Houle, *Meter in Music, 1600–1800* (Bloomington, IN: Indiana Univ. Press, 1987), pp. 62–77. German theories of mode and key are summarized by Joel Lester, *Between Modes and Keys: German Theory, 1592–1802*, Harmonologia Series, 3 (Stuyvesant, NY: Pendragon Press, 1989). German writings on the musical equivalents of rhetorical figures are analyzed and indexed in Dietrich Bartel, *Musica Poetica: Musical-Rhetorical Figures in German Baroque Music* (Lincoln, NE: Univ. of Nebraska Press, 1997).

CHAPTER 12

Sonata and Concerto in
Late Seventeenth-Century Italy

THE ITALIAN TRIO AND SOLO SONATA IN THE SECOND
HALF OF THE SEVENTEENTH CENTURY

During the second half of the seventeenth century, the center for violin making and violin music remained the Po Valley described in Chapter 3. The regions of Emilia, with its main centers of Bologna and Modena, and the Venetian Republic, including Bergamo, Brescia, Cremona, and Venice, continued to produce the most important composers of violin music. The finest string instruments still came from these same cities—from the workshops of Nicolò Amati (1596–1684), Andrea Guarneri (1623–1698), Antonio Stradivari (1644/49–1737), and Carlo Bergonzi (1683–1747) in Cremona; Matteo Goffriller (1659–1742) in Venice; Giovanni Grancino (1637–1709) and Carlo Giuseppe Testore (ca. 1665–1716) in Milan; and Giovanni Tononi (d. 1713) in Bologna.

The leading Italian composers of string ensemble music in this period no longer had close ties to the instrumentalists' guilds or "companies." Their training and careers now generally followed the pattern of the church music director, *maestro di cappella*, even if some of them also played string instruments professionally.

An early example of this new type of composer of string music is Maurizio Cazzati (1616–1678). All of Cazzati's professional positions were at the head of church ensembles: San Pietro in Guastalla when he was seventeen years old, Sant'Andrea in Mantua, the Accademia della Morte in Ferrara, Santa Maria Maggiore in Bergamo, and San Petronio in Bologna. In all these places, he employed instrumental ensembles in the music for Mass and Vespers. He published at least ten collections of instrumental music, nine of them for instruments of the violin family.

The sonata for two violins and basso continuo—the so-called "trio sonata," named for the three written parts, even though often played by four or more musicians—was Cazzati's preferred genre. His works and those of his students helped crystallize the trio sonata as the most common type of sonata in the later Baroque period.

Most of Cazzati's sonatas continue the canzona tradition, with three core movements (*tempi* in Italian): (1) fast, duple meter, and imitative; (2) triple meter and usually homophonic; (3) duple meter, imitative, and motivically related to the first tempo. Avoiding the "quilt sonata" patchwork with many short, contrasting segments in different meters and tempos, Cazzati favored an expansion of the three-tempo plan through the addition of self-contained, slow, expressive movements, which could appear before any or all of the three that he inherited from the canzona tradition. An example of this pattern is Sonata 7, "La Rossella," from Cazzati's Opus 18 of 1656 (A. 101).

Like most Italian trio sonatas of the seventeenth century, Cazzati's Op. 18, no. 7, employs two equally important imitative violin parts with a basso continuo that is given a harmonically and rhythmically supporting role, only occasionally participating in the motivic imitation. The opening slow movement of this sonata conforms to the norms of Mode 1 (transposed to C via a B-flat in the signature with an E-flat as an invariable accidental); it cadences successively on the fifth, third, and final of the mode, using harmony generated to a great extent by parallel thirds between the violins.

The subject of Cazzaati's Allegro, spanning an octave and a fifth with a series of leaps, is typical of the violinistic themes of his sonatas. Likewise typical is the expansion of periods set off by cadences through melodic and harmonic sequences involving imitative exchanges among the three parts.

Cazzati's triple-meter movement breaks with tradition in its $\frac{3}{8}$ meter and a tempo marking of Presto. The movement is a giga, common in the middle sections of Cazzati's Op. 18 sonatas. An important feature of the giga is the extensive elaboration of a small number of rhythmic motives, which together with some scale-wise bass lines conveys the impression of energetic motion directed at cadential goals—an impression that is increasingly common in late seventeenth-century Italian sonata movements.

The Grave inserted before Cazzati's final rapid, duple-meter movement resembles the first movement in its short, cadential phrases on the final and third of the mode, with violins in parallel thirds. The brief final movement makes no obvious reference to the first Allegro: if there is any connection, it would be to measure 24 of the first movement, which the subject of the final Presto resembles somewhat.

When this sonata and the others from Cazzati's early opuses are compared with the earlier works of Marco Uccellini, the differences emerge not so much in the new features introduced by Cazzati as in his avoidance of Uccellini's extravagant and surprising variety, long and rambling elaborations, sharp contrasts, wide range of pacing, exploration of the extreme high register, and vestiges of stock figures from the tradition of improvisation. The relatively small number of tempo-defined segments in Cazzati's sonatas shows that he followed the example of Tarquinio Merula (1594/5–1665) from Cremona, whose last two books of sonatas and canzonas (1637 and 1651) may have been the first to introduce this trait.

The trend of Cazzati's sonatas toward unity and concision is furthered in the works of his student, Giovanni Battista Vitali (1632–1692), a cellist in the orchestra at San Petronio in Bologna, who went on to positions of leadership in the musical chapel of the Este ducal court in nearby Modena.

Vitali's early collections of trio sonatas (1667) and larger-ensemble works (1669) resemble Cazzati's in their expansion of the three-tempo canzona format through the addition of slow movements. The main innovations in these are the creation of even more unity of direction and material by the extensive use of sequences, rhythmic elaborations, and ostinato bass patterns. More important than these canzona-derived sonatas, however, are Vitali's collections of dances and dance-derived sonatas.

Although individual dances are scattered liberally throughout the collections of early Italian violin music—the published collections of Biagio Marini for example—Vitali led the way toward combinations of dances in sonatas *da camera* ("of the chamber," that is, not suitable for the church). Already in his Opus 3 (1667), Vitali included among the usual dance pairs a grouping of a brando in three sections together with a gavotta and its corrente. Such groupings of three dances are standard in Vitali's Opus 4 (1668). There is no question here of French influence; the Italian traits of these dances include the use of imitative counterpoint, sequences, and irregular phrases. In his trio sonatas Opus 8 (1683), Vitali routinely cadences on the fifth of the mode at the end of the first reprise and on the final at the end of each dance (see A. 102). Vitali's *Varie sonate alla francese, e all'italiana* ("Various Sonatas in the French and Italian Manner"), Opus 11 (1684), include a bourrée; seven of these sonatas begin with a non-dance movement (a capriccio or *introduzione*), perhaps under the influence of the sonatas published in Venice by Johann Rosenmüller.

In Modena, Vitali encountered the elderly Marco Uccellini and his most important student, Giovanni Maria Bononcini (1642–1678), who published ten collections of solo and trio sonatas of both the canzona (church) and dance-suite (chamber) types and an important treatise, *Il musico prattico* ("The Practical Musician," 1673).

Bononcini's *Musico prattico* includes the most detailed discussion of mode since the treatises of Adriano Banchieri. Bononcini follows Banchieri in naming the eight modes that are useful in polyphony exactly as shown in Example 3-8, although Bononcini correlates them with certain of the twelve modes of Zarlino's theory, rather than deriving them from a mixture of modal characteristics and psalm tone formulas, as Banchieri did.

Bononcini's *Musico prattico*; *Li primi albori musicali* ("The First Dawn of Music," 1672) and the *Direttorio del canto fermo* ("Directory of Plain Chant," 1689), both by the Bolognese musician Lorenzo Penna (1613–1693); the *Compendio musicale* ("Musical Compendium," 1677) by Bartolomeo Bismantova (before 1675–after 1694) from Reggio Emilia; and the five surviving treatises (1681–93) of Angelo Berardi (ca. 1636–1694), all published in Bologna, would by themselves demonstrate the continuing significance of modal theory in late seventeenth-century solo and trio sonatas from the Po Valley. This should be obvious to us from the music as well as from the fact that a modal designation for each sonata was included in Bononcini's *Sonate da chiesa*, Op. 6 (1672) and in the Opus 4 (1665) sonatas by Giulio Cesare Arresti (1619–1701), also of Bologna.

In his Opus 6 sonatas, Bononcini expands the role of modal pitch structure beyond the formulation, restatement, and transposition of imitated subjects and their correlation to cadence pitches; he also frames a modal octave by the composite melodic activity of the two violin parts in preparation for every cadence. The first movement of Bononcini's Op. 2, no. 11, provides a series of typical examples of this.

In Example 12-1, the score of the first movement of Bononcini's Op. 2, no. 11, is condensed by placing both violin parts on a single staff, thus clarifying the composite melodic line formed by the combination of the two. What we see is a series of modally defined segments, each marked by a complete scalewise descent from the fifth degree in the case of plagal modes or from the octave in the case of authentic modes down to the final pitch of each cadence—always decorated through the addition of abundant surface diminution. In Example 12-1, each of the steps in these descents is marked by a diagonal line and numbered with reference to the eventual cadence pitch. Because the modal octave is thus reframed in preparation for each cadence, each of the segments leading up to a cadence on a pitch other than the original modal final effects a temporary change of mode, identified and marked in the example. The final pitch of each cadence is enclosed within a small box and named with a large, bold letter. Here, as elsewhere in Bononcini's Opus 6, some of the cadences are followed by a few measures of transition, during which the melodic lines of the violin parts rapidly ascend to establish the starting point for a new descent to closure.

Each of the descending melodic segments shown in Example 12-1 is at least partially harmonized by a melodic/harmonic sequence. In sequences 1, 2, 5, 6, and 7, the bass alternately goes down a third and up a step, with figures 5 and 6 in alternation. In sequences 3 and 4, the bass alternately rises by a fourth and descends by a fifth, with implicit or explicit figures of either $\frac{5}{3}$ or 7.

The features described here and illustrated in Example 12-1 are completely typical of Bononcini's Opus 6 sonatas. They can be found occasionally as early as his Opus 1 of 1666, and they are included with increasing frequency in his later dances and chamber sonatas (Opuses 7, 9, and 12), especially in preparation for cadences on the modal fifth degree. This tendency can also be found with increasing frequency in the non–dance trio sonatas (1667, 1669, 1684) by Giovanni Battista Vitali, but not as often or as rigorously as in Bononcini's. This combination of modally structured melodic descent accompanied by harmonic sequences of falling fifths gains significance in an expanding body of music for several decades to come. For that reason, Example 12-1 and the entire sonata from which it is drawn (A. 103) should be studied carefully.

The most significant continuation of the trends represented by the works of Bononcini and Vitali are found in the sonatas for two violins (later one violin), and basso continuo by Arcangelo Corelli, one of the most influential composers in the history of music.

326

EXAMPLE 12-1. Giovanni Maria Bononcini, Op. 2, No. 11, first movement, showing modal pitch structure and sequences

EXAMPLE 12-1. Giovanni Maria Bononcini, Op. 2, No. 11, first movement, showing modal pitch structure and sequences—continued

ARCANGELO CORELLI

Arcangelo Corelli (1653–1713) was born in Fusignano, a small town located about thirty kilometers east of Bologna, and he received his earliest musical instruction in small, nearby centers. Corelli continued his studies in Bologna, where he was admitted (1670) to the prestigious Academia Filarmonica as a composer at the age of seventeen. Only the name of his violin teacher in Bologna is known—Giovanni Benvenuti, a member of the orchestra under Cazzati at the basilica of San Petronio, 1655–1660. Among the sonata composers active in Bologna at that time were Arresti, Cazzati, Vitali, Giovanni Paolo Colonna (1637–1695), and Pietro Degli Antoni (1639–1720). During Corelli's period of study in Bologna, Giovanni Maria Bononcini of nearby Modena published his Opus 6 sonatas and his treatise *Il musico prattico*. Throughout the rest of his life, Corelli called himself "Bolognese."

By 1675 Corelli was established as a violinist in Rome. His early patron there was Queen Christina (1626–1689), who had abdicated the throne of Sweden, a Lutheran country, in 1654, embraced the Catholic religion, and moved to Rome, where she had become a highly influential patron of the arts and learning. The sonata composers Alessandro Stradella, Lelio Colista (1629–1680), Carlo Mannelli (1640–1697), and Carlo Ambrogio Lonati (ca. 1645–1710/15) also belonged to Queen Christina's circle at that time. Their influence, along with what he absorbed from the Bolognese and Modenese composers, can be detected in Corelli's sonatas.

In 1687 Corelli joined the household of Cardinal Benedetto Pamphili, and in 1690 he transferred to the service of the even more powerful Cardinal Pietro Ottoboni, grand-nephew of Pope Alexander VIII and vice-chancellor of the Church. In the service of Queen Christina and the two cardinals, Corelli composed and performed his sonatas for one and two violins with basso continuo and his concerti grossi, to be discussed later. In addition, Corelli led orchestras in performances of concerted church music, oratorios, operas, serenades, sonatas, and concertos, typically with about a dozen musicians but at times with up to 150 string players.

As a result of his playing and especially his composing, Corelli became wealthy and famous—probably the most famous and influential composer of instrumental music up to that time. His published works are contained in six opuses:

Opus 1 (1681), twelve sonatas "a tre" for two violins and violone or archlute with organ continuo, each including a fugal movement but no specified dances.

Opus 2 (1685), twelve sonatas "da camera a tre" for two violins and violone or harpsichord, each of them a series of dances movements, eight beginning with a non-dance prelude.

Opus 3 (1689), twelve sonatas "a tre" for two violins and violone or archlute with organ continuo, each including a fugal movement but no specified dances.

Opus 4 (1694), twelve sonatas "a tre," composed for Cardinal Ottoboni's accademia, for two violins and violone or harpsichord, each of them a series of dance movements preceded by a non-dance prelude.

Opus 5 (1700), twelve sonatas for violin and violone or harpsichord in two parts, the first part consisting of six sonatas, each with a fugal movement, and the second part consisting of six sonatas made up of a suite of dances led off by a non-dance prelude.

Opus 6 (1714), twelve concerti grossi for two violins and violoncello in the concertino group and two violins, viola, and basso, to be doubled optionally, in the concerto grosso group, each group provided with its own basso continuo part; the first eight have fugal movements and no dance titles, while the final four contain a mixture of dance- and non-dance movements preceded by a non-dance prelude.

Corelli's Opus 2 was called *da camera* ("of the chamber"), and his Opus 4 was so titled in its 1695 Roman reprint. None of his collections carries the designation *da chiesa* ("of the church"), and evidence suggests that the Opus 1 and 3 sonatas were intended as chamber music as much as the dance-suite chamber sonatas of Opuses 2 and 4. The *accademia* (literally "academy") mentioned in the title of Opus 4 in its 1695 Venetian reprint would have been a social gathering typically featuring some combination of formal discussion or ritualized debate and musical performance. It is probable that all of Corelli's sonatas were composed for performances at academies of this sort.

Corelli's sonatas appear to be the most frequently reprinted music collections in history. By the end of the eighteenth century, his Opus 1 had been issued in forty editions, his Opus 5 in forty-two. He may have been the first composer whose reputation spread primarily by means of his printed music. Charles Burney did not exaggerate when he wrote, in 1776, "Scarce a contemporary musical writer, historian, or poet, neglected to celebrate his genius and talents."

The trio sonatas of Corelli's Opuses 1 and 3 had the effect of standardizing the non-dance-suite or free sonata as a succession of four movements, slow—fast—slow—fast, typically with a fugue—a movement based upon one or two subjects repeated in imitative counterpoint by all the parts—in the second movement. Corelli's Opus 2 and 4 chamber sonatas also tend to have four movements, often in the same pattern of slow—fast—slow—fast, typically (1) Preludio or Allemanda, (2) Allemanda or Corrente, (3) Sarabanda or non-dance movement, and (4) Giga or Allemanda, Corrente, Gavotta, etc., although several other combinations are found. Although suites opening with a prelude were more typical of German sonatas, suites beginning with a slow allemande were known in Italy during the preceding decades for example in the trio and solo violin sonatas of Bononcini, Vitali, and Giovanni Battista Bassani (ca. 1650–1716) and in the keyboard suites of Corelli's Roman colleague Bernardo Pasquini (1637–1710). The slow prelude may thus be related to the initial allemande found in earlier Italian chamber sonatas.

Corelli is perhaps best remembered today for having normalized harmonic practice, mostly by codifying and selecting from among elements already in use.

THE NORMALIZED HARMONIC STYLE

In his 1708 instruction book on continuo realization, *L'armonico pratico al cimbalo* ("The Practical Harmonist at the Harpsichord"), Francesco Gasparini (1661-1727), a student of Corelli, wrote about the proper method of handling dissonances:

> This is practiced by the good modern composers, and it is found particularly in the very charming *sinfonie* by Arcangelo Corelli, most virtuosic on the violin, true Orpheus of our time, who, with so much artfulness, study, and grace, moves and makes harmonies (*modula*) with those basses of his, with suspensions and [other] dissonances so well regulated and resolved and so well interwoven with a variety of subjects, that it may well be said that he discovered the perfection of a harmony that enraptures. . . . He who will undertake to practice with the [figured] basses of his compositions will derive notable profit from them. . . .

Gasparini's main objective in *L'armonico pratico al cimbalo* is to instruct the reader in the realization of basso continuo accompaniments where specific figures are lacking. As a perhaps unintentional byproduct of this aim, he sets out the main sorts of harmonic sequence and cadence pattern, which form the core of the "perfection of a harmony that enraptures" that Corelli "discovered."

Those patterns shown by Gasparini that are prominent in Corelli's sonatas are illustrated in Example 12-2, along with some other patterns that are not shown in Gasparini's book because, consisting entirely of root-position triads, they present no problems to the "practical harmonist at the harpsichord" when they are notated without figures.

The first pattern shown in Gasparini's "Remarks on Ascending Motion" is the one in which the bass rises by step, with an alternation between the figures 5 and 6 on each note. This may be the most common sequence in the works of Corelli and his Italian contemporaries. Gasparini's example is given as Example 12-2a, while an example from Corelli's Opus 3 is Example 12-2b.

Closely related—by chordal inversion—to the ascending 5–6 sequence is that which takes as its bass the melodic pattern formed by the upper line in the editorial realization of the figured bass in the first measure of Example 12-2b: the pattern down a third then up a fourth. The transference of this pattern to

EXAMPLE 12-2. Types of sequence illustrated in Francesco Gasparini, *L'armonico practico al cimbalo* (1708) and in the trio sonatas by Arcangelo Corelli:
a. Gasparini's 5–6 sequence

5 6 5 6 5 6 5 6 5 6 5 6 5 6 5 6 5 6 5 6

EXAMPLE 12-2b. Corelli, Op. 3, No. 2, second movement, mm. 13–15

the bass is shown in Example 12-2c. Gasparini does not demonstrate this sequence because all the chords are root-position triads, so the bass has no need for the addition of figures. The two closely related patterns shown in Example 12-2a, b, and c are the normal rising sequences used in normalized harmonic style used by Corelli and some of his contemporaries.

The most common descending sequence in the normalized harmonic style is that in which each note of a scalewise descending bass line is harmonized with a sixth and a third, denoted by the single figure 6 (Examples 12-2d and e). Closely related to this is the sequence in which each note of the scalewise descending bass line is harmonized with a 7 and a 6. Gasparini's example is shown in as Example 12-2f, and the same sequence from Corelli's Op. 1, no. 12, is given as Example 12-2g. One might think that the second of these is essentially the same as the first, only decorated with suspensions. But Gasparini appears to consider these two sequences to be distinct.

Gasparini also shows a descending scalewise bass line in tied notes with the figures $\frac{4}{2}$ in alternation (Ex. 12-2h), which is another sequential pattern commonly found in Corelli (e.g., Ex. 12-2i), sometimes with the figure $\frac{6}{5}$ instead of just 6. The same patterns of chords can be found in two other illustrations by Gasparini and are frequently used in the normalized harmonic style: the bass pattern of rising fourths and falling fifths figured with 7 (Exx. 12-2j and k) and the bass pattern of ascending steps and descending third in which the figures $\frac{6}{5}$ and 5 (or no figure) alternate (Ex. 12-2l and m). Gasparini shows (Ex. 12-3a) the bass pattern of falling fourths and rising fifths, the opposite of the pattern illustrated in Exx. 12-2j and k, only with the alternation of the figures $\frac{5}{3}$ and $\frac{6\sharp}{4\sharp}$, as if to indicate a need for the cohesion of a passing harmony of the augmented fourth resolving to a sixth, which mimics one type of cadential progression. This sequence is common enough in the music of Stradella (Ex. 12-3b) and others of the generation preceding Corelli. But it is quite rare in the normalized harmonic style of Corelli and his contemporaries.

Another of Gasparini's rising sequences is completely avoided by Corelli: the rising quarter-note bass shown in Example 12-3c. Considering that the first notes in measures 2, 3, and 4 are A, E, and B, this sequence might be considered a variant of the one mentioned in the previous paragraph, with diminution applied to the bass.

The second sequence shown by Gasparini but not used by Corelli is shown in Example 12-3d. Although Corelli does use the pattern of bass line and figures with the addition of a suspension on the strong beat, shown with the

Text continues on page 334

EXAMPLE 12-2c. Corelli, Op. 2, No. 12, second movement, mm. 97–99

EXAMPLE 12-2d. Gasparini's 6–6 sequence

EXAMPLE 12-2e. Corelli, Op. 2, No. 3, fourth movement, mm. 17–18

EXAMPLE 12-2f. Gasparini's 7–6 sequence

5 6 7 6 7 6 7 6 7 6 7 6 7 6♯

EXAMPLE 12-2g. Corelli, Op. 1, No. 12, second movement, mm. 32–36

5 6 7 6 7 6 7 6 7 6 7 6 7 6

EXAMPLE 12-2h. Gasparini's 4/2–6 sequence

4/2 6 4/2 6 4/2 6 4/2 6 4/2 6 7 6

EXAMPLE 12-2i. Corelli, Op. 5, No. 2, second movement, mm. 46–50

6 4♭/2 6 4/2 6♭ 4/2 6 4/2 6 4/2 6 6/5 5 4/2 6/5

EXAMPLE 12-2j. Gasparini's 7–7 sequence

EXAMPLE 12-2k. Corelli, Op. 4, No. 11, first movement, mm. 2–4

EXAMPLE 12-2l. Gasparini's $^6_5$–$^5_3$ sequence

figure "7" preceding the figure "6" in each case, the plain version of this descending sequence perhaps exposed the consecutive octaves on weak beats too plainly for his taste.

After sequences, the second-most normalized series of harmonies in Corelli's works can be found at cadences. Here, again, Gasparini's examples and cate-

EXAMPLE 12-2m. Corelli, Op. 1, No. 5, fourth movement, mm. 17–22

gories offer a suitable starting point. The focal point for him, as for all theorists preceding him in the seventeenth century, is the conduct of the voice bearing the leading tone (the *cantizans* voice). Gasparini classifies cadences as "compound" if the leading tone is preceded by a suspension with its preparation, "simple" if it is not. Of the compound cadences, those classified as "greater" precede the preparation of the suspension with the leading tone; those classified as "shorter" do not. Example 12-4 illustrates these categories of cadence.

Corelli's occasional simple cadences may appear as in Example 12-4a, mostly with the bass descending by step. Of his far more common compound cadences, there is only one without elaboration in the *cantizans* voice and only slightly more with that voice embellished (Op. 3, no. 1, Grave, mm. 17–19).

In the vast majority of cases, Corelli's cadences, either simple or compound (greater or lesser), have melodic motion in the bass and are, therefore, called "diminished" by Gasparini, in the sense that a hypothetical plain bass line has been subjected to diminution. The majority of Corelli's cadences are in fact greater diminished compound cadences. Example 12-5 contains some typical illustrations.

In creating diminutions for the bass in his greater diminished compound cadences, Corelli introduces additional consonances—new chords—that are not shown in any of Gasparini's examples. Some of the most common harmonizations of greater diminished compound cadences in Corelli's sonatas are shown in Example 12-5, in which the four *cantizans* notes of the greater, compound cadence formula are circled and numbered.

The last of the five key harmonic events of a greater diminished compound cadence can be replaced by an unexpected harmony, creating what Gasparini calls a "deceptive" cadence. Example 12-6 from Gasparini's treatise shows some of them, although Corelli rarely uses any other than the one shown in

EXAMPLE 12-3. Types of sequences discarded by Corelli
a. Gasparini's sequence of falling fourths and rising fifths

EXAMPLE 12-3b. Stradella, Sinfonia for Two Violins and Basso Continuo, fourth movement

EXAMPLE 12-3c. Gasparini's ascending scale sequence

EXAMPLE 12-3d. Gasparini's sequence of interlocking thirds and 6–[5] figures

EXAMPLE 12-4. Gasparini's illustrations of categories of cadence

measure 9 of this example, in which the bass rises by step to form the root of the last harmony.

Oddly, Gasparini completely ignores one further type of cadence that is extremely common in Corelli's music—the Phrygian cadence, in which the *cantizans* voice ascends by whole step, while the bass descends by half step. In occurs frequently at the end of slow movements based on the Phrygian third degree of the major mode that reigns in the other movements, but it can also be found at the end of rapid first movements. Example 12-7 shows some examples.

To a great extent, the movements of Corelli's sonatas, of whatever type, are made up of "periods." A period in this context is defined as a substantial musical segment, usually of more than twelve bars, that concludes with a clear cadence. A period in the works of Corelli and his Italian contemporaries and successors may consist of a harmonic-melodic preparation, central sequences, and an extended greater diminished compound cadence formula. Corelli's repeated use of sequences to focus directional musical processes toward cadences is the culmination of a progressive tendency that can be traced over a period of many decades in the Italian ensemble sonata. To the inherent features of sequences that generate motion—pattern and single-directional contour—Corelli adds suspensions and forward-pressing rhythmic figures far more than any predecessor. More than anyone before him, Corelli consistently introduces, toward the beginning of his sequences, the accidentals that belong to the scale or mode based on the upcoming cadential pitch, thus evoking a specific expectation of the goal. Nearly all of Corelli's descending sequences merge directly into a cadential formula, as, for instance, in all of the Corelli excerpts in Example 12-2. Not even Giovanni Maria Bononcini is as consistent in this regard; of the nine descending sequences by Bononcini, in Example 12-1, for instance, numbers 3, 4, 5, 7, and 9 do not connect directly with cadences, and neither do any of the sequences in the subsequent movements. The sequences in the sonatas by Fontana, Buonamente, Uccellini, Cazzati, and Vitali in the Anthology are even more often not connected to cadences.

Corelli's non-sequential and non-cadential harmonies also contribute to the impression of directed motion. His ever greater concentration on harmonic progression based on the cadence and on descending sequences is part of the explanation, but not all of it. Corelli also uses chordal motion by step and by third, although in far more restricted contexts than his predecessors. It is especially rare for Corelli to string together a series of chords related by step or by third, as Bononcini does in measures 6–8, 14–15, 16–17, and 22 of Example 12-1.

The normalization of harmonic style in which Corelli played such an important role resulted from abandoning chord progressions used by his predecessors, rather than from inventing new ones. Corelli's student Francesco Geminiani (1687–1762) achieved a remarkable insight when he wrote, in the Preface to his *Guida armonica* ("Harmonic Guide," ca. 1752), "*B. Lulli* [i.e., Jean-Baptiste

EXAMPLE 12-5. Samples of greater diminished compound cadences from Corelli's works, with the core pitches of the *cantizans* voice circled and numbered

EXAMPLE 12-6. Gasparini's illustrations of deceptive cadences

Lully], *A. Corelli*, and *J. Bononcini* [i.e., Giovanni Maria Bononcini], were the first Improvers of Instrumental Musick; and had Genius and natural Abilities sufficient to draw from the Ancients, such a Variety of Modulation, as they judge sufficient to render their Compositions delightful and spirituous." Geminiani goes on to criticize these composers for their "narrow and confined Modulation." However, it was the very restriction in the number of possible continuations of any harmonic pattern that gave rise, in the music of Lully, Corelli, Bononcini, and others of their generation, to specific or more narrowly focused expectations where none had existed before. These expectations became the basis of

EXAMPLE 12-7. Examples of Phrygian cadences from the works of Corelli

Op. 4, no. 4, iii, 13-17

musical implications and are, thus, perceived as contributing to the effect of directed motion.

This is not to say that Corelli and his contemporaries replaced earlier methods of pitch organization with something entirely new. There is hardly a composer in the seventeenth century whose works are more regular in their modality than Corelli's. All eight modes described by Banchieri—and, in Corelli's time, by Penna, Berardi, and Bononcini—are found in Corelli's sonatas, some of them in several transpositions. In addition, Corelli, like Bononcini before him, prepares for most cadences by outlining a melodic descent covering the fifth or octave above the eventual cadence pitch, and by the introduction of the accidentals that produce the eventual modal scale. In these respects, the English theorist Roger North (1651–1734) aptly described Corelli's sonatas when he wrote, generally concerning modulation, in his essay "What is Ayre?" (*ca.* 1710):

> It will readily appear that this rule of change will warrant a walk of the aire by note after note all over the scale of tones and semitones:

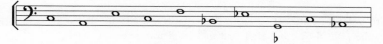

> for if each note sounding is taken for the key in its turne, and the removes not transgressing the rule, there will be no fault in the variety, provided a discretion is used in giving time for each key to hold the aire compleat, that another may not succeed before the former is well worne out.

In this passage, following an established English tradition, "aire" means, approximately, "modal-octave framework." So, when, in *The principles of Musik,* (1634), Charles Butler (ca. 1560–1647) wrote that "air-not's" were "the final Not's of the fowr Cadences proper to the Air," he was referring to the final of the mode, and the third, fifth, and octave above it. Thus, "a walk of the aire" means "a succession of modal changes culminating in cadences." The notes in North's example represent the concluding notes of cadences, each one "taken for the key in its turne." "To hold the aire compleat" means to exploit the fifth above and fourth below the cadential final and possibly to emphasize the reciting tone or repercussion, as well, until the "aire" of the "key" is "well worne out."

This process can be studied in Corelli's Op. 4, no. 4 (A. 104). This sonata takes the form of a four-movement suite: Preludio (slow), Corrente (fast), Adagio (slow), and Giga (fast). The work as a whole is in Mode 6 transposed from a final of F with one flat to a final of D by a signature of two sharps. The basic mode is plagal by virtue of the emphasis on the octave *a'* to *a''* with the final, *d''* in the middle; but the plagal Mode 6 is mixed with the authentic Mode 5, inasmuch as the range of the violin parts extends down to *d'*, notably at the concluding cadences of movements. Also indicative of the reigning plagal mode is the cadence on F-sharp, the third above the final (the reciting tone or repercussion of Mode 6), at the end of the third movement.

Corelli's opening Preludio begins with two similar short cadential phrases on the final and fifth of the mode, respectively. Such an opening has been called a "gambit" in modern writing, with the implication that cadences on these two pitches serve to establish the mode harmonically. Melodically, too, these phrases outline the descending fifth a'' to d''. The additional $c\sharp''$ implies a resolution to the d'', which is, however, withheld until the two last cadences (m. 18), thus binding the movement together.

Corelli's Preludio contains two internal cadences, on A (m. 10) and on B (13), each prepared by a melodic descent from a fifth above, pushed along by a series of suspensions and a recurring three-note upbeat figure in the bass, whose forward-moving tendency is frustrated each time by a rest on the downbeat until the final push to the cadence. The choice of the sixth scale-degree of a major mode as a secondary cadence point after the final and the fifth above the final, instead of a more traditional pitch, like the third above the final, became typical by the late seventeenth century, as Henry Purcell observes in the twelfth edition of John Playford's *An Introduction to the Skill of Musick* (1694), concerning "the Closes [i.e., cadences] proper to each *Key*":

> To a *flat* [i.e., minor] *Key*, the Principal is the *Key* it self, the next in dignity the *Fifth* above, and after that the *Third* and *Seventh* above.
>
> To a *sharp* [i.e., major] *Key* the *Key* it self first, the *Fifth* above, and in stead of the *Third* and *Seventh* (which are not so proper in a *sharp* key) the *Sixth* and *Second* above.

The second and fourth movements of Corelli's Op. 4, no. 4, are dances in the usual binary form (having two reprises), with a cadence on the fifth above the final at the end of the first reprise. In both movements, the first reprise is divided between a phrase cadencing on the overall final, a sequential passage preparing for the cadence on the fifth, and a cadential phrase on the fifth of the mode. This three-part division of a reprise or extended period becomes typical of Italian forms beginning in the last two decades of the seventeenth century. As usual, each cadence in these movements is prepared by a melodic descent from a fifth above and the introduction of accidentals as needed.

The third movement of Corelli's Op. 4, no. 4, is particularly interesting for its extended treatment of Mode 4 transposed from a final of E (with no flats or sharps) or A (with one flat) to a final of F-sharp with a signature of two sharps. As mentioned before, F-sharp is the reciting tone or repercussion of Mode 6 when it is transposed to D. The third movement as a whole is structured exactly as Banchieri and Bononcini outlined for Mode 4; the fifth from B to F-sharp is emphasized as in Mode 5 until the end, where the identity of F-sharp as final is made clear through the Phrygian cadence. Actually, hints that F-sharp is the final and B the reciting tone or repercussion are to be found throughout this movement, even at the beginning.

Thus, the pitch structure of Corelli's sonatas, and that of most Italianate music of the late Baroque, embodies a potent combination of a normalized harmonic style together with the octave-structuring melodic processes from the modal tradition. In effect, chordal composition and modal composition have merged in works of this type. This combination was recognized by Antonio Eximeno in 1774:

> That which is to be noted in the works of Corelli is the natural conduct of the fundamental bass [i.e., the natural progression of chords], the clarity of the modes, the sincerity of the harmonies, the regularity of the mutations of mode, and the perfect resolution of the dissonances.[1]

THE SOLO SONATA AFTER CORELLI

While German, French, and English composers continued to write trio sonatas in the eighteenth century, Italians tended to concentrate on the sonata for one violin (or other treble instrument) and basso continuo after 1700. The most likely reasons for this change include the phenomenal success of Corelli's Op. 5, the careers as violin soloists pursued by several Italian sonata composers of the new generation, and a growing concentration on melody, a style change also evident in the opera and cantata arias of the generation born about 1690.

The first signs of a decisive stylistic break with Corelli can be found in a manuscript collection of twelve solo sonatas in Venice dedicated to the Prince Elector of Saxony in 1716 by the traveling violin virtuoso Francesco Maria Veracini (1690–1768). When Veracini played his and Corelli's sonatas in London in 1714, his compositions were judged "too wild and flighty for the taste of the English at this time, when they regarded the sonatas of Corelli as the models of simplicity, grace, and elegance in melody, and of correctness and purity in harmony," according to Charles Burney (1726–1814). Although Veracini quotes or paraphrases themes from Corelli's sonatas, his departures from the older style are more significant.

Veracini's "neutral" (neither church nor chamber) sonatas have no fugues and no movements titled dances. Instead they have four movements, mostly in binary form, in the order slow—fast—slow—fast. Whereas Corelli never recapitulates themes, Veracini almost always does; his most characteristic form is rounded binary, in which the return to the tonic in the second half of the movement coincides with a recapitulation of the opening theme, and the closing phrase of the first half, originally in the key of the dominant, returns at the end of the second half in the key of the tonic. Veracini also uses exact or varied repetition instead of sequencing as the most common means of expansion in the middle of periods, something Corelli never did. Thus Veracini tends to create short, clearly defined phrase units of equal lengths, as opposed to Corelli's continuously unfolding, sequentially driven periods. And as Burney observed, Veracini's dissonance treatment is radically freer than Corelli's.

---

[1] Antonio Eximeno, *Dell'origine e delle regole della musica colla storia del suo progresso, decadenza, e rinnovazione* (Rome: Barbiellini, 1774), 267.

Veracini's innovations had a decisive influence on Giuseppe Tartini (1692–1770) and Pietro Antonio Locatelli (1695–1664). Early on, Tartini shortened the format of the neutral sonata to the pattern of slow—fast—fast, although the first movement, with its brisk eighth-note pulse and frequent use of thirty-second notes, is not slow in the same sense that Corelli's slow movements are. Both Tartini and Locatelli wrote out elaborate embellishments for the amateur violinists who purchased their collections, initially published mostly in Amsterdam and quickly reprinted in Paris and London. The written-out embellishments make their music appear strikingly different from Veracini's and Corelli's. However, Locatelli's Amsterdam publisher, Estienne Roger, also brought out an edition of Corelli's Opus 5 in 1710 with lavish embellishments "as the composer played them." Several of Locatelli's movements, if stripped of their ornaments, bear a suspicious resemblance to specific movements by Veracini. The opening measures of a sonata by Locatelli, with and without embellishment, is compared with one by Veracini in Example 12-8.

The practice of writing out embellishments for musical amateurs signals an epochal shift in the musical culture of Europe, as do the simpler harmonic style, symmetrical phrases, and new emphasis on melody in the works of Veracini, Tartini, and Locatelli. In effect, their music begins to reflect a marketplace where the influence of middle-class consumers is beginning to have an effect. In these respects, their music may be termed post-Baroque in style and purpose.

THE RISE OF THE CONCERTO GROSSO

Corelli's last published collection, Opus 6 (1712), was entitled *Concerti grossi con duoi violini, e violoncello di concertino obligati, e duoi altri violini, viola e basso di concerto grosso ad arbitrio che si potranno radoppiare* ("Large Ensemble Works with Two Violins and Violoncello Required in the Small [Sub-]Ensemble and Two Other Violins, Viola, and Bass, Optional, in the Large [Sub-]Ensemble, which Can Be Doubled"). Although these concertos were published a year before Corelli's death, there is evidence that he composed at least some of them considerably earlier than that. In the preface to his *Florilegium primum* (1695), Georg Muffat writes, "While in Rome . . . I heard with wonder some of A. Corelli's concertos splendidly performed by a large ensemble." Upon his return to Salzburg in 1682, Muffat published a collection of his own concertos, *Armonico tributo*, which he says had been performed at Corelli's house. These concertos are written for five string parts, but the indications "S[olo]" and "T[utti]" show where contrasts between the *concertino* trio and the full, five-part *concerto grosso* can be deployed at the performers' option. Concertos by Corelli were known in Bologna by at least 1689, since Angelo Berardi mentions them in his *Miscellanea musicale* of that date. In addition, Corelli was known to have revised and polished his works for extended periods before their publication. Therefore, the logical approach would be to look to music written before 1682 for Corelli's models and the genre traditions in which his concertos were situated.

EXAMPLE 12-8. The opening measures of Pietro Antonio Locatelli's Opus 6 (1737), Sonata II, with and without his embellishment, compared with the beginning of Francesco Maria Veracini's Sonata prima from his 1716 manuscript collection

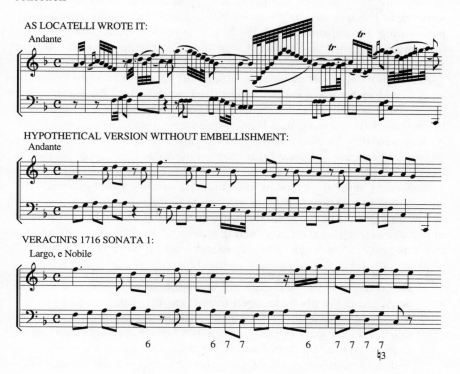

Antiphonal canzonas for two or more choirs of instruments were well known, especially in Venice, during the second half of the sixteenth century. But Corelli's concertos are not antiphonal. Rather, they employ the large ensemble to double or accompany the trio of soloists from time to time. (The exceptions are the fugues, in which the viola of the large ensemble plays an independent part, including statements of the subject.) This approach to orchestration was a Roman specialty. The earliest known instances are found in Johann Hieronymus Kapsberger's *Libro primo di sinfonie a quattro* (Rome, 1615), in which three methods are used to create contrast: (1) marking some passages "tutti" and others "à 4," "à 2," or "solo"; (2) opposing four-part writing against one or two solo parts accompanied by basso continuo; (3) antiphonal exchanges between subgroups of the full ensemble.

Some orchestral rosters of 1666 and 1667 from Rome contain the distinction between concertino and concerto grosso, and the same distinction is built into at least ten works by Corelli's colleague in Rome Alessandro Stradella, including his oratorio *San Giovanni Battista* (A. 72). Indeed, Stradella's *Sonata di viole* ("Sonata for Bowed String Instruments" W. 27) is scored for *concertino di due violini, e leuto* ("small ensemble of two violins and lute") and *concerto grosso di viole* ("large ensemble of bowed string instruments"). Although most of the writing in this work is antiphonal, the penultimate movement contains some rapid passages for the two solo violins supported by the rhythmically punctuating accompaniment of the larger ensemble. In addition, the last movement contains a few scattered instances of doubling between the large and small ensemble.

Although most of the movements in Corelli's Opus 6 concertos are of the types found in his trio sonatas—fugues derived from the canzona tradition, dances in binary form, and homophonic slow movements—the undivided, homophonic (non-binary, non-fugal) movements deserve special comment, both because they have no precedent in Corelli's trio sonatas and because they feature a type of musical period that gains considerable importance during the last two decades of the seventeenth century. This type of period is called the *Fortspinnung* ("spun out") type in some modern writings. Good examples of it are found in two of the movements in Corelli's Op. 6, no. 1 (A. 105).

The first period of the central Allegro in Corelli's Op. 6, no. 1, offers an instructive example of the Fortspinnung type in all its parts. It can be divided into three parts, according to articulation and function (see Ex. 12-9):

1. Eight measures in which a bar-by-bar alternation of the major chords on D and A, enlivened by continuous arpeggiation, is capped by a cadence on A, giving the phrase an open ending and suggesting a corresponding closed ending later on. Such a phrase, stable except for its ending, is often called a *Vordersatz* ("opening phrase"). A Vordersatz might end with a cadence on the fifth degree as this one does, with a cadence on the final, with a harmonic movement from the fifth-degree chord to the final-degree chord, or with a harmonic movement from the final-degree chord to the fifth-degree chord. The conclusion of this one happens to be elided with the second part of the period. That is, the first note of measure 18 serves as the conclusion of the cadence ending of the Vordersatz and, simultaneously, as the first note of the Fortspinnung segment.

2. Eight measures containing two sequences: one that rises by a fourth and descends by a fifth (mm. 8–10) and a second one that descends by a third and rises by a fourth (mm. 10–15). This type of segment is sometimes called the Fortspinnung proper, and it generates motion, rather than stability, because of its sequences and energetic rhythm.

3. A three-measure cadential formula (mm. 16–18), elided with the beginning of the next period. A distinct phrase ending with a cadence that concludes a period is often termed an *Epilog* ("epilogue"). This particular Epilog concludes with a cadence on D, the harmony with which the period and the movement began. Another period of this type might end on a harmony different from its initial chord, producing an open-ended period rather than a closed period.

EXAMPLE 12-9. Corelli, Op. 6, No. 1, central Allegro, mm. 1–18, as an example of a *Fortspinnung*-type period

Many periods of the Fortspinnung type, especially after the beginning of a movement, contain no Vordersatz but begin directly with the sequence(s) that constitute the Fortspinnung. Some have no separate Epilog but run a sequence directly into the cadence; if the cadential formula is then repeated, one usually designates the repeated cadential formula(s) as the Epilog.

In the central Allegro of Corelli's Op. 6, no. 1, there are three periods, ending in measures 18, 31, and 50. The first two have Vordersatz, Fortspinnung, and Epilog; the last has only Fortspinnung and Epilog.

The last Allegro of Corelli's Op. 6, no. 1, contains seven periods, ending in measures 9, 17, 29, 37, 45, 56, and 77, respectively on the first, third, fifth, and sixth degree above the final, in each case with a preparation derived from the techniques of modal change. In this movement, the forward-pressing, rhythmically active, and sequential passages are given to the soloists, while the full ensemble reinforces each of the cadential epilogues, thus outlining in the orchestration the architecture of movement and cadential goals that have a growing importance in music of the late Baroque.

Corelli, of course, did not invent the Fortspinnung period nor the undivided, homophonic movement type. Periods expanded through sequences are found in solo and trio sonatas throughout the seventeenth century. The initial, non-sequential portion of Fortspinnung periods before Corelli's, as in the sonatas of Bononcini and his north Italian contemporaries, provided models and prototypes for Corelli's more expanded and nearly closed type of Vordersatz. Earlier repeated cadence formulas became the prototypes of the Epilog. An early example of these elements in combination is the period from Stradella's *Sonata di viole* (W. 27) contained in measures 122–131. Still earlier instances, perhaps clear only in retrospect, can be found in the sonatas by composers in Bologna and Modena, for examples Cazzati's Sonata "La Rossella" of 1656 (A. 101), measures 11–16; Vitali's "Balletto ottavo of 1683 (A. 102), measures 1–4, 8–11, and 15–18, and Bononcini's Sonata Op. 6, no. 11 of 1672 (A. 103), measures 86–94 and 94–112.

The factors that make Corelli's Fortspinnung period shown in Example 12-9 significantly different from those by Stradella, Cazzati, Vitali, or Bononcini are Corelli's more predicable harmony and greater consistency of rhythmic figuration, which together create the impression of energetic, directed motion toward a goal and thus provide a high degree of cohesion, which enables greater extension. Furthermore, whereas there is just one period of this type in Stradella's sonata, each of Corelli's concertos contains many of them. Although the type of string-instrument figuration that propels Example 12-9 and other passages in Corelli's Op. 6 can be found in earlier works by composers from Bologna, Corelli's role was to combine and codify these existing elements in a way that proved fruitful to composers of the next generation.

THE BOLOGNESE TRUMPET SONATA

Between the early 1680s, when Georg Muffat heard concertos by Corelli in Rome, and the publication of Corelli's Op. 6 in 1714, there arose in northern Italy—principally in Bologna and Venice—another kind of concerto that proved even more influential and lasting: the concerto for one or two solo instruments accompanied by a string ensemble. As usual, this apparent innovation arose by combining existing features in new ways and for new purposes. One of the distinctive features to emerge in this type of concerto was the regular alternation between soloists and the accompanying ensemble, which plays recurring material that is today often called a *ritornello* ("something small that returns"). This alternation gave rise to a ritornello formal procedure that eventually found its way into various other genres, both instrumental and vocal.

The earliest group of concertos for solo instruments that use this ritornello formal procedure are sonatas, concertos, or *sinfonie* for one, two, or four solo trumpets and strings composed during the 1690s by Giuseppe Torelli (1658–1709). Torelli played viola and violin in the orchestra of the Basilica of San Petronio in Bologna from 1686 to his death, except for 1696–1701, when he plied his trade at German courts while the San Petronio orchestra was temporarily disbanded. The immediate background to Torelli's sonatas, concertos, and *sinfonie* with trumpets can be found in the earlier Bolognese repertoire for the same combination of instruments, which began in 1665 with the publication of three sonatas for trumpet and strings included among the Opus 35 sonatas of Maurizio Cazzati, who was then the *maestro di cappella* at the Basilica of San Petronio.

Although the movements (tempi) in Cazzati's trumpet sonatas are very brief, they include several types of non-fugal, non-binary movement. Some consist of a series of short cadential phrases, loosely related by their use of similar melodic and rhythmic material. Others expand such a series through antiphonal exchanges between the trumpet and the violins. A few of Cazzati's movements, such as the second Allegro from the Sonata 11, *La Bianchina*, include some brief elaborations on melodic ideas presented in the opening phrase, interspersed with contrasting flourishes from the trumpet, as shown in Example 12-10.

Johann Schmelzer had already published two trumpet sonatas in his *Sacro-Profanus Concentus Musicus* of 1662, and there are many similar works by Schmelzer and his Vienna colleagues in manuscripts that may date from this time or earlier. Cazzati may have known these works, because Italian and German musicians moved fluidly between the two regions. However, the approach to non-fugal, non-binary movements shown in Example 12-10 has not been found in the early Viennese trumpet sonata repertoire.

From 1679 to 1699 at least one trumpeter was added to the San Petronio orchestra on the annual feast of the patron saint, and the instrumental ensemble of the church, normally only five string players, was expanded to become an orchestra of over a hundred musicians. The works for trumpet written for this holiday are most often entitled *sinfonia*, a term frequently used to designate an instrumental introduction—for example, an opera overture. In fact, one of these trumpet *sinfonie* contains a cue to the Kyrie of the Mass at its end.

Although few of the eighty-three trumpet *sinfonie* in the San Petronio archive are dated, the seven by Domenico Gabrielli (1659–1690) and the one by Petronio Franceschini (1651–1680) must have preceded Torelli's by reason of their composers' death dates. Franceschini's, for two trumpets and strings, is especially notable for distinct thematic material for the trumpets and the strings.

From at least the early 1690s, the Bolognese concerto for trumpets and strings was associated with ritornello formal procedure.

Torelli's *Sinfonia con tromba e violini unissoni* ("Sinfonia with Trumpet and Violins in Unison," A. 106), has the same title and scoring as another of his works that carries the date 1693. The first and last movements can be divided into tutti segments, in which the strings predominate, alternating with passages

EXAMPLE 12-10. Maurizio Cazzati, *La Bianchina*, Op. 35, No. 11 (1665), second Allegro, illustrating a non-fugal, non-binary movement in which recurring material in the orchestra alternates with trumpet flourishes

featuring the solo trumpet. In the first movement, the opening period, which is of the Fortspinnung type, contains three distinct ideas (mm. 1–6, 6–9, 9–12), labeled A, B, and C in the diagram below. These three ideas recur in the other two ritornellos scored primarily for the strings. The segments that do not contain any of these ideas are dominated by the solo trumpet. Today, such solo segments are called "episodes." The alternation of ritornellos and episodes in the first movement of Torelli's *Sinfonia* G 9 is summarized below. Note that the trumpet appears occasionally in the ritornellos, and the strings always accompany the solo episodes.

	Ritornello 1	Episode 1	Ritornello 2	Episode 2		Ritornello 3	
	Strings	Trumpet	Strings	Trumpet		Strings	
Bars:	1	12	19	34	40		53
Ideas:	A B C		A B			A B C	
(Keys) &							
Cadences:	(D) A	D	A (A)	b (D)	A (D) A		D

In a movement like this, one may speak of a ritornello formal procedure, although to call it "ritornello form" at this point in history would be incorrect, because there is no predictable, standardized number or arrangement of the ritornellos in concertos until the 1720s.

The last movement of Torelli's *Sinfonia con tromba e violini unissoni* contains four ritornellos in the following arrangement:

	Ritornello 1	Episode 1	Rit. 2	Ep. 2	Rit. 3	Episode 3	Rit. 4
	Strings	Strings—Trumpet	Strings	Strings	Strings	Strings—Trumpet	Strings
Bars:	68	77	92	104	115	124	139
Ideas:	A B		A B		A B		A
(Keys) &							
Cadences:	(D)	A (D)	A (D)	b (e)	D (D)	A (D) D	D

In this movement, as in the first, the second element of the ritornello, B, recurs in the minor mode on B during the second ritornello. Unlike the first movement, however, the third movement does not exactly recapitulate the first ritornello in its third ritornello. Instead, the first ritornello concludes on A, not D, and the third ritornello is adjusted so as to conclude on the overall final, D. An additional partial ritornello, containing only element A, is added at the end. In this final movement, the trumpet is heard in a solo passage only during the first and third episodes; the second episode features the first violin part.

The Bolognese trumpet sonatas were significant for establishing a standard approach to handling contrast between solo instruments and the rest of the orchestra. Such solo trumpet works continued to be written well into the eighteenth century, but they were not distributed widely through publication. They remained pieces for special occasions restricted to elite ensembles that could be expanded to include one, two, or four trumpeters with rare abilities. The standard approach that they fostered, however, obtained far greater distribution, extending all over Europe and continuing for many decades to come, in the genre of the violin concerto.

THE SOLO VIOLIN CONCERTO

The beginnings of the solo violin concerto are a bit more nebulous than the rise of the trumpet sonata, since the solo violin part does not automatically stand out from the rest of an ensemble the way a solo trumpet part does.

Torelli was one of the earliest to publish works for solo violin and string ensemble in his Op. 5, *Sinfonie a 3 e concerti a 4* (1692), which contains two concertos with a solo violin part and instructions to double the accompanying instruments. Ritornello procedure, however, becomes clearer in Torelli's Op. 6 (1698) and Op. 8, published in 1709 after his death.

The new genre of the violin concerto spread from Bologna first to Venice with the publication of *Sinfonie e concerti a cinque*, Op. 2 (1700) by the wealthy amateur Tomaso Albinoni (1671–1751), and especially with his Op. 5 *Concerti a cinque* (1707), in which the solo violin part is more clearly differentiated from the accompanying ensemble and ritornello procedure is more strongly emphasized. Albinoni's Op. 5 became important for the diffusion of the violin concerto when it was reprinted in Amsterdam in 1708, 1709, ca. 1716, and ca. 1722 for the amateur music market then beginning to flourish in northern Europe.

The most important of the many followers of Torelli and Albinoni was Antonio Vivaldi (1678–1741), whose violin concertos Op. 3, *L'estro armonico* (1711), were published initially in Amsterdam, as were his next eight sets of concertos, Opuses 4, 6–12 (1716–29). Vivaldi's crystallization of ritornello procedure can be summarized as follows:

- The first tutti ritornello usually includes three or more contrasting ideas, of which the last usually recalls the first.
- Subsequent ritornellos normally quote only some of the ideas from the first, often in altered form, until the final ritornello, which usually brings back all the main elements of the first.
- Until the later concertos, solo episodes rarely quote material from the first ritornello and only occasionally relate to one another.
- The main ideas of the opening ritornello, especially the first, tend to be sharply etched in rhythm, played in unison or octaves or simply harmonized and rudimentary in melodic design. The opening ritornello often gives the impression of generating energy to be expended during the following solo episode.
- The solo episodes are almost always dominated by melodic/harmonic sequences with rhythms that are usually faster and more continuous than found in the ritornellos. Hence, the episodes often seem to be unstable and in motion from one relatively stable ritornello to another.
- In the fast movements, the most common number of ritornellos is five—four in the later concertos. In major-mode movements, one of these will normally be set in the minor mode based on the sixth degree of the original scale; in minor-mode movements, one of these will normally be set in the major mode based on the third degree of the original scale.
- Most of Vivaldi's concertos have three movements in the order fast—slow—fast.

Most of these traits are illustrated in Vivaldi's violin concerto Op. 3, no. 3 (A. 107).

Vivaldi's Op. 3, no. 3, adopts the three-movement form (fast—slow—fast) standardized by Albinoni. Its first and last movements use the ritornello procedure developed out of Torelli's models; the first has five ritornellos, the last has four.

The initial ritornello of Vivaldi's first movement contains four elements, labeled A, B, C, and D in Example 12-11. Each of these elements recurs in at least one later ritornello, but none of the later ritornellos includes all four. The relationship between elements A and D—approximate melodic inversion—is underscored in the last ritornello, where they are set side-by-side.

The harmonization of elements A and B in Vivaldi's first-movement opening ritornello is restricted to the chords on G and D, the final and fifth, which establish the principal mode and transposition (key) of the work by a means analogous to a full cadence—a device popularized by Corelli and now completely absorbed into the musical style of several genres. Since element C leads up to a cadence on A with a brief sequence, the first seven measures at first seem to comprise a miniature period of the Fortspinnung type. However, the longer series of sequences that make up element D provide the main Fortspinnung portion of a longer period whose Epilog is the first solo episode (mm. 12–16). The overlapping relationship between the ritornello pattern and the period structure of Vivaldi's first movement is summarized in Figure 12-1.

The second movement of Vivaldi's Op. 3, no. 3, takes the form of one extended Fortspinnung period, with a repeated Epilog. The simple violin figures placed between the repeated chords played by the orchestra may very well represent a generic simplification of more elaborate passages that Vivaldi and other professional violinists were expected to improvise.

The third movement of Vivaldi's concerto has a simpler form than the first, since its ritornello pattern and period structure coincide. As often happens in the final movements of Vivaldi's concertos, the last ritornello presents new material, instead of recapitulating the elements that define the previous ritornellos.

As mentioned earlier, the violin concerto quickly spread to all parts of Europe, and scores of composers of all nationalities wrote them according to Vivaldi's model for use in chamber settings and in church. Vivaldi himself com-

EXAMPLE 12-11. Vivaldi, Concerto for Violin, Op. 3, No. 3, first movement, opening ritornello, melody line with elements labeled

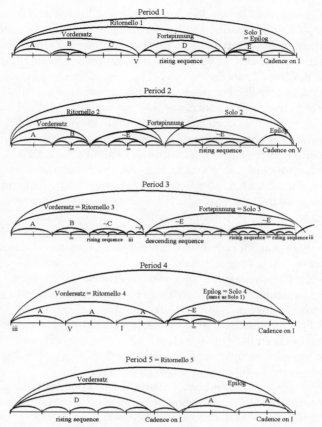

Figure 12-1. A diagram of Vivaldi, Concerto for Violin, Op. 3, No. 3, first movement, showing ritornellos, solo episodes, and periods

posed about 500 concertos, of which about 350 are solo concertos. About 40 are for two solo instruments, and more than 30 are for more than two. Over 230 of Vivaldi's solo concertos are for violin; the others are, in order of frequency, for bassoon, cello, oboe, flute, viola d'amore, recorder, and mandolin. Almost 60 of his concertos are for string orchestra without soloist; in these he tends to string together lengthy and elaborate ritornellos without intervening solo episodes.

Although some of Vivaldi's concertos were written on commission for wealthy amateurs, for the musical ensemble of noble courts such as Dresden, or for his own use as soloist, most of them appear to have been composed for his young female students at the Pio Ospedale della Pietà, one of four Venetian orphanages specializing in musical training for girls, where Vivaldi, a priest, served in various capacities from 1703 to 1740. Masses and Vespers with music, both vocal and instrumental, at these *ospedali* were essentially public concerts, and they attracted large audiences of fashionable visitors and Venetian nobles. Some of the young female performers trained at these *ospedali* became opera singers or music instructors; many of them married well as a consequence of their attainments; and others became nuns.

The phenomenal popularity of the violin concerto all over Northern Europe, which lasted from about 1710 to 1750, signals the beginning of a new era in music history. The voluminous publications of concertos from the music presses of Amsterdam, Paris, and London were aimed at a commercial market in which the consumers must have included substantial numbers of middle-class amateur musicians whose wealth and leisure derived from trade, manufac-turing, and shopkeeping. The size of this market indicates that it did not exist solely for the nobility, and it was centered in the cities where this new mer-chant class first asserted itself in numbers and influence. Wealthy sons of English merchants on the grand tour bought manuscript copies of concertos and opera arias in Venice as cultural souvenirs. Even the musical Masses and Vespers at the Venetian *ospedali* can be viewed as tourist attractions; surely the Venetian gov-ernment lavishly supported these institutions in part for this reason.

The musical style and compositional procedure of Vivaldi's concertos repre-sent a new phase in music history as well. Here we have the first genre in which lengthy and relatively elaborate movements with a substantial variety of material and of musical dynamics—impulse, continuation, moving, waiting, arriving, confirming—unfold in accordance with a conventional procedure that can be summarized in a single, continuous melodic line supported by rel-atively simple normalized harmony revolving around the chords on the first and fifth degrees. The ripieno concertos for strings by Vivaldi and his contem-poraries form an important starting point for the new genre of the symphony, which began to emerge in northern Italy during the 1720s.

For these reasons—social, economic, cultural, and musical—the concertos of Antonio Vivaldi mark the end of the era that we call Baroque and the beginning of a new phase of music history, one that has strong associations with the histori-cal Modern Age, whose beginning may be marked by the death of Louis XIV in 1715, the beginning of the end of absolutism, the rise of parliamentary govern-ment, the age of empirical science, the dramatic growth of trade and commer-cialism, and the dramatic increase of middle-class influence in matters of cultural values and artistic taste. In music, we may speak of a post-Baroque phrase.

These changes arrive in various ways and at various times in each of the major nations of Europe. In the genres of Italian opera, oratorio, and cantata changes par-allel with those in Italian instrumental music took place at the same time and involved some of the same composers. The story of what leads up to these changes will be told in the remaining chapters of this book.

BIBLIOGRAPHICAL NOTES

The Italian Trio and Solo Sonata in the Second Half of the Seventeenth Century
   An overview with a useful listing of composers and general features is William S. Newman, *The Sonata in the Baroque Era,* 4th ed. (New York: W. W. Norton, 1983),

cited earlier. More selective and focused on Italy is Willi Apel, *Italian Violin Music of the Seventeenth Century,* ed. Thomas Binkley (Bloomington, IN: Indiana University Press, 1990). Far more up-to-date and reliable, but more selective than either of these is Peter Allsop, *The Italian "Trio" Sonata from its Origins until Corelli* (Oxford: Clarendon Press, 1992). Important general observations about several composers, in addition to the main figure studied, and many scores of otherwise unavailable works are found in two doctoral dissertations: John Gunther Suess, "Giovanni Battista Vitali and the Sonata da Chiesa," Ph.D. diss., Yale Univ., 1962; and Fred M. Pajerski, "Marco Uccellini (1610–1680) and His Music," Ph.D. diss., New York Univ., 1979. William Klenz, *Giovanni Maria Bononcini of Modena: A Chapter in Baroque Instrumental Music* (Durham, NC: Duke University Press, 1962), is notable for its integration of modal theory and chord patterning.

Arcangelo Corelli

The new standard work on Corelli's life and works is Peter Allsop, *Arcangelo Corelli: "The Orpheus of Our Times"* (Oxford: Oxford University Press, 1999).

The Normalized Harmonic Style

Nothing on this subject can be recommended at present. The approach taken in this book avoids anachronistic involvement with modern tonal theory. The term "tonal harmonic style," or similar, is frequently met but never defined with precision sufficient for a historical investigation.

The Rise of the Concerto Grosso

Allsop's book on Corelli contains the best treatment of this subject to date.

The Bolognese Trumpet Sonata

The entry on Giuseppe Torelli in *The New Grove Dictionary of Music and Musicians,* 2nd ed (London: Macmillan, 2001) with its citation of journal literature, is a good place to begin.

The Solo Violin Concerto

The places to start are Eleanor Selfridge-Field, *Venetian Instrumental Music from Gabrieli to Vivaldi.* 3rd ed. (New York: Dover Publications, 1975); and two books by Michael Talbot: *Tomaso Albinoni: The Venetian Composer and His World* (Oxford: Oxford University Press, 1994), and *Vivaldi,* 2nd ed. (Oxford: Oxford University Press, 2000).

CHAPTER 13

England from the Restoration through the Augustan Age

CHARLES II AND THE MUSICAL INSTITUTIONS OF HIS COURT

Soon after the English Civil War (see Chapter 7) led to the defeat of his father's army in 1646, Charles II fled to Paris, where his mother, Henrietta Maria, had taken refuge at the royal court since 1644. The daughter of the French King Henry IV, Henrietta Maria was the sister of the late King Louis XIII (d. 1643) and the aunt of Louis XIV, then just six years old. France at this time was ruled by Louis's mother, Henrietta Maria's sister-in-law, Anne of Austria, and her prime minister, Cardinal Jules Mazarin. Charles, then sixteen years old, remained with his mother and her entourage at the Louvre Palace until the execution of his father, Charles I, in 1649. After an unsuccessful attempt to defeat Oliver Cromwell's army in England, Charles returned to his mother in Paris, where he lived from 1651 to 1654 on a small pension from the French monarchy. After Cromwell formed an alliance with France against Spain, Charles briefly allied with Spain and moved to Bruges and Brussels in the Spanish Netherlands. Shortly after the death of Cromwell in 1658, Spain and France made peace, Charles regained the support of the French, and chaos reigned in England. General George Monck marched his forces south from Scotland, took control of Parliament, and restored the monarchy in 1660.

When Charles II gained the throne of England at the age of thirty, he had spent most of his early adulthood in Paris among French courtiers, except for some time in Holland and the Spanish Netherlands. His close advisors, followers, and servants, who formed the nucleus of his new court in England, had done the same. His younger brother, James, who would succeed Charles in 1685 also passed his exile years in France and the Spanish Netherlands. By some accounts, Charles secretly practiced the Catholic religion during his exile while officially maintaining allegiance to the Church of England. James, like their mother, was an avowed Catholic, a factor that led to his deposition in the bloodless Glorious Revolution of 1688. By the time of his coronation in 1661, Charles II had reconstituted the Chapel Royal and the King's Musick in imitation of the musical institutions at the court of Louis XIV.

The first person appointed to a position at the English royal court after the Restoration was Captain Henry Cooke (ca. 1615–1672), who in 1660 became Master of the Children of the Chapel Royal. Cooke had been trained and educated in the Chapel Royal of Charles I, and he had fought as a captain with the royalist forces during the Civil War. During the Commonwealth period, Cooke taught and performed as singer and viol player.

The first leading figure in the King's Musick after the Restoration became Matthew Locke (1621/23–1677), who had apparently accompanied Charles in his exile. Back in London by about 1656, Locke composed music for several important stage works, when theatrical production surged following the death of Cromwell. Appointed to the King's Musick in 1660, Locke was at first assigned to the Broken Consort, a group made up of violins, viols, and continuo instruments that played the contrapuntal consort fantasies fashionable at the court of Charles I. Charles II, however, expressed "an utter detestation of Fancys" and reassigned Locke to direct the Twenty-Four Violins, an imitation of the *Vingt-quatre Violons du Roi* of Louis XIV, which played dance music in the French style. He also composed music for His Majesty's Sackbuts & Cornetts, similar to Louis XIV's *Musique de la Grande Ecurie*. The fact that Locke was a practicing Catholic is of some importance for the history of Restoration church music, as is the fact that he wrote out "A Collection of Songs when I was in the Low Countreys 1648," containing Italian concerted motets.

Captain Cooke lost no time in filling out the Chapel Royal with its thirty-two "gentlemen" and twelve boys. Cooke recruited some very talented boys, including Pelham Humfrey (1647/8–1674) in 1660, John Blow (1648/9–1708) in 1661, and Henry Purcell (1659–1695) in 1668 or 1669, all three of whom became important composers.

Pelham Humfrey began composing by the age of fifteen. Within a year he was sent to France and Italy to study the latest Continental music. On his return, in 1666, he became a lutenist in the Private Music (equivalent to the French *Musique de la Chambre*) and a year later a Gentleman of the Chapel Royal. In 1672 he succeeded Cooke as Master of the Children, in which capacity he became the teacher of young Henry Purcell. A prolific and capable composer, he died at the age of twenty-six.

John Blow's compositions were in the Chapel's repertoire by 1664, when he was fifteen years old. In 1668 he became organist of Westminster Abbey, and in 1674 he was made a Gentleman of the Chapel Royal. Later in 1674 he succeeded Humfrey as Master of the Children, recruiting and training future composers Jeremiah Clarke (ca. 1674–1707) and William Croft (1678–1727). Blow, alone among the three young composers, lived a normal life span and left a large body of works, which includes music in all current genres.

Purcell replaced Locke as composer for the Twenty-Four Violins in 1677 on his eighteenth birthday. In 1679 he succeeded Blow as organist of Westminster Abbey. In 1682 he joined the Chapel Royal as an organist, and in 1684 he was given the additional office of Keeper of Instruments. Purcell cultivated every genre typical of the age. Far more than Blow, he wrote for the London theaters, which thrived in the newly permissive atmosphere of the Restoration period, and he composed music for publication—that is, for domestic consumption.

The ranks of the King's Musick were also quickly filled with talented musicians such as John Banister (1624/5–1679), whom the king immediately sent abroad "to see and learn the way of the French compositions." In 1662 Banister was placed at the head of a Select Band, modeled on Lully's *Petits Violons*, and he assumed control of the Twenty-Four Violins until Luis Grabu, who came from Spain via France, supplanted him in 1666.

ANTHEMS AND SERVICES

In the Chapel Royal, as in all cathedrals and collegiate churches in England at this time, there was music at Morning and Evening Prayer every day, and at the Holy Communion, or Second Service, on Sundays and Holy Days. The Anglican liturgy called for musical settings of the Te Deum and Jubilate Deo in the Morning, the Magnificat and Nunc Dimittis in the Evening, and the Kyrie and Creed (occasionally the Sanctus and Gloria) at Communion. These items, sung in English, together constituted a Service. During the period treated here, Services were almost always composed in the "short service" style, with homophonic texture, syllabic text setting, and few, if any, passages for solo voices. Typical in this respect are the sixteen services by William Child (1606/7–1697), one of the few composers from the reign of Charles I to have survived the Commonwealth. Generally the Service was neglected by the court composers who first came to prominence during the Restoration (Purcell is the exception), because anthems now occupied ever more time and attention during English worship services.

An anthem is a setting of an English-language religious text not part of the official liturgy. Like its Catholic counterpart, the motet, the anthem was performed during the Offertory and Postcommunion. As happened in France and Italy toward the end of the seventeenth century, English works of this category became so long that they replaced major portions of the prescribed services.

Due to changes in style and practice, a slightly modified terminology is employed for anthems from the Restoration period onward. Full anthems were traditionally for choir and organ, but when sections for soloists are added, the resulting work is called a "full-with-verse anthem." Works of this category during the Restoration are often in the chordal and syllabic short-service style. The verse anthem at this time featured solos, duets, and trios, with organ continuo, but sections were frequently rounded off by a brief choral interjection or response. Thus, during the Restoration the principal musical difference between the full-with-verse anthem and the verse anthem was the balance between choral and solo sections.

Hear, O heav'ns (ca. 1670) by Pelham Humfrey (A. 108) is a verse anthem for alto, tenor, and bass soloists sung by the men of the Chapel Royal with a response for full chorus, including the boy sopranos, at the end of each of the two halves of the work. The text is from Isaiah 1:2, 4, and 16–18, in the English Bible translation commissioned by King James I and completed in 1611. The musical style, largely declamatory and highly rhetorical, is strongly indebted to the three-voice motets of Giacomo Carissimi, whose music was widely known and imitated in England during the Restoration. Humfrey had additional opportunities to hear Carissimi's music in Italy.

The opening bass solo in *Hear, O heav'ns* is truly in recitative style, scarcely heard before in English church music. Its rising chromatic line creates anticipation (procatascene), while the unexpected interruption by the tenor ("Ah, sinful nation") is an apostrophe, as the words and music suddenly turn to address another party. The auxesis created by the two parallel expressions of mounting intensity, "a seed of evildoers, children that are corrupters," is supported by two phrases forming a rising sequence. Later (m. 44) a sudden rest creates an aposiopesis, which dramatizes the change of tone occasioned by the ameliorating plea (antanagoge), "Come now, let us reason together saith the Lord." This gives rise to a series of antitheses opposing "scarlet" against "white" in one voice against two.

The "symphony anthem" (or "orchestral anthem") is a new type introduced near the beginning of the Restoration period. Its distinguishing feature is the use of a string-centered orchestra, which plays an introduction ("symphony") and interludes ("ritornellos") framing sections for soloists and chorus. This feature was applied to both full (or full-with-verse) and verse anthems. It was introduced to the Chapel Royal by express order of Charles II. The courtier John Evelyn noted (December 21, 1662) in his diary that in the anthem of that day "instead of the antient grave and solemn wind music accompanying the *Organ* was introduced a Consort of 24 Violins betweene every pause, after the *French* fantastical light way. . . ."

This is a challenging observation in 1662, because the period of the French *grand motet* with string ensemble is usually thought to begin in 1663 with the appointment of Henry Du Mont to Louis XIV's Chapelle Royale. However, two surviving motets of Jean Veillot (d. 1662) from about 1659–60 deploy a five-part string ensemble in their interludes. Furthermore, Du Mont learned to combine choirs, soloists, and instruments in the Venetian manner under Hodemont, who had a collection of Italian music and a salaried instrumental ensemble in Liège, a place visited by Charles II and his entourage during their years of exile. Du Mont had highly visible appointments in Paris during those same years, and so it is possible that Charles's musicians heard *grands motets* with strings by Du Mont at that time. Matthew Locke was the one most likely to have brought these innovations from the Continent. His *O Be Joyful in the Lord All Ye Lands* (1664) is representative of the early symphony (verse) anthem.

Locke's *O Be Joyful in the Lord All Ye Lands* (A. 109)—text from Psalm 100 as translated in the *Book of Common Prayer* (1662)—seems to reflect French style in its regularity of phrasing and use of repeating rhythmic modules, such as ♩. ♪ | ♩ ♩ at the beginning. Uncertainty surrounding the chronology of the earliest French *grands motets* makes it difficult to name Locke's probable model for this feature. This type of rhythm is, however, typical of mid-seventeenth-century dances in *ballets de cour*, such as those of 1651 by Michel Mazuel (A. 34). This correspondence may have been what prompted John Evelyn to complain that these new symphony anthems were no longer "grave and solemn ..., better suiting a Tavern or Play-house than a Church."

John Blow's *God Spake Sometime in Visions* (W. 28) is, on the other hand, as "grave and solemn" as one could wish. Composed in 1685 for the coronation of James II, younger brother of Charles II, it applies the features of the symphony anthem to the massive style of the full-with-verses anthem, while reflecting the grandeur of Lully's festive *grands motets* produced in the years since Locke's first trials in this genre. In its introductory symphony, the bursts of loud, dotted figures, set off by soft preparations, contribute to purely instrumental hyperbole. The long rising line, accelerating harmony, and gathering texture of the first choral phrase (mm. 42–60) expands the procatascene, "God spake sometime in visions and said. . . ." The following statement (sententia), "I have laid help upon one that is mighty" (mm. 61–91) gives rise to the central anastrophe, a series of verses for soloists and full statements for the chorus elaborating upon instances of "help" for the "mighty." The final expansion of "amen, allelujah," of course, forms the peroration of the anthem.

Since James II was a Catholic, he maintained a private chapel, and during his reign the Chapel Royal did not perform elaborate music. The Glorious Revolution brought to the throne the devout Anglican Queen Mary II, daughter of James II, and the Calvinist Protestant William of Orange (*Stadholder* of Holland) as co-regents. They ordered daily music in the Chapel Royal to resume, but without orchestra. The succession of Mary's younger sister, Anne (ruled 1702–1714), finally brought the Chapel Royal back to full activity. But in the meantime, John Blow had ceased to compose regularly. He was succeeded as Master of the Children by William Croft, who had been composing for the Royal Chapel since the start of Queen Anne's reign.

Croft wrote a well-received Te Deum in 1709, on the defeat of the French at Malplaquet, in imitation of a 1694 Te Deum by Purcell. He revised and updated its style after he heard another Te Deum for the end of the war with France, which was marked by the first Treaty of Utrecht (1713). That "Utrecht" Te Deum, commissioned by Queen Anne, was the first publicly performed English church work by George Frideric Handel (1685–1759).

ODES AND WELCOME SONGS

The forces of the Chapel Royal and the Twenty-Four Violins were combined also for the performance of odes and welcome songs. Odes were sung for royal birthdays, New Year's Day, St. Cecilia's Day, banquets, other festive occasions, and for funerals. The welcome song is a special type of ode, traditionally performed on the return of the king from a trip abroad or tour of his dominions, most often for his return from Windsor Castle to Whitehall. Odes and welcome songs were performed in a number of locations, but mostly at Whitehall.

The English tradition of singing odes and welcome songs to mark royal occasions can be traced at least to the first Stuart period in the early seventeenth century. These genres, like the anthem, were transformed at the time of the Restoration by the addition of orchestral introductions and interludes and by the division of the work into separate sections or movements featuring solo voices, singly or in combination, or the full chorus.

The texts of Restoration odes were loosely based on the classical models of Horace and Pindar. Although the subject matter is serious, the language is usually not elevated or complex. Regular meter and predictable rhyme schemes are avoided. The texts are almost always divided into stanzas so that the composer can create substantial and well-separated movements.

Although no parallel tradition was known in France, Restoration odes and welcome songs typically incorporate some features of French musical style, such as an overture in the style of Lully and movements dominated by dance rhythms, so that some odes resemble a dance suite with words. Arias with ostinato basses, so-called "ground bass arias," begin to appear in the 1680s, especially in the odes and welcome songs of Purcell. Also in the 1680s, contrapuntal writing, rare in earlier odes, appears in the works of Blow and Purcell, bringing this genre closer to the style of the symphony anthem. A little later, however, the ode diverged from the anthem in its greater length and more varied orchestration.

Chapter 1 began by describing how Henry Purcell's *Sound the Trumpet, Beat the Drum* (W. 29) was performed for King James II's return from a tour of his realm in 1687. This welcome song is notable for its integration of the orchestra with the voices. All of its choruses are laced with short interludes for the strings. Some, like "With Plenty Surrounding," have independent string parts combined with the voices, while the bass aria "While Caesar, Like the Morning Star" uses four string parts to accompany the solo voice throughout. The duet "Let Caesar and Urania Live," with its original ostinato or "ground" in continuous eighth notes, became the model for many similar duets by Purcell and others. Another ostinato—this one an extended version of the passacaglia bass—is found in the long orchestral chaconne near the middle of the work; it has been suggested that it was intended to accompany dancing. Like the chaconne, the overture is French in design, the first part dominated by dotted rhythm and the second, in triple meter, beginning with imitative counterpoint.

Starting in 1683, odes for St. Cecilia's day were produced at Stationers' Hall in London by a group of aristocrats and musicians called the Musical Society. The singers were drawn from the choirs of St. Paul's Cathedral, Westminster Abbey, and the Chapel Royal, the instrumentalists from King's Musick and London's theaters. A leading composer at court was usually chosen to write the ode; Purcell produced two and Blow composed four. The tradition lasted for thirty years and became one element in the creation of the public concert as an innovative institution in London at the end of the seventeenth century.

SONGS AND DOMESTIC VOCAL ENSEMBLES

Three main types of English song can be distinguished in the second half of the seventeenth century: (1) simple, mostly syllabic, strophic songs, with music organized in binary form or in rondeau form (ABACA); (2) more serious songs without a stereotyped musical repetition scheme, some with ground bass, some in recitational style; and (3) songs with two or more contrasting sections or movements.

1. Many of the simplest strophic songs were modeled on the rhythm and phrasing of a court dance such as the minuet, courante, sarabande, or gigue. A representative selection of such songs is contained in the series of five volumes plus expanded editions that began as *Choice Songs and Ayres for One Voyce to Sing to a Theorbo-Lute, or Bass-Viol, Being Most of the Newest Songs Sung at Court, and at the Publick Theatres,* published 1673–84 by the prolific music printer John Playford.

    Matthew Locke's *The Delights of the Bottle* (A. 110) was added to the first volume of Playford's series in its second edition of 1675. In the same year, it was sung by the character Bacchus in the fifth act of Shadwell's *Psyche,* with an added refrain for a chorus of Maenads. Its rhythm and phrasing are those of a minuet. The outline of its voice and bass parts in contrary motion in the first four bars is repeated in the opening of Blow's *God Spake Sometime in Visions* and in numerous works by Purcell and composers of several nations in later decades. It is an example of a module consisting of a melody, bass line, and chord pattern whose repetition and standardization contributed to a new sense of key in the later seventeenth century.

2. Songs that break out of the dance mold become more common in the later volumes in Playford's series. Many of these set poems influenced by Abraham Cowley (1618–1667), who attempted to infuse English verse with the irregular meters and extravagant poetic conceits of the ancient Greek odes by Pindar. John Blow's setting of one such poem, *Lovely Salina* (A. 111), was published in Playford's fourth book of *Choice Songs and Ayres* in 1683.

    The poem *Lovely Selina* contains three stanzas, each with the rhyme scheme ABBA/CC. The number of syllables in the lines of each stanza is 10 8 8 10 / 10 10, but the lines of the same length do not conform to the same metrical patterns. Consequently, the music cannot maintain or elaborate upon a few rhythmic modules, even though the ends of phrases are marked by rhymes.

    As if to heighten the tension already present in the disparity between the poem's rhyme and its meter, Blow chose to set *Lovely Salina* over a passacaglia bass in uniform dotted half notes, the pattern spanning four measures. Inevitably, the vocal phrases go out of phase with the bass pattern. This affords Blow the opportunity to cadence on the third and sixth degrees of the scale in addition to the first and fifth emphasized by the ostinato bass. The lack of rhythmic patterning in the vocal line and the rhetorical inflection imparted by Blow's melodic contours give his setting a recitational quality that constantly pulls against the rhythmic regularity of its ground bass.

3. John Playford's son Henry published two volumes of *Harmonia sacra, or, Divine Hymns and Dialogues* in 1688 and 1693. These volumes contain the devotional counterpart to the repertoire of the *Choice Songs and Ayres*. These religious works were meant to be sung in the same places—at court, in the urban palaces and country manor houses of the nobility, in middle-class homes—and on the same occasions as the secular songs, although some of the sacred works are anthems originally composed for the Chapel Royal, and two of them are solo Latin motets by Carissimi and Gratiani. Most of the compositions in *Harmonia sacra* contain recitative, and almost all are sectional. Therefore, they exemplify one aspect of Category 2, as well as the distinguishing feature of Category 3.

Purcell is the most represented composer in both volumes of *Harmonia sacra*. The majority of his works are for solo voice with continuo accompaniment. One of the more elaborate is *In Guilty Night* (A. 112), a dialogue for three voices, which sing together in the brief opening and closing trios. Purcell seems to have known the text, a paraphrase of I Samuel 28:8–20, from an earlier setting by Robert Ramsey (d. 1644). It dramatizes Saul's visit to the Witch of Endor, who summons the ghost of Samuel to foretell the tragic fate in store for Saul and his son, Jonathan.

Purcell's setting of *In Guilty Night* is far more dramatic than Ramsey's. The opening and closing trios afford Purcell the opportunity to infuse the work with a strong dose of chromaticism and dissonance. Like most English recitative of the Restoration period, Purcell's is derived from models developed in the works of Matthew Locke; it is free of metrical patterning like the Italian kind, precise in rhythmic notation like the French, while more melodically organized than either. Many of its features—angular contours, wide leaps, syncopations, reverse-dotted rhythms, dotted figures followed by rests—derive from the English declamatory air. Purcell's frequent word repetitions and illustrative or emphatic melismas exemplify Restoration innovations in English recitative promoted by John Blow and reveal the influence of the Latin works of Carissimi, Gratiani, and other Italians of that generation. *In Guilty Night* aptly illustrates Henry Playford's assessment (1698) that Purcell had "a peculiar Genius to express the Energy of *English* words, whereby he mov'd the Passions of all his Auditors."

VIOLS AND VIOLINS

Although Charles II detested consort fantasies, Matthew Locke and Henry Purcell continued to compose them, as well as In Nomines, in the specifically English way—having frequent recourse to mixolydian and plagal modes, abundant chromaticism, cross relations, dissonance, canonic imitation, melodic inversion, and rhythmic augmentation and diminution. The harmonic style of these works by now constituted almost a second musical language, distinct from the more modern idiom in which Locke and Purcell couched their other works.

Like the French court's *Vingt-quatre Violons du Roi*, the Twenty-Four Violins consisted of violins, violas, and bass violins (large cellos). An engraved depiction of a banquet celebrating the coronation of James II in 1685 shows the Twenty-Four Violins (only twenty are present) in a balcony (Fig. 13-1).

The Twenty-Four Violins played dances, singly or in suites. In this, of course, the French style was prominent. The diary of Samuel Pepys records that already on November 20, 1660, Charles II was demanding "the French Music" for entertainment. But English tradition was also maintained, perhaps to some extent as a token of political resistance against the geopolitical menace of France and its Catholicism. Anthony Wood reports that in 1667 when His Majesty "called for the Italian [French?] violins," John Banister, the leader of the Twenty-Four Violins, "made answer that he had better have the English." This advice cost Banister his job.

Figure 13-1. The 24 Violins depicted by Francis Standford in *The History of the Coronation of James II* (London, 1687)

Successive editions of the dance anthology *Apollo's Banquet* (1669–1701), compiled and published by John Playford, contain many bourrées, gavottes, and minuets, some traceable to stage works by Lully and Moulinié, along with similar dances by English composers. Other printed anthologies containing French dances by English composers include *Courtly Masquing Ayres* (1662), the *Tripla Concordia* (1676), and *A Collection of Several Simphonies and Airs in Three Parts* (1688). The French features of the dances in these collections, aside from the characteristic rhythms of specific dance types, are the prevalence of dotted rhythms, the avoidance of crossing between the two upper parts, regularity of phrasing, and lack of contrapuntal imitation.

The composers for the Twenty-Four Violins also persisted in writing English-style dance music, which at this time may be defined essentially as music for country-dance. "Country-dance" is a category of social dance of English origin in which a number of couples perform a set pattern of figures. The term arises in the sixteenth century, but the first detailed description is contained in *The English Dancing Master* (1651), a large collection of tunes with dancing instructions for each one compiled by John Playford. Under the title *The Dancing Master*, it went through seventeen further editions between 1652 and 1728, in which new dances are added and some older ones are dropped.

English country-dance includes round dances and dances for two couples or for four couples in a square, but most were danced in two lines, "longwayes for as many as will," a type which gradually displaced all other forms. A typical longways country-dance begins with the two facing lines moving sideways in opposing directions and back. It continues with the lines approaching until opposing individuals are side by side and then returning, and it concludes with partners turning about one another with arms joined. In some country dances the approaching and returning of the lines is repeated as a refrain between other group movements. Whereas a French court dance was defined by specific combinations of elaborate, difficult steps and foot positions, English country-dance required no more than a plain walk. Whereas French court dances could be executed by single couples and even individuals, English country-dance involved the synchronized movements of groups.

Most of the dances tunes in *The Dancing Master* and similar collections are the melodies of ballad songs that had circulated in oral tradition, although a few of them are purely instrumental dance numbers. Among the latter, the most characteristic are hornpipes and jigs, which differ from the other dances in that they require step patterns. Of all English country dances, the hornpipe is the oldest with consistent features. Most hornpipes from the seventeenth century are in triple meter with four-bar phrases divided in half by the characteristic syncopated rhythm $\frac{3}{2}$ ♩ ♩ ♩ ♩, or a variant, in the even-numbered measures. Even the rare duple-meter hornpipe contains a similar syncopation in every second bar.

The English jig involved vigorous stepping and leaping without movement of the body and arms. The music of an English jig at this time typically includes dotted rhythm in the context of compound triple meter, e.g., $\frac{6}{4}$ ♩. ♩. ♪ ♩.

Even hornpipes and jigs involved movement figures in their choreographies. These figures, and especially the movements of lines in longways country-dances, required many repetitions of the music. Hence, English country-dance tunes tend to be shorter than French court dances.

Although English country-dance originated in the outdoor rituals of rural village people, by the second half of the seventeenth century it was widely and enthusiastically embraced by the urban nobility and gentry who, unlike villagers, could read and afford to buy books like *The Dancing Master*. An engraving from the title page of the seventh edition of that collection (Fig. 13-2) depicts a dancing school where middle-class ladies and gentlemen are learning country-dance to the accompaniment of three fiddles without ensemble support. By the end of the seventeenth century, English country-dance was imported to France, where it was called *contredance* or *contredanse*. Vestiges of English country-dance are preserved in the modern square dance of the rural United States.

John Banister's suite of twelve dances called *The Musick att the Bath* (A. 113) contains a corant (courante), two sarabands, a bourrée, a hornpipe, and two jigs. Even the dances with French names have English country-dance characteristics—they are very short, and several of them have cadences on the sixth scale degree instead of the fifth degree. The hornpipe (no. 10) cadences on the sixth degree at the double bar.

The initial Ayre and the untitled tenth movement in Banister's suite resemble any number of items called "march" in *The Dancing Master*. Banister's third dance bears a specific resemblance to "Newmarket" in the fifth edition of *The Dancing Master* (1675), as shown in Example 13-1, but with the rhythm altered by a recurring syncopation that makes the tune into a duple-meter hornpipe. The melody of the last dance was printed as "A Jigg" among the "new tunes" that are country-dances as opposed to the "French dances" (mostly courantes) in the supplement to *The Dancing Master* entitled *The Tunes of the French Dances and Other New Tunes for the Treble-Violin* (1665).

Figure 13-2. "The Dancing Schoole" illustrated on the title page of John Playford, *The Dancing Master*, 7th ed. (London, 1686)

EXAMPLE 13-1. A comparison between the country-dance tune "Newmarket" and the third dance in *The Musick att the Bath* by John Banister

Banister's *The Musick att the Bath* was composed for the subgroup of the Twenty-Four Violins that accompanied the queen and her entourage to Bath in September, 1663. Only the treble and bass of the suite were written out in the surviving score. Presumably the inner parts were filled out by an assistant or copyist, as was often the practice at the French court.

The fashion for French music did not die out in England until the early eighteenth century, but there are signs that it began to abate somewhat by about 1680. French culture was tainted by its association with Catholicism and absolutism in the minds of certain Englishmen. This way of thinking was fueled by the public hysteria surrounding the fictitious "Popish Plot" of 1678, which charged that Jesuit priests, supported by the French army, were plotting to assassinate Charles II in order to crown his Catholic brother, James, King of England. One consequence of this hysteria was a three-year struggle (1679–81) in Parliament to exclude James from the line of succession on religious grounds; James was forced into exile. It was during this debate that the first modern political parties coalesced; the Whigs were opposed to James, and the Tories supported his rights. From this time cultivation of French music could be seen as a sign of Tory sympathies. The same association did not taint Italian music, and the flow of Italian influence coincided with the ebb of the French.

Italian-style solo and trio sonatas for violins had been written by English composers working abroad—e.g., by Henry Butler before 1652 and William Young in 1653—and by Continental composers working in England—e.g., Angelo Notari about 1625, Thomas Baltzar about 1660, and Nicola Matteis about 1670). And sonatas by Italians such as Cazzati, Vitali, Colista, Lonati, and Corelli circulated in England. But among the first English composers to write Italianate violin sonatas for the domestic market was Henry Purcell.

Purcell's *Sonnata's of III Parts* were published in 1683, and his *Ten Sonata's in Four Parts*, although published in 1697 were probably written about 1680 as well. Both are sets of trio sonatas for two violins, bass (bass violin, violoncello, or bass viola da gamba), and basso continuo for organ or harpsichord. In the preface to his 1683 *Sonnata's of III Parts*, Purcell claims to have "faithfully endeavour'd a just imitation of the most fam'd Italian Masters."

Among the Italian trio sonatas found in surviving manuscript copies made in England before 1683, Purcell's most likely models are a set that circulated widely under the name of Lelio Colista. About half of these are actually by Carlo Ambrogio Lonati; both Colista and Lonati were colleagues of Corelli in Rome. Purcell quoted a passage from one sonata by Lonati in his preface to the twelfth edition of *A Breefe Introduction to the Skill of Musick* (1694).

Among the features that link Purcell's sonatas with Colista's and Lonati's are the equal partnership of the bass part in the contrapuntal texture; the division of each sonata into five or more sections or movements, with a substantial slow movement at the beginning; placement of fugal movements in the second and last position; the use of the term "canzona" to designate the second, fugal movement; the use of untitled dance movements in the same sonata together with fugal movements; occasional motivic connections between the two fugal movements; the lack of non-fugal fast movements with concerto-style passage work; and the introduction of two contrasting subjects in the fugal movements. Nearly all of these features are illustrated in Sonata XII from Purcell's *Sonnata's of III Parts* (W. 31).

The harmonic language of Purcell's sonatas is essentially the one which Colista and Lonati shared and Corelli refined. In Chapter 12 we discussed this harmonic language and its conceptualization by Roger North (1651–1734), Purcell's occasional chamber-music partner. This harmonic language contrasts strikingly with that of Purcell's viol fantasies—for example, W. 30—composed at exactly the same time. The reaction to these viol consort works expressed by North reveals an awareness of the emerging norms of harmonic and melodic patterning:

> But in the *In nomines* I never could see a cadence compleat, but proffers and baulks innumerable. That which is properly termed Ayre was an intire stranger to this sort of harmony, and the audience might sitt with all the tranquillity in the world, and hear continuall shiftings of tones (with numberless sincopes and varietys, such as they were), and not be in the least moved; if pleased it was enough.
>
> Now to give a censure of this kind of musick, I must owne my self farr from approving it, because there is no scheme or designe in it; for beginning, midle, and ending are all alike; and it is rather a murmure of accords, than musick. There wants the proper change of keys, without which consort is lame. [Better is] the trumpet, which is confined to its scale, yet sounds the 5th above strong; which profers at a change, and is corresponded by another trumpet sounding a fifth upon that, which makes a cadence.

SOLO KEYBOARD MUSIC

English composers continued to write and publish music for harpsichord or virginals during the Commonwealth period. Although the Puritans did what they could to destroy church organs and abolish their use, they had nothing against playing instruments in the home. Keyboard instruments were found in many homes of the nobility and gentry; Samuel Pepys observed that during the great London fire of 1666 a third of the boats fleeing on the Thames carried virginals.

By the time of the Restoration, two forms of harpsichord music predominated—suites of dances and variations on ground basses.

The style of English keyboard suites at this time derived from that of Chambonnières and Froberger, who visited England in 1651–52. From Chambonnières the English first learned to apply *style brisé* to harpsichord music. Evidence of Froberger's influence includes the English tendency to group dances into suites of three or four movements.

The dances in Matthew Locke's *Melothesia* (1673) and even John Blow's later suites tend to be short and relatively easy to play. The elaborate introductory movements, technical challenges, textural and rhythmic contrasts, and more expressive style of Louis Couperin's suites did not make inroads in England.

English variations on ground basses developed continuously during the seventeenth century in a particular way not influenced by Continental models. Those by John Blow, for instance, are quite long, elaborate, varied, and expressive. His *Ground in E-La-Mi* (W. 32) is based on an eight-bar ostinato of his own invention, which combines two nearly complete descending scales—one on E, ending with a cadence on G, and one on G concluding with a cadence on E. Its twenty-nine variations, covering 232 measures, build to a very high level of energy and intensity.

The principal type of Restoration work for organ is the voluntary. A shorter composition of this type may be termed a verse. The voluntary or verse belongs to the tradition of the keyboard fantasy as represented by the *Fancy* of 1648 by Thomas Tomkins (W. 10). Although English organ music of the Restoration still does not call for pedals, it is distinguished from harpsichord music by its use of sustained tones. Restoration voluntaries and verses could be played before and after any church service or in the middle of Morning and Evening Prayer, between the psalm and the first lesson.

Imitative counterpoint continued to be the typical texture in English organ voluntaries in the Restoration period, but when compared with earlier fantasies, they tend to employ themes with more regular rhythm and less syncopation, and they have more abundant ornamentation, freer part writing, and more frequent figural passages. From about 1670 to 1730 there is a distinct trend in the English voluntary toward a division into two sections or movements defined by tempo and musical material. The Voluntary in D by William Croft is an example from about the mid-point in this period.

The slow introduction in Croft's Voluntary in D (W. 33) is entirely chordal, although contrapuntal opening sections can be found in other voluntaries by him and his contemporaries. This one reveals some of the oddities that persist in English music, even of this late date—the blatant parallel fifths in measure 2, for instance, and the early move to the sixth degree in measure 4. The second section of this voluntary is a double fugue, the two subjects of which are sometimes heard independently of each other. The statements of the second subject on the second, third, and sixth degrees (mm. 44–51) and the extended sequential episodes between subject statements (mm. 54–64, 67–71, 78–86) are features that emerge only tentatively in Corelli's sonatas, especially his solo sonatas of 1700, and are still rare in German organ fugues of the same period.

PLAYS WITH MUSIC—DRAMATICK OPERAS

As mentioned in Chapter 7, the theatrical performance was the cultural activity most violently opposed by the Puritans; public performance of plays was banned in England in 1642. Private productions of masques, however, sometimes escaped this edict because they could be viewed as musical performances. The playwright William Davenant (1606–1667) took advantage of this evasion with his *Cupid and Death* (1653), *The Siege of Rhodes* (1656), and other works, with music by Matthew Locke, Christopher Gibbons, Henry Lawes, and Henry Cooke.

The Restoration of the Stuart monarchy in 1660 opened the way to an unprecedented surge of creative energy and enthusiasm for drama that was repressed during the long years of civil war and Commonwealth. Within the first year of his return to the throne, Charles II issued licences for theater companies to Thomas Killigrew and William Davenant. Although their companies were not part of the royal court establishment, as the Royal Academy of Music was in France, composers and performers in the Chapel Royal and King's Music were always involved in their performances.

The principal theatrical genre, especially during the first twenty years of the Restoration, was the spoken play with extensive instrumental and vocal music. Although music had been an important part of English spoken dramas for at least a century before—for example in Shakespeare's plays—the expanded role for music in Restoration drama and the emergence of conventions governing its placement and usage correspond with contemporaneous developments in France and Spain, the two sources of court experience that Charles II and his circle brought back from exile.

In a Restoration drama, two sets of instrumental music, called the First and Second Music, customarily precede the opening curtain. After the Prologue, which often includes singing and dancing, an Overture and sometimes a separate Curtain Tune are heard. Additional short instrumental numbers or songs are performed as "act-tunes" between the acts. Sometimes these relate to the action just concluded or coming up. Songs that are sung within an act always arise from the action—for example, when entertainment is provided or when a celebration or ceremony is portrayed. These songs were usually sung by minor characters, rarely by an actor with a major speaking role. Finally, in some lavish productions, there might be one or two scenes with a series of musical numbers, either separated by short segments of dialogue or strung together as a continuous staged entertainment. The pretext for such musical complexes is often the appearance of supernatural personages. One such episode was included in *The*

Empress of Morocco (1673), with music by Matthew Locke. Two such musical scenes were included in the 1667 production of Shakespeare's *The Tempest*, adapted for the Restoration stage by William Davenant and John Dryden (1631–1700), the leading playwright of the age. In 1674 their adaptation was expanded to provide for more music, by Thomas Shadwell (1641/42–1692), the Poet Laureate.

The first of the two extended musical scenes in *The Tempest* of 1674 constitutes an extension of an episode in Act II. In Act I, a shipwreck lands Duke Antonio of Milan and his party on the same enchanted island where, twelve years earlier, Prospero, a magician and the former Duke of Milan, and his daughter, Miranda, landed after being set adrift in a small boat by Antonio, who then took over Prospero's dukedom. To punish the usurper and regain his position, Prospero and his fairy sprite, Ariel, conjure up spirits to scare Antonio into repenting. This scene—Shakespeare's Act III, scene 3—was moved to Act II, scene 4, and substantially rewritten by Dryden and Davenant for a 1667 production. In place of the speech of accusation that Ariel, transformed into a harpy, delivers in Shakespeare's play ("You are three men of sin"), the adaptation brings on three devils followed by the personifications of Pride, Fraud, Rapine, and Murder, who accuse and threaten Antonio. For the 1674 production of the play, Shadwell extended this scene, often called the "Masque of Devils" because one of Antonio's group, upon seeing the devils first emerge from the underworld, exclaims, "What horrid Masque will the dire Fiends present?"

The "Masque of Devils" in the 1674 adaptation of *The Tempest* (W. 34) includes music by Pelham Humfrey, Pietro Reggio, and Matthew Locke, all members of the royal musical establishment. An unusual feature is that Humfrey's dialogue for the devils is almost entirely in triple meter, but with syllabic text setting, avoidance of melodic patterning, and frequently static continuo accompaniment. In these respects it resembles Spanish recitative (*recitado*), although it is difficult to imagine how Humfrey could have known Spanish theater music except through Luis Grabu. Reggio's "Arise, ye subterranean Winds" is more typical of Restoration English recitative, derived from Matthew Locke's extension of the English declamatory song tradition.

The Tempest of 1674 included a second extended musical scene, usually called "The Masque of Neptune," in Act V, scene 2. This is an entertainment conjured up by Prospero's magic in celebration of the marriage of his daughter, Miranda, to Prince Ferdinand, the nephew of the now repentant Antonio. In Shakespeare's play, this masque takes place in Act IV and includes entries of Iris, Ceres, and Juno, three goddesses of ancient mythology. In the 1674 adaptation, these deites are replaced by Amphitrite, Neptune, Oceanus, and other mythical beings associated with the sea. In this masque, Humfrey sets the extensive dialogue as normal English recitative in duple meter. The singing is not interrupted by spoken dialogue, as it is in the "Masque of Devils."

The length and number of entirely sung masque-like episodes and the size of the accompanying ensemble were radically increased in Shadwell's and Locke's next collaboration, *Psyche* (1675), which Locke called "an English opera." Locke's

Circe (1677) contained even more music. After Locke's death in 1677 no such lavishly musical plays were written again until Dryden's *King Arthur*, which he called a play in "blank Verse, adorn'd with Scenes, Machines, Songs and Dances." Although written in 1684, *King Arthur* was not produced until later. In the meantime, the theater manager Thomas Betterton adapted a tragicomedy entitled *The Prophetess* for Purcell's music under the title *Dioclesian* (1690).

When *King Arthur*, with music by Purcell, finally reached the stage in 1691, Dryden called it a "dramatick opera," a term that is sometimes applied in retrospect to some of the works just discussed. A modern term for this genre is "semi-opera." The defining features of dramatick opera or English semi-opera are elaborate staging and spoken dialogue in blank verse serving as pretext and framework for several elaborate and extended musical episodes, often containing some dialogue sung as English recitative. Dramatick opera may be considered the English counterpart to French *comédie-ballet* and Spanish semi-opera. By most modern accounts, Purcell composed music for five dramatick operas: *Dioclesian* (1690), *King Arthur* (1691), *The Fairy Queen* (1692), *The Indian Queen* (1695), and *The Tempest* (1695). On the other hand, he wrote music for forty-seven plays that are not considered dramatick operas.

In Purcell's dramatick operas, most of the musical episodes arise out of the action, typically as enhancement of a religious or magical ritual, as a masque offered as entertainment by mortal performers, or as a masque of supernatural beings summoned by magic. In *The Fairy Queen*, however, the musical episodes in the fairy scenes are only loosely connected to the plot.

The Fairy Queen, an anonymous adaptation of Shakespeare's *A Midsummer Night's Dream*, was lavishly produced as a dramatick opera in 1692 and revived with added music in the following year. The original play is based upon a series of hilarious collisions between three sets of characters: four young lovers from the court, four unschooled tradesmen from the town, and a group of fairies in the nearby forest. Hermia and Lysander wish to marry, but Hermia's father wants her to wed Demetrius, who loves her. However, Helena loves Demetrius. All four run off to the forest. In the town, the four comical tradesmen ineptly plan a "Lamentable Comedy." Later they go to the forest to rehearse it. Meanwhile, in the forest, Oberon and Titania, king and queen of the fairies, have quarreled. Oberon seeks to punish Titania by having Puck apply a magic potion to her eyes while she sleeps, which will cause her to fall in love with whomever she first sees upon waking. Puck, however, commits a series of blunders that result in comically misdirected attractions involving the young lovers and Titania, who falls in love with Bottom, one of the uneducated tradesmen, who has been magically fitted with a donkey's head. In the end, Oberon unites the lovers properly and reconciles with his wife. Through his magic, he convinces everyone, including the audience, that everything has taken place in a dream.

If some of Purcell's masque scenes in *The Fairy Queen* are not really part of the action, they at least relate to it through metaphor. The "Masque of Sleep" in Act II prepares Titania for her magic-induced slumber. Titania arranges the masque in Act III in order to seduce Bottom. The "Masque of Seasons" in Act IV symbolizes Oberon's forgiveness of Titania, and the "Masque of Hymen" in Act V celebrates the double wedding of the four young lovers.

It could be said that Purcell's music, also, relates to the drama through metaphor. Whereas earlier English dramatic music, both religious and theatrical, supported the text through elocution and delivery, his music for *The Fairy Queen* supports several dramatic elements (plot, characterization, expression, and scenic effect) through the act of invention, a shift parallel to changes occurring at this time in Italian, French, and German vocal music. Purcell's "Masque of Sleep" in Act II of *The Fairy Queen* (A. 114) will serve as an example.

In the third scene of Act II, Titania magically changes the forest into a "Fairy-Land" and then announces the "Masque of Sleep":

> Let your Revels now begin,
> Some shall Dance, and some shall Sing.
> All Delights this place surround,
> Every sweet Harmonious Sound,
> That e're Charm'd a skilful Ear,
> Meet, and Entertain us here.
> Let Eccho's plac'd in every Grot,
> Catch, and repeat each Dying Note.

The Prelude is a musical summons and a fanfare, but light and delicate, using pyrrhic or anapest rhythms and triadic harmonies, with a gentle overall melodic contour, rising and falling. The fanfare idea continues in the accompaniment to the first song, "Come all ye songsters of the sky," developing the anapest rhythm in several directions suggested by the text. The instrumental trio that follows imitates the birds, the "songsters of the sky," with twittering reverse-dotted figures and fluttering sixteenth-note motives. The second song, "May the God of Wit inspire" and the following instrumental number provide the echoes mentioned in Titania's announcement. The invention in the third song derives from the rhythm of its initial words, "Sing while we trip it."

The "Masque of Sleep," itself, begins after Titania's spoken words,

> Come *Elves,* another Dance, and *Fairy* Song;
> Then hence, and leave me for a while alone.
> Sing me now to Sleep;
> And let the Sentinels their Watches keep.

In the introduction to "See even Night herself is here," sleep is evoked by plain, steady rhythm and the ethereal sound of high strings without bass. Oberon's nefarious plan is reflected in the writhing harmonies and jarring dissonances. Night declaims her words gently, trailing off into ever-more-frequent silences as the song progresses, until the unusually long, soporific instrumental postlude, spiced with typically English cross relations, concludes.

The invention of "I am come to lock all fast," sung by Mystery, is derived from the rhythm of the gavotte in the melody line, which is opposed by the rhythm of the bass. Secresy sings "One charming night gives more delight than a hundred lucky days" to teasing rhythms and harmonies that include diminished and augmented triads. "Hush, no more, be silent all," sung by Sleep and answered by the chorus, features tension between the discontinuity of the melody and rhythm versus the continuity of the harmony, as the music alternately presses forward and is restrained. The concluding "Dance for the Followers of Night" is a double canon with more augmented triads and other harmonic oddities.

ALL-SUNG OPERAS

English patrons and composers were interested in all-sung opera for most of the seventeenth century, and they carried out a number of experiments. The poet Ben Jonson reported that the 1617 setting of his masque *Lovers Made Men* by Nicholas Lanier (1588–1666) was sung throughout and that it incorporated "stylo recitativo." In the absence of surviving music, his claim has been treated with caution. Nevertheless, a long recitative by Lanier from the masque *Hero and Leander* survives. It is thought that Lanier composed this soon after returning from Italy about 1612. In 1656, during the Commonwealth, William Davenant began preparations for a performance of an all-sung stage work entitled *The Siege of Rhodes*, but the music by Henry Lawes, Henry Cooke, and Matthew Locke does not survive. Also during the Commonwealth, two stage works by Richard Flecknoe, *Ariadne Deserted by Theseus* (1654) and *The Marriage of Oceanus and Brittania* (1659), were sung throughout, the first of them entirely in recitative, but again no music survives.

English patrons also imported Continental operas during this period. There is a seventeenth-century manuscript score of Francesco Cavalli's opera *Erismena* (1655) with the text translated into English, although no details of a performance are known. In 1673 Robert Cambert, the pioneer of French opera, moved to London, where he put on a performance of his *Ariane* in 1674, and in 1686 Lully's *Cadmus et Hermione* was staged in London.

The earliest all-sung stage work in English composed in England for which the music survives is John Blow's *Venus and Adonis*, which was performed at court, apparently in 1682 or 1683. In its earliest source, it is called "A Masque for ye entertainment of the King," while in a printed libretto of 1684 it is termed "An Opera Perform'd before the King, afterwards at Mr. Josias Priest's Boarding School at Chelsey By Young Gentlewomen."

In the Prologue to *Venus and Adonis* Cupid sings to the shepherds and shepherdesses, Venus's courtiers, "At Court I find constant and true/ Only an aged lord or two," making it clear that work is an allegory. In Act I, "The Curtain opens and discovers Venus and Adonis sitting together upon a Couch, embracing one another." Adonis offers not to join the hunt, but Venus urges him to go.

Upon hearing a report of a giant boar, Adonis cannot resist the challenge. In Act II, Cupid receives from his mother instruction in the art of love and how "to destroy/ All such as scorn your wanton boy." She tells him to punish them by making them love "the ugly and ill-humour'd." Cupid then, in turn, instructs his "little Cupids" to aim their arrows at "the insolent, the arrogant, the mercenary [he has them spell out the word], the vain and silly, the jealous and uneasy, all such as tease ye," also "one that delights in secret glances and a great reader of romances . . . him that's faithless, wild and gay, who with Love's pain does only play." Presumably, this list should have pretty much covered most of the audience at court. After the Cupids dance, Venus calls the Graces, who also perform a series of dances. In Act III Adonis is brought in, wounded by the boar. He dies and is mourned.

In the first performance, the role of Venus was sung by the actress Moll Davies, the king's former mistress (Fig. 13-3), while Cupid was played by Lady Mary Tudor, their illegitimate daughter. Was this a warning to the king to follow his own counsel, to be wary of faithless courtiers, and to avoid being influenced by love or pride? If this was a reminder of the king's obligation, the tactic worked, for in 1683 he granted Lady Mary an annual income of fifteen hundred pounds. A reference to the plot of *Venus and Adonis* in Purcell's *Dido and Aeneas* hints at a more serious meaning.

Blow's *Venus and Adonis* is unified by a coherent plot motivated by vivid characterizations effectively supported by Blow's music. In these respects it is like an opera. On the other hand, it contains some vestiges of the English masque tradition, particularly the mythological theme, the dance entries, and Cupid's spelling lesson, which resembles a masque episode that might be found in a musical play or dramatick opera.

Charles II may not have been entirely pleased with Blow's *Venus and Adonis*, for shortly after its performance he continued to ask for "something at least

Figure 13-3. Moll Davis, mistress of Charles II, painted by Peter Lely

like an Opera," and he sent Thomas Betterton to Paris in 1683 with instructions to bring back Lully and his opera company. When this proved impossible, Betterton returned with Luis Grabu, a Spaniard trained in France who had been Master of the King's Musick from 1666 to 1673. John Dryden then set about writing what turned out to be *King Arthur*, for which Grabu was to provide an allegorical Prologue praising the king and his brother, James. By 1684, Dryden separated the Prologue from *King Arthur* and developed it into a three-act opera entitled *Albion and Albanius*, which was performed in 1685.

Grabu's setting of *Albion and Albanius* is a full-scale Lullian *tragédie en musique* with an English-language text. The scenes are created out of a continuous mixture of recitative, arioso, air, chorus, and dance; the recitatives even use the French style of meter change. Like most French and English stage works at this time, *Albion and Albanius* has an allegorical plot. It represents the defeat of Democracy and Zelota (Puritan zeal), the return of the brothers Charles (Albion) and James (Albanius), the Popish Plot, various assassination attempts, and the decision to send James into exile. In the end, Democracy and Asebia (atheism) are destroyed.

Henry Purcell's *Dido and Aeneas* followed in the footsteps of both *Venus and Adonis* and *Albion and Albanius*. Like *Venus and Adonis*, it was performed at Josiah Priest's school in Chelsea in 1689. With *Venus and Adonis* Purcell's *Dido and Aeneas* shares its three-act format, the theme of the woman abandoned, the use of a chorus in a variety of roles, the inclusion of dances, and the use of an arioso version of Restoration recitative. As in *Albion and Albanius* and Lully's *Cadmus et Hermione*, the scenes in *Dido and Aeneas* are frequently based upon the pattern recitative—air—chorus—dance.

Nahum Tate's libretto for *Dido and Aeneas* derives from Virgil's *Aeneid* as adapted in Tate's earlier tragedy *Brutus of Alba* (1678). Dido, widowed queen of Carthage, has welcomed Aeneas, a prince who has escaped from the destruction of Troy. Although her courtiers urge her to marry Aeneas, Dido is reluctant. Her response to Aeneas's marriage proposal is "Fate forbids what you pursue." But she gives in to his ardor. In Act II witches plot against Dido by contriving to send Aeneas away. One of them makes a key observation: "That *Trojan* Prince you know is bound / By Fate to seek *Italian* ground," a reference to Virgil's story, in which Aeneas helps to found Rome. The Sorceress helps fate along by sending her "trusty Elf," in the guise of the messenger god, Mercury, who pretends to deliver Jove's command to Aeneas that he sail to the west. The sailors prepare for departure at the beginning of Act III. Aeneas tells Dido of his decision, and she dies of despair.

Like Blow's *Venus and Adonis*, Purcell's *Dido and Aeneas* seems to embody a political allegory, although less obviously than *Albion and Albanius*. In a poem written about 1686, Nahum Tate compares James II to Aeneas, who is misled into abandoning Dido (the English people) to seek "Italian ground" by embracing Rome (Catholicism). According to this allegorical reading, James first participates in the Restoration as Aeneas returns from the hunt with the head of the boar "With Tuskes far exceeding / Those did *Venus'* huntsmen

Tear"—a reference to Adonis's death by goring in Blow's *Venus and Adonis*, that allows us to identify it with the Charles I's execution by the "boar" of democracy. Aeneas (James II) is then sent away (from England) to the embrace of Rome (Catholicism) by a minion of evil pretending to be a messenger from Jove (God). This actually happened to James twice, both times because of his Catholicism; he was exiled from 1679 to 1682 during the Exclusion Crisis and again in 1688 as a consequence of the Glorious Revolution that put William and Mary on the throne. The fact that the libretto of *Dido and Aeneas* expresses more sympathy for Dido (the English people) than for Aeneas (James II) argues for the conclusion that its allegory refers to James's final exile in 1688.

James II was the last Francophile Stuart king. Not long after his deposition, the score of Purcell's *Dioclesian* was published (1691) with a preface by John Dryden, who announced that English music is "now learning *Italian*, which is its best Master, and studying a little of the *French* Air, to give it more Gayety and Fashion." Actually, the musical style of *Dido and Aeneas* (A. 115) already contained a mixture of Italian, French, and English elements.

The most significant Italian features of *Dido and Aeneas* are the intense personal expression in its text and music; the triple-meter, chromatic version of the passacaglia bass ostinato in Dido's lament, "When I am laid in earth;" and the ABA form of the arias "Shake the cloud from off your brow" and "Pursue thy conquest, Love."

The French traits are the plot, which hinges on supernatural intervention that brings on spectacular scenic effects; the chorus and dances that are part of the action; the use of descriptive orchestral music; French court dances such as the gavotte in the chorus "Banish sorrow, banish care," the bourrée in the air "The greatest blessing Fate can give," the minuet in the chorus "When monarchs unite," and the sarabande in the duet with chorus "Fear no danger to ensue"; and the French overture that opens the work.

The dialogues in *Dido and Aeneas* are sung to the kind of English recitative that Matthew Locke developed out of the English declamatory air tradition, as modified in the direction of arioso by John Blow in *Venus and Adonis*. The frequent use of grounds is also an English trait. Beside Dido's lament, grounds appear in her opening air, "Ah, Belinda!," the Triumphing Dance at the end of Act I, and "Oft she visits this lone mountain" in Act II, scene 2. The use of imitative counterpoint in the last two choruses would not be typical of Italian or French opera but can be found in English stage works throughout the period. Finally, the chorus "Come away, fellow sailors" and the following Sailors' Dance have the rhythms of the triple- and duple-meter hornpipes.

After the death of Henry Purcell in 1695, the principal English composers for the theater were John Eccles (ca. 1668–1735), Daniel Purcell (ca. 1660–1717), Jeremiah Clarke (ca. 1674–1707), Gottfried Finger (ca. 1660–1730), and John Weldon (1676–1736). All of them composed for musical plays and dramatick operas comparable to those to which Henry Purcell contributed music. Their airs, however, show more influence from Italian opera in the length and number of melismas and the use of melodic-harmonic sequences. A representative group of works from this period are the four settings of a masque by playwright William Congreve (1670–1729) entitled *The Judgment of Paris* (1701) by Eccles, Daniel Purcell, Finger, and Weldon, who competed for a prize; Weldon won. Today, their efforts are judged inferior to Purcell's in the intrinsic interest of their music and its integration into the drama as a whole.

The activities of the Chapel Royal and King's Musick declined during the reign of William III, 1688–1702, both before and after the death of his consort, Queen Mary, in 1694. William, brought up a Calvinist in Holland, had little interest in music and theater, and he spent a substantial part of his reign commanding his army against the French in Flanders.

William III was succeeded by Queen Anne, the Protestant daughter of James II. Her reign, 1702–1714, is sometimes termed the English Augustan Age—referring by analogy to the period of the Roman Emperor Augustus, ca. 43 B.C.–A.D. 18—because it was marked by domestic peace and a flowering of poetry by such writers as Alexander Pope, Joseph Addison, Sir Richard Steele, John Gay, and Matthew Prior. However, there is no English-born composer of this period who is considered to be their equal.

The Judgment of Paris almost marks the end of Restoration musical theater. After the 1701 production of Weldon's setting of *The Judgment of Paris*, there were practically no new musical stage works produced in London for the next three years. The last dramatick opera was another adaptation of *The Tempest* composed by Weldon in 1712. At the other side of this watershed appeared the first attempt at an all-sung opera in Italian style with English words, *Arsinoe, Queen of Cyprus* (1705) by Thomas Clayton (1673–1725), which was followed quickly by a half dozen similar operas in English, ending with *Camilla*, in an English translation, by Giovanni Bononcini (1670–1747), which received 111 performances in three productions in London from 1706 to 1728. Clearly by 1706 London theatergoers were eager for Italian opera. Its establishment there with the arrival of George Frideric Handel in 1710 will be examined in Chapter 15.

BIBLIOGRAPHICAL NOTES

Charles II and the Musical Institutions of His Court
    The best overview is Ian Spink, ed., *Music in Britain, 3, The Seventeenth Century* (Cambridge: Blackwell, 1992); The introductory essay by Spink, "Music and Society," is especially useful. The experiences of Charles during his exile are summarized by Hester W. Chapman, *The Tragedy of Charles II in the Years 1630–1660* (London: Cape, 1964). A lavishly illustrated account of his reign is Antonia Fraser, *Charles II: His Life and Times* (London: Weidenfeld & Nicolson, 1979).

Anthems and Services
    The chapter "Church Music II: from 1660," by Spink in his volume *The Seventeenth Century* provides a general guide. More detail is available in Ian Spink, *Restoration Cathedral Music, 1660–1714* (Oxford: Oxford University Press, 1995);

Christopher Dearnley, *English Church Music, 1650–1750: In Royal Chapel, Cathedral, and Parish Church* (New York: Oxford University Press, 1970); and Michael Claude Vaughn, "The Restoration Chapel Royal: A Confluence of Traditions and Styles," Ph.D. diss., Northwestern Univ, 1996. Books and dissertations on individual composers include C. G. P. Batchelor, "William Child: An Examination of the Liturgical Sources, and a Critical and Contextual Study of the Church Music," Ph.D. diss., Univ. of Cambridge, 1990; Peter Dennison, *Pelham Humfrey* (Oxford: Oxford University Press, 1986); Watkins Shaw, *The Services of John Blow* (Croydon: Church Music Society, 1988); Fredrick Allen Tarrant, "John Blow's Verse Anthems with Organ Accompaniment," Ph.D. diss., Indiana Univ., 2000; B. Wook, "John Blow's Anthems with Orchestra," Ph.D. diss., Univ. of Cambridge, 1977; Robert Manning, "Purcell's Anthems: An Analytical Study of the Music and Its Context," Ph.D. diss., Univ. of Birmingham, 1979; and Franklin B. Zimmerman, *The Anthems of Henry Purcell* (New York: American Choral Foundation, 1971).

Odes and Welcome Songs
   The genre as a whole is the subject of Rosamond McGuinness, *English Court Odes, 1660–1820* (Oxford: Oxford University Press, 1971); and T. Trowles, "The Musical Ode in Britain c.1670–1800," Ph.D. diss., Univ. of Oxford, 1992) . Specific information about Purcell's odes and welcome songs can be found in Peter Holman, *Henry Purcell* (Oxford: Oxford University Press, 1994); and Franklin B. Zimmerman, *Henry Purcell, 1659–1695: His Life and Times*, 2nd ed. (Philadelphia: University of Pennsylvania Press, 1983).

Songs and Domestic Vocal Ensembles
   An overview of this repertoire is provided by the chapter "Vocal Music II: from 1660," in Spink, *The Seventeenth Century*; and the relevant parts of Ian Spink, *English Song: Dowland to Purcell*, 2nd ed. (London: Batsford, 1986). The sources are listed in Cyrus Lawrence Day and Eleanore Boswell Murrie, *English Song-Books, 1651–1702, and Their Publishers*, reprint (Philadelphia: R. West, 1977).

Viols and Violins
   The relevant chapter in *The Seventeenth Century* is "Consort Music II: from 1660," by Michael Tilmouth and Christopher D. S. Field. Details about the twenty-four Violins are developed in Peter Holman, *Four and Twenty Fiddlers: The Violin at the English Court, 1540–1690*, 2nd ed. (Oxford: Oxford University Press, 1995). Style issues are explored by Mary Monroe, "From 'English Vein' to 'Italian Notes': The Stylistic evolution of Purcell's Chamber Music for Strings," Ph.D. diss., Columbia Univ., 1994.

Solo Keyboard Music
   The best survey is Barry Cooper, *English Solo Keyboard Music of the Middle and Late Baroque* (New York: Garland, 1989).

Plays with Music and Dramatick Operas
   A brief overview can be found in the chapter "Music for the Stage II: from 1650," by Margaret Laurie, in *The Seventeenth Century*. A much more detailed and rewarding treatment is Curtis A. Price, *Music in the Restoration Theatre* (Ann Arbor: UMI Press, 1979). Purcell's theater music is treated specifically by Curtis A. Price,

Henry Purcell and the London Stage (Cambridge: Cambridge University Press, 1984). Several of Purcell's individual stage works have also been treated in monographs, e.g., J. Muller, *Words and Music in Henry Purcell's First Semi-Opera, 'Dioclesian'* (Lewiston, NY: E. Mellen Press, 1990).

All-Sung Operas

In addition to the works cited above, Edward J. Dent, *Foundations of English Opera: A Study of Musical Drama in England during the Seventeenth Century*, rev. ed. (New York: Da Capo Press, 1928), is still useful. Two specific works discussed in detail here are treated in Ellen T. Harris, *Henry Purcell's 'Dido and Aeneas'* (Oxford: Oxford University Press, 1987); and Anthony Lewis, Introduction to *John Blow: 'Venus and Adonis'* (Monaco, 1949). A keen perspective on the beginnings of Italian-style opera in London is offered by Lowell Lindgren, "*I trionfi di Camilla*," *Studi musicali*, 6 (1977), 89–159; and J. Merrill Knapp, "Eighteenth-Century Opera in London before Handel, 1705–1710," *British Theatre and the Other Arts, 1660–1800*, ed. Shirley Strum Kenny (Washington, DC: Folger Shakespeare Library, 1984), 67-91.

Italian Vocal Music, ca. 1680–1730

THE NEOCLASSICAL REFORM OF ITALIAN OPERA, ca.1680–1706

In October 1697 a handwritten Venetian opera newsletter reported, "Truly today operas have become so common in every part of Italy, that not only in its famous cities but even in various towns and villages they are performed incessantly." Indeed, by 1700 opera theaters were found in many towns in Italy so small that today they have neither a railway station nor a cinema. And Italian opera was rapidly becoming an international phenomenon. To judge only by the date of the earliest surviving theatrical librettos, Italian opera, sometimes in translation, arrived for the first time in at least 131 cities and towns of Europe between roughly 1680 and 1730, including Berne (1678), Hanover (1678), Amsterdam (1680), Krakow (1682), Hamburg (1693), Liège (1695), Leipzig (1693), Berlin (1700), Copenhagen (1703), London (1705), Stuttgart (1701), Lisbon (1720), Seville (1729), and Moscow (1731). In any given opera season more than a hundred theaters in virtually every country in Europe were offering Italian opera. This dramatic spread of Italian opera was aided by changes in its form and style that made new works and productions easier and less expensive to create. Paradoxically, these changes began in a neoclassical reform movement aimed at elevating the artistic level of opera; the movement began in Venice.

Venice continued to occupy the central position in the new international world of Italian opera, although Rome and Naples began to challenge its status. During the fifty-year period treated here, Venice normally had six active opera theaters, which were filled with local aristocrats and many of the thousands of wealthy visitors who came to Venice during the carnival season, from December 26 to the beginning of Lent.

The largest of these theaters, named after the church of San Giovanni Grisostomo, was opened in 1678 by the brothers Giovanni Carlo and Vincenzo Grimani. As members of one of the leading noble families of Venice, the Grimani brothers strove to make their theater and its repertoire particularly grand and dignified as a reflection of their social status and in order to appeal to the more prestige-conscious among Venetian operagoers.

The Grimani theater was the largest in Venice: its stage was about twenty meters wide, twenty-six meters deep, and eight meters high; 165 boxes on five levels encircled the floor in a horse-shoe pattern (see Fig. 8-1). It presented mostly premier productions of newly composed operas.

Like most opera theaters in Europe at this time, the Grimani theater was run as a private enterprise by its owners. They paid the singers, scene painters, machinists, librettists, composers, and orchestral musicians. Boxes were rented by the year, but everyone had to buy a ticket for each performance; patrons who did not have a box could either stand or rent a chair on the main floor. Competition among the theaters of Venice was fierce, and profit margins were small. Within their large and luxurious theater, the Grimani brothers met their competition with operas notably elevated in style, different from the Venetian operas of previous years.

The typical Venetian opera libretto of the late seventeenth century was written by a professional theater poet in the complex and fast-paced style introduced about the middle of the century by Giacinto Andrea Cicognini in such operas as *Giasone* and *Orontea*. In librettos of this type, there are usually several parallel plots, at least one of which is comic. Even the serious characters of royal or noble status behave in a ridiculous or immoral way from time to time.

Criticism of this type of libretto can be found in essays, commentaries, and libretto introductions throughout the later seventeenth century, for example in the preface to the libretto of *Epulone* (1675) by Francesco Fulvio Frugoni. Such criticism focused mainly on the concept of decorum and the dramatic unities propounded in such writings from classical antiquity as the *Poetics* of Aristotle and the *Ars Poetica* of Horace. In this view, "decorum" meant both propriety and good taste in conduct or appearance, and consistency of behavior of a dramatic personage, in line with the character's identity and social status. The unities were of time, place, action, and character. Aristotle recommended that the story told in a tragedy cover a time span of no more than a twenty-four-hour day and take place in a space no wider than a javelin throw. Unity of action meant that all events portrayed follow one another without significant breaks and contribute directly to a single outcome. Unity of character meant that a given personage should not appear to be one individual in one scene and someone completely different in another.

The first attempt to revive these classic ideals in an Italian opera came in 1688 with Vincenzo Grimani's libretto for *Orazio*, based directly on the French tragedy *Horace* by Pierre Corneille (1606–1684). From this point onward for a full century, innumerable Italian opera librettos were based on the tragedies of Corneille and of his principal successor, Jean Racine (1639–1699), who more than any playwrights of the seventeenth century pursued the classic ideals of decorum, unity, and elevated language.

In pursuit of these ideals, in 1691 Giovanni Carlo Grimani and his household librarian, Apostolo Zeno (1668–1750), founded the Accademia degli Animosi ("Academy of the Bold"), which sponsored discussions and experiments aimed at a neoclassical reform of the Italian opera libretto. Beginning in 1692, the Grimani theater began to feature operas based on librettos written by members of the Accademia degli Animosi, most of whom were noble dilettantes rather than professional men of the theater. The Paduan count Girolamo Frigimelica Roberti (1653–1732) was notable for strictest adherence to neoclassical ideals of unified plot, elevated language, and elimination of comic scenes and characters—he even wrote operas in five acts in imitation of the tragedies of Corneille and Racine.

Between the extremes of Frigimelica Roberti and such traditionalists as Matteo Noris and Adriano Moreselli, Apostolo Zeno's first libretto, *Gl'inganni felici* (1696), exemplifies a typical opera from the beginning of the neoclassical reform movement. Its musical setting was composed by Carlo Francesco Pollarolo (ca. 1653–1723), the Grimani house composer from 1691 to 1706.

Gl'inganni felici employs only seven characters, as opposed to the nine, ten, or eleven of older-style Venetian operas. Six of these characters are of royal or noble status, and only one, Brenno, is a servant. Brenno's role preserves a mere vestige of the older comic character type, and his light-hearted comments and asides are a dim reflection of the traditional comic scenes that had alternated with serious scenes in earlier Venetian librettos. Although three of the characters in *Gl'inganni felici* appear in disguise, the resulting confusion is moderate, and it is related in the end to the single plot line.

Clistene, King of Siconia, has promised the hand of his daughter, Agarista, to Demetrio, the winner of the Olympic Games. She, however, rejects him unseen, because she is in love with her painting teacher, Armidoro, actually Demetrio in disguise. The loser in the Games, Orgonte, is also in love with Agarista and has gained access to her disguised as her music teacher, Sifalce. He tries to abduct Agarista but is foiled by Armidoro (Demetrio). Demetrio and Agarista are happily united, as are Orgonte and Oronta, a Thessalian princess who, disguised as Alceste, had followed her beloved Orgonte to the court of Siconia.

Pollarolo clearly separates his recitatives and arias, following established conventions for each. He sets the dialogue as plain recitative without aria-style, arioso, or melismatic interjections. The beginning of an aria is signaled by a shift from *versi sciolti* to rhymed, metrical verse. The arias are nearly all found at the ends of scenes. At the end of each aria, the character who sang it exits.

An excerpt from Act I of *Gl'inganni felici* (W. 35) will serve as an example of neoclassical reform opera. In the dialogue at the beginning of Act I, scene 6, King Clistene announces to his daughter, Agarista, that he has promised her hand in marriage to Demetrio. She rejects his decision. In the exit arias that conclude this and the next two scenes Clistene, Agarista, and Alceste in turn express their reactions to this development.

Clistene's words ("A l'offerta d'uno sposo") are firm and measured, almost menacing: "To the offer of a husband your heart will finally yield." Pollarolo's music reinforces this aura with syllables set to steady eighth-note scale segments of moderate speed, limited range, low tessitura, minor mode, mostly descending contours, and avoidance of strong accents.

Agarista's reaction ("Non vedo perché tu speri cor mio") is understandably more agitated: "I do not see why you hope, my heart, if, loving and hoping, hope is vile, and desire is a fault." The word *perché* ("why") is sung three times to a motive set off by rests, as if it were a rhetorical question. The word *speri* ("you hope") is animated by a long melisma. A second melisma on the word *speranza* ("hope") is broken up by rests, as if Agarista were gasping out of anxiety.

Alceste's reaction is intentionally ambiguous because she is really Princess Oronta in disguise. Whereas Brenno thinks that Alceste is pained because Agarista loves someone else, her aria ("Tal'or dico al crudo fato") actually expresses Oronta's concealed longing for Orgonte (disguised as Sifalce, a rival suitor for Agarista): "Sometimes, when I tell cruel fate that I will always be sad, I hear the winged god [Cupid] respond, 'I alone know.'" The musical topic invoked here is the "aria siciliana," identifiable because of its $\frac{12}{8}$ meter, slow tempo, smooth melodic contours, simple and slowly moving harmonies, and mildly melancholy tone, promoted by the minor mode. The word *fato* ("fate") is set to a melisma that struggles painfully upward, and the phrase *io solo il so* ("I alone know") is sung pensively five times.

All three are non-strophic, da capo arias, the formal type that comes to dominate Italian opera by the 1690s. The term *da capo* ("from the head," or "from the beginning") arises from the performance direction often placed at the end of the second part of such an aria. The singer repeats only the first part, completing an ABA scheme. Although arias with an ABA pattern were known as early as the middle of the seventeenth century, their music was usually repeated for a second strophe, and each component section was normally comprised of a single period.

The da capo arias of the 1690s, exemplified by those in Pollarolo's *Gl'inganni felici*, are sung only once, and each section is divided near its midpoint by at least one cadence or half-cadence, often on a harmony different from that of the concluding cadence. Arias of this time frequently include a motto beginning in which the voice states the prevailing motive in a brief phrase which is echoed by the accompaniment and then taken up again by the voice in an expanded treatment leading to the first cadence. The use of the orchestra, not only the basso continuo, in the opening and concluding ritornellos of arias, and within their vocal periods, is another innovation of the 1690s.

In their diversity, these three arias in Pollarolo's *Gl'inganni felici* reflect the greatly expanded range of expressive types and cues available to opera composers at the end of the seventeenth century. In Stradella's and Provenzale's arias we saw the first decisive steps away from the uniform $\frac{3}{2}$ cantabile style that prevailed in the operas of Cavalli and Cesti. By the time of the neoclassical reform of opera, arias were thought capable of suggesting one or two emotions chosen from a wide range of subtly varied passions that helped distinguish characters and contribute to their consistent portrayal—that is, to their dramatic decorum. If the action depicted on stage is slower than in earlier operas, it is because the plot has become more internal, revolving around the interplay of personalities and feelings.

These aims—to express in arias one or two emotions chosen from a wide range of passions and thereby musically to portray individual characters—were explicitly stated in a letter from Alessandro Scarlatti (1660–1725) to the musician-prince Ferdinando de' Medici of Florence in 1706. In this letter, Scarlatti summarizes his aims with respect to his opera *Tamerlano* (Pratolino, 1706) as follows:

> I have woven the modulation with circumscribed easiness, having made a mixture of simple [elements] for the composition, and these are: naturalness, charm, and, at the same time, expression of the passion with which the characters speak, [which is] the most important consideration and circumstance [required] for moving and drawing the spirit of the listener toward the diversity of sentiments that the various events in the plot of the drama express. . . .
> It is impossible, even in merely reading it, not to feel in it the movements of the various passions that it contains. I confess my weakness; in some items, while I was adding the notes to them, I wept.

Although born in Palermo, Sicily, Scarlatti received his training in Rome, where he composed his first operas (1679–1683) for the circle of aristocrats who gathered around the exiled Queen Christina of Sweden. In 1684 Scarlatti moved to Naples, where he was awarded the coveted post of *maestro di cappella* to the Spanish Viceroy and composed at least thirty-two operas for the large San Bartolomeo theater attached to the palace and heavily subsidized by the Viceroy. The upheavals caused by the War of the Spanish Succession (1701–14), however, caused Scarlatti to leave Naples in 1702.

Returning to Rome, Scarlatti received support and commissions from the wealthy and influential Cardinal Chancellor, Pietro Ottoboni, scion of a noble Venetian family. In 1695 Ottoboni had become the protector of the Accademia degli Arcadi ("Academy of the Arcadians"), a group of poets, musicians, and writers concerned with the neoclassical reform of all the arts, including opera, along the same lines advocated by Giovanni Carlo Grimani's Accademia degli Animosi. In fact, Ottoboni and Grimani were friends and corespondents, and in 1698 Grimani's academy became a branch of Ottoboni's Accademia degli Arcadi, whose first and most important published spokesman was Giovanni Mario Crescimbeni (1663–1728). Crescimbeni's *Dell'istoria della volgar poesia* ("Concerning the History of Vernacular Poetry," 1698), *La bellezza della volgar poesia* ("The Beauty of Vernacular Poetry," 1700), and *Commentarii intorno alla sua Istoria della volgar poesia* ("Commentaries upon His History of Vernacular Poetry," 1702) echoed the call for simplicity, decorum, elevation of language, and the classical unities that had issued from Grimani's Venetian circle during the 1690s. When Crescimbeni's ideas about opera and Scarlatti's desire to compose them were frustrated by Rome's lack of a stable public opera theater, Cardinal Ottoboni used his contacts to launch Scarlatti in Venice.

By the time Scarlatti reached Venice via Florence, he had composed or contributed to more than eighty-eight operas, by his own count. The style and outline of these operas generally corresponded to those of Pollarolo.

For Venice, however, Scarlatti composed his most neoclassical opera, *Mitridate Eupatore* (1707), on a libretto by the uncompromising reformer Girolamo Frigimelica Roberti. Cast in five acts like a French tragedy, it contains neither comic characters nor love intrigue. Its music is exceptionally expressive.

By the date of *Mitridate Eupatore*, Scarlatti's style had reached a stable state, advancing over that of Pollarolo principally in the fuller and more varied orchestral accompaniments provided during the vocal periods of arias; longer, more varied, and more difficult melismatic passages; and a further expansion of da capo form.

Although *Mitridate Eupatore* achieved considerable success, Scarlatti, as an outsider, drew satirical attacks in Venice. He returned to Naples in 1708, where he regained his position at the head of the viceregal chapel and continued to compose operas. His influence was felt strongly by a group of highly successful, younger Neapolitan opera composers who helped spread a consistent and somewhat commercialized version of neoclassical reform opera commonly called *opera seria* ("serious opera").

OPERA SERIA, PART 1

When Carlo Francesco Pollarolo temporarily withdrew from opera composition from 1707 to 1714, the Grimani brothers replaced him with Alessandro Scarlatti, Antonio Lotti, Antonio Caldara, and George Frideric Handel. These four may be taken to represent the first generation of opera seria composers.

The term *opera seria* was used occasionally in the eighteenth century to distinguish this type from comic opera, or *opera buffa*. It also reminds us that this type of opera excluded comic characters. The more common (if less descriptive) term for it during the early eighteenth century was *melodramma* ("music drama").

Antonio Lotti (1666–1740) was born in Hannover, Germany, where his father was court music director, but he had been in Venice since 1683, studying with Legrenzi, singing and playing organ in the cappella of San Marco, and directing music at several churches. Between 1706 and 1717 he composed at least sixteen operas for the Venetian theaters, principally for the Grimani theater of San Giovanni Grisostomo.

In 1717, Lotti led a company of singers, including his wife, the soprano Santa Stella, and the librettist Antonio Maria Luchini, to Dresden, where they moved into a newly built opera theater. Although Lotti left after two years, other opera companies continued to operate in Dresden with a few interruptions for most the eighteenth century, under such resident composer-directors as Johann David Heinichen (1683–1729) and Johann Adolf Hasse (1699–1783).

Antonio Caldara (?1671–1736), the only native Venetian among the second group of Grimani composers, had been a colleague of Alessandro Scarlatti under the patronage of Cardinal Ottoboni in Rome. He worked for the Grimani only during the 1707–08 season. After a second period in Rome, he won the post of assistant music director at the imperial court of Vienna in 1717. His duties there including composing six or more operas each year. From 1718 until 1729, his main librettist was the imperial court poet Apostolo Zeno, whose association with the Accademia degli Animosi and the Grimani theater in Venice has been noted. When compared with Scarlatti's arias, Caldara's are somewhat more predictable in formal detail and less individualized in expressive content. Dance rhythms are more common, and the texture of instrumental accompaniment is somewhat more contrapuntal.

The collaboration between Caldara and Zeno contributed substantially to the crystallization of opera seria, a process continued in Vienna after 1720 by Zeno's successor, the librettist Pietro Metastasio (1698–1782).

George Frideric Handel got his start in opera in 1703 at the age of eighteen, when he obtained a position as second violinist (later harpsichordist) in the opera theater of Hamburg, under the leadership of Reinhard Keiser. When Keiser had to flee his creditors in 1704, young Handel was able to step into the breach with two successful Italian operas that imitated and even borrowed from the older master's works. Keiser's mixture of French features (overtures, dance-arias, a variety of aria forms, orchestral action music) and Italian conventions (plain recitative, da capo arias) remained with Handel throughout his opera career.

In 1706 Handel was invited to compose operas for the court of Florence by the visiting Prince Gian Gastone de' Medici, the younger brother of the musician-prince Ferdinando. By 1707 Handel received support and commissions from several cardinals in Rome, including Cardinal Ottoboni, as well as employment in Naples and Florence. In 1709 Handel achieved a resounding success with his satirical, anti-heroic opera *Agrippina* at the Grimani theater in Venice. In the audience were the brother of the Elector of Hannover and the English ambassador to Venice, both of whom would soon generate invitations and opera commissions for Handel.

After the run of *Agrippina*, in 1710 Handel accepted the position of musical director at the electoral court of Hannover, but almost immediately he obtained two leaves to compose operas in London.

Chapter 12 discussed the introduction of Italian-style opera to the general London audience in 1705 with an English-language version of *Arsinoe* by Thomas Clayton and Jakob Greber's *Gli amori d'Ergasto,* followed in 1706 by *Camilla,* composed by Giovanni Bononcini. Handel's *Rinaldo* (1711) was the second Italian opera composed expressly for London. Handel obtained a second leave from the Elector of Hanover to return to London for more opera productions in 1712.

Dismissed from his position at the Hannover court during his prolonged absence, Handel found a variety of employments in England, including the composition of one or two new operas nearly every year through 1741. From 1720 to 1728, he served as the principal composer for a newly created resident opera company, the Royal Academy of Music, which received generous support from the crown.

Handel tended to favor adaptations of librettos by poets of an earlier generation, or poets not associated with the neoclassical reform movement. In these
librettos, he found a variety of scene structure and the inclusion of protagonists
with non-heroic features—features eliminated by the neoclassical reform.
Although he does not completely ignore the exit-aria convention, Handel's
scenes sometimes include short aria-style or arioso interjections, ensemble
singing, and an occasional chorus. He employed orchestrally accompanied recitative (*recitativo accompagnato*, *recitativo obbligato*, or *recitativo stromentato*) far more than
contemporaneous or earlier composers, although some accompanied recitative
can be found as early as Cavalli's operas. Handel's arias are often slightly unconventional in form, with shortened da capo forms, binary forms, and through-
composed numbers among them. It has often been noted that Handel's arias
stand out from his contemporaries' in the richness and detail of their emotional
expression—another feature than can be traced to Keiser's influence. Two
excerpts from Handel's *Tamerlano* (1724) will illustrate these traits.

The first aria in Handel's *Tamerlano*, "Forte, e lieto a morte andrei" (A. 116a),
is sung by Bajazet, emperor of the defeated Turks and prisoner of Tamerlano,
emperor of the victorious Tartars. The scene is the courtyard of Tamerlano's
palace. In the opening recitative, Andronico, Bajazet's Greek ally and espoused
son-in-law, offers the captive emperor his freedom in Tamerlano's name in
return for the hand of Bajazet's daughter. Rejecting this offer out of fierce
pride, Bajazet snatches a guard's dagger and threatens to gain his freedom
through suicide. Andronico reminds Bajazet of his love for his daughter and the
sorrow and distress that she would feel at his death. Bajazet's aria expresses the
conflict that will keep him in check until the end of the opera.

The basis of this interpretation of Bajazet's aria is found in the writings of
composers and theorists of the period who contributed to that branch of
instruction and criticism today often called "The Doctrine of the Affections."
We will examine this doctrine in the following excursus, after which we will
return to Handel's aria and to a summary of opera seria features.

THE DOCTRINE OF THE AFFECTIONS

"The Doctrine of the Affections" and "Theory of the Affects" are alternate
English translations of the German term *Affektenlehre*, a word already in use
during the seventeenth and eighteenth centuries.

The belief that music may inspire emotions was quite old and widespread by
the 1690s. Notions that certain musical details and characteristics may promote
specific passions can be found in the writings of Mersenne and Kircher during
the early and mid-seventeenth century and even earlier in the sixteenth-
century writings of Vicentino, Zarlino, and Galilei. But the idea that a composer may elicit any one of a long list of emotions through the act of musical
invention arises for the first time in writings associated with the German
reception of Italian opera seria shortly after the year 1700.

In the preface to his *Componimenti musicali* of 1706, Reinhard Keiser declared that the principal aim of an aria is the strong and clear expression of the specific emotions embodied in the words and felt by the characters as portrayed in the opera. Keiser's thoughts and practices in this regard had a strong influence on two of his colleagues in the Hamburg opera theater, the librettist Barthold Feind (1678–1721) and the composer Johann Mattheson (1681–1764). Both of them went on to write extensively on this subject.

In his first book, *Das neu-eröffnete Orchestre* ("The Newly Opened Orchestra," 1713), Mattheson names twenty-six emotions and affect-laden concepts that can be imitated in an opera aria—love, jealousy, hate, meekness, impatience, desire, indifference, fear, revenge, courage, timidity, generosity, horror, highness, lowness, splendor, poverty, pride, humility, joy, laughter, crying, lust, pain, bliss, despair—and offers specific suggestions for their musical expression. In his last, most comprehensive guide for music directors, *Der vollkommene Capellmeister* ("The Complete Music Director," 1739), he provides some theoretical explanation of emotions, drawing on a tradition in seventeenth-century philosophy and psychology that originates with *Les Passions de l'âme* (The Passions of the Soul," 1649) by René Descartes (1596–1650) and continues through the writings of Hobbes (1651), Spinoza (1677), Locke (1690), Hutcheson (1728), and Wolff (1732). Although these philosophers differ among one another in many details, the following ideas they held in common may be taken as the main underlying tenets of the early eighteenth century Doctrine of the Affections:

• Affects (affections, emotions, passions) are associated with abnormal conditions of psychological agitation or activity.
• Affects are brought on by outside causes that act upon all persons in a similar way.
• Once aroused to a certain affect, a person will remain in that affective state for a significant time or until acted upon by a different outside cause.
• Affects can be named and classified.
• Each secondary (tertiary, etc.) affect arises from a specific mixture of primary (secondary, etc.) affects, which are fewer in number.
• Among the basic causes of affects, two sets of opposites are the most important—expansion (activity) of the life spirits versus contraction (inactivity) of the life spirits, and pleasure versus pain.

Interest in identifying and characterizing a wide range of specific emotions can be found during the seventeenth century in the visual arts, as shown in the illustration of twelve basic emotions by Charles Le Brun (Fig. 14-1).

Although Descartes and his followers thought that "the life spirits" were tangible and discoverable in the human body, modern students can view their expansion (activity) versus contraction (inactivity) as metaphorical expressions for agitation versus calm.

Among the six primary passions listed by Descartes—joy, sorrow, hate, love, wonder, and desire—it is easy to arrange the first four as extreme combinations

P. 35.

la Joie.

P. 45.

Colere meslée de rage.

P. 19.

l'Amour Simple.

P. 31.

Tristesse

Figure 14-1. Charles Le Brun (1619–1690), illustrations of joy, rage, love, and sorrow

of activity/inactivity and pleasure/pain, as shown in Figure 14-2. Joy is found in the upper left, as an active (expansive) and pleasurable emotion. Sorrow is located at the lower right of the table, combining pain and inactivity (contraction). Hate, an active (expansive) and painful affect, is at the upper right of the table, and love combines pleasure with inactivity (calmness) at the lower left.

The advantage of this approximation is that it helps one comprehend and remember the myriad musical features mentioned by eighteenth-century writers and used by composers of the same period as contributing to the expression of a particular affect. In general, it can be extrapolated from treatises of this period that musical features that were thought to promote expansion or activity were rapid tempo, fast rhythms, ascending rhythmic patterns, high range, wide intervals, loud dynamics, and ascending melodic contours. Their opposites were thought to promote contraction or inactivity. Pain was thought to be caused by minor keys, dissonance, chromaticism, abrupt change of key, mode, or harmony, sharp melodic contours, piercing tone, pointed accents, and so on. Pleasure was thought to be expressed by the opposite features.

A large number of other emotions could be found between the extreme points marked by the four primary emotions shown in Figure 14-2, and would result from some mixture of two or more of them and the musical features that tend to promote them. For example Marpurg (1762) suggests that "jealousy, an affect created out of love, hate, and envy, is introduced by a change from a wavering and rather soft tone, to a very intense, daring and scolding tone and

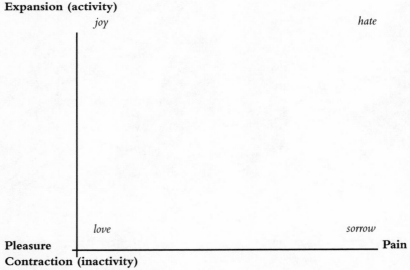

Figure 14-2. A classification of primary emotions following the theories of René Descartes and his followers

again to a moving and sighing tone, while alternating between very slow and very quick movement."

Following an older physiological theory of emotions, the Hamburg librettist Barthold Feind explained the emotional effects of music and poetry with reference to the stimulation of one or a combination of the four cardinal humors, yielding four corresponding states called sanguine (hopeful or confident), choleric (angry), phlegmatic (apathetic; cool, calm, self-possessed), and melancholic (sad). It is easy to see that these four states roughly correspond to the four primary emotions shown in Figure 14-2.

Eighteenth-century writers on musical expression may perhaps seem to exaggerate and over simplify. In that case, the following five warnings or modifications found in the theory of the period will prove useful:

1. The musical features that promote activity, inactivity, pain, or pleasure normally do not occur without some admixture of other features that tend to promote a different or opposite affect. A simple instance is found in C. P. E. Bach's (1753) example of a passage made tender (*affettuoso*) by appoggiaturas whose resolution is played pianissimo (Ex. 14-1). However, the inactive features of the appoggiaturas—small interval, descending motion, diminuendo—are presented together with melodic leaps and dotted rhythms, which tend to promote expansiveness. The solutions to this dilemma are (1) to give attention to those features that are remarkable rather than inevitable and (2) to find, in vocal music, the most plausible match between musical features and expressive meaning of the text, because the universal affirmation of the principle that the music must express the affects of the text leads us to assume that expressive agreement between the music and text was always the composer's intention and the listeners' expectation.

2. We should not believe that early eighteenth century musicians actually believed that a given aria or movement would infallibly arouse one and only one emotion in all listeners. The practice of replacing one aria text with another in Vivaldi's operas, for example, resulted in the same music being used for one text expressing joy and for another expressing fury. In such a case, the expansiveness and high level of activity would support both affects, while the element of pain, which would distinguish fury from joy, is simply absent from the music.

EXAMPLE 14-1. A passage made tender by appoggiaturas, from Carl Philipp Emanuel Bach, *Versuch über die wahre Art das Clavier zu spielen* ("Essay on the True Manner of Playing the Keyboard," 1753), Fig. 82

3. Many arias and examples in treatises relate not directly to affects but to affect-laden concepts, images, or sounds, for example the concept of glory, the image of an ascent to heaven, or the sound of thunder. It is apparent that in these cases the listener was expected to feel a related affect such as pride, triumph, or foreboding.

4. Eighteenth-century writers often name specific features—a short trill, for example—as promoting the expression of a specific affect—happiness, in this case. Here we may assume that the writer has learned to associate a musical feature with a certain affect through repeated experience. If that experience was shared by most listeners and composers of the time, the association between musical feature and emotion could communicate an affect, even if there were nothing intrinsically expressive about the musical feature. And if that feature were to occur in an aria with a text suggesting a quite different emotion, the association would presumably not be activated. Our aim, as modern listeners, should be to focus attention upon notable features of the music that best match significant aspects of the text—affects or concepts, images, or sounds.

5. The affective expression that is perceived by the audience will depend to a large extent on the manner of performance, such as the details of dynamics, accents, articulation, tone production, etc., not specifically notated but provided by the singer or instrumentalist who, ideally, has studied the invention in the aria or movement and has correctly identified the composer's intentions and the listeners' expectations. In fact, much advice about producing affects given in treatises of this period is actually directed at performers. For instance, Marpurg (1762) advises that "longing is expressed by drawn-out, languid tones."

Among musical features whose affective associations were conventional rather than natural, are dance rhythms, evocations of idioms of specific instruments, keys, and a large number of other topics or musical emblems. Thus, Mattheson (1739) makes the following associations between dances and affects, perhaps on the basis of tempo, phrasing, choreography, and the gestures that accompany the steps:

Menuet: moderate cheerfulness	Gigue: ardent and fleeting zeal
Gavotte: jubilation	Loure: pride, arrogance
Bourrée: contentment and pleasantness	Polonaise: frankness and a free manner
Rigaudon: trifling joking	Angloise: stubbornness
March: heroism and fearlessness	Passepied: frivolity
Entrée (i.e., the first part of a French overture, with dotted rhythm): nobility and majesty	Rondeau: confidence
	Sarabande: ambition
Allemande: contentment, satisfaction	Courante: hopefulness
Chaconne: satiating	Intrada: longing

Examples of other conventional affective signals include the bass ostinato outlining a descending fourth through chromatic motion (sorrow, lamenting), dotted anapest or pyrrhico-anapest rhythms (glory, majesty), and trumpet idiom (aggression, courage, valor, glory).

Mattheson places his discussion of musical affective expression in the context of musical rhetoric, distinguishing between musical invention, disposition, elocution, and delivery. He places the expression of specific affects within the compositional act of invention, in which the composer decides upon the basic purposes, features, and motives of a work before planning its form or beginning the actual composition. We can see that delivery was the most important part of musical rhetoric to the earliest opera composers (Peri, Caccini, Monteverdi); elocution—reflection in music of rhetorical figures—was a new preoccupation with composers of the mid-seventeenth century; whereas musical invention is the primary means used for affective expression by the beginning of the eighteenth century.

Placement of affective expression within the act of invention means that a composer should summarize the dominant emotions of the aria in musical features that permeate the whole. As Johann Gottfried Walther wrote in his *Praecepta der Musikalischen Composition* ("Precepts of Musical Composition," 1708), "When, however, an emotion is to be expressed, the composer should look more to it than to the individual words . . . so that he might not observe [the words] in their particularity. . . ." In this sentence, Walther's word for "emotion" is *Gemüths-Regung* (literally, "mind-motion"), a German translation of Descartes's term *action de l'âme* ("action of the soul").

In his *Neu erfundene und gründliche Anweisung . . . zu vollkommener Erlernung des General-Basses* ("Newly Invented and Thorough Instruction for the Complete Understanding of Thorough Bass," 1711), Johann David Heinichen (1683–1729) shows how a composer can find ideas for setting even an unemotional first poetic stanza by mentally reviewing some *loci topici* ("commonplaces"), a classic aid to invention in the lore of rhetoric. Accordingly, he has the composer consider the commonplaces of circumstance, person, time, and causes, as they pertain either to the previous recitative or the second stanza of the aria text. By this means Heinichen is able to demonstrate five quite different but equally appropriate musical settings for the same text. In the 1728 edition of his treatise, published under the title *Der General-Bass in der Composition* ("Thorough Bass in Composition"), he offers a more extended demonstration of the same process applied to several different texts. Later, in *Der vollkommene Capellmeister* of 1739, Mattheson discusses fifteen commonplaces of invention that a composer might use. It is notable that Heinichen in 1711 assumes that if the text has an obvious affective meaning, his readers would be able to grasp it and would know how to express it in music without his help. He affirms that even a dry, unemotional text ought to be set to music that will inspire an affect in listeners.

Thus we may add the following list of general principles common to most musical writings on the affections to the list of commonly held tenets among philosophers offered earlier:

• The overall emotional expression of an aria (or major part thereof), move-ment, or work is the result of musical invention, which produces features that characterize the whole.

• Many expressive features of music can be thought of as promoting activ-ity/inactivity or pleasure/pain.

• Many other expressive features of music are conventional signs or emblems that work through memory and association or by referencing an affect-laden concept, image, or sound.

• Affective features in vocal music are often potentialities that are actualized only when combined with a text containing the right cues.

• A specific emotion or mixture of emotions should be maintained through-out an aria (or major part thereof), movement, or work.

• In finding musical invention that will inspire certain affects, the composer has the option of considering such things as the character of the personage or the situation in which the aria is sung in addition to, or instead of, the specific affective meaning of the words being set.

• The features of the music that define its affect may be found together with other features that do not contribute to the same definition; in that case the features that are the least routine or that accord best with the text are thought to be the most important.

• Usually the music relates only to a portion of the affective content of the text, in which case a different text sharing that portion of the affect may be substituted without breach of propriety.

• Neidhart wrote in 1706 that "The purpose of music is to stimulate all the affections"; Mattheson said in 1739 that "Where there is no passion, no affect to be found, there is also no virtue." Variations on such views were expressed widely during the early eighteenth century, and no contrary view from that period has ever been reported.

With these ideas in mind, we may return to Handel's aria "Forte, e lieto a morte andrei" and the discussion of opera seria.

OPERA SERIA, PART 2

The text of Handel's aria "Forte, e lieto a morte andrei" is

> Forte, e lieto a morte andrei
> Strong and happy to death would I go
>
> Se celassi ai pensier miei
> if were hidden from my thoughts
>
> Della figlia il grande amor.
> my daughter's great love.

Se non fosse il suo cordoglio,
Were it not for her sorrow,

Tu vedresti in me più orgoglio,
you would see in me more pride,

Io morrei con più valor.
I would die with more valor.

Forte, &c.
Strong, etc.

Handel's setting of this aria parallels the mixture of emotions suggested by the words "strong," "happy," "death," "love," "sorrow," "pride," and "valor." In addition, it contains a reference to Bajazet's latent insanity, which according to eighteenth-century belief, his thought of suicide reveals. From the perspective of the Doctrine of the Affections, we can see that this mixture of feelings, some of them conflicting, are encapsulated in the musical details introduced during the opening ritornello (Ex. 14-2); these are the elements of invention that are elaborated in the rest of the aria.

The duple meter, steady eighth-note accompaniment, repeated pitches, and dotted rhythms help to identify the aria as a slow march, which suggests "heroism and fearlessness" according to Mattheson's report.

The opening gesture is an octave leap, an expansive, consonant interval, which is tempered by proceeding downward. When the singer enters, this gesture is sung to the word *forte* ("strong"), an affect that it surely was meant to embody.

Quantz (1752) would interpret the short trill on beat 2 as a suggestion of happiness, and indeed the words sung at this point, when the melody is repeated by the voice, are *e lieto* ("and happy").

The downward leap of a minor sixth on beat 3 would promote a lamenting, mournful expression according to Grassineau (1740), and the appoggiatura on beat 5 would express sorrow in Quantz's view. In the first vocal period, these notes are sung to the words *a morte andrei* ("to death would I go").

The dotted rhythms in the bass of measures 1 and 2 would be associated with pride and magnificence according to Mattheson and many others.

Marpurg's opinion that "gentle and quiet love is expressed with a consonant harmony and soft, flattering melody in broad movements" seems to agree with Handel's decision to drop suddenly to a soft dynamic level with a descending syncopated arpeggio in measure 3.

The brief shift from C major to C minor in measure 4 would represent to Mattheson the interjection of "exceeding loveliness and, at the same time, sadness" into a general context of the "rude and impertinent character" often associated with C major. The harmony associated with the turn to C minor is a diminished-seventh chord on F-sharp superimposed over a G pedal. Rameau

EXAMPLE 14-2. Affective elements in the opening ritornello of George Frideric Handel, "Forte, e lietro," from *Tamerlano* (1724), as they would have been interpreted by eighteenth-century writers

[1]Mattheson (1739)   [6]Marpurg (1762)
[2]Quantz (1752)   [7]Mattheson (1739)
[3]Grassineau (1740)   [8]Rameau ((1722)
[4]Quantz (1752)   [9]Kirnberger (1782)
[5]Mattheson (1739), *et al.*   [10]Mattheson (1739), *et al.*

(1722) associated dissonances of this type with sweetness and tenderness, affects that the soft dynamic level and the slurs tend to reinforce.

The wide leaps in the violin line, which include a diminished seventh and an augmented fourth, would give a hint of insanity in the view of Kirnberger (1782).

Finally, the music of Handel's ritornello regains its air of heroism and valor with a return to the forte dynamic level, C major, dotted rhythm, and short trill toward the end.

All of the interpretations of specific musical features cited in the previous paragraphs come from writings published after the composition of Handel's aria in 1724. Obviously Handel did not learn to deploy these features by reading those treatises. On the contrary, it means that the writers of those treatises learned to associate certain musical features with more or less specific emotions through long experience of the conventions of opera seria and related vocal genres, in which Handel was involved as a creator and performer.

Several months after composing "Forte, e lieto" for *Tamerlano*, Handel reworked the music of the aria for his setting of a devotional text in German. The first vocal period of the original Italian aria and the corresponding passage from the German song are given in Example 14-3. Clearly the German text lacks the affective elements of strength, happiness, love, pride, valor, and derangement found in the libretto of *Tamerlano*. Accordingly, in reworking his music for the German song, Handel eliminated the musical features of his Italian aria that promoted those affects. A close comparison between the two settings would be very instructive.

The many contrasting affective elements introduced in the opening ritornello of "Forte, e lieto a morte andrei" constitute its invention. Handel elaborates on these elements in the rest of the aria; since no new ideas of any significance are added, the whole aria is unified by a single mixture of affects.

In other arias by composers of Handel's generation, one may find that a contrasting or complementary mixture of affects is promoted by the contrasting music of the B section in the ABA scheme of the aria in da capo form.

By the 1720s, composers had expanded the da capo form by increasing, defining, extending, and separating its component periods. When the da capo repeat is taken into account, an aria like "Forte, e lieto a morte andrei" comprises five vocal periods surrounded by six ritornellos—hence the modern term "five-part da capo form." The five vocal periods in this aria trace a pattern of modulation typical of the form:

1. Vocal period 1 (mm. 5–11) cadencing on the dominant.
2. Vocal period 2 (mm. 13–23) visiting the keys of the sixth degree (m. 14) and the second degree (m. 16) and cadencing on the tonic.
3. Vocal period 3 (mm. 28–39) visiting the key of the fourth degree (m. 33) and cadencing on the third degree.
4. Vocal period 4 = vocal period 1 repeated.
5. Vocal period 5 = vocal period 2 repeated.

An aria text at this time normally contains two stanzas, usually with same pattern of lines, scansion, and rhyme scheme. The first stanza is sung once in vocal period 1 and once again in vocal period 2. The second stanza is sung at least once in vocal period 3. Then stanza 1 is sung twice again during the da capo repetition of both vocal periods of part A. Each orchestral ritornello repeats the concluding cadence of the previous vocal period. Mattheson (1739) compared this standard scheme to the rhetorical disposition of an oration, although he was required to redefine the function of the periods in part A when it repeats.

Exordium = the first ritornello, "the introduction and beginning of a melody in which its purpose and intention are shown in order to prepare the listener and to arouse his attention."

Narratio = the first vocal period, containing "a report, a tale in which the meaning and nature of the oration are suggested."

Propositio = the second ritornello, which "briefly contains the meaning and purpose of the musical speech," and the second vocal period, which contains a varied proposition.

Confutatio = part "B" of the aria, containing "everything that goes against the proposition."

Confirmatio = the repetition of part "A" da capo, forming "the clever reinforcement of the proposition."

Peroratio = the final ritornello, which is "the end or conclusion of our musical oration and must, above all else be especially moving."

EXAMPLE 14-3. A comparison between the first vocal periods of Handel's "Forte, e lieto" and "Die ihr aus dunkeln Grüften," transposed from B-flat

EXAMPLE 14-3.—continued

In most arias, excluding those that feature clipped, syllabic declamation, the singer was expected to embellish both vocal periods of part A during the da capo repetition. The final cadences of both part A and part B were normally adorned with cadenzas, during which the singer wove scales, arpeggios, and even motives from the aria proper into a short passage performed without strict time or meter and without accompaniment. Both improvised embellishment and cadenza are illustrated in Example 14-4. The da capo embellishments and cadenzas were supposed to be improvised and different in each performance. However, singers were often accused of memorizing them as written out by their teachers.

"Forte, e lieto a morte andrei" depicts the character of Bajazet in a degree of detail unusual for opera seria. In the rest of this opera, the balance between his strength, pride, courage, and valor on the one hand, and his love of his daughter, Asteria, and the thought of her sorrow in case of his death motivates Bajazet to plot against his captor, Tamerlano, and prevents him from suicide. This balance is tested throughout the opera by Bajazet's interaction with the other personages, whose characters are defined and portrayed by the mixtures of affects projected by the arias they sing. By the end of the opera Bajazet's mental derangement, hinted at in his first aria, tips the balance.

The decisive action of *Tamerlano* unfolds in Act III, scene 10. In it, Bajazet reveals that he has won his freedom and defeated Tamerlano by taking poison.

EXAMPLE 14-4. The conclusion of part "A" in "Sciolta da lido," from *Ambleto* "by Giuseppe Vignati of Milan, sung in that city by Faustina [Bordoni, 1697–1781], with her embellishments, as she sang it during the carnival of 1720"

Asteria asks to join her father in death, and he would willingly help her to that end. As the poison works its effect, he imagines that he can summon the furies from hell to torment Tamerlano for his revenge. In the end, Asteria and Andronico help him off stage, where he dies—an extraordinary end for a noble personage in opera seria.

Handel sets this scene with a nearly seamless succession of segments in plain recitative, (orchestrally) accompanied recitative, arioso, and aria styles. These styles can be found in contemporaneous operas by many composers, but few others would build such an extended scene from so many stylistically diverse sections.

Accompanied recitative, like plain recitative, is normally used in opera seria for dialogue or monologue written in *versi sciolti* but with significantly heightened emotional content. The emotional content is usually unstable, and one affect often follows quickly after another, whereas in an aria one combination of affects is usually maintained throughout each of the three parts (ABA). In Act III, scene 10, of Handel's *Tamerlano*, the orchestral accompaniment tends to alternate with short phrases of recitative for the voice alone. In this way, the orchestra comments upon the emotional content or illustrates the affect-laden imagery contained in the recitative phrases. This practice is typical for accompanied recitative in opera seria. Since it is relatively easy to understand which words, concepts, affects, or images are being reflected in the orchestral responses, the body of accompanied recitative in opera seria provides us with a useful dictionary of expressive musical devices and emblems far more comprehensive than found in period treatises.

The passage marked "Arioso" in Act III, scene 10 (A. 116b, mm. 65–82), of Handel's *Tamerlano* sets a mere three lines of metrical text, like a fragment of an aria text embedded within the *versi sciolti* of a dialogue. The musical setting is also like a fragment of an aria without ritornellos, B section, or da capo. The orchestral accompaniment provides steady rhythm that clearly projects the meter. The vocal writing is mostly syllabic, but is far more melodic than recitative, even if it does not develop musical motives as an aria would. But like an aria, the arioso projects a stable affective state—tenderness mixed with sorrow. And like an aria, the arioso closes with a formal cadence in the original tonic key.

The passage in $\frac{3}{4}$ meter in Act III, scene 10 mm. 94–124, at the words *Su, via, furie e ministre del gran Re dell'ira* ("Up, away, furies and minions of the great king of wrath!") shares features of accompanied recitative and arioso, but it is not exactly either one. Here the orchestra provides continuous melodic content and steady, metrical rhythm while the voice interjects short phrases in recitative style. This is very rare in opera seria. It seems to arise first in forms of comic opera that are stylistically and chronologically beyond the scope of this book.

Handel was in many ways an unconventional composer of operas, since he accorded more importance to drama than to vocal display. This occasionally brought him into conflict with his singers, who were among the most famous in Europe. Such conflicts led Handel's most famous singer, Francesco Bernardi (d. 1759), called "Senesino," to break away and join a rival opera company in London. This Opera of the Nobility rivaled Handel's company from 1733 to

1737 by featuring Farinelli, the most illustrious emerging star singer from Italy, as well as presenting operas by composers who were developing a distinctly new post-Baroque style based on dominance of the vocal melody, extremely simple accompaniments, balanced phrasing rather than sequential Fortspin-nung, and rudimentary, slowly unfolding harmony. Among these were Nicola Porpora (1686–1768), Leonardo Vinci (?1696–1730), and Johann Adolf Hasse (1699–1783).

While opera patrons had been especially interested in female singers during the middle decades of the seventeenth century, the biggest stars of the opera world around 1700 and for decades thereafter were male sopranos and altos, who owed their unnaturally high voices to surgical castration performed before puberty, typically sought by the parents in hopes of future riches. This practice can be traced back to the middle of the sixteenth century, when sopra-nos more capable and experienced than the usual boys were recruited for the papal chapel. Castratos were associated with opera from its beginnings, but their use received a boost when, in 1630, women were banned from singing in public opera performances in Rome and throughout the Papal States of Italy. By 1680, the leading man and often the second man in an Italian opera were usually sung by castrati; in the Papal States and conservative Catholic centers like Vienna, singers of this type were used for the female roles as well, because women were forbidden to take the stage. Among the first castrati to become international opera stars were Giovanni Francesco Grossi (1653–1697), known as "Siface," and Francesco Antonio Maximiliano Pistocchi (1659–1726). They were followed by Senesino and Carlo Broschi (1705–1782), called "Farinelli," one of the most famous singers in history. Although women sometimes sang the male roles written in soprano or alto range, castrati were prized everywhere for the greater strength of their voice and the extreme vocal acrobatics that their strength permitted.

All composers of opera seria were eager to exploit the strengths of the par-ticular singers in a production, and they preferred to know who would sing each part before beginning to compose. Singers also influenced the shape of productions by insisting on singing arias they had learned for roles sung previ-ously in other operas. Since traveling singers carried these arias with them, they were called "suitcase arias" or "baggage arias." When inserted into a new opera production, a baggage aria was often fitted out with a new text to fit a new dramatic context, although sometimes the original text, provided it con-tained a generic expression of love, hate, joy, or sorrow, expressed in language sufficiently abstract or metaphorical, could be used in a variety of situations in various operas. In the best of circumstances, the theater's resident poet could find words appropriate to the new context that also matched the affective content, rhythms, phrasing, and form of the old music. When the range or affective content of a singer's baggage arias was restricted by her stage person-ality or technical limitations, the role or even the plot might be modified and, to accommodate the personality and abilities of the singer and the arias already in her baggage. This certainly was the case with Anna Girò (ca.1710–after 1747), who traveled with Antonio Vivaldi and appeared in over thirty productions of his operas from 1726 to 1739.

The use of baggage arias was one way to facilitate the production of new operas. Another was the reuse of favorite arias from operas by various composers, with either new or old recitatives. Such an opera was termed a *pasticcio* ("pastiche"); they were especially common in London from 1705 to 1717.

Almost all aspects of opera seria reflect a concern for standardization, making all components—libretto, music, and scenery—into interchangeable commodities for the economical production of a commercial product. A list of these standardized aspects of *opera seria* around 1725 will serve as a summary of this discussion.

Typical Features of *opera seria* around 1725

- Three acts.
- The tone of language is universally elevated, the same for all characters, nearly all of whom are of noble status; no comic servants.
- A monarch must choose duty over personal desire to resolve the plot.
- Usually six characters—the first man and first lady, both high voices, who are young and in love; a second man and second lady, also high voices, who must be reunited; and the monarch and his ally or antagonist, high or low voices. There may be a seventh character, usually a messenger.
- Most action takes place offstage and is reported in dialogue sung in plain recitative.
- Favorite librettos are set to music many times over with modifications, especially the substitutions of arias; operas with completely new librettos become increasingly exceptional.
- Arias expressing characters' emotional reactions to dialogue are placed at the ends of scenes; the character exits after singing an aria.
- The librettist Carlo Goldoni and others report that da capo arias were often classified as belonging to one of a small number of standard types:

  Aria di bravura—rapid tempo, fast rhythms, long, difficult melismas, possibly wide leaps; suitable for expressions of joy, rage, and related affects. The end of Act II is the favorite place for an *aria di bravura*.

  Aria cantabile—moderate to slow tempo, major key, mostly conjunct melodic motion, usually narrow range, balanced and stable phrases, slow harmonic rhythm, moderately ornamental and melismatic, mostly consonant harmony, little contrast, often uses appoggiaturas; suitable for expressions of love, peace, contentment, and related affects.

  Aria patetica—slow tempo, minor key, soft dynamics, chromaticism, dissonance, descending melodic and/or bass contours, low register; suitable for expressions of sorrow, lamentation, and related affects.

  Aria parlante—syllabic text setting, rapid tempo, many exclamations and other words set off by rests, and repeated pitches; suitable for expressions of anger, defiance, and related affects.

Aria di mezzo carattere—a mixture or alternation of features of the other types; suitable for setting words that are not strongly affective or that mix various affects through alternating or changing expression.

• Duets normally resemble arias; other ensembles are rare.

• Frequently the only chorus is found at the end of the opera and is sung by the characters in the opera, not by a separate chorus.

• The small orchestra includes two continuo groups (harpsichord, cello, double bass), one at each side of the pit, 6-14 violins and violas in the middle, possibly pairs of horns, trumpets, and oboes, with a bassoon (Fig. 14-3).

• When the last character on stage sings an aria and exits, the scene changes.

• The scenery is painted on wing flats placed in parallel slots on both sides of the stage, on hangings, and on backdrops (Fig. 14-3). Scenery is changed in view of the audience by pulling away one set of flats, hangings, and backdrops to reveal another set, already in place. The first scene in each act tends to depict a small indoor space; subsequent scenes depict increasingly large spaces.

• Settings are highly standardized; common settings include a dungeon, a private chamber, a throne room, a palace antechamber (Fig. 14-3), a garden, a forest, a mountain pass, a battlefield, a harbor's landing place, etc.

"A PERFECT SPIRITUAL *MELODRAMMA*": THE ITALIAN ORATORIO, CA. 1680–1730

The years 1680–1730 mark the peak period for the Italian oratorio in Europe. At some point during these fifty-years, every major city in Italy and many Catholic centers in northern Europe experienced the largest production of oratorios in their history. Oratorios were performed in more cities during these decades than during any other period in the history of the genre. In Florence, for example, between twenty-two and thirty-seven different oratorios were performed each year, versus six or seven operas. For many spectators and musicians, the oratorio provided an experience of dramatic music otherwise denied to them by the exclusivity of the more expensive opera productions.

At this time, the traditional venues of oratorio performances in Italy remained in the forefront: the oratories and churches of the Fathers of the Oratory of St. Philip Neri (the Oratorians) and other teaching and preaching orders, such as the Jesuits, Theatines, and Servites; and the private oratories and chapels of religious lay confraternities. To these were added chapels attached to the palaces of Cardinals; ducal chapels and churches of special uses under the control of the ruling families of various Italian states; the churches of the Venetian *ospedali*, where the girls often sang oratorios in Latin; assembly rooms of learned or artistic academies; banquet halls; and occasionally opera theaters. The trend toward secularization of oratorio performances can be seen in the preparation of performing

Figure 14-3. Pietro Domenico Olivero, The Royal Theater in Turin, 1740

spaces. Figure 14-4 shows the decoration of a salon in the palace of the chancellery in Rome, 1708, which corresponds to a typical decoration of an church
or oratory at this time. Figure 14-5 shows a 1727 oratorio performance in the
private theater that had been added to the chancellery in the meantime.

Oratorios continued to be divided into two parts, but by the end of this
period, the sermon traditionally preached during the interval between the two
parts was replaced in some performances by a sonata or concerto. The favored
sources of stories were the Old Testament and the lives of saints because of the
variety of personages, situations, and themes, including some (mysticism,

asceticism, gruesomeness, eroticism) that were beyond the limits of opera. Changes in the style of oratorio librettos increasingly parallel those of opera.

Like opera, the Italian oratorio was affected by a neoclassical reform movement. As with opera, many changes were underway in the oratorio before they were codified in writing. The principal spokesman for oratorio reform was the librettist Arcangelo Spagna (1632–1726), who published two essays on the oratorio in 1706. In them he celebrated the elimination of the narrator (*Testo*), making the oratorio "a perfect spiritual *melodramma*." Drawing on the precepts of Aristotle and the models of Roman tragedies, Spagna also recommended that oratorio librettists unify their plots and use fewer characters. Although scenery and costumes were not employed in oratorio performances, the printed librettos describe scene changes as they should be imagined by the spectators. As in the realm of opera, the neoclassical reforms of oratorio were promoted above all by the librettist Apostolo Zeno.

Musical settings of Italian oratorios after 1680 continued to call for three to six solo voices but no chorus. The earlier accompanying continuo group, possibly with two violins, expanded to include a full string orchestra, occasionally with oboes, trumpets, and horns. Scenes are usually divided clearly into dialogue, set as plain recitative, leading up to one or more arias, just as in opera. The older aria forms are replaced by the non-strophic da capo aria by the end of the seventeenth century, with the same stereotyped expressive categories found in *opera seria*.

The oratorio *Cain, ovvero Il primo Omidicio* ("Cain, or, The First Homicide") by Alessandro Scarlatti (A. 117) is an example of the oratorio at about the middle of the period under discussion. On the last page of the autograph score, Scarlatti wrote, "End of the oratorio—7 January 1707." It is likely that the oratorio was performed at the ancestral palace of Antonio Ottoboni—the author

Figure 14-4. A stage design for the performance of Alessandro Scarlatti's *Passio Domini Nostri Jesu Christi secondum Joannem* in the Sala Riaria of Cardinal Ottoboni's chancellery palace, 1708

Figure 14–5. The stage setting of Giovanni Battista Costanzi's *Componimento sacro per la festività del SS. Natale* in Cardinal Ottoboni's theater in the chancellery palace, 1727

of the libretto and father of Scarlatti's patron—on the Rio di San Severo in Venice, in imitation of his son's way of producing oratorios in Rome.

In Part I of *Cain, ovvero Il primo Omidicio*, Adam reviews the hard lesson learned from God's punishment for the original sin. As penance, he has his sons, Cain and Abel, offer a sacrifice. The voice of God accepts only Abel's sacrifice. Cain, enraged, listens to the voice of Lucifer and plots his brother's murder. Part II contains the homicide and God's punishment, followed by the lamentations of Adam and Eve. The work calls for six solo voices accompanied by string orchestra, sometimes doubled by winds (probably two oboes and bassoon) and basso continuo.

The use of disembodied voices (God and Lucifer) and the portrayal of a murder are two ways in which *Cain, ovvero Il primo Omidicio* differs from an Italian opera of this time. Another is its frequent interpolation of descriptive instrumental passages such as the one near the beginning of the excerpt in the

Anthology. It is described in the libretto as a "Sinfonia, which imitates the blows [delivered by Cain, and] then is stirred up with wind instruments, which imitate thunder."

On the other hand, the arias in *Cain, ovvero Il primo Omidicio* are all operatic in style, all in da capo form, and all representative of the expressive categories typical of *opera seria*. God's rage on discovering the murder is expressed in an *aria di bravura*, "Come mostro spaventevole" ("Like a frightening monster"). Cain sings of his remorse in "O preservame, per mia pena" (Oh, preserve me for my punishment"), an *aria patetica*. An *aria parlante*, "Vuò il castigo" ("I want punishment"), confirms God's resolve. Cain's aria "Bramo, insieme, e morte e vita" ("I desire, at the same time, death and life") is full of bizarre leaps and jarring cross relations, suggesting that he has become demon-ized. The voice of Lucifer urges Cain to rebel in a typically forceful and expansive bass aria, "Nel poter il Nume immita" ("In power, imitate God"), replete with arpeggios and fanfare figures. Finally, Cain bids his parents farewell in another *aria patetica*, "Miei genitori, addio" ("My parents, farewell"). Scarlatti's oratorio uses arias, ariosos, and accompanied recitatives to portray six distinct characters, who enact the biblical story for the edifica-tion and inspiration of the audience.

THE CHAMBER CANTATA

Like opera, the Italian chamber cantata experienced both wide diffusion and a trend toward standardization during the period 1690–1720. The center from which the genre spread was Rome. Alessandro Scarlatti was by far the most prolific and influential composer of chamber cantatas during these decades. He wrote most of his known cantatas (about six hundred) in the service of Cardi-nals Ottoboni and Pamphili in Rome and for the meetings of the Accademia degli Arcadi in the same city. Most of these works survive in a dozen or so copies preserved in libraries all over Europe. Giovanni Bononcini, another member of the Accademia degli Arcadi, composed about half of his 320 extant cantatas while in the service of Filippo Colonna in Rome, 1691–97. In 1705 François Raguenet declared that more than two hundred of his cantatas were known in Paris by that year. Likewise, George Frideric Handel composed eighty-seven of his cantatas for Marquis Francesco Maria Ruspoli, 1707–09, and other Roman patrons, including Cardinals Pamphili and Ottoboni or the Accademia degli Arcadi.

At this time, cantatas continued to be performed at social occasions by pro-fessional opera singers or by the noble patron. The Sicilian Baron Emanuele d'Astorga (1680–?1751) began composing cantatas in Rome under the influ-ence of Cardinal Ottoboni but continued to write and sing them—about 250 in all—at his various residences in Barcelona, Lisbon, Vienna, and Palermo. Antonio Caldara helped spread the genre from Rome to Venice and Vienna. In

Bologna, Giacomo Perti (1661–1756) left over 140 cantatas, while Giovanni Battista Bassani (ca.1650–1716) published thirteen volumes of them between 1680 and 1713. In Naples, next to Scarlatti the most prolific cantata composer was Francesco Mancini (1672–1737), who left 206 of them for solo voice. In the generation born after 1680, it appears that nearly every composer of Italian opera also wrote chamber cantatas.

The 1690s brought standardization to the chamber cantata. Whereas Scarlatti's earliest cantatas (1672–84) may have up to twelve or more sections, not always clearly defined, and more arias in ABB' form than in da capo form (ABA), the vast majority of them after 1690 have only two or three arias, each preceded by a recitative. By about 1705 the pattern in most composers' cantatas settled into the pattern recitative—aria—recitative—aria, sometimes with arioso transitions between the recitatives and the arias. The majority of these works are written for one voice, most often soprano, with basso continuo accompaniment. A considerable minority of them are written for two voices, and a much smaller number employ ensemble instruments, until about 1730, when the generation of Scarlatti's Neapolitan students introduced a new type of cantata with string-ensemble accompaniment.

The arias in Italian chamber cantatas of the period 1690–1720 are almost invariably cast in da capo form and are not strophic. The expansion and elaboration of da capo form in cantatas generally follows the same path taken by opera arias, except that the ritornellos tend to be shorter, because they are limited to the basso continuo. All the standard types of opera aria are also found in cantatas, but with noticeable restrictions of the most difficult bravura features; long and rapid ornamental melismas, wide leaps, and the like are rare in cantatas.

The text of an Italian chamber cantata of the period 1690–1720 normally consists of words sung by an unnamed shepherd in the Arcadia of Greek mythology, and the subject is most often his unrequited love. As in earlier cantatas, the narrative, dramatic, and lyric modes may be used in a single cantata text, but now the arias set only lyric poetry in rhymed, metrical verse, almost never narrative or dramatic text, which now usually has the form of *versi sciolti* and is set as recitative. Occasionally the narration makes it clear that the words of two different personages are contained in a cantata text. Unless the two personages sing a duet, it is understood that the words of both are sung by one and the same singer. In this way it becomes clear that dramatic and lyrical texts are framed and subsumed by the narrative. The purpose of the text is to define a range of subtly differentiated emotions and literary conceits.

Alessandro Scarlatti's *Il genio di Mitilde* ("The whimsy of Mitilde," dated May 28, 1711, in the autograph) will serve as an example (A. 118). The text, given below, is narrative in the *versi sciolti* (lines 1–7, 16–28) and lyrical in the rhymed and metrical arias (lines 8–15, 29–32). The defining difference in content between the narrative and lyrical text is the emotional level and the use of the subjunctive in the second aria to express a wish.

Alessandro Scarlatti, *Il genio di Mitilde* (May 28, 1711)

1 Il genio di Mitilde,	The whimsy of Mitilde:
2 mente non v'è che penetrar si vanti.	no mind can boast of penetrating it.
3 Si strani, ella hà i pensier, si vari i passi	She has such strange thoughts, such odd
4 che rende stanchi, e lassi	tangents, that they tire and exhaust
5 gli arditi spirti à secondarla intendi.	the daring spirits who try to follow her.
6 Ah che tant'oltre chi poggiar mai crede.	Ah, how much beyond capture!
7 D'onde pria si partì, tornar si vede.	Whence before you left, you see yourself return.
8 Tante il mar non hà procelle,	The sea has not as many storms,
9 tante in Ciel non sono stelle	heaven has not as many stars
10 quante voglie	as Mitilde has desires
11 hà Miltilde nel suo cor.	in her heart.
12 Mite allorché più accarezza	Gentle at first, while she caresses,
13 tutta sdegno poi disprezza,	then, all scorn, she despises.
14 dona, e toglie	She gives and takes away,
15 quando vuole, e speme, e Amor.	when she wishes, both hope and love.
16 Ella muove talor per vie romite	She moves, at times, along solitary paths,
17 solinga i passi	alone,
18 a repirar tra i boschi	to withdraw among the woods.
19 poi sdegnando le selve, e gl'antri foschi	Then, leaving the forests and the dark caves,
20 più ameni soggiorni	for more amusing sojourns,
21 volge le piante à viver lieti i giorni	she leaves the bushes to live happy days.
22 uindi altera, e vezzosa in ricche spoglie	Then, proud and charming, richly dressed,
23 pompa di sua bellezza	she makes her own beauty
24 l guardo altrui si rende.	noticed by others.
25 ortese d'ogni cor gl'ossequi prende	Charmingly, she wins every heart;
26 olce canta, favella, e scherza, e ride,	she sweetly sings, speaks, jokes, laughs.
27 mà allor che di speranza i cuori ingombra,	But while she fills hearts with hope,
28 toglie fuggendo di speranza ogn'ombra.	she flees, removing every shadow of hope.
29 Così d'Amor lo strale fugga	Thus may he flee Love's arrow
30 chi vuol goder tranquilla pace.	whoever would enjoy tranquil peace,
31 Che il dardo suo fatale uccide	since his fatal dart kills
32 col piacer che alletta, e piace.	with pleasure that entices and pleases.

Scarlatti sets the indented rhymed, metrical, lyrical texts as da capo arias. The remaining narrative *versi sciolti* are set as recitative, except that the music for the last sentence in each block of *versi sciolti* (lines 7 and 22–28) contains elements of arioso style. This elevates the emotional interpretation given those sentences, which are summary and transitional in function.

As usual, the meaning of the text in Scarlatti's recitative is projected and clarified by musical parallels to spoken delivery. Thus, for example, his setting of the first sentence yields approximately the following interpretation: "The *whimsy* of Mitilde: no *mind* can boast of *penetrating* it." It is at this time that Scarlatti and his contemporaries begin to use harmonic disjunction after a cadence in order to announce a new line of thought. Examples of this are the first-inversion triads (6 chords) after the conclusions of the first two sentences. Quite often in such cases the bass rises by chromatic half step to form the leading tone of an applied dominant, as in measure 4. If anything, Scarlatti's recitatives in the cantatas are more detailed and nuanced than they are in his operas.

The arioso sections of *Il genio di Mitilde* afford Scarlatti the opportunity to employ musical invention in order to clothe an entire sentence of text in a single emotion. In bars 19–27, for example, he introduces a confused, hurried, helter-skelter bass line beneath the words "before you left, you see yourself return."

Scarlatti develops that bass line into something related but distinct in the first aria, where it illustrates the dramatic image of the storm and a more general suggestion of something overwhelming, like the number of stars in the sky, which could inspire bewilderment. In part B of the aria, he gives the bass a back-and-forth motion, suggesting the concept of fickleness, which could be associated with the feeling of insecurity.

A third variant of the bass line is found in both the bass and vocal lines of the second aria. It would appear that the new variant of the bass line was intended to illustrate the image related to the verb *fuga* ("flee"), which could help to evoke anxiety. A similar melodic configuration is found in the arioso phrase immediately preceding the second aria, where it is used to set the word *fuggendo* ("fleeing").

Thus the two arias and two arioso passages in Scarlatti's *Il genio di Mitilde* are unified by similar passagework. Since variants of this passagework can help promote the related affects of confusion, bewilderment, insecurity, and anxiety, they contribute to the cantata's overall unity. Musical and affective unity of this kind can be found elsewhere among Scarlatti's cantatas and those of his contemporaries, but not in contemporaneous opera.

The vocal periods in the first aria in Scarlatti's *Il genio di Mitilde* are of the Fortspinnung type, as is normal in the da-capo arias in operas, cantatas, and other vocal genres of the decades between 1690 and 1730. The second aria in this cantata is interesting in that only the first ritornello has the form of a Fortspinnung period. The remaining five vocal periods in this aria would be classified as belonging to the *Lied* ("song") type, because they are divided into unequal segments called *Vordersatz* ("antecedent") and *Nachsatz* ("consequent") and contain no sequences.

The *Lied*-type of period is relatively uncommon in the music of Scarlatti's generation, but it becomes the dominant type in the arias of the post-Baroque opera and cantata composers of the younger generation such as Porpora,Vinci, and Hasse. Composers of this generation also tended to replace the pattern recitative—aria—recitative—aria, standardized by Scarlatti, with the pattern aria—recitative—aria. These composers were among the last to write Italian chamber cantatas, since the aristocratic gatherings and ceremonial meetings of academies were gradually replaced by public concerts, where opera scenes became the favored vocal fare.

LATIN CHURCH MUSIC

The same wide variety of instrumental and vocal genres and styles described earlier continued to be heard in Italian churches up to the end of the period treated in this chapter—plain chant, often with organ accompaniment; organ versets, toccatas, and ricercars; strict-style settings of liturgical and motet texts for one or two choirs with organ; concerted settings of liturgical and motet texts for solo voices and choir with instruments. In Italian churches, for the first time in the history of Western music, works by composers of earlier generations continued to be performed. The more elaborate and modern genres and styles were heard in churches with greater resources, those that served the nobility, and those that represented the prestige of a large city; they continued to be heard even in modest urban or rural monastic churches on special days, such as the feast of the patron saint. At the same time, even such a celebrated composer as Antonio Lotti continued to compose church music in strict style, or *stile antico*—with pervasive imitation and learned devices such as canon, rhythmic augmentation, and invertible counterpoint and without diminution or accompaniment by ensemble instruments—for such prestigious venues as San Marco in Venice and the chapel of the electoral court in Dresden.

The practice of using non-liturgical vocal music and instrumental works in place of Proper and Ordinary items in the Mass and antiphons in Vespers and Compline continued and even expanded at the churches and on the days where the more complex and modern music was heard. At the end of this period, in 1749, Pope Benedict XIV complained that "on certain days of the year, sacred buildings are the theater for sumptuous and resounding concerts, which in no way agree with the Sacred Mysteries, which the Church, precisely on those days, offers for the veneration of the faithful."

A typical Venetian concerted Mass at the time of Legrenzi (the 1670s) consisted of a Kyrie, Gloria, Credo, and brief Sanctus, but no Agnus Dei, because non-liturgical motets and instrumental music filled all the time from the Offertory or Elevation to the end of the Mass, just as it did at the Chapelle Royale of Louis XIV in France. But by about 1700, a Venetian concerted Mass often included just the Kyrie and Gloria, leaving all the rest to the "sumptuous and resounding concerts" of which Pope Benedict XIV complained.

Connected with these "concerts," there were three main innovations in the style of concerted church music in Italy in the period from 1680 to 1720: (1) the introduction of concerto style in orchestrally accompanied choral works or movements; (2) the alternation of ritornellos with two or three vocal periods, with or without da capo, in orchestrally accompanied solo movements or works; and (3) the emergence of a standardized sequence of aria—recitative—aria—Alleluia in orchestrally accompanied motets for solo voice. All three innovations appeared first in northern Italy, principally Bologna and Venice, but rapidly spread to Rome and Naples. Since practically every composer of Italian opera seria wrote church works with these three features, these innovations spread throughout Europe wherever Italian opera was performed.

Concerto Style

Until about 1670, the instrumental parts in Italian concerted church music had essentially the same character and content as the vocal parts. That is, the instruments either responded antiphonally to the voices, doubled them, or mixed in with them in contrapuntal or homophonic textures, but in their rhythmic and melodic figures, motives, and general character, the instrumental parts were essentially the same as the vocal parts. The Kyrie of Cavalli's *Messa concertata* (W. 14) illustrates this. But beginning about 1680 one finds choral movements and works in which the orchestral parts are rhythmically and melodically independent of, even contrasting with, the vocal parts. In such choruses, the orchestral parts take on the characteristic motor rhythms, rapid repeated notes, and lively figuration typical of the emerging concerto, while the chorus often declaims the text syllabically and homophonically. It is not surprising that this process can be traced most easily in Bologna, where the essential style and formal procedure of the concerto first emerged.

We see this process, for example, in the printed works (1681–1694) of Giovanni Paolo Colonna (1637–1695), *maestro di cappella* from 1662 to 1695 of the basilica of San Petronio, where Giuseppe Torelli was a string player. It culminates in Colonna's *Messe e salmi concertati*, Op.10 (1691), in which elements of ritornello procedure also begin to appear.

This way of combining chorus and orchestra has often been ascribed incorrectly to "Neapolitan style church music," and Alessandro Scarlatti's St. Cecilia Mass of 1720 is frequently cited as the earliest example. But this feature is not found in any of Scarlatti's earlier Masses, while by 1720 it was already well established in the works of composers in Bologna and Venice. Francesco Durante (1684–1755), the Neapolitan composer often mentioned with Scarlatti as a pioneer in this style, did not embrace it until about 1740. It is true, however, that several important opera composers trained in Naples played a significant role in the spread of this style when they traveled around northern Europe.

Pitting the voices against an orchestra that loudly plays rapid figuration implies the use of a chorus, rather than an ensemble of soloists. Indeed, the basilica of San Petronio in Bologna had three to five salaried singers per part in 1687, but for major feast days the choir typically numbered about sixty-five, between thirteen and twenty singers per part. The orchestra on such occasions would include about ten violins, five violas, four violoncellos, and three double basses. At San Marco in 1714, the *cappella* had twelve sopranos, six altos, ten tenors, and eight basses, with a salaried string group of thirteen violins, seven violas, three cellos, and three double basses.

In connection with the new concerto texture, ritornello procedure emerges in the choral movements of sacred works by Antonio Vivaldi. A good example is found in the first chorus, "Gloria in excelsis Deo," of his Gloria with Intro-duction, RV 588 (A. 119), composed about 1717. The first tutti passage, bars 1–37, contains five distinct elements that recur in various forms throughout the work and help to define five orchestral ritornellos that enclose four vocal episodes. An outline is given on page 417.

Aria Patterns

By the end of the seventeenth century most Latin church works by Italians included regular arias. Arias are found in motets, Psalms, and Mass move-ments. Some of these arias, like the first one in Antonio Vivaldi's Gloria, conform to the operatic da capo form, but most instead have a recapitula-tion that includes a single vocal period or just the introductory instrumental ritornello. By the year 1700, full da-capo arias typically repeat two vocal periods, the first cadencing on the fifth degree, or third degree in minor keys, and the second cadencing on the tonic. Italian church arias that do not bring back two vocal periods in this fashion will typically have one of the following types of recaptiulation: (1) the first vocal period ends on the tonic and is brought back unchanged at the end; (2) only the introductory instru-mental ritornello, ending on the tonic, is brought back at the end, either in written-out form or cued by a sign or instruction such as "da capo"; or (3) the first vocal period ends with a cadence on the fifth or third degree of the overall key and is brought back at the end in a modified form, conclud-ing on the tonic.

Church arias with recapitulations of one of these three types normally consist of a series of instrumental ritornellos that frame a series of vocal periods, just as in da-capo arias. But in church arias, the number of vocal periods and ritornellos is not standardized. In the first aria of the solo motet *Ite Molles* of 1701 (A. 120) by Francesco Antonio Bonporti (1672–1749), the first vocal period (mm. 3–18) ends with a cadence on the fifth degree of the key. This period is brought back (mm. 40–54) at the end in modified form; the music of mm. 15–18 returns in mm. 48–54 extended and transposed upward by a fourth so as to cadence on the tonic. In between, there is an extended vocal period (mm. 21–38) that cadences on the sixth degree. Other Italian church arias of this time might have two or

An outline of Antonio Vivaldi, "Gloria in excelsis Deo" from his Gloria with Introduction, RV 588 of ca. 1717 (Anthology 153)

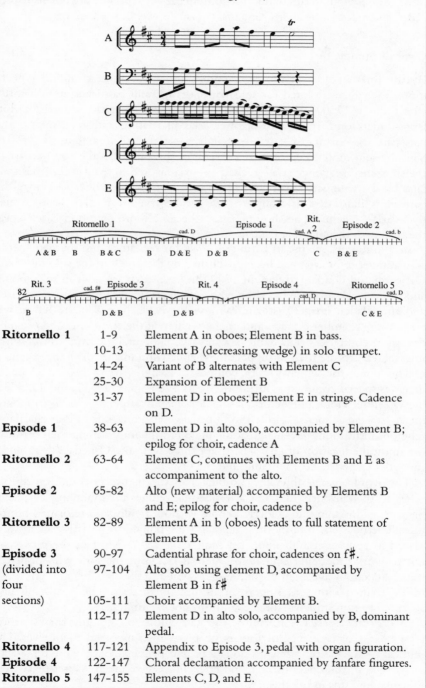

Ritornello 1	1–9	Element A in oboes; Element B in bass.
	10–13	Element B (decreasing wedge) in solo trumpet.
	14–24	Variant of B alternates with Element C
	25–30	Expansion of Element B
	31–37	Element D in oboes; Element E in strings. Cadence on D.
Episode 1	38–63	Element D in alto solo, accompanied by Element B; epilog for choir, cadence A
Ritornello 2	63–64	Element C, continues with Elements B and E as accompaniment to the alto.
Episode 2	65–82	Alto (new material) accompanied by Elements B and E; epilog for choir, cadence b
Ritornello 3	82–89	Element A in b (oboes) leads to full statement of Element B.
Episode 3	90–97	Cadential phrase for choir, cadences on f♯.
(divided into	97–104	Alto solo using element D, accompanied by Element B in f♯
four		
sections)	105–111	Choir accompanied by Element B.
	112–117	Element D in alto solo, accompanied by B, dominant pedal.
Ritornello 4	117–121	Appendix to Episode 3, pedal with organ figuration.
Episode 4	122–147	Choral declamation accompanied by fanfare fingures.
Ritornello 5	147–155	Elements C, D, and E.

three vocal periods in this middle section. All the vocal periods are normally preceded and followed by an instrumental ritornello, even if it is very brief.

Overall Structure

By the early decades of the eighteenth century, the most common type of motet in Italy was scored for solo voice, strings, and basso continuo. Shortly after the year 1700, composers of the post-Scarlatti generation standardized its large-dimension form of two or three arias alternating with recitatives in the pattern: aria—recitative—aria—(recitative—aria)—Alleluia. Nearly all of Vivaldi's solo motets conform to a variant of this plan. It is the counterpart of the shortened sequence aria—recitative—aria favored in secular chamber cantatas by the younger Italian composers at this time. The longer variant of the pattern is illustrated in Bonporti's *Ite molles*: aria—recitative—aria—recitative—aria—Alleluia. The shorter pattern became more common later, as was the case with the chamber cantata.

In solo motets, the use of Latin *versi sciolti* for recitatives and rhymed, metrical Latin verse for arias had been established by the 1660s in the solo motets of Carissimi and Gratiani. By about 1700 the Latin texts for arias in solo motets and larger works include the same range of affects (joy, sorrow, tenderness, etc.) and affect-laden imagery (storm, calm, victory, etc.) found in the Italian aria texts of the chamber cantatas and operas written at the same time and often by the same composers. The same vocabulary of naturalistic and conventional musical features are used to support these affects and images in all three genres.

The venue for which Vivaldi composed a large part of his sacred music deserves special comment. During the years 1703–09, 1711–17, and 1735–38, he was either violin instructor (*maestro di violino*) or supervisor of instrumental music (*maestro de' concerti*) at the Pio Ospedale della Pietà, one of four charitable religious institutions in Venice that included prominently among their missions the musical education of girls. The other three were the Ospedale de' Mendicanti, the Ospedale de' Incurabili, and the Ospedaletto.

The word *ospedale* (literally, "hospital") in the names of these institutions refers to their historic function as residential refuges for foundlings, orphans, beggars, widows, invalids, elderly people without family, and reformed prostitutes. The boys taken in by these *ospedali* were trained to be artisans and were placed in apprenticeships upon reaching adolescence. Most of the girls were put to work producing craft items, such as lace. But the girls who displayed musical talent by age eight or nine were assigned to the *coro* (literally, "chorus"), to be trained either as singers or as instrumentalists. The Incurabili also accepted tuition students, some even from noble families.

Two of the *ospedali* were run by the state, and two were governed by their own boards of laymen. But the music programs supported themselves. The musical performances attracted donations and bequests. Seats were rented for services, as in the opera theater, and collections were taken. Motet texts were sold, like librettos in the theater.

A member of the *coro* could retire at age forty, although some stayed on. At the Pietà, girls who reached adulthood could marry with a dowry of 150 ducats. Upon being accepted into the *coro*, girls had to promise not to enter the music profession outside the *ospedale*.

Beginners studied with older girls, advanced students with adult members or outside teachers. A young woman could become a *sottomaestra* ("assistant instructor") at twenty-four and a *maestra* at thirty. Each division, vocal and instrumental, was headed by its own female *maestra*. Although a male *maestro di coro* headed the whole establishment, his activities were monitored and evaluated by the two female *maestre*.

The *maestro di coro* at the Pietà was required to compose two Masses and two Vespers each year, two motets each month, and other works as required. During Vivaldi's lifetime, the *maestri di coro* at the Pietà were Francesco Gasparini, Carlo Luigi Pietragrua, Giovanni Poreta, Gennaro D'Alessandro, Nicola Porpora, and Andrea Bernasconi—all of them well-known composers. Although Vivaldi's position did not normally require composition, he wrote nearly all of his concertos and much of his sacred vocal music for the girls of the Pietà, especially when there was no *maestro di coro* currently under contract.

At most times and places in Catholic Europe during the Early Modern Era, St. Paul's admonition (I Cor 14:34) that women should be silent in church was interpreted to mean that women should not be heard by men in church, but they could be heard by other women or by men who were not in the same church. Cloistered nuns in many convents, separated by grillwork, performed and composed music. A similar system was used in the *ospedali* of Venice, in which the girls sang in a gallery, separated from the rest of the church by a grill.

It is clear that men did not sing in the choirs of the *ospedali*. The choruses composed for Ospedaletto and the Incurabili are scored SSAA. But the choruses composed for the Mendicanti and Pietà, including Vivaldi's are notated SATB. Although some evidence indicates that occasionally there were women in these choirs who could sing in the tenor and bass ranges, there is more reason to conclude that in most cases the tenor and bass parts were sung an octave higher. When the bass part is written more than an octave below the alto part, this form of transposition does not invert the harmonies, and the cellos and double basses of the orchestra double the vocal bass in the lower octaves. Nicola Porpora scored his sacred works for the Incurabili and the Ospedaletto SSAA but later revised them for mixed choir by transposing the first soprano voice to the tenor range and dropping the alto part to the bass octave.

By the end of the Baroque era, then, Latin church music, like the oratorio and chamber cantata, shared many features of style and expression with opera, which had become the predominant vocal genre in Italy. Still, the motets, Psalms, Magnificats, and Masses of Vivaldi's generation retained distinguishing features, such as non–da-capo aria forms and concerto-like choruses, that influenced composers all over northern Europe and formed the basis for further development in sacred musical genres for generations afterward.

420

BIBLIOGRAPHICAL NOTES

The Neoclassical Reform of Italian Opera, ca. 1680–1706
The most thorough study of this subject is Harris Sheridan Saunders, Jr., "The Repertoire of a Venetian Opera House (1678–1714): The Teatro Grimani di San Giovanni Grisostomo," Ph.D. diss., Harvard Univ., 1985. Robert Freeman, "Apostolo Zeno's Reform of the Libretto," *Journal of the American Musicological Society*, 21 (1968), 321–341, is an excellent study. Patterns of change in revisions and remakes of librettos are the subject of a series of articles by Harold S. Powers, including "*L'Erismena travestita*," *Studies in Music History Essays for Oliver Strunk*, ed. Harold S. Powers (Princeton: Princeton University Press, 1968), pp. 259–324; "*Il Mutio tramutato*, Part I: Sources and Libretto," *Venezia e il melodramma nel seicento*, ed. Maria Teresa Muraro, Studi di musica veneta, 5 (Florence: Olschki, 1976), pp. 227–258; and "*Il Serse trasformato*," *The Musical Quarterly*, 47 (1961), 481–92 and (1962), 73–92. A useful overview of libretto reform is Nathaniel Burt, "Opera in Arcadia," *The Musical Quarterly*, 41 (1955), 145–70. The standard book on Scarlatti's operas is Donald Jay Grout, *Alessandro Scarlatti: An Introduction to His Operas* (Berkeley: University of California Press, 1979). The major study of Pollarolo is Olga Termini, "Carlo Francesco Pollarolo: His Life, Time, and Music with Emphasis on the Operas," Ph.D. diss., Univ. of Southern California, 1970. The spread of Italian opera in northern Europe is treated in several of the essays in Reinhard Strohm, ed., *The Eighteenth-Century Diaspora of Italian Music and* Musicians (Turnhout: Brepols, 2001).

"A Perfect Spiritual Melodramma": The Italian Oratorio, ca. 1680–1730
The general guide is Howard E. Smither, *A History of the Oratorio*, I, *The Oratorio in the Baroque Era: Italy, Vienna, Paris* (Chapel Hill, NC: University of North Carolina Press, 1977). There are several detailed studies of oratorio production in specific Italian cities: Denis Arnold and Elsie Arnold, *The Oratorio in Venice*, Royal Musical Association Monographs, 2 (London: Royal Musical Association, 1986); Arnaldo Morelli, *Il tempio armonico: musica nell'Oratorio dei Filippini in Roma (1575–1705)*, Analecta musicologica, 27 (Laaber: Laaber-Verlag, 1991); Victor Crowther, *The Oratorio in Modena* (Oxford: Clarendon Press, 1992); Victor Crowther, *The Oratorio in Bologna (1650–1730)* (Oxford: Oxford University Press, 1999); John Walter Hill, "Oratory Music in Florence," *Acta Musicologica*, 51 (1979), 108–36, 246–67; and 58 (1986), 129–79. Studies of oratorios by individual composers include David George Poultney, "The Oratorios of Alessandro Scarlatti: Their Lineage, Milieu and Style," Ph.D. diss., Univ. of Michigan, 1968; Ursula Kirkendale, *Antonio Caldara: Sein Leben und seine venezianisch-römischen Oratorien*, Wiener musikwissenschaftliche Beiträge, 6 (Graz: Germann Böhlaus, 1966); and Egils Ozolins, "The Oratorios of Bernardo Pasquini," Ph.D. diss., University of California, Los Angeles, 1987.

Chamber Cantata
There is no book-length treatment of the Italian chamber cantata in its late phase, 1680–1730. Gloria Rose, "The Italian Cantata of the Baroque Period," *Gattungen der Musik in Einzeldarstellungen: Gedenkschrift Leo Schrade*, ed. Wulf Arlt, et al (Bern: Francke, 1973), pp. 655–77, is very brief. The most useful studies are the chapters on the cantatas in books devoted to single composers: Ellen T. Harris, *Handel as Orpheus: Voice and Desire in the Chamber Cantatas* (Cambridge, MA: Harvard University Press, 2001); Michael Talbot, *Tomaso Albinoni: the Venetian Composer*

and his World (Oxford: Oxford University Press, 1990), pp. 115–43; Talbot, *Benedetto Vinaccesi: A Musician in Brescia and Venice in the Age of Corelli* (Oxford: Oxford University Press, 1994), pp. 156–87; Lawrence E. Bennett, "The Italian Cantata in Vienna, 1700–1711: An Overview of Stylistic Traits," *Antonio Caldara: Essays on his Life and Times*, ed. Brian W. Pritchard (Aldershot: Scholar, 1987), pp. 184–211; Colin Timms, "The Dramatic in Vivaldi's Cantatas," *Antonio Vivaldi: teatro musicale, cultura e società*, ed. Lorenzo Bianconi and Giovanni Morelli (Florence: Olschki, 1982), pp. 97–129. Concerning the cantatas of Alessandro Scarlatti, the central figure in this phase of the genre's history, there are two doctoral dissertations: Brian Alan Daw, "Alessandro Scarlatti's Cantatas for Solo Soprano and Continuo, 1708–1717," Ph.D. diss., Univ. of Southern California, 1984; and Edwin Hanley, "Alessandro Scarlatti's *Cantate da camera*: A Bibliographical Study," Ph.D. diss, Yale Univ., 1963.

Latin Church Music

There is no adequate general treatment of Latin church music in Italy during the period 1680–1730. An overview can be found in Otto Ursprung, *Die katholische Kirchenmusik*, Handbuch der Musikwissenschaft, 9 (Potsdam: Akademische Verlagsgesellschaft Athenaion, 1931). Several dissertations make partial inroads: Mary Nicole [i.e., Anne] Schnoebelen, "The Concerted Mass at San Petronio in Bologna, ca. 1660-1730: A documentary and Analytical Study," Ph.D. diss., Univ. of Illinois, 1966; Marc Vanscheeuwijck, "De religieuze muziekproduktie in de San Petronio-kerk te Bologna ten tijde van Giovanni Paolo Colonna (1674–1695): Een onderzoek naar culturele, historische, liturgische en muzikale aspekten uit de Bolognese Hoog-Barok," Ph.D. diss., Univ. of Ghent, 1995; William Michael Hienz, Jr., "The Choral Psalms of Nicola Porpora," D. M. A. diss., Univ. of Illinois, 1980; Gilbert Ambrose Brungardt, "Some Selected Motets of Francesco Durante," D. M. A. diss., Univ. of Illinois, 1967; Paul Allen Brankvik, "Selected Motets of Alessandro Scarlatti," D. M. A. diss., Univ. of Illinois, 1969. Some background to Scarlatti's church music is sketched by Hanns-Bertold Dietz, "Sacred Music in Naples During the Second Half of the Seventeenth Century," *La musica a Napoli durante il seicento*, ed. Domenico Antonio D'Alessandro and Agostino Ziino, Miscellanea musicologica, 2 (Rome: Torre d'Orfeo 1987), pp. 511–27. Vivaldi's church music and its context is masterfully treated by Michael Talbot, *The Sacred Vocal Music of Antonio Vivaldi*, Studi di musica veneta, Quaderni vivaldiani, 8 (Florence: Olschki, 1995). The Venetian *ospedali* are studied by Jane L. Baldauf-Berdes, *Women Musicians of Venice: Musical Foundations, 1525–1855* (Oxford: Clarendon Press, 1993). The problem of SATB scoring for female choirs is tackled by Joan Margaret Whittemore, CSJ, "Revision of Music Performed at the Venetian *ospedali* in the Eighteenth Century," D. M. A. diss., Univ. of Illinois, 1986.

Opera seria

A recent treatment of this genre is Melania Bucciarelli, *Italian Opera and European Theatre, 1680–1720: Plots, Performers, Dramaturgies* (Turnhout: Brepols, 2000). The collection of essays by Reinhard Strohm, *Dramma per musica: Italian Opera seria of the Eighteenth Century* (New Haven, CT: Yale University Press, 1997), provides many useful perspectives. The social, cultural, and material context of Italian opera in this period is explored by several authors in *Opera Production and Its Resources*, ed. Lorenzo Bianconi and Giorgio Pestelli, trans. Lydia G. Cochrane, The History of Italian Opera, Part II, vol. 4 (Chicago: University of Chicago Press,

1987). Several collections of opera seria scene designs have been published in modern times; the best guide to staging practices remains Theon Reading McClure, "A Reconstruction of Theatrical and Musical Practice in the Production of Italian Opera in the Eighteenth Century," Ph.D. diss., Ohio State Univ., 1956. The everyday details of opera production from the perspective of the impresario are revealed through the correspondence of Luca Casimiro degli Albizzi (1664–1745) in William C. Holmes, *Opera Observed: Views of a Florentine Impresario in the Early Eighteenth Century* (Chicago: University of Chicago Press, 1993). A standard study of Handel's operas, useful as a reference tool, is Winton Dean and J. Merrill Knapp, *Handel's Operas, 1704–1726*, rev. ed. (Oxford: Clarendon Books, 1995). Reinhard Strohm, *Essays on Handel and Italian Opera* (Cambridge: Cambridge University Press, 1985), approaches the subject through a selection of topics and issues.

"The Doctrine of the Affections"

The best survey in English of the philosophical writings is found in Rosamond Drooker Brenner, "The Operas of Reinhard Keiser and Their Relationship to the *Affektenlehre*," Ph.D. diss., Brandeis Univ., 1968. An older summary of the musical writings is Frederick T. Wessel, "The *Affektenlehre* in the 18th Century," Ph.D. diss., Indiana Univ., 1955. Mattheson's writings on the subject are translated by Hans Lenneberg, "Johann Mattheson on Affect and Rhetoric in Music," *Journal of Music Theory*, II (1958), 47–84 and 193–236. Mattheson's role in this area is analyzed by George J. Buelow, "Johann Mattheson and the Invention of the *Affektenlehre*," *New Mattheson Studies*, ed. George J. Buelow and Han Joachim Marx (Cambridge: Cambridge University Press, 1983), pp. 393–407. Johann David Heinichen's discussion of musical invention in the composer's reaction to opera libretti is translated by George J. Buelow, "The *Loci Topici* and Affect in Late Baroque Music: Heinichen's Practical Demonstration," *The Music Review*, XXVII (1966), 161–176.

The eighteenth-century treatises cited in Example 14–2 are:

Mattheson (1739)	Johann Mattheson, *Der vollkommene Capellmeister* (Hamburg: Christian Herold, 1739), trans. Ernest C. Harriss (Ann Arbor: UMI Research Press, 1981).
Quantz (1752)	Johann Joachim Quantz, *Versuch einer Anweisung, die Flöte traversiere zu spielen* (Berlin: Johann Friedrich Voss, 1752), trans. Edward R. Reilly, as *On Playing the Flute* (London: Faber and Faber, 1966).
Grassineau (1740)	James Grassineau, *A Musical Dictionary* (London: J. Wilcox, 1740), in part a translation of Sébastien de Brossard, *Dictionnaire de musique* (Paris: Ballard, 1703), but not in the material on musical affects.
Marpurg (1762)	Friedrich Wilhelm Marpurg, "Unterricht von Recitative," *Kritische Briefe über die Tonkunst* (Berlin: Birnstiel, 1762), pp. 262–416.
Rameau (1722)	Jean-Philippe Rameau, *Traité de l'harmonie réduite à ses principes naturels* (Paris: Ballard, 1722), trans. Philip Gossett as *Treatise on Harmony* (New York: Dover, 1971).
Kirnberger (1782)	Johann Philipp Kirnberger, *Anleitung zur Singekomposition* (Berlin: George Jacob Decker, 1782).

CHAPTER 15

French Music from the War of the Grand Alliance to the End of the Regency

FRANCE DECLINES IN THE THEATER OF EUROPE

During the 1680s a series of events combined to bring about important changes in French theater music. Political events led to a decline in the power and wealth of France and to some slippage in the French monarchy's centralized control over the arts. Events in the life of Louis XIV contributed to some of these political changes and to the king's dissociation from musical theater. Events in the musical world also played a role in bringing about changes.

The high water in the fortunes of France and Louis XIV arrived about 1680. France, with the help of England, was victorious in the Dutch War (1672–78) against Spain, the Holy Roman Empire, and Holland. This war, which was fought over territory in the Spanish Netherlands, was referred to allegorically by Lully's *Alceste* (1674). In the Treaties of Nimjegen (1678), France gained several strategic cities along its northern frontier. In 1679, France obtained further territory and concessions through a series of treaties with the Holy Roman Empire, Brandenburg, and Denmark. This marked the furthest extent of European dominions that France ever gained in its history. Afterward the fortunes of France began to recede.

In 1683, the death of Jean-Baptiste Colbert deprived the nation of the architect of the economic development that made it the dominant power in Europe. In 1685, acquiescing to pressure from the Catholic Church and his own growing religious zeal, Louis XIV revoked the Edict of Nantes by which Protestants had enjoyed some measure of religious freedom in France. More than four hundred thousand Protestant Huguenots emigrated to England, Prussia, Holland, and America, depriving France of a large number of its commercial entrepreneurs. This move particularly alienated England, and, after the deposition of the Catholic James II and the accession of Louis's old enemy William of Orange, Great Britain changed from France's friend to her enemy. Thus, when Louis attempted further territorial expansion, he was stopped in the War of the Grand Alliance (1689–97) by England, the United Provinces of the Netherlands, and the Holy Roman Empire. The same alliance opposed

France in the War of the Spanish Succession (1701–14), by which Louis attempted to win Spain and its dominions and colonies for his grandson Philip, later Philip V of Spain, without excluding him from the line of succession to the throne of France. The war ended with the Peace of Utrecht (1713) and two further treaties, leaving Spain with Philip on the throne but deprived of its European dominions, and Louis's desire for the union of France and Spain under one king was thwarted.

The losses and stalemates in these wars also weakened the position of Louis XIV at home. He began to withdraw from public events, no longer dancing in his court spectacles, often not even attending them. After the death of Anne of Austria in 1683, Louis's second wife, Françoise d'Aubigné, marquise de Maintenon, encouraged his turn toward religion and discouraged the production of theatrical spectacles. Jean-Baptiste Lully, the dictator of French opera and friend of Louis XIV since boyhood, died in 1687. In 1697, Madame de Maintenon wrote to a friend, "A taste for pleasure is extinguished in the king's heart. Age and devotion have taught him to reflect seriously on the vanity and emptiness of everything he formerly loved. He makes some progress in the ways of God every day. It is not without reluctance that he attends theaters and festivities." Musical spectacles were now no longer staged at Versailles, but only at the country palaces of Fontainebleau and Marly.

As a consequence of these developments, the production of French opera and other forms of musical spectacle became decentralized about the turn of the eighteenth century. At Versailles, musical productions were organized by other members of the royal family. Two of Louis's younger grandsons built opera theaters in their own palaces. Louis's illegitimate son Louis-Auguste de Bourbon, duc du Maine, and his wife produced lavish musical spectacles at their chateau in Sceaux. Opera also spread to locations far from Paris. In 1683, Lully, the holder of a royal monopoly, granted Pierre Gautier permission to perform operas in Marseilles. After Lully's death, his heirs licensed opera companies in Lyons, Montpellier, Grenoble, Dijon, Chalon, Avignon, Toulouse, and Bordeaux. Performances of Lully's operas also were staged in Rennes, Rouen, Lunéville, Nancy, Metz, Lille, and Strasbourg. Louis XIV had nothing to do with these productions, and even at his own court, he no longer chose the subjects of operas. By about 1690 the function of musical theater as an instrument of statecraft was no longer centrally controlled by the French monarchy.

Upon his death in 1715, Louis XIV was succeeded by his great-grandson, since his eldest son and grandson predeceased him. Since Louis XV was only five years old when he became king, until 1723 France was ruled by a regent, Philippe II, duc d'Orléans, a nephew of Louis XIV. By a provision of his will, Louis XIV also gave roles in the new government to two of his illegitimate sons. Hence, the authority and initiative of the French central government was weakened during the Regency (1715–23).

ITALIAN MUSIC: RAPPROCHEMENT AND RESISTANCE

In previous chapters we saw that Italian music and musical style had political meaning in France from the time of Catherine de' Medici, queen mother and the chief architect of the *Balet comique de la Royne* in 1589. Italian influence intensified when Marie de' Medici reigned as the queen consort of Henry IV (1600–10) and regent (1610–14) for her son, Louis XIII. It was for her wedding that the first surviving opera, *L'Euridice*, was performed in Florence in 1600 and it was she who brought the Caccini family to Paris. Italian music became even more significant while Cardinal Mazarin was prime minister (1642–61) and de facto regent during the minority of Louis XIV. It was he who attempted to introduce Italian opera to the French court.

Among the nobility of Paris, there had been curiosity and interest in Italian music during the second half of the seventeenth century, but largely in the area of church music. A priest and musical amateur named Nicolas Mathieu amassed a library of some two hundred volumes of Italian sacred vocal music from the second half of the seventeenth century and presented weekly performances of this repertoire at his lodgings while he was abbot of Saint-André-des-Arts, 1681–1706. Henry Du Mont based his innovative *grands motets* on Italian models, and the music directors at the Sainte-Chapelle, notably including Marc-Antoine Charpentier (1643–1704), composed in an Italianate style, modeling their works on Carissimi.

The death of Lully in 1687 and the withdrawal of Louis XIV from active participation in opera production opened the way for exploration of Italian style in French musical spectacle. But Lully's operas continued to be performed regularly, and most new French operas for the rest of the seventeenth and first half of the eighteenth century continued the Lully tradition. The continuation of Lullian opera represented the preservation of the political and cultural status quo desired by the upper ranks of the French nobility. They greeted with hostility stage works that included elements of Italian musical style. Although basically Lullian in style, Marc-Antoine Charpentier's *Médée* (1693), a masterpiece of this early Franco-Italian rapprochement, suffered from this hostility.

The libretto of Charpentier's *Médée* was written by Thomas Corneille (1625–1709), a playwright and brother of the more famous Pierre. It is based upon the ancient Greek myth dramatized in Euripides' tragedy *Medea*. Having helped Jason obtain the Golden Fleece and assassinate his usurping uncle, the sorceress Medea has fled with Jason to Corinth. Jason, however, has fallen in love with Creusa. In revenge, Medea kills Creusa with a poisoned robe and murders the children that she has had with Jason.

Both the text and music of *Médée* are powerfully dramatic. Charpentier's score derives its style from Lully's late *tragédies en musique*. However, the *divertissement* at the end of Act II (scene 7) contains an aria in Italian ("Chi teme d'amore") sung by "an Italian lady." Its Italian features are a recurring melisma, a motto beginning, and da capo form, up to the entry of the chorus ("Son gusti i dolori"). However, the aria begins as a continuation of a chaconne, without an introduction of its own, and Part A returns after the first entry of the chorus, forming a typically French rondeau pattern, ABACA. Other than the melisma, the melodic and rhythmic style of the aria could as well be French as Italian.

Far more Italian and certainly more dramatic is Medea's "C'en est fait" in Act IV, scene 4. It begins with a full orchestral introduction, the motives of which recur in several keys during the four successive ritornellos, something never previously found in a French operatic air. Throughout the aria, in both ritornellos and vocal periods, the bass is derived from the relentless, driving rhythm ♩♩♩ and its variants, encapsulating the reigning affect of the aria—vengeance. Thus Charpentier relied for affect on musical invention, as did Italian composers from Stradella onward. Even the form of this aria is Italian, although not from opera; it is the ritornello form typical of Italian solo motets, a genre very familiar to Charpentier.

The context of Medea's "C'en es fait" is supplied in the excerpt in W. 36. It contains the crux of the plot—Medea reflects upon Jason's infidelity, resolves to seek vengeance, and summons infernal demons to her aid. Her soliloquy "Quel prix de mon amour" (Act IV, scene 3) is set as a triple-meter arioso with five-part string accompaniment. Abrupt changes in tempo and meter reflect her conflicted state. After the dialogue with Nerina, in *récitatif ordinaire* with only continuo accompaniment, that frames her aria "C'en est fait," Medea, again alone on stage, summons the infernal demons ("Noires filles du Styx") with orchestrally accompanied *récitatif mesuré*, which Lully pioneered in his late *tragédies en musique*. *Récitatif mesuré* is more lyrical than *récitatif ordinaire*, it has regular meter, and it is meant to be performed in tempo. Charpentier used *récitatif mesuré* more often in this opera than Lully ever did in his. In this instance, the gruesome theme of the action is reflected in horrendous dissonances. The flowing interaction of chorus, solo singing, dance, and descriptive orchestral music that follows (scenes 6 and 7) is another feature modeled on Lully's *tragédies en musique*, which Charpentier uses here for a powerful theatrical effect.

Although Charpentier received praise and support from members of the royal family and from many leaders of informed opinion, his rapprochement with Italian style incited hostility from the more staunch conservatives who were dedicated to the preservation of Lully's stage works and strict adherence to their style. Typical expressions of this hostility are found among the published installments of the *Comparaison de le musique italienne et de la musique françoise* ("Comparison of Italian Music with French Music," 1704–06) by Jean Laurent Le Cerf de la Viéville, seigneur de Freneuse (1674–1707), Keeper of the Seals for the Parliament of Normandy. Le Cerf's *Comparaison* is a vitriolic and sarcastic reply to the pro-Italian *Paralèle des italiens et des françois, en ce qui regarde la musique et les opéra* ("Comparison of the Italians and the French as Regards Music and Opera," 1702) by the priest and physician François Raguenet (ca. 1660–1722). Le Cerf and other writers who opposed Italian influence generally find in French music beauty, calm, charm, delicacy, sweetness, elegance, reason, naturalness, nobility, regularity, and tenderness. In Italian music they discern brilliance, bizarreness, noise, heat, distortion, variety, excess, furor, licentiousness, striving, curiosity, agitation, and violence.

Most French stage works took a middle course between the warring pro- and anti-Italian factions. Typical in this respects is *L'Europe galante* (1697), an *opéra-ballet* by André Campra (1660–1744), a musician of Italian birth but French parentage who at this time was music director at Notre Dame Cathedral in Paris.

L'Europe galante is organized into five *entrées*, entitled "The Gallant Forges of Love," "France," "Spain," "Italy," and "Turkey." In the first *entrée* Discord boasts that he has banished Cupid "from turbulent Europe, at least, if not from the entire world." Venus responds that in spite of war, Cupid "joins two hearts who one day will shape the earth's destiny; the Hero who joins them is starting to untie the knot you fashioned with evil care." Discord understands her meaning and replies, "Do not force me to hear praise of a king who detests you." But Venus prevails, and each of the following *entrées* contains a love scene set in one of the countries named. At the end of the last *entrée*, Discord concedes victory to Venus.

The two hearts mentioned by Venus were Louis, duc de Bourgogne, and Marie Adalaide of Savoy, whose marriage in 1697 coincided with the first production of *L'Europe galante*. As the oldest son of the Grand Dauphin (first-born son of Louis XIV), the groom was considered a future king of France "who one day will shape the earth's destiny." The love scenes in *L'Europe galante* constitute praise of a king in allegory. They symbolize the peace that will ensue from the projected unification of major parts of Europe under the hegemony of France. Part of this plan was the unification of France with Spain and its Italian dominions—hence the *entrées* named "France," "Spain," and "Italy." The *entrée* named "Turkey" refers to the Ottoman Empire, part of Europe inasmuch as it ruled most of what is now Bosnia, Serbia, Albania, Greece, Bulgaria, Romania, and Hungary up to the gates of Vienna. The Habsburg emperors in Vienna were almost continually at war with the Ottomans during the seventeenth and early eighteenth centuries. Between the Ottomans' second siege of Vienna (1683) and the Treaty of Carlowitz (1699), the Habsburgs led the Holy League (Austria, Poland, Venice, and Russia) against them. As an enemy of the Holy Roman Empire, France tried to support the Ottoman Empire—thus the inclusion of "Turkey" within a hoped-for *pax Gallica*.

L'Europe galante includes two Italian arias in the *entrée* "Italy." Both are sung in Italian, although the surrounding recitative uses the French language and musical style. The arias are both in two-strophe da capo form and include such Italian features as extensive melismas and melodic-harmonic sequences; they imitate the style of an Italian aria of the 1680s.

L'Europe galante was called a ballet on the title page of its printed score, but in retrospect it is considered to be the first *opéra-ballet*, using a term introduced in the eighteenth century. The defining features of *opéra-ballet* found in this work are the number, length, and elaborateness of the dance numbers; its organization into *entrées* related only by theme and not by continuous plot, like ballets; the connection of vocal text to dialogue or the depiction of a dramatic scene, as in opera; and the use of recitative for dialogue and the absence of spoken lines, as in opera. Another defining feature of later *opéras-ballets* is the depiction of real-life, present-day situations and characters, instead of the mythological scenarios—vehicles for allegories of the monarchy—that were typical of both opera and ballet in France during the seventeenth century.

The mere presence of two Italian arias in *L'Europe galante* does not signal a change in French musical fashion. The *entrée* entitled "Spain" contains a song in Spanish set to music that imitates the style of Juan Hidalgo and his contemporaries. However, a note at the bottom of the last page of the 1724 edition of the score says, "During the long space of time in which this piece has been performed, many Italian airs have been added, which are found in the *Collection of the Best Italian Airs*; therefore it is not necessary to look for them in the table of contents given above."

Indeed during the "long space of time" between 1697 and 1724, a large number of *tragédies en musique* and *opéras-ballets* show an increasing rapprochement with Italian opera style. The signs of this process are the more intense expression produced by such features of musical invention as prevailing rhythm and unexpected harmony, melismas in arias, da capo aria form, especially in *divertissements*, alongside the typically French binary form, and the idiomatic use of obbligato instruments in arias. On the other hand, French-style recitative, often orchestrally accompanied, with its more varied melodic contours, carefully notated rhythms, and meter changes, was never replaced by Italian *recitativo secco*. The French tradition of orchestral music depicting scenic effect or setting a mood continued, as did the practice of composing continuous scenes that shift freely among recitative, air, ensemble, chorus, and orchestra, as opposed to the scenes of uninterrupted plain recitative with exit arias at the end typical of Italian opera during this period. In addition to Campra, the important composers of French opera during this "long space of time" included Michel Pignolet de Montéclair (1667–1737), the first double-bass player to join the Paris Opéra orchestra, whose *opéra-ballet Les Festes de l'été* (1716) is notable for innovations in orchestration. The bold harmony and orchestration of Montéclair's sacred opera *Jephté* (1732) provided the inspiration for Rameau to enter the field.

The acknowledged masterpiece of French opera from the early eighteenth century is *Hippolyte et Aricie* (1733), a *tragédie en musique* by Jean-Philippe Rameau (1683–1764), organist at the Parisian church of Ste. Croix-de-la-Bretonnerie and a noted theorist, but not at this point known as a composer of theater music. He had never even visited the royal court.

Hippolyte et Aricie is an operatic adaptation by Simon-Joseph Pellegrin of Jean Racine's *Phèdre*, itself derived from the ancient Greek tragedy *Hippolytos* by Euripides, by way of *Phaedra* by the Roman playwright Seneca. The libretto explains that Theseus has become king of Athens by killing off the family of his rival, Pallas—all except for Aricia, whom he forces to take a vow of chastity so that she will not produce heirs.

In Act I, just before she takes her vow in the temple of Diana, the goddess of the hunt, Aricia discovers her love of Hippolytus, the son of Theseus. Phaedra, Theseus's second wife and the stepmother of Hippolytus, discovers this and, in anger, sends her guards into the temple. Diana appears and vows to protect the lovers. A messenger reports that Theseus has descended into the underworld to retrieve his companion, Peirithous, who has been killed in battle. Phaedra reveals that she, too, is in love with her stepson, Hippolytus. Theseus pleads with Pluto in Act II. Afterward he can leave the underworld only through the intervention of his father, Neptune. In Act III, Hippolytus rejects Phaedra's love, but Theseus returns at an awkward moment and receives the mistaken impression that Hippolytus tried to force himself on her. In his rage, Theseus asks Neptune to take revenge on Hippolytus. Neptune sends a sea monster against Hippolytus in Act IV. Phaedra confesses her guilt and commits suicide. Theseus is prevented by Neptune from doing the same in Act V. Hippolytus has been saved by Diana, but Theseus is condemned never to see him again.

The musical style of Rameau's score is predominantly French, in the Lully tradition. Recitatives with continuo or orchestral accompaniment use changing meter and exact rhythmic notation, and they have wider range, more leaps, and more purely musical organization of melodic contours than Italian recitative. The airs are nearly all syllabic, and dance rhythms are found in most of them. The scenes are made up of extended and often unbroken series of recitatives, arioso passages, dances, airs, ensembles, and choruses that participate in the action and dialogue—segments that often connect with one another without a full stop. Descriptive orchestral passages accompany action. The second half of Act IV, in which Neptune's sea monster attacks Hippolytus (A. 121), illustrates these features.

Italian traits are more limited in Rameau's score. Stronger expression, dramatic harmony, wide range, and occasional melismas are found in some of his airs, but none of them resembles an Italian da capo aria. Probably the most pronounced Italian feature is the energetic string writing—with measured tremolando, rapid scales, and arpeggios that could be found in Vivaldi's violin concertos. The excerpt from Act IV also illustrates these features.

The concertos of Antonio Vivaldi had become well known in Paris during the two decades preceding the composition of Rameau's *Hippolyte et Aricie*. The French music publisher Estienne Roger, exiled as a Protestant to Amsterdam, published the first editions of nearly all of Vivaldi's concerto collections that were printed during the composer's lifetime. These works were extremely popular among Parisian string players, amateur and professional, from 1711 onward. The works of Vivaldi's followers and imitators were likewise published in anthologies by Roger and his successors. These collections are the likely source for the highly energetic string writing that Rameau and his predecessors used to depict storms, conflicts, fury, agitation, terror, and the like. In spite of the predominance of French style features, Rameau's *Hippolyte et Aricie* incited a furious reaction from those who upheld the Lully tradition and the politics and cultural values that it represented.

As a consequence of its rapprochement with Italian style, French opera of the period ca. 1690–1735 achieved an estimable integration of music and drama. From Lully's *tragédies en musique* it derived continuity and variety of music during action or plot advancement, participation of the orchestra in establishing scenic effect, and a high level of musical interest during dialogues. From Italian models it gained intense personal expression and musical support of characterization. Works such as Charpentier's *Médée* and Rameau's *Hippolyte et Aricie* must be counted among the monuments of opera regardless of period. And yet it was Italian opera seria, often less impressive as musical drama, that swept Europe. Several reasons for this can be suggested.

An Italian opera seria is made up of separable and somewhat interchangeable modules—*secco* recitatives and da capo arias—that could be assembled, disassembled, and reassembled quickly and inexpensively to suit a particular cast of singers. French operas contain long, musically integrated scenes that cannot be easily altered without a complete rewrite. Italian opera seria is designed to show individual singers to maximum advantage in long, musically interesting arias that require improvised embellishments. French opera contains much less vocal display but requires more coordination among the singers. Italian opera seria uses a smaller, more standardized orchestra; French opera often requires trumpets, horns, oboes, and bassoons, in addition to strings and the continuo group. The scenery for Italian opera seria is much less elaborate than the expensive stage machinery required by most French operas. French opera librettos, usually based on mythology, tend to support the ideology of absolute monarchy through allegory, whereas the typical plot outlines of Italian opera seria better align with the interests of the nobility in suggesting that monarchs need to be restrained from pursuing personal aims and to be reminded of their duty to the nation. Thus Italian opera seria rather than French opera came to dominate theaters across Europe during the first half of the eighteenth century.

THE *CANTATE FRANÇOISE*

The years from about 1706 to 1730 witnessed the rapid rise and precipitous decline of the French secular chamber cantata. In 1714 the *Mercure de France*, the news magazine of the French royal court, reported that cantatas "have inundated all Paris" and are causing the public to grow cool toward Lully's operas. The same journal reported in November 1713:

> Cantatas and sonatas spring up under our very feet. A musician no longer arrives without a sonata or cantata in his pocket, and there are none who do not wish to write a work and have it printed and beat the Italians at their own game. Poets can scarcely keep pace with them, and indeed there are

even some texts that have suffered more than once the torture of Italianate music, so that here we are drowning in cantatas.

While acknowledging the Italian origins of the cantata, the principal poet of the *cantate françoise*, Jean-Baptiste Rousseau (1671–1741), explained the distinctive feature of the new French genre:

> The Italians call these little poems cantatas because they are particularly well suited to being sung. They are usually divided into three recitatives in alternation with the same number of airs. This requires a variety of meter in their verses, whose lines are sometimes long, sometimes short, as in the choruses of ancient tragedy and as in most Pindaric odes. I had heard several such cantatas and resolved to see whether or not one could set an ode to music in imitation of the Greeks. But since I had no model but that of the Italians, who often sacrifice sense in order to accommodate the composers, as we do in France, I realized, after having written some, that the poetry lost what the music gained, and that I could write nothing of value so long as I was content to pile one useless poetic phrase upon another without design or connection with a subject. This was how the idea came to me of giving form to these little poems by basing them upon a clear allegory, in which recitative would form the body of the cantata and the melodious airs the soul or moral. From among the ancient myths I chose those that I believed suitable for my purpose, because not all myths are susceptible to allegory. And this approach of mine succeeded well enough to stimulate other writers to work along similar lines.

Although the text of a French cantata usually portrays a dramatic episode, it is unlike an opera scene inasmuch as narration is always present in addition to dramatic poetry, and only rarely is there more than one voice. On the other hand, the monologue is given to a named personage in a specific situation usually identified in the title of the work and described in the narrative portions of the text. In the typical Italian cantata of this time, on the other hand, the words are sung by a generic shepherd of mythical Arcadia, and they usually do not relate to a story.

Although Rousseau describes Italian cantatas as having three arias and three recitatives, by the time of his writing two arias and one or two recitatives were the norm. The French cantata, on the other hand, is much less predictable in this respect, and it is not uncommon to find more than three airs. In general, the text of the final air draws a moral from the incident portrayed. A French cantata normally includes ensemble instruments such as violins in addition to the continuo group, whereas the Italian cantata normally does not.

Initially, French cantatas were written for and performed at salon gatherings in the palaces and houses of Parisian nobility, away from the royal court. The cantata took the place of the *air de cour*, which flourished in the same surroundings. In fact, an important variety of *air de cour* that flourished toward the end of the seventeenth century, the *air sérieux* ("serious air"), was sometimes written in several distinct movements with solo sections for various voices interspersed with ensemble and chorus movements. *Orphée descendant aux enfers* ("Orpheus Descending into the Underworld," 1683) by Marc-Antoine Charpentier even contains designated dramatic roles. It is the introduction of recitative that distinguishes French cantatas from such *airs sérieux*.

French cantatas were also performed at public concerts for paid admission, a historically significant novelty that arose in Paris, London, and Amsterdam during the late seventeenth and early eighteenth centuries. Beginning in 1725, the court musician Anne-Danican Philidor (1681–1728) organized the *Concerts spirituels*, a series of instrumental and sacred vocal music performances given during Lent and on religious holidays when the opera theater was closed. Indeed, his musicians were the singers and players from the opera. In 1727, Philidor organized a parallel series called the *Concerts français* that included secular vocal music, principally French cantatas. Although the *Concerts spirituels* lasted until 1790, the *Concerts français* endured only as long as the fashion for the cantata, until 1730. While it lasted, the *Concerts français* offered performances twice a week during the winter and once a week during the summer. Similar public concerts, usually called *académies*, soon sprung up in Bordeaux, Lyon, Marseille, Nimes, Nantes, Lille, Montpellier, Aix-en-Provence, Dijon, Amiens, Troyes, Rouen, Orléans, and Strasbourg.

The leading composer of French cantatas at first was Jean-Baptiste Morin (1677–1745), music director for the Regent's daughter, the Abesse de Chellesse. His cantatas were published in three volumes (1706, 1707, and 1712). In the introduction to the first of these, Morin claims, "I have done all that I can to retain the sweetness of our French style of melody, but with greater variety in the accompaniments and employing those tempos and modulations characteristic of the Italian cantata."

Morin's recitatives combine the variety of intervals and precise rhythmic notation of the French tradition with the unchanging duple meter and frequently static continuo part of Italian recitative. The majority of Morin's airs conform to the Italian repetition scheme ABA, in which the last section is an abbreviated version of the first, but a few of them call for a literal repeat of part A. Most of these airs begin with an instrumental introduction, as Italian arias do. Also Italian are Morin's repetitions of words and phrases to accommodate Italianate motivic elaboration, often including sequences and melismas. The rhythmic liveliness of Morin's bass parts, frequently using ostinato patterns, is another Italian feature. The harmonic variety and richness that Morin evidently associated with Italian music is found here and there, but it is not a typical feature of his cantatas.

In the cantatas of André Campra, the longer airs in da capo form with Italian features are called *ariettes*, whereas the shorter binary-form numbers are called *airs*. In several of the cantatas in Campra's second and third published collections (1714, 1728), obbligato instruments (flutes, oboes, trumpets) are added to the strings.

The twenty-five cantatas by Louis-Nicolas Clérambault (1676–1749) were published between 1710 and 1726. He composed many these works for the private performances arranged by Mme de Maintenon for Louis XIV during his last years or for the concerts that Clérambault produced at the homes of Parisian nobility. A widely repeated judgment in the eighteenth century credited Clérambault as the outstanding composer of cantatas in France; *Orphée* ("Orpheus") was his most celebrated work.

Clérambault's *Orphée* (W. 37) was published in his first book of cantatas (1710). Written for soprano, transverse flute (*flûte allemande*, "German flute"), violin, and continuo, its text contains Orpheus's lament, descent into the underworld, and pleading for the return of Euridyce. These dramatic speeches are framed by narratives and are followed by the response of Pluto and the commentary of a chorus, all delivered by the same singer. The cantata consists of five airs, three da capo and one interrupted by recitative, and four recitatives, one of them measured.

Clérambault employs a melodic and rhythmic style that is essentially French. In his airs, melodic contours and rhythms are strongly influenced by syllabic text declamation, but the resulting melodic and rhythmic motives are not extensively developed or varied, as in Italian arias. Wide intervals, arpeggios, and long scale segments are avoided. The musical phrases are mostly short— about four measures—and they are frequently subdivided by the longer notes that conclude the breath phrases of text delivery. The rhythm of the continuo bass often contributes to this segmentation into short phrase units. The small ornaments typical of harpsichord music—trills, mordents, short appoggiaturas, and slides—are abundantly notated. Clérambault's recitatives are of the newer French style described above.

The Italian features in Clérambault's *Orphée* are less evident than the French. They include the expressively expanded harmonic vocabulary and wide range of modulation in both recitatives and airs, and the imitative interplay between voice and accompanying instruments. The da capo designations are misleading; the typical Italian five-part da capo design is not found here, because the A sections consist of only one period rather than two.

The emotional expression that Clérambault's music imparts to Orpheus's words is always touching, but delicate and refined, never violent, in contrast to contemporaneous Italian music. In addition to the features of melody and rhythm mentioned above, the composer's use of rapidly alternating loud and soft (*fort* and *doux*, "strong" and "sweet") contributes to this effect, as does his sparing use of instruments, which often provide a wispy trace of sound or a very transparent background. An extreme example of this delicate transparency is the air "Monarque redouté," in which the violin instead of the bass viol plays the accompanying bass part.

The high point in popularity and elaboration of the French cantata is marked by the three books (1709–1728) of Michel Pignolet de Montéclair, whose operas were mentioned earlier. In his cantatas, Montéclair introduces astonishing instrumental effects, such as triple stops and measured undulation of string tone produced by varied bow pressure. In his *Pan et Sirinx* (ca. 1716), he instructs to singer to "slide imperceptibly from B flat to B natural while inflating the sound of the voice." Two measures later, the violin is instructed to do the same thing on E flat and E natural "if possible."

An important subgenre of the French cantata is the type based upon religious texts. The best examples are the twelve collected in the two volumes of *Cantates françoises sur des sujets tirez de l'Ecriture* ("French Cantatas on Subjects Drawn from the Scriptures," (1708, 1711) by Elisabeth-Claude Jacquet de La Guerre (1665–1729). At the age of five, her harpsichord playing won the admiration of Louis IV, and she was given a place in the household of his mistress, Madame de' Montespan, until she married the organist Marin de La Guerre in 1684. Her opera *Céphale et Procris*, the first by a female composer in France, was performed by the Académie Royale de Musique in 1694.

It is notable that six of Jacquet de La Guerre's scriptural cantatas feature female protagonists ("Esther," "Jacob and Rachel," "Susanna and the Old Men," "Judith," "Adam," and "Jepthe"). It is likely that they were initially performed at her house during the popular concerts at which she improvised brilliantly for up to a half hour at a stretch. She was rather wealthy at the time of her death, and the design for a medal in her honor was displayed in a book honoring the great artists and musicians of France (Fig. 15–1); the motto on the obverse says, "With the great musicians I contended for the prize." Her profile on the face of the medal has been matched to a portrait by François de Troy (1645–1730) that was painted sometime before Jacquet was thirty-nine years old (Fig. 15-2).

Figure 15-1. Design for a medal commemorating Elisabeth-Claude Jacquet de La Guerre published in *Titon du Tillet, Le Parnasse françois* (Paris, 1732)

Figure 15-2. A portrait of
Elisabeth-Claude Jacquet de la
Guerre by François de Troy in
or before 1704

VOCAL CHURCH MUSIC

In 1683 both Henry Du Mont and Pierre Robert retired as co-directors of the
Chapelle Royale. The four musicians who replaced them included one of the
most important composers of the era, Michel-Richard de Lalande
(1657–1726), also known as Delalande. Marc-Antoine Charpentier was among
the candidates, but he became seriously ill just before the final examination
and was not given one of the posts. Lalande and Charpentier were the dominant composers of church music in France during the last quarter of the seventeenth century and until Lalande's death.

Lalande's *grands motets* continue the tradition of Veillot, Formé, Du Mont,
Robert, and Lully, while at the same time expanding the scope of the genre
and updating its style. In addition to choruses in the learned style of imitative
counterpoint and some with a chant melody as cantus firmus, Lalande's *grands
motets* include operatic airs, some with bravura melismatic passages, and homophonic choruses with independent string parts, as in the Italian concerted
motets discussed earlier. Even a few brief recitatives are found in his last works
and revisions.

Lalande's most frequently revised and performed large-scale church work is
his Te Deum, first composed in 1684. Lalande's revisions progress toward
longer, more complete, and more separated movements; expansion of choruses
by means of added contrapuntal elaboration; greater independence of the
orchestra parts during choruses; more frequent use of obbligato solo instruments in dialogue with solo voices; and more operatic or cantata-like airs.

The last version of Lalande's Te Deum (W. 38), published without the inner string parts in a posthumous collection (1729), contains sixteen separate movements—overture, choruses, duets, trios, quartets, airs, and one recitative. The progression of solo—ensemble—chorus within a long, continuous section, established in the *grands motets* of Henry Du Mont, is no longer present, although it was in the first version of this work. The forms of longer movements include fugue, a series of similar periods visiting various cadential goals, rondeau, and binary form. The whole work is unified through the recurrence of similar strings of four to six eighth notes undulating about the D-major scale segment from d'' to a'', with emphasis on f-sharp''. Melodic motives restricted to these notes are idiomatic of the Baroque natural trumpet, appropriate for this majestic text.

Most of the movements in Lalande's Te Deum are characterized by musical inventions that reflect the expressive thrust of their texts. Thus, the first trio for the *petit choeur* (small chorus) and the preceding introductory Symphonie project the concept of "glory"—implied by the words "We praise Thee, oh God, we acknowledge Thee to be the Lord"—through the choice of D major, high registers, brisk tempo, use of trumpets and timpani, end-accented rhythmic grouping, strong word and syllable emphasis, and avoidance of syncopation and ties. The *recit* "Tu devicto mortis aculeo" ("Thou, having overcome the sing of death"), marked *Fierement* ("proudly") resembles the type of operatic bass air expressing defiance through wide-ranging arpeggios, skips over dissonant intervals, strong harmony, and pyrrhico-anapest rhythms. Several movements feature recurring antitheses between opposing expressions, often with marked tempo alternations without corresponding meter changes, something relatively novel at this time. For example, the last chorus repeatedly opposes the supplication "In Thee, O Lord, have I trusted," sung "slowly" (*lentement*), with the demand "Let me not be confounded for ever," in homorhythmic, accented quarter notes marked "rapidly" (*vivement*). In several places in the same chorus, repetitions of the word *non* ("not") are set off by dramatic silences.

The Italian influences detectable in Lalande's *grands motets*—strong expression of the text, melismatic text setting, chromatic harmony, occasional melodic (but not harmonic) sequences—are even more strongly marked in the large-scale Latin church works of his principal successors, Henry Desmarest (1661–1741), André Campra, and Jean-Philippe Rameau.

Because the performance of *grands motets* covered nearly all the words of the liturgy during Mass at the French royal chapel, there are no Mass Ordinary settings from this period that were composed for the Chapelle Royale. The leading composer of Masses in France about the turn of the eighteenth century was Marc-Antoine Charpentier, who was associated with other churches. Most of his surviving Masses date from the late 1680s to the early 1700s. Although some are very simple in style, others are quite elaborate. An example of the latter type is his *Messe de minuit pour Noël* ("Midnight Mass for Christmas"), in which short orchestral interludes introduce the melodies of several popular

Christmas carols, which then become the subject of polyphonic elaboration in the following choral sections.

Whereas the *grand motet* as a genre was conceived for the Chapelle Royale and Charpentier's Masses for other large musical establishments, the solo motet was the standard fare at the majority of churches throughout France in the years surrounding 1700. These include the chapels of convents for women and girls, especially those maintained for the aristocracy.

The most prominent female convent at this time was the Maison Royale de Saint-Louis at Saint-Cyr, founded in 1686 by Mme de Maintenon for the education of young noble women. The first music director at this convent was the organist Guillaume-Gabriel Nivers (ca. 1632–1714), who in 1689 published a collection of sixty-one solo motets in a simple and chaste style for the women to perform. At other convents for the aristocracy professional musicians performed. But since convent churches were designed to permit performance by women by separating them from male auditors by a grillwork or curtain, some Paris convents employed women from the opera theater and charged admission to hear them, as was done in the Venetian *ospedali*:

They [the opera singers] are paid to perform the most pious and solemn motets! We have been going further for several years: we hire actresses who sing a Lesson on Good Friday or a solo motet on Easter behind a curtain that they draw back from time to time to smile at their friends in the audience. One goes to hear them at a certain convent. In their honor one pays the price for a seat at the church that one would pay at the door of the opera. One recognizes [the singers who had been portraying] Urgande and Arcabonne [in Lully's operas] and claps one's hands. I have seen clapping at Tenebrae and Assumption services. I do not remember whether it was for [the singers] la Moreau or for Madame Cheret (Le Cerf, *Comparaison*, 1725, IV:162).

Leçons de ténèbres ("Lessons for Tenebrae") by the famous harpsichordist François Couperin (1668–1733) were written for exactly such a purpose—for the professional female opera singers hired by the nuns of the Abbey of Longchamp near Paris, about 1713–17.

Tenebrae ("darkness") is a name commonly applied to the combined Offices of Matins and Lauds on Thursday, Friday, and Saturday of Holy Week, the end of Lent, immediately preceding Easter Sunday. During each day's Tenebrae service, one of fifteen candles is extinguished after each psalm is sung. After the canticle *Benedictus Dominus*, the last candle is put out, and the rest of that day's service is sung *in tenebris* ("in the dark"). During Matins, as always, nine lessons are sung or recited, three for each of three Nocturns. The musically important texts are the three lessons for the first Nocturn each day, taken from the Lamentations of Jeremiah in the Old Testament.

The lessons that Couperin composed for the nuns of the Abbey of Longchamp were the first three for the third day of Tenebrae, but they are now lost. Later he published a set of three for the first day, with the promise of another three for the second, which are also lost. In the surviving three lessons, which belong to Maundy Thursday, as in the other two sets, Couperin set the first two lessons for solo voice and the third for two voices. He specifies that a bass viol or *basse de violon* can be added to the accompaniment of the organ or harpsichord.

In the Catholic liturgy, each verse from the Lamentations was introduced by an identifying letter from the Hebrew alphabet. In Gregorian chant, the name of this letter, spelled in the Roman alphabet, is sung to a short melismatic formula, and most polyphonic settings also use a melisma. Couperin's introductory melismas are elaborations of the corresponding chant formulas.

After the melismatic setting of the Hebrew letter name, each verse in Couperin's *Leçons* proceeds with a mixture of declamatory and decorative vocal style, most often marked *recitatif*. In most of these French-style recitative segments, the bass is initially static or slow moving, and monotone recitation is usually heard at the beginning, but then more varied intervals, wider contour, short melismas, and a more active bass line are introduced. At the end of each of the first two lessons, Couperin gathers his thoughts into airs, more or less in rondeau form. Extended harmonic resources, unusual intervals, and chains of suspensions for expressive purposes are most in evidence in the third lesson for two voices (W. 39).

Although Le Cerf denounced Couperin as an "eager servant of Italy"—presumably for the usual sins of melismas, dissonance, sequences, and modulation—far more Italian are the five books of solo motets (1695–1720) by André Campra or the two (1704, 1709) by Jean-Baptiste Morin. Campra's solo motets are clearly divided into sections or movements, but true recitative is rarely encountered. The sections that can be compared to airs are Italianate only to the extent that rhythmically defined motives are elaborated, at times through sequences, and the accompanying bass part is active and occasionally imitative of the vocal line. There are also short interludes or ritornellos for the continuo alone. Many of Morin's motets, on the other hand, use a style of recitative that is almost Italian and airs in which ritornellos in various keys are linked by modulating vocal periods, all based on the same motives or phrases. *Ad mensam coelitus paratam* in Morin's Book 1 could pass for a work by an Italian of Vivaldi's generation; the overall format is recitative—aria—recitative—aria—Alleluja, and the first aria is constructed out of a series of ritornellos and vocal periods beginning with a motto phrase with a da capo repetition that modulates from tonic to dominant and back.

ORGAN MUSIC

The organ had little place in Sunday Mass and Vespers at the French royal chapel, since a *grand motet* continued to cover most of the liturgy. Consequently, most French organ music in the decades surrounding 1700 was written for churches in the city of Paris and in other centers. The best representative composers of this repertoire are François Couperin and Nicolas de Grigny (1672–1703).

Although eventually more famous as a composer of harpsichord music, François Couperin began his professional career as organist at the church of St. Gervais, as had his father, Charles, and his uncle Louis. François began as a regular substitute for Michel-Richard de Lalande, who held the title of organist in this and three other churches while he was co-director of the Chapelle Royale. In 1685, at age eighteen, Couperin began to receive a full-time salary for the position. His volume of *Pieces d'orgue*, his first publication of music, was issued in 1690. It consists of two organ Masses, one for parish churches and the other for convents and monasteries. Each set consists of the usual versets (here called "couplets"), meant to alternate with plainchant in the items of the Mass Ordinary, with a longer piece to be played in place of the Offertory. Most of Couperin's couplets carry designations of manuals, stops, mixtures, and musical genres like those used in the suites of organ pieces by composers of the generation of Nivers and Lebègue. But in the opening versets for each item, he revives the use of a plainchant cantus firmus, a technique more typical of sixteenth- and early seventeenth-century organ versets.

The Offertory of Couperin's *Messe à l'usage ordinaire des paroisses* ("Mass for the Ordinary Use of Parish Churches," W. 40) illustrates the continuity, expanse, and topical variety that sets his organ pieces apart from the mercurial miniatures of Nivers and Lebègue. Its three large, highly contrasting sections—a majestic entrée in C major, a fugue in C minor, and a spirited gigue in C major—are subtly related by an initial four-note descent C—B—A—G in the bass of section 1, the second voice of section 2, and the implied harmonization in section 3. The periods that make up each section are even more closely related in content, although they never form exact variations or repetitions. At the smallest dimension, each period is unified by a continuous elaboration of one or two motives.

Like his predecessors, Couperin musters the resources of the classical French organ in carefully indicating the manuals, stops, and mixtures to be used. In most cases, the result is a distinctly layered texture, in which two or three mixtures of very different sonorities and contrasting strengths are used. This is the opposite of a blending of equal voices, and even in passages that appear polyphonic on paper, one or two voices clearly project over the others. Couperin also retains the profusion of small ornaments that had been a hallmark of the French style since the beginning of the seventeenth century. From his uncle, Louis Couperin, he learned to use strong dissonances, unsettling cross relations, shocking chord progressions, and expressive chromaticism to extend and expand his phrases.

Although a student of Lebègue and for three years (1693–95) organist at St. Denis in Paris, Nicolas de Grigny was organist at the cathedral of his native Reims when his *Premier livre d'orgue* was published in 1699. Like Couperin, Grigny combines the typical French dotted rhythms, runs, and repertoire of small ornaments with consistency of part writing and continuity of invention and elaboration, as opposed to the fluctuating and broken style of Nivers and Lebègue. In fact, his textures are even fuller than Couperin's, often including four upper voices supported by a distinct pedal part in the bass. If anything, Grigny's modulations and dissonances are even bolder than Couperin's.

The learned and sometimes weighty style of Couperin and Grigny was rejected by the organ composers of the Regency period, such as Louis Marchand (1669–1732) and Louis-Nicolas Clérambault. In the liturgical suites of this generation, textures, even in the fugues, tend to be homophonic, and the propulsive rhythmic patterns of the earlier style are replaced by a denser application of small ornaments.

PIÈCES DE CLAVECIN

Beginning in the late 1680s, a significant number of the composers of important French harpsichord music did not have appointments at the royal court. This parallels what has already been said about French organ music, cantatas, and even stage music of this period, and it runs contrary to the pattern of the previous decades. Even when a composer held a court position, his harpsichord music was now commercially printed for amateurs of means and education, rather than preserved only in manuscript.

None of Louis Couperin's harpsichord music was printed during his lifetime, and only one collection of D'Anglebert's harpsichord music was published—in 1689, two years before his death. Twelve years passed before the next collection of French harpsichord music was printed. But then the tide of production began to run swiftly, with the 1701 publication of the *Six suites* by Charles Dieupart, two volumes by Louis Marchand in 1699 and 1702, one by Louis-Nicolas Clérambault in 1702, at least one (ca. 1704) by Jean-François Dandrieu, and one by Gaspard Le Roux in 1705—and none of these composers held a position at court.

Some of the changes in style that overtook French harpsichord music by the beginning of the eighteenth century are parallel to those found in vocal and organ music of the same period—greater consistency and continuity in part writing, which moderates the older *style brisé*, and more intensive motivic elaboration, which creates melodic unity. In addition, we find more uniformity in the makeup of the suite, usually a prelude, an allemande, a courante, a sarabande, and a gigue, perhaps with the addition or substitution of a few other dances. In addition, we find more predictable harmony, generally conforming to the harmonic practice embodied in the sonatas of Corelli and later works, vocal and instrumental, by Italian composers. The impression of directed motion that these normalized chordal patterns convey is accentuated by the use of motor rhythms, suspensions, and melodic-harmonic sequences in works of the more Italianate composers, notably Jean-Philippe Rameau.

Rameau's first book of *Pièces de clavecin* (1706) consists of one suite of dances (W. 41)—a half-unmeasured prelude, two allemandes, a courante, a gigue, two sarabandes, the *Vénitienne* ("Venetian Lady"), a gavotte, and a menuet. All but two of the dances are in binary form with two repeated strains. The *Vénitienne* and the gavotte are in rondeau form—ABACA (or A'). These are by far the two most common movement forms for French *pièces de clavecin* of the period. In all the binary movements except for the second allemande, the second strain elaborates on the same motives heard in the first. This correspondence between the two strains is another Italian feature that makes only gradual headway in the *pièces de clavecin* by other French composers. Rameau's bold harmonies, including prominent use of diminished-seventh chords and cross relations were also considered Italian traits at that time. However, traditionally French characteristics, such as a profusion of small ornaments and *style brisé* texture, are still present in Rameau's first book. In his second book (1724) rapid passages requiring hand crossing and rapid motor rhythms suggest the influence of Domenico Scarlatti's sonatas. In other respects, this and his third collection of harpsichord music (1729) reveal the influence of François Couperin.

Couperin's four volumes of *Pièces de clavecin* (1713, 1717, 1722, 1730) quickly became the standard repertoire of French harpsichord music, and many of their features were imitated in France and abroad. With these collections, Couperin popularized the inclusion of descriptive "genre pieces," as they are sometimes called today, pieces that in Couperin's words are *espèces de portraits* ("kinds of portraits"). Such pieces, with their descriptive titles, were found here and there among earlier collections of *pièces de clavecin*. Indeed, music for pantomime dances in *ballets de cour* and other French musical stage works, at least from the middle of the seventeenth century, often is descriptive in title and character. But descriptive pieces are in the majority for the first time in Couperin's first book. They are still arranged in suites (or *ordres*, as Couperin calls them), and many conform to standard dance types. But their range of expressive pictorialization, unencumbered by the limitations of scenic effect and story line, exceeds that of stage dances.

La Ténébreuse ("Darkness") from Couperin's first book of 1713 (A. 122) is identified as an allemande in the publication. It evokes darkness in its first strain through closely spaced chords in the low register, slow tempo, minor mode, octave leaps downward in the bass, and the imposing majesty of its pyrrhico-anapest rhythms (or "fourth paeonic," according to Mersenne). The second strain begins with contrasting light with a sudden shift to a high register and more delicate and graceful melodic and rhythmic materials; this too descends into darkness.

Les Fastes de la grande et ancienne Mxnxstrxndxsx ("The Splendors of the Great and Ancient Minstrelsy") is part of the eleventh *ordre* in Couperin's *Second livre de pièces de clavecin* (1716). A satiric reference to the instrumentalists' guild in Paris, the *Confrérie de Saint-Juilien-des-Ménétriers*, is disguised by replacing the e's with x's in the last word of the title. A suite within a suite (W. 42), it consists of five pieces, each numbered as an *Acte* ("act"), as if to conjure up the shoddy spectacle of the minstrels' street performance.

Act I of *Les Fastes de la grande et ancienne Mxnxstrxndxsx*, *Les Notables et jurés-menestrendeurs* ("The eminent and sworn minstrels"), is called a march, although its rhythm, phrasing, and tempo are those of a gavotte.

Act II, *Les Viéleux et les gueux* ("The hurdy-gurdies and beggars"), also a gavotte, imitates the sound of a hurdy-gurdy, as does Act III, *Les Jongleurs, sauteurs et saltinbanques, avec les ours et les singes* ("The jugglers, jumpers, and tumblers, with bears and monkeys"). The strings of a hurdy-gurdy (Fr. *vielle*) are bowed mechanically by a resin-coated wheel turned by a crank. Melody notes are obtained by fingering a keyboard, while a drone bass is always present. Although Mersenne, in his *Harmonie universelle* (1636–37), associated the instrument with beggars and blind street musicians, it was played during the late seventeenth and early eighteenth centuries by the French aristocracy to evoke rusticity.

Act IV, *Les Invalides, ou gens estropiés au service de la grande mxnxstrxndxsx* ("The disabled persons, or people crippled in the service of the grand minstrelsy") imitates the limp of persons with a dislocation *(les disloqués)* by means of dotted rhythm in the right hand, and the slower, jerky motion of lame people *(les boiteux)* with the widely spaced iambs in the left hand.

Act V depicts the helter-skelter *Desordre et déroute de toute la troupe, causés par les yvrognes, les singes et les ours* ("Disorder and rout of the whole troop, caused by drunkards, monkeys, and bears"), rendered comical by the continuous alternating octaves in the bass, which suggests the stormy measured tremolando of a string orchestra, in the context, however, of innocuous major-key scales moving into a high register in several places.

Le Petit-Rien ("The Little Nothing") from the fourteenth *ordre* in Couperin's third book of *Pièces de clavecin* (1722), A. 123, illustrates the extreme limit of the composer's stylistic range. *La Ténébreuse* (1713) preserves the *style brisé* and series of asymmetrical elaborations on single phrase-length rhythms, one for each of the two strains, typical of the stylized dance music in French harpsichord suites around 1700, together with the expressive harmony, strong dissonance, and dramatic melodic and rhythmic gestures that François learned from the music of his uncle Louis Couperin. *Les Fastes de la grande et ancienne Mxnxstrxndxsx* (1716) reveals Italian influence in the continuous motor rhythms, repetitions of small rhythmic modules, use of melodic sequences, and motivic correspondence between the two strains of the binary-form pieces. *Le Petit-Rien*, by contrast, is in what Couperin thought of as violin-sonata style, in which the bass has the same level of rhythmic activity and melodic importance as the treble, and both parts proceed continuously, without any hint of *style brisé*. The regular two- and four-measure phrases of this piece, its very restricted harmonic vocabulary, and the lack of any striking dissonance or oddities in melodic design reflect the latest fashion of the 1720s in both French and Italian instrumental music, a fashion that can with justification be called post-Baroque or *gallant*.

Like many composers of *pièces de clavecin*, Couperin attached a table of ornamental signs to his first volume (Fig. 15-3). But he also published a short book of instructions, aimed primarily at the well-to-do parents of children beginning to study the harpsichord. Published in 1717, it is entitled *L'art de toucher le clavecin* ("The Art of Playing the Harpsichord"). Selected quotations from this manual are translated on page 445.

Figure 15-3. The table of ornamental signs from François Couperin's first
volume of *Pièces de clavecin* (1713)

The four books of François Couperin's *Pièces de clavecin* inspired a host of
imitators, who often exaggerated his idea of *espèces de portraits*. On the title
page of his collection of 1724, Jean François Dandrieu (1681/82–1738)
advertised "several entertainments, among which the principal ones are *The
Characters of War*, *Those of the Hunt*, and *Village Festivals*." In the first of these,
the piece entitled "Charge" invites the performer to "strike the lowest notes

Figure 15-3A. The second page of the table of ornamental signs in François Couperin's first volume of *Pièces de clavecin* (1713).

of the harpsichord with the entire flat of the hand as many times as desired to express better the discharge of the cannon." Such descriptive and narrative keyboard pieces continued to appear in France throughout the eighteenth and nineteenth centuries. The identity of the dance types that were originally the underlying vehicle for descriptive genre pieces gradually faded away, as they had already begun to dissolve in the works of Couperin. It is impossible

Selected quotations from François Couperin, *L'Art de toucher le clavecin* (1717)

- These principles are absolutely necessary to be able to play my pieces well.
- The thumb of each hand is counted as the first finger.
- The change from one finger to another on the same note will be useful, and that connection contributes to playing.
- The expression that I propose owes its effect to the cessation and the delay of notes done on purpose and according to the characters required by the melodies and pieces.
- On such occasions where bowed instruments swell their tones, the delay of those of the harpsichord seems (by a contrary effect) to produce in the ear what is desired.
- As to the expressive effect of the aspiration, it is necessary to detach the note above which it is places less energetically in pieces that are tender and slow than those that are light and rapid.
- With regard to the delay, it is only used in tender and slow pieces.
- Every mordent (*pincé*) must be fixed upon the note over which it is placed . . . the oscillations and the note on which one stops must all be included in the time value of the principal note.
- Although trills are notated in equal notes in the table of ornaments of my first book, they nevertheless must begin more slowly than they end; but this graduation should be imperceptible.
- On whatsoever note a trill may be marked, it must always begin on the tone or semitone above.
- Trills of any considerable duration consist of three objects, which, in performance, appear to be only the same thing: 1) the appoggiatura, which must be made on the note above the principal note, 2) the oscillations, 3) the stopping place. With regard to other trills, they are variable. There are some with appoggiaturas and other so short that they have neither appoggiatura nor stopping place. One can even make them aspirated.
- The harpsichord . . . has other advantages, which are precision, clarity, brilliance, and range.
- The fact is that we write differently from what we play. This causes foreigners to play our music less well than we play theirs. On the other hand, the Italians write their music with the true time values that they have in mind. For example, we dot the several eighth notes in a scalewise series, and yet we write them as equal. Our custom has enslaved us, and we continue it.
- But all our airs for violins, our pieces for harpsichord and for viols, etc., designate and seem to what to express some feeling. As there are not any images of signs or characters to communicate our specific ideas, we try to remedy this by indicating, at the beginning of our pieces, with some words, like "tenderly," "lively," etc., as far as possible that which we would want to have understood.

to say exactly when the suite of *pièces de clavecin* as a genre recognizable by
Couperin and Rameau came to an end.

SONATAS AND *SONADES*

François Couperin's treatise *L'art de toucher le clavecin* contains a substantial
digression in which the author argues that students of the harpsichord should
be restricted as to the number and types of sonatas (*sonades*) that they play. It is
clear that he is referring to Italian-style violin sonatas, because no other kind of
sonata was known in France at that time, and his discussion of sonatas versus
pièces de clavecin contrasts the violin idiom of the former with the harpsichord
idiom of the latter. This digression suggests that by 1717 it had become a common practice to play sonatas for violin and continuo on the harpsichord alone
by playing the violin part with the right hand and the bass part with the left,
which would have been easy, since violin sonatas were always printed on two
staves, just like harpsichord music.

Couperin warns against playing sonatas on the harpsichord because the rapid
repeated notes (*bateries*) and arpeggios, idiomatic for the violin, are not suited
to the harpsichord, especially since few small ornaments (*agrèmens*) can be introduced in such passages. He allows that the delicate movements of sonatas
(*Légèretés des Sonades*) can be played effectively on the harpsichord, especially
when the upper part and the bass are in constant movement, and he supplies his
own two-voice Allemande with an imitative texture and plenty of mordents to
illustrate this point. Interestingly, the bass part in Couperin's Allemande contains
no figures, and its rapid, leaping passages would be very unusual in the basso
continuo part of an Italian sonata. He seems to have composed this Allemande
as harpsichord music imitating an Italian-style violin sonata.

Couperin warns against playing slow movements from sonatas on the harpsichord because "the basses are not at all made for the addition of lute-style, syncopated inner voices (*parties lutées, et sincopées*), which, he points out, are suited to
the harpsichord. This remark, which underlines an essential difference between
the Italian and French styles, also suggests that unwritten inner parts were customarily added by the performer when Italian sonatas for violin and continuo
were played on the harpsichord in Paris early in the eighteenth century. In
effect, this method of adapting violin sonatas created a new keyboard genre, and
we use Couperin's French word *sonade* to call attention to this novelty.

If harpsichordists played violin music, so violinists played harpsichord music.
In 1729, the court newspaper *Mercure de France* described a performance by
Marguerite-Antoinette Couperin, François's daughter, whose harpsichord was
accompanied by a violin played very softly.

Both crossover methods of performing *pièces de clavecin* and violin sonatas are
illustrated in a 1707 publication by Elisabeth-Claude Jacquet de La Guerre.
The first half of the collection carries the title *Pièces de clavecin qui peuvent se
jouer sur le viollon* ("Harpsichord Pieces that Can Be Played on the Violin"),

while the second half is entitled *Sonates pour le viollon et pour le clavecin* ("Sonatas for the Violin and for the Harpsichord"). The title of the first half means that the single melodic line on the upper staff can be played on the violin, either doubling the harpsichord or alone, while the lower voices are played on the keyboard. The title of the second half of the collection is more ambiguous; if she meant that these violin sonatas should be accompanied by a harpsichord playing the continuo part, the typical wording would be *sonates pour le violon et la basse*. Jacquet's wording suggests that her sonatas were intended equally for the violin with continuo accompaniment and for the harpsichord alone. If this is so, then they are the first of a very important genre.

Jacquet's *pièces de clavecin* are cast in the typical dance meters and styles of the French suite and make extensive use of the broken *parties lutées*, as Couperin termed them. Her sonatas, on the other hand, have unbroken treble (violin) and bass (continuo) lines and continuous elaboration of motives, frequently by means of sequences, in the Italian manner. The first movement of her Sonata 2 (A. 124) preserves the rhythm and phrasing of the gavotte, but the form is binary—the medial cadence without a double bar appears in measure 19—with a bit of recapitulation (mm. 47–55). The form of the last movement of this sonata is remarkable for the long first half, which is divided equally between a period that modulates from the tonic to the dominant—and a period that begins and ends in the dominant.

In 1695 Jacquet gave a manuscript of two of her sonatas for one violin and continuo and four of her trio sonatas to her friend and supporter Sébastien de Brossard (1655–1730), an important theorist, composer, and compiler of a music dictionary. These were among the first violin sonatas written in France. At about the same time, François Couperin composed several trio sonatas that he later revised and retitled for inclusion in *Les nations sonades et suites de simphonies en trio* ("The Nations: Sonatas and Suites of Ensemble Pieces for Trio") of 1726.

Couperin's early trio sonatas that were reused in *Les nations* form sets with introductory movement followed by newly added dance suite. In these introductory sonata movement, the long, continuous melodic lines and sequences with chains of suspensions, supported by steadily marching bass, certainly evoke the style of Corelli, as do the three-voice fugues in the fast movements. Although Couperin cites Corelli as his principal inspiration, the many small ornaments and the dominance of the upper of the two treble parts betray Couperin's French orientation.

A similar combination of Italian and French traits are found in *Les goûts réunis* ("The United Styles"), which Couperin published in 1724. In this collection the combination of French and Italian styles is achieved within each movement rather than by combining Italianate sonata movements with French dances, as in *Les nations*. This combination is especially evident in the two sonatas dedicated to the memory of Corelli and Lully.

Both these commemorative sonatas are programmatic works, the first with seven movements and the second with thirteen, all of which carry descriptive titles. The descriptive features in these movements belong to the French tradition, as do the ornamentation, phrasing, and elaboration on rhythmic extended modules, while the sequences, motor rhythms, and broad melodic contours reflect Couperin's understanding of Italian instrumental styles. Example 15-1 illustrates this combination of features. Although the phrases and melodic contours in this example are relatively long and a melodic/harmonic sequence plays a major role in its expansion, the typically French rhythmic module ♪ ♫ ♫♫ | ♪ is maintained by the complex of voices, while a steady eighth-note pulse—not *notes inégales*—continues as the composite rhythm of the three voices—another Italian trait. The short trills scattered throughout the passage are another French feature.

The most important French composer of violin sonatas in the generation after Couperin was Jean-Marie Leclair the elder (1697–1764). In 1722 Leclair studied in Turin with Giovanni Battista Somis (1686–1763), whose style was comparable to that of Francesco Maria Veracini. Later he worked with Locatelli, whose manner of writing out rapid ornamental runs is reflected in Leclair's Opus 5 (ca. 1734). Like Couperin, Leclair combined French characteristics—dances, extended modular rhythms, and small ornaments—with Italianate

EXAMPLE 15-1. Italian and French features combined the fifth movement of *Le Parnasse; ou L'Apothéose de Corelli* ("Parnassus; or, the Apotheosis of Corelli") from *Les Goûts réunis* (1724) by François Couperin

Corelli, aprés son Entouziasme, s'endort; et sa Troupe jouë le Sommeil suivant
("Corelli, after his rapture, falls asleep, and his ensemble plays following lullaby")

melodic contours, sequences, suspensions, motor rhythms, arpeggios, ornamental runs, and thematically linked binary forms. The clarity of his phrases, the focus on the melody line, and the decorative quality of his ornamentation align Leclair with Tartini and Locatelli as representative of a post-Baroque style adapted to musical amateurs as consumers of published music for home use.

ORCHESTRAL MUSIC

A convenient way to classify French orchestral music of the period 1680–1730 is to divide it into three groups: (1) suites of dances, (2) Italian-style concertos, and (3) hybrid types in which French and Italian styles are joined.

Suites

The repertoire of French orchestral suites can be traced to the practice of extracting dances from stage works for social dancing and for banquet music. Although this practice can be traced back to the middle of the seventeenth century, collections and documentation become abundant only at the beginning of the eighteenth century. Representative of this repertoire are the three large manuscript collections made in 1703, 1727, and 1745 of *Simphonies* by Lalande "which he had performed every fifteen days during the supper of Louis XIV and Louis XV." The first set contains ten suites, 154 movements in all, the second thirteen suites—139 movements—and so on. Although most of the movements are dances from Lalande's stage works, some apparently derive from outdoor festivals with trumpets and still others seem to have been newly composed for the suppers, without reference to dance styles. Some of the latter, with titles like *caprice* or *fantaisie*, feature solo violin and solo oboe.

The general style and format of Lalande's suites are also found in the *Suites de simphonies* (1729) by Jean-Joseph Mouret (1682–1738) and the *Suite de concerts de symphonies en trio* (1730-33) by Jacques Aubert (1689–1753). Similar orchestral suites were assembled, often from the works of Lully, and published in great quantities by the printers of Amsterdam. These were widely circulated all over northern Europe and spawned many imitations, especially in the northern German states.

Programmatic titles and descriptive music are scattered throughout these French orchestral suites in keeping with the origin of the genre in stage music and in parallel with the *pièces de clavecin* by Couperin. Between 1711 and 1737, Jean-Féry Rebel (1666–1747) composed several sets of programmatic music for orchestra or large ensemble. Several of the earlier sets, *Caprice* (1711) and *Les caractères de la danse* ("The Characters of the Dance") originated as music to accompany dance and pantomime performances without scenery but were published as chamber music. The later sets, *Les plaisiers champêtres* (1734) and *Les élémens: simphonie nouvelle* (1737), were apparently conceived as purely instrumental music of a descriptive sort. In the introduction to the last collection, Rebel explains:

To designate each individual element in this confusion, I relied on the most recognized conventions. The bass expresses Earth in notes slurred together and played with tremolos; the flutes, in the rise and fall of their melody, imitate the course and murmur of Water; Air is illustrated by sustained tones followed by trills played on small flutes; in the end, the violins represent Fire by their liveliness and brilliance.

Concertos

Italian concertos were well known in France from their publication in Amsterdam, beginning with Vivaldi's Op. 3 in 1711. In 1727 the Italian expatriate Michele Mascitti (1664–1760) published violin concertos in this style in Paris. These were quickly followed by six flute concertos by Michel Corrette (1707–1795). More similar to Vivaldi's works were the concertos for four violins and cello (1734) by Jacques Aubert and Leclair's violin concertos of 1737 and 1743.

Hybrid Works

A deliberate attempt to combine French and Italian features in works for large ensemble can be found in the *Concerts royaux* ("Royal Ensembles") that François Couperin composed in 1714–15 for chamber performances at Versailles. Although Couperin published only a trio sonata reduction of these works in 1722, he names the players of violin, flute, oboe, viol, and bassoon who joined him in the original performances. Couperin's collection *Les goûts réunis*, mentioned above, were intended as a second volume of this series, and a similar method of combining national styles is found in both collections.

THE HARMONIC THEORIES OF JEAN-PHILIPPE RAMEAU

In 1722 Jean-Philippe Rameau, then known as an organist and composer of harpsichord pieces, published his *Traité de l'harmonie* ("Harmony Treatise"), a work of unprecedented scope and thoroughness. Its genesis can be found in Rameau's search for an easier and more logical way to teach realization of figured-bass accompaniments through the identification of chordal roots and inversions. These concepts had been part of German theory since the early seventeenth century, but Rameau went on to justify them logically and to attempt a theory that would teach and explain normalized chord progressions through reference to chordal roots arranged in a series called the *basse fondamentale* ("fundamental bass").

Rameau explained the major triad and seventh chord by attempting to identify them with partials 2, 3, and 4 or 2, 3, 4, and 5 of the overtone series. Thus he appeared to be relying upon the empirical science of acoustics. To explain the minor triad, however, he invented a series of "undertones," which mirrors the intervals of overtones through melodic inversion, beginning with the fifth of the chord and proceeding downward by major third and minor third—an explanation having nothing to do with acoustics. Even his series of ascending partials were only approximations of the intervals actually used in music, where some form of mean-tone tuning, including equal temperament, was required. To explain diminished chords, ninths, and elevenths, Rameau resorted to even more contrived theories, still further removed from science.

Rameau's theory of chord progressions seems to have begun with the reasonable observation that the new harmonic style coming out of Italy, in the works of such composers as Corelli and Vivaldi, relied heavily on sequences of root movements by ascending fourth or descending fifth. He duly noted that the same root movement is found between the last two chords of what he called a "perfect" cadence. Perhaps by observing that the typical sequence of falling fifths was normally harmonized with chains of suspensions, Rameau theorized that the force that propels such sequences and cadences forward is provided by the dynamic of dissonance and resolution. Thus, wherever the falling fifth or ascending fourth is found in the *basse fondamentale*, Rameau posited a seventh above the first of the two roots, whether or not the interval was actually in the written music. He advised composers to use the *basse fondamentale* progression of the falling or rising fifth above all and, in any case, to use only the consonant intervals of thirds and fifths, ascending or descending, in the *basses fondamentales* of their works. In the normalized harmonic style of the Italians, however, root progressions by step were quite common.

Rameau explained the presence of such typical chord progressions as I^6—ii^6_5—V^7—I by claiming that the first two notes of its *basse fondamentale* actually rise by a fourth, since the second chord should not be considered a first-inversion seventh chord on the second scale-degree but rather a "chord of the added sixth" based on the fourth scale-degree. Then what about the movement to the next chord, based on the fifth scale-degree? Rameau theorized that in relation to the third chord, the second chord in the progression changes from a chord of the added sixth to a the first inversion of a seventh chord based on the second scale degree, through a process he called "double employment." Similarly, he considered the root of the second chord in the common progression I—vi—ii^6_5—V^7—I to be the first scale degree with an added sixth, changing to the first inversion of the chord based on the sixth scale degree through double employment before moving on to the first inversion of the chord on the second scale degree with a seventh. Roman numerals referring to scale degrees have been used to streamline this explanation for students, although this convention was introduced only later in the eighteenth century by Georg Joseph Vogler (1749–1814) and Johann Philipp Kirnberger (1721–1783).

Having identified the driving force of the falling-fifths sequence as the suspension in which the seventh of one chord resolves to the third of the next, Rameau wished to treat all suspensions as chordal events. Hence, he considered the written bass notes of the common suspension shown in Example 15-2 to be part of a "bass by supposition," while the *basse fondamentale* moves by fifths.

EXAMPLE 15-2. An example of bass by supposition from Jean-Philippe Rameau, *Traité de l'harmonie* (1722)

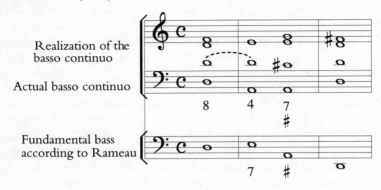

Rameau introduces the terms "tonic" and "dominant." He recognizes the harmonized modal final as the tonic of an entire piece or movement, but he uses the term "dominant" to designate any chord that resolves by movement of the fundamental bass by falling fifth or rising fourth. He privileges the chord built on the fifth degree of the reigning key with the name *tonique dominante*— "the dominant of the tonic."

Although Rameau's theories are important evidence of early eighteenth-century awareness of a normalized harmonic style, the theory of harmony familiar to modern students is actually derived from the opposing and competing theories of Vogler and Kirnberger developed later in the century.

BIBLIOGRAPHICAL NOTES

France in Decline in the Theater of Europe

As noted earlier, the best survey of French music is James R. Anthony, *French Baroque Music from Beaujoyeulx to Rameau,* rev. ed. (Portland, OR: Amadeus Press, 1997), and the political and cultural context is set out admirably in Robert M. Sherwood, *Music in the Service of the King* (Ithaca, NY: Cornell University Press, 1973).

Italian Music: Rapprochement and Resistance

The continuing tradition of Lully's operas is traced in Caroline Wood, *Music and Drama in the 'Tragédie en musique,' 1673–1715: Jean-Baptiste Lully and his Successors* (New York: Garland, 1996). Rameau's operas are treated in detail by Charles William Dill, *Monstrous Opera: Rameau and the Tragic Tradition* (Princeton, NJ: Princeton University Press, 1998). The context for the emergence of Rameau's operas, seen from the perspective of the libretto, is the subject of Catherine Kintzler, *Poétique de l'opéra français de Corneille à Rousseau* (Paris: Minerve, 1991). The controversies surrounding the competition between French and Italian musical styles are scrutinized by Georgia Cowart, *The Origins of Modern Musical Criticism: French and Italian Music 1600–1750* (Ann Arbor: UMI, 1981).

The Cantate Françoise

The master narrative of this subject is David Tunley, *The Eighteenth-Century French Cantata,* 2nd ed. (New York: Clarendon Press, 1997), supplemented by Tunley's seventeen volumes of facsimiles of original prints and manuscript scores published in the series *The Eighteenth-Century French Cantata* (New York, 1990).

Organ Music

The best guides to the French organ of this period are the relevant chapters of Peter Williams, *The European Organ, 1450–1850* (Nashua, NH: Organ Literature Foundation, 1967); and Fenner Douglass, *The Language of the Classical French Organ,* rev ed. (New Haven: Yale University Press, 1995). A more detailed study, including the repertoire, is found in the five volumes of Norbert Dufourcq, *Le Livre de l'orgue français, 1589-1789* (Paris: Picard, 1971–82).

Pièces de clavecin—*Sonatas and* Sonades—*Orchestral Music*

The most detailed survey of the harpsichord repertoire remains David R. Fuller, "Eighteenth-Century French Harpsichord Music," Ph.D. diss., Harvard Univ., 1965. The chapter "French Masters" by Mark Kroll in *Eighteenth-Century Keyboard Music,* ed. Robert L. Marshall (New York: Schirmer, 1994), 124–33, offers a brief overview. A substantial treatment of Couperin's harpsichord music is included in Wilfrid Mellers, *François Couperin and the French Classical Tradition,* rev. ed (London: Faber, 1987). A fascinating study of Jacquet's life and works is Catherine Cessac, *Elisabeth Jacquet de La Guerre: une femme compositeur sous le règne de Louis XIV* (Arles: Actes sud, 1995). Aside from Anthony's *French Baroque Music,* cited above, an overview of French ensemble sonatas of this period can be found in William S. Newman, *The Sonata in the Baroque Era,* 4th ed. (New York: Norton, 1983), cited in earlier chapters.

The Harmonic Theories of Jean-Philippe Rameau

Rameau's first treatise is available in English translation as Jean-Philippe Rameau, *Treatise on Harmony,* trans. Philip Gossett (New York: Dover Publications, 1971). The most recent, authoritative study of Rameau's theory is Thomas Christensen, *Rameau and Musical Thought in the Enlightenment* (Cambridge; Cambridge University Press, 1993).

CHAPTER 16

German Traditions and Innovations, 1690–1750

THE NEW LUTHERAN CANTATA

During the ten years or so surrounding 1700, a new type of Lutheran church vocal work emerged in the western part of Saxony known as Thuringia, located in the north-central part of the German-speaking Empire (Figure 16-1). From there it rapidly spread to most Lutheran cities of the region. This new genre was named the "cantata" by the poet most responsible for its creation; in modern writing it is often called the "madrigal cantata," or "new cantata." It is one of the last two new genres of the Baroque era.

The poet most responsible for the creation of the new Lutheran cantata was Erdmann Neumeister (1671–1756), a theologian from a village near Weissenfels, who was educated at the University of Leipzig. After his graduation in 1695, he remained at the university to deliver a series of lectures, which were published in 1707 by Christian Friedrich Hunold, who falsely claimed authorship, under the title *Die allerneueste Art, zur reinen und galanten Poesie zu gelangen* ("The Very Latest Manner of Mastering Pure and Fashionable Poetry"). In these lectures, Neumeister presented his ideas about a new kind of church cantata, a relatively short work consisting of a few alternating recitatives and arias. In this respect, Neumeister says, "a cantata looks like a segment out of an opera." In fact, his lectures were mostly about how to write German-language opera librettos in imitation of the Italian type, reflecting that fact that German-language operas, a novelty at that time, were currently being produced in Leipzig.

In the verses for recitatives, Neumeister explains, rhyme should be irregular or avoided entirely, and the lines of poetry should have neither caesuras (regular internal breaks) nor regular metrical scansion. Iambs, trochees, and dactyls should follow closely on one another. Expression and meaning should be clear and straightforward. German verse of this kind, resembling Italian *versi sciolti*, was unknown before this time.

Arias, on the other hand, should have regular rhyme and metrical scansion. German poems with these two characteristics had been introduced by Martin Opitz in 1624; they were often called "odes." Neumeister explains that the aria texts for operas and cantatas differed from odes in several important respects. Odes were always multi-strophic, whereas arias should have but a single strophe, so that the composer can match his music to the declamation and expression of a single text. An aria text should express a specific affect in a dramatic or

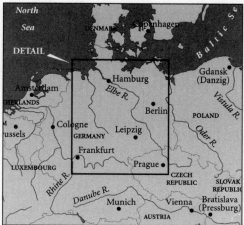

Figure 16-1. Saxony and Thuringia about 1700—detailed and context maps

theatrical manner, and it should be designed to afford the composer opportunities to exercise artistry, whereas ode texts are meant to be sung to "common and easy melodies." The first part of an aria text must have self-contained meaning so that it can be repeated at the end, which is never the case with ode texts. Finally, unlike an ode, which can stand alone, an aria text should be written so as to require a preceding recitative or another aria for context. Neumeister names several genres of vocal music that use arias, the most important of which are opera, oratorio, and cantata.

The German genre that Neumeister calls "oratorio" actually consists of Biblical passages interspersed with arias, like the "concerto-aria" discussed earlier. Since Neumeister's sample oratorios do not contain verses for recitatives, they represented no novelty in 1695.

Although Neumeister compared his new type of church cantata to a segment of an opera, his early cantata texts, unlike an operatic scene, imply the use of only one voice, occasionally two. Their texts contain no dialogue between characters.

At first, Neumeister seems to be describing a German version of an Italian chamber cantata text, like those that Alessandro Scarlatti set. However, he presents, as examples, several cantatas with religious content, cantatas that were eventually published in his collection of church cantata texts in 1716. These texts consist of two to four aria texts alternating with a similar number of texts for recitatives. Whereas the juxtaposition of recitative and aria can be found in earlier concerto-arias, the new features in Neumeister's cantata texts are (1) their exclusive use of newly written recitative and aria texts deliberately linked in content and expression, whereas recitative texts in earlier aria-cantatas were nearly always drawn from the Bible; and (2) the regular alternation between substantial recitatives and arias at the core of the cantata as opposed to earlier works, whose recitatives are generally short.

Neumeister left Leipzig in 1697 to serve as pastor in a succession of other cities, spreading the new cantata genre whereever he went. In 1700–01 he assembled his first complete cycle of new-style cantata texts, all consisting of only recitatives and arias, for the Sundays and major holidays of the entire liturgical year for Weissenfels, near his birthplace. These texts were set to music by Johann Philipp Krieger (1649–1725). These settings are lost, however, and we have only Krieger's music for an earlier Neumeister text without recitatives.

Neumeister's first cycle of new-style cantata texts was reprinted in 1704 under the title *Geistliche Kantaten statt einer Kirchenmusik* ("Religious Cantatas in Place of A Piece of Church Music"), meaning that they were intended to replace church vocal music of the older, traditional types—the concertos, arias, and concerto-arias, with or without chorale texts and melodies.

For Rudolstadt in 1708, Neumeister wrote another cycle of cantata texts that were set by Philipp Heinrich Erlebach (1657–1714) and others. And for Eisenach in 1711 and 1714, he produced two more cantata cycles, most of which were set by Georg Philipp Telemann (1681–1767). After he moved to Hamburg in 1721, Telemann continued to set Neumester's cantata texts. In the meantime, Neumeister's type of cantata text was taken up by a legion of other religious poets, including Neukirch, König, Postel, Richey, Rambach, Lehms, and Franck. Settings of their texts were composed in nearly every Lutheran city of Germany by the mid-1720s.

Beginning with the 1708 cycle, Neumeister began to include texts for short vocal ensemble movements in his cantata librettos. In the 1711 and 1714 sets he added biblical passages and chorale strophes to be sung by ensembles or choirs, always keeping the central core of non-biblical recitatives and arias. A good example of this expanded type of Neumeister cantata is *Gott der Hoffnung erfülle euch* ("May the God of Hope Fill You," W. 43), which Georg Philipp Telemann composed in 1717 for the church at the court of Duke Johann Wilhelm of Saxe-Eisenach.

The text of Telemann's *Gott der Hoffnung erfülle euch* combines biblical passages with Neumeister's original poetry for recitatives and arias. Like many cantatas by Neumeister and his imitators, it follows the outline of a sermon: presentation of a biblical passage, interpretation of the passage, and application of the lesson that it contains, sometimes divided into reflection and exhortation.

The text of the first chorus is the presentation. It is taken from Romans 15:13—"May the God of hope fill you with every joy and peace in faith, so that you may have hope through the power of the Holy Spirit." This text is presented as a *dictum*, that is, an authoritative pronouncement, to which the rest of the text reacts.

The text of Telemann's first aria contains the explanation of the biblical *dictum*: "Faith and hope, consolation and strength are the works of the Holy Spirit. Peace and joy, light and love come from his power. All the good things we have are gifts of the Holy Spirit."

The application proceeds, as often in sermons, in two steps. The first, in the first recitative, is a prayer for ourselves. The second, in second aria and final chorale strophe, contains an admonition directed at others.

It is not surprising that Neumeister's cantata texts resemble sermons, since as a Lutheran clergyman he preached every week. His new type of cantata was performed before the sermon, rather than at the Offertory, as had been traditional with the older types of *Kirchenmusik*. In general, his cantata texts relate to the Gospel and Epistle reading assigned to the Sunday or feast day for which the cantata was written. The sermon was also expected to comment on these biblical readings.

The message of hope and joy contained in the text of the first chorus of *Gott der Hoffnung erfülle euch* is emphasized by Telemann's energetic rhythms, expansive arpeggios played by the two horns, and high tessitura of the voices of the chorus and the violins. For the music of the first aria, Telemann appears to derive most of his invention from the words *Stärke* ("strength") and *Triebe* ("power"), which are reflected in the fanfare figures played by the strings doubling one another in octaves, occasionally reinforced by the horns. The concept of *Freude* ("joy") motivates the rapid runs and short melismas in Telemann's setting. The affect of the second aria is joy and optimism, suggested by the reigning rhythmic figure, energetic tempo, and major key.

Telemann's manner of combining his vocal and instrumental forces in his first chorus draws on the style of Latin church works for chorus and orchestra composed in northern Italy during the decades surrounding 1700; the chorus declaims homophonically while the orchestra plays passages featuring energetic motor rhythms and lively figuration typical of a violin concerto—Vivaldi's *Gloria* is a good example. As in the Italian church works, the full orchestration implies the use of a choir with doubled voices, not merely the quartet of solo singers typical of seventeenth-century Lutheran concerted church music.

Both of Telemann's arias in *Gott der Hoffnung erfülle euch* also reflect the style and form of contemporaneous Italian church music. One can point to at least five ways in which Telemann's cantata arias resemble the arias in Latin church works by Italians at this time: (1) The extended periods in Telemann's arias are propelled by continuous motor rhythms and normalized chord progressions, including sequences; (2) they are structured by alternations between orchestral ritornellos that begin and end with the same harmony and vocal periods that begin in one key and end with a cadence in another; (3) their point of furthest harmonic remove comes near the midpoint; (4) they begin with a short vocal fragment (a motto), which is elaborated after a brief instrumental interjection; and (5) the last vocal period brings back music from the first, but modified and transposed—the first vocal period typically ends in the dominant, whereas the last concludes in the tonic.

It is important to note that neither of the two arias in this cantata is set in operatic da capo form. In the operatic form, the repetition almost always encompasses two vocal periods—the first ending on the dominant, the second concluding on the tonic, and the two periods are separated by a ritornello in the key of the dominant. There is no harmonic adjustment or transposition in the da capo repetition of the typical opera aria at this time. Telemann's two arias, therefore, reflect the *Kirchenarie* form discussed earlier and exemplified by the arias in Bonporti's solo motet *Ite molles ite flores.*

In fact, a Neumeister cantata without chorus, as in his first cycle, with its alternation between recitatives and non-da-capo arias, resembles an Italian solo motet from the same period, except that it does not conclude with an Alleluia, as a solo motet normally does, and its text is in German rather than Latin. A Neumeister cantata with opening and closing choruses is much like a contemporaneous Italian ensemble motet or setting of a liturgical text. Although Neumeister does not mention these resemblances, he did include a "Latin cantata" text, *Me miserum!*, in the 1695 lectures. That text was reprinted in Neumeister's volume of collected cantata texts in 1716, and it was set to music by Telemann. Although Neumeister called it a "Latin cantata," it is hardly different from an Italian solo motet.

The latest church music from Italy reached Telemann and his colleagues in Saxony readily, since Italian and Italian-trained musicians were found in the musical establishment of the Dresden court—especially since the Elector of Saxony converted to the Catholic religion in 1697, in order to become king of Poland. It was natural that composers in Saxony were influenced by the new Italian church music pouring into its capital city, Dresden, after the foundation of a Catholic chapel at the court. To the ordinary Lutheran, however, opera, not Italian church music, appeared to be the inspiration for the new cantata, and this perception generated controversy.

In his 1704 collection of texts, Neumeister anticipated objections to his new type of cantata libretto because of its similarity to opera: "It might almost be supposed that many would be vexed in spirit and ask how sacred music and opera can be reconciled." He answered with a rhetorical question, "May not this kind of poetry, although modeled on theatrical verse, be sanctified by being dedicated to the service of God?" He added three citations from Scripture: I Cor. 14:7, Tim. 4:5, and Phil. 1:18. In the second of these the Apostle Paul confirms Neumeister's point, a central tenet for Lutherans: "For everything created by God is good, and nothing is to be rejected if it is received with thanksgiving; for then it is consecrated by the word of God and prayer." In the first citation, Paul compares the relative usefulness of speaking in tongues and prophecy, emphasizing the need for communication—"Were there a pipe or harp, if they do not produce distinct pitches, how can one know what is piped or harped?" In the last citation, Paul redeems any debt owed by Onesimus, as Christ has redeemed our sins by God's grace. Taken together, the three biblical citations imply that operatic forms may be sanctified if, by their power to communicate, they lead the believer to accept God's grace. By its power to inspire strong emotions, operatic poetry and music can lead members of the congregation to receive the Gospel through the office of the Holy Spirit and thus accept salvation. Johann Schelle's successor as music director of the St. Thomas church in Leipzig, Johann Kuhnau (1660–1722), wrote (1709) that recitatives and arias in church cantatas "seek to stir up in the listener holy devotion, love, joy, sadness, wonderment, and similar things." In his book *Zufällige Gedancken von der Kirchenmusic* ("Incidental Thoughts about Church Music") of 1721, the Lutheran theologian Gottfried Scheibel wrote enthusiastically about the role of music in moving the affections of worshipers in accordance with the Gospel. He even went so far as to approve church performance of opera arias with religious texts substituted for the original poetry.

Opponents of Neumeister's innovation were also heard. When Johann Mattheson (1781–1764) was named music director for the Hamburg Cathedral in 1715, he came into conflict with the older cantor (music director) of the city's Latin school, Joachim Gerstenbüttel (1647–1721), over his use of recitatives and arias in church cantatas. Between 1726 and 1728, Mattheson exchanged two pamphlets on the subject with Joachim Meyer (1661–1732) of Göttingen, even though earlier, in *Das neu-eröffnete Orchester* (1713), Mattheson took a moderate position: "It would be just as well if greater restraint were sometimes shown in these [church] pieces, and if they and the accompaniment, even in arias and recitatives, were composed with altogether more seriousness and solidity than is required in chamber or theatrical music." Johann Sebastian Bach (1685–1750) answered the call for "seriousness and solidity" by emphasizing learned counterpoint in his cantatas.

BACH'S CANTATAS

After succeeding Johann Kuhnau as music director in Leipzig in 1723, Bach composed five annual cycles of cantatas deriving from the new textual type pioneered by Neumeister. The cantatas of the first two cycles were written at the rate of one per week. Most of these include substantial choral movements. "Seriousness and solidity" are the hallmarks of their music.

The Leipzig position was Bach's last. This and his previous posts were located within the areas of Saxony and Thuringia, where he was born and raised, and in which the new cantata had emerged during his youth. He was born in Eisenach, where his father was the chief *Stadtpfeifer* and where Neumeister was to write his third and fourth cycle of cantata texts, set by Telemann. After his father's death in 1695, Bach lived and studied briefly with an older brother in nearby Ohrdruf. In 1700 he won a stipend as choral scholar at the Latin school in far-off Lüneburg, near Hamburg. After graduating in 1702, Bach held a series of posts back in the region of his birth: court musician in Weimar (1703), church organist in Arnstadt (1703–07), church organist at Mühlhausen (1707–08), organist, then concertmaster, at the court of Weimar (1708–17), music director at the court of Cöthen (1717–23), and finally cantor and music director in Leipzig (1723–50). Until he reached Leipzig, a large, cosmopolitan university city and center of book publishing, Bach's positions were in small towns and rural courts. Arnstadt, for instance, had a population of only 3,800, yet it managed to employ three full-time church organists.

The series of Bach's positions outlines a rapid rise in the music profession, aided, especially at first, by a network of family connections that spread over much of Thuringia. Until the move to Leipzig, he obtained each position easily through an overwhelming display of organ virtuosity or the performance of a new or recent piece of vocal church music far more brilliant and elaborate than could have been expected. At Leipzig, however, Bach was the third choice of the town council, and he obtained the position only after it was turned down by Telemann and Christoph Graupner (1683–1760), both of whom possessed university degrees, as had all Leipzig cantors since the sixteenth century. The Leipzig position entailed not only directing or supervising music for all the city's churches and administering the civic instrumentalists but also teaching such subjects as Latin and rhetoric in the St. Thomas School and training its students to sing and play instruments.

In each position, Bach composed more extensively than the job required. The music that he composed usually corresponded roughly with the position he held, more because of performance opportunities than because of employment requirements. Thus, during his time in Arnstadt and Mühlhausen and in his earlier years in Weimar, he composed mostly organ music. Once he gained administrative authority over the court musicians in Weimar as concertmaster, he began to compose more cantatas. Since the prince and his court at Cöthen were Calvinist, Bach composed no church cantatas there, but produced a very large amount of chamber and orchestral music, much of it now lost. At Leipzig, Bach neglected his teaching duties and instead chose to compose and perform many cantatas and other examples of large-scale concerted church vocal music. Later, once his interests turned away from his church duties, he worked in a variety of other genres.

In each position, Bach started off enjoying general good will, and he was always paid substantially more than his predecessor. Eventually friction developed with certain individuals over his ambitious performance program. In each case, Bach was able to move on and upward, until Leipzig, where he remained frustrated by financial limitations and his inability to secure the position he wanted at the court of Dresden.

In Mühlhausen, 1707–08, Bach began composing multi-movement church vocal works with orchestral accompaniment (*Kirchenmusik*) of the older types: concerto-arias with biblical texts and no recitatives and chorale concertos. His first cantatas based on the new type of libretto, with recitatives and arias, were written in Weimar beginning about 1713. In this respect, Bach belonged to the first wave of cantata composers. He set two librettos by Neumeister but preferred texts by the Weimar court poet Salomo Franck (1659–1725), an early convert to the new cantata form. Bach began to strike out in his own direction with the Weimar cantatas, emphasizing extensive choruses, colorful variety of instrumentation, and contrapuntal textures.

Bach continued this tendency in Leipzig. The cantatas written in his first year there generally begin with a long, elaborate, and richly scored chorus on a biblical text, and many include a chorale-based movement near the middle, as well as the usual simply harmonized chorale at the end.

The cycle of cantatas for Bach's second year in Leipzig, 1724–25, is dominated by works based more extensively on chorales. In these chorale cantatas Bach usually set the first and last stanza of the chorale text to music as the first and last movements of the cantata, and these two movements usually also incorporate the chorale melody. Most of the interior movements use texts that are poetic paraphrases of chorale stanzas. These paraphrases normally preserve the meaning of the original chorale stanzas but change their wording so as to create poetic meters for arias and free verse for recitatives. Although the music of these internal movements is usually composed freely, in a few of them Bach incorporates the chorale melody. Earlier German chorale concertos always used the successive stanzas of a chorale text unchanged; they did not include poetry specifically suited for recitatives and arias. Only in eight later chorale cantatas did Bach used only unaltered chorale stanzas, and in those works the few recitatives that he included are rhythmically stilted because the verses of the chorale texts are metrical. Although written later, Bach's *Ein feste Burg ist unser Gott*

Franck's cantata text *Alles, was von Gott geboren* (1715) compared with Bach's *Ein feste Burg ist unser Gott*, BWV 80, final version (ca. 1735–1747)

Franck's text, 1715	*Ein feste Burg ist unser Gott*, BWV 80
	1. "Ein feste Burg," chorale fantasy
"Alles, was von Gott geboren," aria	2. "Alles, was von Gott geboren" and "Mit unsrer Macht" combined in an aria with chorale cantus firmus added
"Erwäge doch," recitative	3. "Erwäge doch," recitative
"Komm in mein Herzenshaus," aria	4. "Komm in mein Herzenshaus," aria
	5. "Und wenn die Welt," chorale chorus
"So stehe denn," recitative	6. "So stehe denn," recitative
"Wie selig sind doch die," aria	7. "Wie selig sind doch die," duet
"Mit unsrer Macht," chorale stanza	8. "Das Wort sie sollen," chorale harmonization

("A Mighty Fortress Is Our God," A. 125) resembles his typical chorale cantatas of 1724–25 in its mixture of movements based on the text and melody of the chorale and recitatives, arias, and a duet not based on the chorale.

The genesis of Bach's *Ein feste Burg ist unser Gott*, BWV 80, covers a span of twenty-five years. The text of the cantata includes three arias and two recitatives from a libretto by Salomo Franck that Bach had set at Weimar in 1715; no music from this setting survives. In Leipzig, sometime between 1727 and 1731, Bach incorporated Franck's text into a larger chorale cantata by adding an opening movement that sets the first stanza of the chorale *Ein feste Burg ist unser Gott* as a straightforward four-voice harmonization of Luther's melody. The second stanza of the chorale text was to be sung as a chorale cantus firmus, simultaneously with the text of Franck's first aria. Only the first movement and beginning of the second survive from this version. Finally, sometime between the mid-1730s and mid-1740s Bach replaced the simple chorale setting of the opening movement with a monumental chorale fantasy for chorus and orchestra. And he placed another chorale-based chorus in the middle of the cantata, either by retaining it from the previous Leipzig version or composing it anew. The box above summarizes the relationship between Franck's cantata text and the final version of Bach's *Ein feste Burg ist unser Gott*.

Cantatas of the new type pioneered by Neumeister were normally connected to the sermon in both placement and content; Bach's *Ein feste Burg ist unser Gott* is no exception.

First, concerning the placement of the cantata, the box on page 463 lists the order of worship observed in Leipzig during Bach's lifetime on Reformation

Order of the Principal Worship Service (*Hauptgottesdienst*) for Reformation Sunday in Leipzig during J. S. Bach's lifetime
Bells rung at 6:00 a.m. Candles set out at 7:00 a.m. Organ prelude Motet Kyrie (concerted music) and Gloria (chanted) Chorale: *Allein Gott in der Höh' sei Ehr* Collect: short prayer in German, text specified Epistle: II Thess. 2: 3–8 Chorale: *O Herre Gott dein göttlich Wort* Gospel: Rev. 14: 6–8 Credo (manner of delivery not specified) Cantata Chorale: *Wir glauben all an einen Gott* Chorale: *Erhalt uns, Herr bei deinem Wort* Sermon: based on the Gospel Te Deum laudamus: sung with drums and trumpets Chorale: *Nun danket alle Gott* Collect: another short prayer in German The Lord's Prayer Prayer of Consecration Chorales (unspecified) Blessing Chorales: *Gott sei uns gnädig, Ein feste Burg ist unser Gott*, and others

Sunday (October 31), the day for which *Ein feste Burg ist unser Gott* was intended. The organ prelude was presumably one of Bach's elaborate chorale settings of the type to be discussed later in this chapter. Typically the motet and Kyrie were drawn from the large collection of sixteenth- and earlier seventeenth-century works in the *stile antico* that Bach maintained for use in the Leipzig churches. The chorales were sung by the congregation with organ accompaniment, possibly preceded by an organ prelude. In this order of service, two chorales come between the cantata and the sermon, but in the orders for other days of the year the cantata precedes the sermon directly. Some longer cantatas were composed in two parts; the first part was performed before the sermon and the second part after it.

Secondly, as to content, Bach's *Ein feste Burg ist unser Gott* was connected to the sermon, which would have expounded the designated biblical readings for the day: the Gospel and the Epistle. The Epistle for Reformation Sunday in Leipzig was II Thessalonians 2:3–8, which reads as follows, translating from Luther's German Bible:

(3) Let no one deceive you in any way! For He will not come, unless the rebellion comes first, and the man of sin is revealed, the son of corruption, (4) who is repugnant and who exalts himself against everything that signifies God or worship, so that he seats himself in the temple of God as a God and presents himself as God. (5) Do you not remember that I told you this when I was still with you? (6) And you know what is restraining Him now so that He may be appear in his time. (7) For malice is already secretly at work, so that he who now permits it must be eliminated. (8) And then the wicked man will be revealed, who the Lord will slay with the spirit of his mouth and will destroy by the manifestation of his eternal life.

The Gospel for the day was Revelation 14: 6–8:

(6) Then I saw another angel flying in the middle of the sky, with an eternal gospel to proclaim to those who live and dwell on earth, to every nation and tribe and tongue and people; (7) and he said with a loud voice, "Fear God and give him glory, for the time of his judgment has come; and pray to him who made heaven and earth, the sea and the fountains of water." (8) And another angel followed, saying, "Fallen, fallen is Babylon, the great city, for it has made all nations drink the wine of its whoring."

Shocking as it may seem to us today, Luther interpreted "the man of sin" to mean the pope and Babylon to represent Rome. These two passages were presented as a prophesy that the second coming will not occur until the Catholic church is overthrown by the Protestant Reformation, whose beginning was commemorated on Reformation Sunday. This interpretation of the biblical readings explains the extended battle metaphor in the text of Bach's *Ein feste Burg ist unser Gott*, in which the "ancient, evil enemy," the devil or anti-Christ, stands for the pope. The text and translation are given in the Web supplement; the words and phrases that relate to the theme of struggle against this evil enemy are easily identified.

Like most cantata texts, *Ein feste Burg ist unser Gott* is organized like a sermon, or perhaps like two sermons. The chorale stanza of the first chorus serves, in place of a biblical reading, as the dictum, the text to be considered. Franck's words for the second movement may be understood as an interpretation of the first chorus text, although they were not originally written for that purpose. The recitative (third movement) contains a reflection ("Consider, Child of God. . . ."), and the fourth movement aria is an exhortation to let Jesus enter one's heart to drive world and Satan out. The middle chorus "And if the world were full of devils," provides a second chorale text in place of a biblical reading, but this one is directly followed by an exhortation ("Then stand beside the bloodstained flag of Christ") and a kind of benediction ("Blessed are they. . . .") and pledge ("They shall cling to the Word of God").

Using the language of the affections, Bach's music emphasizes the emotional dimension of each text, so that the listeners might receive the Word through the office of the Holy Spirit and attain grace. As Bach wrote in the margin of his personal Bible (next to 2 Chronicles 5: 13), "With devotional music, God is always present in his Grace."

The first chorus is powerful and majestic, dominated by the ascending rhythms of the anapest (∪ ∪ —) and pyrrhico-anapest (∪ ∪ ∪ —) feet. The combination of three oboes in unison in canon with the double basses and organ pedals—a canonic presentation of the chorale melody in cantus firmus style, phrase by phrase—contributes to the impression of power and strength, as do the first three notes of the chorale—repetitions of a single pitch, which invite an accented performance. The four voices in the first chorus constantly intertwine with a series of imitative subjects derived from the successive phrases of the chorale, while a principal subject, derived from the first chorale phrase, appears at from time to time throughout. A continuous bass part for the cellos weaves an additional independent strand of counterpoint. This technique—simultaneous presentation of the chorale melody as cantus firmus and as a series of subjects treated imitatively, common in Bach's chorale-based choruses—is borrowed from the tradition of the organ chorale fantasy.

The other concerted chorale chorus, *Und wenn die Welt voll Teufel wär* ("And if the world were full of devils"), sets the chorale cantus firmus, powerfully intoned by the full choir in octaves, against a concerto-style orchestral foreground of swirling, agitated figures plainly intended to evoke a "world full of devils," an affect-laden image of the kind typically treated with musical illustration by German composer's of Bach's generation.

The key affective words and expressions in the text of the aria with chorale cantus firmus, *Alles, was von Gott geboren* ("Everyone who is born of God"), are "victory," "battle," "blood," "conquers," and "hold the field," all of which contribute to the metaphor of warfare against evil. Consequently, Bach gives the violins rapid and incessant triadic arpeggio figures, evoking a trumpet's battle signals, and spiked contours in his relentless elaboration on the fanfare idea, which accompanies the expansive melismas sung by the bass and the unyielding cantus firmus intoned by the soprano. These features of musical invention promote such concepts as vehemence and aggressiveness in the music, matching similar ideas in the text.

Forceful projection of the text's meaning and emotion in the two recitative movements, on the other hand, is accomplished through Bach's highly inflected delivery. This is a type of recitative particular to German vocal works of this period. In his master treatise, *Der vollkommene Capellmeister* (1739), Johann Mattheson gives a precise demonstration of how this detailed, sometimes exaggerated type of declamation is capable of conveying and clarifying the elaborate sentence structure of German, in which inflection holds the key to spoken communication. Speaking the German words of these recitatives with the rhythms and inflections of Bach's setting convincingly demonstrates what must have been the impassioned delivery of the Lutheran preachers of his day.

The text of the soprano aria *Komm in mein Herzenshaus* ("Enter now into my heart") develops the metaphor of romantic love and marriage as a symbol of the union between believer and Christ—a favorite metaphor for arias in the new Lutheran cantata, and one that reflects the influence of Pietist literature. For his setting, Bach borrows a musical *topos* from Italian opera in choosing such aspects of the *aria siciliana* ("Sicilian aria") as $\frac{12}{8}$ meter, moderate tempo, consonant harmonies, and a flowing, melismatic vocal line.

Bach's setting of the relatively relaxed and peaceful text of the duet *Wie selig sind doch die* ("Blessed are they") draws upon another operatic *topos*, the pastoral style, evoked by the use of the oboe da caccia (a type of tenor oboe) that imitates a shepherd's bagpipe, the opening harmonic gambit of I—IV—I, and the gentle melodic and rhythmic contours.

Neither the soprano aria nor the duet, however, use operatic da capo form. Instead, in keeping with the most common practice among Lutheran cantata composers of his generation, Bach casts these items in one or another version of the ritornello form (the *Kirchenarie* formal approach) used earlier in Latin church works by Italians of Vivaldi's generation. The soprano aria, in B minor, contains four modulating vocal periods (moving i→v, v→III, III→iv, and V→i), not counting the introductory vocal motto phrase. The four modulating vocal periods are framed by five tonally stable ritornellos in i, v, III, iv, and i. The return of the first sentence of the text at the end (mm. 28–34) is set to a version of the first vocal period, which is, as usual, modified to replace the original modulation to the dominant with a conclusive tonic ending. The duet, in G major, also has four vocal periods (I→V, I→vi, ii→V, and I→I), not counting motto phrases, framed by five ritornellos (in I, V, vi→iii, V, and I), of which the last is a repetition of the first, cued by the notation *dal segno* ("from the sign").

Although Bach composed about sixty cantatas a year during his first several years in Leipzig, his pace of production fell off in the spring of 1725. The cantatas of Bach's third, fourth, and fifth annual cycles were written at an ever slower pace, in part because he had an ample supply of works to draw on and in part because conflicts with the Leipzig town council lead Bach to turn his interest away from his routine church duties. Although he continued to compose concerted vocal works, including several on a large scale, for the churches of Leipzig for decades afterward, Bach began to devote more of his time to public concerts featuring instrumental music, which will be discussed later.

Elsewhere in Lutheran Germany, beginning in the 1730s, the defining stylistic features of Bach's kind of cantata—strict counterpoint, intensive elaboration of a few motives, promotion of a distinct musical metaphor and associated affective expression in each number, and highly inflected, rhetorically exaggerated recitatives—were losing favor among younger composers and church goers, who were increasingly influenced by such middle-class, Enlightenment ideals as moderation, clarity, and naturalness. In 1737, the Hamburg-based composer and music critic Johann Adolph Scheibe (1708–1776) published an attack on Bach, in which he wrote:

This great man would be admired by whole nations if he had more pleasantness, if he did not remove the natural element in his pieces by giving them a bombastic and confused style, and if he did not obscure their beauty by an excess of art. . . . This not only removes from his pieces the beauty of harmony but completely covers the melody throughout. All the voices must work with each other and be of equal difficulty, and none of them can be recognized as the principal voice. . . . Bombast has led [him] from the natural to the artificial. . . .

Although Bach had many capable defenders, during and after his lifetime, he surely could see that an era was drawing to a close.

PROTESTANT ORATORIOS AND PASSIONS

The Protestant oratorio was, along with the new cantata, the other of the last two innovative genres of the Baroque era. It arose from older Lutheran traditions of Passion music, *historia*, and sacred dialogue, and in turn influenced a fundamental change in Lutheran Passion music.

The Protestant oratorio arose in Germany early in the eighteenth century. It differed from the Catholic oratorio, which originated in Italy, in its inclusion of substantial choruses throughout, not just at the end, performed by choirs, not just an ensemble made up of the soloists. Like the Catholic type, a Protestant oratorio normally differs from a cantata in its greater length, its representation of characters, and its presentation of an event by means of dialogue, narration, or contemplation. All of these distinguishing features were found earlier in Lutheran Passion music.

In Christianity, the term "Passion" (from the Latin *passio*, meaning "suffering") is used to denote the sufferings of Christ between the night of the Last Supper and the crucifixion. The records of these events in the four Gospels were incorporated into the liturgy of Holy Week since medieval times. Early in the Middle Ages, special reciting formulas were used to chant these texts, and separate singers were assigned the words of individual personages in the story, including the narrator, usually designated as one of the evangelists. By the fifteenth century, polyphonic choruses were employed to represent the crowd (*turba*), and Passion plays with singing and additional text were presented on outdoor stages. By the sixteenth century, complete Passion texts were set to polyphony.

After 1600, developments in Passion music were largely concentrated in the Lutheran, German-speaking regions of Europe. The presentation of the Passion story in music belonged to a larger genre called the *historia*—a biblical narrative in music that included some dialogue. At the beginning of the seventeenth century, the genre of the Lutheran *historia* included musical presentations of Easter and Christmas stories, as well as the Passion episode. Early in the seventeenth century, Lutheran composers of *historie* began to add basso continuo accompaniment to chanted recitation. Heinrich Schütz's *historie* for Easter (1623), the Passion story (ca. 1645), and Christmas (1664) show some liberation from the traditions of liturgical chant and the inclusion of a variety of current forms of accompanied solo singing.

About the middle of the seventeenth century, in Saxony and Thuringia, where the cantata originated, non-biblical texts were added to *historie*, and their range of subject matter was increased. The resulting work, often called *actus oratoius* or *actus musicus*, might draw on various events in the life of Christ, an Old Testament story, or the life of a saint. Matthias Weckmann's *Dialogo von Tobia undt Raquel* (1665), for example, is arranged as a series of brief dialogue vignettes set off by instrumental ritornellos. Within the dialogues, the solo voice parts incorporate recitative, arioso, and aria styles in continuous passages, accompanied by continuo. The only ensemble number is the final trio with strings in an imitative texture. The shorter Latin dialogues, or dialogue motets, of Giacomo Carissimi are the obvious models for German works of this kind.

A larger role was evidently given to the chorus in the *Abendmusiken* (weekly evening church concerts) by Dieterich Buxtehude in Lübeck. Although his music is lost, the surviving librettos show that *Die Hochzeit des Lamms* (1678), *Castrum doloris* (1705), and *Templum honoris* (1705) consisted of a mixture of choruses, recitatives, strophic arias, and chorale settings.

Hamburg became the center of German Protestant oratorio production in the early eighteenth century. A new direction was tried in 1704 with Reinhard Keiser's *Der blutige und sterbende Jesus* ("The Bloody and Dying Jesus"), which told the Passion story entirely as dramatic dialogue, without narration, and in newly written, theatrical-style poetry, with no biblical quotations, reflecting features of the new cantata texts of Erdmann Neumeister and the Italian-style Catholic oratorio. The librettist, Christian Friedrich Hunold, met with strenuous opposition from the clergy and civic authorities when the oratorio was performed in the Hamburg cathedral. As a consequence, such works were seldom heard until Johann Mattheson became director of the cathedral's music in 1715.

As director of music at the Hamburg cathedral, 1715–28, Mattheson produced several oratorio performances each year and composed twenty-six oratorios of his own. Their themes are not limited to the Passion story but relate to many other church feast days and biblical episodes. Their texts consist mostly of new poetry, with occasional biblical quotations and chorale strophes. Their music combines operatic recitatives and arias with vocal ensembles and substantial choruses. Mattheson's first oratorio, *Die heilsame Geburt und Menschwerdung unsers Herrn und Heilandes Jesu Christi* ("The Beneficial Birth and Incarnation of Our Lord and Savior, Jesus Christ," 1715; Part II is W. 44) will serve as an example.

The text of this work was arranged by an unnamed author, perhaps Mattheson himself. Divided into two parts like an Italian oratorio of the time, it presents the Christmas story by combining biblical narration (I Kings 11:29 and Luke 2:4-16) with commentary provided by newly written poetry for arias and duets and by chorale strophes. Of the work's three concerted, non-chorale choruses, one (in

Part I) draws its text from Psalm 50 and the other two (in Part II) are the words of the angels and shepherds from the Gospel of Luke.

Of the six arias, all in Part I, five employ a formal design of *Kirchenarie* type, explained earlier. One solo aria and the final duet use operatic da capo form. The arias and ensembles in the oratorio make modest technical demands on the singers, but they effectively project the prevailing emotion of their texts through musical invention, as would be expected in a work by the leading theorist of the Doctrine of the Affections.

The choruses in Mattheson's *Die heilsame Geburt und Menschwerdung unsers Herrn und Heilandes Jesu Christi* are what distinguish it, above all, from an Italian-style oratorio. In the choruses of angels and shepherds in Part II, as in the reflective chorus "Aus Zion bricht an der schöne Glanz Gottes" (text from Psalm 50:2–3) in Part I, Mattheson bases his imitative texture on expansive subjects.

All of Mattheson's later oratorios are based on newly written librettos without biblical text. All but one of them were completed by 1729. Although there is no trend toward longer and more elaborate choruses, substantial choral movements remain prominent in all of them. Apart from the simple, homophonic settings of chorale strophes, Mattheson's choruses tend to be contrapuntal in texture, some employing invertible counterpoint, fugues with one or two countersubjects, or canon. Several of his choruses based on chorale texts and melodies use combinations of cantus firmus and imitation like those found in J. S. Bach's chorale cantatas. Beginning with his Pentecost oratorio *Die gnädige Sendung* (1716), Mattheson frequently combines an aria with a chorus, most often by replacing the aria's recapitulation with a choral rendition of the first section.

Mattheson's principal successors as oratorio composers in Hamburg were Georg Philipp Telemann, who wrote one Passion each year from 1722 to 1767, as well as ten oratorios on other subjects; and Carl Philipp Emanuel Bach (1714–1788), Johann Sebastian's second surviving son, who produced twenty-seven Passions and oratorios for Hamburg's churches. In addition, Georg Frideric Handel's English-language oratorios may be considered a tangential branch of the Hamburg oratorio tradition, at least in some ways.

HANDEL'S ORATORIOS

Although Handel composed two Italian oratorios in 1707–08, before coming to England, his English oratorios are distinguished from the Italian genre by their many choruses. The obvious precedent for this is, of course, the Hamburg oratorio as exemplified in the works of Reinhard Keiser, Handel's mentor, and Mattheson and Telemann, his two closest friends during his early years and throughout his life. Passages from two of Telemann's cantatas printed at Hamburg in 1725–26 turn up later in Handel's *Messiah* (1742) and *Solomon* (1749).

In 1732 Handel produced a privately staged revival of *Esther*, which he had composed in 1718; whether it was originally intended for staged or concert performance is not known. When a public staging of the work later in 1732 was forbidden by a church authority, Handel presented a concert version of it as an oratorio, enlarged by insertions, including two of his earlier coronation anthems and a birthday ode for Queen Anne. The success of this performance prompted Handel immediately to present the oratorio *Deborah*, most of whose movements he hastily scraped together from his earlier works, fitting them out with new texts by the poet Samuel Humphreys. Soon after, in 1733, Handel composed his first work that was specifically intended as an unstaged English oratorio and that consisted mostly of newly composed music—*Athalia*.

Athalia introduces two features new to Handel's oratorios, both characteristic of Mattheson's Hamburg oratorios—airs that lead directly into choruses and non-da capo airs. The Act I air "When storms the proud to terrors doom" is completed by the chorus, "Oh Judah, boast his matchless law," which provides an expanded recapitulation. This creates a combination of air and chorus as in each of Mattheson's oratorios from his second (*Die gnädige Sendung Gottes des Heiligen Geistes*, 1716) onward. In Handel's *Athalia* there are three other airs that are completed by choruses, although not by means of recapitulation. These airs do not use operatic da capo form but rather one of the non-da-capo forms related to the *Kirchenarie* favored by Mattheson and his German Lutheran contemporaries. There are seven other airs in *Athalia* unconnected with choruses that likewise use a non-da-capo form, and five da capo arias.

The proportion of da-capo airs in Handel's oratorios declines as time passes. His non-da-capo airs are mostly binary or in a ritornello form with partial or modified recapitulation. The expressive language of Handel's arias and ensembles is that of Italian opera seria, as is the case with the Hamburg and Italian-style oratorios of this period.

Many of Handel's oratorio choruses resemble those in Hamburg oratorios, since they often feature passages of choral declamation accompanied by concerto-like string writing alternating with fugal expositions, some of them on expansive subjects. These three features—combinations of air and chorus, non-da-capo airs, and declamatory and fugal choruses—are found consistently in Handel's oratorios from this point onward.

In his oratorios, as in his operas, Handel favors the Hamburg customs of beginning with a French overture, rather than the Italian-style opera *sinfonia*, and using instrumental movements to suggest or depict action.

Other typical features of Handel's oratorios are their division into three acts and their use of a dramatic libretto—the exceptions are *Israel in Egypt*, *Messiah*, and the *Occasional Oratorio*—based on the Old Testament or Apocrypha, in which his audiences perceived a parallel between the Israelites and the English nation—people chosen by God. There are also seven works that might be called "secular oratorios."

Although the prominence of the chorus, both in action and in commentary, is a feature found earlier in the Hamburg oratorio repertoire, Handel's longer and more complex choruses certainly owe much to the English anthem, particularly the choruses of praise in scenes of celebration or of religious ceremonies. Of all the types of chorus—simple and homophonic, massive, fugal, ostinato-based, freely imitative, and combinations—those that employ free or episodic imitation, often with only one or two voices singing at a time, bear the most striking resemblance to the oratorio choruses of Keiser, Mattheson, and Telemann.

Beginning in 1732–33, Handel presented his oratorios in opera theaters before a paying audience as a full evening's entertainment. Thus these works are several times longer than a Hamburg oratorio, which was designed to straddle the sermon in a Sunday worship service and to last no more than eighty or ninety minutes. Since his oratorios were not part of a Lutheran church service, Handel dispenses with the Hamburg custom of including chorale settings. Typical performing forces employed by Handel for his oratorios were 4-9 soloists, chorus of 17–24, and an orchestra of 35–40.

The popularity of Handel's oratorios resulted in financial gains for the composer, especially since there were no stage sets, costumes, or expensive Italian singers to drain away profits. But in spite of the success of his oratorio performances of 1732–33, Handel returned to opera composition. Only when his 1738–39 opera season had to be canceled for lack of subscribers did he begin to write his next two biblical oratorios, *Saul* and *Israel in Egypt*, which received repeated performances in the King's Theatre in 1739.

Called "An Oratorio, or Sacred Drama" in the original printed libretto, Handel's *Saul* (A. 126) consists of a series of disconnected dramatic vignettes organized into three acts. The story is based on episodes from the first book of Samuel, with the biblical narration rewritten as dialogue. The same episodes had been included in an earlier oratorio by Keiser, *Der siegende David* ("The Victorious David") in 1717. Handel must have known Keiser's oratorio; *Saul*, like *Der Siegende David*, employs a keyboard-actuated carillon, an extremely rare instrument, at exactly the same place, the women's chorus of praise that greets David's triumphant return from battle.

Throughout *Saul*, Handel's music emphasizes the libretto's contrasts between the tragic older king Saul, driven mad by jealousy, and the younger David, who gains in strength and maturity as the story unfolds, and between Merab, Saul's haughty and scornful older daughter, and Michal, his younger, enthusiastic daughter, who falls in love with David.

At some points in *Saul*, Handel treats the chorus homophonically and concentrates on forceful declamation. In other places he writes contrapuntally, but his fugal subjects are derived from the rhythms and inflections of the text. Sometimes the chorus represents the People of Israel who participate in the action, as in the massive celebration of David's victory over the Philistines that begins the oratorio (A 126a). At other times they offer reflection and commentary, as in "Mourn, Israel" (A. 126c). where Handel's typically well-calculated growth of effect helps to create a rhetorical disposition animated by musically amplified rhetorical figures.

The scene "Saul disguis'd at Endor" (A. 126b), which begins Act III, includes Handel's brilliant portrayals of Saul's tragic downfall in the opening accompanied recitative, and the Witch, with her grotesque, metrically out-of-kilter incantation air.

After 1739, Handel and others produced performances of his oratorios every year until his death. Until 1752, with a few exceptions, Handel composed one new English oratorio each year. His annual performance series always included several revivals of earlier works, as well. The new oratorios did not venture very far into new stylistic realms. Instead, a significant amount of self-borrowing and an increasing use of motives, themes, ritornellos, accompaniments, and entire movements by composers as early as Carissimi and Stradella kept Handel's oratorios stylistically stable. In a period of rapid social, economic, and political change, the stability of Handel's oratorio style must have been reassuring to his audiences. They quickly became icons of English nationhood. John Hawkins (1719–1789), Handel's friend and admirer, rendered a representative evaluation in his book *A General History of the Science and Practice of Music* (1776), which reflects the way the English aristocracy and merchant class viewed themselves and their nation at a time of expanding empire and fortune:

> Till they were taught the contrary by Handel, none were aware of that dignity and grandeur of sentiment which music is capable of conveying, or that there is a sublime in music as there is in poetry. This is a discovery which we owe to the genius and inventive faculty of this great man; and there is little reason to doubt that the many examples of this kind with which his works abound, will continue to engage the admiration of judicious hearers as long as the love of harmony shall exist.

Figure 16-2. The statue of George Frideric Handel erected in Vauxhall Gardens in 1751

Annual performances of Handel's oratorios did not cease with the composer's death in 1759. Instead, they became perhaps the first group of compositions that have remained permanently in the public concert repertoire. Consequently, Handel's fame never faded. Even during his lifetime, Handel was revered as an immortal genius. In 1751 a statue of him (Fig. 16-2) was erected in Vauxhall Gardens, along with a statue of the great seventeenth-century poet John Milton. After his death, Handel was interred in "Poet's Corner" of Westminster Abbey, where another statue of him was placed. A year later John Mainwaring published a biography of him, the first monograph ever devoted to a single composer. And in 1784 Samuel Arnold began to publish a complete edition of Handel's works, the first ever attempted. It reached sixty volumes before it was discontinued.

Thus, Handel's oratorios present us with a historical paradox. Their musical style is rooted firmly in the last decades of the Early Modern Period (the late Baroque), but in retrospect we see in their social and cultural function and in their reception several key features of musical culture in the Modern Era:

• Concert performance for a paying audience
• Music of the past kept permanently in the repertoire as a timeless canon
• A musical genre and style treated as an icon of nationhood
• Music invested with the attributes of genius on a footing with great literature
• A composer enshrined as immortal, even before his death
• A supporting network of traditions, editions, commentary, and biography

BACH'S PASSIONS AND ORATORIOS

Although the production and immediate reception of Johann Sebastian Bach's Passions and oratorios remained within the traditions of Lutheran worship, the size and scope of his Passions represent innovations parallel with Handel's oratorios, and later they too were exalted as icons of a national culture.

Bach's oratorios are similar in length to his cantatas, differing from them only insofar as they contain a plot or narration with dialogue. The extensive use of biblical texts in Bach's oratorios relate them to the Lutheran *historia* and to the Passion. All three oratorios—for Christmas, Easter, and Ascension—rely heavily on music originally composed for cantatas, especially for secular cantatas, with new text replacing the original words. The Christmas Oratorio is actually a set of six cantatas based on six biblical scenes, intended for six different church services between Christmas and Epiphany.

Bach's Passions were also intended as part of a church service, on Good Friday. He composed three of them, based on the Gospels of Sts. Matthew, John, and Mark (only the text survives), and perhaps one other based on St. Luke, although the St. Luke Passion that survives in Bach's handwriting is by another composer.

Bach's St. Matthew, St. John, and St. Mark Passions are today termed "oratorio Passions" because each is a biblical Passion with some features of an oratorio—non-biblical recitatives and arias. They incorporate recitatives, arias, and choruses whose newly written texts comment upon or contemplate the lessons offered by the Gospel verses, which form the narrative and dramatic core of the works. In addition, Bach added a large number of chorales set to the traditional melodies, simply harmonized or elaborated into a chorale fantasy in the manner of an elaborate cantata chorus.

All of Bach's Passions were extended compositions. The St. Matthew Passion is his longest work; modern performances take about two and a half hours. First performed on April 11, 1727, in the St. Thomas church of Leipzig, this work was revised and expanded in 1736 with the addition of a massive chorus at the end of Part I and a division of the performing forces into two groups. The text is a Passion oratorio by the Leipzig poet Christian Friedrich Henrici (his pen name was Picander), expanded through the addition of biblical text and chorales.

Bach's St. Matthew Passion is organized into fifteen scenes grouped into two parts, each with its own introduction, that straddled the sermon (see the following outline). Each scene consists of a biblical passage comprised of narration by the Evangelist and dialogue, the words spoken by the participants, followed by commentary, reflection, and exhortation. Each scene, therefore,

---

J. S. Bach, *St. Matthew Passion*, Outline

Part I

Introduction. 1–3. Choruses introduce the subject. The crucifixion is predicted.
Scene 1. 4–7. The woman anoints Jesus.
Scene 2. 8–10. Judas takes thirty pieces of silver.
Scene 3. 11–17. The Last Supper.
Scene 4. 18–20. Christ on the Mount of Olives.
Scene 5. 21–25. The prayer vigil at Gethsemane.
Scene 6. 26–29. Jesus is betrayed and captured.

Part II

Introduction. 30–32. Jesus is taken to Caiaphas.
Scene 7. 33–37. Jesus is interrogated.
Scene 8. 38–40. Peter denies Jesus.
Scene 9. 41–46. Jesus is taken before Pilate; Judas hangs himself.
Scene 10. 47–50. Pilate finds Jesus innocent, but the crowd calls for his crucifixion.
Scene 11. 51–54. Jesus is scourged.
Scene 12. 55–58. Simon of Cyrene bears His cross.
Scene 13. 59–62. Jesus is taken to Golgotha and crucified.
Scene 14. 63–65. Earthquake; Jesus is taken down from the cross.
Scene 15. 66–68. Jesus is laid to rest in a sealed tomb.

resembles a small-scale cantata or a sermon in miniature. Scene 1 may serve as an example (A. 127).

First, the story is presented through narration by the Evangelist in recitative and direct discourse by the chorus, representing the disciples, and by the bass-baritone, representing Jesus, in recitative. The woman of Bethany pours precious ointment on the head of Jesus. The disciples object to this waste because the ointment might be sold and the money given to the poor. Jesus, however, defends the woman, saying "The poor are always with you, but me you have not always." All these words are from the Gospel according to St. Matthew. Then follows a recitative and aria on Picander's texts. In the recitative, the scene is summarized ("Your disciples foolishly quarrel"), interpreted ("This pious woman with ointment would prepare Your body for the grave"), and applied ("Then grant, meanwhile, that I, with tears streaming from my eyes, may pour water upon Your head"). The aria responds to this lesson with personal feelings ("Penance and remorse grind the sinful heart in two. May the drops of my tears be an acceptable anointing to You, faithful Jesus"), symbolizing emotional reception of the Gospel through the office of the Holy Spirit.

Bach's music for the concluding aria in Scene 1, *Buß und Reu* ("Penance and remorse") reflects the mixture of sorrow and tenderness implied by the text through elements of invention: the choice of F-sharp minor (equally suitable for sadness and love, according to Mattheson); soft dynamics; moderately slow tempo; dissonance; chromaticism; descending contours, including outlines of a chromatically descending fourth; a prevailing middle-accented, amphibrach rhythmic organization (a "descending" poetic foot suggestive of contraction of the life spirits) of individual measures, elaborating upon the rhythm $\frac{3}{8}$ ♪ | ♩ ♪; descending slurred leaps, notably on various kinds of sevenths, dissonant intervals projecting pain; use of two transverse flutes as obbligato (associated with lamentation, according to Mattheson); but parallel thirds (suggesting the pleasure of love). The middle section of this da capo aria presents a different balance, leaning more toward tenderness than sorrow, with more leaps, less dissonance and chromaticism, staccato notes illustrating tear drops, and two cadences on E major. But the emotions of the text were not Bach's only source of invention.

For a broader view of Bach's sources of musical invention in the St. Matthew Passion and other works, it is useful to consider the fifteen commonplaces or topics (*loci topici*) given by Johann Mattheson in *Der vollkommene Capellmeister:*

1. *Locus notationis* ("place of notation"). Features of the music might be suggested to the composer when he considers how the notation will appear on paper—a single note value or a repeating rhythmic pattern, melodic or contrapuntal inversion, repetition or recapitulation, or canonic passages. Almost any piece or movement by Bach will have many examples of these categories of musical structure reflected in notation.

2. *Locus descriptionis* ("place of description"). Features of the music might be suggested to the composer when he considers how to portray the affections implied by the text of vocal music or emotions of his own choosing

in instrumental music. Although Mattheson does not mention it, aspects of the music might also be suggested by things perceivable by the senses, such as objects, actions, and sounds, that can be imitated in music. The aria *Buß und Reu* illustrates the portrayal of both emotions and the dripping of tears.

3. *Locus generis & speciei* ("place of genus and type"). Features of the music might be suggested to the composer when he decides to adhere to the common characteristics of a musical genre and subgenre, especially when it is different from that of the piece being written. For example, Bach's aria *Gebt mir meinen Jesum wieder* ("Give me back my Jesus") in Scene 9 incorporates features of a virtuosic violin concerto.

4. *Locus totius & partium* ("place of whole and part"). Features of the music might be suggested to the composer when he considers what kind of voices or parts will make up an ensemble, or when he treats the left hand differently from the right in a keyboard work. In the chorale-based chorus *O Mensch, bewein' den Sünde groß* ("O Man, bewail your great sin"), which closes Part I of the St. Matthew Passion, the flutes initially play an ascending line with sixteenth notes, the oboes play a descending line with sixteenth notes, the upper strings play a rhythmically augmented version of the oboe's material, and the basses play both ascending and descending figures derived from the chorale melody. In the second phrase, these materials are exchanged among the sections of the orchestra.

5. *Locus causae efficientis* ("place of efficient cause"). Features of the music might be suggested to the composer when he decides to portray or illustrate a story or action. The various effects of an earthquake are described in text and music in Scene 14.

6. *Locus causae materialis* ("place of material cause"). Features of the music might be suggested to the composer when he places emphasis upon certain categories of materials, such as musical motives, tone qualities, consonances, dissonances, textures, media, dynamics, ranges, accents, etc. For example, an insistent repetition of a dotted-rhythm dominates Bach's aria *Gedult, Geduld!* ("Patience, patience") in Scene 7.

7. *Locus causae formalis* ("place of formal cause"). Features of the music might be suggested to the composer when he decides to adopt a specific and recognized musical form, such as da capo, binary, or ritornello form. The choruses in Bach's St. Matthew Passion that use chorale melodies as cantus firmus also adopt the typical AAB form of the chorale. In the first chorus of the work, *Kommt, ihr Töchter* ("Come, you daughters") this AAB design is deeply imbedded within a ritornello procedure, with the additional eccentricity that the chorale cantus firmus is intoned in the key of G major, while the chorus as a whole is in E minor. The formal outline of this remarkable chorus is given as Fig. 16–3. Five of the arias in Bach's St. Matthew Passion use the true operatic da capo, in which the initial two vocal periods, the first cadencing

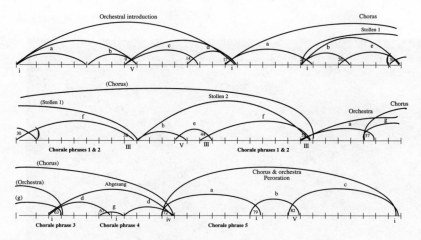

Figure 16-3. An outline of "Kommt, ihr Töchter"

on the fifth degree of a major key or the third degree of a minor key, are repeated at the end without alteration. The other nine arias belong to the *Kirchenarie* category; they limit recapitulation to a ritornello or a single vocal period, or the last vocal period to return is modified to cadence on the tonic.

8. *Locus causae finalis* ("place of final cause"). Features of the music might be suggested to the composer when he considers the overall purpose of the composition. Nearly everything about Bach's St. Matthew Passion seems calculated to achieve the purpose of inspiring emotional acceptance of the Gospel. For example, the mixture of sorrow, love, and thanksgiving are characteristic of Lutheran interpretations of the crucifixion, for which one must feel sincere sorrow and repentance but also gratitude and joy for the salvation it brings.

9. *Locus causae effectorum* ("place of efficient cause"). Features of the music might be suggested to the composer when he considers the effect that the composition might have in a particular setting. When Bach amended his original version by dividing the performing forces of his St. Matthew Passion into two groups, he considered the effect that this disposition would have in the St. Thomas church, with its two organ lofts at opposite ends of the nave (shown in Figures 16-3 and 16-4). In making this division, Bach emphasized the several levels on which the story is told. Choir I, situated in the larger west galleries, included all the speaking roles from the Gospel. When these singers are combined into a chorus, they represent The Daughters of Zion, an allegorical symbol for the eternal city of Jerusalem, which in turn is a symbol for the Christian church through the ages. Choir II, in the smaller eastside "swallow's nest," represents the

Figure 16-4. The eastward view, toward the altar, in the St. Thomas Church, Leipzig, a computer-generated image

Believers of today, both as a chorus and as the soloists in the contemplative recitatives and arias using Picander's texts. When both choirs sing
chorales, they represent all Christians, including the congregation. Each
choir has its own small orchestra, including a continuo group.

10. *Locus adjunctorum* ("place of attributes"). Features of the music might be
suggested to the composer when he considers the personal attributes of

Figure 16-5. The westward view, toward the main entrance, in the St. Thomas Church, Leipzig, a computer-generated image

characters in a drama. Bach's recitatives for Jesus differentiate him through broad but gentle, emotive, and generous voice inflections and through the halo of sound provided by the string accompaniments—a German Lutheran tradition. The Evangelist's recitatives are less broadly inflected, and his delivery is brisker. When the Daughters of Zion sing as a chorus, their music is calm and noble, whereas the interjections of the

Believers, from the other end of the church, are nervous and sharp. Bach's short *turba* choruses represent the crowd as agitated and confused, and a similar characterization is given the disciples when they answer the questions posed by Jesus.

11. *Locus circumstantiarum* ("place of circumstances"). Features of the music might be suggested to the composer when he considers the time of day or season of the year in which the action portrayed or narrated takes place. The most lovely result of invention drawn from this commonplace is Bach's accompanied recitative *Am Abend da es kühle war* ("In the evening, when it was cool"), in which the tranquility of the evening is suggested by the very long bass notes and resultant slow harmonic rhythm, the suppressed attacks indicated by the first-violin bowing, the continuously soft dynamic level, and the slow and steady rhythmic motion.

12. *Locus comparatorum* ("place of comparison"). When dissimilar things are compared—small with large, fiction with reality, day with night, etc.—features of the music might be suggested to the composer that suggest similarities between the apparently dissimilar things.

13. *Locus oppositorum* ("place of opposites"). The composer may derive musical ideas from a consideration of opposing characteristics, such as different meters, contrary motion, juxtaposition of high and low, loud and soft, fast and slow, calm and violent, whether or not suggested by a text. In the aria with chorus *Ich will bei meinem Jesu wachen* ("I will keep watch beside my Jesus"), Bach sets the first sentence to a short musical phrase imitating a trumpet watchtower signal, rising by leaps. In contrast, the chorus's response, "Then our sins go to sleep," is sung to a gently undulating motive suggestive of a lullaby. The opposing characteristics of the Daughters of Zion versus the Believers, and of Jesus versus the Evangelist have already been mentioned. Likewise the G-major chorale in the E-minor chorus in the opening number.

14. *Locus exemplorum* ("place of examples"). A composer has found invention in this commonplace when she/he imitates the style or quotes the music of another composer, nationality, school, period, etc.

15. *Locus testimoniorum* ("place of endorsements"). When a composer quotes a melody known to everyone, such as a chorale, the place of endorsements has yielded up an element of invention. Bach's quotation of chorale melodies is a special feature of the St. Matthew Passion. Altogether it contains two large-scale chorale fantasies for chorus and orchestra and twelve homophonic settings of four different chorale melodies. The chorale melody heard most often—five times—is *O Haupt voll Blut und Wunden* ("O head all blood and wounds"), which is transposed and reharmonized each time, taking on a progressively darker sound. The stanza chosen to be sung to each recurrence of a chorale melody comments upon the episode just narrated.

The *loci topici* of classical rhetorical lore, adapted to music by Mattheson, help one sort through the potentially bewildering variety and richness of Bach's St. Matthew Passion. Approaching the work through this perspective shows how Bach amplifies its text and meanings with musical expression and allusions that are communal and lasting rather than merely personal and time-bound.

Among Bach's other large-scale works for chorus, soloists, and orchestra, the B-Minor Mass deserves mention here, because the music of several of its movements is drawn from cantatas. Its musical style, therefore, is the same as that of Bach's cantatas, Passions, and oratorios. He composed the Kyrie and Credo of this work in 1733 as a typical short Lutheran Mass. In 1748–49 he added the rest of the Catholic Latin Ordinary text, divided into many movements in the custom of that time. The original Kyrie and Gloria were performed in Dresden in honor of the new Elector of Saxony in July, 1733; there is no record of a purpose or performance of the expanded Mass. Toward the end of his life, Bach composed several elaborate works for no apparent practical reason, and the expansion of the B-Minor Mass may be one of these.

BACH'S KEYBOARD WORKS

Bach obtained his earliest positions on the basis of his prowess as organist, and he was widely known as an organist and expert in organ construction during his lifetime. Bach continued to compose music for the organ until his death.

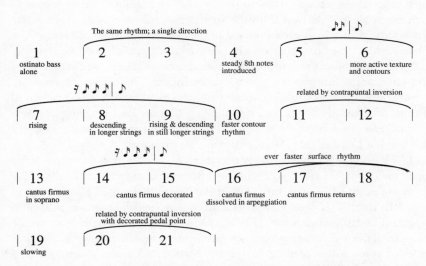

Figure 16-6. An outline of the twenty-one statements of the ostinato in J. S. Bach, Passacaglia, BWV 582

A relatively early organ work that illustrates Bach's engagement with the traditions of northern Germany is his Passacaglia in C minor, BWV 582 (A. 128), which he composed toward the end of his years as organist at the New Church of Arnstadt, 1703–07. The work emulates and competes with the Passacaglia in D minor, BuxWV 161 (A. 94) by Dieterich Buxtehude, whom Bach visited at Lübeck in 1705–06, walking the 250 miles from Arnstadt both ways. The bass ostinato figure in Bach's Passacaglia bears a generic resemblance to Buxtehude's, as both are related to the ciaconna bass, even though the first half of Bach's figure is actually derived from an organ Mass by André Raison printed in 1688. Bach derived from Buxtehude's work the syncopated chords that dominate the second and third statements of Bach's ostinato. Further similarities are the growing energy (increases of surface rhythm, contour rhythm, texture, discontinuity, etc.) within and between groups of ostinato statements. Whereas Buxtehude stated his shorter ostinato figure seven times on D, F, A, and D, Bach's statements tend to fall into seven groups of three (Figure 16-6). At the end of his Passacaglia, Bach adds a fugue whose subject is based on the first half of the ostinato figure.

Of all the categories of Bach's organ works—improvisatory (preludes, toccatas, fantasias), strictly imitative (fugues, fantasias, ricercars, canzonas, capriccios, inventions), combinations (preludes with fugues), sonatas, suites, overtures, chaconnes, passacaglias, pastorales, concertos, and variations—the largest is chorale settings, of which about 169 survive.

Bach wrote every sort of organ chorale setting typical of North German composers—relatively simple harmonizations with plain or embellished melody in the soprano, suitable for accompanying congregational singing; settings with the chorale melody in some other voice, often as cantus firmus in longer note values; sets of variations on the chorale melody; chorale fugues in which the subject is derived from the first phrase of the chorale; motet-style chorale settings in which each imitated motive is derived from a phrase of the chorale melody; canons based on chorale melodies; and chorale fantasies, in which two or more of the above-mentioned techniques are combined, most commonly cantus firmus with motet-style treatment. The chorale fantasies are the most ambitious of Bach's chorale settings; they may have been played before or after the service or as a prelude to a cantata. Bach's setting of *Allein Got in der Höh' sei Ehr*, BWV 663 (A. 129), composed at Weimar, ca. 1708–17 and revised in Leipzig, ca. 1749, may serve as an example.

In BWV 663 Bach places a slowly paced but highly decorated version of the chorale melody in the tenor voice. In the other voices, individual phrases of the melody are outlined in figuration (e.g., at the beginning), stated plainly (e.g., in the pedals, mm. 9–12), or played in canon (e.g., pedals and soprano, mm. 69–72, and pedals and alto, mm. 73–78). Other features of this setting can be summarized from a contemporaneous perspective by taking inventory of its sources of invention according to Johann Mattheson's list of commonplaces (see box on page 483).

Two further points concerning BWV 663. The claim made in Table 16-4 that the work has a joyous character is supported by the report of one of Bach's many students, Johann Gotthilf Ziegler, in a letter of 1746: "As concerns the playing of chorales, I was instructed by my teacher, Kapellmeister Bach, who is still living, not to play the songs merely offhand but according to the affect of the words." If Bach instructed his students to observe the affect of the chorale text in performing an organ chorale setting, surely he would have considered their affect in composing the setting in the first place. The words of *Allein Got in der Höh' sei Ehr* are:

> Glory be to God alone on high,
> and give thanks for his Grace,
> by which we are and will be
> ever more safe from harm.
> God has blessed us by his good will
> with peace without end.
> All strife is now ended.

The second point is that BWV 663 represents a more normalized harmonic style, when compared with a slightly earlier work, the Passacaglia in C Minor. This normalized harmonic style, largely originating in Italy, was created by eliminating certain categories of chord succession while emphasizing others. Example 16-1 shows the fundamental bass of several fragments from Bach's Passacaglia in C Minor, extracted according to the theory of Bach's student Johann Philipp Kirnberger, rather than the theory of Rameau. This example shows that the fundamental bass of Bach's Passacaglia sometimes progresses by step or third in contexts that are not included in the nor-

---

Sources of Invention in Bach's *Allein Gott in der Höh' sei Ehr*, BWV 663

Place of notation: the perpetual motion in the upper voices

Place of description: the joyous character supported by the major key, rapid tempo, fast note values, rising contours, and wide intervals

Place of genre and type: The work imitates a trio sonata with added cantus firmus, a fugue, and a concerto in the use of ritornello form and cadenza, toward the end.

Place of whole and part: There are three levels of rhythmic activity by (1) the upper two parts, (2) the pedal part, and (3) the tenor ornamented cantus firmus.

Place of material cause: The seven motives introduced in the first seven measures provide all the material for all the voices accompanying the cantus firmus for the rest of the work, and none is abandoned.

Place of formal cause: Both bar form (AAB) and ritornello form are in evidence.

Place of final cause: The purpose is to inspire listener with the joy of salvation.

Place of examples: The work imitates, to some extent, the style of a Vivaldi violin concerto.

Place of endorsements: It incorporates a chorale melody known to everyone in the congregation at the time.

EXAMPLE 16-1. The fundamental bass (*alla* Kirnberger) of several fragments of Bach's Passacaglia, BWV 582, showing progressions shummed by the normalized harmonic style of ca. 1700

malized harmonic style of the early eighteenth century, as represented by the works of such composers as Corelli and Vivaldi, by BWV 663, and by later works of Bach.

The probable impetus for Bach's normalization (or "clarification," as it is sometimes called) of harmonic style during his Weimar years was his acquaintance with the collection of the latest Italian concertos that Prince Johann Ernst, one Bach's patrons, brought back from Amsterdam in 1713. Bach made organ transcriptions of several of those concertos—by Antonio Vivaldi, Alessandro and Benedetto Marcello, Giuseppe Torelli, and others—before leaving Weimar. In these concertos, according his son Carl Philipp Emanuel, Bach "studied the chain of ideas, their relation to each other, the variety of the modulations, and many other particulars."

Fugue is another large category of Bach's keyboard music, encompassing works for organ, harpsichord, and undesignated instrument. Considering how often fugues occur in Bach's choral, chamber ensemble, and orchestral works, and in such keyboard works as toccatas and passacaglias, it would be hard to overemphasize the importance of fugal technique in his compositions. Although fugues are found among the keyboard works of Bach's German predecessors, none of them made such a fetish of strict and extended fugal composition.

"Fugue" meant, to German composers of the seventeenth and early eighteenth centuries, an instrumental work, especially for keyboard, with a predominantly imitative texture, in which the voices initially enter, one by one, with a short subject, normally keyed to the first and fifth degrees in regular alternation. Most of Bach's fugues present the subject several more times in various voices of the texture before the end of the piece. In a small number of Bach's fugues, a second subject is introduced at some point.

In many of Bach's fugues, vestiges of the two types of imitative keyboard work of the decades around 1600 can still be found—the ricercar with its slow rhythms and stepwise motion, and the canzona with its typical family of initial rhythms and livelier figuration. In addition, some of Bach's fugues are in the style of a gigue, a dance which, in French keyboard suites, can often be found with an imitative texture.

Two connected features quite common in Bach's fugues but rare in those of his German predecessors and contemporaries are (1) statements of the subject on a variety of scale degrees, notably those that result in a change from major to minor or minor to major; and (2) the insertion of episodes in which motives or figures from the fugue subject, its countersubjects, or connective passages are extended through elaboration, typically in sequences. Both of these features have been compared with the ritornello procedure of Italian violin concertos of the time, although they are found in Bach's fugues even before his exposure to the concertos of Vivaldi in 1713.

Most of Bach's keyboard fugues are preceded by a prelude in a freer style. An example is Prelude and Fugue 21 in B-flat Major (A. 130) from Bach's collection *Das wohltemperirte Clavier, oder Praeludia, und Fugen durch alle Tone und Semitonia sowohl tertiam majorem oder Ut Re Mi anlangend, als auch tertian minorem oder Re Mi Fa betreffend. Zum Nuyzen und Gebrauch der Lehrbegierigen Musikalischen Jugend also auch derer in diesem Studio schon habil . . . Anno 1722* ("The Well-Tempered Keyboard, or Preludes and Fuges through All the Tones and Semitones, both as regards the major third or Ut Re Mi and as concerns the minor third or Re Mi Fa. For the use and profit of the musical youth wishing to learn, as well as for the pastime of those already skilled in this study . . . in the year 1722").

Prelude 21 is divided between a section of arpeggiation and scales, which modulates from B-flat major toward D minor (which is never fully established), and a cadenza-like section alternating between massive chords in dotted rhythms and wide-ranging scales, which outlines an extended full cadence on B-flat, which is afterward confirmed by a plagal cadence.

The subject of Fugue 21, like many of Bach's, begins with a sturdy "head" motive and concludes with a more rapid "tail." In keeping with traditional

modal practices, the interval of a fourth between F and B-flat in the first statement of the subject is answered by the interval of the fifth between B-flat and
F in the "answer form" of the subject, with other notes adjusted to fit in. Thus,
the span of an octave and its division into fifth plus fourth is outlined by adjacent voices, by what today is termed a "tonal answer" (although "modal
answer" would be a better term). After stating the subject for the first time,
each voice proceeds to the same two countersubjects that accompany the
subject at every subsequent appearance. A fugue that begins this way is often
called a "permutation fugue," and the technique that allows the subject or
either of the countersubjects to appear as the bass or as the uppermost voice is
called "invertible (double or triple) counterpoint."

The first episode of Fugue 21 (mm. 17–22) uses the tail of the subject in
the soprano and its melodically inverted head in the bass to effect a modulation, through a sequence, to G minor, the sixth degree of the original key.
The second episode (mm. 30–35) includes a transposed contrapuntal inversion of the first episode, with the tail in the bass and the inverted head in the
soprano. This symmetry is reinforced by the arrangement of the last two
subject statements (mm. 37–45), which form a transposed contrapuntal
inversion of the last two statements before the first episode (mm. 9–17), so
that the movement from tonic to dominant of the earlier two statements is
answered at the end by a reciprocal movement from the subdominant to the
tonic. Every note in Fugue 21 is derived from the subject or one of the
countersubjects.

Although Bach's musical style represents an intensification of traditional fea-
tures rather than the introduction of entirely new ones, he participated in a distinctly new trend in his publication of four volumes of *Clavier-Übung*
("Keyboard Practice") aimed at the commercial market of musical amateurs.
Volume I (1726–31) of this set consists of six suites of dances in a pre-
Couperin French style fortified with the contrapuntal interest typical of all of
Bach's works. Volume II (1735) consists of two solo keyboard works that imitate orchestral music—a French overture with suite of dances and an Italian-
style concerto. Volume III (1739) contains a fugue, nine chorale settings for the
Sunday service, twelve for the catechism service, and four instructive duets,
most of them playable on either harpsichord or organ. Volume IV consists of an
"aria" (actually a sarabande, probably not by Bach) with thirty variations (the
"Goldberg Variations")—all of them conforming to the harmonic and phrase
outline of the aria—in a large-scale symmetrical design based on groups of
three variations, each group ending with a canon (at the unison, second, third,
fourth, fifth, sixth, seventh, octave, and ninth), or at the end a "quodlibet" play-
fully constructed out of folksong fragments. Notable in these variations are
several in the virtuosic style of Domenico Scarlatti (1685–1757), two (nos. 15
and 25) in the intimate and highly expressive *emfindsamer* ("sensitive") style
closely identified with Bach's sons Carl Philipp Emanuel (1714–1788) and
Wilhelm Friedman Bach (1710–1784), and several others in an equally modern, up-to-date style.

It is not true, however, that Bach moved only toward a more modern, up-to-date style in his later keyboard works. If anything, he became more absorbed in writing complex and thorough summations of the contrapuntal art toward the end of his life. The supreme example is *Die Kunst der Fuge* "(The Art of the Fugue"), a collection of didactic keyboard fugues intended to exhaust the possibilities of a single subject, which Bach worked on from 1740 to 1745 and 1748 to 1750 but left unfinished at his death.

INSTRUMENTAL ENSEMBLE MUSIC

Bach's activity in instrumental ensemble music in Leipzig was concentrated in the Collegium Musicum, a group of as many as fifty or sixty musicians, including singers and instrumentalists, many of them university students.

Traditionally, the term "collegium musicum" was used in Germany to denote a voluntary association of amateurs, especially students and educated citizens—town councillors, lawyers, doctors and prosperous merchants. Such groups emerged all over the Empire during its recovery from the Thirty Years' War, in many cases to offset the loss of more traditional musical ensembles of the town, court, and church. These groups sponsored and participated in performances. The repertoire was initially divided between vocal and instrumental music, but during the second half of the seventeenth century, the balance shifted decisively toward instrumental ensemble music.

Adam Krieger formed a student ensemble in Leipzig about 1657, and several more appeared later in the century. Georg Philipp Telemann formed a new collegium musicum in 1701, while he was a law student at the University of Leipzig. This group eventually included forty instrumentalists; it gave weekly performances in coffee houses, a new type of establishment that appeared all over Germany in the years surrounding 1700. After Telemann left Leipzig in 1705, his collegium was taken over by a series of leading musicians. By 1716 the group numbered between fifty and sixty members, and it performed twice weekly. This was the ensemble that Bach inherited in 1729, just when he began to reduce his church-related activities.

Bach's Collegium Musicum performed once a week at Zimmermann's coffeehouse, twice a week during the four annual trade fairs, while a second collegium performed every week at Richter's coffeehouse. These groups presented mostly instrumental music, although they also performed vocal works, such as Bach's secular cantatas. It is unclear whether the performers were paid, although they were occasionally joined by visiting court musicians, who must have received remuneration. Their repertoire featured solo and trio sonatas, concertos, and orchestral suites, the same repertoire used at German courts to accompany banquets and daily dining. Indeed, in 1733 Telemann published three volumes of such works, including some of his 125 orchestral suites and 125 concertos, under the title *Musique de table* ("Table Music," *Tafelmusik* in German), a title used for many other similar collections. In effect, then, these coffeehouse concerts were modeled on the dining-music perform-ances at noble courts. Some of the works that Bach performed with his Col-legium Musicum in Leipzig were new, like his concertos for one or more harpsichords, but many were originally written for his patrons at the courts of Weimar and Cöthen; the four orchestral suites and Brandenburg concertos are well-known examples.

Bach's six Brandenburg concertos were collected into one manuscript volume and dedicated to the margrave of Brandenburg in 1721, while Bach was at Cöthen, although several of the concertos appear to have been composed even earlier, perhaps in Weimar. All of them involve the juxtaposition of passages fea-turing solo instruments or small groups against other segments, often ritornellos, played by the full ensemble. Each of the concertos employs an unusual combina-tion of instruments, and none is limited to the solo violin with four-part string accompaniment that dominates the large Italian repertoire of ensemble music at this time. In this, Bach follows the German practice seen, for example, in the concertos of Telemann and Johann Friedrich Fasch (1688–1758). Bach's approach to concerto formal procedure diverges from the mainstream of Italian style. Bach's first Brandenburg concerto may serve as an example.

Bach's Brandenburg Concerto No. 1 in F Major (A. 131) calls for three oboes, two horns, bassoon, and *violino piccolo* in soloist roles, accompanied by the usual string orchestra in four parts with continuo. The use of horns and the musical material given to them allude to the hunt. The earliest version of this work was called *sinfonia*, and it may have served as the overture to Bach's "Hunt Cantata," BWV 208, in 1713 or 1716. Its original three movements, fast, slow, and fast, are entirely in accord with Italian concerto conventions as regards themes, rhythms, motivic elaboration by means of sequences, and the normal-ized harmonic style. The treatment of form and the contrapuntal texture are another matter.

Bach's two Italian-style fast movements reflect but do not follow exactly typ-ical ritornello formal procedure. Although ritornellos alternate with episodes, the ritornellos often include passages for solo instruments, the episodes often include interjections by the full ensemble, and both ritornellos and episodes are derived from material presented in the first ritornello. In Italian concertos at this time the tutti ritornellos and the solo episodes are usually distinct in both scor-ing and thematic content. However, the ritornello procedure in the first and third movements of Bach's Brandenburg Concerto No. 1 has its own logic and consistency. All their ritornellos begin with a tutti Vordersatz based on the open-ing phrase of the movement, and they all end with a cadence. Nearly all the episodes, on the other hand, begin with Fortspinnung for solo instruments. An outline of the first movement is offered as Figure 16-7.

The second movement is in Mode 4 transposed to A through a one-flat key signature. It is organized into nine phrases related through inexact varia-tion. All but one of these phrases end with a Phrygian cadence. To modern ears, the concluding harmony of this movement may seem like the dominant of D minor, but it is actually the normal harmonization of a Mode 4 final.

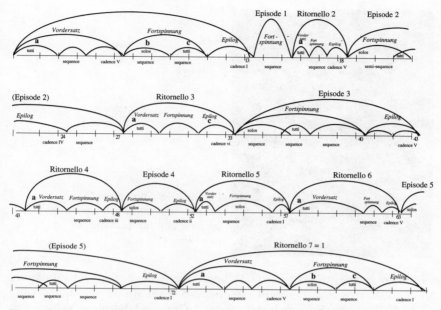

Figure 16-7. An outline of the first movement of Bach's *Brandenburg Concerto no. 1*

Mode 4 continues to appear in the slow movements of concertos by many Italian and German composers of Bach's generation.

The concluding rondeau was added to the end of Bach's concerto in its revised version. It is made up of alternating dances that are French in every respect, including in their avoidance of *Fortspinnung* in favor of *Liedtypus* periods, in which a phrase with implications (the *Vordersatz*) is following by a responding phrase offering at least temporary closure (the *Nachsatz*).

Several other Brandenburg concertos display more modern features, such as clearer overall form, but none of them reflects the latest developments in Italian ensemble music of the 1720s. In his later ensemble works, Bach intensified his interest in contrapuntal techniques and motivic elaboration. Parallel to *Die Kunst der Fuge* is the *Musikalisches Opfer* ("Musical Offering"), a collection of canons and fugues with a trio sonata that Bach composed in 1747 on a theme given him by the musician-king of Prussia, Frederick the Great. In his official portrait of 1746 (Figure 16-8), Bach is pictured with a page containing two canons.

During his lifetime, Bach was widely known and respected, especially by knowledgeable musicians, and he had many successful students. But he did not become a national icon like Handel until after his death. Bach's son Carl Philipp Emanuel Bach and his student Johann Friedrich Agricola published a extended obituary essay in 1754. These two, in addition to other devoted students, such as Johann Philipp Kirnberger and Friedrich Wilhelm Marpurg, kept the memory of Bach alive throughout the eighteenth century. Carl Philipp Emanuel provided Johann Nicolaus Forkel with inspiration

Figure 16-8. The portrait of
Johann Sebastian Bach painted
by Elias Gottlob Haußmann
in 1746

and information that led to Forkel's book about Bach, the first substantial
volume dedicated to a thorough examination of the music of a single composer. Carl Philipp Emanuel also inspired Gottfried Baron von Swieten,
who, beginning in the mid-1780s, organized performances of music by
Bach and Handel in the rooms he occupied as Prefect of the Imperial
Library in Vienna. Toward the end of his life, Mozart studied the music of
Bach in Swieten's collection, but it was not his first encounter with it. That
occurred during Mozart's visit to Leipzig in 1789, as Friedrich Rochlitz, an
eyewitness, later recalled:

On the initiative of the late [Johann Friedrich] Doles, then Cantor of the St.
Thomas School of Leipzig, the choir [of the school] surprised Mozart with the
performance of the double-chorus motet *Singet dem Herrn ein neues Lied* by
[Johann] Sebastian Bach. Mozart knew this master more by hearsay than by his
works, which had become quite rare. . . . Hardly had the choir sung a few
measures when Mozart sat up, startled. A few measures more and he called out,
"What is this?" And now his whole soul seemed to be in his ears. When the
singing was finished he cried out, full of joy, "Now there is something one can
learn from!" He was told that this school, in which Sebastian Bach had been
Cantor, possessed the complete collection of his motets and preserved them as
a sort of sacred relic. "That's the spirit! That's fine!" he cried. "Let's see them!"
There was, however, no score of these songs, so he had the parts given to him.
And then it was a joy for the silent observer to see how eagerly Mozart got
down on hands and knees, with the parts all around him and on the chairs next
to him, and, forgetting everything else, did not get up again until he had
looked through everything of Sebastian Bach's that was there.

THE END OF AN ERA—THE LEGACY OF THE BAROQUE

The rise of the collegium musicum and associated practices—the performance of *Tafelmusik* for middle-class patrons in public places, and concerts for the general public—are symptoms of a fundamental change in European musical culture. Public concerts for paid admission arose principally in London toward the end of the seventeenth and beginning of the eighteenth centuries, usually in the form of a benefit concert for opera singers or instrumental soloists. Gradually this institution spread to the Continent. The Concerts Spirituels that began in Paris in 1725 as a Lenten substitute for opera were part of this new trend.

In public concerts, music was the center of attention, presented to an audience for its own sake and not as an accompaniment to pageantry, drama, dancing, dining, conversation, or worship. It was therefore not primarily intended as a vehicle for the promotion of an ideological or religious agenda. When evening concerts were offered at a church, as with the *Abendmusik* tradition in Lübeck, and when, about the middle of the eighteenth century, hundreds of noble courts in the German-speaking lands began offering musical performances by a small orchestra to an audience that outnumbered the performers, the nobility was beginning to conform to the emerging culture of the middle classes, rather than the reverse. This is a fundamental change.

The repertoire associated with concerts centering around an orchestra included symphonies and keyboard concertos. Both genres emerged initially in the music of Italian composers working for Austro-German patrons, either at home (e.g., Giovanni Battista Sammartini in Milan) or abroad (e.g., Giovanni Benedetto Platti in Würzburg), and were quickly taken up by German-speaking composers. The symphony and keyboard concerto derive from the earlier Italian instrumental genres of the concerto without soloist (*concerto ripieno*) and the violin concerto. The fact that neither the symphony nor the keyboard concerto continued to develop in Italy suggests that these genres emerged in Italy either as tourist fare or as an export commodity—objects of commerce in a new middle-class economy. In many respects, opera seria had become tourist fare in Venice and an export commodity wherever Italian singers, opera composers, librettists, and scene designers were employed north of the Alps.

Music written, printed, and sold in the commercial market for middle-class musical amateurs comprises another large class of post-Baroque repertoire. The prominent genres in this class are sonatas for solo keyboard instrument and keyboard sonatas with the accompaniment of one or more ensemble instruments. The earliest composers of solo keyboard sonatas again appear to have been Italians working for the transalpine market—Francesco Durante, Lodovico Giustini, Giovanni Benedetto Platti, Giovanni Battista Pescetti, Giovanni Battista Martini, Domenico Alberti, etc. They too were quickly followed by German composers. Although the accompanied keyboard sonata emerged first in Paris, its earliest champion, Jean-Joseph Cassanea de Mondonville, tried to imitate Italian models. The sonata for solo violin and basso continuo appears to be the parent genre of both the solo keyboard sonata and, along with the *pièce de clavecin*, the accompanied keyboard sonata.

By the 1750s, the string quartet and similar genres spun off from the symphony, and genres for various chamber-music combinations with keyboard and string ensemble branched off from the two kinds of keyboard sonata.

Thus, the new venue of the public concert and the new commercial market for printed music gave rise to the instrumental genres that have continued to define European art music of the Modern Era. At the same time, musical practices at noble and royal courts increasingly imitated public concerts, and church music quickly faded from prominence. These developments signal the end of the Baroque era, in which monarchy and religion had provided most of the patronage that supported music and had embodied and defined the principal cultural values that music reflected.

The new genres that arose for the public concert and the commercial market shared many new features of style. Above all, this new music was oriented to formal principles derived from melodic organization. No longer guided by the forces of sequence and cadence, this new melody-dominated music relied on hierarchical structures built up from short phrase units, alignment of musical elements to create and sustain discrete dynamic states, variety of topic rather than unity of affect and rhetorical design, and the large-scale rhythm of tension and release created by modulation from the tonic to the dominant and back again. The goals of this new music were neither persuasion nor amusement, but the creation of sustained musical interest for an intently listening audience of consumers, rather than of patrons and clients.

In this context it is understandable that the status of the composer changed. No longer the servant of court or church, as in the Baroque era, the composer gradually became both a commodity and a celebrity. The reinvention of Handel and Bach shortly before or after their deaths dramatizes this change. With the centralization of production and distribution via publication, more and more of Europe's art music was written by fewer and fewer composers. This promoted the creation of a single, international style, initially hailed in the early eighteenth century as the *goûts réunis* (Couperin) or *vermischter Geschmack* (Quantz), the "reunited tastes" or "mixed style," combining features of the French, Italian, and German styles that had been distinct during the seventeenth century.

Many of the innovations of the seventeenth century, however, remained durable features of the European concert music tradition—for example, opera, oratorio, and all other genres making use of recitative; the ensemble sonata; suites of dances; the concerto; works with contrasting sections for solo voices and chorus; the orchestra formed around a core of violin-family instruments; the creation of instrumental idioms capable of being transferred to different instruments and even to voices; the expansion and generalization of poetic scansion (rhythmopoeia) from the level of individual notes to the level of measures and phrases; the purely chordal accompaniment of melody; a normalized harmonic style that coordinates the scale and octave framework of mode, a chordal conception of music, and the diminution practice derived from *contrapunto alla mente*; a rhetorical conception in which invention, disposition, elocution, and delivery might be mirrored, promoted, or controlled by music; a language of musical expression based on a combination of speech characteristics, musical pictorialism, and conventional signs, by which emotions could be communicated by music, even without words. In spite of the many changes that define the end of the era, these and other innovations—along with a vast, varied, fascinating, and exciting repertoire of beautiful music—remain with us as the legacy of the Baroque.

BIBLIOGRAPHICAL NOTES

The New Lutheran Cantata

The overview provided by Friedrich Blume, *Protestant Church Music: A History* (New York: W. W. Norton, 1974) is now out of date. Some new background is provided by G. Webber, *North German Church Music in the Age of Buxtehude* (Oxford: Oxford University Press, 1996). Some studies in German have been published concerning the poet Erdmann Neumeister and a few of the early composers of his librettos; see the bibliographies in the entries in *The New Grove Dictionary of Music and Musicians*, 2nd ed. (London: Macmillan, 2001).

Bach's Cantatas

The best and most recent overview on Bach is found in Christoph Wolff, *Johann Sebastian Bach: The Learned Musician* (New York: W. W. Norton, 2000). Up-to-date information about the chronology, sources, versions, revisions, and text bases of Bach's cantatas is found in Christoph Wolff and Hans-Joachim Schulze, *Bach Compendium: Analytisch-bibliographisches Repertorium der Werke Johann Sebastian Bachs* (Leipzig and Frankfurt: C. F. Peters, 1985–). A useful overview of books on Bach's life and works is Daniel R. Melamed and Michael Marissen, *An Introduction to Bach Studies* (Oxford: Oxford University Press, 1998). A general guide to the musical form and style of Bach's cantatas is W. Murray Young, *The Cantatas of J. S. Bach: An Analytical Guide* (Jefferson, NC: MacFarland, 1989). Commentary that includes references to the biblical readings in the services for which Bach composed individual cantatas is included in Alfred Dürr, *Die Kantaten von Johann Sebastian Bach*, 6th ed. (Kassel: Bärenrieter, 1995). Biblical allusions in Bach's cantata texts are provided by Melvin P. Unger, *Handbook to Bach's Sacred Cantata Texts: An Interlinear Translation with Reference Guide to Biblical Quotations and Allusions* (Lanham, MD.: Scarecrow Press, 1996).

Protestant Oratorios and Passions

The best overview in English is Howard E. Smither, *A History of the Oratorio*, II, *The Oratorio in the Baroque Era: Protestant Germany and England*. A dissertation on the newly recovered oratorios of Johann Mattheson is underway at the University of Hamburg, by Steffen Voss, who generously provided information on this subject.

Handel's Oratorios

The most thorough discussion of Handel's oratorios remains Winton Dean, *Handel's Dramatic Oratorios and Masques* (London: Oxford University Press, 1959). An interdisciplinary perspective is added by R. Smith, *Handel's Oratorios and Eighteenth-Century Thought* (Cambridge: Cambridge University Press, 1995). In addition, there are many detailed studies of individual oratorios listed in the bibliography in *The New Grove Dictionary* listing on Handel.

Bach's Passions and Oratorios

Although there are more recent studies of Bach's St. Matthew and St. John Passions in German, the most extensive treatment of Bach's Passions in English is still B. Smallman, *The Background of Passion Music: J. S. Bach and his Predecessors*, 2nd ed. (London, 1970). An outstanding study of the B Minor Mass is John Butt, *Bach: Mass in B Minor* (Cambridge: Cambridge University Press, 1991). A model study of an individual Passion is Alfred Dürr, *Johann Sebastian Bach, St. John Passion: Genesis, Transmission, and Meaning* (Oxford: Oxford University Press, 2000). Jan Dismas Zelenka (1679-1745) composed Latin music for the court of Dresden during Bach's lifetime, and his works make a worthy comparison; see Janice B. Stockigt, *Jan Dismas Zelenka (1679–1745): A Bohemian Musician at the Court of Dresden* (Oxford: Oxford University Press, 2000).

Bach's Keyboard Works

An informative overview of Bach's keyboard works is provided by David Schulenberg, *The Keyboard Music of J. S. Bach* (New York: Schirmer Books, 1992). The standard overview of Bach's organ works in English is Peter Williams, *The Organ Music of J. S. Bach* (Cambridge: Cambridge University Press, 1980–84). An older study of Bach's organ chorale settings that still has value is Stainton de Boufflers Taylor, *The Chorale Preludes of J. S. Bach: A Handbook* (London: Oxford University Press, 1942). An informative introduction to Bach's fugal technique is provided by Hermann Keller, *The Well-Tempered Clavier by Johann Sebastian Bach* (New York: W. W. Norton, 1976).

Instrumental Ensemble Music

Two recent books with interesting perspectives on Bach's Brandenburg Concertos are Malcolm Boyd, *Bach: The Brandenburg Concertos* (Cambridge: Cambridge University Press, 1993); and Michael Marissen, *The Social and Religious Designs of J. S. Bach's Brandenburg Concertos* (Princeton, NJ: Princeton University Press, 1995). A collection of detailed treatments, mostly in German, is Martin Geck, ed., *Bachs Orchesterwerke*, Dortmunder Bach-Forschung, 1 (Dortmund: Klangfarben Musikverlag, 1997). The smaller-scale works are nicely covered by Hans Vogt, *Johann Sebastian Bach's Chamber Music: Background, Analyses, Individual Works*, trans. Kenn Johnson (Portland, OR: Amadeus Press, 1988). Some broader context is provided by Steven Zohn, "The Ensemble Sonatas of Georg Philipp Telemann: Studies in Style, Genre, and Chronology," Ph.D. diss., Cornell Univ, 1995; Jean Swack, "The Solo Sonatas of Georg Philipp Telemann: A Study of the Sources and Musical Style," Ph.D. diss., Yale Univ, 1988; and Pippa Drummond, *The German Concerto: Five Eighteenth-Century Studies* (Oxford: Oxford University Press, 1980).

Rhetorical Figures that Are Frequently Mirrored in Music

Accumulatio: Heaping up praise or accusation to emphasize or summarize points or inferences already made. Ex.: "He is the betrayer of his own self-respect, and the waylayer of the self-respect of others; covetous, intemperate, irascible, arrogant; disloyal to his parents, ungrateful to his friends. . . ."

Adjunctio: The use of one verb to express two similar ideas at the beginning or end of successive clauses. Ex.: "Fades physical beauty with disease or age"; or "Either with disease or age physical beauty fades."

Admonitio: Reminding, recalling to mind.

Adtenuata: A weakened or reduced utterance.

Alletheta: Substitution of one mood for another.

Amphiboologia: Ambiguity.

Amplificatio: Enlargement, expansion.

Anabasis: Going up, climax.

Anacephalaeosis: A summary or recapitulation, intended to refresh the listener's memory.

Anadiplosis: Repetition of the last word of one line or clause to begin the next. Ex.: "For I have loved long, I crave reward. Reward me not unkindly: think on kindness. Kindness becommeth those of high regard. Regard with clemency a poor man's blindness."

Anaphora: Repetition of the same word at the beginning of successive clauses or verses. Ex.: "To think on death it is a misery. To think on life it is a vanity. To think on the world verily it is. To think that here man hath no perfect bliss."

Anastrophe: The analysis of an issue into its constituent parts, for ease of discussion or clarity of exegesis; dividing and particularizing.

Antanagoge: Ameliorating a fault or difficulty implicitly admitted by balancing an unfavorable aspect with a favorable one. Ex.: "I must needs say, that my wife is a shrew, but such a housewife as I know but a few."

Anthypophora: asking questions and answering them.

Antimetabole: Inverting the order of repeated words to sharpen their sense or to contrast the ideas they convery or both—also chiasmus. Ex.: "I pretty, and my saying apt? or I apt, and my saying pretty?"

Antistasis: Repetition of a word in a different or contrary sense. Ex.: "I wasted time and now doth time waste me."

Antistrophe (epiphora): Repetition of a closing word or words at the end of several successive clauses, sentences, or verses. Ex.: "Where affections bear rule, there reason is subdued, honesty is subdued, good will is subdued, and all things else that withstand evil, for ever are subdued."

Antithesis: Conjoining contrasting ideas. Ex.: "Neither the one hurt her, nor the other help her; just without partiality, might without contradiction, liberal without losing, wise without curiosity. . . ."

Apaetesis: A matter put aside in anger is resumed later.

Apocope: Cutting off discourse abruptly.

Aposiopesis: Stopping suddenly in midcourse, leaving a statement unfinished.

Apostrophe: Breaking off discourse to address directly some person or thing either present or absent.

Apothegm: A short, pithy statement of a general truth.

Assonance: Resemblance or similarity in sound between vowel sounds preceded and followed by differing consonant sounds in words in proximity.

Auxesis: Words or clauses placed in climactic order. Ex.: "I may, I must, I can, I will, I do leave following that which it is gain to miss."

Barbaralexis: Wrenched accent to fit meter or rhyme.

Bomphiologia: Bombastic speech.

Brachylogia: Brevity in speech or writing caused by omission of conjunctions between words. Ex.: "Beguil'd, divorced, wronged, spited, slain!" Hence, disjunction and choppiness of all kinds.

Catacosmesis: Ordering words from the greatest to least in dignity; opposite of Climax. Ex.: "For God, for Country, and for Yale."

Commoratio: Emphasizing a strong point by repeating it several times in different words. Ex.: "Expelled, thrust out, banished, and cast away from the city."

Comparatio: Showing similarities between persons or things, like or seemingly unlike.

Conduplicatio: Repetition of a word or words in succeeding clauses for amplification or to express emotion. Ex.: "You were not moved when his mother embraced your knees? You were not moved?"

Congeries: Word heaps. Ex.: "Who can be wise, amaz'd, temperate and furious, loyal and neutral, in a moment?" (*Macbeth*, I/iii)

Diacope: Repetition of a word or a few words with one or a few words in between. Ex.: "My heart is fixed, O God, my heart is fixed."

Dieremenon: Separation of the elements of a compound word by another word or words. Ex.: "West—by God—Virginia."

Digestion: An orderly enumeration of the points to be discussed, the implications of a question, etc.

Emphasis: Stress of language in such a way as to imply more than is actually stated.

Enumeratio: Division of subject into adjuncts, cause into effects, antecedent into consequents. Ex.: "How do I love thee? Let me count the ways. I love thee to the depth and breadth and height my soul can read, when feeling out of sight for the ends of Being and ideal Grace. I love thee. . . ."

Epandiplosis: Repetition at the end of a clause or sentence of the word with which it began. Ex.: "I might, unhappy word, O me, I might."

Epanodos: A general statement is expanded by discussing it part by part, and the terms used in the initial summary are specifically repeated in the discussion that follows.

Epexegesis: Adding words or phrases to further clarify or specify a statement already made.

Epizeuxis: Emphatic repetition of a word with no other words between. Ex.: "O horror, horror, horror!"

Epimone: Frequent repetition of a phrase or question; dwelling on a point; a refrain.

Erotesis: A rhetorical question implying strong affirmation or denial.

Exclamatio: An exclamation.

Explanatio: Adding words or phrases to further clarify or specify a statement already made: "For I know that in me (that is, in my flesh) dwelleth no good thing."

Exuscitatio: Emotional utterance that moves hearers to like feeling.

Gradatio: Mounting by degrees through words or sentences of increasing weight and in parallel construction. Ex.: "Labor getteth learning, learning getteth fame, fame getteth honor, honor getteth bliss forever."

Homiologia: Tedious, redundant style. Ex.: "Madam, I swear I use no art at all. That he is mad, 'tis true: 'tis true 'tis pity; and pity 'tis 'tis true: a foolish figure; but farewell it, for I will use no art. Mad let us grant him, then: and now remains that we find out the cause of this effect, or rather say, the cause of this defect, for this effect defective comes by cause: thus it remains and the remainder thus."

Homoioleuton: A series of words with like endings.

Hydrographia: Description of water.

Hyperbole: Exaggerated or extravagant terms used for emphasis and not intended to be understood literally; self-conscious exaggeration.

Hypotyposis: Mimicry of acts only, not of manners or feelings.

Hysteron proteron: Syntax or sense out of normal logical order.

Iteratio: Repetition for vehemence.

Mempsis: Complaining against injuries or pleading for help.

Noema: Obscure, subtle speech. Ex.: "In the United States there is more space where nobody is than where anybody is."

Oxymoron: A condensed paradox. Ex.: "Darkness visible."

Parechesis: Repetition of the same sound in words in close succession.

Parenthesis: A word, phrase, or sentence inserted as an aside in a sentence complete in itself.

Peristasis: Amplifying by describing attendant circumstances.

Ploce: Repetition of a word with a new signification after the intervention of another word or words.

Procatascene: Giving an audience a gradual preparation and buildup before telling them about something done.

Pragmatographia: Vivid description of an action or event.

Reditus ad propositum: Return to the proposition after a digression.

Sarcasmus: A bitter gibe or taunt; irony.

Syngnome: Forgiveness of injuries.

Zeugma: One verb governs several congruent words or clauses, each in a different way. Ex.: "Here thou, great Anna! whom three realms obey, dost sometimes counsel take—and sometimes tea."

For further background, see Richard A Lanham, *A Handlist of Rhetorical Terms*, 2nd ed. (Berkeley: University of California Press, 1991), also available in an enhanced version for Macintosh computers; and Dietrich Bartel, *Musica Poetica: Musical-Rhetorical Figures in German Baroque Music* (Lincoln, NE: University of Nebraska Press, 1997).

INDEX